International Olympic Committee

The IOC Official

OLYMPIC COMPANION
1996

Compiled and Edited by
Caroline Searle and Bryn Vaile
Matchtight Media

Published under license from the
INTERNATIONAL OLYMPIC COMMITTEE
by
BRASSEY'S SPORTS
London • Washington

First English Edition 1996

Brassey's Sports is an imprint of Brassey's (UK) Ltd

UK editorial offices: Brassey's Sports, 33 John Street, London WC1N 2AT

North American Orders: Brassey's Inc. PO Box 960, Herndon, VA 22070, USA
UK & Rest of World: Marston Book Services, PO Box 269, Abingdon, OX14 4SD, UK

Caroline Searle and Bryn Vaile have asserted their moral right to be identified as the compilers and editors of this work.

Library of Congress Cataloging in Publication Data
available

British Library Cataloguing in Publication Data
A catalogue record for this book is available from the British Library

ISBN 1 85753 128 0

Origination by Oxprint Design Ltd, Oxford, UK
Printed in Great Britain by BPC (Wheaton) Ltd, Exeter, UK

Preface

A s WE approach the unique occasion of the Games of the XXVI Olympiad, the Centennial Games of the modern era, in Atlanta, United States of America, it is time to reflect on the achievements of the Olympic Movement since the first Olympic Games in Athens in 1896.

What better way to mark this occasion than with a publication which charts the great moments in history of both the Games and the athletes? Moments that warm the heart and defy belief in their sheer quality.

The activity of the Olympic Movement, which is composed of the International Olympic Committee (IOC), the International Sports Federations and the National Olympic Committees, reaches its peak with the bringing together of the athletes of the world at the great sport festival, the Olympic Games.

Juan Antonio Samaranch, President of the IOC

I have no doubt that the people of the United States of America in general, and the people of Georgia and Atlanta in particular, will stage an Olympiad that will represent the pinnacle of all these achievements.

I wish to thank the publishers, Brassey's, and the editors and contributors, for the effort that has gone into this special volume on the Olympic Games.

Juan Antonio Samaranch
President of the International Olympic Committee

Contents

The Sportsfile

A comprehensive guide to each Sport on the Olympic programme including: background information; rules; contemporary stars and sporting legends; Atlanta event schedule and venue guide; current Olympic records; medals table by nation. **Tables of Medallists and results 1896–1992**

Editors' Introduction

THE IOC Official Olympic Companion has been compiled with the aim of providing its readers with essential information covering both a history of the summer Olympic Games since 1896 as well as the work of the IOC, the organization of the Games and the Olympic Movement's work on a four-year cycle.

The Companion is in four Parts. Part 1 takes the reader through the great moments in Olympic history of both the sporting and political variety. An insight is given into the world forces which have shaped the IOC and the Games since the IOC's formation in 1894. The role of women in the Games, and the media, are also explored. A section on the all-time Games' legends is featured here.

Part 2 provides a rapid-reference guide to the Atlanta sports timetable plus a complete list of events and venues. The city's history and attractions are outlined and an Olympic athlete's insight to life in an Olympic village during the Games is included.

The Sportsfile is the major part of the Olympic Companion, occupying some 385 pages in Part 3. It incorporates a sport-by-sport text guide to potential 1996 stars each written by a sports journalist, Olympic medallist or participant. This is an opinion piece followed by a brief history of the sport's origins and development as well as its Olympic involvement under the titles "Retrospective" and "Background". There is a guide to the sport's rules, equipment, 1996 competition format, venue, and schedule.

Within each sport, tables are presented for all-time medals by nation, current Olympic records (for those sports which can be timed or measured in a comparative fashion), and a major tabulation of every medal-winner since 1896. This covers all 1996 programme events. Discontinued events are covered on page 460.

Part 4 comprises an essential section, The Olympic Family and Movement, which sets out to answer questions such as the role of the IOC and the general work of the Olympic movement. Who organises the Games? How are they funded and marketed? What happens to the funds generated for sport? When was drug-testing first introduced?

The Companion concludes with a brief look at the preparations for the Games of Nagano (winter) in 1998 and Sydney (summer) in 2000.

The editors would welcome suggestions for improvement or additional useful features for incorporation in future volumes.

Caroline Searle, Bryn Vaile

PART 1
100 Glorious Years

100 Glorious Years

The Re-birth

Events of great historical and social significance are often shaped by the juxtaposition of a person of vision with a receptive climate. A Frenchman, Baron Pierre de Coubertin, was the man of vision who is widely accepted as having revived the Olympic Games of the modern era in 1896.

Baron Pierre de Coubertin

In his memoirs of 1920 de Coubertin later recalled: "I re-established the Olympic Games to ennoble and strengthen sports and to assure their independence and durability and, moreover, to allow them better to fulfil an educational role which was their duty in the modern world. For the glorification of the individual athlete, whose existence is necessary for the physical activities of the multitude, and whose prowess is essential to continuing general emulation".

At the time he also vowed: "I shall burnish a flabby and cramped youth, its body and its character, by sport, its risks even its excesses...all this is to be for everyone with no discrimination on account of birth, caste, financial standing or occupation". As an educationalist, he saw sport as an arm of education and he was worried about the state of the youth of his nation. "Sport should...be part of physical formation, as well as moral and intellectual development", he said. "It should allow man to know himself, to control himself, and to conquer himself".

His ideas had some philosophical precedence in the late 19th century. He was not the first to think of reviving the Ancient Games of Greece (which, it is thought, ran from 900BC until they were banned by the Roman Emperor Theodosius in 393AD and featured foot races, wrestling matches and other sporting contests). Two Germans, Johann Guts Muths and Ernst Curtius – 50 years apart – had even suggested the same thing. And, in Britain, the Much Wenlock Games, started in 1852 in Shropshire, were a rural replica of the Ancient model whilst Pan-Hellenic Games in Greece had begun in 1859 and were very popular. De Coubertin was further inspired by the role of sport in the English "Public" (really "private") school system as well as German archaeological digs at Olympia in Greece – site of the Ancient Games.

Yet de Coubertin did not, initially, enjoy a particularly welcoming audience for his concept especially in his homeland of the time. He first launched the idea of the Games in 1892 during the closing ceremony of a Congress in France, but he met confusion and a lack of understanding. So he re-doubled his efforts by travelling, writing and organizing meetings.

In 1894, at another Congress, brought together under the guise of an attempt to ratify the rules on amateurism in sport, de Coubertin re-introduced his Olympic revival idea. 2,000 people seated in the "Grande Amphitheatre" at the Sorbonne in Paris had just listened to the "Hyme d'Apollon" and were carried away on a tide of Hellenism. The Congress, with the unanimous support of the 79 delegates and 12 countries present agreed to re-establish the Games, choosing to hold them in Athens in 1896. Other countries soon endorsed the idea.

The Olympic revival had begun. The conference ended on June 23, incidentally on the same day that the French President was assassinated, and toasts were drunk to the new Olympic Movement. The worldwide "Olympic Family" still celebrates Olympic day on June 23 each year to mark the founding conference. And the current IOC's centenary celebrations have spanned the 1994-'96 period to incorporate both the conference and the first Games in 1896.

The Early Years

De Coubertin's struggles were not over, however. There were worries about the financing of those first Games. Crown Prince Constantine of Greece set up a fund-raising committee but an enormous debt of gratitude is owed to George Averoff, the Greek benefactor who paid for the re-building of the stadium in Athens. Winners at those first Games were given silver medals and second-placed athletes bronze medals. There were no awards for third place.

In the meantime, de Coubertin wanted to set an organizational structure for the newly-formed International Olympic Committee. He wanted a group of people who could define general policy and be the guardians of the concept. This group had to be the sovereign power over the Games – one which would be independent and international.

De Coubertin chose the first Committee himself comprising 15 men from 12 nations. Its members were ambassadors from the IOC to their countries and not the reverse. They were selected for their knowledge of sport and their national standing. And the IOC's rules and regulations were based heavily on those for Henley Royal Regatta – a famous rowing event in Great Britain. From these beginnings the IOC has grown to its current membership of 96 from over 80 countries.

De Coubertin always envisaged the IOC as part of an overall movement and encouraged the development of National Olympic Committees and International Federations. These were to be the three pillars working together for world sport and they would meet regularly at the Olympic Congress which took place between 1894 and 1930 before disappearing until 1973 because there were fears that other organizations were encroaching on the IOC's territory.

Early debates at the Olympic Congress revolved around the participation of women at the Games as well as other important issues. The 1906 Olympic Congress first debated the advent of a Cultural Olympiad – a festival of the Arts to run alongside the Games – which was eventually first introduced in 1912. There will be a Cultural Olympiad in Atlanta in 1996.

Meanwhile, the success of the first Games back in 1896 prompted the Greeks to press to stage every subsequent celebration, giving the Games a permanent home – an idea which was revived in the 1980s due to the enormous costs of organization. It was rejected on both occasions as against the principles of universality.

The 1900 Games went to Paris whilst the 1904 Games were staged in St Louis, USA, moves which almost had the fledgling festival floundering before it had really begun. Both Games were linked to international expositions or fairs and were characterized by unsatisfactory organization and officialdom. In 1906 an unofficial "intercalated" Games took place in Greece. They were popular and helped restore the Movement. Two years later, London staged the Games at short notice after the withdrawal of Rome but there were again political disputes and accusations of home bias. So, it was not until Stockholm in 1912 that the Olympic Games registered another successful chapter in its unfolding story. From then onwards, the history of the Games has been inextricably linked with world

forces as outlined in the article by Iain Macleod elsewhere in this book (see page 23).

The original rules of the IOC stated that the registered office should be moved every four years. De Coubertin had done much of the administration from his Paris home. But World War I, which prevented the staging of the 1916 Games in Berlin, brought a change. De Coubertin enlisted in the army and handed over the IOC Presidency to a Swiss, Baron Godefroy de Blonay.

This, combined with de Coubertin's desire to house the IOC in a neutral country, prompted the move to the Swiss city of Lausanne with the IOC taking up its headquarters in a manor called "Mon Repos" in 1922. A year earlier de Coubertin had set up the IOC's first Executive Board.

In 1968 the IOC moved to the Chateau de Vidy on the shore of Lake Geneva in Lausanne, where it remains today apart from the innovative multi-million dollar Olympic Museum which was inaugurated in 1993, fittingly, on June 23. It is based further along the lake at Ouchy in Lausanne and makes the most of current technology to depict the Games. The Museum also incor-porates archival material which has been collected over the last 100 years.

There have been seven presidents of the IOC since its formation – not including De Blonay whose position was temporary (see table). The early rules of the IOC stipulated that the President should come from the nation next hosting the Games. It was natural, therefore, that de Coubertin, until then General Secretary, should take on the role in 1896 as Paris would host the 1900 Games. He remained in office until 1925

The IOC Presidents

1894 – 96	Demetrius Vikelas (Greece)
1896 – 1925	Baron Pierre de Coubertin (France)
1925 – 42	Count Henri de Baillet-Latour (Belgium)
1946 – 52	J Sigfrid Edstrom (Sweden)
1952 – 72	Avery Brundage (USA)
1972 – 80	The Lord Killanin (Ireland)
1980 – to date	The Marques de Samaranch (Spain)

by general acclaim and then became honorary president until his death in 1937.

The Symbolism

Viewers and spectators of the opening ceremony of the 1996 Olympic Games will witness the ceremonial raising of the Olympic flag, the lighting of the Olympic flame with an Olympic torch at the end of its long relay, as well as the athletes and officials reciting an oath and the Olympic hymn will be sung. A giant scoreboard will carry the words of the Olympic motto and quotation. After each event at the Centennial Games, there will be a medal ceremony for the first three-placed athletes who will receive gold, silver and bronze medals. And at the closing ceremony the Olympic flag will be passed on to the next host city and a general invitation will be issued for participation in the year 2000.

These ceremonial trappings and rituals are the culmination of a century of development for the Olympic Movement.

The Olympic flag consists of five interlaced rings of blue, yellow, black, green and red on a white background. De Coubertin found this emblem at Delphi in 1913. The five rings symbolize the five parts (or continents) of the world and the colours are found in the flags of every nation represented. The flag flew for the first time at a Games in Antwerp in 1920. It was made of embroidered satin and was presented by the Belgian Olympic Committee, flying at every subsequent Games until 1988 when it was replaced by a replica made in Korean silk.

The Olympic flame was a sacred flame lit during the Ancient Games in Olympia at the altar of Zeus. In 1928, in Amsterdam, a flame was lit in the main stadium for the first time in the modern Games. But it was not until 1936 in Berlin that this was ignited from the sun's rays at Olympia and travelled to the host city by means of a torch relay – traditions which remain today.

The Olympic motto – Citius, Altius, Fortius (Swifter, Higher, Stronger) – which was subsequently adopted by the IOC first appeared at the 1920 Games. It came from a Domincan monk, Father Henri Didon, who had a great influence over De Coubertin.

There is a secondary quotation which has almost become a motto, too.

"The most important thing in the Olympic Games is not to win but to take part, just as the most important thing in life is not the triumph but the struggle. The essential thing is not to have conquered but to have fought well".

Part of these words were first said by Bishop Ethelbert Talbot of Pennsylvania in his address at an Olympic Service in St Paul's Cathedral, London, on 19 July 1908.

The Olympic hymn which is played so stirringly at each opening and closing ceremony was composed in 1896 by the Greek Spyros Samaras to words by his colleague Costis Palamas. In the 1950s there were calls for a change but they were unsuccessful.

The Olympic oath was first taken by competitors in 1920. The chosen athletes are always from the host country. The competitors vow:

"In the name of all the competitors, I promise that we shall take part in these Olympic Games, respecting and abiding by the rules which govern them in the true spirit of sportsmanship, for the glory of sport and the honour of our teams".

That of the judges is worded:

"In the name of all the judges and officials, I promise that we shall officiate in these Olympic Games with complete impartiality, respecting and abiding by the rules which govern them in the true spirit of sportsmanship".

At the end of each closing ceremony, the Olympic flag is passed between the mayors of the out-going and in-coming Olympic cities and the IOC President "calls on the youth of the world to come together in four years time" in the next Olympic city to participate in the Games of the next Olympiad.

Pigeons or doves were first released at the opening ceremony of 1896 to symbolize peace. They were re-introduced in 1920 and have been a part of the ceremonial ever since. Olympic mascots became popular from 1972 onwards. These have often been animals and Munich began the trend with "Waldi" a dachshund. The mascot for 1996 will be "Izzy", a children's cartoon character.

Olympic winners are awarded a silver-gilt or "gold" medal. This is made of silver, as is the second place medal, but the "gold" medal is heavily gilded and contains at least six grams of pure gold. There is no standard design for the medals, which first included a ribbon or chain in 1960.

Olympic Superlatives

Most golds (men)
10   Ray Ewry (USA), 1900-08, *athletics*

Most golds (women)
9   Larissa Latynina (URS), 1956 – 64, *gymnastics*

Most golds in one Games
7   Mark Spitz (USA) 1972, *swimming*

Most medals
18   Larissa Latynina (URS) 1956 – 64, *gymnastics*

Olympic "Firsts"

The first Olympic Games to be televised were in Berlin in 1936, on a closed circuit throughout the city's cinemas. 80,000 television sets in a 50 mile radius from London carried black-and-white pictures of the 1948 Games. Films of Helsinki (1952) and Melbourne (1956) were flown to countries for TV transmission. The first live transmission came in 1960 in Rome. And the 1964 Tokyo Games were transmitted by satellite with the first live colour pictures from Mexico in 1968. The advent of television meant that competitors in athletics wore their lane numbers on their sides for the first time.

Electric time-keeping and photo-finish equipment were first used officially to decide results in Tokyo in 1964. But they had been used in rudimentary forms at several Games beforehand.

Dope testing at the Games is controlled by the IOC's Medical Commission which was formed in 1967. Testing at the Games came first in the Olympic Winter Games of Grenoble and has taken place at every subsequent Games. Early tests were mainly for amphetamines. The first tests for anabolic steroids came in 1976 in Montreal.

Since 1968, too, female competitors have been required to take "sex" tests to make sure that they were not "males" and therefore deemed to have an unfair advantage. Much debate about the methods and validity of these tests has since followed.

And Next?

Atlanta, Georgia, stages the Olympic Games of 1996 marking the Centenary. It has been a century of tremendous progress as well as of turmoil but one from which the Games and the IOC have emerged bigger and stronger. Firm stewardship is now essential to the continuing well-being of de Coubertin's brainchild.

Nagano, in Japan, will be the home of the 1998 Olympic Winter Games. The Australian city of Sydney has been selected to host the Games of the XXVII Olympiad in the year 2000. Salt Lake City, USA, will be the venue for the 2002 Olympic Winter Games. The process for the selection of the host city of the XXVIII Olympiad in the year 2004 is also underway. Such is the vibrancy of a Movement which rose from the dreams of one man to touch millions in our modern world.

Those Magical Olympic Moments

by Neil Wilson

PEOPLE'S fondest memory of an Olympic Games is a useful guide to their generation. First impressions invariably stay longest, whether it is from the Olympics first attended or watched on television.

It might be a little thing. Mine is the awfulness of Jim Ryun's fall in the heats of the 1,500m at the Munich Games of 1972, the elimination of a great world record holder when at the peak of his powers. Or it might have little to do with sport, like the dazzling smile of gymnast Olga Korbut who in the same Munich Games became the first international personality created out of an Olympic Games by the power of television.

However, there are events in the 100 years of the modern Olympic Movement so critical to the history of sport that they cross all generations and live forever in the popular memory. How many old enough to remember would not choose Bob Beamon's long jump in Mexico City in 1968 as a defining Olympic moment? Or Nadia Comăneci's gymnastic performance in 1976 and the USA's "Dream Team" winning the basketball in 1992?

Baron Pierre de Coubertin, the founder of the Modern Games, chose Citius, Altius, Fortius (Swifter, Higher, Stronger) as the Olympic motto but he could have included as well "Momen-

tous". More than anything, it is those moments that leave the Games of any Olympiad more significant in our minds than other sporting events.

Take Beamon's world record jump. It is not the world record today but it is the record the world remembers. So shattering was it at the time that nothing in that event which follows, not even the first 9m jump, will ever supplant it.

Bob Beamon

In simple terms, Beamon's feat was to jump 8.90m (29ft 2.5in.), which was 55cm or 21.75 in. further than the existing world record. That, in itself, defied

8

credibility but it was the elements surrounding the achievement that lifted it into the realms of fantasy. Beamon won his place in the United States team with a jump of 8.39m (27ft 6.5in.), the longest jump ever recorded but invalid as a record because of the excessive wind assistance. What could he do, people conjectured, in Mexico City where the high altitude meant there was less gravitational pull? Could he, perhaps, become the first to jump more than 28ft?

A 1.96m (6ft 5in) New Yorker who had run 100yds in 9.5 seconds, he had legs so long and slim that they would have graced a stork. But he was wildly inconsistent. "Don't get Bob mad," said the 1960 Olympic champion Ralph Boston jokingly. "He's likely to jump clear out of the pit."

As it was Beamon made himself mad by qualifying for the final with his final attempt after two fouls, and he vowed that in the final he would get it right first time. That way the youngest of the finalists could pressurize the many more experienced, like defending champion, Britain's Lynn Davies, as well as Boston and the Soviet Union's joint world record holder Igor Ter-Ovanesian.

Beamon succeeded beyond his wildest dreams. On a grey, overcast afternoon, three of the minor figures in the final began the competition with fouls. Then came Beamon. He jogged for nearly 30 seconds at the end of the runway, and then began his run into the history books. "There was none of the explosiveness of Davies or Ter-Ovanesian in his take-off," recorded the official British Olympic Association Report. "He appeared simply to stride on into the air."

He managed a one-and-a-half-stride hitchkick in the air, seemingly propelling himself up again in mid-flight, before reaching out for the sand. His momentum carried him in a series of bizarre hops out of the pit. Boston had been right. Beamon had landed beyond the modern measuring device's electronic eye. A steel measure was called for, and Beamon crouched, watching the judges intently.

Suddenly he leaped in the air, arms raised, before kissing the ground. "Gentlemen, I believe we have just witnessed the first 28ft long jump," one athletic correspondent announced in the press box.

He was wrong. In fact, they had witnessed the first 29ft jump. The first 28ft jump was not to happen for another 12 years until the Olympic Games in Moscow. Beamon had ended an Olympic competition in an instant. Rain began to fall almost immediately, and the others lost interest. Beamon himself jumped only once more, a more human 8.04m.

"What happened in Mexico was like a dream, a fantastic dream," he was to say later, and it was a dream that was never to recur for him. He never again jumped even 27 ft, and retired to an administrative post with Dade County in Florida in the mid-'70s. It was to be 23 years before another man, Mike Powell, surpassed his record.

The gymnastic gyrations of Comăneci in Montreal in 1976 had an effect of similar proportion. Never in the history of her sport had any person scored an impeccable "10" in an Olympic Games. This 14 year old Romanian did it not once but on six more occasions. The world's television, alerted by the popularity of Korbut four years earlier, watched in awe as Comăneci achieved

9

Nadia Comăneci

unprecedented perfection, dropping only 0.25 points in the four pieces of apparatus in the Combined Exercises and stimulating a Soviet, Nelli Kim, to achieve two maximum scores herself.

But it is track and field, the sport which was the foundation of the Ancient Olympic Games, that has produced most famous moments. Indeed, Beamon's feat was not alone within Mexico City's Estadio Olimpico even among the jumping events, although the other was not a world record but the introduction of a technique for high jumping that has since replaced all others – the "Fosbury Flop".

High jumpers before 1968 used a variety of techniques for getting over the bar. There was the Eastern cut-off, the Western roll and the belly-roll, also called the straddle. All produced world records in their time but by the '60s the straddle was favoured because it had achieved six world records for the Russian Valeri Brumel.

Fosbury used the Western roll but,

managing only 1.78m, he devised a method of running at the bar from the front, turning at the last moment and taking off from his right leg, the one further from the bar. By twisting in the air as he went over the bar he had his back to it, head first. He named it the 'back float'.

He first achieved 7ft with it early in the year of the Olympic Games but, so new was it, that in the final in Mexico the 12 against him were all using the smoother, apparently more sophisticated straddle. Two of them achieved 2.20m, then American Ed Caruthers alone matched Fosbury at 2.22m. Fosbury assured himself the gold medal at 2.24m but failed in three attempts at the world record height of 2.29m. He was never to break the world record with the technique but in 1973 another American Dwight Stones did and since 1980 the technique that Fosbury created has been responsible for all world records.

One Olympic event which has produced more of its share of memorable occasions is the marathon. The first set the scene, the Greek Spiridon Louïs, a former shepherd who had become a post office messenger, becoming an appropriate inaugural Olympic hero of the modern age when he won an event created to commemorate the mythical feat of a messenger who delivered news of a Greek victory over the Persians in 490BC over what may have been the same route. A lifetime's free supply of clothes, wine, chocolate, bread, shaves and haircuts, as well as cattle, sheep and jewellery, were his reward from a grateful nation but he turned down the hand of a wealthy benefactor's daughter. He was married already with two children!

The marathon produced another classic occasion in 1908 when the Italian Dorando Pietri was disqualified after finishing first for failing to do so under his own power. A well-meaning official had taken his elbow as he staggered on weary legs that refused to obey his mind on the final lap of the White City Stadium. Dorando, a pastrycook from Capri, would have won at previous Games but, at the request of Princess Mary, the race had been extended from 25 miles to start under the windows of the Royal nursery at Windsor Castle, adding 1 mile 385 yds to the distance, an arbitrary distance which 16 years later was accepted as the standard marathon length.

The athletic stadium has been the stage for a host more legendary moments in the Olympic Games' first century. In 1924 the Scot Eric Liddell, who was to become a missionary in China, won the 400m and a bronze in the 200m after refusing to run 100m because the race was on a Sunday.

In 1936 Jesse Owens equalled or lowered 12 Olympic records on his way to gold medals in the 100m, 200m, long jump and sprint relay and only a wind reading fractionally above the permissible limit robbed him of a world 100m record. The exploits of Paavo Nurmi and Emil Zátopek are also legendary and covered elsewhere in this book. So, too, are those of barefoot Ethiopian Abebe Bikila.

In 1972 the Finn Lasse Viren won the 10,000m in a world record time and, after falling, went on to win the 5000m and then did the same double at the 1976 Games. Then in 1984 there was the infamous Decker-Budd clash at the 1984 Games in Los Angeles when the American favourite Mary Decker, a double winner at the 1983 world champion-

ship, fell during the 3000m after running into the 18 year old South African-born Briton Zola Budd, who had stirred controversy in anti-Apartheid circles by her nationality switch prior to the Games.

And who, old enough, will ever forget the classic confrontation in Moscow between the greatest of all British milers, Steve Ovett and Sebastian Coe, where Ovett won the gold at 800m, Coe's world record distance, and Coe responded by winning the gold at 1,500m, where Ovett believed himself supreme.

Other sports have had their legendary occasions. Australian swimmer John Devitt has gone down in Olympic history as the 1960 champion and record breaker at 100m freestyle but contemporary evidence suggested gold should have been awarded to American Lance Larson. A slow-motion television film showed Larson touched first. So did the three electrically-started but manually-stopped timing machines which all put Larson quicker than Devitt. And two of three officials judging second places went for Devitt. Sadly, for the American, two of the three officials judging first place also went for the Australian and the casting vote of a chief judge not seated on the judging rostrum conferred the gold on Devitt.

The greatest of all swimming feats was the seven golds won by Mark Spitz, an American, at the 1972 Games, an Olympic record still. He won the 100m and 200m freestyle, the 100m and 200m butterfly and three sprint relays, and each time he finished it was in a world record time.

At the same Games, an Australian 16-year-old, Shane Gould, the great-great-granddaughter of a man called Fish, won three golds, a silver and a bronze. American rivals devised T-shirts emblazoned with the slogan "All that Glitters is not Gould" but it very nearly was.

Basketball's most famous team was the United States squad in 1992 popularly called the "Dream Team", its players all drawn from the professional National Basketball Association. It won every game by an outrageous margin. The sport's most momentous game, however, was in 1972 when the US, unbeaten in 62 Olympic Games and winners of all six gold medals, finally lost to the Soviet Union. In a dramatic incident, the Americans thought they had won 50-49 with one second remaining. But, an official insisted on an extra period of three seconds. The Soviets scored and won 51-50. America refused to collect their silver medals.

Every sport has its special moment. Japan still smarts from its defeat at home when its own sport of judo was introduced for the first time at the 1964 Olympic Games in Tokyo – and Anton Geesink, a 6ft 6in Dutchman weighing

Anton Geesink

127kg (20st), beat them in the Open category.

Some incidents even characterize the spirit of the Games, like the action of Frenchman Leon Flameng at the first Games who, when the cycle of the only other competitor in the 100km track race, a Greek, broke down waited until it was replaced before continuing towards his victory.

Others are remembered for the courage of the participants. Captain Richard Fanshawe, of Britain, was thrown by his horse when it bolted during the cross country stage of the Three-Day Event and broke his arm. Fanshawe chased the horse, re-mounted and in spite of finishing next to last with 8754.2 penalty points completed Britain's scoring team to win the bronze medals.

Another such hero was American diver Greg Louganis at the 1988 Games. He hit his head on the board in the preliminaries of the springboard but returned with it stitched not only to win that gold medal but the platform event as well.

And has there ever been a more memorable occasion in Olympic boxing than in 1924 when the Briton Harry Mallin, unbeaten in more than 200 bouts, was adjudged to have lost on points in a quarter-final to Frenchman Roger Brousse? A Swedish member of the International Olympic Committee seated at ringside saw Brousse bite Mallin on the chest. He summoned Mallin to an examination and when marks were found disqualified the Frenchman. Mallin went on to retain the Olympic title he won in 1920.

The Olympic Games is full of such moments and such memories. They make the Games so special.

Sporting Legends

Jesse Owens
USA – Athletics

Never mind that he was the greatest athlete of his age and, perhaps, of any other age. Never mind that he was such a genius that it is difficult to assess whether setting six world records in the space of 45 minutes one afternoon at Ann Arbor, Michigan, actually stands as a greater achievement than his four gold medals at the 1936 Berlin Games the following year.

No, even beyond that, the Olympic Movement will always hold up Jesse Owens as the symbol of how the Games should stand above politics, propaganda and prejudice. The story of how this black cotton picker's son visited a nation steadily being brainwashed by Nazi doctrines about negroes being a sub-human race, yet still won the adulation of ordinary Germans, could not be more inspiring.

Owens took the 100m, 200m, long jump and sprint relay golds. He made it look as easy and inevitable, according to one rival, as "water flowing downhill". And he was feted so widely that Berliners even invaded the Olympic village at night to seek his autograph. Hitler, by all accounts, was less delighted, even if the suggestion that he deliberately snubbed Owens was an American myth.

Then, there was Owens' long jump victory over Luz Long – a fair, blue-eyed German who could have passed for a model of supposed Aryan supremacy. Yet Owens struck up an unexpected friendship with him. Long encouraged Owens even when he was in danger of going out in the qualifying round after two fouls and was the first to congratulate him after his win.

"You can melt down all my medals and cups and they would be a plating on the 24-carat friendship I felt for Luz Long at that moment," Owens recalled later. In his own way, then, Long proved as great an Olympian as the man who was to become the most celebrated of them all.

I. C. □

Fanny Blankers-Koen
The Netherlands – Athletics

As a wide-eyed 18 year-old thrilled just to be attending her first Olympic Games with the Dutch team, Fanny Koen reckoned the highlight of her trip to Berlin was managing to land the autograph of Jesse Owens.

A dozen years later at the 1948 Games in London, it was Mrs Fanny Blankers-Koen, the 30 year old housewife and mother of two, who was the target of every autograph hunter. She produced a startling four-gold salvo which emulated the feat of her hero. More than that, the excitement engendered by her exploits transported the standing of the fledgling women's athletics programme from mere sideshow to the centre of the Olympic stage.

She won the 100m, 200m, 80m hurdles and anchored the sprint relay victory. Not bad for a woman who did not even enter the two events at which she was existing world record holder, the high jump and long jump. Yet, earlier that year, she was being written off in many quarters by experts who felt that, having married her coach Jan Blankers and given birth to two children, she had lost her best years to the war. After all, it was now 13 years since she had launched her career as an 800m runner.

However, spurred on by Jan's calculated taunt that "you are too old, Fanny", she won the 100m by three metres, the 200 by seven, overcame a dreadful start to win the hurdles and stormed from fourth to first on her relay leg. All this was achieved from a training programme so undemanding that we can only wonder what she might have achieved under a hard taskmaster.

As it was, the finest natural talent women's sport had ever witnessed took her to world records in seven individual events between 1938 and 1951. The development of women's athletics owes a considerable debt to the "Flying Dutchwoman".

I. C. □

Paavo Nurmi
Finland – Athletics

Other distance athletes have dominated a single Olympic Games. Only one inhabited a plane so far removed from his rivals that, stopwatch in hand, he was almost able to turn the event into a series of personal time trials. That was Nurmi in Paris 1924, at the apogee of a career which saw him earn more Olympic medals (12, including nine gold), break more world records (22 official and 13 unofficial in distances ranging from 1500m to 20,000m) and

Two days later he breezily won the cross country, in such sweltering conditions that many others ended hospitalised, and then added a fourth gold in the 3,000m team race.

Another 10,000m title followed four years later in Amsterdam, and a marathon gold in Los Angeles in 1932 might have been his had he not been banned on the eve of the Games for a supposed breach of amateur rules. His image remains honoured in bronze outside Helsinki's Olympic Stadium but Nurmi's like may never be witnessed again.

I. C. □

Abebe Bikila
Ethiopia – Athletics

As he padded through the torch-lit Roman night en route to victory in the 1960 Olympic marathon, an unknown, barefoot figure was blazing a trail which would signal the emergence of black Africa as a major global athletics

become perhaps more lauded than any athlete before or since.

The carpenter's son from Turku first demonstrated his exceptional ability when, after a spell in the Finnish army, he won the 10,000m and cross country at the 1920 Antwerp Games. Defeat over 5,000m there, though, convinced this cool, calculating perfectionist that he needed to improve his pace judgement. So he began to run with a stopwatch. By Paris, he was unstoppable.

A few weeks beforehand, Nurmi had simulated the challenge of running the 1500 and 5,000m finals within an hour of each other, setting a world record in each. After winning the Paris 1500m he ignored the crowd's cheers, went to the dressing room and emerged to beat his great domestic foe, Vilho Ritola, in the longer race. In both contests he had thrown his watch onto the grass when ready for the kill.

force. Ethiopia's Abebe Bikila, a member of Emperor Haile Selassie's Imperial Bodyguard, explained he had run shoeless "just to make history". But his new world best of 2hr 15:16.2 guaranteed him that anyway.

The novelty value had disappeared come Tokyo when, shoe-clad this time, he became the first two-time winner. But the astonishment remained. Just six weeks after an appendectomy, he destroyed his opponents by over four minutes, again setting a world best, 2hr 12:11.2. His hat-trick attempt in Mexico was foiled by injury after 10 miles and Bikila's career ended tragically in 1969 as a car accident left him wheelchair-bound. Four years later, at 41, he died from a brain haemorrhage but his place in the Olympic pantheon had long since been assured.

I. C. □

Cassius Clay
(later Muhammad Ali)
USA – Boxing

Though Clay, later to become a world famous sporting figure under his Muslim adopted name of Muhammad Ali, only boxed in the 1960 Olympic Games his gold medal winning route and personality outside the ring made him unforgettable.

Having beaten the tough Australian Tony Madigan in the semi-final of the light heavyweight division in Rome, the 18 year-old from Louisville came up against the vastly experienced Pole Zbigniew Pietrzykowski, a triple European amateur champion, twice at middleweight.

Clay seemed to lose the first round clearly as the Pole used all his skills. But in the second round the smoothly-moving but sometimes "show-boating" young American lashed out damagingly four times with rights to the head. In the final round it was nearly all Clay as his linked combination punches exposed the limitations of the stiff, if often effective, East European style.

The first great controversial act of the new Olympic champion, once he had returned home to a hero's welcome and incitement to turn pro with a group of rich white businessmen called the Louisville Sponsoring Group, was not publicized until much later. Clay famously loved his Olympic medal. He was so proud to have won it for America that he carried it around and slept with it on until, one day, he and a friend, Ronnie King, were stopped from eating in a "whites-only" restaurant.

The duo were chased from the scene by a motorbike gang and Clay threw his medal from the Jefferson County bridge into the Ohio river. As he was to say: "I won a gold medal at the Olympics for the US and when I came home I was still treated like a nigger – there were restaurants I couldn't get served in."

Clay – Ali ("I've given up my slave name" he explained) was to reign as professional heavyweight champion of the world three times – from 1964 to 1967, from 1974 to 1978 and finally 1978 to 1979. He won 57 pro fights out of 61, made and spent millions of dollars and gained hundreds of thousands of admirers for his skill, courage and warmth of personality.

Winner of historic battles against Joe Frazier and George Foreman, he never quite forgot the youthful joys of his brief Olympic experience. Just hours before his final, sad last fight, in which he took a ten rounds beating from Trevor Berbick in Nassau in December

1981, he reminisced with me about how he had "fallen" at the 1960 Olympic Games for the graceful American sprinter, Wilma Rudolph who was to win three gold track medals. "I did my best", recalled "The Greatest", "to chase her round that Rome Olympic Village but that, "Skeeter", as we called her, was far too fast for me...."

N. A. □

Lis Hartel
Denmark – Equestrian

In 1952 the Olympic dressage discipline took on a dramatic new dimension. Formerly the exclusive preserve of commissioned officers from the armed forces, it opened itself to other ranks, civilians and, even more radically (for the sport and the time), women. One of these was Lis Hartel, 31, from Denmark. Eight years before, Hartel had fallen victim to polio whilst pregnant. She went on to give birth to a healthy daughter and started slowly but surely to fight the illness until she could ride her horses again, but remained paralyzed below the knees.

Despite this she was selected to compete, in Helsinki in 1952, and finished a remarkable second. When Swedish winner Henri St. Cyr helped her onto the victory platform, it was one of the most emotional moments in Olympic history. Four years later, in Stockholm, most expert spectators said that Hartel had deserved to win gold but the judges thought otherwise and gave the title to St. Cyr leaving the silver once more for this outstanding woman. This time, the riders collected their medals on their horses rather than from a rostrum.

D. H. □

Yasuhiro Yamashita
Japan – Judo

Yasuhiro Yamashita is unanimously regarded as the greatest judo player of all time. Undefeated throughout his eight years of international competition – from 1977 to 1984 – Yamashita capped his career with the title that he prized the most: Olympic champion.

He was too young to be selected for the 1976 Montreal Games, and Japan boycotted the 1980 Moscow Games. The 1984 Los Angeles Games was to be his moment of glory. Yet, it almost did not happen.

During his second bout, against Artur Schnabel of Germany, Yamashita tore his right calf muscle while attempting one of his favourite techniques, "uchimata" (inner thigh throw). This affected his subsequent matches. He nearly lost his semi-final bout against a lanky Frenchman, Laurent del Colombo. Yamashita eventually relied on groundwork to ensure victory. In the final, he faced the big Egyptian, Mohamed Rashwan, who had earlier won all his matches leading to the final, by "ippon".

Rashwan did not hesitate to attack Yamashita's injured leg. Yamashita, fully expecting this, countered Rashwan with a hand technique, and took him straight to the ground where he secured a tight hold-down to gain victory. And thus, he fulfilled his childhood dream of winning an Olympic gold medal. Yamashita's victory made him a popular national hero in Japan.

After his retirement from competition he went abroad for a year, to England, to learn English. He also took the opportunity to study the various training methods and judo styles of the West. Yamashita left Europe with a good impression, stating that he admired some of the European training techniques. He felt they were very scientific and declared that he would try to implement some of the best elements of those techniques in Japan. And, it is Yasuhiro Yamashita who, as manager of the Japanese national squad, leads his country's judo team to Atlanta.

O. O. Y. □

Vera Čáslavská
Czechoslovakia – Gymnastics

The Slavonic name Vera means 'Faith'. Čáslavská has always lived up to her name, both as a gymnast and as a citizen of her own country. "The most important thing in life – is to believe in yourself", was how she described her personal motto. In the annals of women's gymnastics Olympic history only Vera Čáslavská and her predecessor Larissa Latynina remain as twice all-around champions. Neither of the later heroines, Ludmila Turischeva, nor Nadia Comăneci, could emulate this.

In Mexico, 1968, in winning her second all-around title, Čáslavská set another still unbeaten record for a female gymnast – four gold medals from one and the same Games (all-around, vault, uneven bars, floor). But her absolute achievement remains the 1965 and '67 European championships when she literally swept up all the possible gold medals. Inevitably she was also world champion

Born in Prague, Čáslavská was mischievous and dynamic as a child when she played with her two sisters. She took up ballet at five, then tried figure skating until the great Evan Bosakova discovered her talent. With fire and faith in herself Čáslavská turned out to

be the greatest gymnast of the '60s. Her career tally included 11 Olympic medals (four gold), ten world medals (four gold) and 14 European medals (12 gold). Her name became a legend. In 1967 she was pronounced the world's no. 1 sports figure.

In 1968, though, she showed great courage in fighting for the life of her nation by adding her signature to the famous letter of Czechoslovakian intellectuals against the regime. A risky step, which later caused her many troubles. Now Vera Čáslavská is a leading sports figure in the Czech Republic (President of the National Olympic Committee) and in 1995 she was accepted as an IOC member.

V. M. □

Francis 'Conn' Findlay
USA – Rowing

American Conn Findlay, born in 1930, was a sporting hero of the courteous "old school". Olympic coxed pair champion in 1956 and 1964 and a bronze medallist in 1960 – all with different partners – he combines calm dignified modesty with a gritty tenacity. A huge man, nicknamed "man mountain" dean, and with a passion for ice cream, Findlay was renowned as a hard worker. He initiated the long distance 48km plus (30 miles) work loads and weight training techniques which have become the bedrock of training.

From Palo Alto he coached and rowed at Stanford University, California, and founded the Washington Lake Boat Club, staying in touch with the sport after he retired. He accompanied the American team crews abroad as 1968 team manager and then as a rigger and much-respected mentor.

He turned to sailing in the late '60's, winning a Tempest keelboat class bronze medal with legendary Americas Cup skipper Dennis Conner at the 1976 Olympic Games. An engineer by training, he worked for his coach, boatbuilder Stan Pocock, building and renting boats for him. Later he designed and built sailing and catamaran hulls as well as making small remote-controlled toy boats.

D. T. □

Dawn Fraser
Australia – Swimming

Few would have noticed the young swimmer from an industrial suburb of Sydney who was the youngest of eight children and who made her debut in the Australian championships in 1954. But under the watchful eye of her coach Harry Gallagher, Dawn Fraser produced the model front crawl for decades to come.

It took Gallagher several years to develop her stroke to near-perfection whilst also working hard on her mental approach. This arduous training was rewarded with famous victories in the 100m freestyle at the Melbourne, Rome and Tokyo Olympic Games. Her victory in Tokyo was made even more remarkable by the fact that she had spent six weeks with her neck in plaster as the result of a car accident only seven months earlier.

Fraser broke 39 world records in a celebrated career the most significant moment of which was when she became the first female to break the 'magic minute' for the 100m freestyle. This world record stood for the next 15 years. With eight Olympic medals

under her belt and an unbeaten reign in the 100m freestyle between 1956-1964, Fraser became affectionately known as Australia's flying-fish.

A successful all-round swimmer, Fraser was reputed to swim fast butterfly in training but never really tackled the stroke in a major championships until 1960. When she finally gave it a chance Fraser also set a world record in the 100 yards at this stroke.

Despite becoming the holder of 4 Olympic gold medals, the most ever won by an Australian, Fraser never lost sight of her humble Sydney background. She dedicated her swimming to her inspiration and idol, her older brother Don, who died of leukemia a few days after his 21st birthday. Dawn Fraser was a trail-blazer in women's swimming and remains a living legend.

A. J. □

Johnny Weissmuller
USA – Swimming

Coach Bill Bachrach, a well fed 160kg (350lbs), offered to buy his young protege a free dinner if he broke a world record, an offer which proved costly! Fifty one free dinners and ten years later Johnny Weissmuller accepted a professional contract to model swimming suits and his Olympic eligibility ended.

As an amateur his record was impeccable – five swimming gold medals spanning two Olympic Games, all in Olympic record times and fifty one American national championship titles. In fact during his ten year amateur career he never lost a freestyle or backstroke race. "I got bored," quipped Johnny, "so I swam on my back where I could spend more time looking around!"

When he set the 100 yard freestyle world record at the University of Michigan, in a time of 51 seconds, it stood for 17 years. In recognition of this incredible feat in 1950 he was awarded the title of "The Greatest Swimmer Ever".

Even greater fame came in 1932 when, having been bullied by his friends, he auditioned for the role of Tarzan. This arduous task involved climbing a tree and sprinting past the camera whilst carrying a "would-be" Jane. He beat the 150 applicants to win the starring role – an honour which was to save his life on a golf trip to Cuba with friends. As a group of hostile guerrilla troops surrounded their car threatening the American (imperialists) with pointed rifles, Weissmuller slowly pulled himself to a standing position, beat his chest with his fists and bellowed his famous yell. The guerrillas screamed with delight and escorted the entire entourage to the golf course!

As the first human to break the one minute barrier for the 100m freestyle and as Tarzan of the Apes, Johnny Weissmuller is arguably the most celebrated swimmer of all time.

A. J. □

Mark Spitz
USA – Swimming

Few people remember that Mark Spitz won four Olympic medals in the 1968 Mexico Olympic Games, two gold, one silver and one bronze, but even fewer remember him finishing last in the final of his last race, the 200m butterfly.

He had brashly claimed that he would win six golds in Mexico City and he had four years to reflect on his failure. Having had a personal motto instilled in him by his father: "Swimming isn't everything, winning is" this final race was painful.

So what else could he have wished than winning the first final, the men's 200m butterfly, in a new world record, at the Munich Games four years later? He went on to win every race in which he competed, to become an Olympic legend. Even more amazing, every gold medal was won in a new world record time. With Doc Counsilman, the world famous coach guiding him through his glory, Mark Spitz became (and remains) the most successful Olympic athlete that ever lived.

A. J. □

Greg Louganis
USA – Swimming (Diving)

One steamy Korean evening in September, 1988, Greg Louganis won one of the most dramatic Olympic diving contests in the history of the sport. The final margin of victory was a tidy twenty six points but Louganis was far from comfortable.

In the ninth round of qualifying the previous evening, the 45 times American champion took off from the 3m springboard and executed two perfect reverse somersaults. Then in laying out from the pike position Louganis crashed his head against the end of the board. After five emergency stitches and a very restless night, Louganis perfectly performed ten new dives in the Olympic final – including the pike.

He added a second gold to his tally in the platform event by beating the 14 year old Xiong Ni, to become the first man to sweep both 3m and platform gold medals in two consecutive Olympic Games. As double world and Olympic champion, Greg Louganis announced his retirement from the sport on October 2, 1988.

A. J. □

Helen Wills-Moody
USA – Tennis

Suzanne Lenglen's successor as ruler of Wimbledon, Wills-Moody was a relentless baseliner who dominated the tennis world after the French girl had turned professional. Born in Berkeley, California, in 1905, she won Wimbledon eight times (1927 to '30 and 1932, '33, '35 and '38) in nine attempts, losing only in the final to Britain's Kitty McKane in her debut year of 1924 after leading 4-1 in the final set.

Wills-Moody also won the US championships seven times and the French championships four times. She was a sound doubles player, winning Wimbledon three times, the French championships twice and the US title four times, with a variety of partners.

She was also the last woman to win an Olympic gold medal, in Paris in 1924, before tennis was left out of the Games for 64 years. She not only won the singles in Paris but also the women's doubles with Hazel Wightman.

J. O. □

Paul Elvström
Denmark – Sailing

32 years old and already a legend in his own lifetime. Nothing special if you are a swimmer or a gymnast where Olympic talent ripens at a young age. But nothing short of remarkable in the more seasoned sport of yachting.

That was the situation for Danish sailor Paul Elvström in 1960. Having won his fourth consecutive gold medal in the single handed Olympic class (the Finn) in the bay of Naples, he had created a record that will be hard to surpass.

Elvström was 20 when he took part in his first international competition, the Olympic Games of London in 1948. Prior to arriving he had only seen a picture of the newly designed Firefly dinghy, but with a little bit of luck, a lot of hard training and even more talent he managed to win in spite of the fact that he decided to abandon the first race out of youthful shyness.

Elvström later said that winning that gold medal was the biggest thrill of his life as a sportsman. Four years later, at the 1952 Games in Finland, Elvström was so good that his victory was compared to a 100m runner winning by a margin of 25m. Before the Games Elvström was heavily criticized in the Danish press for saying he would win the gold medal. Humility is a virtue he was told. But the Games proved he had the right to be so forthright and optimistic, and he has never been known to brag.

At the 1956 Olympic Games in Melbourne he managed the amazing feat of winning four of the six races on his way to overall victory.

When Paul Elvström won his fourth gold medal in 1960, he also won three races. He chose not to take part in the last race because he had already won and because he did not feel well, a combination of nerves and unfamiliar food.

Back at the start of his career Elvström felt it was all great fun. He was just like a boy playing with his best toy when he was training and trimming his boat. But the strain grew through the years. When he left for an Olympic Games many Danish people only discussed who would win the silver and bronze medal. So when the Olympic Games took place in Tokyo in 1964 Elvström was named only as the team reserve for all classes. He enjoyed watching as a spectator instead of competing.

Four years later he was back. This time taking part in the Star class keel boat, where he ended up finishing fourth. Elvström came to Mexico to have fun. He suddenly discovered that the mental pressure wasn't there this time.

But it certainly came back four years later in Kiel during the 1972 Games. Elvström had a nervous breakdown while sailing in Soling class. Elvström was pushing himself too hard in that period. Not only on the water but also running a world wide sail-making business. The sailing went extremely well until the Olympic Games, but his sail-making company had lost a lot of money and he spent a lot of time talking to bank managers. Elvström felt deeply provoked by a French opponent and simply went home.

He returned to the Olympic arena in 1984, this time with his youngest daughter Trine. To sail the fastest of the Olympic sailing classes, the Tornado catamaran, Paul needed a partner who did not weigh too much. So he asked his four daughters Pia, Gitte, Stine and Trine if any of them would sail with him. Trine said, "Yes." At first she did it for her father's sake, but later she developed the competitive bug. They won the World Cup in 1984 and managed to finish fourth in the 1984 Games, missing the bronze medal by less than a point. Paul also took part in 1988 in Korea with Stine as a substitute as Trine had, by then, decided to concentrate on having a family.

Elvström was first trained as a bricklayer. Suffering from dyslexia had caused him a lot of problems at school. Reading and writing is something he tries to avoid. He had his own building construction company in the '50s, but later went on to develop his marine business. Now he is involved with many aspects of world sailing and seeing how things can be improved for future generations.

Niels Rasmussen ☐

World Forces and the Olympic Games

by Iain Macleod

Introduction

The Olympic Games have always been subject to political influences, even to the extent that Baron Pierre de Coubertin, the founding father of the modern Olympic Movement, is alleged to have threatened, as an alternative measure, to stage the first Games, in 1896, in Hungary. His motive was de-signed to coerce Greece, the home of the Ancient Games, into making a commitment to host the inaugural event.

Marqués de Samaranch (President 1980–)

One hundred years after the rebirth of the Ancient Games, the centennial celebrations in Atlanta will provide an opportunity for reflection on a century of global turmoil which has sometimes threatened the very existence of the Olympic Games, not least after the massacre of 11 Israeli athletes by Palestinian terrorists at the 1972 Games in Munich. Despite such turmoil the International Olympic Committee (IOC) has not only survived but has flourished so much that its turnover in the period 1992-'96 is almost $3 billion. The recent deals for the television rights to the 2000 Games in Sydney and 2002 Olympic Winter Games in Salt Lake City which yielded $1.25 billion offered further evidence of the remarkable growth of a Movement that has been described as the greatest social phenomenon of the 20th century.

There is also the IOC's role in world events to consider and whether the recently-established links with the United Nations and other leading international agencies truly provide succour to the Movement in cases when the IOC and its Games are indirectly drawn into major issues of international significance.

There were times in the past when these type of diplomatic links, so assiduously courted by IOC president, Juan Antonio Samaranch, would have been of inestimable value to his predecessors. The current President may have his critics but his skilful use of diplomacy, as befitting a former Spanish ambassador to Moscow, has been unparalleled in the history of international sports administration.

23

Early History

The first major global breakdown of the modern era was the outbreak of war in 1914, when the IOC was anticipating the sixth Olympiad in Berlin two years later. Germany's militaristic designs manifested themselves in a carnage in which millions lost their lives and an abysmal failure of international goodwill made the Olympic ideal, as de Coubertin saw it, appear almost obsolete in the venomous climate of the time.

Within the IOC the conflict created its own rift. The British member, Theodore Cook, demanded the expulsion of the German members and, when his proposal was rejected, took the only honourable course for an "English gentleman" – he resigned. With German troops on the outskirts of Paris, de Coubertin's sense of outrage – only 44 years had elapsed since the 'hated Boche' had last occupied Paris – was integrated with his lifetime vision that Olympism, and all it stood for, had to be preserved if there was to be any prospect of a world in which war would be diminished and mankind was at peace.

One other aspect of the conflict also had a lasting, and beneficial, effect on the IOC. The organization found the location that to this day remains its home. De Coubertin decided to make his home in the Swiss city of Lausanne – he died there in 1937 – and because the IOC administration was so small, it was a simple mattter to move that there, too.

The 1916 Games naturally did not take place but when hostilities ceased on November 11, 1918, de Coubertin took up the baton again and the IOC, having awarded the 1920 edition of the Games to Antwerp – as a sympathetic gesture to Belgium, whose invasion by Germany had brought Britain into the war – the IOC was immediately faced with the dilemma of whether Germany should be invited to compete.

In hindsight, with Europe ravaged as never before, it is understandable that Germany, Austria and Hungary were not invited. They had been refused membership of the new League of Nations. But this move also marked the beginning of a long chain of events in which the IOC would be riven by political considerations. The Germans did not appear at the 1924 Games in Paris but returned in 1928 and it was not until 1931 that France and Germany met again in a soccer International.

The German influence on world affairs, however, was not to be dormant for long and, by the mid-1930s, the IOC was facing a monumental crisis as inexorably the rise of Hitler and the Nazi party threatened the 1936 Games in Berlin. It was in 1931 that the IOC awarded the Games to Berlin by postal vote but a year later the IOC should have sensed that trouble was in the offing when a German newspaper suggested that the Games should only be for white athletes. Adolf Hitler came to power in January 1933. In June of that year the IOC president, Count de Baillet-Latour, a Belgian who had helped organize the Antwerp Games, sought and was given the guarantee that Germany would respect the Olympic charter otherwise, it was stated, Germany would have to forego the Games.

Nazi ideology was as diametrically opposed to the Olympic ideal as was possible and as the Germans' persecution of the Jews reached appalling proportions, the problems intensified as the Games drew closer. There was little doubt that Hitler intended to use the Games as a massive exercise intent on propagating Nazi virtues. He tried, but failed in the face of IOC pressure, to get rid of the Games' half-Jewish President Dr Theodore Lewald.

The Jewish question, and whether Jewish athletes would be selected for the German Olympic team, was central to the problem and led to the American Olympic Committee being divided on whether or not to boycott the Games. One of the key figures was Avery Brundage, later to become IOC president and who on this occasion opposed the boycott as worldwide opinion about German assurances that Jews would be part of their team began to increase.

Brundage's view that sport and politics should not mix was a trenchant one at the time and would come back to haunt him in 1972 when, at his last Games as IOC President, and ironically, on German soil, he refused to be browbeaten by the Palestinian terrorists atrocity in Munich and famously pronounced that the Games would go on.

In 1936, Brundage's views were equally belligerent. He was concerned that those who opposed the Nazi regime wanted to use the Games as a political tool. His belief that the Games could, instead, be used to reconcile

nations brought the desired result. America participated, and so, therefore, did the other nations who had contemplated a boycott. And the feats of Jesse Owens – a black American – on the athletics track are now the stuff of legends. But it was ironic that Brundage had clearly failed in his efforts to keep politics out of sport – uneasy bedfellows ever since the Hitler era.

Those 1936 Games, though, were the prelude to the greatest catastrophe to befall mankind: World War II. Yet despite the war clouds, and Japan's invasion of Manchuria in 1931, the IOC, at its Session in Berlin, chose Tokyo as the host in 1940. When Japan invaded China in 1937, the IOC did not consider an alternative. The Australians and British agreed to a boycott and the problem was only resolved when Japan withdrew as host because of the huge expense involved. The IOC then designated Helsinki as host but on September 1, 1939, Germany invaded Poland and for the next six years the Games became an irrelevance.

Count Henri de Baillet-Latour died in 1942 and when the IOC executive board had their first post-war meeting in London in August, 1945, the Swede J. Sigfrid Edstrom had assumed the presidency. Should the Games resume? War-ravaged Europe was ill-suited for the cost of staging the Games, but Edstrom and Brundage believed strongly in their role in the new order.

Not for the first time in Olympic history London came to the rescue. In 1906, Rome withdrew as hosts after the eruption on Mt. Vesuvius killed 2,000 people and London hosted, at short notice, the 1908 Games. In 1948, despite the austerity of the times which meant that food and fuel were still being rationed, the

Avery Brundage
(President
1952–1972)

British capital also staged a memorable event.

But the onset of the Cold War era was to provide the IOC with a succession of new political problems. The newly-formed state of Israel was one, though of greater significance was the post-war division of both Germany and Korea each creating two countries. Additional disputes between China and Taiwan contributed to the substantial problems which awaited Brundage, who assumed the IOC presidency in 1952. This Chicago builder often acted with "despotic firmness" but his actions are often thought to have safeguarded the Olympic Games during his 20 years as president.

The animosity between the different factions in Germany and Korea did not engender an easy solution, any more than did China and Taiwan, particularly as the latter claimed jurisdiction over all Olympic sports in China. The Korean War added to the problems, while the growing strength of the Soviet Union (accepted by the IOC in 1951) and its hostility to the West added political complications to virtually every situation.

The IOC, it should be remembered, was not always as politically astute as it has been in recent years. In the post-war years it was not helped by the collective view of members from Warsaw Pact countries who took their cue from the Soviet Union. The IOC temporarily, and after exhaustive work, resolved the situation by recognizing the East German NOC in 1956 but insisting on a joint German team in Melbourne in 1956. This situation continued until 1968 when East Germany was given full recognition and its own team at the Games.

The Democratic People's Republic of China was formed in 1949 by supporters of Mao Tse Tung but its birth was to give the IOC problems across three IOC presidencies. Early on, the rights of the communist and nationalist governments found Edstrom enacting contradictory decisions. The Chinese Olympic Committee, recognized by the IOC, moved to Taiwan in 1951 along with all supporters of Chiang Kai Shek. But it was Peking, not Taiwan, which sent athletes to the 1952 Games in Helsinki and they were allowed to compete despite their doubtful position.

China was so annoyed at the recognition of Taiwan under the banner of the Chinese Olympic Committee that it subsequently withdrew from the Movement and boycotted all summer Games from then until and including 1976. It competed in the 1980 Winter Games but joined the boycott of Moscow only reappearing at the summer Games in 1984 even though a name-change for Taiwan was negotiated in the interim to Chinese Taipei.

It took the influence of Lord Killanin, president from 1972 to 1980, and who had been a journalist in China during the pre-war years, together with Samaranch to orchestrate in 1979 the

The Lord Killanin
(President
1972–1980)

membership of the People's Republic of China, naturally amid contentious circumstances. Killanin worked wonders during his presidency, particularly as he had inherited the Movement in a volatile political situation and with only $2 million in funds compared with the $45 million in the treasury when he was succeeded by Samaranch in 1980.

The Apartheid policy practised by the white South African government also turned out to be a long-running challenge for the IOC. South Africa's team at the 1960 Games was composed of white athletes only. In 1961 South Africa became a Republic, leaving the British Commonwealth and strengthening its racial laws. Within the IOC the Soviet Union's Constantin Andrianov led an offensive against apartheid. The IOC passed a resolution, under the section of its charter which calls for no discrimination on the grounds of race, in Baden Baden in 1963 calling on South Africa to oppose publicly all racial discrimination in sport.

At Innsbruck, in 1964, the IOC registered that the South African National Olympic Committee had not complied and revoked South Africa's invitation to the 1964 Tokyo Games. Four years later in Mexico, the African states threatened a boycott if South Africa participated with an all-white team, while in Munich another four years later, the proposed participation of Rhodesia, over a familiar issue, led to further threats. The Rhodesians were permitted to participate under condition that they had the same flag and anthem as in 1964. They accepted and their athletes, whites and blacks, arrived in Germany. Still almost 20 countries threatened to boycott if Rhodesia took part until the IOC, in a narrow vote, denied Rhodesia's partici-

pation. Rhodesia was to become Zimbabwe in April 1980 and its NOC was recognized in time for them to go to the Moscow Games.

The 1968 Games in Mexico City, the first to be held at altitude, caused many problems to the athletes but will be chiefly remembered for two issues: the student riots (at a meeting ten days before the Games in the Plaza de las Tres Culturas more than 260 died and 1,200 were injured in clashes between students opposed to the government and the military) and the 'Black Power' demonstrations on the medals podium by some of America's black athletes. The era of using the Games continuously to make political statements had arrived and refused to go away.

There is little doubt that the massacre in Munich in 1972 was the Olympic Movement's darkest hour. In the dead of the night on 5 September members of the Black September organization broke into the building housing the Israeli delegation of 21 athletes and officials in the Olympic Village. One Israeli died raising the alarm, some

Hooded terrorist on balcony of Israeli building, Munich, 1972

escaped but 11 were taken hostage. But all later perished along with five terrorists in a gun battle with German security forces at a military airfield. Terrorists and hostages had been taken there by helicopter to board a waiting plane. But the terrorists, suspecting they were being tricked, opened fire. At 10am that morning a memorial ceremony took place in a packed Olympic stadium. And requests came from all parts of the globe to halt the Games. But IOC President, Brundage, said: "We have only the strength of a great ideal. I am sure that the public would agree that we cannot allow a handful of terrorists to destroy this nucleus of international cooperation and goodwill we have in the Olympic Movement... The Games must go on".

Munich massacre – Olympic flag at half-mast

This was a decision which, with hindsight, may have preserved the future of the Games, even if the circumstances suggested that another course of action might have been taken. The Israeli government undoubtedly concurred. It refused to negotiate with terrorists and felt that the cancellation of the Games would have been construed as victory for the PLO.

But having survived the greatest threat to its being, the IOC was subjected four years later in Montreal to the first of three consecutive boycotts.

Yet a year prior to those Canadian Games, the prospect of a trouble-free occasion seemed promising. By May, 1976, the storm clouds had gathered again with the announcement that the New Zealand Rugby Union, which had cancelled a tour to South Africa in 1973, now planned to visit the Republic.

African demands that the IOC exclude New Zealand were rejected and 30 countries boycotted the Games. It took the astonishing political changes in South Africa more than a decade and a half later, and Samaranch's astute diplomacy, to lead to South Africa's participation in Barcelona in 1992 – the first time they had competed since 1960. By then Samaranch was on intimate terms with the occupant of the top office in both the White House and the Kremlin, together with a strong link with the United Nations.

Even Samaranch, however, had been powerless to prevent the Eastern Bloc boycott of Los Angeles in 1984 (a tit-for-tat measure after the American-inspired boycott of Moscow four years earlier following the Soviet invasion of Afghanistan just before the Christmas of 1979).

Samaranch's finest moment was clearly in his handling of the 1988 Games in Seoul, given that South Korea was still in a quasi-state of war with North Korea. The latter sought another Eastern-Bloc boycott if its demands to stage a number of sports were not met. Over a three-year period Samaranch demonstrated remarkable skills and not only did a boycott not materialize, but by the end of the Games, a number of

IOC President Juan Antonio Samaranch with President Nelson Mandela, May 1992.

countries which had no previous diplomatic links with South Korea had established formal relations for the first time.

It is testimony, therefore, to the remarkable aura of the Olympic Games, and the growing diplomatic global influence exerted by Samaranch since 1980, that the Olympic Movement endured potentially fatal situations to emerge on the eve of the Centennial Games in Atlanta in a situation where the five Olympic rings are probably the most recognizable symbol in the world.

For all the problems the IOC and the Olympic Movement have not only survived, but thrived in a manner which would have been unimaginable a century ago. Whether Coubertin would have approved of the commercialization, thought by purists to have corrupted the Games, is another matter, though it has of necessity guaranteed their future.

It was Phillip Noel-Baker, a British athlete who had competed at the 1912 Olympic Games in Stockholm and who won the Nobel Peace Prize in 1959, who probably offered the best summation of what the Olympic ideal has given to the world, throughout a century of unparalleled external evil. "In the nuclear age, sport is man's best hope", he asserted, sagely. It is no less true now than it was then.

Women and the Olympic Games

by Richard Eaton

HAVING safeguarded the financial basis of the Olympic Games as well as fighting to keep sport free of drugs over the past 100 years, the International Olympic Committee is also increasing its involvement in one of the world's great causes – that of women in sport.

Sexual inequality is frequently not understood or noticed because other great inequalities – economic, social and racial – often overshadow it with greater urgency. However, this type of disadvantage is one of the most important because it is one of the major obstacles to human happiness and progress. It is also one of the greatest opportunities. Working within the parameters of existing cultural and political factors, it provides the Olympic Movement with a chance to influence development and change perceptions.

The impetus to do just that has come, over many years, not only from women themselves but from the IOC leadership, too. President Juan Antonio Samaranch, in the first year of his presidency (1980), encouraged the election of the first two women to membership of the IOC, Pirjo Haggman of Finland and the talented, multi-lingual Flor Isava Fonseca of Venezuela. In 1994, in a speech in Atlanta, he made it clear that the aim is still to make bigger efforts to develop women's sport and the structures and organizations which support it.

Another aim is to encourage promotion of images of sporting women who fire the imagination. It is vital to communicate better the great achievements – physical, mental and emotional – by persons who happen to be female. We need as many heroines as heroes.

Atlanta has an equal opportunity plan as part of its Games' organization (showing 52% of those employed are women and 37% of officials and managers are women). It is important that the media tries to match it by recognizing equal opportunities for women in pictures and stories.

For every single high profile female champion like Jackie Joyner Kersee, an outstanding Olympic heptathlete, there have been a host of male equivalents like Carl Lewis, Ed Moses, Daley Thompson and Linford Christie. For every Dawn Fraser, an Australian swimmer who won multiple Olympic gold, there has been a line of men like Mark Spitz, Greg Louganis, Matt Biondi and Adrian Moorhouse. We need to achieve a better balance than this.

Happily, the number of women competing in Atlanta in 1996 will be a Games record of 4,000. Though this is only 60% of the number of men, the number of opportunities for recognizing and communicating heroines has increased with it.

For the first time in 1996, the world's most popular sport, football, now has a women's event. Eight women's teams will play in five stadia around the south-eastern USA. Here, then, is a fascinating chance to see and communicate women's skills and athleticism. It will be interesting, however, to see which attracts more attention – the women's football tournament or beach volleyball in which women will be permitted to wear bathing suits. Whilst it is usually acceptable and often desirable for women to be appreciated for their beauty, this should not be to the detriment of their host of other qualities – at least not in the Olympic Games.

As we approach the end of a century of Olympic Games, we can already expect the women of the wealthier nations to do well in sport. But perhaps the real heroines are those who achieve success from the smaller, poorer or developing nations. There they often

have to do battle against financial as well as sexual disadvantages. Hence the efforts of Hassiba Boulmerka, Olympic 1500m champion, or of the Ethiopian Derartu Tulu, Olympic 10,000m champion, have special merit. There should be others like them in Atlanta. A likely candidate is Ghada Shouaa of Syria, winner of the world heptathlon title in Gothenburg last year.

Part of the problem for women, though, is historical and social and it would be unrealistic to expect the IOC to be able to overcome these barriers at a sweep. The sheer physicality required in sport has often in the past been perceived as a desirable male, but highly undesirable female, quality. The Ancient Games were an all-male affair to the extent that women were not even permitted to spectate – a sort of sexist festival if you like. It was partly this which caused judge David Kenyon to dismiss the case brought by 82 women who lodged a complaint with a Los Angeles court in 1984 to force the IAAF – and through them the IOC – to include a 5,000m and 10,000m race in the women's athletics programme. (12 years later both have been established.)

It may also have been those Ancient origins – as well as prevailing social mores – which contributed to the discouraging fact that the modern Olympic Games began in 1896 without any women at all. In 1900, twelve of the 1,330 competitors were women and Charlotte Cooper of Britain, wearing a tie and starched collar, became the first female Olympic champion in any sport by winning the women's singles gold medal in tennis.

Women's swimming was introduced in 1912 in Stockholm and the first winner of the 100m was Fanny Durack.

Hassiba Boulmerka

However, her biggest struggle had come before the Games, in convincing the men who ran the sport in Australia that it was really worth the time and money to send her.

Five years later Alice Milliat criticized her compatriot, Baron Pierre de Coubertin, for effectively desiring the exclusion of women from the Olympic Games. She renewed her request to have more women included in 1920, and after being turned down, the women began their own competition a year later. This was later called the "Women's Olympics" but after pressure from males the title was changed to the "Women's World Games". The event took place in 1921 and '22 as well as 1926, '30 and '34.

Women's athletics eventually began at the Olympic Games in 1928 in Amsterdam. However, there were only five events and when, at the next Games in Los Angeles, Mildred "Babe" Dikriksen qualified for all five events, she was only allowed to compete in three of them.

Since these early obstacles the number of women competitors and women stars has gradually increased and the main fight has been to achieve equality of event programmes with the men. Fanny Blankers Koen, the Dutch legend who won gold medals in 1948, would probably have won more but for the intervention of World War II. In the '50s and '60s Lia Manoliu became the first athlete to take part in six Olympic Games and 1960 saw the triumphs of the elegantly powerful Wilma Rudolph who set a world record time of 11 seconds for the 100m. At the same time Tamara Press, whose power expressed itself in a totally different way, was overwhelming all other women in the shot put.

The achievements of Dawn Fraser inspired a film. She overcame the difficulties of having been the youngest of eight children from a working class Sydney suburb to win four gold and four silver medals (including the 100m freestyle at three consecutive Games) in 1956, '60 and '64 as well as being the first woman to swim 100m freestyle in under one minute. She was also fun-loving, getting into trouble in Tokyo for climbing a flag-pole in the Village.

Among the great enchantresses have been the gymnasts. The breathtakingly flexible Nadia Comăneci of Romania won golds in 1976 and '80 as well as being the first to record a "perfect ten" score. She was followed by the diminutive Olga Korbut whose personality talked to the TV audience whilst she won two golds in 1972. It must have been hard for Ludmila Turisheva to understand how, despite her four gold, two silver and three bronze medals, the teenager was more popular than her. Larissa Latynina and Vera Čáslavská

32   *Dawn Fraser*

were also legendary champions in this sport.

Munich, too, was the scene of triumph for Mary Peters of Great Britain in the women's pentathlon. Her athletic determination and congenial personality brought her much acclaim – as has her work since in fostering sport in Northern Ireland. But despite the great names such as Steffi Graf and Kristin Otto and infamous incidents – like Mary Decker-Slaney's fall in Los Angeles, Zola Budd's nationality switch, "Flo-jo's" outfits and nail paint – the outline of the women's profile at the Olympic Games still has room for some sharpening.

For women to achieve that, for women to succeed, and for women to change things more quickly, they need a variety of things to happen including better media coverage. Equally, they need better representation in the corridors and committees of sporting power.

It was in 1973 that the IOC first decided that women could be proposed as members. But it took until 1981, the year that President Samaranch took over, that the first two female members were elected. In 1990 one of those – Flor Isava Fonseca – became the first woman to sit on the IOC Executive Board. This trend is likely to be continued.

Although women are still largely absent from sports leadership (as they are from political leadership) the IOC Secretary General is a woman – Françoise Zweifel of Switzerland. And there are four women presidents and four general secretaries of International Federations. Six women are National Olympic Committee presidents and twelve are general secretaries. As a percentage of, for instance, 197 NOCs, it is not much but it is a foundation on which to build.

The funds allocated to women's sport by governments and various other institutions, whether at school or university level, are often derisory and religion and other ancestral traditions are handicaps in other areas. But the IOC is determined to encourage all clubs, NOCs, national and international federations to promote women's sport and to make it easier for them to reach positions with some technical or administrative responsibility. It is seeking by various methods to accelerate this process.

It must only be a matter of time before women have a bigger say not only in their own destiny but in the way sport sees its destiny. In which case we must hope that the words of the French poet Louis Aragon prove true. He said: "women are the future of political men". Most likely of sporting men, too, and of the Olympic Games.

The Olympic Games and the Media

by Michele Verdier

Two worlds, one benefit and future challenge

According to contemporary accounts, at the first Olympic Games in Athens in 1896, a dozen or so journalists reported on the sports competitions involving 280 competitors from 13 countries. In Atlanta, some 17,000 media representatives will provide live coverage of the Games of the XXVI Olympiad, the Centennial Games. They will use the latest technology to reach every corner of the globe instantly, relating the exploits, joys and disappointments of 10,000 athletes representing a possible 197 countries.

Between these two dates, a century. One hundred years of human history. A century during which the world has experienced profound changes and tremendous technological development. The Olympic Movement and sport, which are phenomena rooted in an evolving society, have accompanied and drawn nourishment from these changes.

In those years the Olympic Games have acquired a status, an aura which goes far beyond the simple domain of sport. The Games have become a social, even sociological event, which more or less reflects the state of the world. "The most important social event of the late 20th century", as the IOC President asserts, affects every layer, every fibre, sensibility and mentality, and all levels of global society.

In that time, too, the world has become a global village thanks to technological developments in the field of information and communications. The media have emerged as the fourth power which goes beyond borders, systems and ideologies, establishing its own code and hierarchy. Its representatives form not just a communication tool but also an industry and a financial power.

The television camera is no longer a ponderous piece of machinery. Thanks to a development called a charged couple device, cameras have been able to dispense with large tubing and can be almost any size. This also means they can be placed almost anywhere, too. These micro-cameras (sometimes called "lipstick" cameras) bring the world's sporting TV audience pictures from the top of the pole vault and high jump bars in athletics and the net in badminton and tennis. Their eye-view is as good as any linesman's in the racket sports. And they can also be placed on remote-control tracking devices along the track and poolside to follow races and bring the viewer as close as possible to the action.

Helicopters circle over the marathon running courses and yachting races with cameras mounted on gyro-stabilized platforms, costing millions of dollars, so that the vibrations of the engine are not passed on to the camera. And in the sport of rowing cameras with compressed air devices to keep the lens free of water drops have been used on the stern of boats to show the strain on the rowers' faces.

In the written media stands of any Olympic stadium journalists send their stories in words down data telephone lines to computers in their offices around the world. Photographers can link their mobile telephones to their digital cameras and send instant images back home. There is now often no need to develop and process film.

It is this prodigious evolution that, during its one hundred-year history, the International Olympic Committee has had to incorporate, codify, channel and optimize. For the IOC, and thus for the Olympic Movement, the media, by their nature, perform two essential functions: recounting the Olympic Games and the activities of the Olympic Movement; providing a source of income for the activities of the Olympic Movement.

For while the Games are the key event of the Movement, there is also an underlying structure composed of the International Olympic Committee itself, the International Sports Federations (IFs), the National Olympic Committees (NOCs) and the Organizing Commit-tees (OCOGs) which have their own activities and are also the object of media attention. It is the media who, when the Olympic Games (Games of the Olympiad and Olympic Winter Games) are celebrated, spread the Olympic message across the five conti-nents and ensure the permanent dis-semination before, during and after the Games, of the Olympic ideals and the universal, irreplaceable values of sport, which include tolerance, excellence, self-surpassment and fair play.

In ensuring some of its finances from the media, the IOC, on behalf of the Olympic Movement, has merely accom-panied the development of a new tech-nology which, over the years, has confirmed itself not only as a means of universal communication, but also as a powerful industry, supported by major financial groups for which sport, and particularly big events such as the Olympic Games, are not just an oppor-tunity for reporting – in the first mean-ing of the word – but material for programmes and programming. It is indeed the chance to acquire the exclu-sive broadcasting rights for a given ter-ritory which gives the Olympic contests their monetary value. They then cease to be just an item of current affairs and are transformed into a "product", in the modern marketing sense of the term.

In this field, the IOC has to harmo-nize factors which at first glance appear contradictory to say the least. It must ensure the freedom and plurality of expression which are indispensable, and hence protect freedom of access to information. Equally, it must respect obligations arising from contractual agreements with broadcasters regard-ing the exclusivity of broadcasting the sports programme of the Olympic Games.

Finally, it must ensure that all forms of the media – written and photo-graphic press, general and specialized press, daily press or magazines, radio broadcasters, television broadcasters, exclusive rights-holders or non rights-holders – enjoy optimum and welcom-ing working and living conditions.

Faced with the growth of the media phenomenon, the IOC has had to organize itself and create corresponding structures, composed of professionals, to respond to the needs of all forms of the media and organize their presence at the Olympic Games.

It has done this, firstly, by drawing up a media code – called the Media Guide – incorporating a list of specifications imposed on an organizing committee, describing, managing and organizing the media coverage of the Olympic Games. Secondly it has set up press and radio/television commissions composed of the world's top experts and professionals to play an advisory and accompanying role for media issues.

They make recommendations and give opinions to the executive bodies of the IOC. The full commissions meet at least once a year. Working groups, subcommissions or ad hoc groups may be set up to study specific areas like accreditation, international agencies or access to information. Reports are submitted to each meeting of the Executive Board by the respective chairmen. An overall report is presented as a record of the previous year's activity to the Session, again by the commission chairmen.

The Media Guide, which forms an integral part of the contract signed by the host city immediately after its election by the IOC Session, lists the whole of the structure to be put in place for the media group. This covers written, photographic, radio and TV media both rights and non-rights holding.

This basic document is revised, improved and expanded after each edition of the Olympic Games (winter and summer) to take into account the latest developments in technology

and above all the impact on the media structure of the juridical and contractual framework of the profession. It organizes, delimits and sets the minimum standards in the areas essential to efficient media operation.

Each journalist working at the Olympic Games is given an accreditation card, permitting them to access various facilities and venues. There are more requests for journalists' places than it would be practical to allow at the Games. So the IOC must issue a quota of accreditations to each nation to distribute.

Even though the number of media covering the summer Games is more than double that for the Winter Games (around 17,000 as opposed to 8,000), and even if there is almost no comparison between the number of sports, athletes and officials for the summer and Winter Games (26 sports, 271 events, 15,000 athletes and officials forecast for Atlanta '96 compared with six sports, 61 events and 1738 athletes and officials recorded in Lillehammer '94), the media file at the Olympic Winter Games is just as complex. Specific factors, in particular the ambient weather conditions, venue configuration, often mountainous terrain with a mixed situation of valley floors and high summits, require the implementation of an infrastructure which is just as complicated and costly, requiring a large number of technicians to work outdoors.

In general, however, the media and the Olympic Games are two worlds, that of sport and Olympism, and that of communication, which during their respective history and development have appreciated the advantages to be gained from one another: two worlds whose future lies in living together and maintaining an indispensable dialogue. For while the Olympic Games and sport in general have an absolute need for the media, the media find in the Olympic and sporting phenomenon an extremely powerful vector among the public in general, and the youth of the world in particular.

The challenges which the IOC will have to meet with the media world at the dawn of the third millennium are not financial, but essentially techno-logical and legal. The IOC will have the difficult but vital task of incorporating the advantages of compact, portable and personalized multi-media while eliminating or limiting its potential aberrations; mastering the "information highways", making use of them to serve the de-velopment of sport and promote the Olympic ideal around the world.

Top Television Ratings in Major Markets

	Albertville 1992	Lillehammer 1994
Australia	10.9	17.3
Canada	11.2	12.8
Germany	17.3	20.4
Great Britain	11.0	45.0
Japan	27.3	38.0
USA	25.0	48.5
	(millions of viewers)	

Lillehammer Host Broadcasting Facts

Broadcasting Staff	1,353
Live Programming Hours	330
Cameras	230
Mobile Production Units	26

National Medals Totals in each Olympic Games

1896 Athens	Gold	Silver	Bronze
USA	11	6	2
GRE	10	19	18
GER	7	5	3
FRA	5	4	2
GBR	3	3	1
HUN	2	1	3
AUT	2	-	3
AUS	2	-	-
DEN	1	2	4
SUI	1	2	-
1900 Paris			
FRA	29	41	32
USA	20	14	19
GBR	17	8	10
BEL	8	7	5
SUI	6	2	1
AUS	4	-	4
GER	3	2	2
DEN	2	3	2
ITA	2	2	-
HUN	1	3	2
NED	1	1	3
CUB	1	1	-
CAN	1	-	1
SWE	1	-	1
AUT	-	3	3
NOR	-	2	3
IND	-	2	-
BOH	-	1	-
ESP	-	1	-
1904 St Louis			
USA	80	86	72
GER	5	4	6
CUB	5	3	3
CAN	4	1	1
HUN	2	1	1
AUT	1	1	1
GRE	1	-	1
SUI	1	-	1
IRL	1	-	-
GBR	-	1	1
1908 London			
GBR	56	50	39
USA	23	12	12
SWE	8	6	11
FRA	5	5	9
GER	3	5	5

	Gold	Silver	Bronze
HUN	3	4	2
CAN	3	3	10
NOR	2	3	3
ITA	2	2	-
BEL	1	5	2
AUS	1	2	2
URS	1	2	-
FIN	1	1	3
SAF	1	1	-
GRE	-	3	1
DEN	-	2	3
BOH	-	-	2
NED	-	-	2
AUT	-	-	1
1912 Stockholm			
SWE	24	24	17
USA	23	19	19
GBR	10	15	16
FIN	9	8	9
FRA	7	4	3
GER	5	13	7
SAF	4	2	-
NOR	4	1	5
CAN	3	2	3
HUN	3	2	3
ITA	3	1	2
AUS	2	2	3
BEL	2	1	3
DEN	1	6	5
GRE	1	-	1
URS	-	2	3
AUT	-	2	2
NED	-	-	3
1920 Antwerp			
USA	41	27	28
SWE	19	20	24
GBR	15	15	13
FIN	15	10	9
BEL	14	11	10
NOR	13	7	8
ITA	13	5	5
FRA	9	19	13
NED	4	2	5
DEN	3	9	1
SAF	3	4	3
CAN	3	3	3
SUI	2	2	7
EST	1	2	-
BRA	1	1	1

	Gold	Silver	Bronze
AUS	-	2	1
JPN	-	2	-
ESP	-	2	-
GRE	-	1	-
LUX	-	1	-
CZE	-	-	2
NZL	-	-	1
1924 Paris			
USA	45	27	27
FIN	14	13	10
FRA	13	15	10
GBR	9	13	12
ITA	9	3	5
SUI	7	8	10
NOR	5	2	3
SWE	4	13	12
NED	4	1	5
AUS	3	1	2
DEN	2	5	2
HUN	2	3	4
YUG	2	-	-
CZE	1	4	5
ARG	1	3	2
EST	1	1	4
SAF	1	1	1
URU	1	-	-
AUT	-	3	1
CAN	-	3	1
POL	-	1	1
HAI	-	-	1
JPN	-	-	1
NZE	-	-	1
POR	-	-	1
ROM	-	-	1

/continued on next page

1928 Amsterdam

	Gold	Silver	Bronze
USA	22	18	16
GER	10	7	14
FIN	8	8	9
SWE	7	6	12
ITA	7	5	7
SUI	7	4	4
FRA	6	10	5
NED	6	9	4
HUN	4	5	-
CAN	4	4	7
GBR	3	10	7
ARG	3	3	1
DEN	3	1	2
CZE	2	5	2
JPN	2	2	1
EST	2	1	2
EGY	2	1	1
AUT	2	-	1
AUS	1	2	1
NOR	1	2	1
POL	1	1	3
YUG	1	1	3
SAF	1	-	2
IND	1	-	-
IRL	1	-	-
NZE	1	-	-
ESP	1	-	-
URU	1	-	-
BEL	-	1	2
CHI	-	1	-
HAI	-	1	-
PHI	-	-	1
POR	-	-	1

1932 Los Angeles

	Gold	Silver	Bronze
USA	41	32	31
ITA	12	12	12
FRA	10	5	4
SWE	9	5	9
JPN	7	7	4
HUN	6	4	5
FIN	5	8	12
GER	4	12	5
GBR	4	7	5
AUS	3	1	1
ARG	3	1	-
CAN	2	5	8
NED	2	5	0
POL	2	1	4
SAF	2	-	3
IRL	2	-	-
CZE	1	2	1
AUT	1	1	3
IND	1	-	-
DEN	-	3	3
MEX	-	2	-
LAT	-	1	-
NZE	-	1	-
SUI	-	1	-
PHI	-	-	3
ESP	-	-	1
URU	-	-	1

1936 Berlin

	Gold	Silver	Bronze
GER	33	26	30
USA	24	20	12
HUN	10	1	5
ITA	8	9	5
FIN	7	6	6
FRA	7	6	6
SWE	6	5	9
NED	6	4	7
JPN •	5	4	7
GBR	4	7	3
AUT	4	6	3
CZE	3	5	-
ARG	2	2	3
EST	2	2	3
EGY	2	1	2
SUI	1	9	5
CAN	1	3	5
NOR	1	3	2
KOR	1	-	1
TUR	1	-	1
IND	1	-	-
NZE	1	-	-
POL	-	3	3
DEN	-	2	3
LAT	-	1	1
ROM	-	1	-
SAF	-	1	-
YUG	-	1	-
MEX	-	-	3
BEL	-	-	2
AUS	-	-	1
PHI	-	-	1
POR	-	-	1

1948 London

	Gold	Silver	Bronze
USA	38	27	19
SWE	16	11	17
FRA	10	6	13
HUN	10	5	12
ITA	8	12	9
FIN	8	7	5
TUR	6	4	2
CZE	6	2	3
SUI	5	10	5
DEN	5	7	8
NED	5	2	9
GBR	3	14	6
ARG	3	3	1
AUS	2	6	5
BEL	2	2	3
EGY	2	2	1
MEX	2	1	2
SAF	2	1	1
NOR	1	3	3
JAM	1	2	-
AUT	1	-	3
IND	1	-	-
PER	1	-	-
YUG	-	2	-
CAN	-	1	2
POR	-	1	1
URU	-	1	1
CUB	-	1	-
ESP	-	1	-
TRI	-	1	-

	Gold	Silver	Bronze
SRL	-	1	-
KOR	-	-	2
PAN	-	-	2
BRA	-	-	1
IRN	-	-	1
POL	-	-	1
PUR	-	-	1

1952 Helsinki

	Gold	Silver	Bronze
USA	40	19	17
URS	22	30	19
HUN	16	10	16
SWE	12	13	10
ITA	8	9	4
CZE	7	3	3
FRA	6	6	6
FIN	6	3	13
AUS	6	2	3
NOR	3	2	-
SUI	2	6	6
SAF	2	4	4
JAM	2	3	-
BEL	2	2	-
DEN	2	1	3
TUR	2	-	1
JPN	1	6	2
GBR	1	2	8
ARG	1	2	2
POL	1	2	1
CAN	1	2	-
YUG	1	2	-
ROM	1	1	2
BRA	1	-	2
NZE	1	-	2
IND	1	-	1
LUX	1	-	-
GER	-	7	17
NED	-	5	-
IRN	-	3	4
CHI	-	2	-
AUT	-	1	1
LEB	-	1	1
IRL	-	1	-
MEX	-	1	-
ESP	-	1	-
KOR	-	-	2
URU	-	-	2
TRI	-	-	2
BUL	-	-	1
EGY	-	-	1
POR	-	-	1
VEN	-	-	1

/continued on next page

NATIONAL MEDALS TOTALS IN EACH OLYMPIC GAMES

1956 Melbourne	Gold	Silver	Bronze
URS	37	29	32
USA	32	25	17
AUS	13	8	14
HUN	9	10	7
ITA	8	8	9
SWE	8	5	6
GBR	6	7	11
GER	5	9	6
ROM	5	3	5
JAP	4	10	5
FRA	4	4	6
TUR	3	2	2
FIN	3	1	11
IRN	2	2	1
CAN	2	1	3
NZE	2	-	-
POL	1	4	4
GER	1	4	2
CZE	1	4	1
BUL	1	3	1
DEN	1	2	1
IRL	1	1	3
NOR	1	-	2
MEX	1	-	1
BRA	1	-	-
IND	1	-	-
YUG	-	3	-
CHI	-	2	2
BEL	-	2	-
ARG	-	1	1
KOR	-	1	1
ICE	-	1	-
PAK	-	1	-
SAF	-	-	4
AUT	-	-	2
BAH	-	-	1
GRE	-	-	1
SUI	-	-	1
URU	-	-	1

1960 Rome	Gold	Silver	Bronze
URS	43	29	31
USA	34	21	16
ITA	13	10	13
GER	10	10	6
AUS	8	8	6
TUR	7	2	-
HUN	6	8	7
JPN	4	7	7
POL	4	6	11
GDR	3	9	7
CZE	3	2	3
ROM	3	1	6
GBR	2	6	12
DEN	2	3	1
NZE	2	-	1
BUL	1	3	3
SWE	1	2	3
FIN	1	1	3
AUT	1	1	-
YUG	1	1	-
PAK	1	-	1
ETH	1	-	-
GRE	1	-	-
NOR	1	-	-

	Gold	Silver	Bronze
SUI	-	3	3
FRA	-	2	3
BEL	-	2	2
IRN	-	1	3
NED	-	1	2
SAF	-	1	2
ARG	-	1	1
UAR	-	1	1
CAN	-	1	-
GHA	-	1	-
IND	-	1	-
MOR	-	1	-
POR	-	1	-
SIN	-	1	-
TAI	-	1	-
BRA	-	-	2
BWI	-	-	2
IRQ	-	-	1
MEX	-	-	1
ESP	-	-	1
VEN	-	-	1

1964 Tokyo	Gold	Silver	Bronze
USA	36	26	28
URS	30	31	25
JPN	16	5	8
ITA	10	10	7
HUN	10	7	5
GER	7	14	14
POL	7	6	10
AUS	6	2	10
CZE	5	6	3
GBR	4	12	2
GDR	3	11	5
BUL	3	5	2
FIN	3	-	2
NZE	3	-	2
ROM	2	4	6
NED	2	4	4
TUR	2	3	1
SWE	2	2	4
DEN	2	1	3
YUG	2	1	2
BEL	2	-	1
FRA	1	8	6
CAN	1	2	1
SUI	1	2	1
BAH	1	-	-
ETH	1	-	-
IND	1	-	-
KOR	-	2	1
TRI	-	1	2
TUN	-	1	1
ARG	-	1	-
CUB	-	1	-
PAK	-	1	-
PHI	-	1	-
IRN	-	-	2
BRA	-	-	1
GHA	-	-	1
IRL	-	-	1
KEN	-	-	1
MEX	-	-	1
NGR	-	-	1
URU	-	-	1

1968 Mexico City	Gold	Silver	Bronze
USA	45	28	34
URS	29	32	30
JPN	11	7	7
HUN	10	10	12
GDR	9	9	7
FRA	7	3	5
CZE	7	2	4
GER	5	11	10
AUS	5	7	5
GBR	5	5	3
POL	5	2	11
ROM	4	6	5
ITA	3	4	9
KEN	3	4	2
MEX	3	3	3
YUG	3	3	2
NED	3	3	1
BUL	2	4	3
IRN	2	1	2
SWE	2	1	1
TUR	2	-	-
DEN	1	4	3
CAN	1	3	1
FIN	1	2	1
ETH	1	1	-
NOR	1	1	-
NZE	1	-	2
TUN	1	-	1
PAK	1	-	-
VEN	1	-	-
CUB	-	4	-
AUT	-	2	2
SUI	-	1	4
MON	-	1	3
BRA	-	1	2
KOR	-	1	1
UGA	-	1	1
CAM	-	1	-
JAM	-	1	-
ARG	-	-	2
GRE	-	-	1
IND	-	-	1
TAI	-	-	1

/continued on next page

1972 Munich	Gold	Silver	Bronze
URS	50	27	22
USA	33	31	30
GDR	20	23	23
GER	13	11	16
JPN	13	8	8
AUS	8	7	2
POL	7	5	9
HUN	6	13	16
BUL	6	10	5
ITA	5	3	10
SWE	4	6	6
GBR	4	5	9
ROM	3	6	7
FIN	3	1	4
CUB	3	1	4
NED	3	1	1
FRA	2	4	7
CZE	2	4	2
KEN	2	3	4
YUG	2	1	2
NOR	2	1	1
PRK	1	1	3
NZE	1	1	1
UGA	1	1	-
DEN	1	-	-
SUI	-	3	-
CAN	-	2	3
IRN	-	2	1
BEL	-	2	-
GRE	-	2	-
AUT	-	1	2
COL	-	1	2
ARG	-	1	-
KOR	-	1	-
LEB	-	1	-
MEX	-	1	-
MON	-	1	-
PAK	-	1	-
TUN	-	1	-
TUR	-	1	-
BRA	-	-	2
ETH	-	-	2
GHA	-	-	1
IND	-	-	1
JAM	-	-	1
NIG	-	-	1
NGR	-	-	1
ESP	-	-	1

1976 Montreal	Gold	Silver	Bronze
URS	49	41	35
GDR	40	25	25
USA	34	35	25
GER	10	12	17
JPN	9	6	10
POL	7	6	13
BUL	6	9	7
CUB	6	4	3
ROM	4	9	14
HUN	4	5	13
FIN	4	2	-
SWE	4	1	-
GBR	3	5	5
ITA	2	7	4
FRA	2	3	4
YUG	2	3	3
CZE	2	2	4
NZE	2	1	1
KOR	1	1	4
SUI	1	1	2
JAM	1	1	-
NOR	1	1	-
PRK	1	1	-
DEN	1	-	2
MEX	1	-	1
TRI	1	-	-
CAN	-	5	6
BEL	-	3	3
NED	-	2	3
POR	-	2	-
ESP	-	2	-
AUS	-	1	4
IRN	-	1	1
MON	-	1	-
VEN	-	1	-
BRA	-	-	2
AUT	-	-	1
BER	-	-	1
PAK	-	-	1
PUR	-	-	1
THA	-	-	1

1980 Moscow	Gold	Silver	Bronze
URS	80	69	46
GDR	47	37	42
BUL	8	16	17
CUB	8	7	5
ITA	8	3	4
HUN	7	10	15
ROM	6	6	13
FRA	6	5	3
GBR	5	7	9
POL	3	14	15
SWE	3	3	6
FIN	3	1	4
CZE	2	3	9
YUG	2	3	4
AUS	2	2	5
DEN	2	1	2
BRA	2	-	2
ETH	2	-	2
SUI	2	-	-
ESP	1	3	2
AUT	1	2	1
GRE	1	-	2
BEL	1	-	-
IND	1	-	-
ZIM	1	-	-
PRK	-	3	2
MON	-	2	2
TAN	-	2	-
MEX	-	1	3
NED	-	1	2
IRL	-	1	1
UGA	-	1	-
VEN	-	1	-
JAM	-	-	3
GUY	-	-	1
LEB	-	-	1

1984 Los Angeles	Gold	Silver	Bronze
URS	83	61	30
ROM	20	16	17
GER	17	19	23
CHN	15	8	9
ITA	14	6	12
CAN	10	18	16
JPN	10	8	14
NZE	8	1	2
YUG	7	4	7
KOR	6	6	7
GBR	5	10	22
FRA	5	7	16
NED	5	2	6
AUS	4	8	12
FIN	4	2	6
SWE	2	11	6
MEX	2	3	1
MOR	2	-	-
BRA	1	5	2
ESP	1	2	2
BEL	1	1	2
AUT	1	1	1
KEN	1	-	2
POR	1	-	2
PAK	1	-	-
SUI	-	4	4
DEN	-	3	3
JAM	-	1	2
NOR	-	1	2
GRE	-	1	1
NGR	-	1	1
PUR	-	1	1
COL	-	1	-
EGY	-	1	-
IRL	-	1	-
IVC	-	1	-
PER	-	1	-
SYR	-	1	-
THA	-	1	-
TUR	-	-	3
VEN	-	-	3
ALG	-	-	2
CAM	-	-	1
DOM	-	-	1
ICE	-	-	1
TAI	-	-	1
ZAM	-	-	1

/continued on next page

	Gold	Silver	Bronze
1988 Seoul			
URS	55	31	46
GER	37	35	30
USA	36	31	27
KOR	12	10	11
GER	11	14	15
HUN	11	6	6
BUL	10	12	13
ROM	7	11	6
FRA	6	4	6
ITA	6	4	4
CHN	5	11	12
GBR	5	10	9
KEN	5	2	2
JPN	4	3	7
AUS	3	6	5
YUG	3	4	5
CZE	3	3	2
NZE	3	2	8
CAN	3	2	5
POL	2	5	9
NOR	2	3	-
NED	2	2	5
DEN	2	1	1
BRA	1	2	3
FIN	1	1	2
ESP	1	1	2
TUR	1	1	-
MOR	1	-	2
AUT	1	-	-
POR	1	-	-
SUR	1	-	-
SWE	-	4	7
SUI	-	2	2
JAM	-	2	-
ARG	-	1	1
CHN	-	1	-
CRC	-	1	-
INA	-	1	-
IRN	-	1	-
NLA	-	1	-

	Gold	Silver	Bronze
PER	-	1	-
SEN	-	1	-
VIR	-	1	-
BEL	-	-	2
MEX	-	-	2
COL	-	-	1
DJI	-	-	1
GRE	-	-	1
MON	-	-	1
PAK	-	-	1
PHI	-	-	1
THA	-	-	1
1992 Barcelona			
EUN	45	38	29
USA	37	34	37
GER	33	21	28
CHN	16	22	16
CUB	14	6	11
ESP	13	7	2
KOR	12	5	12
HUN	11	12	7
FRA	8	5	16
AUS	7	9	11
ITA	6	5	8
CAN	6	5	7
GBR	5	3	12
ROM	4	6	8
CZE	4	2	1
PKR	4	-	5
JPN	3	8	11
BUL	3	7	6
POL	3	6	10
NED	2	6	7
KEN	2	4	2
NOR	2	4	1
TUR	2	2	2
INA	2	2	1
BRA	2	1	-
GRE	2	-	-
SWE	1	7	4

	Gold	Silver	Bronze
NZL	1	4	5
FIN	1	2	2
DEN	1	1	4
MOR	1	1	1
IRL	1	1	-
ETH	1	-	2
ALG	1	-	1
EST	1	-	1
LTU	1	-	1
SUI	1	-	-
JAM	-	3	1
NIG	-	3	1
LAT	-	2	1
SAF	-	2	-
AUT	-	2	-
NAM	-	2	-
BEL	-	1	2
CRO	-	1	2
IRN	-	1	2
IOP*	-	1	2
ISR	-	1	1
MEX	-	1	-
PER	-	1	-
TPE	-	1	-
MON	-	-	2
SLO	-	-	2
ARG	-	-	1
BAH	-	-	1
COL	-	-	1
GHA	-	-	1
MAL	-	-	1
PAK	-	-	1
PHI	-	-	1
PUR	-	-	1
QAT	-	-	1
SUR	-	-	1
THA	-	-	1

* Athletes from Serbia, Montenegro and Macedonia

Table of Past Games and Locations

Year	Venue	Nations	Athletes	Sports	No. of sports
1896	Athens	13	311	Athletics, cycling, fencing, gymnastics, shooting, swimming, tennis, weightlifting, wrestling.	9
1900	Paris	22	1,330	Archery, athletics, cricket, croquet, cycling, equestrian, fencing, football, golf, gymnastics, polo, rowing, rugby, shooting, swimming, tennis, yachting.	17
1904	St. Louis	12	625	Archery, athletics, boxing, fencing, football, golf, gymnastics, lacrosse, roque, rowing, swimming, tennis, weightlifting, wrestling.	14
1906	Athens	20	884	Athletics, cycling, fencing, football, gymnastics, rowing, shooting, swimming, tennis, weightlifting, wrestling.	11
1908	London	23	2,035	Archery, athletics, boxing, cycling, fencing, football, gymnastics, hockey, ice skating, jeu de paume, lacrosse, motorboating, polo, rackets, rowing, rugby, shooting, swimming, tennis, wrestling, yachting.	21
1912	Stockholm	28	2,547	Athletics, cycling, equestrian, fencing, football, gymnastics, modern pentathlon, rowing, shooting, swimming, tennis, wrestling, yachting.	13
1920	Antwerp	29	2,692	Archery, athletics, boxing, cycling, equestrian, fencing, football, gymnastics, hockey, ice hockey, ice skating, modern pentathlon, polo, rowing, rugby, shooting, swimming, tennis, weightlifting, wrestling, yachting.	21
1924	Paris	44	3,092	Athletics, boxing, cycling, equestrian, fencing, football, gymnastics, hockey, modern pentathlon, polo, rowing, rugby, shooting, swimming, tennis, weightlifting, wrestling, yachting.	18
1928	Amsterdam	46	3,014	Athletics, boxing, cycling, equestrian, fencing, football, gymnastics, hockey, modern pentathlon, rowing, swimming, weightlifting, wrestling, yachting.	14
1932	Los Angeles	37	1,408	Athletics, boxing, cycling, equestrian, fencing, gymnastics, hockey, modern pentathlon, rowing, shooting, swimming, weightlifting, wrestling, yachting.	14

/continued on next page

43

Year	Venue	Nations	Athletes	Sports	No. of sports
1936	Berlin	49	4,066	Athletics, basketball, boxing, canoeing, cycling, equestrian, fencing, football, gymnastics, handball, hockey, modern pentathlon, polo, rowing, shooting, swimming, weightlifting, wrestling, yachting.	19
1948	London	59	4,099	Athletics, basketball, boxing, canoeing, cycling, equestrian, fencing, football, gymnastics, hockey, modern pentathlon, rowing, shooting, swimming, weightlifting, wrestling, yachting.	17
1952	Helsinki	69	4,925	Athletics, basketball, boxing, canoeing, cycling, equestrian, fencing, football, gymnastics, hockey, modern pentathlon, rowing, shooting, swimming, weightlifting, wrestling, yachting.	17
1956	Melbourne (equestrian in Stockholm)	72	3,342	Athletics, basketball, boxing, canoeing, cycling, equestrian, fencing, football, gymnastics, hockey, modern pentathlon, rowing, shooting, swimming, weightlifting, wrestling, yachting.	17
1960	Rome	83	5,348	Athletics, basketball, boxing, canoeing, cycling, equestrian, fencing, football, gymnastics, hockey, modern pentathlon, rowing, shooting, swimming, weightlifting, wrestling, yachting.	17
1964	Tokyo	93	5,140	Athletics, basketball, boxing, canoeing, cycling, equestrian, fencing, football, gymnastics, hockey, judo, modern pentathlon, rowing, shooting, swimming, volleyball, weightlifting, wrestling, yachting.	19
1968	Mexico City	112	5,531	Athletics, basketball, boxing, canoeing, cycling, equestrian, fencing, football, gymnastics, hockey, modern pentathlon, rowing, shooting, swimming, volleyball, weightlifting, wrestling, yachting.	18
1972	Munich	122	7,156	Archery, athletics, basketball, boxing, canoeing, cycling, equestrian, fencing, football, gymnastics, handball, hockey, judo, modern pentathlon, rowing, shooting, swimming, volleyball, weightlifting, wrestling, yachting.	21
1976	Montreal	88	6,085	Archery, athletics, basketball, boxing, canoeing, cycling, equestrian, fencing, football, gymnastics, handball, hockey, judo, modern pentathlon, rowing, shooting, swimming, volleyball, weightlifting, wrestling, yachting.	21
1980	Moscow	81	5,326	Archery, athletics, basketball, boxing, canoeing, cycling, equestrian, fencing, football, gymnastics, handball, hockey, judo, modern pentathlon, rowing, shooting, swimming, volleyball, weightlifting, wrestling, yachting.	21

/continued on next page

Year	Venue	Nations	Athletes	Sports	No. of sports
1984	Los Angeles	140	7,078	Archery, athletics, basketball, boxing, canoeing, cycling, equestrian, fencing, football, gymnastics, handball, hockey, judo, modern pentathlon, rowing, shooting, swimming, volleyball, weightlifting, wrestling, yachting.	21
1988	Seoul	159	8,465	Archery, athletics, basketball, boxing, canoeing, cycling, equestrian, fencing, football, gymnastics, handball, hockey, judo, modern pentathlon, rowing, shooting, swimming, table tennis, tennis, volleyball, weightlifting, wrestling, yachting.	23
1992	Barcelona	172	10,563	Archery, athletics, badminton, baseball, basketball, boxing, canoeing, cycling, equestrian, fencing, football, gymnastics, handball, hockey, judo, modern pentathlon, rowing, shooting, swimming, table tennis, tennis, volleyball, weightlifting, wrestling, yachting.	25
1996	Atlanta	196*	10,788	Archery, athletics, badminton, baseball, basketball, boxing, canoeing, cycling, equestrian, fencing, football, gymnastics, handball, hockey, judo, modern pentathlon, rowing, shooting, softball, swimming, table tennis, tennis, volleyball, weightlifting, wrestling, yachting.	26

*Number of current NOCs

All-Time Medals Table
1896 – 1992

Country	Gold	Silver	Bronze	Total	Country	Gold	Silver	Bronze	Total
United States	789	603	518	1910	Trinidad & Tobago	1	2	4	7
Soviet Union	442	361	333	1126	Indonesia	2	3	1	6
Germany *	340	358	362	1060	Latvia		4	2	6
Great Britain	177	224	218	619	Colombia		2	4	6
France	161	175	191	527	Uganda	1	3	1	5
Sweden	133	149	171	453	Tunisia	1	2	2	5
Italy	153	126	131	410	Puerto Rico		1	4	5
Hungary	136	124	144	304	Peru	1	3		4
Finland	98	77	112	287	Algeria	1		3	4
Japan	90	83	93	266	Lebanon		2	2	4
Australia	78	76	98	252	Taipei		2	2	4
Romania	59	70	90	219	Ghana		1	3	4
Poland	43	62	105	210	Thailand		1	3	4
Canada	45	67	80	192	Bahamas	1		2	3
Netherlands	45	52	72	169	Croatia		1	2	3
Switzerland	42	63	58	163	IOP		1	2	3
Bulgaria	38	69	55	162	Luxembourg	1	1		2
Czechoslovakia **	49	50	49	149	Lithuania	1		1	2
Demark	26	51	53	128	Surinam	1		1	2
Belgium	35	47	44	126	Namibia		2		2
Norway	43	37	34	114	Tanzania		2		2
China	36	41	37	114	Cameroon		1	1	2
Greece	24	40	39	103	Haiti		1	1	2
Korea (South)	31	27	41	99	Iceland		1	1	2
Cuba	36	25	23	84	Israel		1	1	2
Yugoslavia	26	29	28	83	Panama			2	2
Austria	19	29	33	81	Slovenia			2	2
New Zealand	27	10	28	65	Zimbabwe	1			1
Turkey	26	15	12	53	Costa Rica		1		1
Argentina	13	19	15	47	Ivory Coast		1		1
Spain	17	19	10	46	Netherlands Antilles		1		1
Mexico	9	13	18	40	Senegal		1		1
Brazil	9	10	21	40	Singapore		1		1
Kenya	13	13	13	39	Sri Lanka		1		1
Iran	4	12	17	33	Syria		1		1
South Africa	16	17	20	32	Virgin Island		1		1
Jamaica	4	13	9	26	Barbados			1	1
Estonia	7	6	10	23	Bermuda			1	1
North Korea ***	6	5	10	21	Djibouti			1	1
Egypt	6	6	6	18	Dominican Republic			1	1
Ireland	5	5	5	15	Guyana			1	1
India	8	3	3	14	Iraq			1	1
Ethiopia	6	1	6	13	Malaysia			1	1
Portugal	2	4	7	13	Niger Republic			1	1
Mongolia		5	8	13	Qatar			1	1
Pakistan	3	3	4	10	Zambia			1	1
Morocco	4	2	3	9					
Uruguay	2	1	6	9					
Venezuela	1	2	5	8					
Chile		6	2	8					
Nigeria		4	4	8					
Philippines		1	7	8					

* Includes medals won by Germany 1896-1964, by GDR and FRG 1968-1988 and by Germany in 1992

** Includes Bohemia. Will be two separate nations in 1996 – The Czech Republic and Slovakia.

*** From 1964

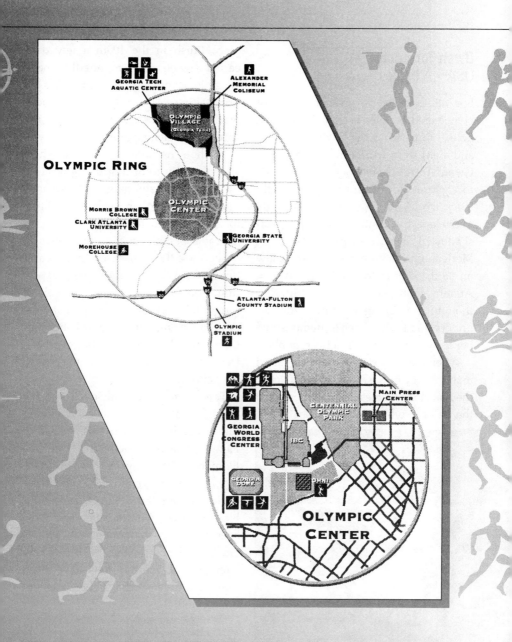

OLYMPIC RING

GEORGIA TECH AQUATIC CENTER

ALEXANDER MEMORIAL COLISEUM

OLYMPIC VILLAGE (GEORGIA TECH)

MORRIS BROWN COLLEGE

CLARK ATLANTA UNIVERSITY

OLYMPIC CENTER

GEORGIA STATE UNIVERSITY

MOREHOUSE COLLEGE

ATLANTA-FULTON COUNTY STADIUM

OLYMPIC STADIUM

MAIN PRESS CENTER

CENTENNIAL OLYMPIC PARK

GEORGIA WORLD CONGRESS CENTER

IBC

GEORGIA DOME

OMNI

OLYMPIC CENTER

Contemporary Heroes and Heroines

Gwen Torrence
USA – Athletics

For all that she is one of the most bemedalled athletes in global track and field – three from the Olympic Games and eight from world championships – Gwen Torrence has somehow failed to capture the imagination of the athletics world. She is always seemingly overtaken by controversy and overshadowed by her ever-popular rival, Merlene Ottey. With the greatest show on earth coming to her home town of Atlanta soon after her 31st birthday, though, the timing is perfect for this undervalued performer to demonstrate her true worth to the American public.

When the subject of Torrence is raised many forget how she won the 200m at the Barcelona Games. Instead they recall the palaver which followed her fourth place finish in the 100m a few days earlier when she reportedly made allegations linking other finalists to drug-taking. At the 1995 Gothenburg world championships, the talk was not so much of her magnificent 100m win as of the sensational 200m final when, after soundly trouncing the opposition by clocking a stunning 21.77 seconds into a headwind, she was disqualified for stepping on the inside line of her lane at least three times around the turn.

She took the setback pretty stoically. But that is what we have come to expect from someone with such a streak of tungsten in her that not even the agony of a hamstring injury stopped her battling through the World Championship trials in Sacramento just to get to Gothenburg.

This time, she intends to make history, not controversy, by joining the select band of six women, from Fanny Blankers-Koen in 1948 to Florence Griffith-Joyner (now threatening a come-back) in 1988, who have achieved the 100m/200m Olympic double at the same Games. Sure, there have been more stylish, more elegant sprinters than Torrence, but, with her raw strength and speed, few have been more effective. Perhaps, her moment has arrived.

I. C. □

Michael Johnson
USA – Athletics

If it were not so awesome, there might be something almost comic about the sight of Michael Johnson at work. Head tilted to the rear, back sergeant-major straight, knees pumping manically and staccato feet creating such a blur that you could convince yourself they were not actually leaving the ground at all. The inimitable Texan might have stepped straight out of a silent movie. For his opponents, though, it has become no laughing matter.

If he was not already out on his own as the most complete sprinter of all time, by the end of 1995 there could be no argument. His unique 200m/400m double in Gothenburg was one of the most extraordinary week's labours the sport has seen. Yet it is a measure of his talent that his 43.39 seconds in the 400m, the second fastest ever, and 19.79 seconds for the half-lap, fifth best of all time, almost provided an anti-climactic feel.

His effort prompted him to suggest he had nothing to prove any more. After all, he holds five world golds, has broken two world indoor records and has not lost a 400m race for six years. He is the only man ever to run a lap in under 43 seconds with his relay anchor leg in Stuttgart in 1993. And, four times, he has achieved the feat of being ranked first at 200m and 400m in the same season. Yet, for all that, his Olympic failure of 1992 when he was defeated by food poisoning and failed to make the 200m final, leaves a critical gap in his curriculum vitae.

It is his dream to make up for it twice over by repeating his Gothenburg double. But an overhaul of the Atlanta track programme would have to be made to accommodate him. A timetable change would be well worth it to see this man on another historic quest.

I. C. □

Noureddine Morceli
Algeria – Athletics

We have come to expect so much from the middle distance wonder who makes the impossible seem possible that it is easy to forget – amid all his extraordinary record-breaking feats and his aura of invincibility – that Noureddine Morceli actually fouled up in his biggest test of all at the Barcelona Olympic Games.

Returning from injury, he ran what even he now ruefully admits was a dismal tactical race to finish seventh in the 1,500m final. "It's just history now," shrugs the man who has not lost a race at the distance since. Yet he clearly has never quite forgotten the humiliation of having to explain this aberration on his return to Algeria.

How he has made up for it, though. Double world champion at 1,500m, holder of world records at 1,500m (3:27.37), mile (3:44.39), 2,000m (4:47.88) and 3,000m (7:25.11). He talks about adding the 5,000m mark – and even, more outlandishly, the 800m and 10,000m records – to his collection with such conviction that there are inevitable echoes of Said Aouita.

Aouita, Morceli's prodigious North African predecessor, was to the '80s what Morceli is to the '90s. "For me, there are no limits," says Morceli. He is the quiet, self-assured figure who always had the more flamboyant Aouita as his inspiration when he pursued his dream as a teenager, slogging up the hills overlooking his little fishing village home of Tenes.

That lad has developed into what has been called the perfect model of mechanical efficiency. He has improbably long legs, abnormally low body fat as well as rare lung capacity, heart efficiency and muscle/weight ratio, plus a remarkable ability to resist injury.

Though he likes to remind us that he is a man, not a machine, his own predictions – ranging from 800m in 1:41.5 to 10,000m in 26:39 – tell of an athlete who inhabits another plane. "In my mind," he says, "I don't believe I have come close to what I can achieve."

I. C. □

Sergei Bubka
Ukraine – Athletics

While the old brigade of superstars appeared to be fading away in Gothenburg, who should buck the trend but the inevitable, indestructible figure of Sergei Bubka. At 31, the "czar" of the pole vault simply sailed on in his own inimitable way, becoming the only competitor to win a gold medal at each of the five editions of the world championship over a 12 year period.

The alarming prospect for his rivals was that, as a millionaire whose attention is increasingly focussed towards his family and business interests, he still looked just as untouchable as that hungry, gymnastically gifted kid who had first surprised everyone by winning the crown in Helsinki in 1983.

Last year might have been a rare world record-free summer for the man who has gleaned 35 of them – of course by a centimetre at a time – but his opponents cannot count on a repeat of Bubka's unthinkable lapse in Barcelona when he surrendered his crown by no-heighting.

I. C. □

Ana Quirot
Cuba – Athletics

Every Olympic Games has its sentimental favourite. In Atlanta, it will surely be

Ana Quirot, the Cuban heroine whose courage and indomitable spirit is already the stuff of legend. Five months after winning 800m bronze in Barcelona, Quirot, by then seven months pregnant, suffered horrendous third-degree burns over her face and upper body when the kitchen stove exploded in her Havana apartment.

She nearly died, she lost her unborn baby but, despite the horrendous psychological and physical scars, despite the seven bouts of plastic surgery (with five more operations to come after Atlanta), Quirot confounded the medics by starting running just four months after the accident.

And, after quietly recuperating and rebuilding her confidence, she took advantage of Maria Mutola's disqualification in the heats to take the two-lap gold at the world championships. "I am not a patient any more; I am an athlete again," she said, but Quirot's most inspiring triumph was simply being able to run in Gothenburg at all.

I. C. □

Omar Linares
Cuba – Baseball

Omar Linares has been considered the best amateur player in the world for nearly a decade. He became the youngest player to make the Cuban national team, aged 17 in 1985, and has been coveted by major league teams nearly ever since. If he were to sign with a team, he probably would command a bonus of upwards of $2 million.

A third baseman with the athletic ability to play shortstop, Linares is a righthanded hitter with both power and speed. A fixture in the no. 3 spot in the Cuban line-up, he dominated pitchers

at the 1992 Olympic Games. He batted .500 with a tournament-best four home runs during the round-robin, and drove in a run in the gold medal 11-1 victory over Chinese Taipei.

He has supplanted Victor Mesa as the greatest player in Cuban history. Virtually every American player who has faced Linares and gone on to reach the big leagues believes that Linares would have no problem becoming a star at that level.

J. C. □

Hakeem Olajuwon
USA – Basketball

His name is Hakeem Olajuwon and he is a player of ineffable grace, a man of unfailing dignity. "Always being on top," that is how his surname translates. And that is just where he will be in Atlanta, where the Olympic Games will provide an exclamation mark to his most amazing tale.

He was born in Lagos, Nigeria, in January of 1963 and for 15 years knew nothing of basketball. He was, in fact, a handball player at the All-Nigeria Teachers Sports Festival in late 1978. There, a friend got him started playing the sport that would make him famous. Just four years later, in 1982, he was starring for the University of Houston and, three years after that, he emerged as a top professional player with his current team, the Houston Rockets.

Yet those facts, as remarkable as they might be, are too dry, too stark to capture the full measure of his journey. For it is only recently, after endless seasons of toiling in relative anonymity, that the multiple talents of Hakeem Olajuwon have come to be fully appreciated and he has come to be embraced as one of

51

his game's finest. He is regarded as that now surely, recognized finally as a mesmerizing dervish, as a 2.13m (7ft) magician able to dip, to feint, to unfurl moves normally associated with performers 30cm (1ft) shorter.

He can be balletic on the court, that is just what he can be. And away from it, he is just as stylish. In this era, when too many basketball players thump their chests and run their mouths and taunt their opponents, he is an anomaly, a gentleman, an act that always reflects class. "I consider myself a citizen of the world," says Hakeem Olajuwon, who was sworn in as an American citizen in 1993, and that makes the world twice blessed. Blessed to have him, and blessed finally to have the opportunity to view him on the Olympic stage.

S. M. □

Teresa Edwards
USA – Basketball

She was born in Atlanta and was a college All-American at the nearby University of Georgia. So the 1996 Olympic Games will be a happy homecoming for forward Teresa Edwards, the grande dame of women's basketball. Two Olympic golds (1984 and '88) and an Olympic bronze (1992); golds at the world championships (1990) and the Pan American Games (1987); a nine-year professional career that has included stops in France, Italy and Japan; a six-figure professional contract. All that is already part of her past, and now, in Atlanta, she will try to become the first basketball player, male or female, to medal in four different Games.

She will do that as part of the USA team that was brought together in the spring of 1995, a pioneering move that made her choose between playing for that team for $50,000 or playing in Europe for at least twice more. For her, it turns out, that was not any choice at all. "I don't feel like it's a sacrifice," says Teresa Edwards. "I feel it's an honour. Everyone on this team is going to be a part of a great historical moment in women's basketball."

S. M. □

Mark Todd
New Zealand – Equestrian

Mark Todd was only 24 years old when he came from New Zealand to Britain and to "Badminton" – the Mecca of three-day eventing – and won the event in 1980. He repeated his success in 1994 and has won the other "big one", Burghley, three times.

In 1984 he became Olympic champion in Los Angeles when he overhauled the leader Karen Stives, of the USA in the final show jumping event. And in 1988, in Seoul, the "Kiwi" was the first rider in half a century to recapture this gold. He failed, however, in his dream of being the first to record three consecutive Olympic wins when, in 1992, his horse was injured during the competition. Regarded as the best eventing rider for more than a decade, he will try for the title again in 1996 in Atlanta, leading a strong New Zealand team which won the 1990 world title but has never won the Olympic gold.

D. H. □

Romario de Souza Farias
Brazil – Football

Romario de Souza Farias could be competing in his second Olympic soccer tournament. He will be hoping that the outcome is different from the first. As a member of the Brazil side in the Seoul Olympic Games in '88, Romario was the Games' top scorer with seven goals – but his country finished second to the former Soviet Union in the championship match.

That mirrored the runner-up performance of the 1984 Brazilians. Winners of every other major prize in the game, the gold medal has eluded Brazil. That's why Romario, among a coterie of veteran Brazilians, has said he will be available for the Olympic Games. A champion with PSV Eindhoven and Barcelona in The Netherlands and Spain, Romario returned to his national team in September, 1993 scoring the two goals that defeated Uruguay and ensured Brazil's place in the 1994 World Cup finals. He proved the dominant player in the 1994 World Cup winning team, scoring vital goals and winning the "Golden Ball" as the tournament's outstanding player.

J. T. □

Svetlana Khorkina
Russia – Gymnastics

Her first name means "light" or "bright". She is as beautiful as a model or a prima ballerina. And anyone who strives to become a crowd favourite in Atlanta will find it difficult whilst she is around.

Svetlana Khorkina combines her beauty with charisma. She is funny, full of life and responsive and brings femininity back to artistic gymnastics. In short she is everything audiences have been longing for during the last decade. And the young Svetlana has already proved herself world class.

It could have all been so different in the beginning. When coach Boris Pilkin saw her for the first time he could only mutter, "She won't be of any use....". At 1.6m (5ft 3in.) she was considered too tall, nothing like the conventional concept of the ideal gymnast. But then he began working with her. And today she is no.1 in the Russian team.

How she is ever able to perform her extremely difficult programme (unique at the uneven bars), nobody is able to understand. Even she cannot explain it. Her gymnastics is risky, progressive and full of style.

Khorkina first appeared on the world stage in 1992 but her success began in 1994; silver medallist on vault and uneven bars at the world championships in Brisbane and European champion and second all-around in Stockholm. In 1995 she won the European cup in Rome.

Khorkina was born on 19 January 1979 in the scarcely-known town of Belgorod. For her, its main advantage was that from there it takes just an hour by train to reach Round Lake – the world famous incubator of champions which functions under the iron hand of the national coach Leonid Arkaev. Khorkina's mother, Lubov, is a doctor. Her father is a businessman working for a Yugoslavian enterprise and her younger sister, by six years, Julia is also involved in gymnastics.

And Khorkina's hobbies? "Music and ... eating", she says. Here, there is no doubt, we are dealing with a joker. The whole world will laugh with her, if Atlanta gold becomes hers.

V. M. □

Stephen Redgrave
Great Britain – Rowing

The career of Steve Redgrave, the British Olympic and world champion, who defends his pairs title with Matthew Pinsent in Atlanta, is one of the finest in rowing history and spans 15 years.

The 34 year old, 105kg athlete is seeking the unprecedented in his sport: a fourth successive Olympic gold medal. His first was in the coxed fours in Los Angeles in 1984 followed by coxless pairs titles in 1988 and 1992. And he has ruled the rowing roost in the pairs unbeaten since 1992.

Stephen Redgrave – right

With six world titles to his credit as well (no-one has achieved such an unbroken reign at the top of the heavyweight disciplines) victory in Atlanta would surpass the remarkable record of Italy's Abbagnale brothers who won six heavyweight championship titles in a row (including two Olympic coxed pairs titles in 1984 and 1988) giving Redgrave a career total of ten championships.

Add an Olympic bronze in the coxed pair in Seoul, as well as two world silvers and a bronze, three Commonwealth Games golds and 15 Henley Royal Regatta titles (plus countless national and international victories), and it becomes clear that he is seemingly untouchable and still going strong.

To maintain motivation and domination over such a long period in an endurance and power event is remarkable but Redgrave's professionalism and focus is legendary. He had, for instance, to overcome a serious digestive tract illness in 1992 to win the Olympic title, but his punishing regime – three sessions a day for 14 years – has put him virtually beyond the reach of his rivals. He lives in Marlow, England, close to the famous Henley regatta course with his doctor wife Ann and their two daughters.

Redgrave does not come from the now outdated traditional rowing background of public school and Oxbridge. The son of a Marlow builder, no one in his family had rowed before.

A dyslexic, he left school at 15 and took an early and, in retrospect, enlightened decision to try to become the best in the world at rowing under the guidance of his mentor Mike Spracklen who now coaches the United States eight.

D. T. ☐

Krisztina Egerszegi
Hungary – Swimming

On September 25, 1988, Krisztina Egerszegi became the youngest swimming gold medallist in Olympic history when she won the 200m backstroke in a new Olympic record time when just 14 years old. Four years later Egerszegi successfully defended her 200m title and also won the 100m backstroke and the 400m individual medley. This was the most gold medals won in individual events by any female competitor at the 1992 Olympic Games. Six months later she was voted "World Female

Swimmer of the Year" for the second year in succession.

Nicknamed "the Mouse" by her legendary coach Lazlo Kiss due to her intense shyness as a youngster, Egerszegi has the ability to make history by defending all three titles in Atlanta should she choose to do so. With the characteristic fingernail paint selected to match her swimming hat, she has a colourful personality and has the perfect physique for a swimming champion. Extremely light, yet deceptively powerful and supremely efficient, the 22 year old from Budapest has retained an almost poetic backstroke technique. It is the closest to perfection that one will ever see in an international swimming pool.

Despite mediocre years in 1994 and 1995 compared to her own remarkable standards (losing in both backstroke races at the 1994 world championships), Krisztina Egerszegi reigns as world record-holder in the 200m backstroke and second fastest ever in the 100m.

If she achieves her goal of three more Olympic gold medals (making a career total of seven) the 400m individual medley world record set by Petra Schneider of the German Democratic Republic 16 years ago, must surely be in danger. With a European championship title at 200m butterfly to add to her successful repertoire, few in Atlanta will be surprised if she is ahead of world record schedule in the 400m individual medley after the butterfly and backstroke legs.

A. J. ☐

Kieren Perkins
Australia – Swimming

The re-emergence of Australia as a world swimming force has much to do with the talents of triple world record holder Kieren Perkins. Since being beaten into the silver medal position by just 16 hundredths of a second in the 400m freestyle in Barcelona, by Evgeni Sadovyi, Perkins has grabbed world distance freestyle swimming by the throat and made it his own.

As the reigning world record holder and world champion at both 400 and 1500m, Perkins is favourite to collect two more Olympic gold medals in Atlanta. This would add to his stunning world record breaking victory in the 1500m final four years ago.

Looking at his lean 1.82m (6ft) body and immaculate freestyle technique, few would believe that there was a time when doctors feared Kieren Perkins may never walk again. Aged nine, he ran through a plate glass door while being chased by his brother. He received injuries that required 86 stitches. At first swimming was a method of rehabilitation, but since then it has become so crucial to him that he has redefined the boundaries of distance freestyle.

Perkins, in partnership with his club and national coach John Carew, has caused the world to rethink their training methods. During workouts of less distance but far higher quality, at his home club in the Western Suburbs of balmy Brisbane, Perkins' attention to stroke technique has made coaches and swimmers sit up and take note.

It should take a super-human performance to prevent Perkins from sweeping the gold medals in both the 400m and 1500m freestyle in Atlanta. The bigger question is whether they will both be world records.

A.J. □

Andre Agassi
USA – Tennis

The most colourful player in the world of tennis today, Agassi attracts large crowds wherever he competes. Born in Las Vegas in 1970, he was introduced to the game before he was four by his father Mike, who boxed in the 1952 Olympic Games in Helsinki. Agassi made great progress and in 1986 emerged as a 16 year old tennis prodigy from the Nick Bollettieri Academy by whom he was coached until three years ago.

A baseliner by inclination with the best service return and ground shots in the game, Agassi can also volley well when necessary and astonished the tennis experts by winning Wimbledon, a volleyer's paradise, in 1992 for his first Grand Slam title.

He had earlier been runner-up in the French Open twice and once in the US

Open. Since his Wimbledon victory Agassi has added the US Open in 1994 and the Australian Open in 1995 to his record. Last year he was ranked world no.1 for the first time.

J. O. □

Naim Suleymanoglü
Turkey – Weightlifting

When a boy called Naim Suleymanoglü was born in the little town of Kircali in Bulgaria in January of 1967 few could have suspected the events which lay in store for him. Aged ten, this Muslim lad started in the sport of weightlifting. He soon excelled.

By the age of 14, he began an international career which had already given him 80 world records before he arrived at the 1988 Olympic Games in Korea. He set his first senior world record at the world junior championships organized in the USA in 1983 and was good enough, but too young, to compete in the 1984 Olympic Games. He started in the 56kg class before moving to the 60kg class in Korea.

Before reaching the Seoul doorstep, however, a lot had happened to the "pocket Hercules" who stood just 1.52m (5ft) and weighed less than 60kg (9st 6lb). His competitive efforts had already seen him acclaimed as a "Hero of Socialist Labour" in Bulgaria. But that all changed when, in 1986, he defected to Turkey to protest over being asked to forego his ethnic Turkish ancestry and being forced to Bulgarianize his name.

The defection took place at the world championships in Melbourne after protracted secret planning. He was flown to Turkey under top-level security and awarded Turkish nationality in record time so that he could compete in Korea for his new land. Once crowned as Olympic champion, Suleymanoglü pleaded via the media for his family to be allowed to join him in Turkey. But it was only when the regime changed in Bulgaria several years later that this took place and the young athlete suffered difficult times along the way.

In Seoul, his main rival was his former countryman Stefan Topourov. Suleymanoglü soon swept him aside and went on to record six world records on the way to the gold medal. His final total meant a lift of over three times his own bodyweight and his gold was Turkey's first for 20 years. Suleymanoglü went on to repeat his golden moment at the Olympic Games in Barcelona in 1992. If he takes a third gold in Atlanta during the Centennial Games, he could become weightlifting's first ever triple Olympic champion in three successive Games. After that, he says, it will be time to retire and, perhaps, take up a role coaching young athletes.

Togay Bayath □

Atlanta Venues

EVERY Olympic athlete dreams of a venue close to the Village to avoid long, hot bus trips to training and competition. The Centennial Olympic Games in Atlanta should, therefore, be an immediate success. There will be 26 sports, 271 events with 1,933 medals in total. And 20 of those sports will take place within metropolitan Atlanta, clustered within the Olympic Ring (see diagram). This is nothing short of remarkable for an Olympic Games which will include 10,000 athletes and 5,000 officials.

The Olympic Ring is an imaginary circle with a radius of 2.5km (1.5 miles) from the Georgia World Congress Center in downtown Atlanta. It includes the Olympic Stadium and Village as well as an "Olympic Center", giving a home to ten sports.

But the centrepiece of any Olympic Games is its Olympic stadium. Few television viewers will forget the flowing lines of the 1988 version in Korea nor the wonderfully atmospheric and restored Montjuic venue in the Barcelona of 1992. Atlanta's Olympic 85,000 seater $209 million "field of dreams", however, is remarkable for its transitory nature.

The city already has a wealth of sports venues. So, once the Olympic flame dims over the Games (and those of the immediately following Paralympic Games) the 1996 Olympic stadium will be reduced to a 45,000 seater new home for the city's baseball team, the Braves, who won last year's world series. Plans for the Olympic Stadium, which will host track and field athletics as well as the opening and closing ceremonies, were first unveiled on October 26, 1992, and a ground breaking ceremony took place on July 10, 1993.

At the heart of the Olympic Center, meanwhile, lies the Georgia Dome which was first opened in August 1992 and is the home of the National Football League's Atlanta Falcons. Its 72,000 seats will be split into two arenas during the Games for gymnastics and basketball. The handball finals will also be held here.

Indoor volleyball will take place at the Omni Coliseum with its 16,400 seats. The venue, built in 1972, is the home of the Atlanta Hawks basketball team and the Atlanta Knights minor league hockey franchise. The halls of the Georgia World Congress Center will witness the fate of 1996 Olympic medals in the sports of fencing, handball, judo, table tennis, weightlifting and wrestling. Modern pentathlon's fencing section will also take place here.

Athletes from the sports of boxing and swimming (including diving, water polo and synchronized swimming) could almost tumble out of bed and into their venues – the Alexander Memorial Coliseum and the Georgia Tech Aquatic Center respectively.

Recently constructed, the Aquatic Center will incorporate all the aquatic disciplines during the Games – a remarkable feat. It has a diving pool, water polo pool and a 14,000 seater outdoor main pool. Construction began in 1993 and the venue was inaugurated in late 1995.

To the south-west of the Olympic Center lies a group of venues within the Atlanta University Center which will host field hockey and some of the basketball preliminaries.

For many of the outlying venues, however, there will be satellite "athlete villages". Preliminary Olympic football matches will take place in a variety of locations some as far apart as Washington DC in the North and Miami in the South. And yachting, as at so many previous Games, will take place far from the Olympic hub in the waters off Savannah. Whitewater canoeing will be based at the Ocoee river in Tennessee and flatwater canoeing will be organized on Lake Lanier, together with rowing, to the north-east of Atlanta. Women's softball will be located at Columbus, Georgia.

Tennis, archery and cycling will be hosted in the picturesque setting of Stone Mountain park to the east of the city. A stark granite monolith – the largest exposed of its kind in the world – looms over the park which is an area of outstanding beauty. So, too, is Georgia International Horse Park, the venue for the equestrian disciplines together with mountain biking. Right across the city, to the south-west, lies the Wolf Creek shooting complex.

A total of 27 venues, without mentioning hundreds of training and pre-Games acclimatization centres. All waiting to witness the Centennial Games of the modern Olympic era.

Olympic Program 1996

SPORT	VENUE
OPENING CEREMONY	Olympic Stadium
Aquatics	
Diving	Georgia Tech Aquatic Center
Swimming	Georgia Tech Aquatic Center
Synchro Swimming	Georgia Tech Aquatic Center
Water Polo	Georgia Tech Aquatic Center
Archery	Stone Mountain Park
Athletics	Olympic Stadium
Marathon	Atlanta (course to be set)
Race Walk	Summerhill/Grant Park
Badminton	Georgia State University
Baseball	Atlanta - Fulton County Stadium
Basketball	Georgia Dome/Morehouse College
Boxing	Alexander Memorial Coliseum
Canoe/Kayak	
Slalom	"Ocoee Whitewater Center, Tennessee"
Sprint	Lake Lanier
Cycling	
Mountain Bike	Georgia International Horse Park
Road	Atlanta
Track	Stone Mountain Park
Equestrian	Georgia International Horse Park
Fencing	Georgia World Congress Center
Football	
Semifinals/Finals	"Sanford Stadium, Athens, Georgia"
Prelim/Quarterfinals	"Birmingham, Alabama/Miami, Florida"
Preliminaries	"Orlando, Florida/Washington, D.C."
Gymnastics	
Artistic	Georgia Dome
Rhythmic	University of Georgia
Handball	Georgia World Congress Center/Georgia Dome
Hockey	Morris Brown College/Clark Atlanta University
Judo	Georgia World Congress Center
Modern Pentathlon	Multiple sites
Rowing	Lake Lanier
Shooting	Wolf Creek Shooting Complex
Softball	"Golden Park, Columbus, Georgia"
Table Tennis	Georgia World Congress Center
Tennis	Stone Mountain Park
Volleyball	
Beach	Atlanta Beach
Indoor	Omni Coliseum/University of Georgia
Weightlifting	Georgia World Congress Center
Wrestling	Georgia World Congress Center
Yachting	"Wassaw Sound, Savannah, Georgia"
CLOSING CEREMONY	Olympic Stadium

ns = no spectators; *T* = ticketed training; * = gala event.

JULY													AUGUST					
F	S	Su	M	T	W	Th	F	S	Su	M	T	W	Th	F	S	Su	No.of	Event
19	20	21	22	23	24	25	26	27	28	29	30	31	1	2	3	4	days	Finals
19																	1	0
							26	27	28	29	30	31	1	2			8	4
	20	21	22	23	24	25	26										7	32
											30			2			2	1
	20	21	22	23	24		26	27	28								8	1
									28ns	29	30	31	1	2			6	4
							26	27	28	29		31	1	2	3		8	39
									28							4	2	2
							26							2			2	3
					24	25	26	27	28	29	30	31	1				9	5
	20	21	22	23	24	25		27	28	29	30		1	2			12	1
	20	21	22	23	24	25	26	27	28	29	30	31	1	2	3	4	16	2
	20	21	22	23	24	25	26	27	28		30	31	1	2	3	4	15	12
							26T	27	28								3	4
											30	31	1	2	3	4	6	12
											30						1	2
		21										31			3		3	4
					24	25	26	27	28								5	8
		21	22	23	24	25ns	26	27	28	29		31	1		3	4	13	6
	20	21	22	23	24	25											6	10
									28			31	1	2	3		5	2
	20	21	22	23	24	25		27	28								8/8	0
	20	21	22	23	24	25											6/6	0
	20	21	22	23	24	25			28	29	30*						9	14
													1	2	3	4	4	2
					24	25	26	27	28	29	30	31	1	2	3	4	12	2
	20	21	22	23	24	25	26	27	28	29	30	31	1	2			14	2
	20	21	22	23	24	25	26										7	14
											30						1	1
		21	22	23	24	25	26	27	28								8	14
	20	21	22	23	24	25	26	27									8	15
		21	22	23	24	25	26	27		29	30						9	1
				23	24	25	26	27	28	29	30	31	1				10	4
				23	24	25	26	27	28	29	30	31	1	2	3		12	4
				23	24	25	26	27	28								6	2
	20	21	22	23	24	25	26	27	28	29	30	31	1	2	3	4	16	2
	20	21	22	23	24		26	27	28	29	30						10	10
	20	21	22	23							30	31	1	2			8	20
			22	23	24	25	26	27	28	29	30	31	1				11	10
																4	1	0

World Time Chart

International Time Zones

Hours ahead (+) or behind (–) Greenwich Mean Time – no account is taken of Summer Time

Afghanistan	+4	Bolivia	−4	Cuba	−5
Albania	+1	Bosnia Herzegovina	+1	Cyprus:	+3
Algeria	+1	Botswana	+2	North	+2
Angola	+1	Brazil		South	
Antigua	−4	West	−4	Czech Republic	+1
Argentina	−3	East	−3	Denmark	+1
Armenia	+3	Acre	−5	Djibouti	+3
Aruba	−4	Brunei	+8	Dominica	−5
Australia:		Bulgaria	+2	Dominican Republic	−4
Canberra, NSW	+10	Burkina Faso	GMT	Ecuador	−5
Victoria,		Burundi	+2	Egypt	+2
Queensland	+10	Cameroon	+1	Equatorial Guinea	+1
Tasmania	+10	Canada:		Estonia	+3
Northern Territory	+10	Newfoundland	−3	Ethiopia	+3
South Australia	+9	Atlantic	−4	Fiji	+12
Western Australia	+8	Eastern	−5	Finland	+2
Austria	+1	Central	−6	France	+1
Azerbaijan	+4	Mountain	−7	Gabon	+1
Bahamas	−5	Pacific	−8	Gambia	GMT
Bahrain	+3	Yukon	−8	Georgia	+4
Bangladesh	+6	Cape Verde Islands	−1	Germany	+1
Barbados	−4	Cayman Islands	−5	Ghana	GMT
Belarus	+3	Central African		Gibraltar	+1
Belgium	+1	Republic	+1	Great Britain	GMT
Belize	−6	Chad	+1	Greece	+2
Benin	+1	Chile	−4	Grenada	−4
Bermuda	−4	China, People's		Guam	+10
Bhutan	+6	Republic	+8	Guatemala	−6
		Colombia	−5	Guinea	GMT
		Comoro Islands	+3	Guyana	−3
		Congo	+1	Haiti	−5
		Cook Islands	−10	Honduras	−6
		Costa Rica	−6	Hong Kong	+8
		Cote d'Ivoire	GMT	Hungary	+1
		Croatia	+1	Iceland	GMT

India	+5	Mozambique	+2	Spain	+1
Indonesia:		Myanmar	+6	Sri Lanka	+5
West Zone	+7	Namibia	+2	Sudan	+2
Central Zone	+8	Nepal	+5	Surinam	−3
East Zone	+9	Netherlands	+1	Swaziland	+2
Iran, Islamic Republic	+3	Netherlands Antilles	−4	Sweden	+1
Iraq	+3	New Zealand	+12	Switzerland	+1
Ireland	GMT	Nicaragua	−6	Syria	+2
Israel	+2	Niger	+1	Taiwan	+8
Italy	+1	Nigeria	+1	Tajikistan	+5
Jamaica	−5	Norway	+1	Tanzania	+3
Japan	+9	Oman	+4	Thailand	+7
Jordan	+2	Pakistan	+5	Togo	GMT
Kazakhstan		Palestine	+2	Tonga	+13
Ama-Ata	+6	Panama	−5	Trinidad & Tobago	−4
Ouralsk	+5	Papua New Guinea	+10	Tunisia	+1
Kenya	+7	Paraguay	−4	Turkey	+3
Korea	+9	Peru	−5	Turkmenistan	+5
Korea DPR	+9	Philippines	+8	Turks & Caicos	
Kuwait	+3	Poland	+1	Islands	−5
Kyrgyzstan	+6	Portugal	GMT	Uganda	+3
Lao	+7	Puerto Rico	−4	Ukraine	+3
Latvia	+3	Qatar	+3	United Arab Emirates	+4
Lebanon	+2	Romania	+2	USA:	
Lesotho	+2	Russia:		Eastern	−5
Liberia	GMT	Moscow	+2	Central	−6
Libya	+1	St. Petersburg	+3	Mountain	−7
Liechtenstein	+1	Omsk	+6	Pacific	−8
Lithuania	+2	Vladivostock	+10	Alaska	−9/10
Luxembourg	+1	Rwanda	+2	Hawaii	−10
Macedonia	+1	Saint Lucia	−4	Uruguay	−3
Madagascar	+3	Saint Vincent	−4	Uzbekistan	+5
Malawi	+2	Salvador (El)	−6	Venezuela	−4
Malaysia	+8	Samoa	−11	Vietnam	+7
Maldives	+5	San Marino	+1	Virgin Islands	−4
Mali	+1	Saudi Arabia	+3	Yemen	+3
Malta	+1	Senegal	GMT	Yugoslavia	+1
Marshall Islands	+12	Seychelles	+4	Zaire:	
Mauritania	GMT	Sierra Leone	GMT	Kinshasa	+1
Mauritius	+4	Singapore	+8	Shaba	+2
Mexico	−6	Slovakia	+1	Zambia	+2
Moldova	+3	Slovenia	+1	Zimbabwe	+2
Monaco	+1	Solomon Islands	+11		
Mongolia	+8	Somalia	+3		
Morocco	GMT	South Africa	+2		

Atlanta: A Personal View

by Bert Roughton Jr

THE ONLY hero in Atlanta's history to merit a statue on a downtown boulevard is neither a general nor a literary giant but a newspaperman who was honoured for raising civic "boosterism" to a fine art and providing the city with its first slogan.

To this day, respectful Atlantans carry Henry W. Grady's century-old words on their bumper stickers: "We Have Raised a Brave and Beautiful City."

It was the first of a rich line of boasts that over the years have kept Atlanta perpetually scrambling to match, sometimes successfully, its own hype. The most recent and most daunting: Olympic City. Grady must be smiling from the grave.

The editor of *The Atlanta Constitution* at the close of the last century, Grady today stands on Marietta Street facing East, his back to "CNN Center". Thousands of tourists stream by him daily to experience what, next to Coca-Cola, is Atlanta's most identifiable product: Ted Turner's Cable News Network.

Grady's phrase was delivered during a famous New York speech he made in 1886 – the year Coca-Cola was created. Ironically, William T. Sherman, the general who 22 years earlier ordered his Union soldiers to burn the key Confederate transportation hub of Atlanta, was in the audience.

Sherman had enjoyed the blaze from the vantage point of Copenhill, just East of the city and a place that 120 years later Jimmy Carter selected for his presidential library. While surely entertaining, the fire was considerably less spectacular than David O. Selznick's technicolor portrait of a metropolis smouldering to its redbrick foundations – a Hollywood hyperbole of the already exaggerated image conjured by Margaret Mitchell in her opus, "Gone With the Wind."

When Sherman's troops stormed through in early September of 1864, Atlanta's population was only about 10,000, much smaller than Charleston, Savannah or New Orleans.

Even so, it is impossible to understand Atlanta today without taking note of the way this fire marked the city's soul and psyche. Atlanta has been building and tearing down at a frightful rate ever since – as if trying to escape its own ashes. Not blessed with a harbour or navigable river or, really any other natural advantage, Atlanta had no reason to exist apart from the random decision to lay two major railroad lines here in the 1830s. Sherman's fire changed that. It gave Atlanta an obsessive will to survive and expand. The Phoenix of Greek mythology, the golden-winged bird that rose from its own ashes, became its symbol and central myth.

To help fuel the rebirth Grady went to New York seeking Yankee dollars. In his already-mentioned speech he also coined the term "New South" and, by implication, made Atlanta the capital. Noting that Sherman was in the audience, Grady could not resist a joke. "I want to say to General Sherman, who is considered an able man in our parts – though some people think he is a kind of careless man about fire – that from the ashes he left us in 1864 we have raised a brave and beautiful city; that somehow or other we have caught the sunshine in the bricks and mortar therein not one ignoble prejudice or memory."

In a way this is the essence of Atlanta; to forgive and forget, particularly when remembering interferes with turning a profit.

While many Southerners retained their bitterness toward the North after the war, Atlantans – not unlike the Japanese and Germans of later generations – regarded being crushed by the US Army as a moment pregnant with opportunity. Instead of damning the Yankees, Atlantans like Grady sought instead to entice them to build their factories in the South. They waved the carrots of low-paid, non-union workers – eager to trade their ploughs for welders' goggles – before their noses.

This same pragmatism extended to the issue of race. Grady himself was rare among Southerners in his support of the notion that blacks needed to be educated, trained and provided decent circumstances. Not because he was a saint but because he was an opportunist who knew that marshalling such a huge labour force would aid the cause of attracting Yankee dollars.

This is the environment that made it possible for a black preacher in the first half of this century to raise among his children Martin Luther King Jr. The tolerant, polite segregation of Atlanta contrasted sharply with the open hostility King encountered as an adult in such cities as Birmingham, Montgomery and Memphis.

While other Southern cities seethed during the '60s, Grady's heirs in Atlanta, black and white, went quietly about building political bridges to keep the peace and maintain real estate values. In the '60s, former Mayor William B. Hartsfield, declared Atlanta: "A City too Busy to Hate."

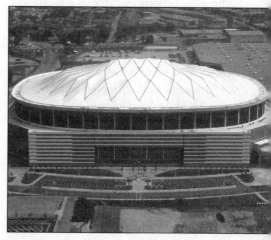

Georgia Dome

Busy it was. After growing quietly during the first half of the century, sprouting fine old mansions built on the fortunes raised from banking, insurance and the Coca-Cola empire, Atlanta boomed after World War II. The city adopted and discarded slogans to match its evolving PR positioning: "Atlanta: The City Without Limits"; "Atlanta: The Next Great International City"; "Atlanta: Hometown of the American Dream"; and, now, "Atlanta: Come Share Our Dream."

65

Although one local favourite – though certainly not with the city fathers – is: "Atlanta: Not bad for Georgia."

Atlanta became a magnet and today teems with people from elsewhere, most sharing the common culture of commerce. Forty percent of the area's residents did not live here 20 years ago.

In many ways, Atlanta has much more in common with newer cities like Dallas, Phoenix or Los Angeles than with other traditional Southern cities such as Richmond or Charleston. Within the South, Atlanta often seems out of place and it elicits mixed feelings from Southerners. One Southern historian, unimpressed with Atlanta's pushy, big-city ways, once described the city as "what 100,000 Confederate soldiers died to prevent."

Business was attracted here by railroads, highways, air conditioning and, finally, the airport. Before the city decided in the '60s to become an air power, Atlanta and Birmingham were roughly the same size. Today with a metro population of three million people, Atlanta dwarfs Birmingham and virtually all other Southern cities outside of those in Texas. Atlanta's Hartsfield International Airport is the world's second largest and third busiest.

Yet, because Atlanta grew up in the automobile age, it has no real centre. Rem Koolhass, the famed Dutch architect/philosopher, describes the city this way: "Atlanta does not have the classic symptoms of city: It is not dense, it is a sparse, thin carpet of habitation."

That's about right. Atlanta invented its Downtown in the '70s and '80s as a comfortable place to sequester conventioneers until they have exhausted their expense accounts. Sadly, Atlanta has also been a city too busy – and, perhaps too young – to care enough about art and culture. This year's Olympic Games present the best chance to retrofit the city with the makings of a vibrant centre. To prepare for the Games the city is spending nearly $2 billion to build a new stadium, aquatic centre, housing, parks and the like downtown.

Although Atlanta lacks the obvious attractions of older, better known cities, it still has its charms and a few sights. The weather is obscenely fine, with the exception of a hellish late July and early August, which, incidentally, happen to coincide with the dates of the 1996 Olympic Games. The city is built on interesting, hilly terrain with rich forests and established gardens.

Atlanta's High Museum of Art is as good as whatever travelling exhibit passes through it. And its Symphony Orchestra is routinely splendid. The Zoo is superior to just about any in Europe or North America. Next to the Zoo, in Grant Park, is the Cyclorama, an odd yet interesting painting-in-the-round depicting the battle of Atlanta. No city offers better golfing or tennis. (There are 60,000 members of the Atlanta Lawn Tennis Association – easily the largest such group in the world.)

There are a number of artsy neighbourhoods such as Little Five Points, Midtown and Virginia Highland, where visitors can tour small galleries and shops and mingle with Atlanta's very proud and well-pierced avant garde.

Atlanta also has some of the world's friendliest taverns to stop in for a beer or burger. In Virginia Highland are "George's", "Moe's and Joe's" and "Manuel's", where local politicians and journalists meet to swap outrageous lies and gallons of draft beer.

Perhaps no city offers the political diversity of Atlanta. The same city is home to pacifist Martin Luther King Jr., liberal populist Jimmy Carter and ultra-conservative House Speaker Newt Gingrich.

Honest to its commercial soul, few cities have as much in sheer shopping opportunity. The millions of square feet of shopping space at Phipps Plaza and Lenox Square, which stand on opposite sides of the same street in utter defiance of one another in the fashionable Buckhead district, are alone worth a visit.

In the past 20 years, Atlantans have also learned one of the greatest reasons to acquire disposable incomes: food. Once a city happy to provide a decent steak, Atlanta has become one of America's sleeping giants for dining.

Atlantans have become enthusiastic, free-spending fans of away-from-home dining. According to a recent study by the National Restaurant Association, Atlantans use almost half their total food budget – 47.2 percent – on eating out. That's a higher percentage than any other US city. And the biggest reason is that Atlanta restaurants are cheap.

Since Atlanta was named host to the Centennial Olympic Games in 1990, an unprecedented build-up of restaurants, bars and clubs has occurred. Local entrepreneurs, national and international chains, celebrities and aspiring moms-and-pops have all jumped in.

Downtown, the superhyped Hard Rock Cafe has been joined by megahyped Planet Hollywood. We like our food both trashy – check out the chilli dogs at the "Varsity", the world's largest fast food restaurant or the incendiary hot wings at "Taco Mac" in

Virginia Highland – and elegant, such as the eclectic California-European fare at "Bacchanalia" in Buckhead or the authentic – we dare you – French cuisine at "Ciboulette" in Ansley Park.

You can also get "homey": At the "Colonnade" genteel old ladies sit back-to-back with aging gay couples scarfing fried chicken, collard greens and rutabagas. Or "bluesy": At "Fat Matt's" in Morningside, you can get huge, tender ribs cooked, it seems forever, in the hot breath of barbecue gods and served with beans baked in onions and bourbon. In the background some local blues band shares an awful lot of misery.

In Buckhead, there are: "Pano's & Paul's", "Bone's", "Chops and Buckhead Diner" – great places to spend someone else's money. For fancy Cajun: "A Taste of New Orleans"; or "French Quarter". For Great Mexican: "Nuevo Laredo" or "Mexico City Gourmet".

There is even something called "Nouveau Southern" with traditional dishes dressed up with a little European flare at such establishments as "Kudzu Cafe" in Buckhead and "South City Kitchen" in Midtown. These places offer such dishes as blue crab and lemon basil salad on fried green tomatoes or wood-roasted Hiawassee mountain trout with wild mushroom whipped potatoes and sage browned butter. Maybe this is what Grady really meant by New South.

Maybe the best way to think of Atlanta is to think of it as an adolescent, deceptively young for its size, gawky and eager to please. At times, it is brash, shallow and arrogant. But all in all, it is worth a little time, some patience and worthy still of great expectations.

The Cultural Olympiad

by Caroline Searle

WHEN THE Olympic Games took place in Ancient Greece the sports events were part of an overall festival which included the arts. Once the Olympic Games were revived in the modern era, starting in 1896, it did not take long before the desire to emulate those ancient festivals came to the fore. The Olympic Congress of 1906 discussed the role of art and literature. And in 1912 a "Cultural Olympiad" was introduced to run alongside the Games. The Cultural Olympiad has been a tradition ever since. It is hosted every four years in the same city as the Olympic Games.

For Atlantans, the current Cultural Olympiad began almost as the Olympic flame dimmed after the closing ceremony in Barcelona in 1992. It has been a four-year, multi-disciplinary arts and culture festival which is set to peak between June and October of 1996. And, in celebration of the unique Centennial Games, the organizers have promised that it will be the most "expansive" Cultural Olympiad in history.

The aim is to permit outside audiences to appreciate the diverse cultural experiences of the American South whilst, at the same time, affording the local audience (including Olympic and other visitors) the opportunity to savour a variety of international artists and experiences – expanding people's vision in both ways through concerts, exhibitions and theatrical performances.

In 1993 Atlanta embarked on a cultural exchange with its immediate Olympic predecessor, Lillehammer, the Norwegian hosts of the 1994 Olympic Winter Games. The highlight of the exchange came with the world premiere of composer James Oliverio's "The Explorer", a new symphonic work commissioned by the Cultural Olympiad. In that same year there were exhibitions and concerts with Mexican and Swiss themes – the latter to celebrate the inauguration of the Olympic Museum in

Lausanne.

In 1994 Atlanta met Africa in the shape of "Celebrate Africa" a ten-day feast of drama and music featuring 600 performers from 27 African nations which attracted almost a million visitors. Last year, the Carter Presidential Center in the city played host to a gathering called "The Nobel Laureates of Literature". Eight Laureates from around the world were joined by ex-President Carter and others to hear a series of public readings and panel discussions.

The American South has also been enjoying a series of on-going programmes. These include a cinematic celebration of the 100th anniversary of film (1995), concerts given by the Atlanta Olympic Band drawn from local high school and college musicians, dance master-classes, and performances by the Atlanta Symphony Orchestra (which celebrated its 50th anniversary season in 1994/95).

An unparalleled series of events, however, awaits once the Games is upon the world around the twin themes of "Southern Connections" and "International Connections – Celebrating the Centennial". This will incorporate over 50 major pop, rock, country, rhythm and blues, gospel and other musical acts. There will be performances by more than 20 theatre and dance companies as well as exhibitions of painting, sculpture, contemporary art and Olympic memorabilia. An array of orchestra, opera and chamber-music performances will take place. And on the large, outdoor site of the Southern Crossroads Festival hundreds of regional artists, artisans and performers will gather each day.

For music lovers the highlight could well be 21 nights of Olympic Amphitheater Concerts in Centennial Olympic Park featuring a variety of musical disciplines from Willie Nelson's country music to performances by artists from China and Africa. These will be linked with works such as the Atlanta Opera performing Gershwin's political satire "Of thee I sing" as well as an International Opera Gala.

The role of women in the Olympic Games will also be featured in a multimedia presentation including rare archival film. As will the musical genius of Duke Ellington through photographs, period instruments and interactive audio and video material. Atlanta awaits to welcome the world both within, and without, its sporting arenas.

Olympic Village Life

An athlete's eye-view of the Olympic Village

by Nicola Fairbrother

THE OLYMPIC VILLAGE is the epicentre of any Games. It is the nucleus of a fantastic fire, that burns away, fuelling itself on the athletes' dreams and desires until the last battle has been won and lost. Until then, until the very last medal has been presented, the Village bursts with vitality. You can taste the apprehension in the air, sense the hopes and the dreams.

We arrived in Barcelona on July 21, 1992, three days before that archer fired his lit arrow into the night sky and officially declared the 1992 Olympic Games open. It is difficult now, four years on, to lift myself back to that first warm, dusky evening. But I remember the stillness of the Village. It seemed much quieter than I had expected, probably because athletes were sleeping and teams from different nations and sports were yet to arrive. I remember the noise of the sea and the quiet buzz of tension in the air and inside my mind going into over-drive.

Team-mates who had been to Seoul had warned me that an Olympic Games would blow my mind. They were right. I had been sure that I could handle it. After all, I thought, it was just going to be like any other major tournament, just like a world championships. But that

first night, waiting to receive my official accreditation pass, and then walking along the seafront to the judo apartments, I realized that it was bigger than anything ever before. And not just a little bit bigger but way, way off-the-scale bigger.

If I had fought that next day, or anytime in that next week, I would almost certainly have lost. But, luckily I had ten days before I fought. Ten days to acclimatize. You need that time to surface because being a competitor in an Olympic Village is rather like being a pebble in a tidal wave – you need a while to get your bearings. And the next morning, after the quietness of the first evening, I woke up to find out what it was really about.

The first thing to hit me was the size. The Village was actually more like a town with training facilities, gyms, saunas, shops, the arcades, music and video rooms, launderettes, chemists ... everything you can imagine ... and it stretched for a couple of miles along the seafront.

I do not know exactly the distances but you could do a healthy ten minute run and not get to the last gate. Our apartment overlooked the harbour, coloured with its yachts from the many nations and edged with restaurants, free drink machines, free ice-cream containers. All food in the Village was free. You could eat when, and as much as you liked. Soon the main food hall, which was situated inland, away from the harbour, became like a magnet for socializing.

It sat thousands and offered every type of food you can imagine. A bit of a nightmare before I fought, with judo being fought in weight divisions and every last 100 grams being monitored.

For the ten days before I remember craving the new white "Magnum" - an ice cream – that had only just been brought out. I promised myself as soon as I had fought I could have as many as I liked. But they ran out. Somehow the 10,000 athletes were on average eating three of these Magnums a day each and although after I had finished, and won my silver medal, I searched every ice-cream container in the Village, the white ones were long gone. Devastated, I had to make do with the milk and dark ones.

I also have vivid memories of the atmosphere walking about the Village. It was like a bond that existed through every competitor in the Village, regardless of colour, size, shape or sport. You could watch African runners lope by, followed by a group of the tiny Hungarian gymnasts and the Chinese volleyball team and there would be the same look in all of their faces. Everyone in the Village seemed united by the incredible experience, everyone seemed ALIVE. It was great to walk about in this company, to be a part of this elite group of sportsmen and women, and very easy to get carried along by it all, enjoy it too much and forget the reason for being a part of it all. But outside the Village there were constant reminders.

Outside the security gates, reality hit you hard in the face. Outside came the Olympic "pin" (lapel badge) collectors and the autograph hunters. Then, worst of all, came the media with their incessant questioning. "How do you think you are going to do?" "Who are you worried about?" Enough to get the adrenalin pumping ready for the big day.

It seemed to me like my day was never going to come. On the walls in the judo apartment at the Village, our team manager (Roy Inman) had pinned up each of the weight division draws. They were pinned in weight order, with the heavyweights first (as the judo started with the heavyweights, with one division fighting each day).

Every evening, when the fighting had finished, Roy would remove that day's draw. Fighting at under-56kgs, I was the fourth bit of paper out of the seven. It was like being on death row, slowly watching the papers being pulled down and your weight division creep to the front of the queue! And then, suddenly, it was my turn. I remember looking at the wall on July 31, the day I fought, and there only being three pieces of paper up there and mine was at the front. I remember thinking tonight that is going to come down and it is all going to be over, so let's enjoy it, every minute of it !

But then at the stadium things changed. All the nerves, the incredible tension of the past ten days nearly took their toll in my first fight. I was fighting badly, the nerves were suffocating me and stopping me from attacking, but somehow I scraped through on a minor score.

I got off the mat, shaking, desperately scared of losing and not wanting to return one little bit for my next fight against a class opponent, the twice world champion, Cathy Arnaud from France. I wobbled around the warm-up room trying to sort it all out, and then suddenly something clicked in my head. The nerves began to settle and I began to enjoy it all again. The more I enjoyed it, the less the nerves played a part and thirty minutes later I jumped back onto the mat and threw Arnaud twice, ending the contest before time.

From that moment on I enjoyed it all. The final was incredible, with the noise of 6,000 Spaniards behind my opponent, Miriam Blasco, of the host nation. It was close with Blasco scoring a "yuko" (five points) to my "koka" (three points). A tiny difference but the difference for me between the silver medal and being the Olympic Champion.

Of course, when I came off the mat, I was bitterly disappointed for I had come within a whisker of taking the gold. Still, the next few days that followed in the Village and the Closing Ceremony were fantastic. It was like floating off a huge mountain and gliding down to earth, enjoying the amazing last few days of the 1992 Olympic Games, content knowing I had won an Olympic medal. It certainly took a long time until I hit the ground again.

1996 Sports and Events List

Archery

Men
Individual
Team

Women
Individual
Team

Athletics

Men (24 events)
100m
200m
400m
800m
1,500m
5,000m
10,000m
110m hurdles
400m hurdles
3,000m
  steeplechase
20km walk
50km walk
4x100m relay
4x400m relay
Marathon
High jump
Long jump
Triple jump
Pole vault
Shot put
Discus
Javelin

Hammer throw
Decathlon

Women (20 events)
100m
200m
400m
800m
1,500m
5,000m
10,000m
100m hurdles
400m hurdles
10km walk
4x100m relay
4x400m relay
Marathon
High jump
Long jump
Triple jump
Shot put
Discus
Javelin
Heptathlon

Badminton

Men
Singles
Doubles

Women
Singles
Doubles

Mixed doubles

Baseball

Men - team

Basketball

Men - team
Women - team

Boxing

Men (12 events)
– 48kg
  Light flyweight
– 51kg
  Flyweight
– 54kg
  Bantamweight
– 57kg
  Featherweight
– 60kg
  Lightweight
– 63.5kg Light
  welterweight
– 67kg
  Welterweight
– 71kg Light
  middleweight
– 75kg
  Middleweight
– 81kg Light
  heavyweight
– 91kg
  Heavyweight
+ 91kg Super
  heavyweight

Canoeing

Men (12 events)

Kayak
K1 500m
   1,000m
K2 500m
   1,000m
K4 1,000m

Canadian
C1 500m
   1,000m
C2 500m
   1,000m

Slalom
K1
C1
C2

Women (4 events)

Kayak
K1 500m
K2 500m
K4 500m

Slalom
K1

Cycling

Men (8 events)

Track
1km time trial
Sprint

/ continued on next page

4,000m individual
pursuit
4,000m team
pursuit
Individual points
race

Road
Individual road
race
Individual road
time trial

Mountain Bike
Cross-country

Women (6 events)

Track
Sprint
3,000m individual
pursuit
Individual points
race

Road
Individual road
race
Individual road
time trial

Mountain Bike
Cross-country

Equestrian

Mixed (6 events)

Show jumping
Individual
Team

Dressage
Individual
Team

3-day event
Individual
Team

Fencing

Men (6 events)

Foil
Individual
Team

Sabre
Individual
Team

Epée
Individual
Team

Women (4 events)

Foil
Individual
Team

Epée
Individual
Team

Football

Men - team
Women - team

Gymnastics

Men (8 events)

Artistic

Team
Individual all
round
Floor exercise
Pommel horse
Rings
Vault
Parallel bars
Horizontal bar

Women (8 events)

Artistic

Team
Individual all
round
Vault
Asymmetric bars
Beam
Floor exercises

Rhythmic
Individual
Team

Handball

Men - team
Women - team

Hockey

Men - team
Women - team

Judo

Men (7 events)
– 60kg Extra
lightweight
– 65kg Half
lightweight
– 71kg
Lightweight
– 78kg Half
middleweight
– 86kg
Middleweight
– 95kg Half
heavyweight
+ 95kg
Heavyweight

Women (7 events)
– 48kg Extra
lightweight
– 52kg Half
lightweight
– 56kg

Lightweight
– 61kg Half
middleweight
– 66kg
Middleweight
– 72kg Half
heavyweight
+ 72kg
Heavyweight

Modern Pentathlon

Men - individual

Rowing

Men (8 events)
Double sculls
Coxless pairs
Single scull
Coxless fours
Quadruple sculls
Coxed eights

Lightweight
Coxless fours
Double sculls

Women (6 events)
Coxless pairs
Double sculls
Single scull
Quadruple sculls
Coxed eights

Lightweight
Double sculls

Shooting

Men (10 events)
Rapid fire pistol
25m
Free pistol 50m

/continued on next page

Air pistol 10m
Running target
  10m
Smallbore rifle
  3 positions 50m
Smallbore rifle
  prone 50m
Air rifle 10m
Double trap
Olympic trap
Skeet

Women (5 events)
Sport pistol 25m
Air pistol 10m
Air rifle 10m
Smallbore rifle
  3 positions 50m
Double trap

Softball

Women - team

Swimming

Men (19 events)

Freestyle
50m
100m
200m
400m
1,500m

Backstroke
100m
200m

Breaststroke
100m
200m

Butterfly
100m
200m

Medley
200m
400m

Relays
Freestyle 4x100m
Freestyle 4x200m
Medley 4x100m

Diving
Springboard 3m
Platform 10m

Waterpolo - team

Women (19 events)

Freestyle
50m
100m
200m
400m
800m

Backstroke
100m
200m

Breaststroke
100m
200m

Butterfly
100m
200m

Medley
200m
400m

Relays
Freestyle 4x100m
Freestyle 4x200m
Medley 4x100m

Diving
Springboard 3m
Platform 10m

**Synchronized
swimming**
Team

Table Tennis

Men (2 events)
Singles
Doubles

Women (2 events)
Singles
Doubles

Tennis

Men (2 events)
Singles
Doubles

Women (2 events)
Singles
Doubles

Volleyball

Men (2 events)
Indoor - team
Beach - pairs

Women (2 events)
Indoor - team
Beach - pairs

Weightlifting

Men (10 events)
– 54kg
– 59kg
– 64kg
– 70kg
– 76kg
– 83kg
– 91kg
– 99kg
– 108kg
+ 108kg

Wrestling

Men (20 events)

**Freestyle &
Greco-roman**

– 48kg
– 52kg
– 57kg
– 62kg
– 68kg
– 74kg
– 82kg
– 90kg
– 100kg
+ 100kg

Yachting

Men (3 events)
470
Finn
Mistral

Women (3 events)
470
Europe
Mistral

Mixed (4 events)
Soling
Star
Laser
Tornado

List of Country Abbreviations

The following is a list of abbreviations which have been used either in the text passages or data sections of this Companion.

AFG	Afghanistan
AHO	Netherlands Antilles
ALB	Albania
ALG	Algeria
AND	Andorra
ANG	Angola
ANT	Antigua
ARG	Argentina
ARM	Armenia
ARU	Aruba
ASA	American Samoa
AUS	Australia
AUT	Austria
BAH	Bahamas
BAN	Bangladesh
BAR	Barbados
BDI	Burundi
BEL	Belgium
BEN	Benin
BER	Bermuda
BHU	Bhutan
BIH	Bosnia & Hercegovina
BIR	Burma
BIZ	Belarus
BOL	Bolivia
BOT	Botswana
BRA	Brazil
BRN	Bahrain
BRU	Brunei
BUL	Bulgaria
BUR	Burkina Faso
CAF	Central African Republic
CAM	Cambodia
CAN	Canada
CAY	Cayman Islands
CGO	Congo
CHA	Chad
CHI	Chile
CHN	China
CIV	Ivory Coast
CMR	Cameroun
COK	Cook Islands
COL	Colombia
COM	Comoros
CPV	Cape Verde
CRC	Costa Rica
CRO	Croatia
CUB	Cuba
CYP	Cyprus
DEN	Denmark
DJI	Djibouti

DMA	Dominica
DOM	Dominican Republic
ECU	Ecuador
EGY	Egypt
ESA	El Salvador
ESP	Spain
EST	Estonia
ETH	Ethiopia
FIJ	Fiji
FIN	Finland
FRA	France
FRG	Germany (West)*[1]
GAB	Gabon
GAM	Gambia
GBR	Great Britain
GDR	Germany (East)*[1]
GEO	Georgia
GEQ	Equatorial Guinea
GER	Germany*[1]
GHA	Ghana (ex-Gold Coast)
GRE	Greece
GRN	Grenada
GUA	Guatemala
GUI	Guinea
GUM	Guam
GUY	Guyana
HAI	Haiti
HKG	Hong Kong
HON	Honduras
HUN	Hungary
INA	Indonesia
IND	India
IRL	Ireland
IRN	Iran
IRQ	Iraq
ISL	Iceland
ISR	Israel
ISV	Virgin Islands
ITA	Italy
IVB	British Virgin Islands
JAM	Jamaica
JOR	Jordan
JPN	Japan
KAZ	Kazakhstan
KEN	Kenya
KGZ	Kyrgyzstan
KOR	Korea
KSA	Kingdom of Saudi Arabia
KUW	Kuwait
LAO	Laos
LAT	Latvia
LBA	Libya
LBR	Liberia
LCA	Saint Lucia
LES	Lesotho
LIB	Lebanon

LIE	Liechtenstein
LTU	Lithuania
LUX	Luxembourg
MAD	Madagascar
MAL	Malaysia
MAR	Morocco
MAW	Malawi
MDA	Republic of Moldava
MDV	Maldives
MEX	Mexico
MGL	Mongolia
MKD	Republic of Macedonia
MLI	Mali
MLT	Malta
MON	Monaco
MOZ	Mozambique
MRI	Mauritius
MTN	Mauritania
MYA	Myanmar
NAM	Namibia
NCA	Nicaragua
NED	Netherlands
NEP	Nepal
NGR	Nigeria
NGU	Papua New Guinea
NIG	Niger
NOR	Norway
NRU	Nauru
NZL	New Zealand
OMA	Oman
PAK	Pakistan
PAN	Panama
PAR	Paraguay
PER	Peru
PHI	Philippines
PLE	Palestine
POL	Poland
POR	Portugal
PRK	Democratic People's Republic of Korea
PUR	Puerto Rico
QAT	Qatar
ROM	Romania
RSA	South Africa*[2]
RUS	Russian Federation
RWA	Rwanda
SAF	South Africa*[2]
SAM	Western Samoa
SEN	Senegal
SEY	Seychelles
SIN	Singapore
SKN	St Kitts and Nevis
SLE	Sierra Leone
SLO	Slovenia
SMR	San Marino
SOL	Solomon Islands
SOM	Somalia

SRI	Sri Lanka
STP	Sao Tome and Principe
SUD	Sudan
SUI	Switzerland
SUR	Surinam
SVK	Slovakia
SWE	Sweden
SWZ	Swaziland
SYR	Syria
TAN	Tanzania
TCH	Czechoslovakia*[3]
THA	Thailand
TJK	Tajikistan
TKM	Turkmenistan
TOG	Togo
TGA	Tonga
TPE	Taipei (formerly Formosa/Taiwan)
TRI	Trinidad & Tobago
TUN	Tunisia
TUR	Turkey
UAE	United Arab Emirates
UGA	Uganda
UKR	Ukraine
URS	Soviet Union
URU	Uruguay
USA	United States of America
UZB	Uzbekistan
VAN	Vanuatu
VEN	Venezuela
VIE	Vietnam
VIN	St Vincent and the Grenadines
VOL	Upper Volta
YEM	Yemen
YUG	Yugoslavia
ZAI	Zaire
ZAM	Zambia (ex Northern Rhodesia)
ZIM	Zimbabwe (ex Rhodesia)

[1] Germany from 1896 to 1964 inclusive, German Democratic Republic and Federal Republic of Germany from 1968 to 1988 inclusive. Germany from 1992.

[2] South Africa prior to 1992. RSA from 1992 onwards.

[3] Czechoslovakia up to and including 1992. Henceforth two separate nations - Slovakia (SVK) and the Czech Republic (CZE).

PART 3
The Sportsfile

Weights and Measures

g	grams
kg	kilograms
st	stones (= 14 lbs)
lb	pounds
mm	millimetres
cm	centimetres
m	metres
km	kilometres
yds	yards
ft	feet
in.	inches

Scores and Times

pts	Points
NS	Non starter
DQ	Disqualified
2:11:46.23	– hours: minutes: seconds. divisions of seconds

Event Categories

(m)	Men
(w)	Women
(op)	Open
ind.	Individual
-52kg etc.	Under 52kg
100+ kg etc.	Over 100kg
K1	Single-handed kayak (canoeing)
K2	two-person kayak
K4	four-person kayak
C1	single-handed Canadian canoe
C2	two-person Canadian canoe
Cox	Coxswain (rowing)
pos	Positions i.e. smallbore rifle three positions
4x100m etc.	A relay of four legs each covering 100m.

Archery

Stars to Watch

by Richard Perelman

Not for the Feint of Heart

A S THE 1996 Olympic Games draws near, there are certain events for which the favourite is well established, well known and for whom the competition may just as well be a coronation. Archery is not one of them.

The thrilling, unpredictable and nerve-rattling excitement of archery's Olympic Round has tossed the sport into a period of arising interest and enthusiasm as never before. Unlike the past years, where all archers shot more than 100 arrows and the winner was singled out from the crowd only at the end, the Olympic Round pits archers against each other in a sudden-death format in six separate rounds of matches.

Who, then, will wear the title of Olympic champion after the competitions at Stone Mountain are completed? Judging by the results of the 1992 Olympic Games and the subsequent world championships, it could be almost anyone. The man or woman who is best able to concentrate under pressure will win.

Kim Soo Nyung

Sebastien Flute of France, the 1992 champion, is amongst the men's favourites. He also won the European men's title in 1992 and followed that with silver in the same event in 1994. Korea, meanwhile, have a new shooting star in the guise of Lee Kyung Chul. He won the 1995 world championships as an unknown. His compatriot and bronze medallist in the same event, Oh Kyo Moon, is the current world record holder for the "FITA Round" (144 arrows at four different distances).

Finland's 23 year old Jari Lipponen, as 1995 European champion, must have a chance. So does Taipei's Wu Tsung-yi, the silver medallist at last year's world championships. 1988 Olympic champion Jay Barrs, of the USA, will also be part of the starting line-up.

Korea's female archers have been totally dominant since the mid-'80s and four names could feature amongst the 1996 medallists – Youm Youn Ja, the highest ranked Korean of 1995, together with world junior medallists Kang Hyun Ji, Hwang Jin Hae and Park Woon Joo. But the Olympic Round is proving a great equalizer and Germany's 1995 world silver medallist, Barbara Mensing must have a chance. If a favourite were named, however, it would have to be Elena Toutachikova of Russia who won the 1995 world championships.

★★★★★★★★★★★★★★★★★★★★★★★★★★ **A Contemporary Heroine**

Kim Soo Nyung (Korea)

Great champions come to the field expecting to win. Legends, however, are expected to win. So it was for Kim Soo Nyung, the unperturbable Korean who completely dominated women's archery from 1988 – '91.

Kim rose to international attention as a 16 year old in 1987 and set a world record for the 30m segment of the FITA Round with 356 out of a possible 360 points. By 1988 she had become the world's best, setting three world records and winning the Olympic tournament with consummate ease.

In 1989 she set three more world records (including her third mark in the challenging 144-arrow FITA Round) and destroyed an outstanding field to win her first world championship – a title she successfully defended in 1991.

Kim completed her outstanding "run" with a silver medal at the 1992 Olympic Games where even her hot shooting proved no match for 22 year old Cho Youn Jeong. In honour of Kim's achievements the Koreans named one of the finest archery fields in the world – just outside Seoul – after her.

In the team competitions, where three archers must work quickly to fire 27 arrows per match (nine per archer) in just nine minutes, the depth of the Korean women's team gives them the favourite's role. But they will be challenged by balanced teams from Indonesia, Sweden, the USA and the surprise of the 1995 world championships, Turkey.

Will Spain pull off another miracle in the men's division as they did in winning the men's title in 1992? Not likely, with strong teams from Korea (the favourite), the United States, Italy, Sweden, France and Finland all in contention.

R. P. □

Retrospective

Archery introduced a new head-to-head format (where archers compete side by side and shoot alternately) called the

"Olympic Round" for its final stages four years ago in Barcelona and it proved an immediate and resounding success. After a qualifying round of 144 arrows at four distances, the top 32 men and top 32 women went forward to knock-out stages decided by 12 arrow contests. Korea, so dominant in 1988, adapted well to the format winning two gold and two silver medals.

The Games Spanish hosts, however, provided the shock results by winning the men's team event after France had disposed of the favourites, Korea, in the quarter-finals. Britain won its first individual medal for 84 years when unemployed roofer, Simon Terry, took bronze in the men's competition. Terry needed a sudden-death one arrow shoot-out to beat reigning Olympic champion Jay Barrs in the last eight after they had tied on 108 points apiece.

Korea and America have tended to dominate the Olympic archery scene in recent Games. Few champions, however, could be more diverse than John Williams and Doreen Wilber who took their respective individual titles for the USA in 1972 – a year in which archery returned to the Olympic Games after an absence of 52 years in the idyllic setting of the "Englischer Garden".

Williams stood 1.89m (6ft 2in.) tall and was a private in the army whose training was a revolution in the sport and could be likened to a long distance runner. He was still only 18 when he arrived in Munich despite having won a world silver medal in 1969. In the first round he scored a world record 1,268 points and followed that with a total of 2,528 points by the end of the second round – the first man to break the magic 2,500 points barrier. He knew he had won with three arrows to spare in the second round.

Wilber, meanwhile, was an Iowa housewife aged 42. Staggeringly, she managed to recover from a 26 point deficit to Pole Irena Szydłowska after the first round to win by 17 points on the final day.

Archery has also created two Olympic "firsts". William Dod won the 1908 men's singles event and Charlotte Dod was silver medallist in the women's competition of that year. They

Charlotte (Lottie) Dod

were brother and sister, the first siblings to win Olympic medals in any sport at the Games. Charlotte was a remarkable athlete having won the Wimbledon tennis singles five times, the British Ladies golf title and represented England at hockey.

At the 1984 Games New Zealand's Neroli Fairhall competed in the women's event finishing 35th. In doing so, she became the first wheelchair athlete to compete in an Olympic Games.

Background

Archery made its Olympic debut in 1900. It returned in 1904, 1908 and 1920 before vanishing from the programme until 1972. Team events were added in 1988. The Olympic rumour machine claims that there was once an event in the sport called "shooting the live pigeon" but this is extremely difficult to verify from any official source.

There is much legend surrounding the sport. This includes a considerable amount of literature about a celebrated English outlaw and popular hero called Robin Hood who lived in Nottinghamshire's Sherwood Forest in about 1160. He is alleged to have robbed the rich to give to the poor and defended his people against the "wicked" Sheriff of Nottingham.

Moreover, he is always described as having outstanding skill in archery. In fact, the title page of an early ode to the hero "A Mery Geste of Robyn Hoode" (1550) pictures him preparing to shoot an arrow from a longbow of at least 6ft (1.83m) in height.

The use of the bow first appears in Ancient Egyptian artworks and is reported in the accounts of famous battles throughout history to the 1500s. Ghengis Khan conquered massive territories using a short, powerful bow for his Mongol hordes. British monarchs, including Henry VIII, were archers of considerable renown and English literature honours the longbow for famous victories at Agincourt, Crecy and Poitiers.

International competitions in archery began with Anglo-French matches around 1900, leading to its appearance in the Olympic Games of that year. Belgian Hubert van Innis won six gold and three silver medals in the Games of 1900 and 1920 – still the most for any archer at the Games. Archery's international federation, FITA, was formed in 1931 to standarize rules and the first world championships were held in

A Sporting Legend ★★★★★★★★★★★★★★★★★★★★★★★★★★★★★★★★★★★★★★

Hubert van Innis *(Belgium)*

The skill and concentration demanded by archery makes repeating a championship – or even a medal – difficult. Consider then the ability of one man who won gold medals in different events in two different Games, spaced 20 years apart. That is Hubert van Innis of Belgium.

As a 34 year old, in 1900, he performed brilliantly in Paris to win two individual gold medals (Au cordon dore: 33m and Au chapelet: 33m) and a silver medal (Au cordon dore: 50m).

Archery took place at the 1904 and 1908 Games but van Innis did not compete. He returned in 1920, in Antwerp, to win the Moving Bird Target class at 28m and 33m, and the 28m and 50m team events. He also won two silver medals. His medal haul qualifies him as one of the most decorated of all Belgian Olympians. This sporting legend died in 1961 aged 95.

Lvov, Poland, in that year. Poland, Czechoslovakia, USA, Great Britain, Denmark, Germany and Sweden were early forces within the sport.

Equipment

The simple "whippy" wood and string bows of childhood games, together with the longbows of yore, bear little resemblance to the high-tech bows of today's Olympic archer (see diagram). They can be made from laminations of wood with carbon fibre, fibreglass, ceramic (boron) or hard foam. Competitors can use a sighting device on their bows as long as it does not contain a lens or other magnifying device. Binoculars are only used to see how particular arrows have scored. Bows also have stabilizers with shock absorbing weights.

Each arrow has a shaft made of carbon or aluminium with a steel head (or point) and "fletchings" (vanes to assist in flight) normally of thin plastic. The targets used in the Olympic Games are of 122cm (48in.) and 80cm (31.4in.) in diameter and are marked into coloured zones which each score differently (see diagram). The bullseyes or centres are 12.2cm (4.8in.) and 4.0cm (1.57in.).

Rules

At the 1996 Games archers will first compete in a "ranking round" of 72 arrows each at 70m on the larger of the two targets (see below) in ends of six arrows each. From this first round, the leading 64 men and 64 women will advance to a knock-out phase consisting of 18 arrows at 70m until eight archers emerge for the final rounds. In the quarter-finals, semi-finals and final – as well as the bronze medal shoot-off – archers will have 12 arrows each, shooting alternately with a time limit of 40 seconds per arrow. Any ties will be broken by a sudden death encounter of a single arrow.

The top 16 three-person teams, selected from the results of the individual event, compete in the knock-out team event. Each team must shoot a total of 27 arrows within nine minutes – three at a time per archer.

The target is marked out in separate colours each of which has an inner and outer ring. They score as follows from inner to outer: gold – 10 and 9 points, red 8 and 7 points, blue 6 and 5 points, black 4 and 3 points, white 2 and 1 points.

Bow and arrow

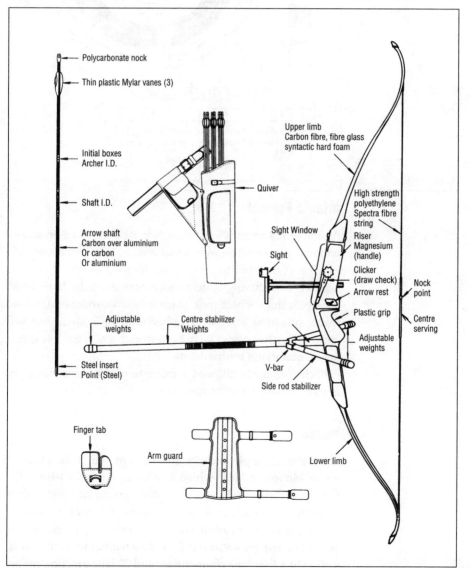

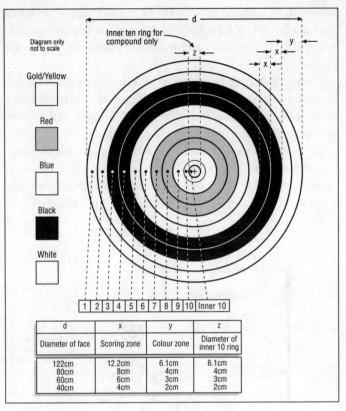

1	2	3	4	5	6	7	8	9	10	Inner 10

d	x	y	z
Diameter of face	Scoring zone	Colour zone	Diameter of inner 10 ring
122cm	12.2cm	6.1cm	6.1cm
80cm	8cm	4cm	4cm
60cm	6cm	3cm	3cm
40cm	4cm	2cm	2cm

Diagram only not to scale

Inner ten ring for compound only

Gold/Yellow

Red

Blue

Black

White

Archery target

Atlanta Format

A total of 128 archers will compete in Atlanta – 64 men and 64 women. There will be individual men's and women's as well as team events. For the first time, the road to the Games has been via a qualifying system based heavily on the 1995 world championships which took place in Jakarta, Indonesia, where teams qualified for places rather than individually-named archers. Further places have been won through the five continental qualifying tournaments.

Each country is allowed a maximum of three archers per gender in the Olympic tournament.

Venue

The 1996 Olympic archery tournament will take place at Stone Mountain Park which is 25.6km (16 miles) from the Olympic Village and has a spectator capacity of 5,200. This is a dramatic venue as it is set against the world's largest exposed granite monolith – one of Atlanta's top tourist attractions. The archery arena itself will be a temporary facility consisting of a four lane competition, and 22 lane practice, range.

Stone Mountain Archery Site

MEDALLISTS (by nation)

	Men's			Women's			
	Gold	Silver	Bronze	Gold	Silver	Bronze	Total
United States	7	5	4	4	2	3	25
France	6	10	6	-	-	-	22
Belgium	10	6	3	-	-	-	19
Korea	1	2	-	5	2	2	12
Soviet Union	-	1	1	1	2	4	9
Great Britain	1	1	3	1	1	1	8
Finland	1	1	1	-	-	1	4
Japan	-	1	1	-	-	-	2
China	-	-	-	-	2	-	2
Italy	-	-	2	-	-	-	2
Netherlands	1	-	-	-	-	-	1
Spain	1	-	-	-	-	-	1
Indonesia	-	-	-	-	1	-	1
Poland	-	-	-	-	1	-	1
Sweden	-	1	-	-	-	-	1
	28[1]	28	21[2]	11	11	11[3]	110

[1] Only a gold medal awarded in two 1920 events
[2] No bronze medals in one 1900 and six 1920 events
[3] No bronze medal in 1904 team event

ATLANTA SCHEDULE

Venue: Stone Mountain Park

Date	Description	Round	Start	End
28 Jul	ind (w)	ranking	9:00	11:30
	ind (m)	ranking	14:00	16:30
29 Jul	ind (w)	Last 64	9:00	12:20
	ind (w)	Last 32	14:00	17:20
30 Jul	ind (m)	Last 64	9:00	12:20
	ind (m)	Last 32	14:00	17:20
31 Jul	ind (w)	Last 16	9:00	12:20
	ind (w)	FINAL	14:00	17:00
1 Aug	ind (m)	Last 16	9:00	12:20
	ind (m)	FINAL	14:00	17:00
2 Aug	team (w)	Last 16	9:00	11:00
	team (w)	q/finals		
	team (w)	s/finals		
	team (m)	Last 16		
	team (m)	q/finals		
	team (m)	s/finals		
	team (w)	s/finals	12:15	17:00
	team (w)	FINALS		
	team (m)	s/finals		
	team (m)	FINALS		

MEDALLISTS

ARCHERY (Men)

Year	Gold	C'ntry	Points	Silver	C'ntry	Points	Bronze	C'ntry	Points
Individual									
1972*	John Williams	USA	2528	Gunnar Jervill	SWE	2481	Kyösti Laasonen	FIN	2467
1976	Darrell Pace	USA	2571	Hiroshi Michinaga	JPN	2502	Giancarlo Ferrari	ITA	2495
1980	Tomi Poikolainen	FIN	2455	Boris Isatchenko	URS	2452	Giancarlo Ferrari	ITA	2449
1984	Darrell Pace	USA	2616	Richard McKinney	USA	2564	Hiroshi Yamamoto	JPN	2563
1988	Jay Barrs	USA	2605	Park Sung Soo	KOR	2614	Vladimir Echejev	URS	2600
1992	Sebastien Flute	FRA	110	Chung Jae Hun	KOR	107	Simon Terry	GBR	109
1996									

Year	Gold	C'ntry	Points	Silver	C'ntry	Points	Bronze	C'ntry	Points
Team									
1988	Chun In Soo	KOR	986	Jay Barrs	USA	972	Steven Hallard	GBR	968
	Lee Han Sup			Richard McKinney			Richard Priestman		
	Park Sung Soo			Darrell Pace			Leroy Watson		
1992	Juan Carlos Holgado	ESP	238	Ismo Falck	FIN	236	Steven Hallard	GBR	233
	Romero			Jari Lipponen			Richard Priestman		
	Alfonso Ménendez			Tomi Poikolainen			Simon Terry		
	Vallín								
	Antonio Vásquez Megido								
1996									

ARCHERY (Women)

Year	Gold	C'ntry	Points	Silver	C'ntry	Points	Bronze	C'ntry	Points
Individual									
1972	Doreen Wilber	USA	2424	Irena Szydłowska	POL	2407	Jemma Gaptchenko	URS	2403
1976	Luann Ryon	USA	2499	Valentina Kovpan	URS	2460	Zebinoso Rustamova	URS	2407
1980	Ketevan Losaberidse	URS	2491	Natalia Butusova	URS	2477	Päivi Meriluoto-Aaltonen	FIN	2449
1984	Seo Hyang Soon	KOR	2568	Li Lingjuan	CHN	2559	Kim Jin Ho	KOR	2555
1988	Kim Soo Nyung	KOR	1352	Wang Hee Kyung	KOR	2612	Yung Young Sook	KOR	2603
1992	Cho Youn Jeong	KOR	112	Kim Soo Nyung	KOR	105	Natalia Valejeva	EUN	104
1996									

Year	Gold	C'ntry	Points	Silver	C'ntry	Points	Bronze	C'ntry	Points
Team									
1988	Kim Soo Nyung	KOR	982	Lilies Handayani	INA	952	Deborah Ochs	USA	952
	Wang Hee Kyung			Nurfitriyana Saiman			Denise Parker		
	Yun Young Sook			Kusuma Wardhani			Melanie Skillman		
1992	Cho Youn Jeong	KOR	236	Ma Xiangjun	CHN	228	Ludmila Archannikova	EUN	240
	Kim Soo Nyung			Wang Hong			Katuna Kvrivichvili		
	Lee Eun Kyung			Wang Xiaozhu			Natalia Valejeva		
1996									

* Archery also took place in different formats in the years 1900–1908 and 1920.

Athletics (Track & Field)

Stars to Watch

by Ian Chadband

The Class of '96

THEY have a lot to live up to but, if their previous examination results are anything to go by, the cream of the athletics class of '96 should graduate from Atlanta with flying colours. Their names will rest comfortably alongside any of the revered alumni who illuminated the previous century of Olympic track and field competition.

The roll call promises an intoxicating mix. There are the long-time playground idols like Carl Lewis, Heike Drechsler, Jackie Joyner-Kersee, Sergei Bubka, Javier Sotomayor and Merlene Ottey. They are preparing for perhaps one final prize-giving day, while precocious students like Ivan Pedroso, Maria Mutola and Haile Gebrselassie wait to fill their shoes.

Linford Christie

Then we have the supremely gifted like Noureddine Morceli, Michael Johnson and Jonathan Edwards, who flunked their last Olympic exams. And Dan O'Brien and Moses Kiptanui, who missed out on the chance to even sit them. They are all desperate not to mess up their retakes. From the mercurial Jan Zelezny to the miraculous Gail

Devers and the "magnifique" Marie-Jose Perec, the assembly is overflowing with rare talent.

One thing is for sure; the class will be the most cosmopolitan we have seen. Athletes from a record 35 countries won medals at the last Games in Barcelona. But the evidence from the 1995 world championships in Gothenburg, where the figure rose to 43, indicates the spoils will be shared more widely than ever before.

That promises to be the great thing about these Olympics. From Tajikistan to Trinidad, from the Bahamas to Burundi, from Syria to Saudi Arabia, a host of previously unlikely nations can harbour realistic dreams of gold, some of which could never before have imagined seeing one of their own on the podium.

After Jerome Romain, from Dominica, won triple jump bronze in Gothenburg, he spent most of his time afterwards explaining that he did not come from the Dominican Republic and telling everyone just exactly where in the Caribbean his beautiful little island lay. In July, you can guarantee others will be putting their unsung countries on the map, too.

A Contemporary Heroine ★★★★★★★★★★★★★★★★★★★★★★★★★★★★★★

Ghada Shouaa (Syria)

Nothing exemplified the nature of track and field's expanding global village quite like the sight of a powerful 21 year-old from an Arab nation with no previous athletics pedigree ascending to the title of the world's best all-round woman athlete in Gothenburg. In the absence of the injured American Jackie Joyner-Kersee, Ghada Shouaa took the opportunity to become Syria's first world champion in any sport amid great celebrations back in Damascus.

When the increasingly vulnerable Joyner-Kersee returns to defend her heptathlon crown in Atlanta, she will find an opponent who, despite lacking her natural speed and finesse, has enviable raw talent. Shouaa is national record holder in six of her seven heptathlon events and is improving at such a startling rate (with the help of money-no-object funding from her government and expert coaching from former Soviet discus star Kim Bukhantsev) that it is surely only a matter of time before she becomes only the third woman to top the 7,000pt mark.

For the likes of Romain, a medal from Gothenburg was quite something. One from Atlanta would represent the ultimate. The move to biennial world championships (which has led some athletes to feel its medals have already become slightly devalued) has only served to heighten the importance and mystique of the Games.

After Kiptanui (the great Kenyan steeplechaser who missed out on Barcelona when he failed to qualify from the trials) won in Gothenburg, he reckoned he could not get too excited because it was his third world gold in six years; but the Olympics? Ah, he said, that was different, that was his dream.

Indeed, it is remarkable how many of the world's premier athletes have so far failed to realise that same dream. O'Brien, the world decathlon record holder and three-times world champion, blew out in the last US Olympic trials. He no-heighted in the pole vault. Morceli, who ran wretchedly in the Barcelona 1,500m final, believes he could never stake his claim to being the finest middle-distance runner of all unless he mounts that Olympic gold medal podium.

Michael Johnson (USA)

Likewise, Johnson, whose four years of almost unprecedented sprinting success was rudely interrupted by his failure even to reach the 200m final in Barcelona. Will Jamaica's marvellous 36 year old Ottey feel her dazzling career is somehow unfulfilled if she cannot add a gold to the four consolation bronzes she owns? She is seeking, in her fifth Games, to become the only woman track and field athlete ever to win medals over a 16-year span.

As he attempts to hop, step and jump his way to glory, will Edwards, Britain's world triple jump champion, recall how he could not even reach the final last time around? Can his compatriot Colin Jackson, the finest sprint hurdler of all time who has achieved everything else in the sport, shake off the memory of how he could only finish seventh in the 1992 final?

Being world champion is certainly no guaranteed passport to Olympic success. Only three of the athletes who won individual titles at the 1991 Tokyo world championships went on to repeat the feat in the following year's Games. Barcelona was a champions' graveyard and who is to say Atlanta will be different?

After all, it certainly gets no easier for the old favourites like Joyner Kersee in the heptathlon, Drechsler in the long jump and Zelezny in the javelin. Bubka, of pole vault fame, who had an off-day in Barcelona, has seen off more 'new Sergeis' than he's had world records. But, in Okkert Brits (a daredevil young vaulter from South Africa who last year

A Contemporary Hero ★★★★★★★★★★★★★★★★★★★★★★★★★★★★★

Jonathan Edwards *(Great Britain)*

There are, says Jonathan Edwards, performers who are convinced of their own sporting destiny, who know they were born to greatness. "I", he hastens to add, "am not one of them". Which is why the Briton's ascent to athletic greatness in Gothenburg with a baffled smile and a shrug of incomprehension was so refreshing.

He is, he reckons, an ordinary, skinny guy without the talent, strength and speed of many of his rivals. Yet, in one glorious summer, he graduated from the 38th best triple jumper of all time to become the man who, "à la Beamon", has forced a redefinition of a venerable event's limits.

First, the two longest jumps ever seen, a wind-assisted 18.43m and 18.39m at the European cup in Lille. Then, a world record 17.98m in Salamanca and, ultimately, the breaking of triple jump's most cherished landmarks – the first legal 18m and 60ft jumps – in Gothenburg where he became the first field event athlete ever at a major championship to shatter two world records in successive attempts (18.16m and 18.29m).

A revamped coaching set-up and a modified technique (which sees him use both arms instead of one to propel him through the three phases of the jump) may lie at the root of his incredible improvement. Even he, though, is not quite sure. "People must look at me and think 'If he can do it, anyone can do it'", says Edwards.

His strong faith – he once would not compete on a Sunday because of his religious beliefs – have prompted light-hearted suggestions that divine help must have been at hand. But it is that faith which helps him put his overnight fame into perspective. "God has given me this ability but it's only jumping three times into a pit. The things that matter to me are being a good Christian, husband and family man".

became only the third man to clear six metres) he perhaps sees his genuine heir, a man producing the same fearless aggression which he also used to display as a championship novice.

Ana Quirot

Nothing warmed the heart more in Gothenburg than seeing Ana Quirot, Cuba's incredible comeback woman, take the 800m gold. But her title of world's best may just be on loan. Mutola, the powerhouse from Mozambique who had been unbeaten – and had looked just about unbeatable – in three years of two-lap racing was left in tears in Gothenburg. She was sensationally disqualified in her semi-final for running out of her lane. Lightning cannot be expected to strike twice.

Meanwhile Kiptanui is already seen as some sort of elder statesman for Kenyan athletics, even though he is still

★★★★★★★★★★★★★★★★★★★★★★★★★★★★★★★ A Contemporary Hero

Moses Kiptanui *(Kenya)*

Seven world records, three successive world titles and the historic first sub-eight minute 3,000m steeplechase put Moses Kiptanui on that pedestal reserved for only the finest Kenyan runners – the likes of Keino, Jipcho, Ngugi and Rono. Yet, this quiet, dignified individual will tell you it is still not enough for him. Deprived of his chance for Olympic glory in 1992 when, hampered by injury, he could only finish fourth in the Kenyan steeplechase trial, Kiptanui vowed his career would be unfulfilled unless he put the matter straight in Atlanta.

After completing his world championship hat-trick in Gothenburg, then lowering his record to 7:59.18 in Zurich a few days later, the steeplechase remains his target at the Games. Such is his talent, he could have aimed for the 5,000m following his world record 12:55.30 in Rome in 1995, but his serious assault on the flat will have to wait until 1997 when he will still be only 25.

only 24. He will no doubt have a new crop of compatriots snapping at his heels. Led, perhaps, by Christopher Koskei. He is the barefoot steeplechaser whose bizarre leaps over the barriers and extraordinary mid-race surges in the Gothenburg final stamped him as a real "one-off".

With East African pride at stake, Daniel Komen (another protege of Kiptanui who almost beat the master to the 5,000m world record in Rome in 1995) and Ismael Kirui (whose 5,000m win in Gothenburg was one of the performances of the championships) could turn out to be the best bets to put Kenyan spokes in Ethiopian Gebrselassie's bid for double glory at 5,000 and 10,000m.

Who can beat Morceli, though? If not himself then maybe Burundi's Venuste Niyongabo or Morocco's Hicham El Guerrouj. The two gifted youngsters chased the Algerian home in the Gothenburg 1,500m.

In a Games where there will be few certainties, one is that the host nation will finish top of the track and field medals table – just as in Gothenburg where the USA took 12 golds. No other nation could muster more than two. Atlanta is seen by the movers and shakers in American athletics as a critical opportunity to revive a sport which is treated, for the most part, with indifference at home compared to the likes of pro baseball, basketball and football.

The search for star-spangled heroes and heroines to spark the renaissance leads to champions like Devers, the woman who survived a life-threatening illness to win 100m gold in Barcelona, and Allen Johnson, the smooth high hurdles technician.

A Contemporary Hero ★★★★★★★★★★★★★★★★★★★★★★★★★★★★★★★

Haile Gebrselassie *(Ethiopia)*

Away from the competitive arena, there is an innocence and joviality about Haile Gebrselassie. On the track, his personality is somehow reflected in the way he bounces over the track with a stylish lightness of step which always identified him as something out of the ordinary. For the world's top distance men, it must be like running into a smiling assassin.

This modest young farmer's son is doing a murderous job on the record books, too. At just 22, he could boast four world titles at junior and senior level, and four world records, the last two of which in 1995 represented astonishing new landmarks for the 10,000m and 5,000m. "I am not a God; the only athlete whose image is still revered in my country is Abebe Bikila", says Gebrselassie, yet everyone in Ethiopia is already convinced he is creating a legend all of his own.

The Dutch-based phenomenon, having set a 5,000m record of 12:56.96 in Hengelo in June 1994, returned a year later to clock 26:43.53 for 10,000m. He sliced almost 8.5 seconds off the record thus becoming the first athlete since Henry Rono to hold both marks simultaneously.

That was just the hors d'oeuvre, though. In August, he majestically retained his world 10,000m title, covering the last 200m in a remarkable 25 seconds. And, eight days later, produced a quite epic 5,000m in Zurich. He recorded 12:44.39, removing almost 11 seconds from the record he had lost to Moses Kiptanui earlier in the summer. It marked the single greatest advance in the record for 63 years!

The appetizing prospect for Atlanta is that Gebrselassie will attempt to emulate the 5,000/10,000m double last achieved by his compatriot, Miruts Yifter, in 1980. "I am not interested in silver; the one and only aim of my career is to win Olympic gold," he smiles. We have been warned.

Indeed, the good folk of Atlanta need only look on their own doorstep at Gwen Torrence to find an athlete capable of a golden sprint double. Although the by-now familiar challenge from Ottey and Russia's Irina Privalova makes it anything but a foregone conclusion.

But a demanding public will be looking for something out of the ordinary, something like sprinter and long-jumper Carl Lewis's four-gold masterpiece in Los Angeles. Step forward, Michael Johnson. If the timetable is rearranged to allow him the chance, he could replace Lewis as the American icon by winning both the 200m and 400m as he did in Gothenburg.

Again, though, the hosts cannot count on boasting the fastest man on earth. That holds true even if Britain's Linford Christie, the reigning 100m champion, sticks to his decision not to defend his title. Almost unthinkably, no American made the first three in Gothenburg. Instead, we saw a takeover of Caribbean-born athletes headed by Jamaican-born Canadian, Donovan Bailey, a brilliant sprint late-comer who will be urged on by a nation to exorcise the memory of Ben Johnson and all that.

John Smith, one of the top American coaches, was not alone in pointing out how this new athletics force (17 Caribbean-born athletes, headed by high jump champion, Bahamian

Troy Kemp, won medals in Barcelona) was rapidly eating into traditional USA strongholds. What is the betting, for instance, that Cuba's Ivan Pedroso, homing in on the first nine metre long jump, finally brings down the curtain on Lewis and Mike Powell's long-running double act? And will Javier Sotomayor, also of Cuba and beaten in the Gothenburg final, restore his pride with a successful high jump defence?

As for Smith's star pupil, the Guadeloupe-born Marie-Jose Pérec, she is blessed with such divine ability that either the 400m or one-lap hurdles crown could be hers. If she decides to target the latter after her relentless progress in her first serious campaign at the event in 1995, the company of reigning Olympic champion Sally Gunnell and Gothenburg's most surprising world record breaker, Kim Batten, should ensure another landmark race.

But as one force emerges, another disappears. Whither the Chinese and their one-summer wonder women of 1993? The world awaits the possibility of a return of the amazing Wang Junxia or a remodelled "Ma's Army". But three formidable champions in Algeria's Hassiba Boulmerka (1,500m), Ireland's Sonia O'Sullivan (5,000m) and Portugal's Fernanda Ribeiro (10,000m) are not holding their breath.

The athletics world, though, may be forced to catch its breath if the class of '96 deliver as much as they promise. These centenary Games demand nothing less.

I. C. ☐

★★★★★★★★★★★★★★★★★★★★★★★★★★★ A Contemporary Heroine

Sonia O'Sullivan (Ireland)

Thousands of Irish adventurers have sailed out of Cobh en route to a new life. But few from this beautiful harbour town have gone on to conquer their new world in the single-minded fashion of Sonia O'Sullivan.

Her athletics finishing school was at college in the USA, her home life is divided between a London suburb and Philadelphia and her workaholic racing career has made her a globe-trotting citizen of the world. But when that steely determination powered her to the inaugural 5,000m crown in Gothenburg, she was nobody's but Ireland's. The country's first woman world track champion has succeeded the one-off Chinese wonders, who prevented her collecting two golds at the Stuttgart World Championships, as the complete middle-distance runner.

Equipped with unmatched endurance and speed for the 5,000m in particular, she is planning to double up in the Olympic Games at 1,500m, the event at which she was the world's fastest in 1995. The Irish are ready to turn Atlanta green.

Retrospective

American James Brendan Connolly assured himself of a place in Olympic history when he won the hop, step and jump (now the triple jump) in Athens in 1896 becoming the first Olympic gold medallist of the modern era. Indeed the USA were dominant in many events at the inaugural Games. Thomas Burke won the men's 100m using a "crouch" start, something which fascinated the spectators.

For the Greek hosts, however, the newly-introduced marathon race was the most important of all. It was based on an unverified but legendary run by Greek messenger Pheidippides bringing news of a victory over the Persians in 490 BC. And the Greeks badly wanted to win it. A local shepherd, Spiridon Louis, duly obliged and became a national hero, feted by the King and showered with gifts by a grateful populace. It is even alleged that he stopped for a glass of wine en route.

The marathon also provided a colourful story from the 1908 Games when Italian Dorando Pietri entered the stadium first but on the point of collapse. He was assisted across the line by two well-meaning officials but was later disqualified. Queen Alexandra presented him with a consolation gold cup. The marathon distance had earlier been extended so that the start could be viewed from the Royal nursery at Windsor Castle. It has since remained at the distance of 26 miles 385yds (42.263km instead of the original 42km).

1936 marathon winner Son Kitei (Sohn Kee Chung), of Korea, won his title under the Japanese flag as his country was occupied by Japan at the time. Over fifty years later, in a poignant moment of Olympic history, he carried the Olympic torch into the stadium during the opening ceremony of the Games in South Korea.

Frenchman Alain Mimoun-O-Kacha won the 1956 marathon. He proceeded to donate money raised for him in a collection by the "Equipe" newspaper to the 1928 winner Boughera El Ouafi – also Algerian born – who had been found as a "down-and-out". Four years later barefoot Ethiopian Abebe Bikila signalled the emergence of Africa by winning the marathon – a title he was to defend successfully four years later. The first man in history to do so. The 1972 marathon was marred by a student "prankster" who entered the stadium first and ran a lap before it was discovered that he was not officially entered nor had he run the complete race.

In those 1972 Games Finland's Lasse Viren won the 5,000 and 10,000m double before doing the same in 1976 – a unique double "double". In the 1972 10,000m final he fell during the race but picked himself up and still won in a world record time. The Munich medal rostrum was moved during the Games due to danger from the hammer-throwing competition. And Germany's Ulrike Meyfarth became the youngest ever track and field medallist, aged 16, when she won the high jump to the delight of the home crowd. Meyfarth won the title again in 1984.

Soviet athlete Valeri Borzov won the 1972 100 and 200m sprint double, the first European to achieve the feat at the Games. Haitian, Anilus Joseph, was not quite as competent, however. He was lapped in the 10,000m heats but thought that the final lap bell for the others was also for him. Joseph sprinted a lap before he realized he had at least another lap to run.

Back in 1900 America's track athletes had been shocked, on arrival, to learn that the athletics events in Paris were to be

★★★★★★★★★★★★★★★★★★★★★★★★★★★★★★★★ **A Sporting Legend**

Carl Lewis *(USA)*

Eight gold medals, four of which in one Games. An unprecedented, consecutive three golds in the long jump. The first man successfully to defend a 100m crown. Yet there still remains some unfinished Olympic business for Carl Lewis.

Maybe the prospect that another gold in his fourth Games would bring him level with Nurmi's tally of nine? That two would see him equal Ray Ewry's record of ten? Perhaps that is what persuades him to give it another go. But, he does not have to make another claim on being the finest performer in athletics history. For many that is taken as read as Lewis approaches the close of a career which has also seen him scoop eight world championship titles, equal or better four world records at 100m and set eight low-altitude world bests at 100m, 200m and long jump.

The statistics illustrate as much. But mere statistics could never convey the poetry of Lewis in full cry. In Los Angeles, in 1984, he clocked 9.99 seconds to win the 100m by the biggest-ever margin, recorded a 19.80 seconds 200m into a headwind, jumped 8.3m (28ft) at his first long jump attempt and produced a sprint relay anchor leg timed at 8.94 seconds.

Fantastic, but emulating Owens was apparently not enough for an American audience who felt him just too brash, perhaps almost too good. That has always been his problem. Expectations of his genius have been such that the dual feats of retaining his 100m crown (following Ben Johnson's disqualification) in Seoul and adding two more long jump titles, went largely under-appreciated.

It is only after a few years with his star on the wane that Lewis has begun to earn the admiration (and even affection) back home that his talent always merited. At 35, even if his LA heyday proves a distant memory, Atlanta could provide the USA with a last chance to give a proper salute to a towering figure.

run on grass. They had never before competed on the surface but still managed to dominate the medal tables. Four years later George Page of the USA became the first black man to compete in the Olympic Games when he ran in the heats of the 60m. Page later won a bronze medal in the 400m hurdles. Some sources, however, say that Joseph Stadler, also of the USA, who came second in the standing high jump on the same day, was also black.

Undoubtedly, though, the most famous black American track and field athlete was Jesse Owens. His four golds in the 1936 Olympic Games were won against a backdrop of a pre-War Nazi Germany.

Owens' feats were not matched until the 1984 Games when Californian Carl Lewis also won four golds. Needless to say, Owens had been Lewis's childhood hero.

Lewis went on to re-capture his 1984 100m title four years later in Seoul, South Korea, after one of the most notorious moments in Olympic history. Race winner, Ben Johnson of Canada, was disqualified after giving a sample for drug-testing which showed that he had been using anabolic steroids. Johnson turned from Canadian hero to villain overnight.

Returning, however, to 1912 and a Games where automatic timing was used for the first time. Those Games will be remembered more for the exploits of Jim Thorpe who won both the pentathlon and decathlon. Thorpe, who came from a North American Indian reservation, was later disqualified because it was alleged that he had received money for playing baseball prior to 1912 thus damaging his amateur status. His medals were stripped by the IOC but were later, posthumously, reinstated. Ironically, Avery Brundage competed in the 1912 Games, too. The American was to become IOC President in 1952.

Another American decathlon winner was Bob Mathias in 1948 during the London Games at the tender age of just 17. Those Games were dubbed the "austerity Games" because Britain was still recovering from World War II and many items such as food and petrol were still being rationed.

The 1952 Games, meanwhile, belonged to Emil Zátopek. The Czech won the 5,000 and 10,000m as well as the marathon – all in Olympic record times. His wife, Dana, also won the javelin at the same Games. Remarkably, they were born on the same day as each other.

Zátopek also competed in the 1956 Olympic Games – an act which for the European competitors meant a six-week sea

★★★★★★★★★★★★★★★★★★★★★★★★★★★★★★★ **A Sporting Legend**

Emil Zátopek *(Czechoslovakia)*

He sounds like the stuff of schoolboy fiction. A figure so dramatic that, despite a permanent grimace and hunched style which made him always look as if he was running racked with agony, could win an impossible treble of Olympic 5,000m, 10,000m and marathon golds in the space of eight days. Yet a figure who so embodied the finest values of sportsmanship that his rivals could not help but adore the man who was grinding them into the track.

Zátopek's tale, though, was not fiction: "18 year old Czech from a humble background works in local shoe factory...gets press ganged into running local race...starts taking running seriously...gets called crazy for his revolutionary experiments in pushing back training limits...sometimes slogs himself to near-exhaustion round the track lap after lap in army boots...becomes almost unbeatable at 10,000m...rewrites the record books...sets 18 world marks over six years across the board from 5,000m to 30,000m...ends up a national hero who plays a big part in his country's freedom fight in 1968".

A fantastic tale of which the centrepiece was Zátopek's trip to the Helsinki Games of 1952. First, he successfully defended the 10,000m crown he had won in London. Then, after chatting to and cajoling his opposition in the heats of the 5,000m, prevailed in one of the great Olympic finals, winning a celebrated last lap battle against Alain Mimoun-O-Kacha, Herbert Schade and Christopher Chataway.

Finally, unthinkably, came the marathon, at which he was a complete novice. Thinking Britain's Jim Peters was the man to beat, he introduced himself on the start line, ran alongside him and at 10 miles asked: "Jim, the pace – it is too fast?" Peters, already struggling, jokily replied: "Emil, the pace – it is too slow". Taking him at his word, Emil soon hared off towards immortality.

journey to the Australian city of Melbourne. In the 3,000m steeplechase of that year, Britain's Christopher Brasher (who with Christopher Chataway had helped pace Sir Roger Bannister to the first sub four minute mile) won the steeple-chase but only after having his disqualification for alleged "interference" quashed.

Bannister, Brasher and Chataway's achievements at the Iffley Road track, Oxford, were captured on film and will live forever. So, too, will the stories of Harold Abrahams and Eric Liddell the 1924 100m and 400m winners, respectively, immortalized in the film "Chariots of Fire". Liddell was a deeply-religious Scot, son of a missionary, who was born in China and returned there after the Games. He competed occasionally in Asia but was interned by the Japanese during World War II and died in 1945 of a brain tumour.

Sisters Irina (80m hurdles) and Tamara (shot put) Press both won gold medals at the 1960 Olympic Games. But the crowd was also enchanted by the performances of American

A Sporting Legend ★★★★★★★★★★★★★★★★★★★★★★★★★★★★★★★★★★

Herb Elliott *(Australia)*

"There's only one way to beat him", pondered the 1956 Olympic champion, Ron Delany, after watching the back of a young Australian powering to a new world mile record in Dublin in 1958, "and that's to tie his legs together".

Those who tackled Herb Elliott in his brief but utterly brilliant career understood the sentiment. From when he started training seriously at 16, nobody could beat him in 44 races at 1,500m or the mile. Honed to unprecedented levels of fitness, urged on in fiendish sessions up the sand dunes by his visionary mentor Percy Cerutty, Elliott embodied his master's voice in one fantastic 1,500m run at the 1960 Rome Games when he kicked with 600m left, forged home 20m clear of the field and broke his own world record in 3:35.6. Soon after, at 22, Elliott retired with nothing left to prove. He already had a persuasive claim to being the finest middle distance man of them all.

sprinter Wilma Rudolph who had been a polio victim as a child. Rudolph won three gold medals.

Irina Press, meanwhile, went on to win the pentathlon in 1964 in a Games which will also be remembered for the wonderful and unique double victory for New Zealander Peter Snell in the 800 and 1,500m.

Four years later, in Mexico, during a sometimes turbulent but always spectacular Games, all eyes turned briefly to American Al Oerter who won the discus title for the fourth consecutive time. Mexico provided the environment for Bob Beamon's truly amazing long jump world record and gave the Soviet Union's Victor Saneev the first of his three con-secutive triple jump victories. And those were also the Games in which Americans Tommie Smith and John Carlos won gold and bronze respectively in the 200m. But they proceeded to give their infamous black-gloved, closed-fist salute in a black-power protest on the victory rostrum.

Montreal might have had its African boycott and financial

A Sporting Legend ★★★★★★★★★★★★★★★★★★★★★★★★★★★★★★★★★★

Bob Beamon *(USA)*

The record has gone now, but the moment will never be eclipsed. "Tell me I'm not dreaming", said Bob Beamon, a gangling 1.9m (6ft 3in.), 22 year old New Yorker, when the enormity dawned on him.

He had just taken off into Mexico City's thin air and delivered the single most spectacular feat in Olympic history, not to mention the entire history of track and field.

It had taken 33 years for the world long jump record to progress 8.5in. But with one space-age leap, Beamon improved it by another 21.75in., completely bypassing the 28ft barrier and recording a 29ft 2.5in. (8.90m) monster. "You", the defending champion Lynn Davies told the incredulous record-breaker, "have destroyed this event".

Beamon retired soon after. How, after all, could he top that? His record did eventually disappear 23 years later to Mike Powell in Tokyo at the world championships. But nobody ever forced the sports world to take a leap of the imagination quite like Beamon.

troubles but the Canadian city played host to a unique moment when Hungary's Miklos Nemeth won the javelin with a world record of 94.58m. His father, Imre, won the hammer in 1948. They were the first father and son Olympic gold double.

★★★★★★★★★★★★★★★★★★★★★★★★★★★★★★★ **A Sporting Legend**

Sebastian Coe *(Great Britain)*

Forget his 11 world records; what best identified Sebastian Coe as such a special individual were two extraordinary Olympic comebacks – one mental, one physical.

First, in Moscow 1980, at the height of frenzied speculation about his rivalry with fellow British giant Steve Ovett, Coe, overwhelming favourite to take the 800m, was crestfallen to run a shocker and let in Ovett. Six days later, he brilliantly turned the tables in the 1,500m, handing Ovett his first defeat at the distance for three years.

His hopes of becoming the first man to defend successfully his crown had been written off after he suffered a rare infection which made him wonder in late 1983 whether he might never run again. But, in Los Angeles, he was back to break the Olympic record in the final. "You've seen an athlete come back from the dead", Coe's father and coach Peter said after Moscow. Nobody expected to witness the miracle twice.

Another Olympic relationship which proved very successful in 1980 was that of Britain's Alan Wells and his wife. Wells, who won the 100m gold and silver in the 200m, could not have succeeded without his wife who doubled as his coach.

Both the 1980 and '84 Games, hosted by Moscow and Los Angeles, were marred by tit-for-tat boycotts. In 1984 the women's 3,000m was added to the programme for the first time. It provided one of the most gripping incidents of the Games when the darling of the home crowd, American Mary Slaney, clashed during the race with the diminutive South-African turned Briton, Zola Budd. Budd had been painted a villain for her change of nationality. Both had been pre-race favourites. Slaney tripped and fell and had to be helped away from the track. Budd continued the race but could only finish seventh. Needless to say, a media frenzy of recriminations ensued.

In 1988 the Games moved to Seoul, South Korea, and the emergence of the African nations as an athletics power was thrust to the fore when Africans won all the men's gold medals from 800 to 10,000m. An American woman, however, managed to steal the show. Florence Griffith Joyner (she of the painted, long finger nails, flowing locks and bizarre running outfits) won the 100 and 200m, setting a world record in the 200m twice in 90 minutes. Britain's Daley Thompson, however, failed in his attempt to win the decathlon for a third consecutive Games.

The last Olympic Games in Barcelona were spectacular for their setting as well as their achievements. South Africa returned to the fold for the first time since 1960 leading to one of the most poignant post-race embraces of Games history when the women's 10,000m was won by black Africa's Derartu Tulu of Ethiopia in an epic battle from silver medallist and white South African, Elana Meyer.

Linford Christie became the oldest men's 100m champion at 32 turning the table on the Americans who had beaten him at the 1991 world championships in Tokyo when four men had crossed the line in under ten seconds.

American Gail Devers' story also brought tears to the eyes. She won the 100m just a year after an illness had brought her close to having both legs amputated. Devers might also have won the 100m hurdles but for a dramatic tumble. She fell when leading just a stride or two from the line which allowed Greece's Paraskevi Patoulidou to take victory.

Another square in the patchwork of Olympic human interest stories was provided by Britain's Derek Redmond who had fought injury to make it to the Games. Just into his 400m semi-final, however, his hamstring tore leaving him in agony. But he was determined to cross the line on his own two legs, angrily pushing away the proffered stretcher. His father watched for a while from the crowd before, overcome with emotion, leaping the barrier to help his son limp to the line. The Olympic history books await Atlanta and the chance to add to these rich historical anecdotes.

Background

Athletics has its origins in antiquity. There are records of foot races and throwing competitions which date back as far as the thirteenth century BC as part of the Greek Olympic Games. All the events, of course, were for men. Women were forbidden from even spectating. And it took until 1928 before women's track events, only five (which remained the same until 1972), were permitted as part of the athletics programme of the modern Olympic Games as well as the discus and high jump.

In Europe, competitions have been recorded as far back as 1154 and there were races in both Robert Dover's "Olympick Games", between 1612 and 1852, as well as the Much Wenlock Olympian Games from 1850 onwards – both in Britain. The first athletics club, Necton Guild, was formed in Britain in 1817 and the first English athletics championships were in 1866. After that time, however, America became the leading athletics power internationally.

Early competitions were often held on open fields although they were to be supplanted by clay and "cinder" tracks before the advent of modern synthetic surfaces. Automatic timing of races began as early as the 1912 Olympic Games and in 1948 the first photo-finish camera was installed. The camera was not used, however, until 1960 as a means of recording official times. By 1952 electronic scoreboards, so much a part of modern spectator sports, had emerged.

In 1956 the Soviet Union, after the re-drawing of post-War Europe, won its first track and field gold medals with Vladimir Kouts in the 5,000 and 10,000m. In that same year, the Federal Republic of Germany and the German Democratic Republic competed as one nation after protracted negotiations with the IOC.

The 1960 Games were remarkable for the fact that Olympic records were set in every men's event except the 5,000m, 20km walk, 110m hurdles and javelin. There were also qualifying standards for the first time for track and field events.

Athletes from Ethiopia, Kenya and Morocco emerged as leading forces in those Rome Games, too. And the women's 800m was re-instated after an absence of 32 years. Four years later the Olympic programme included a 400m for women for the first time.

★★★★★★★★★★★★★★★★★★★★★★★★★★★★★★★ **A Sporting Legend**

Irena Szewińska *(Poland)*

No woman athlete achieved so much over such a long span as Poland's majestic queen of the track. And nobody provided more pleasure over an incredible journey which took in five Games and a record seven medals in five different events.

It started in Tokyo where the 18 year old Leningrad girl of Polish parentage, Irena Kirszenstein, took long jump silver behind Mary Rand, then helped her relay team to a world record. It forged on to Mexico, where the now-married Mrs Szewińska won the 200m in a world record (22.5 seconds).

Two years after the birth of her son, it stuttered on to Munich where, unfit, she still landed a 200m bronze, but revived miraculously in Montreal where she smashed her own 400m world record (49.29 seconds). It ended with injury in Moscow. But no matter. The mind's eye could still recall those long flowing strides of an all-rounder who always delighted in a challenge and exemplified grace under pressure.

In 1968 American Dick Fosbury unveiled his revolutionary high jump technique called the Fosbury "flop" where athletes twist at the last moment to sail over the bar backwards. It has since passed into universal use. Mexico City also witnessed the introduction of the still controversial "sex testing" for female athletes.

Meanwhile confidence in women's ability to run longer distances was marked in 1972 by their first Olympic 1,500m race – that at a time when the 10,000m was being introduced to the men's programme. The female athlete of the 1972 Games was Ludmila Bragina who set a world and Olympic record in winning the 1,500m. And another woman, Lia Manoliu, of Romania, a discus thrower competed in her sixth Games.

In 1976 Cuban Alberto Juantorena re-wrote the record books by winning the 400m and 800m – the first man ever. And certainly the first to win an 800m title as a virtual international novice at the distance. The Games were marred, however, by Poland's Danuta Rosani who became the first track and field athlete to test positive for drugs at the Games.

Sebastian Coe

Sebastian Coe of Great Britain became the first man to defend successfully the 1,500m title in Los Angeles in 1984. In that same year Valerie Brisco-Hooks of America became the first woman to win the 200m and 400m in one Games. And in Los Angeles a new style javelin was introduced because throwing distances with the old javelin were beginning to endanger the spectators.

Another two "firsts" in Los Angeles came with the introduction of a women's marathon and 400m hurdles. The latter was won by Morocco's Nawal El Moutawakel who became the first Arabic woman to take track gold. She was swiftly followed by Said Aouita, her compatriot, who was the first Arabic man to win a medal with gold in the 5,000m.

In 1988, reflecting the modern era, a women's 10,000m event was added for the first time and was won by Olga Bondarenko of the Soviet Union. Whilst Carl Lewis will be remembered for his 100m victory in Seoul (after Ben Johnson's disqualification) he also won the long jump for the second time. Amazingly, in 1992, he was to add a third consecutive long jump title taking his place in the record books as the first man ever to do so.

Lewis is still a possible contender for Atlanta where he would also become remarkable for his Olympic longevity. It may be left to others, however, to continue to add to the annals of Olympic history and superlatives.

Equipment

America's sprinters were already using "crouch starts" at the first Games of the modern era in Athens. Today's sprinters must, however, use starting blocks for events up to and including the 400m as these are wired as part of the timing device and to detect false starts through the pressure pads on them.

All the hurdles events have ten barriers varying in height from 106.7cm (3ft 6in.) for the men's 110m hurdles to 76.2cm (2ft 6in.) for the women's 400m hurdles. In the 3,000m steeplechase there are 28 barriers 3.96m (12ft 11in.) wide and 91.4cm (3ft) high and seven water jumps 3.66m (12ft) in length and never more than 0.7m (2ft 4in.) in depth to negotiate during the race.

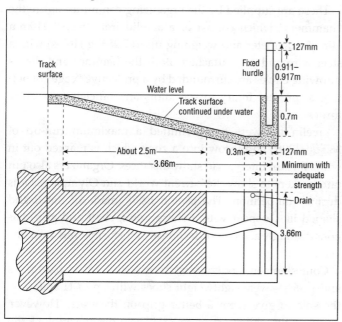

Water jump

A throwing circle of 2.135m (7ft) in diameter is used for the shot and hammer and 2.50m (8ft 2in.) for the discus. These have a wooden stop board at the front edge. The shot is made of solid iron, brass or any metal not softer than brass and

Shot put circle

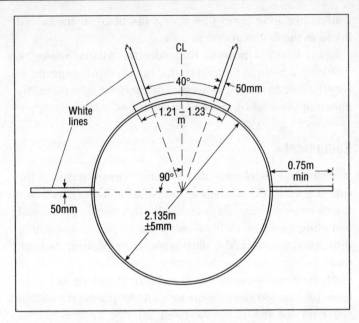

weighs up to 7.285kg (16lbs) for men and 4.025kg (8–9lbs) for women. The discus is composed of wood or other suitable materials with metal plates and weighs up to 2.025kg (4lb 7oz) for men and 1.025kg (4lb 4oz) for women.

These are supplied by the organizing committee as are the "hammers" which consist of a a solid iron "head" 110mm (4in.) in diameter and weighing up to 7.285kg (16lbs) with a steel wire and grip attached. Both the hammer and discus throwing circles are surrounded by a protective "cage" of netting to prevent injury to spectators and officials from stray throws.

Javelin throwers are permitted a maximum run-up of 36.5m (120ft) and throw into a zone which is marked out in white lines at intervals to show distances. Organizers also put out markers to show the current world and Olympic records during competition. The javelin itself (made of metal and shaped like a spear with a sharp point, shaft and grip) has gone through a series of technical transformations over the years.

Contestants in modern track races – rather than road races and walks – wear lightweight shoes with up to 11 spikes on the sole to give them a better grip on the track. However, these are not obligatory as several "barefoot" champions can testify. The old running vest and shorts have been replaced in many cases by tight, lycra running suits. Competitors must wear their running number on both their back and chests (only either the back or chest for high jump and pole vault) as well as adhesive numbers on the sides of their shorts to help the photo-finish cameras.

The track itself is 400m long and has 8 lanes which are between 1.22 (4ft) and 1.25m (4ft 1in.) wide. Modern tracks are made of synthetic surfaces. They have replaced the old grass and cinder versions and have a raised concrete kerb on the inside.

Competitors in the high jump are permitted a maximum 25m run-up to the bar where conditions permit. The upright posts of the high jump barrier are four metres apart and the bar itself must not weigh more than 2kg (4lbs 6oz). Generally, it is made of lightweight metal. And the landing area is soft cushioning unlike the sand pits of history.

In the long jump and triple jump the run-up is a maximum of 45m (148ft) and competitors still land in a sand pit but jumps are measured at international events with an electronic device rather than measuring tape. And if a competitor no-jumps by putting a part of a foot beyond the take-off board this registers when the spikes pierce a plasticine indicator board just in front of the take-off board.

The pole vault, it is believed, developed as a sporting event from its Dutch origins where farmers used long wooden poles to vault over drainage ditches. Considerable changes have taken place in the landing area (now a soft cushion) and the pole itself (now generally made of carbon fibre) to allow flexibility and spring. The runway for the pole vault is around 45m (148ft) and, on take-off, the end of the pole is placed into a "box". Vaulters attempt to clear the cross bar which is 4.52m (14ft 3in.) wide and weighs a maximum of 2.5kg.

Timekeepers at modern athletics events are now able to time races to the nearest one hundredth of a second. Their equipment is linked to the starter's gun, or similar apparatus, with less than a millisecond of delay between the report of the muzzle and the start of the timing device. The finish must be recorded through a stills camera, with a vertical slit, positioned at the finish line on a continuous film by a photo-finish procedure. Or by a video camera with a minimum of 50 frames per second. The film must also be synchronized with a uniformly marked time-scale graduated in thousandths of a second. The times and places are read from the film with a special device. They are then relayed to the scoreboards via a computer system.

Cameras, of course, are not only used for timing at the Olympic Games. TV cameras are now so sophisticated, and so small, that they can be placed in the uprights of the high jump and pole vault, for instance, giving close-ups of the action. Track race coverage is also enhanced by a camera placed on the back of a golf-cart type vehicle which rolls ahead of the action and by cameras placed in tracks down the finish straight – either at ground level or along the stadium roof. For road races, cameras are carried on the back of vehicles and motor-cycles.

Rules

Track races take place in an anti-clockwise direction and each athlete has a separate lane for all races up to and including 400m. They must remain in that lane at all times – stepping on the inside of the white line between lanes on the bend leads to disqualification.

There are "staggered" starts for the 200m, 400m, 800m and 400m hurdles races as well as the 4 x 400m relays. This is to take into account the curvature of the track. In the 800m competitors run in their lanes as far as the end of the first bend at which point they "break" for the inside lane. In the 4 x 400m relay teams run in their lanes for a complete lap and one complete curve before they are allowed to break. For both the 4 x 100m and 4 x 400m relays the athletes must pass the baton to each other within designated changeover boxes on the track. There are complicated formulae for the measurement and marking out of the different staggers and relay change-over boxes.

In all the shorter distances competitors are drawn in lanes. At the start no part of their hands must pass beyond the starting line. Both hands and one knee must be in contact with the ground and both feet with the starting blocks. For races up to 400m the starter gives the commands "on your marks", "set" and then the gun is fired. For races longer than 400m he simply says "on your marks" and then the gun is fired.

If a competitor starts to move before the gun sounds, a false start is registered. This is indicated by a marker on that athlete's lane box. Two false starts (three in combined events) means disqualification. In races which are not run in lanes – such as the longer distances of 5,000 and 10,000m – the starting line is curved so that runners start at the same distance from the finish.

In close finishes the winner of a race is the athlete whose body crosses the line first. By "body", the rules mean the torso as distinguished from the head, arms, neck, legs, hands or feet. Athletes in hurdles races can knock over any number of barriers without being disqualified as long as they are judged not to have done so deliberately with their hands or feet. In the steeplechase it is permissible to stand on the barrier in making a clearance. Athletes must also go over or through, rather than around, the water jump.

In the field events, a no-throw is registered if an athlete steps out of the throwing circle (or across the throwing line in the javelin). Each athlete is allowed three throws to qualify for the final of 12 athletes – consisting of three throws each from which the best eight athletes go forward for another three throws. Competitors are allowed two practice throws before the competition begins. The javelin must land tip first within the designated area.

There have been few more harrowing sights than that at the 1993 world championships when, literally, dozens of walkers were disqualified as they entered the stadium for infringements which occurred earlier in the race. Basically, walkers must maintain unbroken contact with the ground – i.e the front foot must touch the ground before the back foot is lifted. Competitors are warned if they infringe the rule and then are disqualified for a second infringement.

In the high jump a starting height is chosen for the competition and thereafter the bar is raised at pre-designated levels after each round. Competitors can decide at which height they enter the competition. After a failure at one height a competitor can forego his other two attempts and try at the next height. A competitor is eliminated after three consecutive failed attempts regardless of the height. The winner is the athlete who jumps the highest. In the event of athletes recording the same height a "count-back" system on attempts at each height is used to determine the winner and other placings. The same basic rules apply for the pole vault.

Athletes are drawn in the order in which they compete for both the long and triple jumps. Each athlete has three attempts to reach the final of 12 athletes which consists of three more jumps from which the best eight athletes go forward for a further three jumps. Competitors are disqualified if their take-off foot goes over the board, if they land outside the pit and if they employ any form of somersaulting!

There are two combined events in the Olympic Games – the decathlon for men and the heptathlon for women. These are decided by a system of points attributed for each performance. The athlete with the highest number of points wins.

Atlanta format

1,300 men and 776 women are expected to take part in the track and field athletics events in Atlanta. All competition will be according to International Amateur Athletics Federation rules.

Since 1992, a women's 5,000m and triple jump competition have been added to the programme whilst the 3,000m for women has been deleted. There are qualifying standards in all events. A country may enter up to three athletes per event provided that they have achieved the international "A" standard.

Venue

Athletics will take place at the Olympic Stadium in Atlanta. This is situated 4.7km (2.9 miles) from the Olympic Village and has a capacity of over 83,000. It was constructed specially for the Games and will later become the home of the Atlanta Braves baseball team and the track itself will be modified and given to Clark Atlanta University. Construction began in 1993 and finished in 1996. The cost of the entire project is $209 million.

ATHLETICS – current Olympic records

Event	Name	Country	Time/Result	Games	Year
Men					
100m	Carl Lewis	USA	9.92	Seoul	1988
200m	Mike Marsh	USA	19.73	Barcelona	1992
400m	Quincy Watts	USA	43.50	Barcelona	1992
800m	Joaquim Cruz	BRA	1:43.00	Los Angeles	1984
1,500m	Sebastian Coe	GBR	3:32.53	Los Angeles	1984
5,000m	Said Aouita	MAR	13:05.59	Los Angeles	1984
10,000m	Moulay Brahim Boutayeb	MAR	27:21.46	Seoul	1988
Marathon (42,195m)	Carlos Lopes	POR	2:09:21.00	Los Angeles	1984
3,000m steeplechase	Julius Kariuki	KEN	8:05.51	Seoul	1988
110m Hurdles	Roger Kingdom	USA	12.98	Seoul	1988
400m Hurdles	Kevin Young	USA	46.78	Barcelona	1992
20km walk	Jozef Pribilinec	TCH	1:19.57	Seoul	1988
50km walk	Vyacheslav Ivanenko	URS	3:38.29	Seoul	1988
4x100m relay	Mike Marsh	USA	37.40	Barcelona	1992
	Leroy Burrell				
	Dennis Mitchell				
	Carl Lewis				
4x400m relay	Andrew Valmon	USA	2:55.74	Barcelona	1992
	Quincy Watts				
	Michael Johnson				
	Steve Lewis				
High Jump	Gennadi Avdeenko	URS	2.38	Seoul	1988
Pole Vault	Sergei Bubka	URS	5.90	Seoul	1988
Long Jump	Bob Beamon	USA	(A) 8.90	Mexico City	1968
Triple Jump	Mike Conley	USA	17.63	Barcelona	1992
Shot	Ulf Timmermann	GDR	22.47	Seoul	1988
Discus	Jurgen Schult	GDR	68.82	Seoul	1988
Hammer	Sergei Litvinov	URS	84.80	Seoul	1988
Javelin[1]	Miklós Németh	HUN	94.58	Montreal	1976
	Jan Železný	TCH	89.66	Barcelona	1992
Men Decathlon[2]	Daley Thompson	GBR	8847	Los Angeles	1984

[1]In 1986 the javelin was technically changed to reduce the risk incurred by very long throws
[2]Under the 1962 tables - 8798 points

Event	Name	Country	Time/Result	Games	Year
Women					
100m	Florence Griffith Joyner	USA	10.62	Seoul	1988
			10.54(w)		
200m	Florence Griffith Joyner	USA	21.34	Seoul	1988
400m	Olga Bryzguina	URS	48.65	Seoul	1988
800m	Nadezhda Olizarenko	URS	1:53.43	Moscow	1980
1,500m	Paula Ivan	ROM	3:53.96	Seoul	1988
3,000m	Tatiana Samolenko	URS	8:26.53	Seoul	1988
10,000m	Olga Bondarenko	URS	31:05.21	Seoul	1988
Marathon (42,195m)	Joan Benoit	USA	2:24.52	Los Angeles	1984
10km walk	Chen Yueling	CHN	43:32.00	Barcelona	1992
100m Hurdles	Jordanka Donkova	BUL	12.38	Seoul	1988
400m Hurdles	Debra Flintoff-King	AUS	53.17	Seoul	1988
4x100m relay	Romy Muller	GDR	41.60	Moscow	1980
	Barbel Wockel				
	Ingrid Auerswald				
	Marlies Gohr				
4x400m relay	Tatiana Ledovskaia	URS	3:15.18	Seoul	1988
	Olga Nazarova				
	Maria Piniguina				
	Olga Bryzguina				
High Jump	Louise Ritter	USA	2.03	Seoul	1988
Long Jump	Jackie Joyner-Kersee	USA	7.40	Seoul	1988
Shot	Ilona Slupianek	GDR	22.41	Moscow	1980
Discus	Martina Hellmann	GDR	72.30	Seoul	1988
Javelin	Petra Felke	GDR	74.68	Seoul	1988
Heptathlon	Jackie Joyner-Kersee	USA	7291	Seoul	1988

MEDALLISTS (by nation)

	Men's			Women's			
	Gold	Silver	Bronze	Gold	Silver	Bronze	Total
United States[1]	251	189	157	36	24	14	671
Soviet Union	37	37	42	34	29	35	214
Great Britain	44	57	43	5	20	13	182
Finland	47	33	29	-	2	-	111
GDR	14	14	14	24	23	21	110
Sweden	19	25	42	-	-	3	89
Germany	7	22	24	7	12	13	85
Australia	6	9	12	11	8	12	58
France	7	20	19	4	1	3	54
Canada	10	10	16	2	5	7	50
Italy	13	7	19	3	4	2	48
FRG	4	8	12	8	6	5	43
Poland	9	7	5	6	8	7	42
Hungary	6	13	16	3	1	2	41
Kenya	12	12	8	-	-	-	32
Greece	3	8	14	1	-	-	26
Czechoslovakia	8	7	3	3	2	2	25
Romania	-	-	1	9	9	6	25
Jamaica[2]	4	10	4	-	3	4	25
Cuba	3	6	3	2	1	4	19
New Zealand	7	1	7	1	-	2	18
Japan	4	5	6	-	2	-	17
South Africa	4	4	4	1	2	1	16
Bulgaria	1	-	1	2	7	5	16
Netherlands	-	1	5	6	2	1	15
Ethiopia	5	1	6	1	-	-	13
Norway	3	2	7	-	1	-	13
Belgium	2	6	3	-	-	-	11
Brazil	3	2	5	-	-	-	10
Switzerland	-	6	2	-	-	-	8
Morocco	3	2	1	1	-	-	7
Mexico	3	3	-	-	-	-	6
Spain	2	2	2	-	-	-	6
China	-	-	1	1	1	3	6
Ireland	4	1	-	-	-	-	5
Argentina	2	2	-	-	1	-	5
Portugal	1	1	1	1	-	1	5
Austria	-	-	-	1	1	3	5
Tunisia	1	2	1	-	-	-	4
Denmark	1	1	1	-	-	1	4
Trinidad	1	1	2	-	-	-	4
Nigeria	-	1	1	-	-	1	3
Chile	-	1	-	-	1	-	2
India	-	2	-	-	-	-	2
Tanzania	-	2	-	-	-	-	2
Yugoslavia	-	2	-	-	-	-	2
Estonia	-	1	1	-	-	-	2
Latvia	-	1	1	-	-	-	2
Taipei	-	1	-	-	-	1	2
Namibia	-	2	-	-	-	-	2
Panama	-	-	2	-	-	-	2
Philippines	-	-	2	-	-	-	2
Algeria	-	-	-	1	-	-	1
Korea	1	-	-	-	-	-	1
Lithuania	1	-	-	-	-	-	1
Luxembourg	1	-	-	-	-	-	1
Uganda	1	-	-	-	-	-	1
Haiti	-	1	-	-	-	-	1
Iceland	-	1	-	-	-	-	1
Ivory Coast	-	1	-	-	-	-	1
Senegal	-	1	-	-	-	-	1
Sri Lanka	-	1	-	-	-	-	1
Bahamas	-	-	1	-	-	-	1

	Men's			Women's			
	Gold	Silver	Bronze	Gold	Silver	Bronze	Total
Barbados[2]	-	-	1	-	-	-	1
Colombia	-	-	-	-	-	1	1
Djibouti	-	-	1	-	-	-	1
Qatar	-	-	1	-	-	-	1
Turkey	-	-	1	-	-	-	1
Venezuela	-	-	1	-	-	-	1
	555	555	551	174	176	173	2184

[1]Includes 2 additional golds awarded when Jim Thorpe reinstated to 1912 decathlon/pentathlon titles
[2]Two bronzes counted for joint British West Indies 4x400m relay team in 1960

ATLANTA SCHEDULE

Venue: Olympic Stadium

Date	Description	Round	Start	End
26 Jul	20km walk (m)	FINAL	8:00	12:15
	shot (m)	Q/fying		
	100m (w)	Rd 1		
	100m (m)	Rd 1		
	800m (w)	Rd 1		
	javelin (w)	Q/fying	17:30	22:15
	100m (m)	Rd 2		
	high jump (m)	Q/fying		
	100m (m)	Rd 2		
	800m (m)	Rd 1		
	5000m (w)	Rd 1		
	shot (m)	FINAL		
	10,000m (m)	Rd 1		
27 Jul	heptathlon (w)	100m hurdles	9:15	14:30
	triple jump (w)	Q/fying		
	400 m (m)	Rd 1		
	heptathlon (w)	high jump		
	400m (w)	Rd 1		
	hammer (m)	Q/fying		
	heptathlon (w)	shot	17:30	22:20
	triple jump (m)	Q/fying		
	100m (w)	s/finals		
	100m (m)	s/finals		
	800m (m)	Rd 2		
	javelin (w)	FINAL		
	800m (w)	s/finals		
	100 (w)	FINAL		
	100m (m)	FINAL		
	heptathlon (w)	200m		
	10,000m (w)	Rd 1		
28 Jul	marathon (w)	FINAL	7:30	12:00
	heptathlon (w)	long jump		
	discus (w)	Q/fying		
	110m hurdles (m)	Rd 1		
	400m hurdles (w)	Rd 1		
	hammer (m)	FINAL	15:30	21:50
	high jump (m)	FINAL		
	heptathlon (w)	javelin		
	110m hurdles (m)	Rd 2		
	400m (m)	Rd 2		
	400m (m)	Rd 2		
	triple jump (w)	FINAL		
	800m (m)	s/finals		
	5,000m (w)	FINAL		
	heptathlon	800m FINAL		

Date	Description	Round	Start	End
29 Jul	10km walk (w)	FINAL	8:30	12:55
	discus (m)	Q/fying		
	200m (m)	Rd 1		
	200m (w)	Rd 1		
	1,500m (m)	Rd 1		
	400m hurdles (m)	Rd 1		
	110m hurdles (m)	s/finals	18:00	22:30
	200m (w)	Rd 2		
	200m (m)	Rd 2		
	discus (w)	FINAL		
	400m (w)	s/finals		
	triple jump (m)	FINAL		
	400m (m)	s/finals		
	800m (w)	FINAL		
	110m hurdles (m)	FINAL		
	3,000m steeple (m)	Rd 1		
	400m hurdles (w)	s/finals		
	10,000m (m)	FINAL		
31 Jul	decathlon (m)	100m	9:00	12:55
	pole vault (m)	Q/fying		
	1,500m (w)	Rd 1		
	decathlon (m)	long jump		
	100m hurdles (w)	Rd 1		
	decathlon (m)	shot		
	shot (w)	Q/fying	17:15	23:00
	decathlon (m)	high jump		
	100m hurdles (w)	Rd 2		
	200m (m)	s/finals		
	long jump (m)	Q/fying		
	200m (w)	s/finals		
	400m hurdles	s/finals		
	discus (m)	FINAL		
	400m hurdles (w)	FINAL		
	3,000m steeple (m)	s/finals		
	400m (m)	FINAL		
	400m (w)	FINAL		
	800m (m)	FINAL		
	decathlon (m)	400m		
	5,000m (m)	Rd 1		
1 Aug	decathlon (m)	110m hurdles	8:00	11:35
	high jump (w)	Q/fying		
	decathlon (m)	discus		
	800m w/chair (w)	FINAL		
	1,500m w/chair (m)	FINAL		
	long jump (w)	Q/fying		
	decathlon (m)	pole vault	14:00	22:30
	decathlon (m)	javelin		
	100m hurdles (w)	s/finals		
	long jump (m)	FINAL		
	1,500m (w)	s/finals		
	1,500m (m)	s/finals		
	400m hurdles (m)	FINAL		
	200m (w)	FINAL		
	200m (m)	FINAL		
	100m hurdles (w)	FINAL		
	decathlon (m)	1,500m FINAL		
	5,000m (m)	s/finals		
2 Aug	50km walk (m)	FINAL	7:30	11:05
	4x100m relay (m)	Rd1		
	javelin (m)	Q/fying		
	4x100m relay (w)	Rd 1		
	4x400m relay (m)	Rd 1		
	pole vault (m)	FINAL		
	shot put (w)	FINAL		

Date	Description	Round	Start	End
	4x100m relay (w)	s/finals		
	4x100m relay (m)	s/finals		
	long jump (w)	FINAL		
	4x400m relay (w)	Rd 1		
	4x400m relay (m)	s/finals		
	3,000m steeple (m)	FINAL		
	10,000m (w)	FINAL		
3 Aug	high jump (w)	FINAL	18:30	21:55
	javelin (m)	FINAL		
	4x100m relay (w)	FINAL		
	4x100m relay (m)	FINAL		
	1,500m (w)	FINAL		
	1,500m (m)	FINAL		
	5,000m (m)	FINAL		
	4x400m relay (w)	FINAL		
	4x400m relay (m)	FINAL		
4 Aug	marathon (m)	FINAL	18:30	21:30

MEDALLISTS

ATHLETICS (Men)

Year	Gold	C'ntry	Time	Silver	C'ntry	Time	Bronze	C'ntry	Time
100m									
1896	Thomas Burke	USA	12.0	Fritz Hoffmann	GER	12.2	Alajos Szokolyi	HUN	12.6
1900	Francis Jarvis	USA	11.0	Walter Tewksbury	USA	11.1	Stanley Rowley	AUS	11.2
1904	Archie Hahn	USA	11.0	Nathan Cartmell	USA	11.2	William Hogenson	USA	11.2
1908	Reginald Walker	SAF	10.8	James Rector	USA	10.8	Robert Kerr	CAN	11.0
1912	Ralph Craig	USA	10.8	Alvah Meyer	USA	10.9	Donald Lippincott	USA	10.9
1920	Charles Paddock	USA	10.8	Morris Kirksey	USA	10.8	Harry Edward	GBR	10.9
1924	Harold Abrahams	GBR	10.6	Jackson Scholz	USA	10.7	Arthur Porritt	NZL	10.8
1928	Percy Williams	CAN	10.8	Jack London	GBR	10.9	Georg Lammers	GER	10.9
1932	Eddie Tolan	USA	10.3	Ralph Metcalfe	USA	10.3	Arthur Jonath	GER	10.4
1936	Jesse Owens	USA	10.3	Ralph Metcalfe	USA	10.4	Martinus Osendarp	NED	10.5
1948	Harrison Dillard	USA	10.3	H Norwood Ewell	USA	10.4	Lloyd Labeach	PAN	10.6
1952	Lindy Remigino	USA	10.4	Herbert McKenley	JAM	10.4	Emmanuel McDonald Bailey	GBR	10.4
1956	Bobby Morrow	USA	10.5	Walter Baker	USA	10.5	Hector Hogan	AUS	10.6
1960	Armin Hary	GER	10.2	David Sime	USA	10.2	Peter Radford	GBR	10.3
1964	Robert Hayes	USA	10.0	Enrique Figuerola	CUB	10.2	Harry Jerome	CAN	10.2
1968	James Hines	USA	9.9	Lennox Miller	JAM	10.0	Charles Greene	USA	10.0
1972	Valeri Borzov	URS	10.14	Robert Taylor	USA	10.24	Lennox Miller	JAM	10.33
1976	Hasely Crawford	TRI	10.06	Donald Quarrie	JAM	10.08	Valeri Borzov	URS	10.14
1980	Allan Wells	GBR	10.25	Silvio Leonard	CUB	10.25	Petr Petrov	BUL	10.39
1984	Carl Lewis	USA	9.99	Sam Graddy	USA	10.19	Ben Johnson	CAN	10.22
1988	Carl Lewis	USA	9.92	Linford Christie	GBR	9.97	Calvin Smith	USA	9.99
1992	Linford Christie	GBR	9.96	Frank Fredericks	NAM	10.02	Dennis Mitchell	USA	10.04
1996									
200m									
1900	Walter Tewksbury	USA	22.2	Norman Pritchard	IND	22.8	Stanley Rowley	AUS	22.9
1904	Archie Hahn	USA	21.6	Nathan Cartmell	USA	21.9	William Hogenson	USA	—
1908	Robert Kerr	CAN	22.6	Robert Cloughen	USA	22.6	Nathan Cartmell	USA	22.7
1912	Ralph Craig	USA	21.7	Donald Lippincott	USA	21.8	William Applegarth	GBR	22.0
1920	Allen Woodring	USA	22.0	Charles Paddock	USA	22.1	Harry Edward	GBR	22.2
1924	Jackson Scholz	USA	21.6	Charles Paddock	USA	21.7	Eric Liddell	GBR	21.9
1928	Percy Williams	CAN	21.8	Walter Rangeley	GBR	21.9	Helmuth Körnig	GER	21.9
1932	Eddie Tolan	USA	21.2	George Simpson	USA	21.4	Ralph Metcalfe	USA	21.5
1936	Jesse Owens	USA	20.7	Matthew Robinson	USA	21.1	Martinus Osendarp	NED	21.3
1948	Melvin Patton	USA	21.1	H Norwood Ewell	USA	21.1	Lloyd Labeach	PAN	21.2
1952	Andy Stanfield	USA	20.7	Walter Baker	USA	20.8	James Gathers	USA	20.8
1956	Bobby Morrow	USA	20.6	Andy Stanfield	USA	20.7	Walter Baker	USA	20.9
1960	Livio Berruti	ITA	20.5	Lester Carney	USA	20.6	Abdoulaye Seye	FRA	20.7
1964	Henry Carr	USA	20.3	Otis Drayton	USA	20.5	Edwin Roberts	TRI	20.6
1968	Tommie Smith	USA	19.8	Peter Norman	AUS	20.0	John Carlos	USA	20.0
1972	Valeri Borzov	URS	20.00	Larry Black	USA	20.19	Pietro Mennea	ITA	20.30
1976	Donald Quarrie	JAM	20.23	Millard Hampton	USA	20.29	Dwayne Evans	USA	20.43
1980	Pietro Mennea	ITA	20.19	Allan Wells	GBR	20.21	Donald Quarrie	JAM	20.29
1984	Carl Lewis	USA	19.80	Kirk Baptiste	USA	19.96	Thomas Jefferson	USA	20.26
1988	Joe Deloach	USA	19.75	Carl Lewis	USA	19.79	Robson Silva	BRA	20.04
1992	Mike Marsh	USA	20.01	Frank Fredericks	NAM	20.13	Michael Bates	USA	20.38
1996									
400m									
1896	Thomas Burke	USA	54.2	Herbert Jamison	USA	—	Charles Gmelin	GBR	—
1900	Maxwell Long	USA	49.4	William Holland	USA	49.6	Ernst Schultz	DEN	—
1904	Harry Hillman	USA	49.2	Frank Waller	USA	49.9	Herman Groman	USA	50
1908	Wyndham Halswelle	GBR	50						
	John Carpenter	USA	DQ	William Robbins	USA	NS	John Taylor	USA	NS
1912	Charles Reidpath	USA	48.2	Hanns Braun	GER	48.3	Edward Lindberg	USA	48.4
1920	Bevil Rudd	SAF	49.6	Guy Butler	GBR	49.9	Nils Engdahl	SWE	50.0
1924	Eric Liddell	GBR	47.6	Horatio Fitch	USA	48.4	Guy Butler	GBR	48.6
1928	Raymond Barbuti	USA	47.8	James Ball	CAN	48.0	Joachim Büchner	GER	48.2
1932	William Carr	USA	46.2	Ben Eastman	USA	46.4	Alexander Wilson	CAN	47.4

ATHLETICS (TRACK & FIELD)

Year	Gold	C'ntry	Time	Silver	C'ntry	Time	Bronze	C'ntry	Time
1936	Archie Williams	USA	46.5	Godfrey Brown	GBR	46.7	James LuValle	USA	46.8
1948	Arthur Wint	JAM	46.2	Herbert McKenley	JAM	46.4	Malvin Whitfield	USA	46.9
1952	Vincent George Rhoden	JAM	45.9	Herbert McKenley	JAM	45.9	Ollie Matson	USA	46.8
1956	Charles Jenkins	USA	46.7	Karl Haas	GER	46.8	Ardalion Ignatiev	URS	47.0
							Voitto Hellsten	FIN	47.0
1960	Otis Davies	USA	44.9	Carl Kaufmann	GER	44.9	Malcolm Spence	SAF	45.5
1964	Michael Larrabee	USA	45.1	Wendell Mottley	TRI	45.2	Andrzej Badeński	POL	45.6
1968	Lee Evans	USA	43.8	Larry James	USA	43.9	Ronald Freeman	USA	44.4
1972	Vincent Matthews	USA	44.66	Wayne Collett	USA	44.8	Julius Sang	KEN	44.92
1976	Alberto Juantorena	CUB	44.26	Fred Newhouse	USA	44.4	Herman Frazier	USA	44.95
1980	Viktor Markin	URS	44.60	Richard Mitchell	AUS	44.84	Frank Schaffer	GDR	44.87
1984	Alonzo Babers	USA	44.27	Gabriel Tiacoh	CIV	44.54	Antonio McKay	USA	44.71
1988	Steven Lewis	USA	43.87	Harry Reynolds	USA	43.93	Danny Everett	USA	44.09
1992	Quincy Watts	USA	43.50	Steve Lewis	USA	44.21	Samson Kitur	KEN	44.24
1996									

800m

Year	Gold	C'ntry	Time	Silver	C'ntry	Time	Bronze	C'ntry	Time
1896	Edwin Flack	AUS	2:11.0	Nándor Dani	HUN	2:11.8	Demitrios Golemis	GRE	—
1900	Alfred Tysoe	GBR	2:01.2	John Cregan	USA	2:03.0	David Hall	USA	—
1904	James Lightbody	USA	1:56.0	Howard Valentine	USA	1:56.3	Emil Breitkreutz	USA	1:56.44
1908	Melvin Sheppard	USA	1:52.8	Emilio Lunghi	ITA	1:54.2	Hans Braun	GER	1:55.2
1912	James Edward Meredith	USA	1:15.9	Melvin Sheppard	USA	1:52.0	Ira Davenport	USA	1:52.0
1920	Albert Hill	GBR	1:53.4	Earl Eby	USA	1:53.6	Bevil Rudd	SAF	1:54.0
1924	Douglas Lowe	GBR	1:52.4	Paul Martin	SUI	1:52.6	Schuyler Enck	USA	1:53.0
1928	Douglas Lowe	GBR	1:51.8	Erik Byléhn	SWE	1:52.8	Hermann Engelhard	GER	1:53.2
1932	Thomas Hampson	GBR	1:49.8	Alexander Wilson	CAN	1:49.9	Phillip Edwards	CAN	1:51.5
1936	John Woodruff	USA	1:52.9	Mario Lanzi	ITA	1:53.3	Phillip Edwards	CAN	1:53.6
1948	Malvin Whitfield	USA	1:49.2	Arthur Wint	JAM	1:49.5	Marcel Hansenne	FRA	1:49.8
1952	Malvin Whitfield	USA	1:49.2	Arthur Wint	JAM	1:49.4	Heinz Ulzheimer	GER	1:49.7
1956	Thomas Courtney	USA	1:47.7	Derek Johnson	GBR	1:47.8	Audun Boysen	NOR	1:48.1
1960	Peter Snell	NZL	1:46.3	Roger Moens	BEL	1:46.5	George Kerr	ANT	1:47.1
1964	Peter Snell	NZL	1:45.1	William Crothers	CAN	1:45.6	Wilson Kiprugut	KEN	1:45.9
1968	Ralph Doubell	AUS	1:44.3	Wilson Kiprugut	KEN	1:44.5	Thomas Farrell	USA	1:45.4
1972	David Wottle	USA	1:45.9	Evgeni Arzhanov	URS	1:45.9	Mike Boit	KEN	1:46.0
1976	Alberto Juantorena	CUB	1:43.50	Ivo Vandamme	BEL	1:43.86	Richard Wohlhuter	USA	1:44.12
1980	Steven Ovett	GBR	1:45.40	Sebastian Coe	GBR	1:45.90	Nikolai Kirov	URS	1:46.00
1984	Joaquim Cruz	BRA	1:43.00	Sebastian Coe	GBR	1:43.64	Earl Jones	USA	1:43.83
1988	Paul Ereng	KEN	1:43.45	Joaquim Cruz	BRA	1:43.90	Said Aouita	MAR	1:44.06
1992	William Tanui	KEN	1:43.66	Nixon Kiprotich	KEN	1:43.70	Johnny Gray	USA	1:43.97
1996									

1,500m

Year	Gold	C'ntry	Time	Silver	C'ntry	Time	Bronze	C'ntry	Time
1896	Edwin Flack	AUS	4:33.2	Arthur Black	USA	4:33.6	Albin Lermusiaux	FRA	4:36.0
1900	Charles Bennett	GBR	4:06.2	Henri Deloge	GRA	4:06.6	John Bray	USA	4:07.2
1904	James Lightbody	USA	4:05.4	William Verner	USA	4:06.8	Lacey Hearn	USA	—
1908	Melvin Sheppard	USA	4:03.4	Harold Wilson	GBR	4:03.6	Norman Hallows	GBR	4:04.0
1912	Arnold Jackson	GBR	3:56.8	Abel Kiviat	USA	3:56.9	Norman Taber	USA	3:56.9
1920	Albert Hill	GBR	4:01.8	Philip Baker	GBR	4:02.4	Lawrence Schields	USA	4:03.1
1924	Paavo Nurmi	FIN	3:53.6	Wilhelm Scharer	SUI	3:55.0	Henry Stallard	GBR	3:55.6
1928	Harry Larva	FIN	3:53.2	Jules Ladoumègue	FRA	3:53.8	Eino Purje	FIN	3:56.4
1932	Luigi Beccali	ITA	3:51.2	John Cornes	GBR	3:52.6	Phillip Edwards	CAN	3:52.8
1936	John Lovelock	NZL	3:47.8	Glenn Cunningham	USA	3:48.4	Luigi Beccali	ITA	3:49.2
1948	Henry Eriksson	SWE	3:49.8	L Strand	SWE	3:50.4	Willem Slijkhuis	NED	3:50.4
1952	Joseph Barthel	LUX	3:45.2	Robert McMillen	USA	3:45.2	Werner Lueg	GER	3:45.4
1956	Ronald Delany	IRL	3:41.2	Klaus Richtzenhain	GER	3:42.0	John Landy	AUS	3:42.0
1960	Herbert Elliott	AUS	3:35.6	Michel Jazy	FRA	3:38.4	István Rózsavölgyi	HUN	3:39.2
1964	Peter Snell	NZL	3:38.1	Josef Odložil	TCH	3:39.6	John Llewellyn Davies	NZL	3:39.6
1968	Hezakieh Keino	KEN	3:34.9	James Ryun	USA	3:37.8	Bodo Tümmler	FRG	3:39.0
1972	Pekka Vasala	FIN	3:36.3	Kipchoge Keino	KEN	3:36.8	Rod Dixon	NZL	3:37.5
1976	John Walker	NZL	3:39.17	Ivo Vandamme	BEL	3:39.27	Paul Wellmann	GER	3:39.33
1980	Sebastian Coe	GBR	3:38.40	Jurgen Straub	GDR	3:38.80	Steven Ovett	GBR	3:39.00
1984	Sebastian Coe	GBR	3:32.53	Steve Cram	GBR	3:33.40	José Abascal	ESP	3:34.30
1988	Peter Rono	KEN	3:35.96	Peter Elliot	GBR	3:36.15	Jens-Peter Herold	GDR	3:36.21
1992	Fermin Cacho Ruiz	ESP	3:40.12	Rachid El-Basir	MAR	3:40.62	Mohamed Sulaiman	QAT	3:40.69
1996									

5,000m

Year	Gold	C'ntry	Time	Silver	C'ntry	Time	Bronze	C'ntry	Time
1912	Hannes Kolehmainen	FIN	14:36.6	Jean Bouin	FRA	14:36.7	George Hutson	GBR	15:07.6
1920	Joseph Guillemot	FRA	14:55.6	Paavo Nurmi	FIN	15:00.0	Erik Backman	SWE	15:13.0
1924	Paavo Nurmi	FIN	14:31.2	Vilho Ritola	FIN	14:31.4	Edwin Wide	SWE	15:01.8
1928	Vilho Ritola	FIN	14:38.0	Paavo Nurmi	FIN	14:40.4	Edwin Wide	SWE	14:41.2
1932	Lauri Lehtinen	FIN	14:30.0	Ralph Hill	USA	14:30	Lauri Virtanen	FIN	14:44.0
1936	Gunnar Höckert	FIN	14.22.2	Lauri Lehtinen	FIN	14:25.8	John Jonsson	SWE	14:29.0
1948	Gaston Reiff	BEL	14:17.6	Emil Zátopek	TCH	14:17.8	Willem Slijkhaus	NED	14:26.8
1952	Emil Zátopek	TCH	14:06.6	Alain Mimoun-O-Kacha	FRA	14:07.4	Herbert Schade	GER	14:08.6
1956	Vladimir Kouts	URS	13:39.6	Gordon Pirie	GBR	13:50.6	Derek Ibbotson	GBR	13:54.4
1960	Murray Halberg	NZL	13:43.4	Hans Grodotzki	GER	13:44.6	Kazimierz Zimny	POL	13:44.8
1964	Robert Keyser Schul	USA	13:48.8	Harald Norpoth	GER	13:49.6	William Dellinger	USA	13:49.8
1968	Mohamed Gammoudi	TUN	14:05.0	Hezakieh Keino	KEN	14:05.2	Nabiba Temu	KEN	14:06.4
1972	Lasse Viren	FIN	13:26.4	Mohamed Gammoudi	TUN	13:27.4	Ian Steward	GBR	13:27.6
1976	Lasse Viren	FIN	13:24.76	Dick Quax	NZL	13:25.16	Klaus Hildenbrand	GER	13:25.38
1980	Miruts Yifter	ETH	13:21.0	Suleiman Nyambui	TAN	13:21.6	Kaarlo Maaninka	FIN	13:22.0
1984	Said Aouita	MAR	13:05.59	Markus Ryffel	SUI	13:07.54	Antonio Leitão	POR	13:09.20
1988	John Ngugi	KEN	13:11.70	Dieter Baumann	FRG	13:15.52	Hansjoerg Kunze	GDR	13:15.73
1992	Dieter Baumann	GER	13:12.52	Paul Bitok	KEN	13:12.71	Fita Bayisa	ETH	13:13.03
1996									

10,000m

Year	Gold	C'ntry	Time	Silver	C'ntry	Time	Bronze	C'ntry	Time
1912	Hannes Kolehmainen	FIN	31:20.8	Louis Tewanima	USA	32:06.6	Albin Stenroos	FIN	32:21.8
1920	Paavo Nurmi	FIN	31:45.8	Joseph Guillemot	FRA	31:47.2	James Wilson	GBR	31:50.8
1924	Vilho Ritola	FIN	30:23.2	Edwin Wide	SWE	30:55.2	Eero Berg	FIN	31:43.0
1928	Paavo Nurmi	FIN	30:18.8	Vilho Ritola	FIN	30:19.4	Edwin Wide	SWE	31:00.8
1932	Janusz Kusociński	POL	30:11.4	Volmari Iso-Hollo	FIN	30:12.6	Lauri Virtanen	FIN	30:35.0
1936	Ilmari Salminen	FIN	30:15.4	Arvo Askola	FIN	30:15.6	Volmari Iso-Hollo	FIN	30:20.2
1948	Emil Zátopek	TCH	29:59.6	Alain Mimoun-O-Kacha	FRA	30:47.4	Bertil Albertsson	SWE	30:53.6
1952	Emil Zátopek	TCH	29:17.0	Alain Mimoun-O-Kacha	FRA	29:32.8	Alexander Anufrijev	URS	29:48.2
1956	Vladimir Kouts	URS	28:45.6	József Kovács	HUN	28:52.4	Allan Cleve Lawrence	AUS	28:53.6
1960	Piotr Bolotnikov	URS	28:32.2	Hans Grodotzki	GER	28:37.0	David William Power	AUS	28:38.2
1964	William Mills	USA	28:24.4	Mohamed Cammoudi	TUN	28:24.8	Ronald Clarke	AUS	28:25.8
1968	Nabiba Temu	KEN	29:27.4	Mamo Wolde	ETH	29:28.0	Mohamed Gammoudi	TUN	29:34.2
1972	Lasse Viren	FIN	27:38.4	Emiel Puttemans	BEL	27:39.6	Miruts Yifter	ETH	27:41.0
1976	Lasse Viren	FIN	27:40.38	Carlos Sousa Lopes	POR	27:45.17	Brendan Foster	GBR	27:54.92
1980	Miruts Yifter	ETH	27:42.70	Kaarlo Maaninka	FIN	27:44.30	Mohammed Kedir	ETH	27:44.70
1984	Alberto Cova	ITA	27:47.54	Michael McLeod	GBR	28:06.22	Mike Musyoki	KEN	28:06.46
1988	Brahim Boutaib	MAR	27:21.46	Salvatore Antibo	ITA	27:23.55	Kipkemboi Kimeli	KEN	27:25.16
1992	Khalid Skah	MAR	27:46.70	Richard Chelimo	KEN	27:47.72	Addis Abebe	ETH	28:00.07
1996									

Marathon

Year	Gold	C'ntry	Time	Silver	C'ntry	Time	Bronze	C'ntry	Time
1896	Spiridon Louïs	GRE	2:58:50	Charilaos Vassilakos	GRE	3:06.03	Gyula Kellner	HUN	3:06:35
1900	Michel Theatro	FRA	2:59:45	Emile Champion	FRA	3:04.17	Ernst Fast	SWE	3:37:14
1904	Thomas Hicks	USA	3:28:53	Albert Corey	FRA	3:34:52	Arthur Newton	USA	3:47:33
1908	John Hayes	USA	2:55:18.4	Charles Hefferon	SAF	2:56:06.0	Joseph Forshaw	USA	2:57:10
1912	Kenneth McArthur	SAF	2:36:54.8	Christian Gitsham	SAF	2:37:52.0	Gaston Strobino	USA	2:38:42
1920	Hannes Kolehmainen	FIN	2:32:35.8	Yüri Lossmann	EST	2:32:48.6	Valerio Arri	ITA	2:36:32
1924	Albin Stenroos	FIN	2:41:22.6	Romeo Bertini	ITA	2:47:19.6	Clarence De Mar	USA	2:48:14
1928	Boughèra El Ouafi	FRA	2:32:57.0	Miguel Plaza	CHL	2:33:23.0	Martti Marttelin	FIN	2:35:02
1932	Juan Carlos Zabala	ARG	2:31:36.0	Samuel Ferris	GBR	2:31:55.0	Armas Toivonen	FIN	2:32:12
1936	Son Kitei	JPN	2:29:19.2	Ernest Harper	GBR	2:31:23.2	Shoryu Nan	JPN	2:31:42
1948	Delfo Cabrera	ARG	2:34:51.6	Thomas Richards	GBR	2:35:07.6	Etienne Gailly	BEL	2:35:33
1952	Emil Zátopek	TCH	2:23:03.2	Reinaldo Gorno	ARG	2:25:35.0	Gustaf Jansson	SWE	2:26:07
1956	Alain Mimoun-O-Kacha	FRA	2:25.00	Franjo Mihalić	YUG	2:26.32	Veikko Leo Karvonen	FIN	2:27.47
1960	Abebe Bikila	ETH	2:15:16.2	Ben Abdesselem Rhadi	MOR	2:15:41.6	Barry Magee	NZL	2:17:18
1964	Abebe Bikila	ETH	2:12:11.2	Benjamin Heatley	GBR	2:16:19.2	Kokichi Tsuburaya	JPN	2:16:22
1968	Mamo Wolde	ETH	2:20:26.4	Kenji Kimihara	JPN	2:23:31.0	Michael Ryan	NZL	2:23:45
1972	Frank Shorter	USA	2:12:19.8	Karel Lismont	BEL	2:14:31.8	Mamo Wolde	ETH	2:15:08

Year	Gold	C'ntry	Time	Silver	C'ntry	Time	Bronze	C'ntry	Time
1976	Waldemar Cierpinski	GDR	2:09.55	Frank Shorter	USA	2:10:45	Karel Lismont	BEL	2:11:12
1980	Waldemar Cierpinski	GDR	2:11:03	Gerard Nijboer	NED	2:11:20	Setymkul Dzhumanazarov	URS	2:11:35
1984	Carlos Lopes	POR	2:09.21	John Treacy	IRL	2:09.56	Charles Spedding	GBR	2:09.58
1988	Gelindo Bordin	ITA	2:10:32	Douglas Wakiihuri	KEN	2:10:47	Houssein Ahmed Saleh	DJI	2:10:59
1992	Hwang Young Cho	KOR	2:13:23	Koichi Morishita	JPN	2:13:45	Stephan Freigang	GER	2:14:00
1996									

110m Hurdles

Year	Gold	C'ntry	Time	Silver	C'ntry	Time	Bronze	C'ntry	Time
1896	Thomas Curtis	USA	17.6	Grantley Goulding	GBR	17.6			
1900	Alvin Kraenzlein	USA	15.4	John McLean	USA	15.5	Frederick Moloney	USA	15.6
1904	Frederick Schule	USA	16.0	Thaddeus Shideler	USA	16.3	Lesley Ashburner	USA	16.4
1908	Forrest Smithson	USA	15.0	John Garrels	USA	15.7	Arthur Shaw	USA	—
1912	Frederick Kelly	USA	15.1	James Wendell	USA	15.2	Martin Hawkins	USA	15.3
1920	Earl Thomson	CAN	14.8	Harold Baron	USA	15.1	Frederick Murray	USA	15.2
1924	Daniel Kinsey	USA	15.0	Sidney Atkinson	SAF	15.0	Sten Pettersson	SWE	15.4
1928	Sydney Atkinson	SAF	14.8	Stephen Anderson	USA	14.8	John Collier	USA	14.9
1932	George Saling	USA	14.6	Percy Beard	USA	14.7	Donald Finlay	GBR	14.8
1936	Forrest Towns	USA	14.2	Donald Finlay	GBR	14.4	Frederik Pollard	USA	14.4
1948	William Porter	USA	13.9	Clyde Scott	USA	14.1	Craig Dixon	USA	14.1
1952	Harrison Dillard	USA	13.7	Jack Davis	USA	13.7	Arthur Barnard	USA	14.1
1956	Lee Calhoun	USA	13.5	Jack Davis	USA	13.5	Joel Shankle	USA	14.1
1960	Lee Calhoun	USA	13.8	Willie May	USA	13.8	Hayes Wendell Jones	USA	14.0
1964	Hayes Wendell Jones	USA	13.6	Harold Blaine Lindgren	USA	13.7	Anatoli Mikhailov	URS	13.7
1968	Willie Davenport	USA	13.3	Ervin Hall	USA	13.4	Eddy Ottoz	ITA	13.4
1972	Rodney Milburn	USA	13.24	Guy Drut	FRA	13.34	Thomas Hill	USA	13.48
1976	Guy Drut	FRA	13.30	Alejandro Casañas	CUB	13.33	Willie Davenport	USA	13.38
1980	Thomas Munkelt	GDR	13.39	Alejandro Casañas	CUB	13.40	Alexander Puchkov	URS	13.44
1984	Roger Kingdom	USA	13.20	Gregory Foster	USA	13.23	Arto Bryggare	FIN	13.40
1988	Roger Kingdom	USA	12.98	Colin Jackson	GBR	13.28	Anthony Cambell	USA	13.38
1992	Mark McKoy	CAN	13.12	Tony Dees	USA	13.24	Jack Pierce	USA	13.26
1996									

400m Hurdles

Year	Gold	C'ntry	Time	Silver	C'ntry	Time	Bronze	C'ntry	Time
1900	Walter Tewksbuy	USA	57.6	Henri Taulin	FRA	58.3	George Orton	USA	—
1904	Harry Hillman	USA	53.0	Frank Waller	USA	53.2	George Poage	USA	—
1908	Charles Bacon	USA	55.0	Harry Hillman	USA	55.3	Leonard Tremeer	GBR	57.0
1920	Frank Loomis	USA	54.0	John Norton	USA	54.3	August Desch	USA	54.5
1924	Frederick Morgan Taylor	USA	52.6	Erik Vilén	FIN	53.8	Ivan Riley	USA	54.2
1928	David Burghley*	GBR	53.4	Frank Cuhel	USA	53.4	Frederick Morgan Taylor	USA	53.6
1932	Robert Tisdall	IRL	51.7	Glenn Hardin	USA	51.9	Frederick Morgan Taylor	USA	52.0
1936	Glenn Hardin	USA	52.4	John Loaring	CAN	52.7	Miguel White	PHI	52.8
1948	Roy Cochran	USA	51.1	Duncan White	CEY	51.8	Rune Larsson	SWE	52.2
1952	Charles Moore	USA	50.8	Yuri Litujev	URS	51.3	John Holland	NZL	52.2
1956	Glenn Davis	USA	50.1	Silas Southern	USA	50.8	Josh Culbreath	USA	51.6
1960	Glenn Davis	USA	49.3	Clifton Cushman	USA	49.6	Richard Howard	USA	49.7
1964	Warren Cawley	USA	49.6	John Cooper	GBR	50.1	Salvatore Morale	ITA	50.1
1968	David Hemery	GBR	48.1	Gerhard Hennige	FRG	49.0	John Sherwood	GBR	49.0
1972	John Akii-Bua	UGA	47.82	Ralph Mann	USA	48.51	David Hemery	GBR	48.52
1976	Edwin Moses	USA	47.64	Michael Shine	USA	48.69	Evgeni Gavrilenko	URS	49.45
1980	Volker Beck	GDR	48.70	Vasili Arkhipenko	URS	48.46	Gary Oakes	GBR	49.11
1984	Edwin Moses	USA	47.75	Danny Harris	USA	48.13	Harald Schmid	FRG	48.19
1988	Andre Phillips	USA	47.19	El Hadj Dia Ba	SEN	47.23	Edwin Moses	USA	47.56
1992	Kevin Young	USA	46.78	Winthrop Graham	JAM	47.66	Kriss Akabusi	GBR	47.82
1996									

*Lord Burghley

Year	Gold	C'ntry	Time	Silver	C'ntry	Time	Bronze	C'ntry	Time

3,000m Steeplechase

1900 (2,500)

	George Orton	USA	7:34.4	Sidney Robinson	GBR	7:38.0	Jacques Chastanie	FRA	—

1904 (2,590)

	James Lightbody	USA	7:39.6	John Daly	IRL	7:40.6	Arthur Newton	USA	—

1908 (3,200)

	Arthur Russell	GBR	10:47.8	Archie Robertson	GBR	10:48.4	John Eisele	USA	—
1920	Percy Hodge	GBR	10:00.4	Patrick Flynn	USA	—	Ernesto Ambrosini	ITA	—
1924	Vilho Ritola	FIN	9:33.6	Elias Katz	FIN	9:44.0	Paul Bontemps	FRA	9:45.2
1928	Toivo Loukola	FIN	9:21.8	Paavo Nurmi	FIN	9:31.2	Ove Andersen	FIN	9:35.6

1932 (3,460)

	Volmari Iso-Hollo	FIN	10:33.4	Thomas Evenson	GBR	10:46.0	Joseph McCluskey	USA	10:46.2
1936	Volmari Iso Hollo	FIN	9:03.8	Kaarlo Tuominen	FIN	9:06.8	Alfred Dompert	GER	9:07.2
1948	Thore Sjöstrand	SWE	9:04.6	Erik Elmsäter	SWE	9:08.2	Göte Hagström	SWE	9:11.8
1952	Horace Ashenfelter	USA	8:45.4	Vladimir Kazantsev	URS	8:51.6	John Disley	GBR	8:51.8
1956	Christopher Brasher	GBR	8:41.2	Sándor Rozsnyói	HUN	8:43.6	Ernst Larsen	NOR	8:44.0
1960	Zdislaw Krzyszkowiak	POL	8:34.2	Nikolai Sokolov	URS	8:36.4	Semyon Rzhistchin	URS	8:42.2
1964	Gaston Roelants	BEL	8:30.8	Maurice Herriott	GBR	8:32.4	Ivan Beliaev	USR	8:33.8
1968	Amos Biwott	KEN	8:51.0	Benjamin Kogo	KEN	8:51.6	George Young	USA	8:51.8
1972	Kipchoge Keino	KEN	8:23.6	Benjamin Jipcho	KEN	8:24.6	Tapio Kantanen	FIN	8:24.8
1976	Anders Gärderud	SWE	8:08.02	Bronisław Malinowski	POL	8:09.11	Frank Baumgartl	GDR	8:10.36
1980	Bronisław Malinowski	POL	8:09.70	Filbert Bayi	TAN	8:12.50	Eshetu Tura	ETH	8:13.60
1984	Julius Korir	KEN	8:11.80	Joseph Mahmoud	FRA	8:13.31	Brian Diemer	USA	8:14.06
1988	Julius Kariuki	KEN	8:05.51	Peter Koech	KEN	8:06.79	Mark Rowland	GBR	8:07.96
1992	Mathew Birir	KEN	8:08.84	Patrick Sang	KEN	8:09.55	William Mutwol	KEN	8:10.74
1996									

20km Walk

1956	Leonid Spirine	URS	1:31:27.4	Antanas Mikenas	URS	1:32.03.0	Bronno Iounk	URS	1:32:12
1960	Vladimir Golubnichi	URS	1:34:07.2	Noel Freeman	AUS	1:34:16.4	Stanley Vickers	GBR	1:34:56
1964	Kenneth Matthews	GBR	1:29:34.0	Dieter Lindner	GER	1:31:13.2	Vladimir Golubnichi	URS	1:31:59
1968	Vladimir Golubnichi	URS	1:33:58.4	José Pedraza	MEX	1:34:00.0	Nikolai Smaga	URS	1:34:03
1972	Peter Frenkel	GDR	1:26:42.4	Vladimir Golubnichi	URS	1:26:55.2	Hans Reimann	GDR	1:27:16
1976	Daniel Bautista	MEX	1:24:40.6	Hans Reimann	GDR	1:25:13.8	Peter Frenkel	GDR	1:25:29
1980	Maurizio Damilano	ITA	1:23:35.5	Piotr Pochinchuk	URS	1:24:45.4	Roland Wieser	GDR	1:25:58
1984	Ernesto Canto	MEX	1:23:13	Raúl González	MEX	1:23:20	Maurizio Damilano	ITA	1:23:26
1988	Jozef Pribilinec	CZE	1:19:57	Ronald Weigel	GDR	1:20:00	Maurizio Damilano	ITA	1:20:14
1992	Daniel Plaza	ESP	1:21:45	Guillaume Leblanc	CAN	1:22:25	Giovanni de Benedicts	ITA	1:23:11
1996									

50km Walk

1932	Thomas Green	GBR	4:50.10.0	Jánis Dalinsh	LAT	4:57.20.0	Ugo Frigerio	ITA	4:59.06
1936	Harold Whitlock	GBR	4:30:41.4	Arthur Schwab	SUI	4:32.09.2	Adalberts Bubenko	LAT	4:32:42
1948	John Ljunggren	SWE	4:41.52.0	Gaston Godel	SUI	4:48.17.0	Terence Johnson	GBR	4:48.31
1952	Giuseppe Dordoni	ITA	4:28:07.8	Josef Doležal	TCH	4:30.17.8	Antal Róka	HUN	4:31:27
1956	Norman Read	NZL	4:30:42.8	Evgeni Maskinskov	URS	4:32:57.0	John Arthur Ljunggren	SWE	4:35:02
1960	Donald Thompson	GBR	4:25:30.0	John Ljunggren	SWE	4:25:47.0	Abdon Pamich	ITA	4:27:55
1964	Abdon Pamich	ITA	4:11:12.4	Vincent Nihill	GBR	4:11:31.2	Ingver Albin Pettersson	SWE	4:14:17
1968	Christoph Hohne	GDR	4:20:13.6	Antal Kiss	HUN	4:30:17.0	Larry Young	USA	4:31:55
1972	Bernd Kannenberg	FRG	3:56:11.6	Veniamin Soldatenko	URS	3:58:24.0	Larry Young	USA	4:00:46
1980	Hartwig Gauder	GDR	3:49:24.0	Jorge Llopart	ESP	3:51:25.0	Evgeni Ivchenko	URS	3:56.32
1984	Raúl González	MEX	3:47:26	Bo Gustafsson	SWE	3:53:19	Sandro Bellucci	ITA	3:53:45
1988	Viacheslav Ivanenko	URS	3:38:29	Ronald Weigel	GDR	3:38:56	Hartwig Gauder	GDR	3:39:45
1992	Andrei Perlov	EUN	3:50:13	Carlos Mercenario Carbajal	MEX	3:52:09	Ronald Weigel	GER	3:53:45
1996									

4 × 100m

1912	William Applegarth Vicktor d'Arcy David Jacobs Henry Macintosh	GBR	42.4	Knut Lindberg Karl Luther Ivan Möller Ture Persson	SWE	42.6	Max Herrmann Erwin Kern Richard Rau Otto Röhr	GER	DQ

Year	Gold	C'ntry	Time	Silver	C'ntry	Time	Bronze	C'ntry	Time
1920	Morris Kirksey Loren Murchison Charles Paddock Jackson Scholz	USA	42.2	Emile Ali Khan René Lorrain René Mourlon René Tirard	FRA	42.6	Agne Holmström Sven Malm William Petersson Nils Sandström	SWE	42.9
1924	Louis Clarke Francis Hussey Alfred LeConey Loren Murchison	USA	41.0	Harold Abrahams William Nichol Walter Rangeley Lancelot Royle	GBR	41.2	Marinus van den Berge Jacobus Boot Henricus Broos Jan de Vries	NED	41.8
1928	Charles Borah James Quinn Henry Russell Frank Wykoff	USA	41.0	Richard Corts Hubert Houben Helmuth Körnig Georg Lammers	GER	41.2	Cyril Gill John London Walter Rangeley Edward Smouha	GBR	41.8
1932	Hector Dyer Robert Kiesel Emmett Toppino Frank Wykoff	USA	40.0	Erich Borchmeyer Walter Hendrix Arthur Jonath Helmuth Körnig	GER	40.9	Giuseppe Castelli Luigi Facelli Ruggero Maregatti Edgardo Toetti	ITA	41.2
1936	Foy Draper Ralph Metcalfe James Owens Frank Wykoff	USA	39.8	Gianni Caldana Tullio Gonnelli Orazio Mariani Elio Ragni	ITA	41.1	Erich Borchmeyer Erwin Gillmeister Gerd Hornberger Wilhelm Leichum	GER	41.2
1948	William Harrison Dillard Harold Norwood Ewell Melvin Patton Lorenzo Wright	USA	40.6	John Archer John Gregory Kenneth Jones Alastair McCorquodale	GBR	41.3	Carlo Monti Enrico Perucconi Antonio Siddi Michele Tito	ITA	41.5
1952	William Harrison Dillard Lindy Remigino Finis Dean Smith Andrew Stanfield	USA	40.1	Levan Kaljajev Levan Sanadze Vladimir Soukharev Boris Tokarev	URS	40.3	György Csányi Béla Goldoványi Géza Varasdi László Zarándi	HUN	40.5
1956	Walter Baker Leamon King Robert Morrow Ira Murchison	USA	39.5	Leonid Bartenev Yuri Konovalov Vladimir Soukharev Boris Tokarev	URS	39.8	Heinz Fütterer Manfred Germar Lothar Knörzer Leonard Pohl	GER	40.3
1960	Bernd Cullmann Armin Hary Martin Lauer Walter Mahlendorf	GER	39.5	Leonid Bartenyev Yuri Konovalov Gusman Kosanov Edvins Ozolin	USR	40.1	David Jones Peter Radford David Segal Neville Whitehead	GBR	40.2
1964	Gerald Ashworth Otis Paul Drayton Robert Hayes Richard Stebbins	USA	39.0	Marjan Dudziak Marjan Foik Wiesław Maniak Andrzej Zieliński	POL	39.3	Josselyn Delecour Paul Genevay Bernard Laidebeur Claude Piquemal	FRA	39.3
1968	Charles Greene James Hines Mel Pender Ronald Smith	USA	38.2	Enrique Figuerola Pablo Montes Juan Morales Hermes Ramírez	CUB	38.3	Roger Bambuck Josselyn Delecour Gérard Fénouil Claude Piquemal	FRA	38.4
1972	Larry Black Eddie Hart Robert Taylor Gerald Tinker	USA	38.19	Valeri Borzov Alexander Korneliuk Vladimir Lovetski Yuri Silov	URS	38.50	Klaus Ehl Jobst Hirscht Karlheinz Klotz Gerhard Wucherer	FRG	38.79
1976	Harvey Glance Millard Hampton John Jones Steven Riddick	USA	38.33	Manfred Kokot Klaus-Dieter Kurrat Jorg Pfeifer Alexander Thieme	GDR	38.66	Alexander Aksinin Valeri Borzov Nikolai Kolesnikov Yuri Silovs	URS	38.78
1980	Alexander Aksinin Vladimir Muraviov Andrei Prokofiev Nikolai Sidorov	URS	38.26	Leszek Dunecki Zenon Licznerski Marian Woronin Krzysztof Zwoliński	POL	38.33	Pascal Barré Patrick Barré Herman Panzo Antoine Richard	FRA	38.53
1984	Ron Brown Sam Graddy Carl Lewis Calvin Smith	USA	37.83	Albert Lawrence Gregory Meghoo Donald Quarrie Ray Stewart	JAM	38.62	Sterling Hinds Ben Johnson Tony Sharpe Desai Williams	CAN	38.70

/continued on next page 117

Year	Gold	C'ntry	Time	Silver	C'ntry	Time	Bronze	C'ntry	Time
1988	Viktor Bryzgine	URS	38.19	Elliot Bunney	GBR	38.28	Bruno Marie-Rose	FRA	38.40
	Vladimir Krylov			Linford Christie			Max Morinière		
	Vladimir Mouraviev			Michael Mcfarlane			Giles Quénéhervé		
	Vitali Savine			John Regis			Daniel Sangouma		
1992	Leroy Burrell	USA	37.40	Olapade Adeniken	NGR	37.98	Andres Gomez	CUB	38.00
	Carl Lewis			Davidson Ezinwa			Joel Gonzalez		
	Mike Marsh			Chidi Imoh			Joel Loaces		
	Dennis Mitchell			Oluyemi Kayode			Jorge Ruiz		
1996									

4 × 400m

Year	Gold	C'ntry	Time	Silver	C'ntry	Time	Bronze	C'ntry	Time
1908	Nathan Cartmell	USA	3:29.4	Hanns Braun	GER	3:32.4	Ödön Bodor	HUN	3:32.5
(Medley	William Hamilton			Hans Eicke			József Nagy		
(Relay)	Melvin Sheppard			Arthur Hoffmann			Vilmos Racz		
	John Taylor			Otto Trieloff			Pál Simon		
1912	Edward Lindberg	USA	3:16.6	Pierre Failliot	FRA	3:20.7	Ernest Henley	GBR	3:23.2
	James Meredith			Charles Lelong			George Nicol		
	Charles Reidpath			Charles Poulenard			Cyril Seedhouse		
	Melvin Sheppard			Robert Schurrer			James Tindal Soutter		
1920	John Ainsworth-David	GBR	3:22.2	Harry Davel	SAF	3:24.2	Georges André	FRA	3:24.8
	Guy Butler			Clarence Oldfield			Maurice Delvart		
	Cecil Griffiths			Johannes Oosterlaak			Jean Devaux		
	Robert Lindsay			Bevil Rudd			Gaston Féry		
1924	Shelton Cochran	USA	3:16.0	Erik Byléhn	SWE	3:17.0	Guy Butler	GBR	3:17.4
	Alan Helffrich			Nils Engdahl			George Renwick		
	Oliver McDonald			Arthur Svensson			Richard Ripley		
	William Stevenson			Gustaf Weijnarth			Edward Toms		
1928	Frederick Alderman	USA	3:14.2	Hermann Engelhard	GER	3:14.8	James Ball	CAN	3:15.4
	George Baird			Richard Krebs			Philip Edwards		
	Raymond Barbuti			Otto Neumann			Stanley Glover		
	Emerson Spencer			Werner Storz			Alexander Wilson		
1932	Edgar Ablowich	USA	3:08.2	David Burghley*	GBR	3:11.2	James Ball	CAN	3:12.8
	William Carr			Thomas Hampson			Philip Edwards		
	Ivan Fuqua			Godfrey Rampling			Raymond Lewis		
	Karl Warner			Crew Stoneley			Alexander Wilson		
1936	Arthur Godfrey Brown	GBR	3:09.0	Harold Cagle	USA	3:11.0	Helmut Hamann	GER	3:11.8
	Godfrey Rampling			Alfred Fitch			Rudolf Harbig		
	William Roberts			Edward O'Brien			Friedrich von Stülpnagel		
	Frederick Wolff			Robert Young			Harry Voigt		
1948	Clifford Bourland	USA	3:10.4	Robert Chef d'Hotel	FRA	3:14.8	Folke Alnevik	SWE	3:16.0
	Roy Cochran			Jean Kerebel			Rune Larsson		
	Arthur Harnden			Jacques Lunis			Kurt Lundqvist		
	Malvin Whitfield			François Schewetta			Lars-trik Wolfbrandt		
1952	Leslie Lang	JAM	3:03.9	Gerrard Cole	USA	3:04.0	Hans Geister	GER	3:06.6
	Herbert McKenley			Oliver Matson			Karl-Friedrich Haas		
	Vincent George			Charles Moore			Günther Steines		
	Rhoden			Malvin Whitfield			Heinz Ulzheimer		
	Arthur Wint								
1956	Thomas Courtney	USA	3:04.8	Graham Gipson	AUS	3:06.2	Francis Peter Higgins	GBR	3:07.2
	Charles Jenkins			Richard Kevan Gosper			Derek Johnson		
	Louis Jones			Leonard Gregory			John Salisbury		
	Jesse Mashburn			David Lean			Michael Wheeler		
1960	Glenn Davis	USA	3:02.2	Johannes Kaiser	GER	3:02.7	Keith Gardner	ANT	3:04.0
	Otis Davis			Carl Kaufmann			George Kerr		
	John Yerman			Manfred Kinder			Malcolm Spence		
	Earl Young			Hans-Joachim Reske			James Wedderburn		
1964	Henry Carr	USA	3:00.7	Robbie Brightwell	GBR	3:01.6	Kent Bernard	TRI	3:01.7
	Ollan Cassell			John Cooper			Wendell Mottley		
	Michael Larrabee			Timothy Graham			Edwin Roberts		
	Ulis Williams			Adrian Metcalfe			Edwin Skinner		
1968	Lee Evans	USA	2:56.1	Charles Asati	KEN	2:59.6	Gerhard Hennige	FRG	3:00.5
	Ronald Freeman			Naftali Bon			Martin Jellinghaus		
	Larry James			Munyoro Nyamau			Manfred Kinder		
	Vincent Matthews			Daniel Rudisha			Helmar Müller		

Year	Gold	C'ntry	Time	Silver	C'ntry	Time	Bronze	C'ntry	Time
1972	Charles Asati	KEN	2:59.8	David Hemery	GBR	3:00.5	Gilles Bertould	FRA	3:00.7
	Hezahiah Nyamau			David Jenkins			Jacques Carette		
	Robert Ouko			Alan Pascoe			Francis Kerbiriou		
	Julius Sang			Martin Reynolds			Daniel Velasques		
1976	Benjamin Brown	USA	2:58.65	Zbigniew Jaremski	POL	3:01.43	Bernd Herrmann	FRG	3:01.98
	Herman Frazier			Jerzy Pietrzyk			Franz-Peter Hofmeister		
	Fred Newhouse			Ryszard Podlas			Lothar Krieg		
	Maxie Parks			Jan Werner			Harald Schmid		
1980	Nikolai Chernetski	URS	3:01.10	Volker Beck	GDR	3:01.30	Stefano Malinverni	ITA	3:04.30
	Mikhail Linge			Andreas Knebel			Pietro Mennea		
	Viktor Markin			Frank Schaffer			Roberto Tozzi		
	Remigius Valiulis			Klaus Thiele			Mauro Zuliani		
1984	Ray Armstead	USA	2:57.91	Kriss Akabusi	GBR	2:59.13	Innocent Egbunike	NGR	2:59.32
	Alonzo Babers			Todd Bennett			Rotimi Peters		
	Antonio McKay			Philip Brown			Moses Ugbusien		
	Sunder Nix			Gary Cook			Sunday Uti		
1988	Danny Everett	USA	2:56.16	Bertland Cameron	JAM	3:00.30	Norbert Dobeleit	FRG	3:00.56
	Steven Lewis			Howard Davis			Edgar Itt		
	Harry Reynolds			Winthrop Graham			Raif Lubke		
	Kevin Robinzine			Devon Morris			Jorg Vaihinger		
1992	Michael Johnson	USA	2:55.74	Lázaro Despaigne	CUB	2:59.51	Kriss Akabusi	GBR	2:59.73
	Steve Lewis			Hector Ortiz			Roger Black		
	Andrew Valmon			Roberto Prendes			David Grindley		
	Quincy Watts			Norberto Tellez			John Regis		
1996									

*Lord Burghley

High Jump

Year	Gold	C'ntry	Time	Silver	C'ntry	Time	Bronze	C'ntry	Time
1896	Ellery Clark	USA	1.81	James Connolly	USA	1.65	Robert Garrett	USA	1.65
1900	Irving Baxter	USA	1.90	Patrick Leahy	GBR	1.78	Lajos Gönczy	HUN	1.75
1904	Samuel Jones	USA	1.80	Garrett Serviss	USA	1.77	Paul Weinstein	GER	1.77
1908	Harry Porter	USA	1.905	Georges André	FRA	1.88			
				Cornelius Leahy	GBR	1.88			
				Istvan Somody	HUN	1.88			
1912	Alma Richards	USA	1.93	Hans Liesche	GER	1.91	George Horine	USA	1.89
1920	Richmond Landon	USA	1.935	Harold Muller	USA	1.90	Bo Ekelund	SWE	1.90
1924	Harold Osborn	USA	1.98	Leroy Brown	USA	1.95	Pierre Lewden	FRA	1.92
1928	Robert King	USA	1.94	Benjamin Hedges	USA	1.91	Claude Ménard	FRA	1.91
1932	Duncan McNaugthon	CAN	1.97	Robert Van Osdel	USA	1.97	Simeon Toribio	PHI	1.97
1936	Cornelius Johnson	USA	2.03	David Albritton	USA	2.00	Delos Thurber	USA	2.00
1948	John Winter	AUS	1.98	Björn Paulson	NOR	1.95	George Stanich	USA	1.95
1952	Walter Davis	USA	2.04	Ken Wiesner	USA	2.01	José Telles Da Conceição	BRA	1.98
1956	Charles Dumas	USA	2.12	Charles Michael Porter	AUS	2.10	Igor Kachkarov	URS	2.08
1960	Robert Shavlakadze	URS	2.16	Valeri Brumel	URS	2.16	John Thomas	USA	2.14
1964	Valeri Brumel	URS	2.18	John Thomas	USA	2.18	John Rambo	USA	2.16
1968	Richard Fosbury	USA	2.24	Edward Caruthers	USA	2.22	Valentin Gavrilov	URS	2.20
1972	Yuri Tarmak	URS	2.23	Stefan Junge	GDR	2.21	Dwight Stones	USA	2.21
1976	Jacek Wszola	POL	2.25	Greg Joy	CAN	2.23	Dwight Stones	USA	2.21
1980	Gerd Wessig	GDR	2.36	Jacek Wszoła	POL	2.31	Jörg Freimuth	GDR	2.31
1984	Dietmar Mögenburg	FRG	2.35	Patrik Sjöberg	SWE	2.33	Zhu Jianhua	CHN	2.31
1988	Gennadi Avdeenko	URS	2.38	Hollis Conway	USA	2.36	Rudolf Povarnitsyne	URS	2.36
							Patrik Sjöberg	SWE	2.36
1992	Javier Sotomayor	CUB	2.34	Patrik Sjöberg	SWE	2.34	Artur Partyka	POL	2.34
1996									

Pole Vault

Year	Gold	C'ntry	Time	Silver	C'ntry	Time	Bronze	C'ntry	Time
1896	Wílliam Welles Hoyt	USA	3.30	Albert Tyler	USA	3.20	Evangelos Damaskos	GRE	2.85
1900	Irving Baxter	USA	3.30	Meredith Colket	USA	3.25	Carl Albert Andersen	NOR	3.20
1904	Charles Dvorak	USA	3.50	LeRoy Samse	USA	3.43	Louis Wilkins	USA	3.43
1908	Edward Cooke	USA	3.71				Edward Blake	CAN	3.58
	Alfred Gilbert	USA	3.71						

/continued on next page 119

Year	Gold	C'ntry	Time	Silver	C'ntry	Time	Bronze	C'ntry	Time
1912	Harry Babcock	USA	3.95	Frank Nelson	USA	3.85			
				Marcus Wright	USA	3.85			
1920	Frank Foss	USA	3.80	Henry Petersen	DEN	3.75	Edwin Myers	USA	3.60
1924	Lee Barnes	USA	3.95	Glenn Graham	USA	3.95	James Brooker	USA	3.90
1928	Sabin Carr	USA	4.20	William Droegemueller	USA	4.10	Charles McGinnis	USA	3.95
1932	William Miller	USA	4.31	Shuhei Nishida	JPN	4.30	George Jefferson	USA	4.20
1936	Earle Meadows	USA	4.35	Shuhei Nishida	JPN	4.25	Sueo Oe	JPN	4.25
1948	O Guinn Smith	USA	4.3	Erkki Kataja	FIN	4.2	Robert Richards	USA	4.2
1952	Robert Richards	USA	4.55	Donald Laz	USA	4.50	Ragnar Lundberg	SWE	4.40
1956	Robert Richards	USA	4.56	Robert Gutowski	USA	4.53	Georges Roubanis	GRE	4.50
1960	Donald Bragg	USA	4.70	Ronald Morris	USA	4.60	Eeles Landström	FIN	4.55
1964	Fred Hansen	USA	5.10	Wolfgang Reinhardt	GER	5.05	Klaus Lehnertz	GER	5.00
1968	Robert Seagren	USA	5.4	Claus Schiprowski	FRG	5.4	Wolfgang Nordwig	GDR	5.4
1972	Wolfgang Nordwig	GDR	5.50	Robert Seagren	USA	5.40	Jan Johnson	USA	5.35
1976	Tadeusz Ślusarski	POL	5.5	Antti Kalliomäki	FIN	5.5	David Roberts	USA	5.5
1980	Władysław Kozakiewicz	POL	5.78	Konstantin Volkov	URS	5.65	Tadeusz Ślusarski	POL	5.65
1984	Pierre Quinon	FRA	5.75	Mike Tully	USA	5.65	Earl Bell	USA	5.60
							Thierry Vigneron	FRA	5.60
1988	Sergei Bubka	URS	5.90	Radion Gataoulline	URS	5.85	Grigori Egorov	URS	5.80
1992	Maxim Tarassov	EUN	5.80	Igor Trandenkov	EUN	5.80	Javier Garcia	ESP	5.75
1996									

Long Jump

Year	Gold	C'ntry	Time	Silver	C'ntry	Time	Bronze	C'ntry	Time
1896	Ellery Clark	USA	6.35	Robert Garrett	USA	6	James Connolly	USA	5.84
1900	Alvin Kraenzlein	USA	7.185	Myer Prinstein	USA	7.175	Patrick Leahy	GBR	6.95
1904	Meyer Prinstein	USA	7.34	Daniel Frank	USA	6.89	Robert Stangland	USA	6.88
1908	Francis Irons	USA	7.48	Daniel Kelly	USA	7.09	Calvin Bricker	CAN	7.08
1912	Albert Gutterson	USA	7.60	Calvin Bricker	CAN	7.21	Georg Åberg	SWE	7.18
1920	William Peterssen	SWE	7.15	Carl Johnson	USA	7.095	Erik Abrahamsson	SWE	7.08
1924	William de Hart-Hubbard	USA	7.445	Edward Gourdin	USA	7.275	Sverre Hansen	NOR	7.26
1928	Edward Hamm	USA	7.73	Silvio Cator	HAI	7.58	Alfred Bates	USA	7.40
1932	Edward Gordon	USA	7.64	Charles Lambert Redd	USA	7.60	Chuhei Namabu	JPN	7.45
1936	Jesse Owens	USA	8.06	Luz Long	GER	7.87	Naoto Tajima	JPN	7.74
1948	Willie Steele	USA	7.825	Thomas Bruce	AUS	7.555	Herbert Douglas	USA	7.545
1952	Jerome Biffle	USA	7.57	Meredith Gourdine	USA	7.53	Ödön Földesi	HUN	7.30
1956	Gregory Bell	USA	7.83	John Bennett	USA	7.68	Jorma Rainer Valkama	FIN	7.48
1960	Ralph Boston	USA	8.12	Irvin Roberson	USA	8.11	Igor Ter-Ovanesian	URS	8.04
1964	Lynn Davies	GBR	8.07	Ralph Boston	USA	8.03	Igor Ter-Ovanesian	URS	7.99
1968	Robert Beamon	USA	8.90	Klaus Beer	GDR	8.19	Ralph Boston	USA	8.16
1972	Randy Williams	USA	8.24	Hans Baumgartner	FRG	8.18	Arnie Robinson	USA	8.03
1976	Arnie Robinson	USA	8.35	Randy Williams	USA	8.11	Frank Wartenberg	GDR	8.02
1980	Lutz Dombrowski	GDR	8.54	Frank Paschek	GDR	8:21	Valeri Podluzhnyi	URS	8.18
1984	Carl Lewis	USA	8.54	Gary Honey	AUS	8.24	Giovanni Evangelisti	ITA	8.24
1988	Carl Lewis	USA	8.72	Mike Powell	USA	8.49	Larry Myricks	USA	8.27
1992	Carl Lewis	USA	8.67	Mike Powell	USA	8.64	Joe Greene	USA	8.34
1996									

Triple Jump

Year	Gold	C'ntry	Time	Silver	C'ntry	Time	Bronze	C'ntry	Time
1896	James Connolly	USA	13.71	Alexandre Tuffère	FRA	12.70	Ioannis Persakis	GRE	12.52
1900	Myer Prinstein	USA	14.47	James Connolly	USA	13.64	Lewis Sheldon	USA	13.64
1904	Myer Prinstein	USA	14.35	Fred Englehardt	USA	13.90	Robert Stangland	USA	13.36
1908	Timothy Ahearne	GBR	14.92	Garfield MacDonald	CAN	14.76	Edvard Larsen	NOR	14.39
1912	Gustaf Lindblom	SWE	14.76	Georg Åberg	SWE	14.51	Erik Almlöf	SWE	14.17
1920	Vilho Tuulos	FIN	14.505	Folke Jansson	SWE	14.48	Erik Almlöf	SWE	14.275
1924	Anthony Winter	AUS	15.525	Luis Bruneto	ARG	15.425	Vilho Tuulos	FIN	15.37
1928	Mikio Oda	JPN	15.21	Levi Casey	USA	15.17	Vilho Tuulos	FIN	15.11
1932	Chuhei Nambu	JPN	15.72	Eric Svensson	SWE	15.32	Kenkichi Ohshima	JPN	15.12
1936	Naoto Tajima	JPN	16.00	Masao Harada	JPN	15.66	John Metcalfe	AUS	15.50
1948	Ame Åhman	SWE	15.40	George Avery	AUS	15.365	Ruhl Sarialp	TUR	15.025
1952	Adhemar Ferreira da Silva	BRA	16.22	Leonid Scherbakov	URS	15.98	Arnoldo Devonish	VEN	15.52
1956	Adhemar Ferreira da Silva	BRA	16.35	Vilhjálmur Einarsson	ICL	16.26	Vitold Kreer	URS	16.02
1960	Jósef Szmidt	POL	16.81	Vladimir Goriaev	URS	16.63	Vitold Kreer	URS	16.43

Year	Gold	C'ntry	Time	Silver	C'ntry	Time	Bronze	C'ntry	Time
1964	Jósef Szmidt	POL	16.85	Oleg Fedoseev	USR	16.58	Viktor Kravchenko	URS	16.57
1968	Viktor Saneev	URS	17.39	Nelson Prudencio	BRA	17.27	Giuseppe Gentile	ITA	17.22
1972	Viktor Saneev	URS	17.35	Jörg Drehmel	GDR	17.31	Nelson Prudencio	BRA	17.05
1976	Viktor Saneev	URS	17.29	James Butts	USA	17.18	João Carlos de Oliviera	BRA	16.90
1980	Yaak Uudmäe	URS	17.35	Viktor Saneev	URS	17.24	João Carlos de Oliviera	BRA	17.22
1984	Al Joyner	USA	17.26	Mike Conley	USA	17.18	Keith Connor	GBR	16.87
1988	Hristo Markov	BUL	17.61	Igor Lapchine	URS	17.52	Alexander Kovalenko	URS	17.42
1992	Michael Conley	USA	18.17	Charles Simpkins	USA	17.60	Frank Rutherford	BAH	17.36
1996									

Shot Put

Year	Gold	C'ntry	Time	Silver	C'ntry	Time	Bronze	C'ntry	Time
1896	Robert Garrett	USA	11.22	Miltiades Gouskos	GRE	11.2	Georgios Papasideris	GRE	10.36
1900	Richard Sheldon	USA	14.10	Josiah McCracken	USA	12.85	Robert Garrett	USA	12.37
1904	Ralph Rose	USA	14.10	William Coe	USA	14.40	Leon Feuerbach	USA	13.37
1908	Ralph Rose	USA	14.21	Dennis Horgan	GBR	13.62	John Garrels	USA	13.18
1912	Patrick McDonald	USA	15.34	Ralph Rose	USA	15.25	Lawrence Whitney	USA	13.93
1920	Frans Pörhölä	FIN	14.81	Elmer Niklander	FIN	14.155	Harry Liversedge	USA	14.15
1924	Lemuel Clarence Houser	USA	14.995	Glenn Hartranft	USA	14.895	Ralph Hills	USA	14.64
1928	John Kuck	USA	15.87	Herman Brix	USA	15.75	Emil Hirschfeld	GER	15.72
1932	Leo Sexton	USA	16.00	Harlow Rothert	USA	15.67	František Douda	CZE	15.61
1936	Hans Woellke	GER	16.2	Sulo Bärlund	FIN	16.12	Gerhard Stöck	GER	15.66
1948	Wilbur Thompson	USA	17.12	F James Delaney	USA	16.68	James Fuchs	USA	16.42
1952	William Parry O'Brien	USA	17.41	Clarence Hooper	USA	17.39	James Fuchs	USA	17.06
1956	William Parry O'Brien	USA	18.57	William Nieder	USA	18.18	Jiři Skobla	CZE	17.65
1960	William Nieder	USA	19.68	William Parry O'Brien	USA	19.11	Dallas Crutcher Long	USA	19.01
1964	Dallas Long	USA	20.33	James Randel Matson	USA	20.20	Vilmos Varju	HUN	19.39
1968	Randy Matson	USA	20.54	George Woods	USA	20.12	Eduard Gushchin	URS	20.09
1972	Władysław Komar	POL	21.18	George Woods	USA	21.17	Hartmut Briesenick	GDR	21.14
1976	Udo Beyer	GDR	21.05	Evgeni Mironov	URS	21.03	Alexander Barisnikov	URS	21.00
1980	Vladimir Kiselev	URS	21.35	Alexander Baryshnikov	URS	21.08	Udo Beyer	GDR	21.06
1984	Alessandro Andrei	ITA	21.26	Michael Carter	USA	21.09	Dave Laut	USA	20.97
1988	Ulf Timmermann	GDR	22.47	Randy Barnes	USA	22.39	Werner Günthör	SUI	21.99
1992	Michael Stulce	USA	21.70	James Doehring	USA	20.96	Viacheslav Lykho	EUN	20.94
1996									

Discus

Year	Gold	C'ntry	Time	Silver	C'ntry	Time	Bronze	C'ntry	Time
1896	Robert Garrett	USA	29.15	Panagiotiss Paraskevopoulo	GRE	28.955	Sotirios Versis	GRE	27.78
1900	Rezsö Bauer	HUN	36.04	František Janda	BOH	35.25	Richard Sheldon	USA	34.60
1904	Martin Sheridan	USA	39.28	Ralph Rose	USA	39.28	Nicolaos Georgantas	GRE	37.68
1908	Martin Sheridan	USA	40.89	Merritt Giffin	USA	40.70	Marquis Horr	USA	39.45
1912	Armas Taipale	FIN	45.21	Richard Byrd	USA	42.32	James Duncan	USA	42.28
1920	Elmer Nicklander	FIN	44.685	Armas Taipale	FIN	44.19	Augustus Pope	USA	42.13
1924	Lemuel Clarence Houser	USA	46.155	Vilho Niittymaa	FIN	44.95	Thomas Lieb	USA	44.83
1928	Lemuel Clarence Houser	USA	47.32	L Antero Kivi	FIN	47.23	James Corson	USA	47.1
1932	John Anderson	USA	49.49	Henri Jean Laborde	USA	48.47	Paul Winter	FRA	47.85
1936	Kenneth Carpenter	USA	50.48	Gordon Dunn	USA	49.36	Giorgio Oberweger	ITA	49.23
1948	Adolfo Consolini	ITA	52.78	Giuseppe Tosi	ITA	51.78	Fortune Gordien	USA	50.77
1952	Sim Iness	USA	55.03	Adolfo Consolini	ITA	53.78	James Dillion	USA	53.28
1956	Alfred Oerter	USA	56.36	Fortune Gordien	USA	54.81	Desmond Koch	USA	54.40
1960	Alfred Oerter	USA	59.18	Richard Babka	USA	58.02	Richard Cochran	USA	57.16
1964	Alfred Oerter	USA	61.00	Ludvik Daněk	TCH	60.52	David Lawson Weill	USA	59.49
1968	Alfred Oerter	USA	64.78	Lothar Milde	GDR	63.08	Ludvik Daněk	TCH	62.92
1972	Ludvik Daněk	TCH	64.4	Jay Silvester	USA	63.5	Rickard Bruch	SWE	63.4
1976	Mac Wilkins	USA	67.5	Wolfgang Schmidt	GDR	66.22	John Powell	USA	65.6
1980	Viktor Rashchupkin	URS	66.64	Imrich Bugár	TCH	66.38	Luis Delis	CUB	66.32
1984	Rolf Danneberg	FRG	66.60	Mac Wilkins	USA	66.30	John Powell	USA	65.46
1988	Jurgen Schult	GDR	68.82	Romas Oubartas	URS	67.48	Rolf Danneberg	FRG	67.38
1992	Romas Ubartas	LTU	65.12	Jurgen Schult	GER	64.94	Roberto Moya	CUB	64.12
1996									

Year	Gold	C'ntry	Time	Silver	C'ntry	Time	Bronze	C'ntry	Time

Hammer

Year	Gold	C'ntry	Time	Silver	C'ntry	Time	Bronze	C'ntry	Time
1900	John Flanagan	USA	49.73	Thomas Truxtun Hare	USA	49.13	Josiah McCracken	USA	42.46
1904	John Flanagan	USA	51.23	John DeWitt	USA	50.26	Ralph Rose	USA	45.73
1908	John Flanagan	USA	51.92	Matthew McGrath	USA	51.18	Cornelius Walsh	CAN	48.51
1912	Matthew MacGrath	USA	54.74	Duncan Gillis	CAN	48.39	Clarence Childs	USA	48.17
1920	Patrick Ryan	USA	52.875	Carl Johan Lindh	SWE	48.430	Basil Benett	USA	48.230
1924	Frederick Tootell	USA	53.295	Matthew MacGrath	USA	50.840	Malcolm Nokes	GBR	48.875
1928	Patrick O'Callaghan	IRL	51.39	Ossian Sköld	SWE	51.29	Edmund Black	USA	49.03
1932	Patrick O'Callaghan	IRL	53.92	Ville Pörhöiä	FIN	52.27	Peter Zaremba	USA	50.33
1936	Karl Hein	GER	56.49	Erwin Blask	GER	55.04	Oscar Warngård	SWE	54.83
1948	Imre Németh	HUN	56.07	Ivan Gubijan	YUG	54.27	R Bennett	USA	53.73
1952	József Csermák	HUN	60.34	Karl Storch	GER	58.86	Imre Németh	HUN	57.74
1956	Harold Connolly	USA	63.19	Mikhail Krivonossov	URS	63.03	Anatoli Samotsvetov	URS	62.56
1960	Vasily Rudenkov	URS	67.10	Gyula Zsivótsky	HUN	65.79	Tadeusz Rut	POL	65.64
1964	Romuald Klim	URS	69.74	Gyula Zsivótsky	HUN	69.09	Uwe Beyer	GER	68.09
1968	Gyula Zsivótzky	HUN	73.36	Romuald Klim	URS	73.28	Lázár Lovász	HUN	69.78
1972	Anatoli Bondarchuk	URS	75.5	Jochen Sachse	GDR	74.96	Vasili Khmelevski	URS	74.04
1976	Yuri Sedykh	URS	77.52	Alexei Spiridonov	URS	76.08	Anatoli Bondarchuk	URS	75.48
1980	Yuri Sedykh	URS	81.80	Sergei Litvinov	URS	80.64	Yuri Tamm	URS	78.96
1984	Juha Tiainen	FIN	78.08	Karl-Hans Riehm	FRG	77.98	Klaus Ploghaus	FRG	76.68
1988	Sergei Litvinov	URS	84.80	Yuri Sedykh	URS	83.76	Iouri Tamm	URS	81.16
1992	Andrei Abduvaliyev	EUN	82.54	Igor Astapkovich	EUN	81.96	Igor Nikulin	EUN	81.38
1996									

Javelin

Year	Gold	C'ntry	Time	Silver	C'ntry	Time	Bronze	C'ntry	Time
1908	Eric Lemming	SWE	54.83	Arne Halse	NOR	50.57	Otto Nilsson	SWE	47.11
1912	Eric Lemming	SWE	60.64	Julius Juho Saaristo	FIN	58.66	Mór Kovacs	HUN	55.5
1920	Jonni Myyrä	FIN	65.78	Urho Peltonen	FIN	63.50	Paavo Johansson	FIN	63.095
1924	Jonni Myyrä	FIN	62.96	Gunnar Lindström	SWE	60.92	Eugene Oberst	USA	58.35
1928	Erik Lundkvist	SWE	66.60	Béla Szepes	HUN	65.26	Olav Sunde	NOR	63.97
1932	Matti Järvinen	FIN	72.71	Matti Sippala	FIN	69.80	Eino Penttilä	FIN	68.70
1936	Gerhard Stöck	GER	71.84	Yrjö Nikkanen	FIN	70.77	Kaarlo Toivonen	FIN	70.72
1948	Kai Rautavaara	FIN	69.77	Steve Seymour	USA	67.56	József Várszegi	HUN	67.03
1952	Cy Young	USA	73.78	William Miller	USA	72.46	Toivo Hyytiäinen	FIN	71.89
1956	Egil Danielsen	NOR	85.71	Janusz Sidło	POL	79.98	Viktor Tsibulenko	URS	79.50
1960	Viktor Tsibulenko	URS	84.64	Walter Krüger	GER	79.36	Gergely Kulczár	HUN	78.57
1964	Pauli Nevala	FIN	82.66	Gergely Kulczár	HUN	82.32	Yanis Lusis	URS	80.57
1968	Yanis Lusis	URS	90.10	Jorma Kinnunen	FIN	88.58	Gergely Kulczár	HUN	87.06
1972	Klaus Wolfermann	FRG	90.48	Yanis Lusis	URS	90.46	William Schmidt	USA	84.42
1976	Miklós Németh	HUN	94.58	Hannu Siitonen	FIN	87.92	Gheorghe Megelea	ROM	87.16
1980	Dainis Kula	URS	91.20	Alxander Makarov	URS	89.64	Wolfgang Hanisch	GDR	86.72
1984	Arto Häkönen	FIN	86.76	David Ottley	GBR	85.74	Kenth Eldebrink	SWE	83.72
1988	Tapio Korjus	FIN	84.28	Jan Železný	TCH	84.12	Seppo Raty	FIN	83.26
1992	Jan Železný	TCH	89.66	Seppo Räty	FIN	86.60	Steve Backley	GBR	83.38
1996									

Decathlon

Year	Gold	C'ntry	Time	Silver	C'ntry	Time	Bronze	C'ntry	Time
1912	Hugo Wieslander	SWE	7724	Charles Lomberg	SWE	7414	G Holmer	SWE	7348
	Jim Thorpe	USA							
1920	Helge Lövland	NOR	5970	Brutus Hamilton	USA	5940	Bertil Olsson	SWE	5825
1924	Harold Osborn	USA	7740.78	Emerson Norton	USA	7350.90	Alexander Klumberg	EST	7329.33
1928	Paavo Yrjölä	FIN	8053	Akilles Järvinen	FIN	7932	John Kenneth Doherty	USA	7707
1932	James Bausch	USA	8462	Akilles Järvinen	FIN	8292	Wolrad Eberle	GER	8031
1936	Glenn Morris	USA	7900	Robert Clark	USA	7601	Jack Parker	USA	7275
1948	Robert Mathias	USA	7139	Ignace Heinrich	FRA	6974	Floyd Simmons	USA	6950
1952	Robert Mathias	USA	7887	Milton Campbell	USA	6975	Floyd Simmons	USA	6788
1956	Milton Campbell	USA	7937	Rafer Johnson	USA	7587	Vassili Kouznetsov	URS	7465
1960	Rafer Johnson	USA	8392	Yan Chuan Kwang	CHI	8334	Vassili Kouznetsov	URS	7809
1964	Willi Holdorf	GER	7887	Rein Aun	USR	7842	Hans-Joachim Walde	FRG	7809
1968	William Toomey	USA	8193	Hans-Joachim Walde	FRG	8111	Kurt Bendin	FRG	8054
1972	Nikolai Avilov	URS	8454	Leonid Litvinenko	URS	8035	Ryszard Katus	POL	7984
1976	Bruce Jenner	USA	8618	Guido Kratschmer	FRG	8411	Nikolai Avilov	URS	8369
1980	Daley Thompson	GBR	8495	Yuri Kutsenko	URS	8331	Sergei Zhelanov	URS	8135
1984	Daley Thompson	GBR	8797	Jurgen Hingsen	FRG	8673	Siegfried Wentz	FRG	8412
1988	Christian Schenk	GDR	8488	Torsten Voss	GDR	8399	Dave Steen	CAN	8328
1992	Robert Zmelik	TCH	8611	Antonio Peñalver	ESP	8412	David Johnson	USA	8309
1996									

ATHLETICS (Women)

Year	Gold	C'ntry	Time	Silver	C'ntry	Time	Bronze	C'ntry	Time
100m									
1928	Elizabeth Robinson	USA	12.2	Fanny Rosenfeld	CAN	12.3	Ethel Smith	CAN	12.3
1932	Stanisława Walasiewicz	POL	11.9	Hilde Strike	CAN	11.9	Wilhelmina Von Bremen	USA	12.0
1936	Helen Stephens	USA	11.5	Stanisława Walasiewicz	POL	11.7	Käthe Krauss	GER	11.9
1948	Francina Blankers-Koen	NED	11.9	Dorothy Manley	GBR	12.2	Shirley Strickland	AUS	12.2
1952	Marjorie Jackson	AUS	11.5	Daphne Hasenjager	SAF	11.8	Shirley Strickland	AUS	11.9
1956	Elizabeth Cuthbert	AUS	11.5	Christa Stubnick		11.7	Marlene Judith Mathews	AUS	11.7
1960	Wilma Rudolph	USA	11.0	Dorothy Hyman	GBR	11.3	Guiseppina Leone	ITA	11.3
1964	Wyomia Tyus	USA	11.4	Edith McGuire	USA	11.6	Ewa Kłobukowska	POL	11.6
1968	Wyomia Tyus	USA	11.0	Barbara Ferrell	USA	11.1	Irena Kirszenstein-Szewinska	POL	11.1
1972	Renate Stecher	GDR	11.07	Raelene Boyle	AUS	11.23	Silvia Chivás	CUB	11.24
1976	Annegret Richter	FRG	11.08	Renate Stecher	GDR	11.13	Inge Helten	FRG	11.17
1980	Ludmila Kondratieva	URS	11.06	Marlies Göhr	GDR	11.07	Ingrid Auerswald	GDR	11.14
1984	Evelyn Ashford	USA	10.97	Alice Brown	USA	11.13	Marlene Ottey-Page	JAM	11.16
1988	Florence Griffith-Joyner	USA	10.54	Evelyn Ashford	USA	10.83	Heike Drechsler	GDR	10.85
1992	Gail Devers	USA	10.82	Juliet Cuthbert	JAM	10.83	Irina Privalova	EUN	10.84
1996									
200m									
1948	Francina Blankers-Koen	NED	24.4	Audrey Williamson	GBR	25.1	Audrey Patterson	USA	25.2
1952	Marjorie Jackson	AUS	23.7	Bertha Brouwer	NED	24.2	Nedežda Hnykina	URS	24.2
1956	Elizabeth Cuthbert	AUS	23.4	Christa Stubnick	GER	23.7	Marlene Judith Mathews	AUS	23.8
1960	Wilma Rudolph	USA	24.0	Jutta Heine	GER	24.4	Dorothy Hyman	GBR	24.7
1964	Edith Marie McGuire	USA	23.0	Irena Kirszenstein	POL	23.1	Marilyn Black	AUS	23.1
1968	Irena Kirszenstein	POL	22.5	Raelene Boyle	AUS	22.7	Jennifer Lamy	AUS	22.8
1972	Renate Stecher	GDR	22.4	Raelene Boyle	AUS	22.45	Irena Szewińska	POL	22.74
1976	Bärbel Eckert	GDR	22.37	Annagret Richter	FRG	22.39	Renate Stecher	GDR	22.47
1980	Bärbel Wöckel	GDR	22.03	Natalia Bochina	URS	22.19	Merlene Ottey	JAM	22.20
1984	Valerie Brisco-Hooks	USA	21.81	Florence Griffith-Joyner	USA	22.04	Merlene Ottey-Page	JAM	22.09
1988	Florence Griffith-Joyner	USA	21.34	Grace Jackson	JAM	21.72	Heike Drechsler	GDR	21.95
1992	Gwen Torrence	USA	21.81	Juliet Cuthbert	JAM	22.02	Merlene Ottey-Page	JAM	22.09
1996									
400m									
1964	Elizabeth Cuthbert	AUS	52.0	Ann Packer	GBR	52.2	Judith Amoore	AUS	53.4
1968	Colette Besson	FRA	52.0	Lillian Board	GBR	52.1	Natalia Pechenkina	URS	52.2
1972	Monika Zehrt	GDR	51.08	Rita Wilden	FRG	51.21	Kathy Hammond	USA	51.64
1976	Irena Szewińska	POL	49.29	Christina Brehmer	GDR	50.51	Ellen Streidt	GDR	50.55
1980	Marita Koch	GDR	48.88	Jarmila Kratochvilova	TCH	49.46	Christina Lathan	GDR	49.66
1984	Valerie Brisco-Hooks	USA	48.83	Chandra Cheeseborough	USA	49.05	Kathryn Cook	GBR	49.42
1988	Olga Bryzguina	URS	48.65	Petra Müller	GDR	49.45	Olga Nazarova	URS	49.90
1992	Marie-Jose Perec	FRA	48.83	Olga Bryzguina	EUN	49.05	Ximena Restrepo Gaviria	COL	49.64
1996									
800m									
1928	Lina Radke	GER	2:16.8	Kinue Hitomi	JPN	2:17.6	Inga Gentzel	SWE	2:17.8
1960	Ludmila Shevcova	URS	2:04.3	Brenda Jones	AUS	2:04.4	Ursula Donath	GER	2:05.6
1964	Ann Packer	GBR	2:01.1	Maryvonne Dupureur	FRA	2:01.9	Ann Chamberlain	NZL	2:02.8
1968	Madeline Manning	USA	2:00.9	Ilona Silai	ROM	2:02.5	Maria Gommers	NED	2:02.6

/continued on next page 123

Year	Gold	C'ntry	Time	Silver	C'ntry	Time	Bronze	C'ntry	Time
1972	Hildegard Falck	FRG	1:58.6	Nione Ssabaite	URS	1:58.7	Gunhild Hoffmeister	GDR	1:59.2
1976	Tatiana Kazankina	URS	1:54.94	Nikolina Chtereva	BUL	1:55.42	Elfi Zinn	GDR	1:55.60
1980	Nadezhda Olizarenko	URS	1:53.50	Olga Mineeva	URS	1:54.90	Tatiana Providokhina	URS	1:55.50
1984	Doina Melinte	ROM	1:57.60	Kim Gallagher	USA	1:58.63	Fita Lovin	ROM	1:58.83
1988	Sigrun Wodars	GDR	1:56.10	Christine Wachtel	GDR	1:56.64	Kim Gallagher	USA	1:56.91
1992	Ellen van Langen	NED	1:55.54	Lilia Nurutdinova	EUN	1:55.99	Ana Quirot Moret	CUB	1:56.80
1996									

1,500m

Year	Gold	C'ntry	Time	Silver	C'ntry	Time	Bronze	C'ntry	Time
1972	Ludmila Bragina	URS	4:01.04	Gunhild Hoffmeister	GDR	4:02.8	Paola Cacchi	ITA	4:02.9
1976	Tatiana Kazankina	URS	4:05.48	Gunhild Hoffmeister	GDR	4:06.02	Ulrike Klapezynski	GDR	4:06.09
1980	Tatiana Kazankina	URS	3:56.60	Christiane Wartenberg	GDR	3:57.80	Nadezhda Olizarenko	URS	3:59.60
1984	Gabriella Dorio	ITA	4:03.25	Doina Melinte	ROM	4:03.76	Maricica Puică	ROM	4:04.15
1988	Paula Ivan	ROM	3:53.96	Lailoute Baikauskaite	URS	4:00.24	Tatiana Samolenko	URS	4:00.30
1992	Hassiba Boulmerka	ALG	3:55.30	Ludmila Rogacheva	EUN	3:56.91	Qu Yunxia	CHN	3:57.08
1996									

5,000m

Year
1996

10,000m

Year	Gold	C'ntry	Time	Silver	C'ntry	Time	Bronze	C'ntry	Time
1988	Olga Bondarenko	URS	31:05.21	Elizabeth McColgan	GBR	31:08.44	Elena Joupieva	URS	31:19.82
1992	Derartu Tulu	ETH	31:06.02	Elana Meyer	RSA	31:11.75	Lynn Jennings	USA	31:19.89
1996									

Marathon

Year	Gold	C'ntry	Time	Silver	C'ntry	Time	Bronze	C'ntry	Time
1984	Joan Benoit	USA	2:24:52	Grete Waitz	NOR	2:26:18	Rosa Mota	POR	2:26:57
1988	Rosa Mota	POR	2:25:40	Lisa Martin	AUS	2:25:53	Kathrin Doerre	GDR	2:26.21
1992	Valentina Yegorova	EUN	2:32:41	Yuko Arimori	JPN	2:32:49	Lorraine Moller	NZL	2:33:59
1996									

10km Walk

Year	Gold	C'ntry	Time	Silver	C'ntry	Time	Bronze	C'ntry	Time
1992	Chen Yueling	CHN	44:32	Elena Nikolaeva	EUN	44:33	Li Chunziu	CHN	44:41
1996									

100m Hurdles

Year	Gold	C'ntry	Time	Silver	C'ntry	Time	Bronze	C'ntry	Time
1972	Annelie Ehrhardt	GDR	12.59	Valeria Bufanu	ROM	12.84	Karin Balzer	GDR	12.90
1976	Johanna Schaller	GDR	12.77	Tatiana Anisimova	URS	12.78	Natalia Lebedeva	URS	12.80
1980	Vera Komisova	URS	12.56	Johanna Klier	GDR	12.63	Lucyna Langer	POL	12.65
1984	Benita Fitzgerald-Brown	USA	12.84	Shirley Strong	GBR	12.88	Kim Turner	USA	13.06
							Michele Chardonnet	FRA	13.06
1988	Jordanka Donkova	BUL	12.38	Gloria Siebert	GDR	12.61	Claudia Zackiewicz	FRG	12.75
1992	Paraskevi Patoulidou	GRE	12.64	La Vonna Martin	USA	12.69	Yordanka Donkova	BUL	12.70
1996									

400m Hurdles

Year	Gold	C'ntry	Time	Silver	C'ntry	Time	Bronze	C'ntry	Time
1984	Nawal El Moutawakel	MAR	54.61	Judi Brown	USA	55.20	Cristina Cojocaru	ROM	55.41
1988	Debra Flintoff-King	AUS	53.17	Tatiana Ledovskaia	URS	53.18	Ellen Fiedler	GDR	53.63
1992	Sally Gunnell	GBR	53.23	Sandra Farmer-Patrick	USA	53.69	Janeene Vickers	USA	54.31
1996									

4 × 100m

Year	Gold	C'ntry	Time	Silver	C'ntry	Time	Bronze	C'ntry	Time
1928	Myrtle Cook	CAN	48.4	Jessica Cross	USA	48.8	Anny Holdmann	GER	49.0
	Fanny Rosenfeld			Loretta McNeil			Helene Junker		
	Ethel Smith			Elizabeth Robinson			Rosa Kellner		
	Jean Thompson			Mary Washburn			Helene Schmidt		
1932	Wilhemina Von Bremen	USA	47.0	Mary Frizzell	CAN	47.0	Nellie Halstead	GBR	47.6
	Mary Carew			Mildred Frizzell			Eileen Hiscock		
	Evelyn Furtsch			Lillian Palmer			Gwendoline Porter		
	Annette Rogers			Hilda Strike			Violet Webb		

Year	Gold	C'ntry	Time	Silver	C'ntry	Time	Bronze	C'ntry	Time
1936	Harriet Bland Elizabeth Robinson Annette Rogers Helen Stephens	USA	46.9	Audrey Brown Barbara Burke Eileen Hiscock Violet Olney	GBR	47.6	Dorothy Brookshaw Hilda Cameron Mildred Dolson Aileen Meagher	CAN	47.8
1948	Francina Blankers- Koen Gerda van der Kade- Koudijs Xenia Stad-de Jong Jeanette Witziers- Timmer	NED	47.5	Joyce King June Maston Elizabeth McKinnon Shirley Strickland	AUS	47.6	Dianne Foster Patricia Jones Nancy MacKay Viola Myers	CAN	47.8
1952	Mae Faggs Catherine Hardy Barbara Jones Janet Moreau	USA	45.9	Helga Klein Ulla Knab Marga Petersen Maria Sander	GER	45.9	Heather Armitage Sylvia Cheeseman Jean Desforges June Foulds-Paul	GBR	46.2
1956	Norma Croker Elizabeth Cuthbert Fleur Mellor Shirley Strickland	AUS	44.5	Heather Armitage Anne Pashley June Foulds-Paul Jean Scrivens	GBR	44.7	Isabelle Daniels Mae Faggs Margaret Matthews Wilma Rudolph	USA	44.9
1960	Martha Hudson Barbara Jones Wilma Rudolph Lucinda Williams	USA	44.5	Anni Biechel Jutta Heine Brunhilde Hendrix Martha Langbein	GER	44.8	Barbara Janiszewska Celina Jesionowska Halina Richter Teresa Wieczorek	POL	45.0
1964	Teresa Ciepla Halina Górecka Irena Kirszenstein Ewa Kłobukowska	POL	43.6	Edith McGuire Wyomia Tyus Marilyn White Willye White	USA	43.9	Daphne Arden Dorothy Hyman Mary Rand Janet Simpson	GBR	44.0
1968	Margaret Bailes Barbara Ferrell Mildrette Netter Wyomia Tyus	USA	42.8	Miguelina Cobián Marlene Elejarde Violeta Quesada Fulgencia Romay	CUB	43.3	Galina Bukharina Vera Popkova Ludmila Samotesova Ludmila Zharkova	URS	43.4
1972	Christiane Krause Ingrid Mickler Annegret Richter Heidemarie Rosendahl	FRG	42.81	Christina Heinich Evelyn Kaufer Renate Stecher Bärbel Struppert	GDR	42.95	Silvia Chivás Marlene Elejalde Fulgencia Romay Carmen Valdes	CUB	43.36
1976	Carla Bodendorf Bärbel Eckert Marlis Oelsner Renate Stecher	GDR	42.55	Inge Helten Annegret Kroniger Elvira Possekel Annegret Richter	FRG	42.59	Vera Anisimova Nadezhda Besfamilnaya Ludmila Maslakova Tatiana Prorochenko	URS	43.09
1980	Ingrid Auerswald Marlies Göhr Romy Müller Bärbel Wöckel	GDR	41.60	Vera Anisimova Natalia Bochina Vera Komisova Ludmila Maslakova	URS	42.10	Beverley Goddard Heather Hunte Sonia Lannaman Kathryn Smallwood	GBR	42.43
1984	Evelyn Ashford Jeanette Bolden Alice Brown Chandra Cheeseborough	USA	41.65	Angela Bailey France Gareau Marita Payne Angella Taylor	CAN	42.77	Beverley Callender Kathryn Cook Simone Jacobs Heather Oakes	GBR	43.11
1988	Evelyn Ashford Alice Brown Sheila Echols Florence Griffith- Joyner	USA	41.98	Kerstin Behrendt Marlies Göhr Ingrid Lange Silke Möller	GDR	42.09	Marina Jirova Ludmila Kondratieva Galina Maltchougina Natalia Pomochtchnikova	URS	42.75
1992	Evelyn Ashford Carlette Guidry Esther Jones Gwen Torrence	USA	42.11	Olga Bogoslovskaya Galina Malchugina Irina Privalova Marina Trandenkova	EUN	42.16	Faith Idehen Mary Onyali Christy Thompson Beatrice Utondu	NIG	42.81
1996									

4 × 400m

| 1972 | Dagmar Käsling
Rita Kühne
Helga Seidler
Monika Zehrt | GDR | 3:23.0 | Mable Fergerson
Kathy Hammond
Madeline Manning
Cheryl Toussaint | USA | 3:25.2 | Inge Bödding
Hildegard Falck
Anette Rückes
Rita Wilden | FRG | 3:26.5 |

/continued on next page 125

Year	Gold	C'ntry	Time	Silver	C'ntry	Time	Bronze	C'ntry	Time
1976	Christina Brehmer	GDR	3:19.23	Rosalyn Bryant	USA	3:22.81	Ludmila Aksenova	URS	3:24.24
	Doris Maletzki			Sheila Ingram			Nadezhda Ilyina		
	Brigitte Rohde			Pam Jiles			Inta Klimovoch		
	Ellen Streidt			Debra Sapenter			Natalia Sokolova		
1980	Tatiana Goishchik	URS	3:20.20	Marita Koch	GDR	3:20.40	Joslyn Hoyte-Smith	GBR	3:27.50
	Irina Nazarova			Barbara Krug			Linsey MacDonald		
	Tatiana Prorochenko			Christina Lathan			Janine Macgregor		
	Nina Ziuskova			Gabriele Löwe			Michelle Probert		
1984	Valerie Brisco-Hooks	USA	3:18.29	Charmaine Crooks	CAN	3:21.21	Gaby Bussmann	FRG	3:22.98
	Chandra Cheeseborough			Molly Killingbeck			Heide Gaugel		
	Sherri Howard			Marita Payne			Heike Schulte-Mattler		
	Lillie Leatherwood			Jillian Richardson			Ute Thimm		
1988	Olga Bryzguina	URS	3:15.18	Valerie Brisco	USA	3:15.51	Sabine Busch	GDR	3:18.29
	Tatiana Ledovskaia			Diane Dixon			Kirsten Emmelmann		
	Olga Nazarova			Florence Griffith-			Petra Muller		
	Maria Piniguina			Joyner			Dagmar Neubauer		
				Denean Howard					
1992	Olga Bryzguina	EUN	3:20.20	Natasha Kaiser	USA	3:20.92	Sandra Douglas	GBR	3:24.23
	Ludmila Dzhigalova			Jearl Miles			Sally Gunnell		
	Olga Nazarova			Rochelle Stevens			Phylis Smith		
	Elena Ruzina			Gwen Torrence			Jennifer Stoute		
1996									

High Jump

Year	Gold	C'ntry	Time	Silver	C'ntry	Time	Bronze	C'ntry	Time
1928	Ethel Catherwood	CAN	1.59	Carolina Gisolf	NED	1.56	Mildred Wiley	USA	1.56
1932	Jean Shiley	USA	1.65	Mildred Didriksen	USA	1.64	Eva Dawes	CAN	1.60
1936	Ibolya Csák	HUN	1.6	Dorothy Odam	GBR	1.6	Elfriede Kaun	GER	1.6
1948	Alice Coachman	USA	1.68	Dorothy Tyler	GBR	1.68	Micheline Ostermeyer	FRA	1.61
1952	Esther Brand	SAF	1.67	Sheila Lerwill	GBR	1.65	Aleksandra Tshudina	URS	1.63
1956	Mildred Louise McDaniel	USA	1.76	Thelma Elizabeth Hopkins	GBR	1.67	Maria Pissareva	URS	1.67
1960	Iolanda Balaş	ROM	1.85	Jaroslawa Jóźwiakowska	POL	1.71	Dorothy Shirley	GBR	1.71
1964	Iolanda Balaş	ROM	1.90	Michele Brown	AUS	1.80	Taisia Chenchik	URS	1.78
1968	Miloslová Režk	TCH	1.82	Antonina Okorokova	URS	1.80	Valentina Kozyr	URS	1.80
1972	Ulrike Meyfarth	FRG	1.92	Yordanka Blagoeva	BUL	1.88	Ilona Gusenbauer	AUT	1.88
1976	Rosemarie Ackermann	GDR	1.93	Sara Simeoni	ITA	1.91	Yordanka Blagoeva	BUL	1.91
1980	Sara Simeoni	ITA	1.97	Urszula Kielan	POL	1.94	Jutta Kirst	GDR	1.94
1984	Ulrike Meyfarth	FRG	2.02	Sara Simeoni	ITA	2.00	Joni Huntley	USA	1.97
1988	Louise Ritter	USA	2.03	Stefka Ostadinova	BUL	2.01	Tamara Bykova	URS	1.99
1992	Heike Henkel	GER	2.02	Galina Astafei	ROM	2.00	Joanet Quintero	CUB	1.97
1996									

Long Jump

Year	Gold	C'ntry	Time	Silver	C'ntry	Time	Bronze	C'ntry	Time
1948	Olga Gyarmati	HUN	5.695	Noëmi De Portela	ARG	5.600	Ann-Britt Leyman	SWE	5.575
1952	Yvette Williams	NZL	6.24	Aleksandra Tshudina	URS	6.14	Shirley Cawley	GBR	5.92
1956	Elżbieta Krzesińska	POL	6.35	Willie White	USA	6.09	Nadejda Dvalichvil	URS	6.07
1960	Vera Krepkina	URS	6.37	Elżbieta Krzesińska	POL	6.27	Hildrun Claus-Laufer	GER	6.21
1964	Mary Rand	GBR	6.76	Irena Kirszenstein	POL	6.60	Tatiana Schelkanova	URS	6.42
1968	Viorica Viscopoleanu	ROM	6.82	Sheila Sherwood	GBR	6.68	Tatiana Talysheva	URS	6.66
1972	Heidemarie Rosendahl	FRG	6.78	Diana Yorgova	BUL	6.77	Eva Šuranová	TCH	6.67
1976	Angela Voigt	GDR	6.72	Kathy McMillan	USA	6.66	Lidiya Alfeeva	URS	6.60
1980	Tatiana Kolpakova	URS	7.06	Brigitte Wujak	GDR	7.04	Tatiana Skachko	URS	7.01
1984	Anisoara Stanciu	ROM	6.96	Vali Ionescu	ROM	6.81	Susan Hearnshaw	GBR	6.80
1988	Jackie Joyner-Kersee	USA	7.40	Heike Drechsler	GDR	7.22	Galina Tchistiakova	URS	7.11
1992	Heike Drechsler	GER	7.14	Inessa Kravets	EUN	7.12	Jackie Joyner-Kersee	USA	7.07
1996									

Triple Jump

Year									
1996									

Year	Gold	C'ntry	Time	Silver	C'ntry	Time	Bronze	C'ntry	Time

Shot Put

Year	Gold	C'ntry	Time	Silver	C'ntry	Time	Bronze	C'ntry	Time
1948	Micheline Ostermeyer	FRA	13.75	Amelia Piccinini	ITA	13.095	Ine Schäffer	AUT	13.08
1952	Galina Zybina	URS	15.28	Marianne Werner	GER	14.57	Klavdija Totshenova	URS	14.50
1956	Tamara Tychkevitch	URS	16.59	Galina Zybina	URS	16.53	Marianne Werner	GER	15.61
1960	Tamara Press	URS	17.32	Johanna Lüttge-Hübner	GER	16.61	Earlene Brown	USA	16.42
1964	Tamara Press	URS	18.14	Renate Garisch-Culmberger-Boy	GER	17.61	Gaalina Zybina	USR	17.45
1968	Margitta Gummel	GDR	19.61	Marita Lange	GDR	18.78	Nadezhda Chizhova	URS	18.19
1972	Nadezhda Chizhova	URS	21.03	Margitta Gummel	GDR	21.22	Ivanka Hristova	BUL	19.35
1976	Ivanka Christova	BUL	21.16	Nadezhda Chizhova	URS	20.96	Helena Fibingerová	TCH	20.67
1980	Ilona Slupianek	GDR	22.41	Svetlana Krachevskaia	URS	21.42	Margitta Pufe	GDR	21.20
1984	Caudia Losch	FRG	20.48	Mihaela Loghin	ROM	20.47	Gael Martin	AUS	19.19
1988	Natalia Lisovskaya	URS	22.24	Kathrin Neimke	GDR	21.07	Li Meisu	CHN	21.06
1992	Svetlana Kriveleva	EUN	21.06	Huang Zhihong	CHN	20.47	Kathrin Neimke	GER	19.78
1996									

Discus

Year	Gold	C'ntry	Time	Silver	C'ntry	Time	Bronze	C'ntry	Time
1928	Halina Konopacka	POL	39.62	Lillian Copeland	USA	37.08	Ruth Svedberg	SWE	35.92
1932	Lillian Copeland	USA	40.58	Ruth Osburn	USA	40.12	Jadwiga Wajsowna	POL	38.74
1936	Gisela Mauermayer	GER	47.63	Jadwiga Wajsówna	POL	46.22	Paula Mollenhauer	GER	39.80
1948	Micheline Ostermeyer	FRA	41.92	Edira Cordiale Gentile	ITA	41.17	Jacqueline Mazeas	FRA	40.47
1952	Nina Romashkova	URS	51.42	Elizabeta Bagrjantseva	URS	47.08	Nina Dumbadze	URS	46.29
1956	Olga Fikotova	TCH	53.69	Irina Begliakova	URS	52.54	Nina Ponomareva	URS	52.02
1960	Nina Ponomareva	URS	55.10	Tamara Press	URS	52.59	Lia Manoliu	ROM	52.36
1964	Tamara Press	USR	57.27	Ingrid Lotz	GER	57.21	Lia Manoliu	ROM	56.97
1968	Lia Manoliu	ROM	58.28	Liesel Westermann	FRG	57.76	Jolan Kleiber	HUN	54.90
1972	Faina Melnik	URS	66.62	Argentina Menis	ROM	65.06	Vassilka Stoeva	BUL	64.34
1976	Evelin Schlaak	GDR	69.00	Maria Vergova	BUL	67.30	Gabriele Hinzmann	GDR	66.84
1980	Evelin Jahl	GDR	69.96	Maria Petkova	BUL	67.90	Tatiana Lesovaia	URS	67.40
1984	Ria Stalman	NED	65.36	Leslie Deniz	USA	64.86	Florenta Craciunescu	ROM	63.64
1988	Martina Hellmann	GDR	72.30	Diana Gansky	GDR	71.88	Tzvetanka Hristova	BUL	69.74
1992	Maritza Marten	CUB	70.06	Tzvetanka Hristova	BUL	67.78	Daniela Costian	AUS	66.24
1996									

Javelin

Year	Gold	C'ntry	Time	Silver	C'ntry	Time	Bronze	C'ntry	Time
1932	Mildred Didriksen	USA	43.68	Ellen Braumüller	GER	43.49	Tilly Fleischer	GER	43.00
1936	Tilly Fleischer	GER	45.18	Luise Krüger	GER	43.29	Marja Kwaśniewska	POL	41.80
1948	Herma Bauma	AUT	45.57	Kaisa Parviainen	FIN	43.79	Lily Carlstedt	DEN	42.08
1952	Dana Zátopková	TCH	50.47	Aleksandra Tshudina	URS	50.01	Elena Gorchakova	URS	49.76
1956	Inessa Iaounzem	URS	53.86	Marlene Ahrens	CHL	50.38	Nadejda Koniaeva	URS	50.28
1960	Elvira Ozolina	URS	55.98	Dana Zátopková	TCH	53.78	Birute Kaledene	URS	53.45
1964	Mihaela Penes	ROM	60.54	Antal Márta Rudas	HUN	58.27	Elena Gorchakova	URS	57.06
1968	Angéla Németh	HUN	60.36	Mihaela Peneş	ROM	59.92	Eva Janko	AUT	58.04
1972	Ruth Fuchs	GDR	63.88	Jacqueline Todten	GDR	62.54	Kathryn Schmidt	USA	59.94
1976	Ruth Fuchs	GDR	65.94	Marion Becker	GER	64.7	Kathryn Schmidt	USA	63.96
1980	Maria Colon	CUB	68.40	Saida Gunba	URS	67.76	Ute Hommola	GDR	66.56
1984	Tessa Sanderson	GBR	69.56	Tiina Lillak	FIN	69.00	Fatima Whitbread	GBR	67.14
1988	Petra Felke	GDR	74.68	Fatima Whitbread	GBR	70.32	Beate Koch	GDR	67.30
1992	Silke Renk	GER	68.34	Natalia Shikolenko	EUN	68.26	Karen Forkel	GER	66.86
1996									

Heptathlon

Year	Gold	C'ntry	Time	Silver	C'ntry	Time	Bronze	C'ntry	Time
1984	Glynis Nunn	AUS	6390	Jackie Joyner	USA	6385	Sabine Everts	FRG	6363
1988	Jackie Joyner-Kersee	USA	7291	Sabine John	GDR	6897	Anke Behmer	GDR	6858
1992	Jackie Joyner-Kersee	USA	7044	Irina Belova	EUN	6845	Sabine Braun	GER	6649
1996									

Badminton

Stars to Watch

by Hans Møller

Even easier for Indonesia?

GOING into the 1992 Olympic Games the Republic of Indonesia had but a single silver medal to its name in the record books. When the badminton players returned, however, from Barcelona Indonesia's harvest had been considerably enriched with two gold, two silver and one bronze medal. Can the Indonesians repeat that feat?

The answer is yes. With a little luck they may do even better. At the last world championships Indonesia captured two gold, one silver and one bronze medal. More notably, their silver medal was won in the women's doubles where Indonesians were far from dominant in Barcelona. The male players are of the same strength as in 1992. And Susi Susanti, the defending Olympic women's singles champion, is still one of the all-time "greats" even if she has met some recent turbulence.

Indeed, in the men's singles, the Indonesians have such strength in depth that any four on the national ranking list could win Olympic gold. But a country is only allowed three participants in each category of the Games and a hard internal fight has taken place to reach the "Promised Land". Allan Budi Kusuma – Susanti's fiancé – won gold in Barcelona but a man worth watching is the dynamic world champion Heryanto Arbi with his powerful and spectacular jump smashes. His closest challenger could be his complete opposite in playing style – the 1992 silver medal winner, Ardy Wiranata, who is admired for his patience and improvizations.

However, whilst the Indonesians are favourites they are not "bankers". Their challengers could be Park Sung Woo, of South Korea, the two Danes Poul-Erik Hoyer and 1992 Olympic

Susi Susanti

bronze medallist, Thomas Stuer-Lauridsen, without mentioning the two young Chinese, Sun Jun and Dong Jiong.

Park won silver at the world championships even if some considered it a gift. He was trailing 8-15, 1-5 in the semi-final when his opponent Stuer-Lauridsen, the only European medallist in 1992, twisted a foot and was taken to hospital.

Hoyer, who will turn 31 on 20 September 1996, is also a man to watch. His elegance, anticipation and disciplined game earned him the All England title (badminton's equivalent to the Wimbledon tennis championships) in 1995 when beating Arbi in the final. Sun Jung copied Hoyer's

---

★★★★★★★★★★★★★★★★★★★★★★★★★★★★ A Contemporary Heroine

Susi Susanti *(Indonesia)*

On meeting Susi Susanti you are struck immediately by, well, her "ordinariness". She has an open, friendly face and could pass for the girl next door if you happened to live in downtown Jakarta.

But Susanti is far from "ordinary" in badminton terms. She has already, at 25, won every major title that badminton has to offer – many of them several times over. This deceptively slight girl, from an island nation, has conquered the world championships, world cup, world grand prix, All England championships and a host of other major Open titles. Most observers consider her the best female singles player of all time.

Even the legendary Gillian Gilks, of Britain, admitted recently that in her heyday she would have needed to be at her very best "to even stand a chance against Susi". And Susanti's achievements are all the more remarkable for the gruelling schedules of current top badminton players which put them on a par with their jet-setting tennis counterparts.

Perhaps it is not just her determined, winning ways but also her engaging smile which have helped Susanti capture the imagination of spectators and TV cameras around the world. Undoubtedly, however, it was her triumph in the inaugural Olympic women's singles tournament which made her a heroine in her home land.

In the final she beat Bang Soo Hyun of South Korea 5-11, 11-5, 11-3. And she was greeted on her return to Indonesia from Barcelona in 1992 with the kind of victory parade which would not have shamed the Beatles on an American tour in the '60s. Dignitaries lined up to shake her hand and the crowd chanted her name.

And love had a lot to do with increasing the general fervour. Because in one of those Olympic fairytales which are enough to bring tears to the eyes, Susanti was engaged to marry Allan Budi Kusuma – also of Indonesia and winner of the men's singles gold medal in Barcelona.

The couple are still engaged and Susanti has been hinting recently at a wedding date in 1997, possibly after retiring from the sport. Not until, though, she has had a good stab at defending her title with the help of her consistency of shot and smooth, fast footwork about the court.

And whereas she seemed unbeatable four years ago, the same is not the case now. During a disastrous three months in 1995, Susanti lost both her All England and world championships crowns. The first to Sweden's Chinese import Lim Xiao Qing and the second to China's Ye Zhaoming. And she fell from the world no.1 slot which she had seen as her own. After, literally, years of winning the shock could have been fatal. But Susanti bounced back with some great results in the ensuing major grand prix Opens in Malaysia and Indonesia. Ye is still likely to be her main rival in Atlanta. The Chinese girl has a wider variety of shots than Susanti. But there is also a threat from Bang, the 1992 silver medallist, to Susanti's wish for a potentially "golden" wedding present.

achievement during the world team tournament (Sudirman Cup) in Switzerland last year.

25 year old Susi Susanti, meanwhile, has for years been badminton's – and Kusuma's – darling. Her feminine style, her graceful movements and her outstanding skill have delighted sports lovers far beyond mere badminton circles. A few unexpected defeats have only served to prove that she is not a winning machine but a human being.

Last year Susanti lost both her world and her All England titles to Ye Zhaoming, of China, and Lim Xiao Qing, of Chinese birth but Swedish nationality, respectively. Both Ye and Lim are strong contenders for Olympic medals but the strongest could be Bang Soo Hyun from South Korea who has won almost everything but a world and Olympic title.

Contemporary Heroes ★★★★★★★★★★★★★★★★★★★★★★★★★★★★★★★★★★

Thomas Lund and **Jon Holst-Christensen** *(Denmark)*

Thomas Lund and Jon Holst-Christensen ended a 23 year wait when they won the All England men's doubles title in 1993. They were the first Danes to take the title since Bacher and Petersen in 1970. And, as Atlanta approaches, they are two of the very few Europeans who have a chance of stopping the Asian medal train in its tracks.

Both start as major contenders in the men's doubles (together) and the mixed doubles with Marlene Thomsen and Lotte Olsen respectively. Holst-Christensen is smaller, stockier but bursting with energy and power whilst Lund is long, lean and deceptively cool under pressure.

But their biggest plus is that they move around the court as a pair and can take on both European and Asian styles of play. Lund is the tactician, making the openings and is also very fast about the court. And they are consistently good in the big events. They do not come bigger than the centenary Games.

28 year old Rexy Mainaky and Ricky Subagja, three years his junior, expect to convert their men's doubles quarter-final placing in Barcelona to another first place for Indonesia in Atlanta and, all things being equal, leave the other contenders to fight for the remaining places. Among them could be Cheah Soon Kit and Yap Kim Hock (Malaysia), Peter Axelsson and Par Gunnar Jonsson (Sweden) and Thomas Lund with Jon Holst-Christensen (Denmark) – or another Indonesian pair!

South Korea and China will fight for the top places in the women's doubles with Indonesia as outsiders. The favourites are the outstanding pairing of Gil Young Ah and Jang Hye Ock, the current world champions. The non-Asian players seem to have little chance of success here in contrast with the mixed doubles which appears on the Olympic programme for the first time.

Denmark's duo of Thomas Lund and Marlene Thomsen will, most likely, leave the others to fight for silver and bronze. Their closest rivals will be compatriots Jon Holst-Christensen and Lotte Olsen and Jan-Eric Antonsson and Astrid Crabo, of Sweden. Just for a change in this event it will be the Asians who struggle to get a place on the podium.

H. M. □

Thomas Lund

Retrospective

Romance seemed to be in the air when the fledgling sport of badminton graced the Olympic stage for the first time in 1992. Not only were the eventual men's and women's singles champions engaged to be married but men's bronze medallist Hermawan Susanto, also of Indonesia, unexpectedly beat world champion Zhao Jianhua of China in the quarter-finals after seeing his girlfriend, Sarwendah Kusumawhardani, lose in the quarter-finals to eventual women's beaten finalist Bang Soo Hyun of Korea.

A measure of Asian dominance of this sport, though, came with the fact that only Thomas Stuer-Lauridsen, an English-based Dane, could manage a medal – a bronze – for Europe. And he had to work hard for his passage with wins over China's former All-England champion Liu Jun as well as one-time world grand prix winner Rashid Sidek.

For China, though, Barcelona spelt disaster as they failed to reach any of the four finals. On the eve of the Games that would have seemed unthinkable. No doubt, the Chinese squad will wish to make amends in Atlanta.

But the player who, perhaps, deserved the crowd's sympathy as well as praise was beaten men's singles finalist Ardy Wiranata. Son of the Indonesian manager, Ardy was the player in form throughout the tournament. But the scheduling gave him less time to recover from a gruelling semi-final than his compatriot and opponent Allan Budi Kusuma. He led 9-1 in a dramatic second game of the final but ran out of steam and was overhauled and defeated.

A cruel fate, meanwhile, waited for Helen Troke of Great Britain (who as former European and Commonwealth champion was one of Europe's hopes of breaking the Asian stranglehold in the women's singles). She had remained in the sport to compete at the Olympic Games but was drawn in the first round against world champion Tang Jiuhong of China only to lose in two, very quick games. She retired after the Games.

Elegant and dynamic Korean, Park Joo Bong, joined forces with Kim Moon Soo to win the men's doubles title whilst their compatriots Hwang Hye Young and Chung So Young won the women's equivalent – not bad for a nation who only burst onto the international scene in the early '80s.

Background

Badminton returned some of the highest television ratings for any sport from the 1992 Olympic Games in Barcelona. Hardly surprising, perhaps, as the sport is so fundamentally popular in Asia where there are massive centres of the world's population.

China, Malaysia, Indonesia and Korea are all leading nations in a sport which is characterized by a need for quick reflexes, speed of foot and stamina. Thailand and Japan are not far behind. And one of the most avid badminton fans is the Sultan of Brunei who stages his own international tournament every year.

In Europe there have always been battles for supremacy between England and Denmark. And Sweden is also a strong nation. Further afield, some of the most graceful and skilful

A Sporting Legend ★★★★★★★★★★★★★★★★★★★★★★★★★★★★★★★★★

Morten Frost *(Denmark)*

Morten Frost, who finished his active playing career after the 1991 world championships, is often dubbed the "nearly man". Certainly, he was the best player never to win a world championships and he will be in Atlanta as coach/manager to the Danish team.

The Dane, who suffered badly from asthma as a child, reached the final of both the 1985 and '87 world championships. Two Chinese players denied him the title. He lost the first final to Han Jian and the second final to Yang Yang (the latter being the only man to win the title twice following his success in Beijing two years later in Jakarta).

Apart from the world title, Frost won every title you care to mention in the sport during his career. His successes included: four All England crowns (in 1982 against Luan Jin of China, in 1984 against Liem Swie King of Indonesia, in 1986 against Misbun Sidek of Malaysia and in 1987 against Icuk Sugiarto of Indonesia). And, for an astounding eight consecutive years, Frost featured as an All England finalist.

Frost's play was characterized by a head as cool as his name as well as unsurpassed footwork and defence. He will, no doubt, be more than pleased if his successors produce similar results at the 1996 Olympic Games.

players have come from India.

The USA, however, has not enjoyed world prominence since Judy Devlin (later Judy Hashman) won ten All England singles titles in the late '50s and early '60s. America also won the first three world team championships for women, called the Uber Cup, from the 1956/57 season onwards.

China is such an exciting and integral part of the current world scene that it is easy to forget that their players only emerged internationally in the '70s. Until that time, Denmark, Indonesia and Malaysia had generally shared out the post World War II major men's titles. South Korea are international newcomers, too, despite their current strength in depth. They first came into the spotlight in 1981 when the previously unknown Hwang Sun Ai won the All England women's singles event.

Agreement on the definitive origins of badminton are difficult to find as there are games with similar characteristics from countries such as China, India and England. However, the name of the sport comes from "Badminton House" in England which had one of the original courts but which, today, is better known as a venue for the famous equestrian three-day event. And badminton was played by army officers in India in the late 1800s, where the sport's first rules were registered. It is thought that the game was then brought back to England where the first national badminton association was formed in 1893.

★★★★★★★★★★★★★★★★★★★★★★★★★★★★★★ **A Sporting Legend**

Rudy Hartono *(Indonesia)*

Whilst the current Indonesian favourites battle for the 1996 Olympic gold debate still ranges over who is the all-time greatest badminton player. Ask three experts and you'll get three different names. Ask five and you'll get five names. But everybody agrees that the Indonesian Rudy Hartono was indisputably "the best" in a decade starting at the end of the sixties. He also won badminton's Olympic demonstration event in 1972.

Hartono came into the limelight in 1968 when, as a 20 year-old, he won the All England at the first attempt, a victory which the badminton world became familiar with as he took the same title for the next six years.

He won his last and record-breaking eighth title in 1976. Failure came only in 1975 when his greatest rival and good friend, the late Svend Pri from Denmark, beat him and also achieved the accolade of being the only player in the world to beat Hartono on his home ground in Jakarta.

Before retiring from the international scene the legend rounded off his career by winning the world championships in 1980 when he beat another of the all-time greats, his compatriot Liem Swie King, in the final.

Hartono was the first person to be presented with the International Badminton Federation's (IBF) highest award, The Herbert Scheele Trophy, and is now a member of the IBF's council.

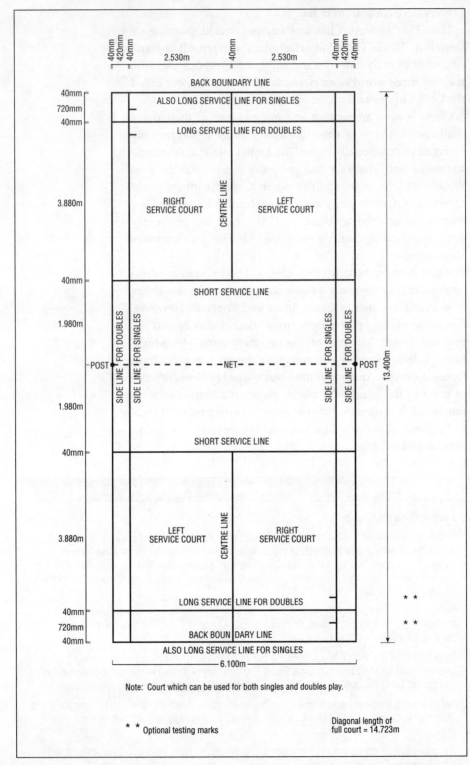

Note: Court which can be used for both singles and doubles play.

* * Optional testing marks

Diagonal length of
full court = 14.723m

Badminton court

The sport's first international championship, the All England Open, began in 1899. Kitty Godfree, winner of several Olympic tennis medals as well as the Wimbledon tennis title, was champion three times in the 1920s. A men's world team championships, the Thomas Cup, took place for the first time in 1949 – named after the first President of the International Badminton Federation (formed in 1934), Sir George Thomas. The women's equivalent is the Uber Cup. Badminton's first world championships – including men's and women's singles and doubles events – were held in 1977. This also incorporates a mixed team event called the Sudirman Cup.

Equipment

Early badminton rackets were not dissimilar to those used in table tennis matches of the same era – only larger. They were wooden with a hollow head covered by two sheets of velum. Later versions developed with the use of gut and synthetic stringing instead of the velum. They were followed by rackets with metal shafts before more recent models which have incorporated modern technology and materials such as graphite and carbon fibre to make them strong but exceptionally light.

The shuttlecock has a rounded cork base and is made of 16 goose feathers fixed so that they form a circle of 68mm (2.68in.) in diameter. For top international matches different speeds of shuttlecock are available for differing environmental conditions and tournament organizers will test them in advance of each session of play to make sure that they are correct. If a shuttlecock becomes damaged during play, either player can request permission from the umpire for it to be replaced.

Until the turn of the century badminton courts came in two types – "hour-glass" shaped, and rectangular. But the former was then dropped in favour of the latter which has become today's standard (see diagram). For events such as the Olympic Games, the organizers will use courts marked out on special synthetic mats which are designed to give some "spring" and protect the players from injury in such a demanding physical sport.

The badminton net is 1.524m (5ft) high at the centre and 1.55m (5.08ft) high over the side lines. It is made of a fine mesh and is edged at the top by a white tape. There must be no gap between the ends of the net and its supporting posts.

Rules

Winning and keeping the right to serve is of fundamental importance in badminton as a player, or pair, can only score a point for a rally won if they are serving. Otherwise, if the server loses an exchange in singles, the serve simply "changes hands" – i.e. it goes over to the opponent without a point being scored. In doubles both players in a pair can serve before the serve changes hands but, as in singles, if they continue to win rallies a pair keeps the serve.

Matches are played over the best of three games. In doubles and men's singles a game is won by the first player or pair to reach 15 points and in women's singles it is won by the first player to reach 11 points.

There is also a system of "setting" – similar to the tie-break in tennis – if the score reaches 13-all or 14-all in men's singles and doubles and nine-all or ten-all in women's singles. This is optional. The player or pair which first reached the relevant score (e.g. 13 in men's doubles) can choose whether to set or not. If they do, the score reverts to 0-0 and the first player or pair to score five points, from 13-all, or three points from 14-all and nine-all, or two points from ten-all wins the game.

The rules of badminton state that play must be continuous. So the players change ends without rest at the end of each game unless the match goes to a third game when there is a five minute interval. The players also change ends in the middle of the third game.

Play is controlled by the match umpire who sits on a raised chair looking over the net. He is helped by the service judge, who sits at ground level below the umpire and who interprets the sport's strict service rules. When serving, players must stand in the correct box, must not lift either foot completely off the ground, must ensure that their racket head is below the level of their hand and that the shuttlecock is held at a level below their waist and is hit with one, continuous action. Any infringement of these rules means that the player is faulted and loses that opportunity to score. There are different service courts for singles and doubles and a pair, or player, serves from alternate sides of the court.

Atlanta format

A maximum of 192 players will compete in the Atlanta badminton tournament: 36 in each of the men's and women's singles and 20 pairs in each of the men's, women's and mixed doubles. The mixed doubles event is an addition to the programme since 1992. Each competition will be based on a knock-out draw. The finalists will play for the gold and silver medals with the losing semi-finalists playing-off for the bronze medal.

Most players will have qualified for the 1996 Olympic Games through their computer ranking based on results gained at international tournaments between April 1995 and March '96. But the selection system ensures that there is one player from each continent for each of the five events. One nation is permitted to enter a maximum of three players or pairs in each event, if they are ranked 1-16 in the world, and two players or pairs per event, if they are ranked from 17 to 64. The host nation is entitled to have two players in the overall Olympic competition regardless of their ranking.

Venue

The Atlanta badminton competition will take place downtown in the gymnasium at Georgia State University which is 4km (2.5 miles) from the Olympic Village. It has a capacity of 4,800 spectators. 24,000 students attend the University which is the second largest institute of higher education in the State of Georgia.

MEDALLISTS (by nation)

| | Men's | | | Women's | | | |
	Gold	Silver	Bronze	Gold	Silver	Bronze	Total
Indonesia	1	2	1	1	-	-	5
China	-	-	1	-	1	3	5
Korea	1	-	-	1	1	1	4
Denmark	-	-	1	-	-	-	1
Malaysia	-	-	1	-	-	-	1
	2	2	4	2	2	4	16

ATLANTA SCHEDULE

Venue: Georgia State University

Date	Description	Round	Start	End
24 Jul	Singles (m&w)	Rd 1	9:00	11:30
			14:00	16:30
			20:00	23:00
25 Jul	Doubles (m&w)	Rd 1	9:00	12:45
	Singles (m)	Rd 2	14:00	17:00
	Doubles (m)	Rd 1		
	Singles (m)	Rd 2	20:00	22:15
26 Jul	Singles (w)	Rd 2	9:00	12:30
	Singles (m)	Last 16		
	Singles (m)	Last 16	14:00	17:00

Date	Description	Round	Start	End
	Singles (w)	Rd 2		
	Singles (w)	Rd 2	20:00	23:59
	Mixed Doubles	Rd 1		
27 Jul	Singles (w)	Last 16	9:00	13:00
	Doubles (m)	Last 16		
	Doubles (m)	Last 16	14:00	18:00
	Mixed Doubles	Last 16		
	Doubles (w)	Last 16	20:00	23:00
28 Jul	Doubles (m&w)	q/finals	9:00	12:00
	Singles (m&w)	q/finals	20:00	23:00
29 Jul	Mixed Doubles	q/finals	9:00	12:15
	Doubles (w)	s/finals		
	Doubles (m&w)	s/finals	20:00	23:45
30 Jul	Singles (m&w)	s/finals	9:00	11:45
	Mixed Doubles	s/finals	14:00	17:45
	Singles (m)	s/finals		
	Doubles (m&w)	play-off		
		(bronze)	20:00	23:00
31 Jul	Doubles (m&w)	FINALS	9:00	12:30
	Singles (m&w)	play-off		
		(bronze)	19:00	23:30
	Mixed Doubles	play-off		
		(bronze)		
1 Aug	Singles (m&w)	FINALS	9:00	14:00
	Mixed Doubles	FINAL		

MEDALLISTS

BADMINTON (Men)

Singles

Year	Gold	C'ntry	Points	Silver	C'ntry	Points	Bronze	C'ntry	Points
1992	Allan Budi Kusuma	INA	15:12, 18:13	Ardy Wiranata	INA		Hermawan Susanto	INA	
							Thomas Stuer-Lauridsen	DEN	
1996									

Doubles

Year	Gold	C'ntry	Points	Silver	C'ntry	Points	Bronze	C'ntry	Points
1992	Kim Moon Soo Park Joo Bong	KOR	15:11,15:7	Rudy Gunawan Eddy Hartono	INA		Jalani Sidek Razif Sidek	MAS	
							Li Yongbo Tian Bingyi	CHN	
1996									

BADMINTON (Women)

Singles

Year	Gold	C'ntry	Points	Silver	C'ntry	Points	Bronze	C'ntry	Points
1992	Susi Susanti	INA	5:11,11:5, 11:3	Bang Soo Hyun	KOR		Hua Huang	CHN	
1996							Tang Jiuhong	CHN	

Doubles

Year	Gold	C'ntry	Points	Silver	C'ntry	Points	Bronze	C'ntry	Points
1992	Chung So Young Hwang Hye Young	KOR	18:16, 12:15, 15:13	Guan Weizhen Nong Qunhua	CHN		Lin Ying Yao Fen	CHN	
							Gil Young Ah Shim Eun Jung	KOR	
1996									

Mixed Doubles

Year	Gold	C'ntry	Points	Silver	C'ntry	Points	Bronze	C'ntry	Points
1996									

Baseball

Stars to Watch

by Jim Callis

Can the USA crack Cuba?

IT WAS considered a foregone conclusion that perennial power Cuba would win the first official Olympic baseball competition in Barcelona four years ago. The chances that the Cubans will successfully defend their gold medal in Atlanta are far less certain.

Cuba has won 108 consecutive games at major international tournaments since 1987 but cracks are beginning to show in their armour. The Cubans had never lost more than three games in a row or been swept in a series until the United States of America defeated them in four straight games during the summer of 1995.

"The no. 1 thing about Cuba is their hubris," American team head coach Skip Bertman said. "They're certain they're going to win. Now there's a chink that's going to be in place in the Cuban national team's thinking."

The defections of national team pitchers Osvaldo Fernández, who started twice against the USA at the 1992 Olympic Games, and Livan Hernández, a key reliever, may also hurt Cuba's chances. Fernández left during Cuba's series against the USA in Millington, Tennessee, in July. Hernández departed while training in Mexico City two months later.

But Cuba still has a nucleus of players responsible for the

A Contemporary Hero ★★★★★★★★★★★★★★★★★★★★★★★★★★★★★★★

Victor Mesa *(Cuba)*

Cuba had boycotted the two previous demonstration tournaments but there was no way it would miss the first fully-fledged Olympic baseball competition. The Cubans won all seven of their games during the round-robin, then beat the United States of America and Chinese Taipei in the medal round to win the gold medal.

Longtime star Victor Mesa, nicknamed 'El Loco' for his swaggering style of play, was instrumental in all this. A centre fielder, Mesa led all hitters during the round-robin with a .545 average, and also contributed two homers and eight RBIs. He drove in four runs in a 6-1 victory over the USA in the semifinals, and added two more RBIs in an 11-1 win over Chinese Taipei in the final.

Though he is slowing down with age, Mesa is likely to start in left field for the Cubans in Atlanta. It may be his farewell to international competition.

winning streak in third baseman Omar Linares, shortstop Germán Mesa, second baseman Antonio Pacheco and righthander Lazaro Valle. And while veterans such as Lourdes Gurriel and outfielder Victor Mesa are ageing, they provide plenty of international experience.

The USA's surprising performance showed that it has the talent to avenge its disappointing fourth-place finish in 1992. After leaving Barcelona without a medal, USA Baseball changed its approach, making the formation of its 1996 Olympic team a two-year process.

*Cuban team –
Barcelona 1992*

As a result, several of the stars from the 1995 team that beat Cuba and won its final 21 games should be in Atlanta. Among them are Stanford University catcher "A J" Hinch, University of Southern California outfielder Jacque Jones, California State University outfielder-lefthander Mark Kotsay and San Diego State University first baseman Travis Lee.

The two other teams with a realistic hope of competing for a medal are Japan and South Korea, who gained Olympic berths by finishing first and second at the Asian Games in September. Both Asian teams usually combine their college-level stars with experienced players who do not participate in their nation's professional leagues.

Japan won the Olympic bronze in 1992 and is the only nation to medal in each of the three previous Olympic tournaments. They defeated the USA for the Olympic demonstration sport title in 1984, and the two teams reversed roles four years later.

★★★★★★★★★★★★★★★★★★★★★★★★★★★★★★ **A Contemporary Hero**

Mark Kotsay *(USA)*

After leading Cal State University-Fullerton to the 1995 college world series title, Mark Kotsay would like nothing more than to follow up with an Olympic gold medal in 1996. With his reputation for clutch play, it would not be a surprise if he carried the United States to a championship in Atlanta.

Kotsay is a pure hitter from the left side with good power, especially to the outfield gaps. He is not the most gifted athlete, but he is a base-stealing threat and an effective outfielder. He also doubles as a lefthanded relief pitcher with a decent repertoire and impressive competitiveness.

In 1995, Kotsay batted .422 with 21 homers, 90 RBIs and 15 steals for Fullerton, and allowed only one run in 21 pitching appearances while saving 11 games. He set six college world series records as Fullerton won the national championship. He continued to star during the summer, earning MVP honours at the National Baseball Congress world series, a national tournament won by Team USA.

A Contemporary Hero ★★★★★★★★★★★★★★★★★★★★★★★★★★★★★★

Shinji Kurano *(Japan)*

Japan relies heavily on industrial league players for its Olympic teams, but a few college stars always crack the roster, usually on their way to stardom in Japan's professional leagues. A likely candidate for that role in 1996 is Shinji Kurano, a righthanded pitcher from Aoyama Gakuin University.

In 1995, Kurano was named to the 'Best Nine', an all-star team for the Tokyo University League. He is expected to be an early pick in the November 1996 Japanese baseball draft, and probably will begin his professional career the following year. He is not overpowering, but has an excellent curveball.

Kurano excelled in international play during the summer of 1995. He pitched twice in a five-game series won 3-2 by the United States of America, picking up a victory and allowing just two runs in nine innings. At the world university games in August, he allowed one hit and struck out seven in four innings against a Florida State University team representing the USA, prompting Seminoles coach Mike Martin to compare Kurano to major league star Orel Hershiser.

Holland and Italy are the top two European nations having faced each other in the final of the European championships last year with Holland emerging the victors. Nicaragua, which gained Olympic entry by finishing second to Cuba at the Americas Baseball Challenge in August, could also be a contender.

But the notable absentee in Atlanta will be 1992 silver medallists, Chinese Taipei. To gear up for Barcelona, the nation's top 40 prospects were frozen out of Taiwan's professional league and trained together for two years. The players received significant cash bonuses for qualifying for the Olympic Games, and another $200,000 each for winning the silver.

The Chinese Taipei Olympic Committee did not put as much effort into preparing for Atlanta, and it showed as they were unable to unseat Japan or South Korea at the Asian Games.

J. C. □

Retrospective

Baseball's 1992 Barcelona Games venue had an appropriate name – "Hospitalet" or the hospital ground. It was the scene for America to nurse its wounded pride. In the first full-programme Olympic baseball tournament of all time, the nation who gave the sport to the world was beaten by Cuba 6-1 in the semi-final. Back home the folks were stunned. Cuba went on to beat Chinese Taipei in the final.

Perhaps the American audiences should have remembered the 1984 Olympic demonstration baseball tournament which

★★★★★★★★★★★★★★★★★★★★★★★★★★★★★★★★★★★★ **A Sporting Legend**

Tino Martinez *(USA)*

In 1988, in Seoul, South Korea, a first baseman sparked his team to the Olympic demonstration sport gold medal. The University of Tampa's Tino Martinez drilled two home runs and drove in four of the United States of America's five runs in a 5-3 victory over Japan.

Martinez batted .471 in Seoul, led all players with his two home runs and tied team-mate Ted Wood for the RBI lead with eight. In the final, Martinez became the only player to clear the centre-field fence during the demonstration tournament with a two-run homer in the fourth innings, and added an RBI single in the fifth and a solo homer in the eighth.

Martinez has since become a major league star with the Seattle Mariners, whom he joined in 1990. He had his best season in 1995, batting .293 with 31 home runs and 111 RBIs to help the Mariners make their first play-off appearance in their 18-year history.

Japan won by beating the USA – a result the Americans reversed with a win in 1988. Baseball was a demonstration sport several times prior to 1984, under many guises and in front of record crowds such as the 114,000 who saw the States beat Australia, 11-5, in 1956. American teams for these demonstration events were often composed of servicemen. A demonstration of Finnish baseball also featured in 1952.

Background

Baseball conjures up America, the movies, the top pros and big money – and in recent years lock-outs. But a sport considered as American as apple pie is directly descended from the old English game of "rounders" now played mainly by girls in British schools.

A man called Cartwright of the New York Knickerbockers is generally thought to have written the first set of modern rules for baseball in 1845. The sport soon became popular and turned professional. A National League started in America in 1876. This marked the beginning of a number of trade wars and cartels surrounding various leagues until a settlement in 1903 brought about the National Commission which led the sport until 1920. During that time the World Series was born – a series of games played between the champions of the major American leagues to decide the "world champion".

After World War II, aided by the advent of air travel, the sport continued to grow. It became the biggest participation sport for American men and boys. And the major league clubs built new, extended concrete stadia to increase gate numbers. But baseball also spread to other nations around the globe with the help of Americans who travelled or settled abroad. Today, it has multi-million dollar status in the USA

A Sporting Legend ★★★★★★★★★★★★★★★★★★★★★★★★★★★★★★★

Katsumi Hirosawa *(Japan)*

A USA team loaded with future major league stars such as Will Clark, Barry Larkin and Mark McGwire was expected to cruise to a gold medal in the 1984 Olympic baseball demonstration tournament. But Japan stopped those plans with a 6-3 victory in the championship game at Los Angeles.

Providing the key blow was first baseman Katsumi Hirosawa, who blasted a three-run home run in the eighth innings to put the game out of reach. He batted .438 for the tournament, topping all players with nine RBIs and tying Clark for the home run lead with three. Hirosawa also contributed an RBI single early in the gold-medal game to help Japan jump to a 3-1 lead.

Since the Olympic Games, Hirosawa has gone on to become a star in Japan's major leagues with the Yakult Swallows and Yomiuri Giants. He led the Central League in RBIs in 1991 and 1993, and batted .240 with 20 homers and 72 RBIs in 1995. He is the iron man among current Japanese players, not missing a game since 1987.

but is also widely played in the Far East and Central and South America.

Equipment

The baseball pitch is divided between a diamond-shaped infield containing four "bases" at each corner and a larger outfield. A baseball infield is 8.36 sq m (90 sq ft). The pitcher's plate is 25.4cm (10in.) above the home plate. Home base and the pitcher's plate are marked by a five-sided slab of whitened rubber whilst the other three bases are marked by white canvas bags which are securely attached to the ground. A baseball ball is formed by yarn wound around a small core of cork, rubber or similar material and then covered with two strips of white leather tightly stitched together.

The bat is a smooth round stick made from one piece of solid wood which is not more than 6.98 cm (2.75in.) in diameter and 106.68cm (42 in.) in length. Each team member wears a uniform and the catcher wears a specially-padded leather "mitt" or glove as well as a chest-protector, shin-guards and a metal mask. All other fielders may use a leather glove if they wish and the first baseman normally wears a large mitt, too. Each player, when in bat, must wear protective headgear.

Rules

Two teams of nine players compete over nine innings with the aim of winning by scoring the most runs. A run is scored when a batsman successfully hits the ball safely and runs around the four bases to get "home" before the ball is fielded by the opponents. This does not have to be achieved in one movement. A batsman can make any number of bases before stopping and waiting for the next batsman on his team to hit the ball and run.

An innings means that both teams are given the chance to bat. A team remains in bat and can keep scoring until three of its members are "out". Batsmen are either caught out, run out or struck out – the latter when the pitcher beats them with three successful throws over the "plate" or strike zone. A batsman scores only when he gets "home". However, he can also score more runs if he brings preceding batsmen, already on bases, home with him. Very rarely, he can score a "grand-slam homer". This happens if all three bases are loaded and the hit is good enough to bring four people home including the batsman.

Batsman in action with catcher behind

If the score is level after nine innings, extra innings are played until one team pulls ahead at the end of an innings.

Atlanta format

160 athletes – all male – will take part in the 1996 Olympic baseball tournament. The competition consists of one pool of eight teams playing in a round-robin format with the top four teams progressing to the semi-finals and final. There will also be a bronze medal match between the losing semi-finalists. Teams qualified for Atlanta by means of the Asian Games, Americas Baseball Challenge and zonal qualifying events in Europe and Oceania.

Venue

Baseball will be located at the Atlanta-Fulton County Stadium which has a spectator capacity of 52,000. This is 4.3km (2.7 miles) from the Olympic Village and is home to the city's major league baseball team – the Atlanta Braves.

MEDALLISTS (by nation)

	Gold	Silver	Bronze	Total
Cuba	1	-	-	1
Chinese Taipei	-	1	-	1
Japan	-	-	1	1

ATLANTA SCHEDULE

Venue: Atlanta – Fulton County Stadium

Date	Description	Round	Start	End
20 Jul	team	prelims	10:00	13:00
			15:00	18:00
			20:00	23:00
21 Jul	team	prelims	15:00	18:00
			20:00	23:00
22 Jul	team	prelims	10:00	13:00
			15:00	18:00
			20:00	23:00
23 Jul	team	prelims	10:00	13:00
			15:00	18:00
			20:00	23:00

Date	Description	Round	Start	End
24 Jul	team	prelims	15:00	18:00
			20:00	23:00
25 Jul	team	prelims	10:00	13:00
			15:00	18:00
			20:00	23:00
27 Jul	team	prelims	10:00	13:00
			15:00	18:00
			20:00	23:00
28 Jul	team	prelims	10:00	13:00
			15:00	18:00
			20:00	23:00
29 Jul	team	prelims	10:00	13:00
			15:00	18:00
			20:00	23:00
30 Jul	team	prelims	10:00	13:00
			15:00	18:00
			20:00	23:00
1 Aug	team	s/finals	14:00	17:00
			19:00	22:00
2 Aug	team	play-off (bronze)	14:00	17:00
		FINAL	19:00	22:20

Competition in this sport is open to men only

MEDALLISTS

BASEBALL

Year	Gold	C'ntry	Score	Silver	C'ntry	Score	Bronze	C'ntry	Score
1992	Omar Ajete Iglesias	CUB	11-1	Chang Cheng-hsien	TPE		Tomohito Ito	JPN	8-3
	Rolando Arrojo Ávila			Chang Wen-chung			Shinichiro Kawabata		
	José Raul Delgado Diez			Chang Yaw-teing			Masahito Kohiyama		
	Giorge Díaz Lorén			Chen Chi-hsin			Hirotami Kojima		
	José Antonio Estrada			Chen Wei-chen			Hiroki Kokubo		
	González			Chiang Tai-chuan			Takashi Miwa		
	Osvaldo Fernández			Huang Chung-yi			Hiroshi Nakamoto		
	Rodríguez			Huang Wen-po			Masafumi Nishi		
	Lourdes Gurriel Delgado			Jong Yeu-jeng			Kazutaka Nishiyama		
	Orlando Hernández Pedroso			Ku Kuo-chian			Koichi Oshima		
	Alberto Hernández Pérez			Kuo Lee Chie-fu			Hiroyuki Sakaguchi		
	Orestes Kindelán Olivares			Liao Ming-hsiung			Shinichi Sato		
	Omar Linares Izquierdo			Lin Chao-huang			Yasuhiro Sato		
	Germán Mesa Fresneda			Lin Kun-han			Masanori Sugiura		
	Victor Mesa Martínez			Lo Chen-jung			Kento Sugiyama		
	Antonio Pacheco Masso			Lo Kuo-chong			Yasunori Takami		
	Juan Padilla Alfonso			Pai Kun-hong			Akihiro Togo		
	Juan Carlos Pérez Rondón			Tsai Ming-hung			Koji Tokunaga		
	Luis Ulacia Álvarez			Wang Kuang-shih			Shigeki Wakabayashi		
	Ermidelio Urrutia Quiroga			Wu Shih-hsih			Katsumi Watanabe		
	Jorge Luis Valdes Berriel								
	Lazaro Vargas Álvarez								
1996									

Basketball

Stars to Watch

by Skip Myslenski

Biggest, brightest, gaudiest and glitziest

I T WAS the ultimate novelty item back in Barcelona. The biggest and brightest, gaudiest and glitziest bauble on the Olympic shelf. It was an original, the first men's basketball team from the United States of America to include professionals. It was memorable, counting among its members the legendary names of Magic Johnson and Larry Bird, Michael Jordan and Charles Barkley. And it was overwhelming, running off to its gold medal without ever encountering a threat.

It resembled the world's greatest rock'n'roll band, this group called "The Dream Team". And everywhere it set down, every place it appeared, it inspired madness and created chaos. Opponents collected the autographs of its members, rushed to pose for pictures with them, and – after receiving their inevitable beating – smiled and said how it had been such an honour to simply share the court with those members.

In Monte Carlo, where it practised and played an exhibition in advance of Barcelona, the young Prince Albert exchanged high fives with his dad Prince Rainier while watching it perform. And in Barcelona itself, it stayed in a private hotel, arrived for games under police escort and always played in front of full and adulating houses.

Magic Johnson

Never, ever, will there again be another like that original "Dream Team". Nor will Atlanta fall under the thrall of its successor, "DT III". ("DT II" won the world championships in Toronto in 1994.) That city, after all, is the home of the National Basketball Association Hawks and quite familiar with the names on that team. But, once more, the United States will surely dominate the men's basketball competition and leave

147

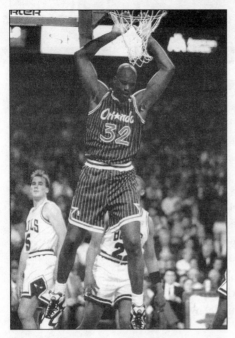

Shaquille O'Neal

Hakeen Olajawon

all others playing for silver, bronze and personal pride.

This is a certainty. The world just has not yet caught up with the USA in this sport. Even though Johnson and Bird, Jordan and Barkley will be absent from Atlanta another quartet from the original "Dreamers" – John Stockton, Karl Malone, David Robinson and Scottie Pippen – has chosen to return for an encore. And joining it is enough talent to assure the USA another basketball gold.

The 2.13m (7ft 1in), 136kg (300lbs) Shaquille O'Neal is the most daunting member of DT III. He is sure to cast his multi-faceted personality (actor, rapper, adman as well as basketball player) over the Games. Anfernee "Penny" Hardaway, a slick passing guard, and Reggie Miller, a sweet-stroking three-point shooter, are sure to be noticed as well. As are two of basketball's brightest young stars, Grant Hill and Glenn Robinson. But the most fascinating Dreamer of them all is 32 year old Hakeem Olajawon, native of Nigeria, a terror once known as "The Nigerian Nightmare," a man of rare dignity who received his US citizenship in 1993.

Together they should dominate Atlanta as the original "Dreamers" dominated Barcelona, and leave Croatia and Yugoslavia, Greece and Lithuania fighting for silver and bronze. Croatia, the silver medallists a quadrennium ago, suffered a terrible loss when Dražen Petrović was killed in an automobile accident in 1993. But they still feature current NBA players Toni Kukoč and Dino Radja. Yugoslavia, a non-participant in Barcelona, has its own NBA presence in centre Vlade Divac, as does Lithuania with Sarunas Marciulionis. A meeting between Croatia and Yugoslavia would, of course, generate interest far beyond the bounds of the basketball court.

Interest of a different sort will

surround the USA women's team which in Barcelona was as heavily-favoured as the "Dreamers" but ultimately settled for a bronze. That failure, and the desire for redemption, prompted the USA to abandon its past policy of putting its team together just before the Games. Instead it named them in the spring of 1995, and so they will land in Atlanta to face the world's challengers after playing together for a year under national team coach Tara VanDerveer.

"There are about ten countries capable of winning the gold medal in Atlanta. We have a lot of work to do," says VanDerveer, and the result of that work, that is the most intriguing question surrounding this basketball competition. For, again, when it comes to the men, there is neither question nor intrigue about who will once more reign.

S. M. □

Retrospective

Probably one of the most infamous Olympic incidents of all time happened in the sport of basketball. And it all began at the surreal, almost "witching", hour of a quarter to midnight in Munich during the 1972 Games. The Soviet Union faced the USA in the basketball final and they were making a good fist of beating the previously untouchable Americans.

Until, that is, the dying seconds when Doug Collins of the USA sunk two free throws to put the USA ahead for the first time by 50-49. Then, with a second remaining, a stoppage of

★★★★★★★★★★★★★★★★★★★★★★★★★★★★★ **A Contemporary Hero**

Sarunas Marciulionis *(Lithuania)*

When Lithuania earned its freedom from the Soviet Union and was welcomed back into the Olympic family, it was Sarunas Marciulionis who led its basketball team to Barcelona. He helped organize it. He helped raise funds for it (from, among others, the band called the 'Grateful Dead' who contributed both money and the team's memorable warm-up suits). And he starred for it, leading it to an emotional, bronze medal game victory over The Unified Team that was representing the former Soviet Union.

"It was an inspiration for the people going through all the difficulties of changes in their life," he said of that win.

Now a member of the Seattle SuperSonics, Marciulionis had earlier become the first Soviet player to sign an NBA contract when he joined the Golden State Warriors in 1989, a year after winning an Olympic gold as a member of the Soviet team in Seoul. That was the last time he would play in an international competition for anyone but Lithuania, his homeland, a homeland where he is both a hero and a nation's most recognized personality.

A Contemporary Hero ★★★★★★★★★★★★★★★★★★★★★★★★★★★★★★

Toni Kukoč *(Croatia)*

It did not matter then that he was considered the finest player in Europe. It did not matter that he was making over $3 million starring in Italy for Benetton Treviso. Or that he lived in a luxury apartment, or that he drove a specially-remodelled BMW, or that he was draped with a plethora of nicknames. "The Pink Panther" was one of those, coined because of his long and lean body.

"The Waiter" was another, the one he earned by serving up deft passes to his team mates for easy baskets. "The Alien" was a third, picked up from those who felt he played as if he were from a different planet.

None of that mattered then in Barcelona, where the 2.10m (6ft 11in) Toni Kukoč was performing for his native Croatia against the "Dream Team" of the United States. There, instead, he was just an untested draftee of the Chicago Bulls, an unknown commodity who had been munificently praised by officials of the Chicago Bulls even though he had yet to play for them. A mystery figure who would now be challenged by the two Chicago Bulls on that USA team, Scottie Pippen and Michael Jordan.

They, in fact, presented him with challenges he had never before encountered and on this afternoon they just smoked him, holding him to a single field goal in the first half, holding him to a mere four points for the game. "I have never seen defence like that before," a dazed Kukoč said later. But then he added a postscript that clearly manifested his mettle. For right there, in the wake of the worst game of his life, he declared he wanted to play for the Bulls, to play in the NBA, to play against the best.

He did, a week later, rebound from that performance to score 16 points and hand out nine assists in Croatia's loss to the USA in the gold medal game, and then – after one more season in Italy – he did, indeed, join the Bulls. Now, in stark contrast to his state a quadrennium ago, he is a team mate of Jordan and Pippen, and an NBA veteran who is certain not to be intimidated if he and Croatia face off against "DT III" in Atlanta. He has survived, survived that terrible introduction he received from the NBA, and is now, quite simply, part of it himself.

play was called for technical reasons and the Americans, thinking they had won, began celebrating. The referee seemed to agree that one second did, indeed, remain but he was over-ruled by William Jones of Great Britain, an official of FIBA (the International Basketball Federation), who insisted that the clock should be re-set to give three seconds remaining.

Bizarrely, the Soviets now had a second chance. They grabbed it by sending a long throw from Ivan Edeshko to Alexander Belov. Belov "blatantly", according to American observers, pushed past two defenders and scored to give his team victory by 51-50. Inevitably the USA protested, only to be over-ruled by 3-2.

A batch of Olympic silver medals still lie somewhere in a Munich bank vault. The disgruntled Americans flew out of town without bothering to collect them. Twenty years later, in Barcelona, American coach Chuck Daly played his team a video of his country's defeat in that 1972 final.

★★★★★★★★★★★★★★★★★★★★★★★★★ **A Contemporary Heroine**

Tara VanDerveer *(USA)*

Tara VanDerveer's current college team, Stanford, has won two national championships. Her career record as a college coach, which she has been for 17 years, is 403-113 (.781). Her resumé includes six stints coaching international teams and three "National Coach of the Year" awards. Yet, in Atlanta and despite this impressive background, Tara VanDerveer will clearly be put on the spot and asked to satisfy her country's grand expectations.

She will be there as coach of the USA women's team, the first American basketball team ever to be pulled together a year in advance to prepare for the Games. This is a grand experiment in the USA – one openly aimed at reclaiming the gold medal. And by the time the Atlanta competition opens, her group will have lived together for a year, trained together for a year and spent a year touring and playing not only in the USA but in Asia, Australia and Europe as well.

This preparation is recognition of the fact that the USA can no longer throw a team together a month before the Games and expect to be successful. This preparation also means Tara VanDerveer is now burdened with expectations that only a gold medal can satisfy.

Inevitably, basketball has provided the Games with some of its tallest Olympians and medallists. A trip to the Olympic Village whilst it is being set up will reveal workers installing bed extensions in all the quarters which will house the basketball players. Normal beds are just not long enough. It might have all been different, however, if the early organizers had succeeded in their desire to ban all players over the height of 1.90m (6ft 2¾in.).

★★★★★★★★★★★★★★★★★★★★★★★★★★★★ **A Sporting Legend**

Julijana Semenova *(Soviet Union)*

Think of Michael Jordan and Magic Johnson and the rest of The Dream Team that represented the USA at the Barcelona Games. Recall how they dominated their opponents, how clearly superior they were, how their talents far outshone those of their opponents. Do that, and you have some idea of just how Julijana Semenova loomed over women's basketball through all of the '70s.

She was a centre who stood 2.18m (7ft 1.75in.), the tallest female gold medallist ever. And an intimidating presence who won 45 medals in a career that would span 18 years. In 1976, when women's basketball was introduced to the Olympic Games, she led the Soviets to the gold, averaging 19.4 points and 12.4 rebounds even though she rarely played more than half of any game. She, in fact, went 18 years without ever losing a game in international competition, an amazing streak the USA finally ended in 1986, the last year of Julijana Semenova's equally amazing career.

The opening Olympic basketball tournament, of 1936, was played outdoors on sand courts which turned decidedly muddy in the rain. Spain's team withdrew from its matches to return home because of the outbreak of the Spanish Civil War. The USA men's team began a winning streak in the tournament which was to last 62 matches until they were finally defeated by the Soviet Union in the 1972 final. Women's basketball was added to the Olympic programme for the first time in 1976.

In 1960 a Soviet player pulled down the stand and smashed the glass backboard in a preliminary game against Puerto Rico. Erecting a new stand delayed the match until 2.30am.

A Sporting Legend ★★★★★★★★★★★★★★★★★★★★★★★★★★★★★★★★★★★★★

Alexander Gomelsky *(Soviet Union)*

His career began quietly in 1947 with a woman's team in the city then known as Leningrad and ended gloriously in 1988 in the Olympic city of Seoul. In the interim, Alexander Gomelsky came to be known as "The Godfather" of basketball in the Soviet Union, a wily fox who led that country to silver in the Games of 1960 and '64 and to bronze in those of '68.

Two years later, after his national team managed only a bronze at the world championships, he was replaced as its coach, but, a half-dozen years after that, he reclaimed his position. Boycotts precluded his taking on the USA in the next two Games ('80 and '84), and at those of Seoul, his team looked sorely overmatched against that long-time basketball power.

But in their meeting in one of the semi-finals, he coached it to a most shocking win, to a most unexpected 82-76 victory. Two days later, with its dismantling of Yugoslavia, the Soviet Union had its second basketball gold and Alexander Gomelsky had his rightful place in the record books.

Background

Any image of modern basketball conjures up all things American. Yet the sport's inventor, James Naismith, was Canadian-born. In 1891 he introduced basketball to add variety to sports lessons at Springfield College, Massachusetts, USA. His gymnasium had a 3m (10ft) balcony and he suspended peach baskets from it to make goals. And the first games were played with a normal football (of the British "Association Football" variety). Soon Naismith was showered with requests for copies of the sport's rules because of its immediate popularity with other sports institutions.

Backboards, allowing rebound shots, and better nets were added at a later stage and basketball today is played by millions worldwide – spread in many cases by American servicemen living overseas.

The sport was demonstrated at the Olympic Games in 1904 and FIBA was formed in 1932, holding its inaugural world championships in 1950.

In America, meanwhile, the sport was also developing a professional arm. The National Basketball Association (NBA) achieved major league status in 1949. It was not until the 1992 Olympic Games tournament, however, that a change in FIBA rules allowed American professionals to play at the Games. Previously, the USA had relied on college players many of whom, inevitably, went on to play in the NBA.

America has always been one of the dominant forces in basketball both professional and amateur. Their record is second to none. Other top amateur nations have included, inevitably, the Soviet Union but also Yugoslavia, Italy, Uruguay and Brazil for the men, as well as Bulgaria, Korea and China for the women.

Equipment

Basketball is played on a rectangular court (see diagram) which has a flat, hard surface – often sprung wood – and above which there should be at least 7m (23ft) of clear height. A centre circle with a radius of 1.80m (5ft 9in.) is marked on the court as are two "keyhole" shaped zones at

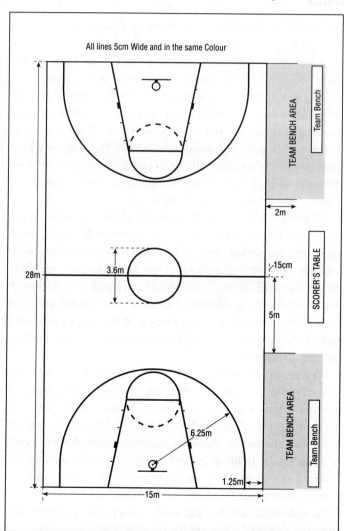

Basketball court

each end stretching out from under each basket incorporating the free throw line (from which any free shots at the basket are taken as a result of certain types of foul).

The "baskets" themselves are solid iron rings, 45cm (1ft 5in.) in diameter from which a white cord net is suspended and behind which are mounted backboards. The sport is played with a pressurized synthetic or leather ball weighing a maximum of 650g (1.43lb) and with a circumference of 78cm (1ft 6.5in.)

Each player wears a number on the front and back of their vest to help identification. Opposing teams must wear different coloured kit – one light-coloured and the other dark.

Rules

Basketball is played by two teams of five players each. A team's aim is to score into the opponents' basket and to prevent the other team from securing the ball or scoring. The team with the highest number of points wins the game.

Only five players are allowed on court per team at any one time but each team can have up to seven substitutes. Games last 40 minutes – played in two halves of 20 minutes each. There is a 15 minute interval at half-time. Play begins with a "jump ball" (when the ball is tossed by the referee between two opposing players who must leap up and attempt to tap it to one of their team) at the centre circle.

All goals score two points except for those taken from the free throw line after a foul. These score one point. Long range shots into the basket (thrown from outside a semi-circle with a 6.25m (20ft 6in.) radius from the basket) count for three points. The ball can be thrown with one hand or two to score but it can also be "dunked" (forced downwards into the basket) or "tapped" into the basket. When a goal has been scored the opposition are given a throw-in from the endline for play to resume.

Players can throw, tap or dribble – but not kick – the ball. Players dribble the ball by tapping it against the floor with one hand whilst moving. Immediately the player puts two hands on the ball again, the dribble is over and the player must pass the ball or make an attempt at goal. A player cannot run whilst holding the ball in two hands and must not remain for more than three seconds in the opponents' restricted area (the "keyhole" beneath the basket).

Basketball is a fast moving sport. A team must move the ball from the back to the front of the court within ten seconds once they have possession and a closely guarded player must either shoot or pass the ball within five seconds. Teams cannot pass back to the backcourt from the front court. Basketball is also a non-contact sport so that players cannot deliberately push, block, charge, hold or handcheck an opponent. If they do, during normal play, a foul is recorded and the opposing team is awarded a throw-in. If contact occurs during a shot on goal then free throws at goal are awarded. A player who has committed five fouls in a game must automatically leave the court.

Court officials include a referee and an umpire – dressed in black trousers and grey shirt – a timekeeper, scorer, assistant scorer and 30-second operator. The referee and umpire stop play if a violation or foul is committed and award the relevant penalty. It is the scorer's job to supervise substitutions and record all incidents, goals scored and free throws taken. Once it gains control of the ball in live play, a team must make an attempt at goal within 30 seconds. If it does not, a violation occurs. It is the job of the 30-second operator to monitor play for this rule.

Each team is allowed a coach and an assistant coach. They alone can call for "time-outs" – periods when the clock is stopped and a team can consult on tactics. Each team is allowed two time-outs per half – each of one minute – and one time-out in any period of extra time.

Atlanta format

12 men's and 12 women's teams will contest the 1996 Olympic basketball tournament, divided into two groups of six for a preliminary round-robin stage. The top teams will emerge from this to play quarter-finals, semi-finals and a final. There will also be a play-off between the losing semi-finalists for the bronze medal. And classification matches will rank the teams from 5-12 place.

All the teams booked their Atlanta slot by means of five continental qualifying events covering Africa, Asia, the Americas, Europe and Oceania. The host nation also automatically gets a place in the tournament. There are four more women's teams in the 1996 tournament than there were in Barcelona.

Venue

Basketball preliminaries will take place at Morehouse College, part of Atlanta University Center. A new $8 million gymnasium (completed last Autumn) has been built on the site and will be passed from the Organizing Committee to the Center after the Games. The college has a spectator capacity of 5,700 and is 4.8km (3 miles) from the Olympic Village.

35,500 spectators, however, can be accommodated at the Georgia Dome – host venue for the later stages. The Dome is the home of the National Football League's Atlanta Falcons and was opened in 1992. During the Games it will be split in two to house both the basketball and part of the gymnastics competition as well as the handball finals.

MEDALLISTS (by nation)

	Men's			Women's			
	Gold	Silver	Bronze	Gold	Silver	Bronze	Total
United States	10	1	1	2	1	1	16
Soviet Union	2	4	3	3	-	1	13
Yugoslavia	1	3	1	-	1	1	7
Brazil	-	-	3	-	-	-	3
Bulgaria	-	-	-	-	1	1	2
China	-	-	-	-	1	1	2
Uruguay	-	-	2	-	-	-	2
Canada	-	1	-	-	-	-	1
Croatia	-	1	-	-	-	-	1
France	-	1	-	-	-	-	1
Italy	-	1	-	-	-	-	1
Korea	-	-	-	-	1	-	1
Spain	-	1	-	-	-	-	1
Cuba	-	-	1	-	-	-	1
Lithuania	-	-	1	-	-	-	1
Mexico	-	-	1	-	-	-	1
	13	13	13	5	5	5	54

ATLANTA SCHEDULE

Venue: Georgia Dome = GD   Morehouse College = MC

Date	Round	Start	End	Venue
20 Jul	prelims (m)	10:00	13:30	MC
		15:00	18:30	MC
		20:00	23:30	GD
21 Jul	prelims (w)	10:00	13:30	MC
		15:00	18:30	MC
		20:00	23:30	GD
22 Jul	prelims (m)	10:00	13:30	MC
		15:00	18:30	MC
		20:00	23:30	GD
23 Jul	prelims (w)	10:00	13:30	MC
		15:00	18:30	MC
		20:00	23:30	GD
24 Jul	prelims (m)	10:00	13:30	GD
		15:00	18:30	MC
		20:00	23:30	GD

Date	Description	Start	End	Venue
25 Jul	prelims (w)	10:00	13:30	GD
		15:00	18:30	MC
		20:00	23:30	GD
26 Jul	prelims (m)	10:00	13:30	GD
		15:00	18:30	GD
		20:00	23:30	GD
27 Jul	prelims (w)	10:00	13:30	GD
		15:00	18:30	
		20:00	23:30	
28 Jul	prelims (m)	10:00	13:30	GD
		17:00	18:30	GD
		20:00	23:59	MC
29 Jul	prelims (w)	10:00	13:30	GD
		15:00	18:30	GD
		20:00	23:30	MC
30 Jul	q/finals (m)	10:00	13:30	GD
	classification (m)	15:00	18:30	MC
	q/finals (m)	20:00	23:30	GD
31 Jul	classification (w)	10:00	13:30	GD
	q/finals (m)	15:00	18:30	
	q/finals (m)	20:00	23:30	
1 Aug	classification (m)	10:00	13:30	GD
	classification (w)	15:00	18:30	
	s/finals (m)	20:00	23:30	
2 Aug	play-off (7-8 place) (m)	10:00	13:30	GD
	play-off (5-6 place) (m)			
	s/finals (w)	15:00	18:30	GD
	play-off (11-12 place) (m)	20:00	23:30	GD
	play-off (9-10 place) (m)			
3 Aug	play-off (7-8 place) (w)	10:00	10:30	GD
	play-off (5-6 place) (w)			
	play-off (11-12 place) (w)	15:00	18:30	GD
	play-off (9-10 place) (w)			
	play-off (bronze) (m)	20:00	23:30	GD
	FINAL (m)			
4 Aug	play-off (bronze) (w)	9:30	13:00	GD
	FINAL (w)			

MEDALLISTS

BASKETBALL (Men)

Year	Gold	C'ntry	Score	Silver	C'ntry	Bronze	C'ntry	Score
1936	Samuel Balter	USA	19-8	Gordon Aitchison	CAN	Carlos Borja Morca	MEX	26-12
	Ralph Bishop			Jan Allison		Viktor Hugo Borja Morca		v POL
	Joe Fortenberry			Arthur Chapman		Rodolfo Choperena Irizarri		
	John Gibbons			Charles Chapman		Luís Ignacio de la Vega Leija		
	Francis Johnson			Edward Dawson		Raúl Fernández Robert		
	Carl Knowles			Irving Meretsky		Andrés Gómez Dominguez		
	Frank Lubin			Douglas Peden		Silvio Hernandez del Valle		
	Arthur Mollner			James Stewart		Francisco Martinez Cordero		
	Donald Piper			Malcolm Wiseman		Jesús Olmoz Moreno		
	Jack Ragland					José Pamplona Lecuanda		
	Willard Schmidt					Greer Skousen Spilsbury		
	Carl Shy							
	Duane Swanson							
	William Wheatley							
1948	Clifford Barker	USA	65-21	André Barrais	FRA	Alfonso Azevedo Evora	BRA	52-47
	Donald Barksdale			Michel Bonnevie		João Francisco Braz		v MEX
	Ralph Beard			André Buffière		Alfredo Rodrigues da Motta		
	Lewis Beck			René Chocat		Zenny de Azevedo		
	Vincent Boryla			René Dérency		Rui de Freitas		
	Gordon Carpenter			Maurice de Saymonnet		Nilton Pacheco de Oliveira		
	Alexander Groza			André Even		Marcus Vinicius Dias		
	Wallace Jones			Maurice Girardot		Alexandro Gemignani		
	Robert Kurland			Fernand Guillou		Alberto Marson		
	Raymond Lumpp			Raymond Offner		Massinet Sorcinelli		
	Robert Pitts			Jacques Perrier				
	Jesse Renick			Yvan Quénin				
	Robert Robinson			Lucien Robuffic				
	Kenneth Rollins			Pierre Thiolon				
1952	Ronald Bontemps	USA	36-25	Stiapas Butautas	URS	Martin Acosta y Lara	URU	68-59
	Marcus Freiberger			Nodar Dzordzikija		Enrique Baliño		v ARG
	Victor Wayne Glasgow			Anatoli Konev		Victorio Cieslinskas		
	Charles Hoag			Otar Korkija		Héctor Costa		
	William Hougland			Heino Kruus		Nelson Demarco		
	John Keller			Ilmar Kullam		Héctor García Otero		
	Melvin Dean Kelley			Justinas Lagunavitshius		Tabaré Larre Borges		
	Robert Kenney			Jogan Lysov		Adesio Lombardo		
	Robert Kurland			Alexander Moisejev		Roberto Lovera		
	William Lienhard			Yuri Ozerov		Sergio Matto		
	Clyde Lovelette			Kasis Petkjavitshus		Wilfredo Pelaez		
	Frank McCabe			Stasis Stonkous		Carlos Rosselló		
	Daniel Pippin			Majgonis Valdmanis				
	Howard Williams			Viktor Vlasov				
1956	Carl Cain	USA	88-59	Arkadi Botchkarev	URS	Carlos Blixen	URU	71-62
	Charles Darling			Janis Kroumigne		Nelson Chelle		v FRA
	William Evans			Algirdas Laouritenas		Ramiro Cortes		
	Gilbert Ford			Valdis Mouijnieks		Héctor Costa		
	Burdette Haldorson			Yuri Ozerov		Nelson Demarco		
	William Hougland			Kasis Petkiavitchous		Héctor García Otero		
	Robert Jeangerard			Mikhail Semenov		Carlos González		
	Kenneth Jones			Stasis Stonkous		Sergio Matto		
	Richard Boushka			Mikhail Stoudenetsku		Raúl Mera		
	William Russell			Vladimir Torban		Oscar Moglia		
	Ronald Tomsic			Majgonis Valdman		Ariel Olascoaga		
	James Walsh			Viktor Zoubkov		Milton Scarón		

/continued on next page 157

Year	Gold	C'ntry	Score	Silver	C'ntry	Bronze	C'ntry	Score
1960	Jay Arnette	USA	81-57	Yuri Korneev	URS	Edson Bispo dos Santos	BRA	78-75
	Walter Bellamy			Janis Kruminj		Moyses Blas		v ITA
	Robert Boozer			Valdis Minaschvili		Waldemar Blatkauskas		
	Terry Dischinger			Valdis Muizhniek		Waldyr Geraldo Boccardo		
	Burdette Haldorson			Caesar Ozers		Zenny de Azevedo		
	Darrall Imhoff			Alexander Petrov		Carmo de Souza		
	Allen Kelley			Mikhail Semenov		Wlamir Marques		
	Lester Lane			Vladimir Ugrekhlidze		Carlos Domingo Massoni		
	Jeremy Lucas			Majgonis Valdman		Amaury Antonio Pasos		
	Oscar Robertson			Albert Valjtin		Fernando Pereira de Freitas		
	Adrian Smith			Gennadi Voljnov		Jatyr Edúardo Schall		
	Jeremy West			Viktor Zubkov		Antonio Salvador Sucar		
1964	James Barnes	USA	73-59	Armenak Alachachian	URS	Edson Bispo dos Santos	BRA	76-60
	William Bradley			Nikolai Bagley		Friedrich Braun		v PUR
	Lawrence Brown			Yuris Kalninsh		Carmo de Souza		
	Joseph Caldwell			Viacheslav Khrynin		Sergio de Toledo Machado		
	Mel Counts			Yuri Korneev		Wlamir Marques		
	Richard Davies			Janis Krumins		Carlos Domingo Massoni		
	Walter Hazzard			Yaak Lipso		Viktor Mirshawka		
	Lucius Jackson			Levan Moseshvili		Amaury Antonio Pasos		
	John McCaffrey			Valdis Muizhniek		Ubiratan Pereira Maciel		
	Jeffrey Mullins			Alexander Petrov		Jatyr Eduardo Schall		
	Jerry Shipp			Alexander Travin		José Edvar Simões		
	George Wilson			Gennadi Volnov		Antônio Salvador Sucar		
1968	Michael Barrett	USA	65-50	Dragutin Čermak	YUG	Vladimir Andreev	URS	70-53
	John Clawson			Krešimir Ćosić		Sergei Belov		v BRA
	Donald Dee			Vladimir Cvetković		Vadim Kapranov		
	Calvin Fowler			Ivo Daneu		Sergei Kovalenko		
	Spencer Haywood			Radivoje Korać		Anatoli Krikun		
	William Hosket			Zoran Maroević		Yaak Lipso		
	James King			Nicola Plećas		Modestas Paulauskas		
	Michael Silliman			Tajko Rajković		Anatoli Polivoda		
	Glynn Saulters			Dragoslav Ražnjatović		Zurab Sakandelidze		
	Charles Scott			Petar Skansi		Yuri Selikhov		
	Kenneth Spain			Damir Solman		Priit Tomson		
	Joseph White			Aljoša Zorga		Gennadi Volnov		
1972	Sergei Belov	URS	51-50	Michael Bantom	USA	José Miguel Alvarez	CUB	66-65
	Alexander Belov			James Brewer		Miguel Calderon Gomez		v ITA
	Alexander Boloshev			Tommy Burleson		Rafael Canizares Poey		
	Ivan Dvorni			Douglas Collins		Pedro Chappé Garcia		
	Ivan Edeshko			Kenneth Davis		Juan Domecq		
	Mikhail Korkia			James Forbes		Ruperto Herrera		
	Sergei Kovalenko			Thomas Henderson		Tomas Herrera		
	Modestas Paulauskas			Dwight Jones		Conrado Perez Armenteros		
	Anatoli Polivoda			Robert Jones		Juan Roca		
	Alshan Sharmukhamedov			Kevin Joyce		Franklin Standard		
	Gennadi Volnov			Thomas McMillen		Alejandro Urgelles		
	Zurab Sakandelidze			William Edward Ratleff		Oscar Varona		
1976	Michel Armstrong	USA	95-74	Krešimir Ćosić	YUG	Vladimir Arzamaskov	URS	100-72
	William Buckner			Dražen Dalipagić		Sergei Belov		v CAN
	Kenneth Carr			Mirza Delibašić		Alexander Belov		
	Adrian Dantley			Blagoje Georgijevski		Ivan Edeshko		
	Walter Davis			Vinko Jelovać		Mikhail Korkiya		
	Phil Ford			Željko Jerkov		Andrei Makeev		
	Ernie Grunfeld			Dragan Kićanović		Valeri Miloserdov		
	Philip Hubbard			Andro Knego		Anatoli Mychkin		
	Mitchell Kupchak			Zoran Slavnić		Alexander Salnikov		
	Thomas La Garde			Damir Solman		Vladimir Tkachenko		
	Scott May			Žarko Varajić		Alzhan Zharmukhamedov		
	Steve Sheppard			Rajko Žižić		Vladimir Zhigiliy		

Year	Gold	C'ntry	Score	Silver	C'ntry	Bronze	C'ntry	Score
1980	Krešimir Ćosić	YUG	86-77	Marco Bonamico	ITA	Alexander Belostenny	URS	117-94
	Dražen Dalipagić			Roberto Brunamonti		Sergei Belov		v ESP
	Mirza Delibašić			Fabrizio Della Fiori		Nikolai Deruguin		
	Željko Jerkov			Pietro Generali		Stanislav Eremin		
	Dragan Kićanović			Enrico Gilardi		Sergejus Jovaisa		
	Andro Knego			Pierluigi Marzorati		Andrei Lopatov		
	Duje Krstulović			Dino Meneghn		Valeri Miloserdov		
	Mihovil Nakić-Vojnović			Romeo Sacchetti		Anatoli Myshkin		
	Ratko Radovanović			Marco Solfrini		Alexander Salnikov		
	Branko Skroče			Michael Sylvester		Sergei Tarakanov		
	Zoran Slavnić			Renzo Vecchiato		Vladimir Tkachenko		
	Rajko Žižić			Renato Villalta		Vladimir Zhigily		
1984	Steve Alford	USA	96-65	Fernando Arcega	ESP	Dražen Dalipagić	YUG	88-82
	Patrick Ewing			José Manuel Beiran		Sabit Hadžić		v CAN
	Vern Fleming			Juan Antonio Corbalan		Andro Knego		
	Michael Jordan			Juan Domingo De La Cruz		Emir Mutapčić		
	Joseph Kleine			Andres Jimenez		Mihovil Nakić-Vojnović		
	Jon Koncak			José Luis Llorente		Alexander Petrović		
	Chris Mullin			Juan Maria Lopez		Dražen Petrović		
	Samuel Perkins			José Maria Margall		Ratko Radovanović		
	Alvin Robertson			Fernando Martin		Ivan Sunara		
	Wayman Tisdale			Fernando Romay		Branko Vukicević		
	Jeffrey Turner			Juan Antonio San Epifanio		Rajko Žižić		
	Leon Wood			Ignacio Solozabal		Nebojša Zorkić		
1988	Alexander Belostennyi	USR	76-63	Franjo Arapović	YUG	Willie Anderson	USA	78-49
	Valdemaras Chomicius			Zoran Čutura		Stacey Augmon		v AUS
	Valeri Goborov			Danko Cvjetičanin		Vernell Coles		
	Rimas Kurtinaitis			Vlade Divac		Jeffrey Grayer		
	Sarunas Marciulionis			Toni Kukoč		Hersey Hawkins		
	Igors Miglinieks			Želimir Obradović		Daniel Majerle		
	Viktor Pankracskin			Žarko Paspalj		Danny Manning		
	Arvydas Sabonis			Dražen Petrović		Herman Reid		
	Tiit Sokk			Dino Radja		Mitchell Richmond		
	Sergei Tarakanov			Zdravko Radulović		David Robinson		
	Vadim Tikhonenko			Stojan Vranković		Charles Daniel Smith		
	Alexander Volkov			Jurij Zdovc		Charles Edward Smith		
1992	Charles Barkley	USA	117-85	Vladan Alanović	CRO	Romanas Brazdauskis	LTU	82-78
	Larry Bird			Franjo Arapović		Valdemaras Chomicius		v CIS
	Clyde Drexler			Danko Cvjetićanin		Darius Dimavicius		
	Patrick Ewing			Alan Gregov		Gintaras Einikis		
	Earvin 'Magic' Johnson			Arijan Komazec		Sergejus Jovaisa		
	Michael Jordan			Toni Kukoč		Arturas Karnisovas		
	Christian Laettner			Aramis Naglic		Gintaras Krapikas		
	Karl Malone			Velimir Perasović		Rimas Kurtinaitis		
	Chris Mullin			Dražen Petrović		Sarunas Marciulionis		
	Scottie Pippen			Dino Radja		Alvydas Pazdrazdis		
	David Robinson			Zan Tabak		Arvydas Sabonis		
	John Stockton			Stojko Vranković		Arunas Visockas		
1996								

/continued on next page

BASKETBALL (Women)

Year	Gold	C'ntry	Score	Silver	C'ntry	Bronze	C'ntry	Score
1976*	Tamara Daunene	URS		Cindy Brogden	USA	Krasimira Bogdanova	BUL	79-95
	Nelli Ferjabnikova			Nancy Dunkle		Dijana Dilova-Brajnova		v TCH
	Natalia Klimova			Lusia Harris		Krasimira Giurova		
	Olga Barisheva-Korosteleva			Patricia Head		Nadka Goltcheva		
	Raisa Kurvijakova			Charlotte Lewis		Todorka Jordanova		
	Tatiana Ovetchkina			Nancy Lieberman		Petkana Makavejeva		
	Angele Rupsene			Gail Marquis		Penka Metodieva		
	Nadesjda Schuvajeva- Olkhov			Ann Meyers		Sneziana Mikailova		
	Julijana Semenova			Mary Anne O'Connor		Margarita Sjtarkelova		
	Olga Sukarnova			Patricia Roberts		Girgina Skerlatova		
	Tatiana Zakarova-Nadivova			Susan Rojcewicz		Marija Stojanova		
	Nadesjda Zakarova			Julienne Simpson		Penka Stojanova		
1980	Vida Beselene	URS	104-73	Krasimira Bogdanova	BUL	Mrdsada Becirspahić	YUG	68-65
	Nelli Ferjabnikova			Vanja Dermendchieva		Mira Bjedov		v HUN
	Tatiana Jvinskaia			Dijana Dilova-Brajnova		Vesna Despotović		
	Olga Barisheva-Korosteleva			Silvja Germanova		Vera Djurašković		
	Tatiana Ovetchkina			Nadka Goltcheva		Zorica Djurković		
	Ludmila Rogoschina			Petkana Makavejva		Jelica Komnenović		
	Angele Rupsene			Penka Metodieva		Biljana Majstorović		
	Liubov Scharmai			Angelina Mikailova		Vukica Mitić		
	Nadesjda Schuvajeva- Olkhov			Snezjana Mikailova		Sanja Ožegović		
	Julijana Semenova			Kostadinka Radkova		Sofija Pekić		
	Olga Sukarnova			Jevladia Slavtcheva-Stefanova		Jasmina Perazić		
	Tatiana Zakarova-Nadivova			Penka Stojanova		Marija Tonković		
1984	Catherine Boswell	USA	85-55	Choi Aei Young	KOR	Ba Yan	CHN	63-57
	Denise Curry			Choi Kyung Hee		Chen Yuefang		v CAN
	Anne Donovan			Jeong Myung Hee		Cong Xuedi		
	Teresa Edwards			Kim Eun Sook		Li Xiaoqin		
	Ludi Lea Henry			Kim Hwa Soon		Liu Qing		
	Janice Lawrence			Kim Young Hee		Qui Chen		
	Pamela McGee			Lee Hyung Sook		Song Xiaobo		
	Carol Menken-Schaudt			Lee Mi Ja		Wang Jun		
	Cheryl Miller			Moon Kyung Ja		Xiu Lijuan		
	Kimberley Mulkey			Park Chan Sook		Zhang Hui		
	Cindy Noble			Sung Jung A		Zhang Yueqin		
	Lynette Woodard					Zheng Haixia		
1988	Cynthia Brown	USA	77-70	Andjelija Arbutina	YUG	Olessia Barel	URS	68-53
	Victoria Bullett			Vesna Bajkuša		Olga Buriakina		v AUS
	Cynthia Cooper			Polona Dornik		Irina Gerlits		
	Anne Donovan			Sladjana Golić		Olga Jakovleva		
	Teresa Edwards			Kornelija Kvesić		Olga Jevkova		
	Mary Ethridge			Mara Lakić		Elena Kudaschova		
	Jennifer Gillom			Žana Lelas		Aleksandra Leonova		
	Bridgette Gordon			Bojana Milosević		Irina Mink		
	Andrea Lloyd			Razija Mujanović		Galina Savitskaia		
	Katrina McClain			Danira Nakić		Irini Sumnikova		
	Suzanne McConnell			Stojna Vangelovska		Vitalija Tuomaite		
	Teresa Weatherspoon			Eleonora Vild				
1992	Elena Baranova	EUN	76-66	Cong Xuedi	CHN	Victoria Bullett	USA	88-74
	Elen Bunatiants			He Jun		Daedra Charles		v CUB
	Irina Gerlits			Li Dongmei		Cynthia Cooper		
	Elena Jirko			Li Xin		Clarissa Davis		
	Elena Kudaschova			Liu Jun		Medina Dixon		
	Irina Mink			Liu Qing		Teresa Edwards		
	Elena Shvaibovitch			Peng Ping		Tammy Jackson		
	Irina Sumnikova			Wang Fang		Carolyn Jones		
	Marina Tkatchenko			Zhan Shuping		Katrina McClain		
	Elena Tornikidou			Zheng Dongmei		Suzanne McConnell		
	Svetlana Zabolueva			Zheng Haixia		Victoria Orr		
	Natalia Zasulskaia			Zheng Xiulin		Teresa Weatherspoon		
1996								

*Medals decided on group points basis

Boxing

Stars to Watch

by Neil Allen

America seeks to recapture Olympic Glory

A RE THE great Cuban amateur boxing teams of the '80s no more? Can the United States recapture some of its former Olympic ring glory, highlighted at Montreal in 1976, now that its selected team will be fighting at home in the 10,000 seater Alexander Memorial Coliseum?

Finally, will the historic Olympic boxing tournament be able to maintain its place in the Olympic schedule? After all, mounting criticism during the past few years has been aimed at controversial refereeing, judging and scoring as well as the

★★★★★★★★★★★★★★★★★★★★★★★★★★★★★★★ **A Contemporary Hero**

Felix Savon *(Cuba)*

Felix Savon Fabre, to give him his full name, is the arrow head of a powerful Cuban boxing squad which has dominated the international boxing scene for well over a decade.

Born on 22 November 1967 in Guantanamo City, Savon has always boxed as a heavyweight with a divisional limit of 91kg (13st 8lb). He became world junior champion at Bucharest in 1985 and the following year, in Reno, Nevada, was crowned for the first time as world senior heavyweight champion. An inspiration for the young Savon was the presence on the same team, and winner of the super heavyweight title for the third time, Teófilo Stevenson.

Savon, like Stevenson, had to miss the 1984 and 1988 Games because of his country's boycotts. But he came back to top international competition in 1989 in the politically welcoming atmosphere of Moscow and was to win three more world championships in 1991 (Sydney), 1993 (Tampere) and 1995 (Berlin).

By the time of the 1992 Barcelona Games, Savon was a thoroughly seasoned international competitor as he proved with his progress through the rounds while his team-mates were winning six titles in eight of the finals. Savon stopped Poland's Krzysztop Rojek in the second round of his opening bout and then out-pointed a German and an American before winning his semi-final clearly on points against Holland's Van Der Lijde. In the final the Cuban beat Nigerian David Izonritei by 14-1.

Noted for his patriotism, there seems no chance that Savon will ever turn professional. In the last world championships in Berlin he won his fifth title by stopping Germany's Laun Krasniqi in the second, having looked a little less impressive in a 9-6 semi-final win over Christopher Mendy of France.

generally-acknowledged potential risk of brain damage through punches to the head.

To address the third, and surely most important question, first. The future of boxing in the Olympic ring, post-1996, may be by no means a lost cause judging from a brief but amiable interview I had with IOC President Juan Antonio Samaranch in London.

The President rather shyly confirmed to me that he, in student days, had had a brief but successful amateur boxing career. Obviously a former diplomat with a "dig" in either hand, the President was at that time waiting for further medical reports on a sport which, over the years, has included several vital safeguards, including the compulsory though also controversial use of headguards and stricter medical control. A final decision on the year 2000 will come during programme commission meetings post-Atlanta.

In the meantime, though, there are bound to be many new faces competing for the 1996 Games boxing medals. This sport, compared with all the up-to-the-minute statistical information available in track and field athletics and swimming, can never fully reflect current form. Even with zonal qualification the Olympic entry will be a mixture of enormous natural talent and sometimes disturbingly inadequate opposition in the early rounds.

We have some evidence to go by from the international ranking lists supplied to AIBA (the International Amateur Boxing Association) by Rainer Scharf of Germany. He issues his own scoring table, adjudging and awarding points for boxers who compete in a number of multi-nations tournaments as well as major championships like the Pan-American Games and the world championship.

Last year, Scharf rated the top ten boxers in each of the 12 amateur weight categories, ranging from light flyweight to super heavyweight. The top man in each weight consisted of six Cubans and one boxer each from Bulgaria, Kazakhstan, Thailand, Romania, Ukraine and the USA.

The 1995 world championships in Berlin was the occasion which suggested that the remarkable domination of the sport by Cuba might just be on the wane. Compared with the eight gold medals they won in 1993, the Cubans were successful in only four weights though they also won two silver and three bronze medals.

That, though, was still an outstanding team performance compared with the Americans who had their worst world showing since 1978. Uncle Sam's only winner in Berlin was southpaw light heavyweight Antonio Tarver from Orlando who beat Cuba's Diosvani Vegas on a 7-3 decision. The only other American medallist was super heavyweight Lawrence Clay-Bey with a bronze.

Cuba's four world amateur champions in Berlin were heavyweight Felix Savon, his fifth title, middleweight Ariel Hernàndez, welterweight Juan Hernández, his third title, and light welterweight Hector Vinent who also won in 1993. But Cuban coach Julian Gonzalez called it the "toughest world championships I've been to...... The titles used to be just between us, Russia, America and the Germans. Now there are so many countries that the hunt for medals gets very, very hard."

Expect then to see another wide share out of the honours in Atlanta, especially since the former Communist bloc has split up into many smaller countries, most of them with such strong nationalistic urges that former eastern style Government sports backing may not be quite a thing of the past. As a post-script watch out for the American professional managers who have already been making overtures to the Cuban squad to forget Marxism and follow the dollar.

N. A. ☐

Retrospective

That Olympic boxing champions, particularly in the heavier divisions, should turn professional after their Games victories is almost automatic. Indeed the first heavyweight champion,

★★★★★★★★★★★★★★★★★★★★★★★★★★★★★ A Sporting Legend

Johnny Douglas *(Great Britain)*

Known from his initials, JWHT as "Johnny Won't Hit Today". This nickname was not a reference to boxing passivity but to Douglas's stonewalling tactics as a batsman when he was cricket captain of both Essex and England. Also an England soccer player, Douglas won the 1908 London Olympic middleweight title after scoring two stoppages in the early rounds.

The London final was against Australia's Reginald "Snowy" Baker, arguably as fine an all-rounder as Douglas for Baker also competed in the Games springboard diving and 4 x 200m swimming relay and, during his life, competed in nearly 30 other sports and games.

The Douglas-Baker match was regarded at the time as a classic. Even though the official 1908 report says that Baker was down in the second round other later sources from Australia state that the exchanges were so even that a fourth, deciding round was called for.

A Sporting Legend ★★★★★★★★★★★★★★★★★★★★★★★★★★★★★★★★★★★

Eddie Eagan *(USA)*

First ever Olympic boxing winner at light heavyweight when the division was introduced at Antwerp in 1920, Eagan is also the only boxing competitor in Olympic history to have won an Olympic Winter Games gold medal as well.

Eagan, whose father died when he was only one, lived an austere enough life as a teenager in Colorado but he ended up winning the heavyweight titles of Yale, Harvard and Oxford University with a considerable education to boot. Not quite 1.82m (6ft) tall, he won both the light heavyweight and heavyweight bouts on the same night in Oxford's annual Varsity match against Cambridge.

Eagan made his name internationally by winning the middleweight title at the 1919 Inter-Allied Games in Paris. Having won the US Olympic trials as a light heavyweight Eagan went to Antwerp and beat a South African, a Frenchman and a Briton before winning the final on points against Sverre Sörsdal of Norway.

Twelve years later, by now a successful businessman, Eagan was asked at the last minute to join the US four man bobsleigh team at the Winter Games of 1932 at Lake Placid. After totalling 7min 53.68sec., Eagan and his team-mates, including Jay O'Brien, aged 48 years 359 days (the oldest ever Olympic Winter Games gold medallist) were triumphant.

Samuel Berger of the USA (1904) did just that. And of all the past great Olympic boxing winners, two middleweights (Floyd Patterson and Michael Spinks), two light heavyweights (Cassius Clay and Leon Spinks), three heavyweights (Joe Frazier, George Foreman and Ray Mercer) and one super heavyweight (Lennox Lewis) have gone on to win a version of the professional world heavyweight title – sometimes called the "richest prize in sport".

Teófilo Stevenson of Cuba is one exception. He won the Olympic heavyweight crown three times from 1972 – '80. In doing so, he became only the second man to win three boxing gold medals and the first man to win them in the same weight class. Hungary's László Papp also won three gold medals in 1948 (middleweight), '52 and '56 (light middleweight). But whereas Papp briefly turned professional at the end of his career, Stevenson remained staunchly amateur and could well have won a fourth medal in 1984 if his country had not boycotted the Los Angeles Games.

Meanwhile Michael and Leon Spinks of the USA were brothers. Michael won the Olympic middleweight title in Montreal in 1976 moments before his elder brother, Leon, began the light heavyweight final which he won. Leon went on to fight and beat Muhammad Ali as a professional heavyweight.

In the Olympic arena, boxing has never been short on controversy. Harry Mallin, a London policeman, was the first man to defend successfully a title, winning the middleweight gold medal in 1920 and '24. In his 1924 quarter-final, in Paris, Mallin was seemingly beaten by Frenchman Roger Brousse until bite marks were found on Mallin's chest and Brousse was later disqualified by the jury of appeal.

The incident made for a marred final in the French capital. "The crowd", says the official British Olympic Association report of those Games, "kept up a continuous series of cat-calls and varied noises signifying its disapproval of Mallin's presence. Mallin eventually won a close fight but we are unable to give a more detailed description owing to the fact that we were seated in the centre of a group of excited and gesticulating Frenchmen who...refused to allow anyone in their proximity to get a view of the fight".

Another Briton, Chris Finnegan, who won the middle-weight title in Mexico in 1968, provides an amusing anecdote. After his final the boxer had so much trouble providing a urine sample for the dope testers that they had to accompany him to a local restaurant for his victory meal until he finally "performed" for them in the small hours of the night.

Boxing has also been marked by a series of dramatic protests against refereeing and judging decisions. The 1988 Olympic Games in Seoul, South Korea, were no exception. Keith Parker, a referee from New Zealand, was attacked by Korean team official, Lee Heung Soo, after the two points he deducted for alleged head-butting by boxer Byun Jong Il proved crucial in Byun's defeat by Bulgarian Alexander

★★★★★★★★★★★★★★★★★★★★★★★★★★★★★★ **A Sporting Legend**

Ingemar Johansson *(Sweden)*

Ingemar Johansson is an almost bizarre exception to the list of great Olympic champions who have gone on to win world professional boxing titles. His nightmare Olympic boxing experience came in Helsinki in 1952 when he was disqualified in the heavyweight final against American Ed Sanders for "inactivity in the ring". Yet, seven years later, in June 1959, "Ingo" became undisputed pro champion by stopping Patterson in the third round in New York.

Johansson still claims a rare place in Olympic history. On 9 May 1982, at the trotting ground in his home city of Gothenburg, the Swede was finally awarded the silver medal of which he had been officially deprived 30 years earlier. This miracle, still inexplicable to some, was accomplished only by strenuous lobbying from Don Hall of AIBA and Swedish journalist Sven Ekstron.

In 1952 the Swedish Olympic Committee had cabled "sincere and unreserved regret for the unsportsmanlike way in which the Swedish boxer Johansson performed." But 30 years later "after long and careful study" by the IOC, Johansson received his medal from President Samaranch who had been lobbied on a visit to Stockholm the previous year.

Johansson, who now works as a boxing commentator for Swedish TV, had a total of only 28 fights as a professional, losing the world title to Patterson in a return in June 1960 by a fifth round knockout and then losing the rubber match in the sixth the following year. But the three matches earned the genial Swede $1.5m.

Hristov. Korean officials filled the ring after the fight and Parker had to be escorted out of the stadium under protection before catching one of the earliest flights home.

Meanwhile Byun staged his own sit-in protest in the ring in silence for over an hour before leaving when the organizers switched off all the venue lights. But if that protest seemed original, it was not. Byun's compatriot, Dong Kih Choh had done it all before, 24 years earlier. In 1964 he refused to leave the ring for a full 51 minutes after a decision went against him.

But, perhaps, the worst incident of the 1988 Games came when Roy Jones, the youngest member of the American squad, clearly outpunched the Korean Park Si Hun in the light middleweight final, only to be judged to have lost the contest 3-2. When announced, the result was greeted with total disbelief as an unofficial scoring device had given Jones 86 scoring punches to Park's 32. Even the Korean apologized to Jones and asked him to join him on the victory rostrum. Jones was later awarded the Val Barker Cup – a trophy which is given by AIBA at each Games to the boxer "who shows the best style and is the most proficient boxer at the Games".

America has been one of the dominant forces in Olympic boxing since its inception – although in Barcelona in 1992 the USA had its worst tournament since the London Olympic Games of 1948, winning just one gold medal. Cassius Clay – later to become Muhammad Ali – was probably one of the most famous American Olympic winners of all time. But even Clay added to boxing folklore when he threw away the gold medal of which he had been so proud because he was later incensed by what he saw as racism back home.

Another American, Paul Gonzales, won the light flyweight title at the Los Angeles Games just four miles from where he lived. One of eight children, he joined one of the district's notorious gangs and was shot in the head at the age of 12. He was charged with murder at the age of 15 but had a good alibi – he had been boxing at the time.

The Games of 1964 in Tokyo also had its fair share of boxing "colour". Valentin Loren, a Spaniard, was so disgruntled at being disqualified for repeated fouls that he promptly punched the Hungarian referee. Needless to say he was banned for life from the amateur code. In the heavyweight final of that year a young American called Joe Frazier fought and won his final against Hans Huber of Germany with a broken hand which was all the more ironic as he had been a

★★★★★★★★★★★★★★★★★★★★★★★★★★★★★★★★ **A Sporting Legend**

Teófilo Stevenson *(Cuba)*

Born on 29 March 1952 at Las Junas, Oriente, he is the only man to have won three Olympic titles at the same weight, being heavyweight champion in 1972, '76 and '80 - the latter being the last Games before the super heavyweight division at over 91kg (13st 8lb) was added.

The powerfully-built Cuban was still only 20 when he won the first of his three gold medals at Munich but he went on to take the world amateur heavyweight titles in 1974, '78 and '86 as well. Stevenson was so far in advance of his contemporaries that it was not until the Moscow 1980 semi-final that any Olympic rival managed to survive three rounds against him. The delighted István Lévai of Hungary was the proud survivor. All of Stevenson's previous nine opponents in three Games had failed to hear the final bell.

In his 1976 Olympic semi-final Stevenson knocked out American John Tate in the first round. Three years later Tate became WBA pro heavyweight champion. Winner of an astounding 309 out of 321 bouts, and 72 international gold medals, Stevenson had many offers, amounting to $2 million, to box professionally including a title fight with champion Muhammad Ali but insisted: "I want to remain an amateur athlete."

last-minute replacement in the American team for Buster Mathis who had broken a knuckle.

Background

Boxing, the so-called "noble art of self-defence", was part of the Ancient Olympic Games. Contestants, in those days, squared up with simple leather straps tied round their hands and trained with primitive versions of today's punch bags. During Roman times metal studs were added to the leather with increasingly violent results until the sport was banned.

Boxing's modern, organized revival began in England in the 17th and 18th centuries with wealthy patrons backing their own prize-fighters. Glove fighting, rather than the bare-fisted variety, grew in popularity at the end of the 19th century, and, in 1865, the Marquess of Queensberry drew up his famous rules to standardize competition and ensure fairness and safety where possible. Professional boxing became popular in Britain and America first before gaining a toe-hold in Europe.

The Amateur Boxing Association was set up in England in 1880 and led the way for the amateur version of the sport internationally. The ABA staged internationals with America, South Africa, Australia and France in the early part of the century. World amateur boxing later came under the control of the Federation Française de Boxe which was replaced by the International Amateur Boxing Association (AIBA) in 1946.

When the Olympic Games of the modern era began in 1896, however, boxing, despite support from the Games' founding father, Baron Pierre de Coubertin, was not on the programme. The Athens organizers ruled boxing out because it was "ungentlemanly, dangerous and practised by the dregs of the population". Boxing was introduced to the Games in 1904 (when there was a demonstration of women's boxing as well as the men's event) and has been part of the programme ever since.

The USA, Cuba, the former Soviet Union and the German Democractic Republic have been dominant forces in Olympic boxing over the years. The last Olympic tournament, in Barcelona four years ago, was marked by the return of a highly professional Cuban squad who, after an absence of 12 years through boycotts, won seven of the 12 gold medals after contesting nine finals.

A Sporting Legend ★★★★★★★★★★★★★★★★★★★★★★★★★★★★★★★★★★★★

László Papp *(Hungary)*

This former railway clerk is, together with the Cuban heavyweight Teófilo Stevenson, the only triple Olympic boxing champion. His three gold medals were won in 1948, '52 and '56 in a feat of consistency which is unlikely to be equalled let alone surpassed.

At the 1948 Games in London, when he said his hardest fight ever was probably that with Britain's Johnny Wright in the Games final, Papp won the middleweight division. Four years later, when the light middleweight division was introduced at Helsinki, Papp moved down a division and defeated South Africa's Theunis van Schalkwyk for his second gold. That he needed the extra division to find physical comfort is underlined by the fact that, back in 1947, Papp had won a silver medal in the European championships as a welterweight.

Also a European winner in 1949 as a middleweight and in 1951 as a light middleweight, Papp seemed to be past his best when it was reported that in the 1953 European championships in Warsaw he was beaten in the second series of the light middleweights by Boris Tishin of the Soviet Union.

But what makes Papp's third Olympic victory, at Melbourne in 1956, so extraordinary was the background. Those Games looked to be almost completely overshadowed by an uprising in Hungary against the Soviet Union overlords with tank battles and street sniping in the capital, Budapest. Most of the Hungarian Olympic team waiting to fly to Melbourne were lodged in the cellar of a hotel.

How thrilling then it was for Papp to win his third gold medal against the American José Torres, talented enough later to become professional world light heavyweight champion. All through the three rounds of the final, Papp's team-mates from a wide range of sports, many of them already planning to seek political asylum, roared him on. Papp himself went back home, eventually gaining permission from a shell-shocked government to turn professional. He won the European pro title in 1962 and subsequently defended it six times. In 1964, however, his travel permit was cancelled and he was forced to retire, undefeated, later becoming Hungarian national coach.

The Games boxing weight categories have changed over the Olympiads including the introduction of a super-heavyweight division since 1984. Compulsory headgear was also introduced in that year and doctors were given the right to halt contests – part of a package of changes which were designed to increase safety.

Two rings have been used at the venue three times – 1936, '52 and '88 – but have been criticized for causing confusion for both boxers and referees who are often distracted by the bell sounding in the other ring. Electronic scoring machines were at ringside for the first time at the 1989 world under-19 championships in Puerto Rico. They were subsequently adopted by the Barcelona Games in 1992 but caused some "human problems".

According to *Sports Illustrated* magazine one inexperienced judge, apparently overcome by nerves at the technical challenge of using the machine, never hit the electronic button at all.

In Barcelona, too, boxers had to qualify for the Games for the first time via a series of world zonal qualifying tournaments. This will also be the practice for Atlanta.

Equipment

Boxing takes place in a "ring" which is, paradoxically, a raised square platform at least 91cm (36in.) above the ground and 6.10 metres square (65.63 sq ft). The ring floor is covered with canvas laid over a felt or rubber padding – hence the phrase "hitting the canvas". There are four corner posts. Two are white but one is red and the other blue. The coloured posts are diagonally opposite each other at the "corners" in which the boxers sit during rests between rounds. Three or four lines of ropes are secured horizontally between the posts to delineate the ring.

Boxers wear leather, padded gloves which are standardized and provided by the Organizing Committee. Each glove weighs 283gm (10 ounces) and has a white strip, introduced in 1972, to mark the main hitting area. In some of the lighter weight categories gloves used to be 226gm (8 ounces). Competitors can also bandage their hands beneath the gloves to give support and stop bones spreading. These are also provided as standard by the organizers.

For all international competitions, including the Olympic Games, each boxer wears either a blue or red vest to denote his "corner" and the shorts he wears must be at least mid-thigh length. All boxers must wear headguards, gumshields and cup protectors. And any budding Olympian must give up all thoughts of sporting a beard as the rules say that each boxer must be clean-shaven. Only a thin moustache is permitted.

Rules

Before they step into the ring all boxers must have both passed their medical examination and "made the weight" for their chosen category. There is an official weigh-in on the opening day and on every subsequent day of competition for each boxer. Boxers are weighed naked and have only one chance to be under the limit otherwise they are disqualified or must fight in a higher weight category if a space is available in the draw.

Olympic boxing bouts are controlled by a referee – he's the man in the ring with the white shirt and trousers and black bow-tie – five judges and a jury. The referee controls the actual contest. He can terminate the proceedings if, for instance, a boxer is being outclassed, is badly injured, is knocked out or decides to retire – an event which can be signalled by a boxer's two "seconds" (a coach and/or other official) throwing a towel into the ring. He can also issue cautions and warnings – for the latter two points are awarded against a boxer.

And the referee can disqualify boxers for misconduct or other rule infringements. As well as the more obvious offences such as kicking, biting, holding and using the ropes unfairly these include "passive defence" and "aggressive utterances", particularly when directed at the referee himself.

If a boxer is knocked down the referee begins a count to ten – with one second between each number concluding with the word "out" if the boxer fails to resume the contest. A referee can also insist on a mandatory count of eight even if the boxer gets up and wants to resume the contest immediately after he is knocked down. Three mandatory counts in one round mean disqualification.

The judges, meanwhile, score the contest. Points are recorded by a boxer for hits with the knuckled part of the glove on the front or sides of his opponent's head or body above the belt. At the Olympic Games there is an electronic scoring machine and a boxer only records a scoring blow if three of the five judges push their buttons within one second of the punch being landed. The jury verifies the scoring of the

judges once the bout is finished and then instructs the referee
to indicate the winner by raising his hand.

Atlanta format

364 male competitors will take part in the 1996 Olympic
Games. There is no female boxing contest at the Games. All
boxers will have qualified for the Atlanta tournament
through continental qualifying competitions. For each of the
12 weight categories there will be preliminary rounds followed by quarter-finals, semi-finals and finals in a direct
elimination draw.

Each bout will consist of three rounds of three minutes
with a one minute interval between rounds. (This will change
at the 2000 Olympic Games to five rounds of two minutes.)
All boxers must have reached a minimum age of 17. And,
would-be "George Foremans" take note, the upper age-
limit is 34.

The winning and losing finalists will receive gold and silver medals whilst the losing semi-finalists, as at every Games
since 1952, will be awarded bronze medals. This is because it
was considered unsafe, and unfair, to ask the two losing semi-
finalists to box-off against each other, particularly as they
may have suffered severe punishment in losing their previous
bout.

Venue

The 1996 Olympic boxing tournament will take place at the
Alexander Memorial Coliseum which is next door to the
Olympic Village and has a spectator capacity of 9,300. It is
normally the home of Georgia Tech's basketball teams.

MEDALLISTS (by nation)

Country	Gold	Men Silver	Bronze	Total
United States	46	21	29	96
Soviet Union	14	20	19	53
Great Britain	12	10	21	43
Poland	8	9	26	43
Italy	14	12	13	39
Cuba	19	10	5	34
Argentina	7	7	9	23
Germany	5	11	5	21
Romania	1	8	11	20
South Africa	6	4	9	19
Hungary	9	2	7	18
Canada	3	6	7	16
Korea	3	5	7	15
Finland	2	1	11	14
GDR	5	2	6	13
France	3	4	6	13
Bulgaria	3	3	7	13
Denmark	1	5	6	12
Yugoslavia	3	2	6	11
Mexico	2	3	6	11
Sweden	-	5	6	11
Ireland	1	3	5	9
Kenya	1	1	5	7
Czechoslovakia	3	1	2	6
North Korea (PRK)	2	2	2	6
Netherlands	1	1	4	6
FRG	1	-	5	6
Norway	1	2	2	5
Venezuela	1	2	2	5
Nigeria	-	3	2	5
Australia	-	2	3	5
Puerto Rico	-	1	4	5
Belgium	1	1	2	4
Uganda	-	3	1	4
Philippines	-	1	3	4
Thailand	-	1	3	4
Japan	1	-	2	3
Chile	-	1	2	3
Ghana	-	1	2	3
Algeria	-	-	3	3
Colombia	-	-	3	3
New Zealand	1	1	1	3
Cameroon	-	1	1	2
Spain	-	1	1	2
Mongolia	-	-	2	2
Morocco	-	-	2	2
Turkey	-	-	2	2
Estonia	-	1	-	1
Bermuda	-	-	1	1
Brazil	-	-	1	1
Dominican Republic	-	-	1	1
Egypt	-	-	1	1
Guyana	-	-	1	1
Niger	-	-	1	1
Pakistan	-	-	1	1
Tunisia	-	-	1	1
Uruguay	-	-	1	1
Zambia	-	-	1	1
	180	180	298	658

The official 1908 report only notes a single bronze medal awarded

ATLANTA SCHEDULE

Venue: Alexander Memorial Coliseum at Georgia Tech

Date	Description	Round	Start	End
20-24 Jul	Various rounds	Rd 1	13:30	17:00
			20:00	23:30
25 Jul	bantamweight	Rd 2	13:30	16:30
	welterweight		and	
	heavyweight		20:00	23:00
26 Jul	light flyweight	Rd 2	13:30	16:30
	lightweight		and	
	middleweight		20:00	23:00
27 Jul	featherweight	Rd 2	13:30	16:30
	light middleweight		and	
	super heavyweight		20:00	23:00
28 Jul	flyweight	Rd 2	13:30	16:30
	light welterweight		and	
	light heavyweight		20:00	23:00
30 Jul	light flyweight	q/finals	13:30	16:30
	bantamweight		and	
	lightweight		20:00	23:00
	welterweight			
	middleweight			
	heavyweight			
31 Jul	flyweight	q/finals	13:30	16:30
	featherweight		and	
	light welterweight		20:00	23:00
	light middleweight			
	light heavyweight			
	super heavyweight			
1 Aug	light flyweight	s/finals	20:00	23:00
	bantamweight			
	lightweight			
	welterweight			
	middleweight			
	heavyweight			
2 Aug	flyweight	s/finals	20:00	23:00
	featherweight			
	light welterweight			
	light middleweight			
	light heavyweight			
	super heavyweight			
3 Aug	light flyweight	FINALS	13:30	15:47
	bantamweight			
	lightweight			
	welterweight			
	middleweight			
	heavyweight			
4 Aug	flyweight	FINALS	13:30	15:47
	featherweight			
	light welterweight			
	light middleweight			
	light heavyweight			
	super heavyweight			

MEDALLISTS

BOXING

Year	Gold	C'ntry	Silver	C'ntry	Bronze	C'ntry

−48kg Light Flyweight*

Year	Gold	C'ntry	Silver	C'ntry	Bronze	C'ntry
1968	Francisco Rodriguez	VEN	Jee Young Ju	KOR	Hubert Skrzypczak	POL
					Harlan Marbley	USA
1972	György Gedó	HUN	U Gil Kim	PRK	Enrique Rodriguez	ESP
					Ralph Evans	GBR
1976	Jorge Hernández	CUB	Byong Uk Li	PRK	Payao Pooltarat	THA
					Orlando Meldonado	PUR
1980	Shamil Sabirov	URS	Hípolito Ramos	CUB	Byong Uk Li	PRK
					Ismail Mustafov	BUL
1984	Paul Gonzales	USA	Salvatore Todisco	ITA	Keith Mwila	ZAM
					José Marcelino Bolivar	VEN
1988	Ivailo Hristov	BUL	Michael Carbajal	USA	Róbert Isaszegi	HUN
					Leopoldo Serantes	PHI
1992	Rogelio Marcelo	CUB	Daniel Bojinov	BUL	Roel Velasco	PHI
					Jan Quast	GER
1996						

−51kg Flyweight

Year	Gold	C'ntry	Silver	C'ntry	Bronze	C'ntry
1904	George Finnegan	USA	Miles Burke	USA		
1920	Frank Di Genaro	USA	Anders Petersen	DEN	William Cuthbertson	GBR
1924	Fidel La Barbara	USA	James MacKenzie	GBR	Raymond Fee	USA
1928	Antal Kocsis	HUN	Armand Appell	FRA	Carlo Cavagnoli	ITA
1932	István Énekes	HUN	Francisco Cabañas	MEX	Louis Salica	USA
1936	Willi Kaiser	GER	Gavino Matta	ITA	Louis Laurie	USA
1948	Pascual Perez	ARG	Spartaco Bandinelli	ITA	Han Soo An	KOR
1952	Nate Brooks	USA	Edgar Basel	GER	Anatoli Bulakov	URS
					William Toweel	SAF
1956	Terence Spinks	GBR	Mircea Dobrescu	ROM	John Caldwell	IRL
					René Libeer	FRA
1960	Gyula Török	HUN	Sergei Sivko	URS	Kyoshi Tanabe	JPN
					Abdelmoneim Elguindi	UAR
1964	Fernando Atzori	ITA	Artur Olech	POL	Robert Carmody	USA
					Stanislav Sorokin	URS
1968	Ricardo Delgardo	MEX	Artur Olech	POL	Leo Rwabwogo	UGA
					Servilio Oliveira	BRA
1972	Giorgi Kostadinov	BUL	Leo Rwabwogo	UGA	Douglas Rodriguez	CUB
					Leszek Błażyński	POL
1976	Leo Randolph	USA	Ramon Duvalon	CUB	David Torosyan	URS
					Leszek Błażyński	POL
1980	Petr Lesov	BUL	Viktor Miroshnichenko	URS	Hugh Russell	IRL
					Janos Varadi	HUN
1984	Steven McCrory	USA	Redžep Redžepovski	YUG	Eyup Can	TUR
					Ibrahim Bilali	KEN
1988	Kim Kwang Sun	KOR	Andreas Tews	GDR	Mario González	MEX
					Timofei Skriabin	URS
1992	Chol Choi	PRK	Raul Gonzalez	CUB	István Kovács	HUN
					Timothy Austin	USA
1996						

−54kg Bantamweight

Year	Gold	C'ntry	Silver	C'ntry	Bronze	C'ntry
1904	Oliver Kirk	USA	George Finnegan	USA		
1908	Henry Thomas	GBR	John Condon	GBR	William Webb	GBR
1920	Clarence Walker	SAF	Clifford John	CAN	James McKenzie	GBR
1924	William Smith	SAF	Salvatore Tripoli	USA	Jean Ces	FRA
1928	Vittorio Tamagnini	ITA	John Daley	USA	Harry Isaacs	SAF
1932	Horace Gwynne	CAN	Hans Ziglarski	GER	José Villanueva	PHI
1936	Ulderico Sergo	ITA	Jackie Wilson	USA	Fidel Oritz	MEX
1948	Tibor Csík	HUN	Giovanni Zuddas	ITA	Juan Venegas	PUR
1952	Pentti Hämäläinen	FIN	John McNally	IRL	Kang Joon Ho	KOR
					Gennadi Garbuzov	URS

*All boxing weight divisions have varied slightly over the years.

/continued on next page

Year	Gold	C'ntry	Silver	C'ntry	Bronze	C'ntry
1956	Wolfgang Behrendt	GER	Song Soon Chun	KOR	Frederick Gilroy	IRL
					Claudio Barrientos	CHI
1960	Oleg Grigoryev	URS	Primo Zamparini	ITA	Brunon Bendig	POL
					Oliver Taylor	AUS
1964	Takao Shakurai	JPN	Chung Shin Cho	KOR	Juan Mendoza	MEX
					Washington Rodriguez	URU
1968	Valeri Sokolov	URS	Eridadi Mukwanga	UGA	Eiji Morioka	JPN
					Chang Kyou Chull	KOR
1972	Orlando Martinez	CUB	Alfonso Zamora	MEX	George Turpin	GBR
					Ricardo Carreras	USA
1976	Yong Jo Gu	PRK	Charles Mooney	USA	Patrick Cowdell	GBR
					Viktor Rybakov	URS
1980	Juan Hernandez	CUB	Bernardo José Piñango	VEN	Michael Anthony	GUY
					Dumitru Cipere	ROM
1984	Maurizio Stecca	ITA	Hector Lopez	MEX	Dale Walters	CAN
					Pedro J Nolasco	DOM
1988	Kennedy McKinney	USA	Alexander Hristov	BUL	Phajol Moolsan	THA
					Jorge Julio Rocha	COL
1992	Joel Casamayor	CUB	Wayne McCullough	IRL	Gwang Li	PRK
					Mohamed Achik	MAR
1996						

−57kg Featherweight

Year	Gold	C'ntry	Silver	C'ntry	Bronze	C'ntry
1904	Oliver Kirk	USA	Frank Haller	USA	Fred Gilmore	USA
1908	Richard Gunn	GBR	Charles Morris	GBR	Hugh Roddin	GBR
1920	Paul Fritsch	FRA	Jean Gachet	FRA	Edoardo Garzena	ITA
1924	John Fields	USA	Joseph Salas	USA	Pedro Quartucci	ARG
1928	Lambertus van Klaveren	NED	Viktor Peralta	ARG	Harold Devine	USA
1932	Carmelo Robledo	ARG	Josef Schleinkofer	GER	Carl Carlsson	SWE
1936	Oscar Casanovas	ARG	Charles Catterall	SAF	Josef Miner	GER
1948	Ernesto Formenti	ITA	Dennis Shepherd	SAF	Alexsy Antkiewicz	POL
1952	Ján Zachara	TCH	Sergio Caprari	ITA	Joseph Ventaja	FRA
					Leonard Leisching	SAF
1956	Vladimir Safronov	URS	Thomas Nicholls	GBR	Henryk Niedzwiedzki	POL
					Pentti Hämäläinen	FIN
1960	Francesco Musso	ITA	Jerzy Adamski	POL	Jorma Limmonen	FIN
					William Meyers	SAF
1964	Stanislav Stepashkin	URS	Anthony Villanueva	PHI	Charles Brown	USA
					Heinz Schulz	GER
1968	Antonio Roldan	MEX	Albert Robinson	USA	Ivan Michailov	BUL
					Philip Waruingi	KEN
1972	Boris Kusnetsov	URS	Philip Waruinge	KEN	Clemente Rojas	COL
					András Botos	HUN
1976	Angel Herrera	CUB	Richard Nowakowski	GDR	Leszek Kosedowski	POL
					Juan Parades	MEX
1980	Rudi Fink	GDR	Adolfo Horta	CUB	Viktor Rybakov	URS
					Krzysztov Kosedowski	POL
1984	Meldrick Taylor	USA	Peter Konyegwachie	NGR	Turgut Aykac	TUR
					Omar Catari Peraza	VEN
1988	Giovanni Parisi	ITA	Daniel Dumitrescu	ROM	Abdelhak Achik	MAR
					Lee Jae Hyuk	KOR
1992	Andreas Tews	GER	Faustino Reyes	ESP	Hocine Soltani	ALG
					Ramazi Paliani	EUN
1996						

−60kg Lightweight

Year	Gold	C'ntry	Silver	C'ntry	Bronze	C'ntry
1904	Harry Spanger	USA	Jack Eagan	USA	Russell Van Horn	USA
1908	Frederick Grace	GBR	Frederick Spiller	GBR	Harry Johnson	GBR
1912	not held					
1920	Samuel Mosberg	USA	Gotfred Johansen	DEN	Clarence Newton	CAN
1924	Hans Nielsen	DEN	Alfredo Copello	ARG	Frederick Boylstein	USA
1928	Carlo Orlandi	ITA	Stephen Halaiko	USA	Gunnar Berggren	SWE
1932	Lawrence Stevens	SAF	Thure Ahlqvist	SWE	Nathan Bor	USA
1936	Imre Harangi	HUN	Nikolai Stepulov	EST	Erik Ågren	SWE
1948	Gerald Dreyer	SAF	Joseph Vissers	BEL	Svend Wad	DEN

Year	Gold	C'ntry	Silver	C'ntry	Bronze	C'ntry
1952	Aureliano Bolognesi	ITA	Alexsy Antkiewicz	POL	Erkki Pakkanen	FIN
					Gheorghe Fiat	ROM
1956	Richard McTaggart	GBR	Harry Kurschat	GER	Anthony Byrne	IRL
					Anatoli Laguetko	URS
1960	Kazimierz Pazdużior	POL	Sandro Lopopolo	ITA	Richard McTaggart	GBR
					Abel Laudonio	ARG
1964	Józef Grudzień	POL	Vellikton Barannikov	URS	James McCourt	IRL
					Ronald Harris	USA
1968	Ronnie Harris	USA	Józef Grudzień	POL	Catistrat Cutov	ROM
					Vujin Zvonimir	YUG
1972	Jan Szczepański	POL	Laszlo Orbán	HUN	Alfonso Pérez	COL
					Samuel Mbugua	KEN
1976	Howard Davis	USA	Simion Cutov	ROM	Vasily Solomin	URS
					Ace Rusevski	YUG
1980	Angel Herrera	CUB	Viktor Demianenko	URS	Kazimierz Adach	POL
					Geofrey Nyeko	UGA
1984	Pernell Whitaker	USA	Luis Ortiz	PUR	Martin Ndongo Ebanga	CMR
					Chun Chil-Sung	KOR
1988	Andreas Zuelow	GDR	George Cramne	SWE	Nerguy Enkhbat	MGL
					Romallis Ellis	USA
1992	Oscar De La Boya	USA	Marco Rudolph	GER	Namjil Bayarsaikhan	MGL
					Hong Sung-Sik	KOR
1996						

-63.5kg Light welterweight

1952	Charles Adkins	USA	Viktor Mednov	URS	Erkki Mallenius	FIN
					Bruno Visintin	ITA
1956	Vladimir Enguibarian	URS	Franco Nenci	ITA	Henry Loubscher	SAF
					Constantin Dumitrescu	ROM
1960	Bohumil Němeček	TCH	Clement Quartey	GHA	Quincey Daniels	USA
					Marian Kasprzyk	POL
1964	Jerzy Kulej	POL	Eugeny Frolov	USR	Habib Galhia	TUN
					Eddie Blay	GHA
1968	Jerzy Kulej	POL	Enrique Regueiferos	CUB	Arto Nilsson	FIN
					James Wallington	USA
1972	Ray Seales	USA	Angel Angelov	BUL	Zvonimir Vujin	YUG
					Issaka Daborg	NIG
1976	Ray Leonard	USA	Andrés Aldama	CUB	Vladimir Kolev	BUL
					Kazimiar Szczerba	POL
1980	Patrizio Oliva	ITA	Serik Konakbaev	URS	Anthony Willis	GBR
					José Aguilar	CUB
1984	Jerry Page	USA	Dhawee Umponmaha	THA	Mircea Fulger	ROM
					Mirko Puzovic	YUG
1988	Viatcheslav Janovski	URS	Grahame Cheney	AUS	Reiner Gies	FRG
					Lars Myrberg	SWE
1992	Hector Vinent	CUB	Mark Leduc	CAN	Jyri Kjall	FIN
					Leonard Doroftei	ROM
1996						

-67kg Welterweight

1904	Albert Young	USA	Harry Spanger	USA	Joseph Lydon	USA
1920	Julius Albert Schneider	CAN	Alexander Ireland	GBR	Frederick Colberg	USA
1924	Jean Delarge	BEL	Héctor Méndez	ARG	Douglas Lewis	CAN
1928	Edward Morgan	NZL	Raúl Landini	ARG	Raymond Smillie	CAN
1932	Edward Flynn	USA	Erich Campe	GER	Bruno Ahlberg	FIN
1936	Sten Suvio	FIN	Michael Murach	GER	Gerhard Petersen	DEN
1948	Julius Torma	TCH	Horace Herring	USA	Alessandro D'Ottavio	ITA
1952	Zygmunt Chychła	POL	Sergei Scherbakov	URS	Viktor Jörgensen	DEN
					Günter Heidemann	GER
1956	Nicolae Linca	ROM	Fred Tiedt	IRL	Kevin Hogarth	AUS
					Nicholas Gargano	GBR
1960	Giovanni Benvenuti	ITA	Yuri Radonyak	URS	James Lloyd	GBR
					Leszek Drogosz	POL
1964	Marian Kasprzyk	POL	Richardas Tamulis	URS	Perrti Purhonen	FIN
					Silvano Bertini	ITA

/continued on next page 175

Year	Gold	C'ntry	Silver	C'ntry	Bronze	C'ntry
1968	Manfred Wolke	GDR	Joseph Bessala	CAM	Mario Guilloti	ARG
					Vladimir Musalinov	URS
1972	Emilio Correa	CUB	János Kajdi	HUN	Jesse Valdez	USA
					Dick Tiger Murunga	KEN
1976	Jochen Bachfeld	GDR	Pedro J Gamarro	VEN	Reinhard Skricek	GER
					Viktor Zilberman	ROM
1980	Andrés Aldama	CUB	John Mugabi	UGA	Karl-Heinz Krüger	GDR
					Kazimierz Szczerba	POL
1984	Mark Breland	USA	An Young Su	KOR	Joni Nyman	FIN
					Luciano Bruno	ITA
1988	Robert Wangila	KEN	Laurent Boudouani	FRA	Jan Dydak	POL
					Kenneth Gould	USA
1992	Michael Carruth	IRL	Juan Hernandez	CUB	Arkom Chenglai	THA
					Anibal Acevedo	PUR
1996						

–71kg Light middleweight

Year	Gold	C'ntry	Silver	C'ntry	Bronze	C'ntry
1952	László Papp	HUN	Theunis van Schalkwyk	SAF	Boris Tishin	URS
					Eladio Herrera	ARG
1956	László Papp	HUN	José Torres	USA	Zbgniew Pietrzykowski	POL
					John McCormack	GBR
1960	Wilbert McClure	USA	Carmelo Bossi	ITA	Boris Lagutin	URS
					William Fisher	GBR
1964	Boris Lagutin	URS	Joseph Gonzales	FRA	Józef Grzesiak	POL
					Nojim Maiyegun	NIG
1968	Boris Lagutin	URS	Rolando Garbey	CUB	Günther Meier	FRG
					John Baldwin	USA
1972	Dieter Kottysch	GER	Wiesław Rudkowski	POL	Alan Minter	GBR
					Peter Tiepold	GDR
1976	Jerzy Rybicki	POL	Tadija Kačar	YUG	Viktor Savchenko	URS
					Rolando Garbey	CUB
1980	Armando Martinez	CUB	Alexander Koshkin	URS	Ján Franek	TCH
					Detlef Kästner	GDR
1984	Frank Tate	USA	Shawn O'Sullivan	CAN	Manfred Zielonka	FRG
					Christophe Tiozzo	FRA
1988	Park Si Hun	KOR	Roy Jones	USA	Raymond Downey	CAN
					Richard Woodhall	GBR
1992	Juan Lemus	CUB	Orhan Delibas	NED	György Mizsei	HUN
					Robin Reid	GBR
1996						

–75kg Middleweight

Year	Gold	C'ntry	Silver	C'ntry	Bronze	C'ntry
1904	Charles Mayer	USA	Benjamin Spradley	USA		
1908	John Douglas	GBR	Reginald Baker	AUS	William Philo	GBR
1920	Harry Mallin	GBR	George Prud'Homme	CAN	Montgomery Herscovitch	CAN
1924	Harry Mallin	GBR	John Elliott	GBR	Joseph Beecken	BEL
1928	Piero Toscani	ITA	Jan Heřmánek	TCH	Leonard Steyaert	BEL
1932	Carmen Barth	USA	Amado Azar	ARG	Ernest Pierce	SAF
1936	Jean Despeaux	FRA	Henry Tiller	NOR	Raúl Villareal	ARG
1948	László Papp	HUN	John Wright	GBR	Ivano Fontana	ITA
1952	Floyd Patterson	USA	Vasile Tită	ROM	Stig Sjölin	SWE
					Boris Nicoloff	BUL
1956	Gennadi Chatkov	URS	Ramón Tapia	CHI	Gilbert Chapron	FRA
					Viktor Zalazar	ARG
1960	Edward Crook	USA	Tadeusz Walasek	POL	Ion Monea	ROM
					Evgeni Feofanov	URS
1964	Valer Popenchenko	URS	Emil Schulz	GER	Tadeusz Walasek	POL
					Franco Valle	ITA
1968	Christopher Finnegan	GBR	Alexei Kiselev	URS	Agustin Zaragoza	MEX
					Alfred Jones	USA
1972	Viatcheslav Lemechev	URS	Reima Virtanen	FIN	Prince Amartey	GHA
					Marvin Johnson	USA
1976	Michael Spinks	USA	Rufat Riskiev	URS	Alec Nastac	ROM
					Luis Martinez	CUB
1980	José Gomez	CUB	Viktor Savchenko	URS	Valentin Silaghi	ROM
					Jerzy Rybicki	POL

Year	Gold	C'ntry	Silver	C'ntry	Bronze	C'ntry
1984	Shin Joon Sup	KOR	Virgil Hill	USA	Mohamed Zaoui	ALG
					Aristides Gonzalez	PUR
1988	Henry Maske	GDR	Egerton Marcus	CAN	Chris Sande	KEN
					Hussain Shah Syed	PAK
1992	Ariel Hernández	CUB	Chris Byrd	USA	Chris Johnson	CAN
					Lee Seung-Bae	KOR
1996						

−81kg Light heavyweight

Year	Gold	C'ntry	Silver	C'ntry	Bronze	C'ntry
1920	Edward Eagan	USA	Sverre Sörsdal	NOR	Harold Franks	GBR
1924	Harry Mitchell	GBR	Thyge Petersen	DEN	Sverre Sörsdal	NOR
1928	Viktor Avendaño	ARG	Ernst Pistulla	GER	Karl Leendert Miljon	NED
1932	David Carstens	SAF	Gino Rossi	ITA	Peter Jörgensen	DEN
1936	Roger Michelot	FRA	Richard Vogt	GER	Francisco Risiglione	ARG
1948	George Hunter	SAF	Donald Scott	GBR	Maurio Cia	ARG
1952	Norvel Lee	USA	Antonio Pacenza	ARG	Anatoli Perov	URS
					Harry Siljander	FIN
1956	James Boyd	USA	Gheorghe Negrea	ROM	Romoualdas Mouraouskas	URS
					Carlos Lucas	CHI
1960	Cassius Clay	USA	Zbigniew Pietrzykowski	POL	Anthony Madigan	AUS
					Giulio Sabaudi	ITA
1964	Cosimo Pinto	ITA	Alexei Kiseliov	URS	Zbigniew Pietrzykowski	POL
					Alexander Nicolov	BUL
1968	Dan Pozdniak	URS	Ion Monea	ROM	Gueorgui Stankov	BUL
					Stanislaw Dragan	POL
1972	Mate Parlov	YUG	Gilberto Carrillo	CUB	Isaac Ikhouria	NGR
1976	Leon Spinks	USA	Sixto Soria	CUB	Costica Dafinoiu	ROM
					Janausz Gortat	POL
1980	Slobodan Kačar	YUG	Paweł Skrzecz	POL	Herbert Bauch	GDR
					Ricardo Rojas	CUB
1984	Anton Josipović	YUG	Kevin Barry	NZL	Mustapha Moussa	ALG
					Evander Holyfield	USA
1988	Andrew Maynard	USA	Nourmgomed Chanavazov	URS	Henryk Petrich	POL
					Damir Škaro	YUG
1992	Torsten May	GER	Rostislav Zaoulitchnyi	EUN	Zoltan Beres	HUN
					Wojciech Bartnik	POL
1996						

−91kg Heavyweight*

Year	Gold	C'ntry	Silver	C'ntry	Bronze	C'ntry
1904	Samuel Berger	USA	Charles Mayer	USA	William Michaels	USA
1908	Albert Oldman	GBR	Sydney Charles Evans	GBR	Frederick Parks	GBR
1920	Ronald Rawson	GBR	Sören Petersen	DEN	Xavier Eluere	FRA
1924	Otto von Porat	NOR	Sören Petersen	DEN	Alfredo Porzio	ARG
1928	Arturo Rodriguez Jurado	ARG	Nils Ramm	SWE	Jacob Michaelsen	DEN
1932	Santiago Lovell	ARG	Luigi Rovati	ITA	Frederick Feary	USA
1936	Herbert Runge	GER	Guillermo Lovell	ARG	Erling Nilsen	NOR
1948	Rafael Iglesias	ARG	Gunnar Nilsson	SWE	John Arthur	SAF
1952	Edward Sanders	USA	Ingemar Johansson	SWE	Andries Nieman	SAF
					Ilkka Koski	FIN
1956	Peter Rademacher	USA	Lev Moukhine	URS	Daniel Bekker	SAF
					Giacomo Bozzano	ITA
1960	Franco De Piccoli	ITA	Daniel Bekker	SAF	Josef Němec	TCH
					Günter Siegmund	GER
1964	Joseph Frazier	USA	Hans Huber	GER	Vadim Yemelyanov	URS
					Giuseppe Ros	ITA
1968	George Foreman	USA	Jonas Chepulis	URS	Joaquin Rocha	MEX
					Giorgio Bambini	BUL
1972	Teófilo Stevenson	CUB	Ion Alexe	ROM	Hasse Thomsén	SWE
					Peter Hussing	GDR
1976	Teófilo Stevenson	CUB	Mircea Simon	ROM	Johnny Tate	USA
					Clarence Hill	BER
1980	Teófilo Stevenson	CUB	Piotr Zaev	URS	István Lévai	HUN
					Jürgen Fanghänel	GDR

/continued on next page 177

Year	Gold	C'ntry	Silver	C'ntry	Bronze	C'ntry
1984	Henry Tilman	USA	Willie Dewit	CAN	Angelo Musone	ITA
					Arnold Vanderlijde	NED
1988	Ray Mercer	USA	Baik Hyun Man	KOR	Andrzej Golota	POL
					Arnold Vanderlijde	NED
1992	Felix Savon	CUB	David Izonritei	NGR	David Tua	NZL
					Van Der Lijde	NED
1996						

*There has been a variety of weight limits over the years

+91kg Superheavyweight

Year	Gold	C'ntry	Silver	C'ntry	Bronze	C'ntry
1984	Tyrell Biggs	USA	Francesco Damiani	ITA	Robert Wells	GBR
					Salihu Azis	YUG
1988	Lennox Lewis	CAN	Riddick Bowe	USA	Alexander Mirochnichenko	URS
					Janusz Zarenkiewicz	POL
1992	Roberto Balado	CUB	Richard Igbineghu	NGR	Brian Nielsen	DEN
					Svilen Roussinov	BUL
1996						

Canoeing

Stars to Watch

by Ivan Lawler (flatwater) *and Myriam Jerusalemi* (slalom)

Hungarian honours and a spectacular whitewater course

Honours at the 1996 Olympic flatwater competition will be more hotly contended than ever before because, with the newly enforced qualification system, only the best of the best will be in attendance.

Both history and recent form show that the strongest nations are Hungary and Germany, between them taking 15 of the 36 medals (a medal in every event and gold in all but one) at the 1995 world championships. Only the exceptional talent of Nikolai Boukhalov (Bulgaria) and Ivans Klementjevs (Latvia), who between them hold three Olympic and ten world titles spanning ten years, can challenge this supremacy.

In the men's kayaks, however, there is no overwhelming power, the six golds last year were spread among five nations, only Italy picking up two. The 1000m singles will see continued rivalry between Knut Holmann (Norway) and Clint Robinson (Australia). Over the last five years they have alternated in taking the available gold medals but Robinson starts as Olympic champion. Mikko Kolehmainen of Finland holds the title for the 500m but will have to race well to hold off Poland's Piotr Markiewizc, current world champion. Even then, in races with the majority of the field finishing within one second, nothing is predictable.

Barcelona 1992

The doubles events are also wide open; crews to watch for are the Germans, current Olympic champions in both distances, the Italians, current world champions over both distances, and the Danes, unbeaten last year until illness took them out of the world championships. The fours, historically, have been a two-horse race between Hungary and Germany but neither the Russians nor Poles can be discounted.

A Contemporary Heroine ★★★★★★★★★★★★★★★★★★★★★★★★★★★★★★★

Rita Kőbán (Hungary)

Born in Budapest in 1965, Rita began canoeing at the age of 12. Having won age-group titles in her first year of the sport, she progressed rapidly to the national junior team where, in 1980, she won two bronze medals at the world junior championships. Success at senior level first came at the 1985 world championships in Belgium where she won silver and bronze medals in the pairs and fours respectively.

From this point she has never looked back. Gold in the four in Barcelona, silver in the pairs. And this was only a beginning. Since that time she has taken women's canoeing by storm. In Mexico, in 1994, she was nominated athlete of the world championships winning three gold and two silver medals. At the Duisburg world championships of 1995 her 500m victory was the most decisive and emphatic declaration of supremacy of the whole event.

With two Olympic and 22 world championship medals to her credit Rita Kőbán must now be planning to take Atlanta by storm.

Meanwhile, the women's events will again be a showdown between Hungary and Germany. The Germans are dominant in crew events, but Rita Kőbán (Hungary), current world champion, will be hard to beat in the singles, even for Birgit Schmidt, the most prolific medal-winning canoeist in history with over twenty world titles. Other big names to watch for in the singles are Caroline Brunet (Canada) and Susanne Gunnarsson (Sweden). And, finally, it would be foolish to underestimate the Chinese women's four.

In the slalom canoeing events competition will be in a spectacular setting. The course, on the Ocoee River, in Tennessee, is natural, fast and powerful with some of the more difficult features coming towards the end of the course. Lukáš Pollert, the Olympic champion from Prague and Gareth Marriott of Great Britain, the 1992 Olympic silver medallist, should clock fast times in the Canadian singles. But another fast and skilful paddler to watch out for is Frenchman, Emmanuel Brugvin. The home country favourites, though, will be the veteran American duo of David Hearn, from Maryland, the current world champion, and Jon Lugbill, five times world champion who is never more at home than on the waters of the Ocoee.

Lynn Simpson, of Britain, as the reigning world champion must start as favourite in the women's kayak event. She was also world cup champion in 1994 and '95 and pre-Olympic cham-

Gareth Marriott

pion a year ago. Her strongest challenge will come from the French, led by 1995 world silver medallist Anne Boixel and the Czechs, Stepanka Hilgertova and Irena Pavelkova. Germany, meanwhile, won the 1992 title with Lisa Micheler. This time round, with Kordula Striepecke, the 1995 world bronze medallist, they have further medal aspirations.

A year ago, in Nottingham, England, the men's Canadian doubles was the most fiercely-contested event of the world championships. The young Polish duo of Kryzstof Kolomanski and Michel Staniszewski put in a brilliant performance to take the title whereas this event has traditionally been a tussle between the French, Czech, German and American crews. The USA won the 1992 title with Joe Jacobi and Scott Strasbaugh but they have since retired, leaving the other Barcelona medallists, Miroslav Šimek and Jiři Rohan of the Czech Republic, and Franck Adisson and Wilfrid Forgues, of France, still very much in contention.

The final race on the Atlanta programme will be the men's kayak singles. In this fastest of all slalom events the favourites – depending on selection – must include the 1995 world champion Oliver Fix who leads a strong German team. He will be chased by America's world silver medallist Scott Shipley. But Slovenia's Fedja Marusic is a dark horse whilst Italy's Pierpaolo Ferrazzi will be hoping to challenge for a second Olympic gold medal.

I. L./M. J. □

Retrospective

Slalom canoeing makes only its third appearance at the Olympic Games in 1996 following its prior inclusion at

★★★★★★★★★★★★★★★★★★★★★★★★★★★★★★ A Sporting Legend

Gert Fredriksson *(Sweden)*

When it comes to choosing the world's greatest ever canoe racer, there are several strong contenders. But it is the longevity as well as the quality of Gert Fredriksson's competitive career that set him apart.

His prolific medal-winning reign began in 1948 at the London Olympic Games. Here he won both individual titles, contested over 1,000m and 10,000m. Olympic success was repeated in Helsinki, Melbourne and Rome where he also took two medals and brought his tally to an incredible six gold, one silver and one bronze, a feat made all the more remarkable as by the Rome Games he was in his early 40s.

During this reign of Olympic dominance he was no less successful in the world championships, amassing seven gold, two silver and two bronze medals over the four championship events contested between 1948 and '58.

the Games of 1972 and '92. For the Munich Games of 1972, a special and costly artificial course was built in Lech. The events were dominated by Germans, both East and West.

1948 1,000m Kayak singles won by Gert Fredriksson

East Germans also made a dramatic mark on the 1976 Games in flatwater canoeing because they designed a new type of kayak which was allegedly much faster than previous versions. Eventually they won three of the seven kayak medals on offer.

Flatwater racing has a longer Olympic pedigree, beginning in 1936. Women first raced at the Games in 1948 in a kayak singles 500m event. And Britain's 31 year old Liz Sharman, world slalom champion, swapped disciplines to compete in the 1988 Olympic Games flatwater events just so that she could become an Olympian before it was too late.

Those Games also provided one of the most dramatic finishes to a race when Grant Davies of Australia and America's Gregory Barton seemed to finish completely together in the kayak singles 1,000m event. Davies was awarded victory and celebrated for a few minutes until the photo-finish camera and the judges decided to reverse the decision giving the gold to Barton.

Four years ago, in Barcelona, the German team took six of the 12 flatwater gold medals on offer at the Games with just 14 athletes. The former East Germany and Soviet Union have dominated this sport in recent Games along with Hungary.

Background

Many primitive civilizations used hollowed-out logs as "canoes" of a fashion. But the version which developed into that which is used in the modern Canadian disciplines originated with the North American Indians who used it for hunting and fishing. Conversely, the kayak style of canoe can be traced back to the eskimos. 1984 kayak pairs 1,000m winner Alwyn Morris came from an Indian Reserve in Canada and wore an eagle's feather to his victory ceremony to symbolize the sharing of his triumph with all native Americans.

Canoeing as a competitive sport emerged first in Britain in 1866 with the Royal Canoe Club whose members used clinker-built canoes to race on the Thames river in London. By 1870 the American Canoe Association had also been formed. In 1907 a German called Klepper designed a lightweight, folding canoe which popularized the sport in Europe. Later, in Eastern Europe, a kayak with a rigid frame was designed and became the blueprint for future competitive craft. The first world championships took place in 1930, leading to Olympic integration six years later.

Equipment

There are two types of craft used at the Games: Canadian canoes and Kayaks. The former is open-decked (for flatwater racing) but closed for slalom and is paddled by competitors in a kneeling position with a single-bladed paddle. Kayaks have closed decks, a pointed bow and stern and are propelled by competitors in a sitting position with a long, double-bladed paddle. Kayaks also have a rudder for flatwater races. Today's canoes, for both disciplines, are made of lightweight composite materials and all slalom competitors wear protective headgear as well as a rubber "skirt" or spray deck to keep the water out of the craft.

The flatwater, or sprint canoe courses, are marked out in lanes of 9m (29ft 6in.) wide by buoys or floats and the water must be still but at least 2m (6ft 6in.) deep. Automatic start, and photo-finish, equipment are both used at the Games.

Slalom canoeists need good timing and control to keep the boat on the fastest line through the 25 gates (at least six of which must be upstream) of the 300 – 500m (328 – 547yds) course of turbulent water. They are timed by photo-electric timing. Each gate consists of two suspended thin poles (painted in green and white stripes for downstream, and red and white stripes for upstream) set up to 3.5m (11ft 6in.) apart and finishing 15cm (6in.) above the surface of the water.

Rules

The object of flatwater racing is to be the first across the finish line in head-to-head racing with other boats. There are umpires at the start, finish and on the course to make sure that the races are fair in all aspects. A seven-person jury handles any disputes but the photo-finish camera is the final arbiter in any close finish.

In slalom a competitor must negotiate each of the 25 gates on the course. This means crossing the line between the two poles with the body and head and all, or part, of the boat. If a competitor touches the gate five penalty points are incurred. 50 penalty points are given if a competitor fails to go through a gate. The winner is the paddler, or pairing, with the best combination of fastest time and the lowest or no penalty points.

Atlanta Format

Each of the flatwater, or sprint, racing events at the 1996 Olympic Games consists of a series of heats, repechage (or second chance) and semi-final races from which the top nine boats contest the final. In all but the heats (in which lanes are drawn) the fastest boats are placed in the middle lanes. In slalom, each competitor, or pairing, is given two runs down the course with the better of the two counting towards the final result.

A total of 485 competitors (343 men and 142 women) will take part – 135 in slalom and 350 in flatwater. There are events in both kayak and Canadian canoes for the men in both slalom and flatwater disciplines. There are no Canadian canoeing events for women.

Venue

Flatwater racing at the 1996 Olympic Games takes place at Lake Lanier which is 88km (55 miles) from the Olympic Village and north-east of Atlanta near Gainesville in Hall County. It is a popular weekend destination for Atlantans and during the Games will have a spectator capacity of 20,000. The lake's lane markers will retract into the lake outside of future competition times to allow recreational use of the lake.

Slalom competition, meanwhile, will take place at the Ocoee Whitewater Center which is located in the Cherokee National Forest in Tennessee. Athletes and officials will be housed in their own Olympic Village in nearby Cleveland. The competition site is 209km (130 miles) north of Atlanta.

CANOEING – current Olympic records

Event	Name	Country	Time/Result	Games	Year
Men					
Kayak 1 – 500m	Mikko Kolehmainen	FIN	1:40.34	Barcelona	1992
Kayak 1 – 1,000m	Gregory Barton	USA	3:32.34	Barcelona	1992
Kayak 2 – 500m	Kay Bluhm	GER	1:28.11	Barcelona	1992
	Torsten Gutsche				
Kayak 2 – 1,000m	Gunnar Olsson	SWE	3:12.19	Barcelona	1992
	Karl Sundqvist				
Kayak 4 – 1,000m	Attila Ábrahám	HUN	2:54.08	Barcelona	1992
	Ferenc Csipes				
	Lásló Fidel				
	Zsolt Gyulay				
Canadian 1 – 500m	Nikolai Boukhalov	EUN	1:15.15	Barcelona	1992
Canadian 1 – 1,000m	Jan Bartunek	TCH	4:02.48	Barcelona	1992
Canadian 2 – 500m	Ulrich Papke	GER	1:40.53	Barcelona	1992
	Ingo Spelly				
Canadian 2 – 1,000m	Ulrich Papke	GER	3:32.08	Barcelona	1992
	Ingo Spelly				
Women					
Kayak 1 – 500m	Rita Kőbán	HUN	1:50.97	Barcelona	1992
Kayak 2 – 500m	Ramona Portwich	GER	1:40.29	Barcelona	1992
	Anke von Seck				
Kayak 4 – 500m	Kinga Czigány	HUN	1:32.94	Barcelona	1992
	Eva Dónusz				
	Rita Kőbán				
	Erika Meszáros				

CANOEING

MEDALLISTS (by nation)

	Men's			Women's			
	Gold	Silver	Bronze	Gold	Silver	Bronze	Total
Soviet Union	22	12	6	8	2	3	53
Hungary	7	18	13	1	4	5	48
Germany	9	8	9	4	5	1	36
GDR	8	5	8	6	2	1	30
Romania	8	8	8	1	1	3	29
Sweden	11	8	2	2	2	1	26
France	1	6	13	-	-	-	20
United States	5	2	4	-	1	2	14
Bulgaria	3	1	6	1	2	1	14
Austria	3	4	4	-	1	1	13
Canada	3	5	3	-	1	1	13
Czechoslovakia	7	4	1	-	-	-	12
Denmark	2	4	4	1	-	1	12
Finland	4	2	3	1	-	-	10
Poland	-	3	4	-	-	3	10
Australia	1	2	4	-	1	-	8
Netherlands	-	1	3	-	2	2	8
New Zealand	5	1	1	-	-	-	7
FRG	1	1	1	1	2	1	7
Norway	1	2	3	-	-	-	6
Yugoslavia	2	2	1	-	-	-	5
Spain	-	2	2	-	-	-	4
Italy	1	1	1	-	-	-	3
Great Britain	-	1	-	-	-	-	1
Latvia	-	1	-	-	-	-	1
	104	104	104	26	26	26	390

ATLANTA SCHEDULE

SLALOM

Venue: Ocoee Whitewater Center, Ocoee River, Cherokee National Forest, Tennessee

Date	Description	Round	Start	End
27 Jul	kayak single (w)	run 1	10:00	17:05
	canoe single (m)			
	kayak single (w)	FINAL		
	canoe single (m)			
28 Jul	canoe double (m)	run 1	10:00	17:05
	kayak single (m)			
	canoe double (m)	FINAL		
	kayak single (m)			

SPRINT

Venue: Lake Lanier, Gainesville/Hall County, Georgia

Date	Description	Round	Start	End
30 Jul	kayak double 1,000m (m)	prelims	9:00	12:30
	canoe single 1,000m (m)			
	kayak fours 500m (w)			
	kayak single 1,000m (m)			
	canoe double 1,000m (m)			
	kayak fours 1,000m (m)			
	kayak double 1,000m (m)	repechage	14:30	16:50
	canoe single 1,000m (m)			
	kayak fours 500m (w)			
	kayak single 1,000m (m)			
	canoe double 1,000m (m)			
	kayak fours 1,000m (m)			
31 Jul	kayak double 500m (m)	prelims	9:00	12:20
	canoe single 500m (m)			
	kayak single 500m (w)			
	kayak single 500m (m)			
	canoe double 500m (m)			
	kayak double 500m (w)			
	kayak double 500m (m)	repechage	14:30	16:50
	canoe single 500m (m)			
	kayak single 500m (w)			
	kayak single 500m (m)			
	canoe double 500m (m)			
	kayak double 500m (w)			
1 Aug	kayak double 1,000m (m)	s/finals	9:00	11:10
	canoe single 1,000m (m)			
	kayak fours 500m (w)			
	kayak single 1,000m (m)			
	canoe double 1,000m (m)			
	kayak fours 1,000m (m)			
2 Aug	kayak double 500m (m)	s/finals	9:00	11:10
	canoe single 500m (m)			
	kayak single 500m (w)			
	kayak single 500m (m)			
	canoe double 500m (m)			
	kayak double 500m (w)			
3 Aug	kayak double 1,000m (m)	FINALS	9:00	11:20
	canoe single 1,000m (m)			
	kayak fours 500m (w)			
	kayak single 1,000m (m)			
	canoe double 1,000m (m)			
	kayak fours 1,000m (m)			
4 Aug	kayak double 500m (m)	FINALS	9:00	10:50
	canoe single 500m (m)			
	kayak single 500m (w)			
	kayak single 500m (m)			
	canoe double 500m (m)			
	kayak double 500m (w)			

MEDALLISTS

CANOEING (Men)

Year	Gold	C'ntry	Time	Silver	C'ntry	Time	Bronze	C'ntry	Time

FLATWATER

Kayak Single 500m

Year	Gold	C'ntry	Time	Silver	C'ntry	Time	Bronze	C'ntry	Time
1976	Vasile Diba	ROM	1:46.41	Zoltán Sztanity	HUN	1:46.95	Rüdiger Helm	GDR	1:48.30
1980	Vladimir Parfenovich	URS	1:43.43	John Sumegi	AUS	1:44.12	Vasile Dîba	ROM	1:44.90
1984	Ian Ferguson	NZL	1:47.84	Lars-Erik Moberg	SWE	1:48.18	Bernard Bregeon	FRA	1:48.41
1988	Zsolt Gyulay	HUN	1:44.82	Andreas Stähle	GDR	1:46.38	Paul MacDonald	NZL	1:46.46
1992	Mikko Kolehmainen	FIN	1:40.34	Zsolt Gyulay	HUN	1:40.64	Knut Holmann	NOR	1:40.71
1996									

Kayak Double 500m

Year	Gold	C'ntry	Time	Silver	C'ntry	Time	Bronze	C'ntry	Time
1976	Joachim Mattern Bernd Olbricht	GDR	1:35.87	Sergei Nagorny Vladimir Romanovski	URS	1:36.81	Policarp Malihin Larion Serghei	ROM	1:37.43
1980	Sergei Chukhrai Vladimir Parfenovich	URS	1:32.38	Herminio Menendez Guillermo del Riego	ESP	1:33.65	Rüdiger Helm Bernd Olbricht	GDR	1:34.00
1984	Ian Ferguson Paul MacDonald	NZL	1:34.21	Per-Inge Bengtsson Lars-Erik Moberg	SWE	1:35.26	Hugh Fisher Alwyn Morris	CAN	1:35.41
1988	Ian Ferguson Paul MacDonald	NZL	1:33.98	Viktor Denissov Igor Nagaev	URS	1:34.15	Attila Ábrahám Ferenc Csipes	HUN	1:34.32
1992	Kay Bluhm Torsten Gutsche	GER	1:28.27	Maciej Freimut Wojciech Kurpiewski	POL	1:29.84	Bruno Dreossi Antonio Rossi	ITA	1:30.00
1996									

Canadian Single 500m

Year	Gold	C'ntry	Time	Silver	C'ntry	Time	Bronze	C'ntry	Time
1976	Alexander Rogov	URS	1:59.23	John Wood	CAN	1:59.58	Matija Ljubek	YUG	1:59.60
1980	Sergei Postrekhin	URS	1:53.37	Liubomir Liubenov	BUL	1:53.49	Olaf Heukrodt	GDR	1:54.38
1984	Larry Cain	CAN	1:57.01	Henning Jakobsen	DEN	1:58.45	Costica Olaru	ROM	1:59.86
1988	Olaf Heukrodt	GDR	1:56.42	Mikhail Slivinski	URS	1:57.26	Martin Marinov	BUL	1:57.27
1992	Nikolai Boukhalov	BUL	1:51.15	Mikhail Slivinski	EUN	1:51.40	Olaf Heukrodt	GER	1:53.00
1996									

Canadian Double 500m

Year	Gold	C'ntry	Time	Silver	C'ntry	Time	Bronze	C'ntry	Time
1976	Sergei Petrenko Alexander Vinogradov	URS	1:45.81	Andrzej Gronowicz Jerzy Opara	POL	1:47.77	Tamás Buday Oszkár Frey	HUN	1:48.35
1980	László Foltán István Vaskuti	HUN	1:43.39	Petre Capusta Ivan Patzaichin	ROM	1:44.12	Borislav Ananiev Nikolai Ilkov	BUL	1:44.83
1984	Matija Ljubek Mirko Nišović	YUG	1:43.67	Ivan Patzaichin Toma Simionov	ROM	1:45.68	Enrique Miguez Narcisco Suárez	ESP	1:47.71
1988	Viktor Reneiski Nikolai Zouravski	URS	1:41.77	Marek Dopierała Marek Lubik	POL	1:43.61	Joël Bettin Philippe Renaud	FRA	1:43.81
1992	Dmitri Dovgalenok Alexander Masseikov	EUN	1:41.54	Ulrich Papke Ingo Spelly	GER	1:41.68	Martin Marinov Blagovest Stoyanov	BUL	1:41.94
1996									

Kayak Single 1000m

Year	Gold	C'ntry	Time	Silver	C'ntry	Time	Bronze	C'ntry	Time
1936	Gregor Hradetzky	AUT	4:22.9	Helmut Cämmerer	GER	4:25.6	Jacob Kraaier	NED	4:35.1
1948	Gert Fredriksson	SWE	4:33.2	John Andersen	DEN	4:39.9	Henri Eberhardt	FRA	4:41.4
1952	Gert Fredriksson	SWE	4:07.9	Thorvald Strömberg	FIN	4:09.7	Louis Gantois	FRA	4:20.1
1956	Gert Fredriksson	SWE	4:12.8	Igor Pissarev	URS	4:15.3	Lajos Kiss	HUN	4:16.2
1960	Erik Hansen	DEN	3:53.00	Imre Szöllösi	HUN	3:54.02	Gert Fredriksson	SWE	3:55.89
1964	Rolf Peterson	SWE	3:57.13	Mihály Hesz	HUN	3:57.28	Aurel Vernescu	ROM	4:00.77
1968	Mihály Hesz	HUN	4:02.63	Alexander Shaparenko	URS	4:03.58	Erik Hansen	DEN	4:04.39
1972	Alexander Shaparenko	URS	3:48.06	Rolf Peterson	SWE	3:48.35	Géza Csapó	HUN	3:49.38
1976	Rüdiger Helm	GDR	3:48.20	Geza Csapó	HUN	3:48.84	Vasile Diba	ROM	3:49.65
1980	Rüdiger Helm	GDR	3:48.77	Alain Lebas	FRA	3:50.20	Ion Birladeanu	ROM	3:50.49
1984	Alan Thompson	NZL	3:45.73	Milan Janić	YUG	3:46.88	Greg Barton	USA	3:47.38
1988	Gregory Barton	USA	3:55.27	Grant Davies	AUS	3:55.28	André Wohllebe	GDR	3:55.55
1992	Clint Robinson	AUS	3:37.26	Knut Holmann	NOR	3:37.50	Greg Barton	USA	3:37.93
1996									

Kayak Double 1000m

Year	Gold	C'ntry	Time	Silver	C'ntry	Time	Bronze	C'ntry	Time
1936	Alfons Dorfner Adolf Kainz	AUT	4:03.8	Fritz Bondroit Ewald Tilker	GER	4:08.9	Nicolaas Tates Willem Frederik van der Kroft	NED	4:12.2
1948	Hans Berglund Lennart Klingström	SWE	4:07.3	Ejvind Hansen Bernhard Jensen	DEN	4:07.5	Thor Axelsson Nils Björklöf	FIN	4:08.7
1952	Yrjö Hietanen Kurt Wires	FIN	3:51.1	Lars Glassér Ingemar Hedberg	SWE	3:51.1	Maximilian Raub Herbert Wiedermann	AUT	3:51.4
1956	Meinrad Miltenberger Michael Scheuer	GER	3:49.6	Anatoli Demitkov Mikhail Kaaleste	URS	3:51.4	Maximilian Raub Herbert Wiedermann	AUT	3:55.8
1960	Gert Fredriksson Sven-Olov Sjödelius	SWE	3:34.73	György Mészáros András Szente	HUN	3:34.91	Stefan Kapłaniak Władysław Zieliński	POL	3:37.44
1964	Sven-Olov Sjödelius Nils Gunnar Utterberg	SWE	3:38.54	Antonius Geurts Paul Hoekstra	NED	3:39.30	Heinz Büker Holger Zander	GER	3:40.69
1968	Vladimir Morozov Alexander Shaparenko	URS	3:37.54	Csaba Giczi István Timár	HUN	3:38.44	Günther Pfaff Gerhard Seibold	AUT	3:40.71
1972	Nikolai Gorbachev Viktor Kratassyuk	URS	3:31.23	József Deme János Rátkai	HUN	3:32.00	Rafał Piszcz Władysław Szuszkiewicz	POL	3:33.83
1976	Sergei Nagorny Vladimir Romanovski	URS	3:29.01	Joachim Mattern Bernd Olbricht	GDR	3:29.33	Zoltan Bakó István Szabó	HUN	3:30.36
1980	Sergei Chukhrai Vladimir Parfenovich	URS	3:26.72	István Joós István Szabó	HUN	3:28.49	Herminio Menendez Luis Ramos-Misione	ESP	3:28.66
1984	Hugh Fisher Alwyn Morris	CAN	3:24.22	Bernard Bregeon Patrick Lefoulon	FRA	3:25.97	Barry Kelly Grant Kenny	AUS	3:26.80
1988	Gregory Barton Norman Bellingham	USA	3:32.42	Ian Ferguson Paul MacDonald	NZL	3:32.71	Peter Foster Kelvin Graham	AUS	3:33.76
1992	Kay Bluhm Torsten Gutsche	GER	3:16.10	Gunnar Olsson Karl Sundqvist	SWE	3:17.70	Dariusz Białkowski Grzegorz Kotowicz	POL	3:18.86
1996									

Kayak Fours 1000m

Year	Gold	C'ntry	Time	Silver	C'ntry	Time	Bronze	C'ntry	Time
1964	Nikolai Chuzhikov Anatoli Grischin Viacheslav Ionov Vladimir Morozov	URS	3:14.67	Günther Perleberg Bernhard Schulze Friedhelm Wentzke Holger Zander	GER	3:15.39	Simion Cuciuc Atanase Sciotnic Mihai Turcaş Aurel Vernescu	ROM	3:15.51
1968	Steinar Admundsen Tore Berger Jan Johansen Egil Søby	NOR	3:14.38	Anton Calenic Dimitrie Ivanov Haralambie Ivanov Mihai Turcaş	ROM	3:14.81	István Csizmadia Csaba Giczi Imre Szöllösi István Timár	HUN	3:15.10
1972	Valeri Didenko Yuri Filatov Vladimir Morozov Yuri Stezenko	URS	3:14.02	Atanase Sciotnic Roman Vartolomeu Aurel Vernescu Mihai Zafiu	ROM	3:15.07	Steinar Amundsen Tore Berger Jan Johansen Egil Søby	NOR	3:15.27
1976	Sergei Chuhrai Alexander Degtiarev Yuri Filatov Vladimir Morozov	URS	3:08.69	José Celorrio José Diaz-Flor Herminio Menendez Luis Ramos Misione	ESP	3:08.95	Peter Bischof Bernd Duvigneau Rüdiger Helm Jürgen Lehnert	GDR	3:10.76
1980	Bernd Duvigneau Rüdiger Helm Harald Marg Bernd Olbricht	GDR	3:13.76	Vasile Dîba Nicuşor Eşeanu Ion Geantă Mihai Zafiu	ROM	3:15.35	Borislav Borisov Lazar Kristov Ivan Manev Bozhidar Milenkov	BUL	3:15.46
1984	Grant Bramwell Ian Ferguson Paul MacDonald Alan Thompson	NZL	3:02.28	Per-Inge Bengtsson Tommy Karls Lars-Erik Moberg Thomas Ohlsson	SWE	3:02.81	François Barouh Philippe Boccara Pascal Boucherit Didier Vavasseur	FRA	3:03.94
1988	Attila Ábrahám Ferenc Csipes Zsolt Gyulay Sándor Hódosi	HUN	3:00.20	Viktor Denissov Sergei Kirsanov Alexander Motouzenko Igor Nagaev	URS	3:01.40	Hans-Jörg Bliesener Kay Bluhm Andreas Stähle André Wohllebe	GDR	3:02.37
1992	Oliver Kegel Thomas Reineck Mario Von Appen Andre Wohllebe	GER	2:54.18	Attila Ábrahám Ferenc Csipes László Fidel Zsolt Gyulay	HUN	2:54.82	Ramon Andersson Kelvin Graham Ian Rowling Steven Wood	AUS	2:56.97
1996									

Year	Gold	C'ntry	Time	Silver	C'ntry	Time	Bronze	C'ntry	Time

Canadian Single 1000m

Year	Gold	C'ntry	Time	Silver	C'ntry	Time	Bronze	C'ntry	Time
1936	Francis Amyot	CAN	5:32.1	Bohuslav Karlík	TCH	5:36.9	Erich Koschik	GER	5:39.0
1948	Josef Holeček	TCH	5:42.0	Douglas Bennett	CAN	5:53.3	Robert Boutigny	FRA	5:55.9
1952	Josef Holeček	TCH	4:56.3	János Parti	HUN	5:03.6	Olavi Ojanperä	FIN	5:08.5
1956	Leon Rottman	ROM	5:05.3	István Hernek	HUN	5:06.2	Guennadii Boukharine	URS	5:12.7
1960	János Parti	HUN	4:33.03	Alexander Silayev	URS	4:34.41	Leon Rottman	ROM	4:35.87
1964	Jürgen Eschert	GER	4:35.14	Andrei Igorov	ROM	4:37.89	Eugeni Peniaev	URS	4:38.31
1968	Tibor Tatai	HUN	4:36.14	Detlef Lewe	FRG	4:38.31	Vitali Galkov	URS	4:40.42
1972	Ivan Patzaichin	ROM	4:08.94	Tamás Wichmann	HUN	4:12.42	Detlef Lewe	GER	4:13.63
1976	Matija Ljubek	YUG	4:09.51	Vasili Urchenko	URS	4:12.57	Tamás Wichmann	HUN	4:14.11
1980	Liubomir Liubenov	BUL	4:12.38	Sergei Postrekhin	URS	4:13.53	Eckhard Leue	GDR	4:15.02
1984	Ulrich Eicke	FRG	4:06.32	Larry Cain	CAN	4:08.67	Henning Jakobsen	DEN	4:09.51
1988	Ivans Klementjevs	URS	4:12.78	Jörg Schmidt	GDR	4:15.83	Nikolai Bukhalov	BUL	4:18.94
1992	Nikolai Boukhalov	BUL	4:05.92	Ivans Klementjevs	LAT	4:06.60	György Zala	HUN	4:07.35
1996									

Canadian Double 1000m

Year	Gold	C'ntry	Time	Silver	C'ntry	Time	Bronze	C'ntry	Time
1936	Jan Brzák-Felix Vladimír Syrovátka	TCH	4:50.1	Alois Edletitsch Josef Kampfl	AUT	4:53.8	Harvey Charters Frank Saker	CAN	4:56.7
1948	Jan Brzák-Felix Bohumil Kudrna	TCH	5:07.1	Steven Lysak Stephen Macknowski	USA	5:08.2	Georges Dransart Georges Gandil	FRA	5:15.2
1952	Finn Haunstoft Bent Peder Rasch	DEN	4:38.3	Jan Brzák-Felix Bohumil Kudrna	TCH	4:42.9	Egon Drews Wilfried Soltau	GER	4:48.3
1956	Alexe Dumitru Simion Ismailciuc	ROM	4:47.4	Gratsijan Botev Pavel Kharine	URS	4:48.6	Ferenc Mohácsi Károly Wieland	HUN	4:54.3
1960	Leonid Geyshter Sergei Makarenko	URS	4:17.04	Aldo Dezi Francesco La Macchia	ITA	4:20.77	Imre Farkas András Törö	HUN	4:20.89
1964	Andrei Khimich Stepan Oschephov	URS	4:04.65	Jean Boudehen Michel Chapuis	FRA	4:06.52	Peer Norrbohm Nielsen John Sörensen	DEN	4:07.48
1968	Serghei Covaliov Ivan Patzaichin	ROM	4:07.18	Gyula Petrikovics Tamás Wichmann	HUN	4:08.77	Naum Prokupets Mikhail Zamotin	URS	4:11.30
1972	Vladas Chessyunas Yuri Lobanov	URS	3:52.60	Serghei Covaliov Ivan Patzaichin	ROM	3:52.63	Ivan Bourtchin Fedia Damianov	BUL	3:58.10
1976	Sergei Petrenko Alexander Vinogradov	URS	3:52.76	Gheorghe Danielov Gheorghe Simionov	ROM	3:54.28	Tamás Budai Oszkár Frey	HUN	3:55.66
1980	Ivan Patzaichin Toma Simionov	ROM	3:47.65	Olaf Heukrodt Uwe Madeja	GDR	3:49.93	Yuri Lobanov Vasili Urchenko	URS	3:51.28
1984	Ivan Patzaichin Toma Simionov	ROM	3:40.60	Matija Ljubek Mirko Nišović	YUG	3:41.56	Didier Hoyer Eric Renaud	FRA	3:48.01
1988	Nikolai Jouravski Viktor Reneiski	URS	3:48.36	Olaf Heukrodt Ingo Spelly	GDR	3:51.44	Marek Dopierała Marek Lubik	POL	3:54.33
1992	Ulrich Papke Ingo Spelly	GER	3:37.42	Christian Frederiksen Arne Nielsson	DEN	3:39.26	Olivier Boivin Didier Hoyer	FRA	3:39.51
1996									

SLALOM

Kayak Single

Year	Gold	C'ntry	Time	Silver	C'ntry	Time	Bronze	C'ntry	Time
1972	Siegbert Horn	GDR	268.56	Norbert Sattler	AUT	270.76	Harald Gimpel	GDR	277.95
1992	Pierpaolo Ferrazzi	ITA	106.89	Sylvain Curinier	FRA	107.06	Jochen Lettmann	GER	108.52
1996									

Canadian Single

Year	Gold	C'ntry	Time	Silver	C'ntry	Time	Bronze	C'ntry	Time
1972	Reinhard Eiben	GDR	315.84	Reinold Kauder	FRG	327.99	Jamie McEwan	USA	335.95
1992	Lukáš Pollert	TCH	113.69	Gareth Marriott	GBR	116.48	Jacky Avril	FRA	117.18
1996									

Canadian Double

Year	Gold	C'ntry	Time	Silver	C'ntry	Time	Bronze	C'ntry	Time
1972	Rolf-Dieter Amend Walter Hofmann	GDR	310.68	Wilhelm Baues Hans Otto Schumacher	FRG	311.9	Jean-Claude Olry Jean-Louis Olry	FRA	315.1
1992	Joe Jacobi Scott Strausbaugh	USA	122.41	Jiří Rohan Miroslav Šimek	TCH	124.25	Franck Adisson Wilfrid Forgues	FRA	124.38
1996									

CANOEING (Women)

Year	Gold	C'ntry	Time	Silver	C'ntry	Time	Bronze	C'ntry	Time

FLATWATER
Kayak Single 500m

Year	Gold	C'ntry	Time	Silver	C'ntry	Time	Bronze	C'ntry	Time
1948	Karen Hoff	DEN	2:31.9	Alida van der Anker-Doedans	NED	2:32.8	Fritzi Schwingl	AUT	2:32.9
1952	Sylvi Saimo	FIN	2:18.4	Gertrude Liebhart	AUT	2:18.8	Nina Savina	URS	2:21.6
1956	Elisaveta Dementieva	URS	2:18.9	Therese Zenz	GER	2:19.6	Tove Goltermann Soby	DEN	2:22.3
1960	Antonia Seredina	URS	2:08.08	Therese Zenz	GER	2:08.22	Daniela Walkowiak	POL	2:10.46
1964	Ludmila Khvedosiuk	URS	2:12.87	Hilde Lauer	ROM	2:15.35	Marcia Ingram Jones	USA	2:15.68
1968	Ludmila Pinaeva	URS	2:11.09	Renate Breuer	FRG	2:12.71	Viorica Dumitru	ROM	2:13.22
1972	Yulia Ryabchinskaya	URS	2:03.17	Mieka Jaapies	NED	2:04.03	Anne Pfeffer	HUN	2:05.50
1976	Carola Zirzow	GDR	2:01.05	Tatiana Korshunova	URS	2:03.07	Klára Rajnai	HUN	2:05.01
1980	Birgit Fischer	GDR	1:57.96	Vania Gesheva	BUL	1:59.48	Antonina Melnikova	URS	1:59.66
1984	Agneta Andersson	SWE	1:58.72	Barbara Schüttpelz	FRG	1:59.93	Annemiek Derckx	NED	2:00.11
1988	Vania Gesheva	BUL	1:55.19	Birgit Schmidt	GDR	1:55.31	Izabella Dylewska	POL	1:57.38
1992	Birgit Schmidt	GER	1:51.60	Rita Kőbán	HUN	1:51.96	Izabella Dylewska	POL	1:52.36
1996									

Kayak Double 500m

Year	Gold	C'ntry	Time	Silver	C'ntry	Time	Bronze	C'ntry	Time
1960	Maria Chubina Antonina Seredina	URS	1:54.76	Ingrid Hartmann Therese Zenz	GER	1:56.66	Vilma Egresi Klára Fried	HUN	1:58.22
1964	Roswitha Esser Annemarie Zimmermann	GER	1:56.95	Francine Fox Gloriane Perrier	USA	1:59.16	Hilde Lauer Cornelia Sideri	ROM	2:00.25
1968	Roswitha Esser Annemarie Zimmermann	FRG	1:56.44	Anna Pfeffer Katalin Sagi	HUN	1:58.60	Ludmila Pinaeva Antonina Seredina	URS	1:58.61
1972	Ekaterina Kuryshko Ludmila Pinayeva	URS	1:53.50	Petra Grabowsky Ilse Kaschube	GDR	1:54.30	Viorica Dumitru Maria Nichiforov	ROM	1:55.01
1976	Nina Gopova Galina Kreft	URS	1:51.15	Anna Pfeffer Klára Rajnai	HUN	1:51.69	Bärbel Köster Carola Zirzow	GDR	1:51.81
1980	Martina Bischof Carsta Genäuss	GDR	1:43.88	Galina Alekseeva Nina Trofimova	URS	1:46.91	Eva Rakusz Mária Zakariás	HUN	1:47.95
1984	Agneta Andersson Anna Olsson	SWE	1:45.25	Alexandra Barre Sue Holloway	CAN	1:47.13	Josefa Idem Barbara Schüttpelz	FRG	1:47.32
1988	Anke Nothnagel Birgit Schmidt	GDR	1:43.46	Vania Gesheva Diana Paliiska	BUL	1:44.06	Annemarie Cox Annemiek Derckx	NED	1:46.00
1992	Ramona Portwich Anke von Seck	GER	1:40.29	Agneta Andersson Susanne Gunnarsson	SWE	1:40.41	Eva Dónusz Rita Kőbán	HUN	1:40.81
1996									

Kayak Fours 500m

Year	Gold	C'ntry	Time	Silver	C'ntry	Time	Bronze	C'ntry	Time
1984	Agafia Constantin Nastasia Ionescu Tecla Marinescu Maria Stefan	ROM	1:38.34	Agneta Andersson Eva Karlsson Anna Olsson Susanne Wiberg	SWE	1:38.87	Alexandra Barre Lucie Gray Sue Holloway Barbara Olmsted	CAN	1:39.40
1988	Anke Nothnagel Ramona Portwich Birgit Schmidt Heike Singer	GDR	1:40.78	Erika Géczi Rita Kőbán Erika Meszáros Eva Rakusz	HUN	1:41.88	Vania Gesheva Borislava Ivanova Diana Paliiska Ogniana Petkova	BUL	1:42.63
1992	Kinga Czigány Eva Dónusz Rita Kőbán Erika Meszáros	HUN	1:38.32	Katrin Borchert Ramona Portwich Brigit Schmidt Anke von Seck	GER	1:38.47	Agneta Andersson Maria Haglund Anna Olsson Susanne Rosenqvist	SWE	1:39.79
1996									

SLALOM
Kayak Single

Year	Gold	C'ntry	Time	Silver	C'ntry	Time	Bronze	C'ntry	Time
1972	Angelika Bahmann	GDR	364.50	Gisela Grothaus	FRG	398.15	Magdalena Wunderlich	FRG	400.50
1992	Elisabeth Micheler	GER	126.41	Danielle Woodward	AUS	128.27	Dana Chladek	USA	131.75
1996									

Cycling

Stars to Watch

by Peter Bryan

Return of the Professionals

THE EARLY Olympic concept, espoused by Baron de Coubertin, of the supreme importance of preserving "the noble and chivalrous character of athletics against professionalism" has had a succession of little chips taken from it in modern times. Inevitably so, as sport has progressed.

For cycling, the centenary Games in Atlanta will mark the end of both amateurism and "shamateurism" as the sport goes fully "open". Track racing went that way in 1993. Road racing, a billion dollar industry, approached the idea of an open licence less enthusiastically but will conform in 1996.

If all men – and women – are equal, in Atlanta some will be more equal than others: the former professionals. Their inclusion in the Olympic programme will shake the majority of amateur aspirations for gold just as state-funded sport, particularly from the eastern bloc nations, did 20 years ago.

That will be especially applicable to the road race which, in theory, is an individual event although each nation is allowed four riders. It will be fascinating to watch this event, always one of the most difficult to predict and whose outcome can be something of a lottery. Each country will select its best quartet, many of whom will have raced against each other in rival professional teams all year. They will have to put those rivalries behind them and may have to sacrifice their own chances to get the "rider-in-form" over the line first on the day.

Sadly, Italy's Fabio Casartelli will not

Miguel Indurain

A Contemporary Hero ★★★★★★★★★★★★★★★★★★★★★★★★★★★★★★★

Chris Boardman *(Great Britain)*

Chris Boardman, Britain's first gold medallist in any sport at the 1992 Barcelona Games and who won his country's first individual Olympic cycling title since Vic Johnson's victory in London 84 years earlier, is virtually certain not to defend his 4,000m title.

Now a professional, he accepts that his paymasters (Gan, a French assurance company) play a major role in determining his 1996 programme aims. One will be to lead his team in the Tour de France which ends only a week before the pursuit competition starts.

"It's impossible to contemplate the pursuit after three weeks of the Tour," says Boardman, but he plans to be in Atlanta for the 52km individual road time trial – at which discipline he is world champion – on August 3. The time trial is known as 'the race of truth'. There are no team tactics from which a rider can benefit. It's just man against the watch.

The 27 year old Briton, who lives on the Wirral, won the opening time trial in the 1993 Tour de France to take the traditional yellow jersey of race leader.

be there to defend his Barcelona crown. He was killed in a crash during the 1995 Tour de France. The possible outcome at the 1996 Games, though, is likely to bear some relation to 1995 performances.

Spain's Miguel Indurain, who won his fifth Tour de France in 1995 tops the list of gold medal contenders, even though he finished second to compatriot Abraham Olano in the 1995 world road race in Colombia. Indurain had nothing to prove. A few days earlier he had taken the world time trial crown – in the absence, through injury, of Britain's reigning champion Chris Boardman.

Italy, France, Spain and Belgium remain the consistently major international performers and must be top-ranked for Atlanta: expect Claudio Chiappucci, Laurent Jalabert, Indurain and Johan Museeuw to be among the medallists – if

A Contemporary Hero ★★★★★★★★★★★★★★★★★★★★★★★★★★★★★★★

Marty Nothstein *(USA)*

Marty Nothstein was glad to see the back of 1995, the climax of which should have been the world track championships in Colombia. A year earlier, the 1.93m (6ft 4in) American had won both the sprint and keirin titles and was favourite to repeat the double.

It was not to be. Four weeks before the championships Nothstein crashed heavily, breaking a knee-cap. Yet, with his injury only partially healed, he insisted (against doctor's orders) on going to the line in Bogota to defend his two titles.

He managed to get through the first four rounds of the sprint but went down in the quarter finals to eventual gold medal winner Darryn Hill (Australia). Nothstein reached the final of the keirin, finishing a creditable fourth in an eight-man field.

"It was better to be there than sitting around at home wondering what might have been," said the American after his defeats, adding that the only thing that now mattered was July 26 – the opening day of the 1996 Olympic sprint competition.

their sponsors release them for selection.

Boardman, because of his commitment to the 1996 Tour de France, is unlikely to defend his 4,000m pursuit title but Scotland's Graeme Obree, the world record holder and champion, could yet again prove faster than Italy's Andrea Collinelli.

Expect Australia's amateurs to feature strongly in the individual track sprint, one kilometre time trial and the 4,000m team pursuit. They are the most improved nation on the international circuit. Darryn Hill (sprint), Shane Kelly (kilometre time trial) and Bradley McGee, Rod McGee, Stuart O'Grady and Tim O'Shannessy (4,000m team pursuit) qualify for the description of poetry in motion. And it has to be said, the USA cannot be ignored.

P. B. □

Retrospective

The pyschology of technology has inevitably played its part in top-class cycling over the years. A recent example is that of Britain's Chris Boardman, gold medallist in the 1992 individual pursuit, and his "dream machine" made of carbon fibre and designed with the use of a wind tunnel by motor-racing manufacturers Lotus. Back in 1976 Dutchman Herman Ponsteen won silver in the same event with an allegedly "special lightweight" machine sprayed in silver paint. At those Games, too, Germany's track cyclists claimed that putting helium in their tyres gave them an advantage.

Top Olympic cyclists in the past often turned professional after their first appearance at the Games. These have included Eddy Merckx of Belgium and Jacques Anquetil of France who each finished 12th in the road races of 1964 and 1952 respectively and who jointly hold the record number of wins (five) in the Tour de France with Spain's Miguel Indurain – although Indurain has the opportunity to win a record sixth title on the eve of the 1996 Games.

In 1960 tragedy struck Olympic cycling with the death of Denmark's Knut Jensen who collapsed during the road race. His death was first attributed to sunstroke. Only later did it transpire that he had taken a stimulant.

The 4,000m individual pursuit at the 1972 Games in Munich was unexpectedly won by Norway's Knut Knudsen – a remarkable achievement for a man whose country only possessed one cycling track and even that was flat and saucer-

A Sporting Legend ★★★★★★★★★★★★★★★★★★★★★★★★★★★★★★★★★

Eddy Merckx *(Belgium)*

Haohioji, 30 miles north of Tokyo, offers no particular attractions in the rain. Certainly not to the 150 riders who lined up for the start of the 1964 Olympic 194km (120.5 miles) road race. Not only was it wet but also chillingly cold.

Among those waiting for the gun to signal the off was Eddy Merckx, a 19 year old Belgian who only a few weeks earlier had become world road race champion at Sallanches, France. Possibly the youngest rider racing for the Olympic title, Merckx was still considered a dangerman. And he was soon to show that his world championship victory was no fluke.

He launched a succession of attacks in the final hour, the last of which took him clear with Mike Cowley, of Great Britain, and the Dutchman, Henri Steevens. Merckx had the lead on the final bend, a left-hander, 1,000m from the finish but Steevens tried to 'cut' the corner, going inside the Belgian only to lose control of his bike. Both crashed heavily as did Cowley who could not avoid the fallen pair.

No medals for any of them. Merckx, however, proved his talent over and over again: three world professional road titles, five Tours de France, five Tours of Italy and one Tour of Spain.

From Olympic disaster came triumph. In his career, Merckx won 525 races from 1,800 starts. The name Merckx may feature in the Atlanta road race. His son Axel shows a fine turn of speed.

shaped unlike the steeply-banked Olympic tracks. Knudsen used wheels lent to him by the Danish team. Tandem races were last seen in the Olympic Games of that year.

Four Swedish brothers – Gosta, Sture, Erik and Tomas – made the 1968 Olympic Games a family affair by winning the silver medal in the road team time trial.

Background

Cycling was first introduced to the Olympic programme in 1896 when six cyclists went from Athens to Marathon where they had to sign their names for verification purposes before returning. Surprisingly, women had to wait until 1984 before their inclusion at the Games in a road race which was won by the American Connie Carpenter-Phinney by just half a wheel's length from her compatriot Rebecca Twigg. Carpenter-Phinney had competed in the 1972 Olympic Winter Games as a speed skater.

Christa Luding Rothenburg, of the former German Democratic Republic, won a women's cycling sprint silver in 1988 to add to her world title in the same discipline from 1986. This outstanding athlete, however, had also won Olympic speed skating gold in both 1984 and '88.

★★★★★★★★★★★★★★★★★★★★★★★★★★★★★★ **A Sporting Legend**

Reg Harris *(Great Britain)*

Looking down on the new, magnificent £9 million Manchester Velodrome, in the northern British city, is an impressive life-size sculpture of Reg Harris, five times sprint champion of the world, in action.

He was a soldier who escaped, injured, from a burning tank in the World War II North African campaign, won his first world title in 1947 and should have been odds-on favourite for the Olympic title in London a year later.

It was not to be. Harris, driving to London for the traditional Good Friday meeting, broke two bones in his spine in a car accident. A month later he was back on his bike. Two weeks on, he had returned to winning form. Two months later, in what appeared a minor racing crash, it transpired that he had broken a bone in his right wrist. In the four weeks remaining before the Olympic Games, Harris's injury did not heal completely and he had the added burden of an unhappy contretemps with British officials which, initially, saw him dropped from the squad.

It was, therefore, neither a fit nor a confident Harris who reached the Olympic sprint final – decided by a best-of-three series – against Italy's Mario Ghella, an 18 year old revelation. The masterly tactics, the famous sudden surge of power were absent. As was an Olympic gold. For Harris it was silver.

Track cycling was held indoors at the Games for the first time in 1976. In 1936 the road race featured its first mass start. And the longest Olympic cycling race took place in 1912 at a distance of 320km (199 miles). The 100km road team time trial was added to the programme in 1960, followed by the 4,000m individual pursuit in 1964.

Cycling as a mode of transport and as a recreational pursuit is almost universal. The first official cycle race is thought to have taken place in Paris in 1868. This was followed soon afterwards by the advent of long distance races such as that from Paris to Rouen. But there have been informal races almost since the invention of the bicycle.

Professional events began in Britain in 1871. These were initially held in enclosed areas such as city parks. Later, purpose built cycle tracks appeared. The USA, Australia, France and Germany – together with Great Britain – were early forces within the sport. The International Cycling Union (UCI) was formed in 1900.

Equipment

Dateline Los Angeles, 1984. Cycling entered the era of space-age technology. Cyclists wore aerodynamic helmets and racing suits and rode bikes with "low profiles" and solid graphite wheels. In 1992 Chris Boardman, of Great Britain, rode a "super-bike" developed by racing car manufacturers, to win the 4,000m individual pursuit title. He was also a superb athlete but each rider continues to strive, within the rules, to make technological changes to give them a competitive edge at the Games.

Racing bikes in general weigh around 8.16kg (18lbs) and are often made of titanium. The road race bike has at least 15 gears – or more if a double chain wheel is used. Its pedals are flat and specially designed to allow a rider's shoes to clip in. Road time trial machines have triathlon "bars" attached to the handlebars to allow a rider to tuck in their elbows (just like a skier in a tuck position for long downhill glides) to become more aerodynamic. They can also have disc rear wheels and carbon fibre front wheels with just three spokes.

On the track, there are generally two types of bikes. The first is more traditional in design and is used for sprints and points races. It has a fixed gear ratio and no brakes. The second, is more dramatically modern and is used for individual and team pursuits as well as time trials. It sometimes has disc wheels at the front and rear but often the front wheel is smaller than the rear wheel to pitch the rider forward over the front wheel in riding style. The frame tubing is likely to be moulded in an aerodynamic fashion.

Meanwhile, mountain bikes are built to cope with the terrain. They are sturdier than their road or track counterparts and have triple chain wheels with a large selection of gears and wide tyres. They can have hydraulic suspension over the front forks.

Riders in all disciplines on the track wear shaped helmets made of fibreglass and polystyrene as well as one-piece, tight-fitting racing suits in Lycra or similar material. Their shoes can have clips to fit into the pedals of some road and track bikes.

The 1996 Olympic cycling track is 250m long, oval shaped, and is made of wood with steep banking. Cyclists will travel around it in an anti-clockwise direction. The track has a finish line at the end of the home straight which continues up the safety fence. Photo-finish equipment will be used.

Rules and regulations

The 1,000m sprint is the "blue-riband" event of track cycling in which riders need both explosive speed and skill. Lots are drawn for each race and the rider who draws the inside of the track at the start must lead for the first lap. A tactical battle then ensues in which the riders play "cat and mouse" with each other neither wishing to take the lead and leave themselves open to an attack from behind. This often results in both riders coming to a standstill high on the banking in a battle of wills during which a rider must not roll backwards more than 20cm (8in). Finally, with the last lap to go, one rider will normally make a sprint for the line opening up a dramatic finish. In the early stages of this competition there are repechages to give the riders a second chance to qualify for the later stages where contests are the best of three rides.

For the kilometre time trial, cyclists are pitted one at a time against the clock. The fastest cyclist wins. The individual and team pursuits are "chases". Cyclists start on opposite sides of the track and attempt to catch up with each other. A cyclist wins the race if he or she overtakes his or her opponent or crosses the finish line first. The qualification round is a time trial to seed cyclists for matches which pit the fastest against the slowest. There are then later rounds, semi-finals and finals. In the team event four riders race in each team. A team wins if its third rider overtakes the opposition no.3 or if its third rider is fastest than his opposite number over the line.

The final track event is the points race in which cyclists accumulate points for designated sprint laps. Every eight laps a sprint is signalled for the end of the next lap and the first four riders over the line score points. The sprint over the final lap is worth double points. A fascinating series of attacks and counter-attacks is a feature of this event.

On the road at the Games, the men's and women's races both feature a mass start with cyclists completing a number of circuits of the course. The men complete more circuits than the women. In each race the first cyclist to cross the line wins. For the individual time trial, cyclists start from a ramp at intervals of 60 seconds and race against the clock. The cyclist with the fastest time is declared the winner.

Mountain biking, a new discipline for the 1996 Games, consists of two cross country races – one each for men and women. Both take place over a series of loops on an identical course but the men's race is longer. The first rider to cross the finish line is the winner.

Atlanta Format

611 cyclists will take part in the cycling events of the 1996 Olympic Games – 169 women and 442 men. The programme consists of road and track cycling as well as mountain biking. A women's points race has been added to the track

disciplines since the 1992 Games and mountain biking is making its Olympic debut in Atlanta.

The road race cycling courses for men and women cover approximately 240km (149 miles) and 110km (68 miles) respectively. On the track, the points race consists of a 24km (14.9 miles) ride for women and a distance of 40km (24.8 miles) for men.

Venue

Stone Mountain Park lies 25.6km (16 miles) east of Atlanta's Olympic Center and will play host to the track cycling events at the 1996 Games. It is one of the region's top tourist attractions and is an area of outstanding natural beauty. The velodrome will be a 250m wooden track housed within a temporary stadium incorporating 6,000 spectator seats and ancillary facilities.

The road race circuits will be in and around the city of Atlanta whilst mountain biking will take place in Georgia International Horse Park situated 53km (33 miles) from the Olympic village and with a spectator capacity of 25,000.

CYCLING – current Olympic records

Event	Name	Country	Time/Result	Games	Year
Men					
1km Time Trial	José Moreno Periñan	ESP	1:03.342	Barcelona	1992
Individual Sprint[1]	Jens Fiedler	GER	10.252	Barcelona	1992
4,000m Team Pursuit	Germany	GER	4:08.791	Barcelona	1992
4,000m Individual Pursuit	Chris Boardman	GBR	4:24.496	Barcelona	1992
Women					
Individual Sprint	Ingrid Haringa	NED	11.419	Barcelona	1992
Individual Pursuit	Petra Rossner	GER	3:41.509	Barcelona	1992

[1] Time measured only for last 200m

MEDALLISTS (by nation)

Country	Men Gold	Silver	Bronze	Women Gold	Silver	Bronze	Total
France	27	15	21	-	1	-	64
Italy	28	15	6	-	-	-	49
Great Britain	9	21	14	-	-	-	44
United States[1]	10	9	13	1	1	2	36
Netherlands	8	13	4	1	-	2	28
Soviet Union	10	4	8	1	-	1	24
Germany	6	8	8	1	1	-	24
Belgium	6	6	10	-	-	-	22
Australia	5	9	4	1	1	-	20
Denmark	6	6	8	-	-	-	20
GDR	6	5	4	-	1	-	16
FRG	3	4	4	-	1	1	13
Sweden	3	2	8	-	-	-	13
South Africa	1	4	3	-	-	-	8
Poland	-	5	3	-	-	-	8
Czechoslovakia	2	2	2	-	-	-	6
Switzerland	1	3	2	-	-	-	6
Greece	1	3	1	-	-	-	5
Canada	-	2	2	-	-	-	4
Austria	1	-	2	-	-	-	3
Norway	1	-	1	-	-	-	2
Estonia	-	-	-	1	-	-	1
Spain	1	-	-	-	-	-	1
Jamaica	-	-	1	-	-	-	1
Japan	-	-	1	-	-	-	1
Latvia	-	-	1	-	-	-	1
Mexico	-	-	1	-	-	-	1
New Zealand	-	-	1	-	-	-	1
	135	136	133[2]	6	6	6	422

[1] Includes 7 events in 1904 formerly excluded
[2] No bronzes in 1896 100km, 1972 road team trial and individual road race

ATLANTA SCHEDULE

Cycling – Mountain Bike
Venue: Georgia International Horse Park

Date	Description	Round	Start	End
30 Jul	ind cross country (m&w)	FINALS	10:00	17:30

Cycling – Road
Venue: Atlanta (course to be decided)

Date	Description	Round	Start	End
21 Jul	road race (w)	FINAL	11:00	14:30
31 Jul	road race (m)	FINAL	8:30	14:30
3 Aug	ind time trial (m&w)	FINALS	8:30	15:30

Cycling – Track
Venue: Stone Mountain Park

Date	Description	Round	Start	End
24 Jul	ind pursuit (m)	Q/fying	10:00	13:30
	sprint (w)	Q/fying		
	1 km time trial (m)	FINAL		
	ind pursuit (m)	q/finals		
	sprint (m)	Q/fying	16:30	18:55
		Rd 1		
		repechage		
25 Jul	ind pursuit (w)	Q/fying	9:00	12:10
	ind pursuit (m)	s/finals		
	sprint (m)	Rd 2		
	sprint (w)	Last 16		
	sprint (m)	repechage		
	sprint (w)	repechage		
	ind pursuit (m)	FINAL		
26 Jul	team pursuit (m)	Q/fying	8:30	13:00
	sprint (w)	q/finals		
	sprint (m)	Last 16		
	sprint (m)	repechage		
	sprint (w)	tiebreak		
	team pursuit (m)	q/finals		
	sprint (w)	s/finals		
	ind pursuit (w)	q/finals		
	sprint (w)	ride-off 7-8 place		
	sprint (w)	ride-off 5-6 place		
	sprint (w)	s/finals tiebreak		
27 Jul	sprint (m)	q/finals	11:15	14:10
	ind pursuit (w)	s/finals		
	team pursuit (m)	s/finals		
	sprint (w)	ride-off (bronze)		
	sprint (w)	FINAL		
	sprint (m)	q/finals		
	sprint (m)	q/finals tiebreak		
	sprint (w)	FINAL tiebreak		
	sprint (m)	s/finals		
	sprint (m)	ride-off 7-8 place		
	sprint (m)	ride-off 5-6 place		
	team pursuit (m)	FINAL		
	sprint (m)	s/finals tiebreak		
28 Jul	points race (m)	FINAL	11:15	14:30
	sprint (m)	ride-off (bronze)		
	sprint (m)	FINAL		
	ind pursuit (w)	FINAL		
	sprint (m)	FINAL		
	points race (w)	FINAL		

MEDALLISTS

CYCLING (Men)

Year	Gold	C'ntry	Time	Silver	C'ntry	Time	Bronze	C'ntry	Time

1000m Time Trial

Year	Gold	C'ntry	Time	Silver	C'ntry	Time	Bronze	C'ntry	Time
1896	Paul Masson	FRA	24.0	Stamatios Nikolopoulos	GRE	25.4	Adolf Schmal	AUT	26.6
1908	Victor Louis Johnson	GBR	1:27.4	Karl Neumer	GER		F D Venter	SAF	
1928	Willy Falck Hansen	DEN	1:14.2	Gerard Bosch van Drakestein	NED	1:15.1	Edgar Gray	AUS	1:15.3
1932	Edgar Laurence Gray	AUS	1:13.0	Jacobus van Egmond	NED	1:13.3	Charles Rampelberg	FRA	1:13.4
1936	Arie van Vliet	NED	1:12.0	Pierre Georget	FRA	1:12.8	Rudolph Karsch	GER	1:13.2
1948	Jacques Dupont	FRA	1:13.5	Pierre Nihant	BEL	1:14.5	Thomas Godwin	GBR	1:15.0
1952	Russell Mockridge	AUS	1:11.1	Marino Morettini	ITA	1:12.7	Raymond Robinson	SAF	1:13.0
1956	Leandro Faggin	ITA	1:09.8	Ladislav Fouček	TCH	1:11.4	Alfred James Swift	SAF	1:11.6
1960	Sante Gaiardoni	ITA	1:07.27	Dieter Gieseler	GER	1:08.75	Rostislav Vargashkin	URS	1:08.86
1964	Patrick Sercu	BEL	1:09.59	Giovanni Pettenella	ITA	1:10.09	Pierre Trentin	FRA	1:10.42
1968	Pierre Trentin	FRA	1:03.91	Niels Fredborg	DEN	1:04.61	Janusz Kierzkowski	POL	1:04.63
1972	Niels Fredborg	DEN	1:06.44	Daniel Clark	AUS	1:06.87	Jürgen Schütze	GDR	1:07.02
1976	Klaus-Jürgen Grünke	GDR	1:05.927	Michel Vaarten	BEL	1:07.516	Niels Fredborg	DEN	1:07.617
1980	Lothar Thoms	GDR	1:02.955	Alexander Panfilov	URS	1:04.845	David Weller	JAM	1:05.241
1984	Fredy Schmidtke	FRG	1:06.10	Curtis Harnett	CAN	1.06.44	Fabrice Colas	FRA	1:06.65
1988	Alexandre Kiritchenko	URS	1:04.499	Martin Vinnicombe	AUS	1:04.784	Robert Lechner	FRG	1:05.114
1992	José Moreno Periñan	ESP	1:03.342	Shane Kelly	AUS	1:04.288	Erin Hartwell	USA	1:04.753
1996									

1000m Sprint

Year	Gold	C'ntry	Time	Silver	C'ntry	Time	Bronze	C'ntry	Time
1896	Paul Masson	FRA	4:56.0	Stamatios Nikolopoulos	GRE	5:00.2	Leon Flameng	FRA	
1900	Georges Taillandier	FRA	2:52.0	Fernand Sanz	FRA		John Lake	USA	
1908	declared void								
1920	Mauritius Peeters	NED	1:38.3	Horace Thomas Johnson	GBR		Harry Ryan	GBR	
1924	Lucien Michard	FRA	12.8*	Jacob Meijer	NED		Jean Cugnot	FRA	
1928	Roger Beaufrand	FRA	13.2	Antoine Mazairac	NED		Willy Falck Hansen	DEN	
1932	Jacobus Van Egmond	NED	12.6	Louis Chaillot	FRA		Bruno Pellizzari	ITA	
1936	Toni Merkens	GER	11.8	Arie van Vliet	NED		Louis Chaillot	FRA	
1948	Mario Ghella	ITA	12.0	Reginald Harris	GBR		Axel Schandorff	DEN	
1952	Enzo Sacchi	ITA	12.0	Lionel Cox	AUS		Werner Potzernheim	GER	
1956	Michel Rousseau	FRA	11.4	Guglielmo Pesenti	ITA		Richard Francis Ploog	AUS	
1960	Sante Gaiardoni	ITA	11.1	Leo Sterckx	BEL		Valentino Gasparella	ITA	
1964	Giovanni Pettenella	ITA	13.69	Sergio Bianchetto	ITA		Daniel Morelon	FRA	
1968	Daniel Morelon	FRA	10.68	Giordano Turrini	ITA		Pierre Trentin	FRA	
1972	Daniel Morelon	FRA	11.25	John Michael Nicholson	AUS		Omar Phakadze	URS	
1976	Anton Tkáč	TCH	10.78	Daniel Morelon	FRA		Hans-Jürgen Geschke	GDR	
1980	Lutz Hesslich	GDR	11.4	Yavé Cahard	FRA		Sergei Kopylov	URS	
1984	Mark Gorski	USA	10.49	Nelson Vails	USA		Tsutomu Sakamoto	JPN	
1988	Lutz Hesslich	GDR		Nikolai Kovche	URS		Gary Neiwand	AUS	
1992	Jens Fiedler	GER		Gary Neiwand	AUS		Curtis Harnett	CAN	
1996									

*Times from 1924 over the last 200m only.

4000m Individual Pursuit

Year	Gold	C'ntry	Time	Silver	C'ntry	Time	Bronze	C'ntry	Time
1964	Jiři Daler	TCH	5:04.75	Giorgio Ursi	ITA	5:05.96	Preben Isaksson	DEN	5:01.90
1968	Daniel Rebillard	FRA	4:41.71	Mogens Jensen	DEN	4:42.43	Xaver Kurmann	SUI	4:39.42
1972	Knut Knudsen	NOR	4:45.74	Xaver Kurmann	SUI	4:51.96	Hans Lutz	FRG	4:50.80
1976	Gregor Braun	FRG	4:47.61	Herman Ponsteen	NED	4:49.72	Thomas Huschke	GDR	4:52.71
1980	Robert Dill-Bundi	SUI	4:35.66	Alain Bondue	FRA	4:42.96	Hans-Henrik Ørsted	DEN	4:36.54
1984	Steve Hegg	USA	4:39.35	Rolf Gölz	FRG	4:43.82	Leonard Harvey Nitz	USA	4:44.03
1988	Gintaoutas Umaras	URS	4:32.00	Dean Woods	AUS	4:35.00	Bernd Dittert	GDR	4:34.17
1992	Christopher Boardman	GBR	3:21.649	Jens Lehmann	GER	3:27.357	Gary Anderson	NZL	4:31.061
1996									

Year	Gold	C'ntry	Time	Silver	C'ntry	Time	Bronze	C'ntry	Time

Individual Points Race

Year	Gold	C'ntry	Time	Silver	C'ntry	Time	Bronze	C'ntry	Time
1984	Roger Llegems	BEL		Uwe Messerschmidt	FRG		José Manuel Youshimatz	MEX	
1988	Dan Frost	DEN		Leo Peelen	NED		Marat Ganeev	URS	
1992	Giovanni Lombardi	ITA		Leon van Bon	NED		Cedric Mathy	BEL	
1996									

4000m Team Pursuit

Year	Gold	C'ntry	Time	Silver	C'ntry	Time	Bronze	C'ntry	Time
1908	Benjamin Jones Clarence Kingsbury Leonard Meredith Ernest Payne	GBR	2:18.6	Bruno Goetze Richard Katzer Hermann Martens Karl Neumer	GER	2:28.6	William Anderson Walter Andrews Frederick McCarthy William Morton	CAN	2:29.6
1920	Arnoldo Carli Ruggero Ferrario Franco Giorgetti Primo Magnani	ITA	5:20.0	Cyril Alden Horace Johnson William Stewart Albert White	GBR		Harry Goosen Henry Justaves Kaltenbrun William Smith James Walker	SAF	
1924	Angelo De Martino Alfredo Dinale Aurelio Menegazzi Francesco Zucchetti	ITA	5:15.0	Józef Lange Jan Lazarski Tomasz Stankiewicz Franciszek Szymczyk	POL		Gustave Daghelinckx Henri Hoevenaers Ferdinand Saive Jean van den Bosch	BEL	
1928	Cesare Facciani Giacomo Gaioni Mario Lusiani Luigi Tasselli	ITA	5:01.8	Adriaan Braspennin Johannes Maas Johannes Pijnenburg Petrus van der Horst	NED	5:06.2	Michael Southall Frederick Wyld Leonard Wyld Percy Wyld	GBR	
1932	Nino Bosari Marco Cimatti Alberto Ghilardi Paolo Pedretti	ITA	4:53.0	Paul Chocque Amédée Fournier René Legrèves Henri Mouillefarine	FRA	4:55.7	William Harvell Charles Holland Ernest Johnson Frank Southall	GBR	4:56.0
1936	Robert Charpentier Jean Goujan Guy Lapébie Roger Le Nizerhy	FRA	4:45.0	Bianco Bianchi Mario Gentili Armando Latini Severino Rigoni	ITA	4:51.0	Harry Hill Ernest Johnson Charles King Ernest Mills	GBR	4:53.6
1948	Pierre Adam Serge Blusson Charles Coste Fernand Decanali	FRA	4:57.8	Arnaldo Benfenati Guido Bernardi Anselmo Citterio Rino Pucci	ITA	5:36.7	Robert Geldard Thomas Godwin David Ricketts Wilfrid Waters	GBR	4:55.8
1952	Loris Campana Mino De Rossi Guido Messina Marino Morettini	ITA	4:46.1	George Estman Robert Fowler Thomas Shardelow Alfred Swift	SAF	4:53.6	Donald Burgess George Newberry Alan Newton Ronald Stretton	GBR	4:51.5
1956	Antonio Domenicali Leandro Faggin Franco Gandini Valentino Gasparella	ITA	4:37.4	René Bianchi Jean Graczyk Jean-Claude Lecante Michel Vermeulin	FRA	4:39.4	Donald Burgess Michael Gambrill John Geddes Thomas Simpson	GBR	4:42.2
1960	Luigi Arienti Franco Testa Mario Vallotto Marino Vigna	ITA	4:30.90	Bernd Barleben Peter Gröning Manfred Klieme Siegfried Köhler	GER	4:35.78	Arnold Beljgardt Leonid Kolumbet Stanislav Moskvin Viktor Romanov	URS	4:34.05
1964	Lothar Claesges Karl Heinz Henrichs Karl Link Ernst Streng	GER	4:35.67	Vincenzo Mantovani Carlo Rancati Luigi Roncaglia Franco Testa	ITA	4:35.74	Hendrik Cornelissen Gerard Koel Jacob Oudkerk Cornelis Schuuring	NED	4:38.99
1968	Gunnar Asmussen Mogens Jensen Per Lyngemark Reno Olsen	DEN	4:22.44	Udo Hempel Karl Heinz Henrichs Jürgen Kissner Karl Link	FRG	4:18.94	Lorenzo Bosisio Cipriano Chemello Giorgo Morbiato Luigi Roncaglia	ITA	4:18.35
1972	Jürgen Colombo Günter Haritz Udo Hempel Günther Schumacher	FRG	4:22.14	Thomas Huschke Heinz Richter Herbert Richter Uwe Unterwalder	GDR	4:25.25	Michael Bennett Ian Hallam Ronald Keeble William Moore	GBR	4:23.78
1976	Gregor Braun Hans Lutz Günther Schumacher Peter Vonhof	FRG	4:21.06	Vladimir Osokin Alexander Perov Vitali Petrakov Viktor Sokolov	URS	4:27.15	Ian Banbury Michael Bennett Robin Croker Ian Hallam	GBR	4:22.41

/continued on next page 201

Year	Gold	C'ntry	Time	Silver	C'ntry	Time	Bronze	C'ntry	Time
1980	Viktor Manakov	URS	4:15.70	Gerald Mortag	GDR	4:19.67	Teodor Černý	TCH	2:10.01
	Valeri Movchan			Uwe Unterwalder			Martin Penc		
	Vladimir Osokin			Matthias Wiegand			Jiří Pokorný		
	Vitali Petrakov			Volker Winkler			Igor Sláma		
1984	Michael Grenda	AUS	4:25.99	David Grylls	USA	4:29.85	Reinhard Alber	FRG	4:25.60
	Kevin Nichols			Steve Hegg			Rolf Gölz		
	Michael Turtur			Patrick McDonough			Roland Gunther		
	Dean Woods			Leonard Harvey Nitz			Michael Marx		
1988	Viacheslav Ekimov	URS	4:13.31	Steffen Blochwitz	USA	4:14.09	Brett Dutton	AUS	4:16.02
	Artouras Kasputis			Roland Hennig			Wayne McCarney		
	Dimitri Nelubine			Dirk Meier			Stephen McGlede		
	Gintaoutas Umaras			Carsten Wolf			Dean Woods		
1992	Guido Fulst	GER	4:08.791	Brett Aitken	AUS	4:10.218	Dan Frost	DEN	4:15.860
	Michael Gloeckner			Stephen John McGlede			Jimmi Madsen		
	Jens Lehmann			Shaun William O'Brien			Klaus Kynde Nilsen		
	Stefan Steinweg			Stuart Peter O'Grady			Jan Bo Petersen		
1996									

ROAD
Individual Road Race

1896	Aristidis Konstantinidis	GRE	3:22:31	August Goedrich	GER	3:42:18	E Battel	GBR	
1912	Rudolph Lewis	SAF	10:42:39	Frederick Grubb	GBR	10:51:24	Carl Schutte	USA	10:52:38
1920	Harry Stenqvist	SWE	4:40:01	Henry Kaltenbrun	SAF	4:41:26	Fernand Canteloube	FRA	4:42:54
1924	Armand Blanchonnet	FRA	6:20:48	Henri Hoevenaers	BEL	6:30:27	René Hamel	FRA	6:30:51
1928	Henry Hansen	DEN	4:47:18	Frank Southall	GBR	4:55:06	Gösta Carlsson	SWE	5:00:17
1932	Attilio Pavesi	ITA	2:28:05	Guglielmo Segato	ITA	2:29:21	Bernhard Britz	SWE	2:29:45
1936	Robert Charpentier	FRA	2:33.05	Guy Lapébie	FRA	2:33:05	Ernst Nievergelt	SUI	2:33:05
1948	José Beyaert	FRA	5:18:12	Geradus Voorting	NED	5:18:16	Lode Wouters	BEL	5:18:16
1952	Andre Noyelle	BEL	5:06:03	Robert Grondelaers	BEL	5:06:51	Edi Ziegler	GER	5:07:47
1956	Ercole Baldini	ITA	5:21.17	Arnaud Geyre	FRA	5:23.16	Alan Jackson	GBR	5:23.16
1960	Viktor Kapitonov	URS	4:20:37	Livio Trapé	ITA	4:20:37	Willy van den Berghen	BEL	4:20:57
1964	Mario Zanin	ITA	4:39:51	Kjell Åkerström Rodian	DEN	4:39:51	Walter Godefroot	BEL	4:39:51
1968	Pierfranco Vianelli	ITA	4:41:25	Leif Mortensen	DEN	4:42:49	Gösta Pettersson	SWE	4:43:15
1972	Hennie Kuiper	NED	4:14.37	Kevin Clyde Sefton	AUS	4:15.04			
1976	Bernt Johannson	SWE	4:46:52	Giuseppe Martinelli	ITA	4:47:23	Mieczysław Nowicki	POL	4:47.23
1980	Sergei Sukhoruchenkov	URS	4:48:28	Czesław Lang	POL	4:51:26	Yuri Barinov	URS	4:51.29
1984	Alexi Grewal	USA	4:59.57	Steve Bauer	CAN	4:59.57	Dag Otto Lauritzen	NOR	5:00.18
1988	Olaf Ludwig	GDR	4:32.22	Bernd Groene	FRG	4:32.25	Christian Henn	FRG	4:32.46
1992	Fabio Casartelli	ITA	4:35.21	Erik Dekker	NED	4:35.22	Dainis Ozols	LAT	4:35.24
1996									

Individual Road Time Trial

1996

Mountain Bike Cross Country

1996

CYCLING (Women)

Year	Gold	C'ntry	Time	Silver	C'ntry	Time	Bronze	C'ntry	Time

ROAD
Individual Road Race

1984	Connie Carpenter-Phinney	USA	2:11:14	Rebecca Twigg	USA	2:11:14	Sandra Schumacher	FRG	2:11:14
1988	Monique Knol	NED	2:00:52	Jutta Niehaus	FRG	G	Laima Zilporitee	URS	G
1992	Kathryn Watt	AUS	2:04:42	Jeannie Longo-Ciprelli	FRA	2:05:02	Monique Knol	NED	2:05:03
1996									

Year	Gold	C'ntry	Time	Silver	C'ntry	Time	Bronze	C'ntry	Time

Individual Road Time Trial

1996

TRACK

3000m Individual Pursuit

| 1992 | Petra Rossner | GER | 3:41.753 | Kathryn Watt | AUS | 3:43.438 | Rebecca Twigg | USA | 3:52.429 |
| 1996 | | | | | | | | | |

Sprint

| 1988 | Erika Saloumiae | URS | | Christa Luding Rothenburg | GDR | | Connie Paraskevin-Young | USA | |
| 1992 | Erika Saloumiae | EST | | Annett Neumann | GER | | Ingrid Haringa | NED | |

Individual Points Race

1996

Cross Country Mountain Bike

1996

Equestrian

Stars to Watch

by Dieter Hennig

A musical addition to this unique sport

THE equestrian disciplines are, for two reasons, unique to the Olympic Games. They are the only ones in which male and female athletes compete head-to-head in all events and in which (one section of modern pentathlon excepted) athlete and animal participate as a couple.

And the Atlanta Games will pose the severest of tests for both horses and riders in the three-day event as, for the first time, they will have to face the cross-country course twice. This is because the individual and team medals will not be decided in one single event any more. There will be two separate competitions.

Riders can enter both tests with different horses but predictions of success in this discipline are now extremely difficult. And there have always been occasions when horses have been protected from further strain by being forced to retire after the horse inspection on any of the days, as happened, in 1992, to Mark Todd on his way to what would have been an unprecedented third consecutive individual victory.

A Contemporary Hero ★★★★★★★★★★★★★★★★★★★★★★★★★★★★★★★★

Mark Todd *(New Zealand)*

Mark Todd was only 24 years old when he came from New Zealand to Britain and to "Badminton" – the Mecca of three-day eventing – and won the event in 1980. He repeated his success in 1994 and has won the other "big one", Burghley, three times.

In 1984 he became Olympic champion in Los Angeles when he overhauled the leader Karen Stives of the USA in the final show jumping event. And in 1988, in Seoul, the "Kiwi" was the first rider in half a century to recapture this gold. He failed, however, in his dream of being the first to record three consecutive Olympic wins when, in 1992, his horse was injured during the competition. Regarded as the best eventing rider for more than a decade, he will try for the title again in 1996 in Atlanta, leading a strong New Zealand team which won the 1990 world title but has never won the Olympic gold.

Therefore, the prospects seem brightest for teams with strength in depth, such as the defending Olympic champions, Australia, world champions, Great Britain, or New Zealand (going for a first gold after winning silver in 1992). And for the hosts, the USA, trying to repeat their 1984 home victory.

★★★★★★★★★★★★★★★★★★★★★★★★★★★ **A Contemporary Heroine**

Dorothy Trapp *(USA)*

Dorothy Trapp, a blonde from Kentucky, proved the rising star of the 1994 world championships, finishing a close runner-up to Vaughan Jefferis. She lost the gold on the endurance phase when her horse, "Molkai", sprang a shoe. In 1995 both riders rationed their appearances at top events because of their preparation for Atlanta where newcomer Trapp might well become the first female Olympic eventing champion.

One of her main contenders should be her compatriot from Pennsylvania, Bruce Davidson. The 45 year old celebrated an unexpected comeback in 1995, winning for the first time the ultimate challenge at Badminton – 21 years after gaining his first of two world titles (1974 and '78) and well past his two 1976 and '84 Olympic team golds.

In the individual event, women, for many years, have competed on equal terms with the men in this most demanding discipline. New Zealand's Vaughan Jefferis might have won the 1994 world championships but he was followed swiftly by American Dorothy Trapp and Britons Karen Dixon and Mary King-Thomson in second, third and fourth places respectively. It would not be a big upset if they, or others such as Ireland's European Champion, Lucy Thompson, should become the first individual female Olympic champion.

Of the two most prestigious trophies in 1995, 45 year old Bruce Davidson of the USA captured "Badminton" – the most famous three-day event competition which takes its name from the stately home on the estate which houses the course. While "Burghley" – another top event based in Britain – saw a first win for popular "Kiwi", Andrew Nicholson. But defending Olympic champion, Matt Ryan, of Australia, also looked as strong as he did when winning in Barcelona.

Post-1992, meanwhile, the equestrian discipline of dressage faced the Olympic question: "To be or not to be?". Should it remain as part of the Games or not? The sport came up with the answer in the shape of a new format. Now, for the first time in Olympic history, dressage looks set to be a popular "hit" at the Games.

Cross Country action – Barcelona Games

This Cinderella story has come true because of the new freestyle final "Kur to music" – a formula which should also guarantee top TV ratings. The new era started at the 1995 European championships in Mondorf, Luxembourg, with a three day thriller featuring Holland's Anky van Grunsven and Germany's Isabelle Werth, leaving the latter to triumph narrowly. Werth's team-mate Nicole Uphoff-Becker, double Olympic champion from 1988 and '92, missed the medals because her famous mount Rembrandt, already 18 years of age, seemed to be past its peak. This might well also give 60 year old Reiner Klimke a medal chance, in Atlanta, in his seventh Games. So far he has collected six gold and two bronze medals.

The new artistic showdown of the individual event, however, does not mean that a "circus rider" has a medal chance. The top twelve still have to qualify for the final via the traditional tests: Grand Prix and GP Special. And all three parts count equally in the scoring. The Grand Prix test also remains the basis of the team competition. This is where the long-term dominance of Germany is, even in silence, likely to be challenged by the Dutch.

Unlike the other equestrian disciplines no Olympic show jumping champion has ever been able successfully to defend the title. Few would give more than short odds against Ludger Beerbaum of Germany winning in 1996. His top Atlanta challenger could be his countryman Franke Sloothaak, the Dutch-born world champion. Or Nick Skelton, the 1995 world cup winner from Britain. Or Ireland's Peter Charles. Or any of the American riders, who can always

Contemporary Heroines ★★★★★★★★★★★★★★★★★★★★★★★★★★★★★★

Anky van Grunsven *(Netherlands)*
Isabelle Werth *(Germany)*

In what may become almost the top "soap-opera" style story of the Atlanta Games, two blonde, good-looking, charming and eminently skilled horsewomen could battle for the gold in dressage. They are Anky van Grunsven, from the Netherlands, and Isabelle Werth, from Germany, both of whom live in the same lower Rhine area.

Werth, now 27, won the dress rehearsal at the 1995 European championships. It was an exciting event and a tight decision – but one close enough to leave hopes for van Grunsven, 27, too. Both could compete on top 13 year old horses at the Games: van Grunsven's "Bonfire" and Werth's "Gigolo".

In 1992, Werth took Olympic silver behind team-mate Nicole Uphoff. Van Grunsven, meanwhile, was fourth. At the 1994 world championships, when for the last time two titles were at stake, van Grunsven won the freestyle and Werth took the traditional Grand Prix Special. But now there is no room left to share and only one can be crowned "queen of dressage".

peak in front of a home crowd as in 1984 when Joe Fargis and Conrad Homfeld finished first and second.

Meanwhile Lesley McNaught-Maendli, from Switzerland, third in the 1995 world cup final, could have an outside chance of becoming the discipline's first female Olympic champion. Some of the all-time greats have never become Olympic champions. John Whitaker, of Britain, is amongst those who may, at least, still have the opportunity of changing his Olympic fortunes in 1996.

In the 1992 team show jumping event, the Netherlands surprisingly took the gold with underdogs Austria as runners-up. But experts would name the world champions from Germany as well as the Netherlands amongst the favourites – this time. Or the USA, perhaps, winning at home as in 1984. And why not Great Britain, for the first time since 1952? Or Switzerland, double European champions in 1993 and '95?

★★★★★★★★★★★★★★★★★★★★★★★★★★★★★ **A Contemporary Hero**

John Whitaker *(Great Britain)*

Of all the top equestrian nations, Britain has never won the Olympic show jumping competition. In 1992 the time seemed to be right for John Whitaker. For the first time he had been allowed by the horse's owners to present "Milton" to the Games. Dubbed the "white wonder horse" Milton and Whitaker had won the world cup twice in a row. In Barcelona both cleared the first round without penalty but returned a disastrous second round with 19.25 penalty points. Milton retired in 1995.

Whitaker, however, now 40 but still in good shape, will try to make history again in Atlanta. As will his younger brother, Michael, and the 1995 world cup winner Nick Skelton. All of them are members of the teams which have already won three European championships.

D. H. □

Retrospective

The unique combination of athlete and animal has provided some of the most emotive Olympic stories. In 1936, in Berlin, Konrad Freiherr von Wangenheim, from Germany, was thrown to the ground and broke his collarbone during the cross-country section of the three day event. He remounted and completed the course – including over 30 more obstacles, because he knew that his team would be disqualified if he did not finish. The next day the 26 year-old started the jumping final with his arm in a sling. The horse reared up, landed on the rider who again remounted and again completed without another fault, winning gold for the German team in front of a home crowd of 100,000.

A Sporting Legend ★★★★★★★★★★★★★★★★★★★★★★★★★★★★★★★★★★★★

Hans-Günther Winkler with **"Halla"** *(Germany)*

On the final day of the 1956 Games, Hans-Günther Winkler led the show jumping competition after the first round. With his mare "Halla" he had become world champion in 1954 and in 1955.

During that first round Winkler injured his groin badly. Even after an injection he could not move and had to be helped onto "Halla". But the horse, with no assistance from the rider at all, cleared the course without any penalty, giving Winkler an individual gold as well as another for the German team. "Halla" became a legend.

Winkler won three more team golds, one team silver and a team bronze, in a career which finished in 1976 with him as the most decorated Olympic show jumper of all time.

The 1936 three day event course proved extremely difficult. Of 50 horses, only 27 finished. And one British competitor, called Richard Gennys Fanshawe, accumulated 8,000 penalty marks for being over time. He lost his horse after falling at a pond and had to run two and a half miles to catch it. That paled into insignificance, however, beside the $2\frac{3}{4}$ hours it took Czech Otomar Bures to find his horse. On a more sobering note, three horses died in their efforts to complete the course.

America's Helen Dupont made three day event Olympic history in 1964 when she became the first female competitor in the discipline. The first women to compete in equestrian disciplines, in general, at the Games took part in the 1952.

No rider has ever won consecutive gold medals in show jumping. Pierre Jonquères D'Oriola is the only one to have come close, winning in 1952 and again in 1964, when, on the last day, he gave France its only golden moment. Germany's Reiner Klimke has won the most gold medals – six during the Games from 1964 – 1988.

No rider and horse combination completed the show jumping course without fault between 1928 and '76. In 1972 the team jumping competition was altered to allow four horses per team with the top three scores only counting towards the final result.

A famous equestrian Olympic "family" is that of the Roycrofts from Australia. Bill Roycroft competed at the Olympic Games of 1960 – '76. He had three sons of whom Wayne took part in 1968 and '76, Clarke in 1972 and Barry in 1976 and '88. Wayne's wife Vicki also competed in the Games of 1984 and '88.

In 1956 Stockholm, Sweden, played host to the equestrian events whilst the rest of the Olympic Games were taking place in Melbourne, Australia. This unusual state of affairs

Raimondo and Piero D'Inzeo *(Italy)*

In the dramatic 1956 individual Olympic show jumping contest, Italian brothers Raimondo and Piero D'Inzeo finished second and third and took silver in the team event, beaten only by the German "wonderhorse", "Halla", ridden by Hans Günther Winkler.

But, four years later, on home ground in Rome, both dominated the individual event. Raimondo, already world champion in 1956 and 1960, took the gold, leaving silver to his elder brother, by two years, Piero. It was a regular supporting role for Piero, who only clinched a big title once – at the 1959 European championships when Raimondo could not take part.

In equestrian sport, there have been a lot of brothers competing at top level. But 1960 was the only time that such siblings battled for Olympic gold. In the team event, now decided separately, they also won bronze in 1964 and in 1972 when they finished their successful career as the most famous Olympic jumping "double". But Raimondo went on to compete in 1976, appearing in a record eight Games.

came about because of Australia's strict animal quarantine rules. In Stockholm the severity of the cross-country course for the three day event was criticized as was the 1960 version.

Back in 1912 prizes were given to the victors as well as medals and two of the events were actually called "prize riding" and "prize jumping" although, of course, prize-money was not allowed. In 1936 the Spanish team had to return home before competition began because of the outbreak of the Spanish Civil War. And in that same year, the dressage competition included a 70 year old Austrian – General von Pongracz.

In general, the dressage event has often included some of the oldest competitors in any sport at the Games. 1948 was an unusual year for dressage, however. The event was made shorter and easier because of the lack of preparation

Henri St Cyr (centre)

EQUESTRIAN

time available to riders after World War II. Henri St Cyr of Sweden (1952 and '56) and Nicole Uphoff of Germany (1988 and '92) are the only two riders to have won the Olympic dressage title twice.

Arrangements for transporting horses to the Games, and feeding and stabling them once there, provide Olympic organizers with some of their most complex logistical problems. This has even included transporting trays of special grass to the 1992 Games. At those Games there were fears that an outbreak of a type of equine influenza in the area might prevent the competition from taking place at all. Those fears were allayed when the epidemic disappeared several months before the Games.

Background

Early attempts were made to include an equestrian event in the 1896 Olympic Games but these were abandoned due to organizational problems. Show jumping was the first equestrian discipline to appear on the Olympic programme – in 1900 – but the sport only became a regular feature from 1912 onwards. Horses, however, had seen it all before in the chariot races of the Ancient Games. There is also evidence of the partnership between horse and man in the literature of ancient China, Egypt and Persia. And equine competitions have allowed riders through the ages to hone the skills used by generations for survival, farming, hunting, travel and battle.

Yet military practices ultimately dictated the development of the sport towards its current Olympic formats. Dressage – which appears both as an individual and team sport at the Games as well as forming a section of the three day event – comes from the French generic term for the gymnastic training of horses. Originally, this training was used for war horses.

Show jumping, meanwhile, became popular towards the end of the nineteenth century with simple competitions during agricultural shows. The first of these was the Royal Dublin Show of 1864. Britain, Russia and Sweden led the way in the development of this equestrian discipline in which there were, originally, different penalties scored for fences brought down by the horses' fore and hind legs.

Parallel development took place in the USA at the Upperville and Springfield shows in Virginia and Massachusetts respectively. An international circuit soon grew and the

FEI (International Equestrian Federation) was formed in 1921 in response to a need to standardize competition regulations. As course builders became more imaginative jumping events developed into major spectator and TV attractions.

Modern three day event competitions owe their origins to endurance tests set for the cavalry. Initially, these tests were mainly on the flat but fences were added towards the late eighteenth century. The first all-round international competition (including dressage, cross country and jumping events) was held in 1902 in France and was called the "Championnat du Cheval d'Armes".

From that time a variety of formats have been tried at both major international and Olympic competitions. The most famous current three day event, "Badminton", was introduced by the Duke of Beaufort in 1949. Until that time, the discipline had not been popular in Britain, a nation which is now one of the world's best.

Equipment

Six complete pages of the FEI's rule book are devoted to the stabling and training area requirements for the equestrian disciplines at the Olympic Games. All that before the horses and riders even reach the competition arena, such is the inevitable logistical complexity of this sport. This includes stable boxes, grass and sand schooling areas, seven jumping areas with water jumps to the same specification as the competition arena, one rectangular dressage training area for every 20 competitors and a 2,000m galloping track.

Isabelle Werth (GER) on Gigolo at Barcelona Games (dressage)

EQUESTRIAN

During competition there are also strict dress codes for the riders. Take, for instance, the dressage event where it is compulsory to wear a black or dark blue tail coat, top hat, white breeches, hunting stock, gloves, black riding boots and spurs. Equally the type of saddle, bridles, bits and nosebands also come under scrutiny for each event.

The dressage arena is 60m x 20m (197ft x 66ft), predominantly of sand and with a clearly marked centre line. Its surface is rolled after every five or six riders. In show jumping, however, there is no standard course. There is a register of suitably-qualified course designers for both this discipline and the three day event courses.

Show jumping fences must not exceed 1.60m (5ft 3in.) in height whilst solid fences, in the three day event, must not be higher than 1.20m (3ft 9in.) and natural fences not higher than 1.40m (4ft 6in.). In both disciplines there is a water jump and show jumping fences can be arranged in groups of two or three called double and triple combinations.

Rules

There are three disciplines which form the Olympic competition – dressage, three day event and show jumping. All three have a team, as well as an individual, competition.

The horses' owners must be of the same nationality as the riders. Each horse must be at least seven years old and have along with its rider a certificate of "capability" indicating experience in top international competition.

The individual dressage consists of an initial grand prix test from which the top one third of riders qualify for the grand prix special. From there, a further reduction in competitors is made for the freestyle final to music.

Competitors must memorize a series of required movements to be performed in a set sequence (except in the freestyle) and are marked out of ten for each move and out of a further ten for elements such as overall pace and the rider's position. Penalty points are deducted for any error and the competitor with the highest total number of points from all three stages wins. There are an immense variety of movements and figures which include walks, trots, canters, gallops, flying changes of legs and pirouettes. The results from the grand prix competition decide the team event.

The team show jumping competition consists of 12-15 obstacles spread over a distance of 600m – 700m. The running order is drawn and one rider from the first nation is followed by the first rider from the next nation and so on. Each nation's riders jump the same course twice.

A rider is penalized four faults for a knock down, three for the first refusal at an obstacle and six for the second. A third refusal results in elimination. There are also penalties for going over the time limit. The three best riders' scores for each team are added together to ascertain the winner. In the event of a draw, a jump off against the clock over six obstacles is held to decide the medal placings.

The individual show jumping event consists of two rounds.

45 riders begin the first round of 10-12 obstacles with only 20 – scoring the least faults – qualifying for the second round over a different course. Final placings are decided by adding together the penalties incurred in both rounds. A jump off is used in the case of a draw.

Equestrian's three day event was once called the "complete test". It involves three separate elements – dressage, an endurance test (comprising four phases – two of road and tracks (16 – 20km each), a steeplechase (of over 3,000m) and a cross country (of over 7,400m)), and show jumping. Each element takes place on a different day (with two days for the dressage section). Final results are obtained by adding together the penalty points incurred in each of the three elements. The winner is the competitor with the lowest number of points. During the event the horses, to safeguard their well-being, must undergo three fitness inspections as well as two veterinary tests.

For the separate team event the winner is decided by adding together the penalties of the top three riders in each team with the team scoring the least penalties winning.

Atlanta format

Riders must be at least 18 years old to take part in the show jumping and three day event competitions but they can compete in the dressage from the age of 16. A total of 225 riders and 255 horses are eligible for the Games and have reached minimum qualifying standards at major international events including the world equestrian games of 1994. Riders and horses can qualify as combinations for the three day event and dressage and as either a combination, or separately, for the show jumping. There are also some combinations who have qualified by means of "wild cards" issued by the IOC.

Each country can enter a maximum of seven competitors and seven horses in the three day event, four competitors and six horses in the show jumping and four competitors and four horses in the dressage. In the dressage and three day event team competitions nations compete with either three or four horses and three or four riders. 11 nations compete in the dressage team event and 16 in the three day event team competition (which for the first time in 1996 will be decided as a separate event). Further nations are represented in the individual events. The show jumping team event features 17 nations with teams of four riders and six horses with further nations represented in the individual competition.

Equestrian venue at the Georgia International Horse Park.

Venue

All the equestrian events in Atlanta take place at Georgia International Horse Park in Conyers which is 53km (33 miles) east of town. There is a spectator capacity of 29,700 in the main stadium but further spectator capacity along the cross country course of the three day event. The 461 hectare (1,139 acre) site, at Conyers, will become a permanent equestrian centre after the Games, featuring stables, dressage and jumping arenas, a track course, trails, a steeplechase oval and training facilities. The new Olympic event of mountain biking will also be held at the same venue as well as some elements of the modern pentathlon.

MEDALLISTS (by nation)

	Gold	Men's Silver	Bronze	Total
Sweden	17	8	14	39
Germany	16	12	11	39
United States	8	15	11	34
France	11	12	9	32
FRG	11	5	9	25
Italy	7	9	7	23
Great Britain	5	7	9	21
Switzerland	4	8	7	19
Soviet Union	6	5	4	15
Netherlands	6	5	1	12
Belgium	4	2	6	12
Mexico	2	1	4	7
Australia	4	1	2	7
Poland	1	3	2	6
Denmark	-	4	1	5
New Zealand	2	1	2	5
Canada	1	1	2	4
Austria	1	1	1	3
Portugal	-	-	3	3
Spain	1	1	-	2
Chile	-	2	-	2
Romania	-	1	1	2
Czechoslovakia	1	-	-	1
Japan	1	-	-	1
Argentina	-	1	-	1
Bulgaria	-	1	-	1
Norway	-	1	-	1
Hungary	-	-	1	1
	109[1]	107	107[2]	323

[1] Two golds in 1900 high jump
[2] No bronze in 1932 three day team event

ATLANTA SCHEDULE

Venue: Georgia International Horse Park

Date	Description	Round	Start	End
Dressage				
27 Jul	team (op)	Rd 1	8:30	17:05
		Rd 2		
28 Jul	team (op)	Rd 3	8:30	17:45
		Rd 4 (FINAL)		
31 Jul	ind (op)	Rd 1	8:30	17:30
		Rd 2		
3 Aug	ind freestyle (op)	FINAL	9:00	12:20
Jumping				
29 Jul	ind (op)	Q/fying	8:00	12:30
1 Aug	team	Rd 1	8:30	19:00
		Rd 2 (FINAL)		
4 Aug	ind (op)	s/finals	10:00	16:00
	ind (op)	FINAL		
Three Day				
21 Jul	team dressage (op)	Rd 1	9:00	17:50
22 Jul	team dressage (op)	Rd 2	9:00	17:50
23 Jul	team endurance (op)		7:00	11:30
	ind dressage (op)	Rd 1	15:00	18:00
24 Jul	team jumping (op)		9:00	12:30
	ind dressage (op)	Rd 2	15:00	18:00
25 Jul	ind endurance (op)		7:30	11:00
26 Jul	ind jumping (op)	FINAL	11:00	13:00

MEDALLISTS

EQUESTRIAN*

* all equestrian events are open to men and women

Dressage Individual

Year	Gold	C'ntry	Points	Silver	C'ntry	Points	Bronze	C'ntry	Points
1912	Carl Bonde	SWE	15	Gustaf Adolf Boltenstern	SWE	21	Hans von Blixen-Finecke	SWE	32
1920	Janne Lundblad	SWE	27.937	Bertil Sandström	SWE	26.312	Hans von Rosen	SWE	25.125
1924	Ernst De Linder	SWE	276.4	Bertil Sandström	SWE	275.8	Xavier Lesage	FRA	265.8
1928	Carl Friedrich Freiherr von Langen	GER	237.42	Charles Marion	FRA	231	Ragnar Olson	SWE	229.78
1932	François Lesage	FRA	343.75	Charles Marion	FRA	305.42	Hiram Tuttle	USA	300.5
1936	Heinz Pollay	GER	1760	Friedrich Gerhard	GER	1745.5	Alois Podhajsky	AUT	1721.5
1948	Hans Moser	SUI	492.5	André Jousseaume	FRA	480	Gustaf Boltenstern	SWE	477.5
1952	Henri St Cyr	SWE	561	Lis Hartel	DEN	541.5	André Jousseaume	FRA	541
1956	Henri St Cyr	SWE	860	Lis Hartel	DEN	850	Liselotte Linsenhoff	GER	832
1960	Sergei Filatov	URS	2144	Gustav Fischer	SUI	2087	Josef Neckermann	GER	2082
1964	Henri Chammartin	SUI	1504	Harry Boldt	GER	1503	Sergei Filatov	URS	1486
1968	Ivan Kizimov	URS	1572	Josef Neckermann	FRG	1546	Reiner Klimke	FRG	1537
1972	Liselotte Linsenhoff	FRG	1229	Elena Petushkova	URS	1185	Josef Neckermann	FRG	1177
1976	Christine Stückelberger	SUI	1468	Harry Boldt	FRG	1435	Reiner Klimke	FRG	1395
1980	Elisabeth Theurer	AUT	1370	Yuri Kovshov	URS	1300	Viktor Ugriumov	URS	1234
1984	Reiner Klimke	FRG	1504	Anne Grethe Jensen	DEN	1442	Otto Hofer	SUI	1364
1988	Nicole Uphoff	FRG	1521	Margitt Otto-Crépin	FRA	1462	Christine Stückelberger	SUI	1417
1992	Nicole Uphoff	GER	1626	Isabelle Werth	GER	1551	Klaus Balkenhol	GER	1515
1996									

Dressage Team

Year	Gold	C'ntry	Points	Silver	C'ntry	Points	Bronze	C'ntry	Points
1928	Hermann Linkenbach Carl Friedrich Freiherr von Langen Eugen von Lotzbeck	GER	669.72	Carl Bonde Janne Lundblad Ragnar Olson	SWE	650.86	Gérard Le Heux Jan van Reede Pierre Versteegh	NED	642.96
1932	André Jousseaume François Lesage Charles Marion	FRA	2818.75	Gustaf-Adolf Boltenstern Jr Thomas Byström Bertil Sandström	SWE	2678	Isaac Kitts Alvin Moore Hiram Tuttle	USA	2576.75
1936	Friedrich Gerhard Heinz Pollay Hermann von Oppeln-Bronikowski	GER	5074	Gerard de Ballore Daniel Gillois André Jousseaume	FRA	4846	Gregor Adlercreutz Sven Colliander Folke Sandström	SWE	4660.5
1948	Maurice Buret André Jousseaume Jean Saint-Fort Paillard	FRA	1269	Robert Borg Frank Henry Earl Thomson	USA	1256	Luis Mena e Silva Fernando Pais Franciso Valadas	POR	1182
1952	Gustaf-Adolf Boltenstern Jr Henri St Cyr Gehnäll Persson	SWE	1597.5	Henri Chammartin Gustav Fischer Gottfried Trachsel	SUI	1579	Heinz Pollay Fritz Thiedemann Ida von Nagel	GER	1501
1956	Gustaf-Adolf Boltenstern Jr Henri St Cyr Gehnäll Persson	SWE	2475	Anneliese Küppers Liselotte Linsenhoff Hannelore Weygand	GER	2346	Henri Chammartin Gustav Fischer Gottfried Trachsel	SUI	2346
1964	Harry Boldt Reiner Klimke Josef Neckermann	GER	2558	Henri Chammartin Gustav Fischer Marianne Gossweiler	SUI	2526	Sergei Filatov Ivan Kalita Ivan Kizimov	URS	2311
1968	Reiner Klimke Liselotte Linsenhoff Josef Neckermann	FRG	2699	Ivan Kalita Ivan Kizimov Elena Petuchkova	URS	2657	Henri Chammartin Gustav Fischer Marianne Gossweiler	SUI	2547
1972	Ivan Kalita Ivan Kizimov Elena Petuchkova	URS	5095	Liselotte Linsenhoff Josef Neckermann Karin Schlüter	FRG	5083	Ulla Håkansson Ninna Swaab Maud Von Rosen	SWE	4849

/continued on next page

Year	Gold	C'ntry	Points	Silver	C'ntry	Points	Bronze	C'ntry	Points
1976	Harry Boldt	FRG	5155	Ulrich Lehmann	SUI	4684	Hilda Gurney	USA	4647
	Gabriela Grillo			Doris Ramseier			Edith Master		
	Reiner Klimke			Christine Stückelberger			Dorothy Morkis		
1980	Yuri Kovshov	URS	4383	Georgi Gadzev	BUL	3580	Anghelache Donescu	ROM	2945
	Viktor Ugriumov			Svetoslav Ivanov			Petre Rosca		
	Vera Misevich			Peter Mandadzhiev			Dumitru Veliku		
1984	Reiner Klimke	FRG	4955	Amy-Cathérine de	SUI	4673	Ingamay Bylund	SWE	4630
	Herbert Krug			Bary			Ulla Håkanson		
	Uwe Sauer			Otto Hofer			Louise Nathhorst		
				Christine Stückelberger					
1988	Ann-Kathrin	FRG	4302	Otto Hofer	SUI	4164	Cynthia Ishoy	CAN	3969
	Linsenhoff			Daniel Ramseier			Ashley Nicoll		
	Monica Theodorescu			Christine Stückelberger			Gina Smith		
	Nicole Uphoff								
	Reiner Klimke								
1992	Klaus Balkenhol	GER	5224	Tineke Bartels	NED	4742	Charlotte Bredahl	USA	4643
	Monica Theodorescu			Ellen Bontje			Robert Dover		
	Nicole Uphoff			Annemarie Sanders			Carol Lavell		
	Isabelle Werth			Anky van Grunsven			Michael Poulin		
1996									

Three Day Event Individual

Year	Gold	C'ntry	Points	Silver	C'ntry	Points	Bronze	C'ntry	Points
1912	Axel Nordlander	SWE	46.59	Friedrich von Rochow	GER	46.42	Jean Cariou	FRA	46.32
1920	Helmer Mörner	SWE	1775	Åge Lundström	SWE	1738.75	Ettore Caffaratti	ITA	1733.75
1924	Adolph van der Voort	NED	1976	Frode Kirkebjerg	DEN	1853.5	Sloan Doak	USA	1845.5
	van Zijp								
1928	Charles Pahud de	NED	1969.82	Gerard de Kruijf	NED	1967.26	Bruno Neumann	GER	1944.42
	Mortanges								
1932	Charles Pahud de	NED	1813.83	Earl Thomson	USA	1811	Clarence von Rosen	SWE	1809.42
	Mortanges								
1936	Ludwig Stubbendorff	GER	37.7	Earl Thomson	USA	99.9	Hans Mathiesen-	DEN	102.2
							Lunding		
1948	Bernard Chevallier	FRA	4	Frank Henry	USA	21	Robert Selfelt	SWE	25
1952	Hans Blixen-Finecke	SWE	28.55	Guy Lefrant	FRA	54.1	Willi Büsing	GER	55.5
1956	Petrus Kastenman	SWE	66.53	August Lütke-	GER	84.87	Francis Weldon	GBR	85.48
				Westhues					
1960	Lawrence Morgan	AUS	7.15	Neale Lavis	AUS	16.5	Anton Bühler	SUI	51.21
1964	Mauro Checcoli	ITA	64.4	Carlos Alberto	ARG	56.4	Fritz Ligges	GER	49.2
				Moratorio					
1968	Jean-Jacques Guyon	FRA	38.46	Derek Allhusen	GBR	41.61	Michael Page	USA	52.31
1972	Richard Meade	GBR	57.73	Alessandro Argenton	ITA	43.33	Jan Jönsson	SWE	39.67
1976	Edmund Coffin	USA	114.99	John Plumb	USA	125.85	Karl Schultz	FRG	129.45
1980	Frederico Euro Roman	ITA	108.6	Alexander Blinov	URS	120.8	Yuri Salnikov	URS	151.6
1984	Mark Todd	NZL	51.6	Karen Stives	USA	54.2	Virginia Holgate	GBR	56.8
1988	Mark Todd	NZL	42.60	Ian Stark	GBR	52.80	Virginia Leng	GBR	62.00
1992	Matthew Ryan	AUS	70.00	Herbert Blocker	GER	81.30	Robert Blyth Tait	NZL	87.60
1996									

Three Day Event Team

Year	Gold	C'ntry	Points	Silver	C'ntry	Points	Bronze	C'ntry	Points
1912	Nils Adlercreutz	SWE	139.06	Eduard von Lütcken	GER	138.48	Guy Henry	USA	137.33
	Ernst Casparsson			Friedrich von Rochow			Benjamin Lear		
	Axel Nordlander			Richard Graf von			John Montgomery		
				Schaesberg-Tannheim					
1920	Åge Lundström	SWE	5057.5	Giulio Cacciandra	ITA	4735	Jules Bonvalet	BEL	4560
	Helmer Mörner			Ettore Caffaratti			Roger Moeremans d'Emaus		
	Georg von Braun			Garibaldi Spighi			Oswald Lints		
1924	Gerard de Kruijf	NED	5297.5	Gustaf Hagelin	SWE	4743.5	Alessandro Alvisi	ITA	4512.5
	Charles Pahud de			Claës König			Emanuele di Pralormo		
	Mortanges			Carl Torsten Sylvan			Beraudo		
	Adolf van der Voort						Alberto Lombardi		
	van Zijp								

Year	Gold	C'ntry	Points	Silver	C'ntry	Points	Bronze	C'ntry	Points
1928	Gerard de Kruijf	NED	5865.68	Wilhelm Johansen	NOR	5395.68	Michał Antoniewicz	POL	5067.92
	Charles Pahud de			Bjart Ording			Karol Rómmel		
	Mortanges			Arthur Qist			Józef Trenkwald		
	Adolf van der Voort								
	van Zijp								
1932	Edwin Argo	USA	5038.083	Charles Pahud de	NED	4689.08			
	Harry Chamberlin			Mortanges					
	Earl Thomson			Karel Johan					
				Schummelketel					
				Aernout van Lennep					
1936	Rudolf Lippert	GER	676.65	Zdzisław Kawecki	POL	991.7	Richard Fanshawe	GBR	9195.5
	Ludwig Stubbendorff			Seweryn Kulesza			Edward Howard-Vyse		
	Konrad Freiherr von			Henryk Rojcewicz			Alec Scott		
	Wangenheim								
1948	Charles Anderson	USA	161.5	Robert Selfeldt	SWE	165	Raúl Campero	MEX	305.25
	Frank Henry			Olof Stahre			Humberto Mariles Cortés		
	Earl Thomson			Sigurd Svensson			Joaquin Solano Chagoya		
1952	Folke Frölén	SWE	221.94	Wilhelm Büsing	GER	235.49	Charles Hough	USA	587.16
	Olof Stahre			Otto Rothe			Walter Staley		
	Hans von Blixen-Finecke Jr			Klaus Wagner			John Wofford		
1956	Albert Hill	GBR	355.48	August Lütke-	GER	475.91	James Elder	CAN	572.72
	Arthur Rook			Westhues			Brian Herbison		
	Francis Weldon			Otto Rothe			John Rumble		
				Klaus Wagner					
1960	Neil Lavis	AUS	128.18	Anton Bühler	SUI	386.02	Jack Le Goff	FRA	515.71
	Laurence Morgan			Rudolf Günthardt			Jehan Le Roy		
	James Roycroft			Hans Schwarzenbach			Guy Lefrant		
1964	Paolo Angioni	ITA	85.8	Kevin Freeman	USA	65.86	Horst Karsten	GER	56.73
	Mauro Checcoli			Michael Page			Fritz Ligges		
	Giuseppe Ravano			Michael Plumb			Gerhard Schulz		
1968	Derek Allhusen	GBR	175.93	Michael Page	USA	245.87	Brien Cobcroft	AUS	331.36
	Reuben Jones			Michael Plumb			Wayne Roycroft		
	Richard Meade			James Wofford			William Roycroft		
1972	Mary Gordon-Watson	GBR	95.53	Bruce Davidson	USA	10.81	Ludwig Goessing	FRG	18
	Richard Meade			Kevin Freeman			Harry Klugmann		
	Bridget Parker			Michael Plumb			Karl Schultz		
1976	Edmund Coffin	USA	441	Herbert Blocker	FRG	584.6	Mervyn Bennett	AUS	599.54
	Bruce Davidson			Helmut Rethemeier			Wayne Roycroft		
	Michael Plumb			Karl Schultz			William Roycroft		
1980	Alexander Blinov	URS	457	Anna Casagrande	ITA	656.2	David Barcena Rios	MEX	1172.85
	Yuri Salnikov			Euro Federico Roman			Manuel Mendivil Yocupicio		
	Valeri Volkov			Mauro Roman			José Luis Perez Soto		
1984	Torrance Fleischmann	USA	186	Lucinda Green	GBR	189.2	Claus Erhorn	FRG	234
	Michael Plumb			Virginia Holgate			Dietmar Hogrefe		
	Karen Stives			Ian Stark			Bettina Overesch		
1988	Matthias Baumann	FRG	225.95	Virginia Leng	GBR	256.80	Andrew Bennie	NZL	271.20
	Ralf Ehrenbrink			Mark Phillips			Marges Knighton		
	Claus Erhorn			Ian Stark			Tinks Pottinger		
	Thies Kaspareit			Karen Straker			Mark Todd		
1992	David Green	AUS	288.60	Victoria Latta	NZL	290.80	Matthias Baumann	GER	300.30
	Andrew Hoy			Andrew Nicholson			Herbert Blocker		
	Gillian Rolton			Blyth Tait			Ralf Ehrenbrink		
	Matthew Ryan			Mark Todd			Cord Hermann Mysegaes		
1996									

Jumping Individual

Year	Gold	C'ntry	Time/ Faults	Silver	C'ntry	Time/ Faults	Bronze	C'ntry	Time/ Faults
1900	Aimé Haegeman	BEL	2:16.0	Georges van de Poele	BEL	2:17.6	M de Champsavin	FRA	2:26.0
1912	Jean Cariou	FRA	186	Rabod Wilhelm von	GER	186	Emanuel de	BEL	185
				Kröcher			Blommaert		
1920	Tommaso Lequio Di	ITA	2	Alessandro Valerio	ITA	3	Carl-Gustaf	SWE	4
	Assaba						Lewenhaupt		

/continued on next page 217

Year	Gold	C'ntry	Time/Faults	Silver	C'ntry	Time/Faults	Bronze	C'ntry	Time/Faults
1924	Alphonse Gemusens	SUI	6	Tommaso Lequio	ITA	8.75	Adam Królikiewicz	POL	10
1928	František Ventura	TCH	0	Pierre Bertran	FRA	2	Charley Kuhn	SUI	4
1932	Takeichi Nishi	JPN	8	Harry Chamberlin	USA	12	Clarence van Rosen	SWE	16
1936	Kurt Hasse	GER	4	Henri Rang	ROM	4	Joseph von Platthy	HUN	8
1948	Humberto Mariles Cortés	MEX	6.25	Rubén Urizac	MEX	8	Jean François D'Orgeix	FRA	8
1952	Pierre Jonquères D'Oriola	FRA	0	Oscar Cristi	CHL	4	Fritz Thiedemann	GER	8
1956	Hans-Günther Winkler	GER	4	Raimondo D'Inzeo	ITA	8	Piero D'Inzeo	ITA	11
1960	Raimondo D'Inzeo	ITA	12	Piero D'Inzeo	ITA	8	David Broome	GBR	23
1964	Pierre Jonquères D'Oriola	FRA	9	Hermann Schridde	ITA	13.75	Peter Robeson	GBR	16
1968	William Steinkraus	USA	4	Marion Coakes	GBR	8	David Broome	GBR	12
1972	Graziano Mancinelli	ITA	8	Ann Moore	GBR	8	Neal Shapiro	USA	8
1976	Alwin Schockemöhle	FRG	0	Michel Vaillancourt	GBR	12	François Mathy	BEL	12
1980	Jan Kowalczyk	POL	8	Nikolai Korolkov	CAN	9.5	Joaquin Perez Heras	MEX	12
1984	Joe Fargis	USA	4	Conrad Homfeld	USA	4	Heidi Robbiani	SUI	0
1988	Pierre Durand	FRA	1.25	Greg Best	USA	4	Karsten Huck	FRG	4
1992	Ludger Beerbaum	GER	0.00	Piet Raymakers	NED	0.25	Norman Dello Joio	USA	4.75
1996									

Jumping Team

Year	Gold	C'ntry	Time/Faults	Silver	C'ntry	Time/Faults	Bronze	C'ntry	Time/Faults
1912	Gustaf Kilman Carl-Gustaf Lewenhaupt Hans von Rosen	SWE	25	Michel d'Astafort Jean Cariou Bernard Meyer	FRA	32	Ernst-Hubertus Deloch Sigismund Freyer Wilhelm von Hohenau	GER	40
1920	Claes König Daniel Norling Hans von Rosen	SWE	14	André Coumans Herman de Gaiffier d'Hestroy Henri Laame	BEL	16.25	Alessandro Alvisi Giulio Cacciandra Ettore Caffaratti	ITA	18.75
1924	Åge Lundström Axel Ståhle Åke Thelning	SWE	42.25	Hans Bühler Alphonse Gemuseus Werner Stüber	SUI	50	José Mouzsinho d'Albuquerque Antonio Borges d'Almeida Hélder de Sousa Martins	POR	53
1928	Marquis de los Trujillos Julio Garcia Fernandez José Navarro Morenes	ESP	4	Michał Antoniewicz Kazimierz Gżowski Kazimierz Szosland	POL	8	Carl Björnstjerna Ernst Hallberg Karl Hansen	SWE	10
1932	no riders completed course								
1936	Heinz Brandt Kurt Hasse Marten von Barnekow	GER	44	Jan Adrianus de Bruine Johan Jacob Greter Henri Louis van Schaik	NED	51.5	José Baltrão Luis Marquéz de Funchal Luis Mena e Silva	POR	56
1948	Humberto Mariles Cortés Rubén Uriza Castro Alberto Valdes Lacarra	MEX	34.25	Jaime Garcia Cruz Marcelino Gavilán y Ponce de Leon José Navarro Morenes	ESP	56.5	Arthur Carr Harry Llewellyn Henry Nicoll	GBR	67
1952	Harry Llewellyn Douglas Stewart Wilfred White	GBR	40.75	Oscar Cristi Ricardo Echeverria Cesar Mendoza	CHL	45.75	Arthur McCashin John Russell William Steinkraus	USA	52.25
1956	Alfons Lütke-Westhues Fritz Thiedemann Hans-Günther Winkler	GER	40	Piero D'Inzeo Raimondo D'Inzeo Salvatore Oppes	ITA	66	Peter Robeson Patricia Smythe Wilfred White	GBR	69
1960	Alwin Schockemöhle Fritz Thiedemann Hans-Günther Winkler	GER	46.5	Frank Chapot George Morris William Steinkraus	USA	66	Piero D'Inzeo Raimondo D'Inzeo Antonio Oppes	ITA	80.5
1964	Kurt Jarasinski Hermann Schridde Hans-Günther Winkler	GER	68.5	Pierre Jonquères D'Oriola Janou Lefevre Guy Lefrant	FRA	77.75	Piero D'Inzeo Raimondo D'Inzeo Graziano Mancinelli	ITA	88.5
1968	James Day James Elder Thomas Gayford	CAN	102.75	Pierre Jonquères D'Oriola Janou Lefevre Jean Rozier	FRA	110.25	Alwin Schockemöhle Hermann Schridde Hans-Günther Winkler	FRG	117.25

Year	Gold	C'ntry	Time/Faults	Silver	C'ntry	Time/Faults	Bronze	C'ntry	Time/Faults
1972	Fritz Ligges Hartwig Steenken Gerhard Wiltfang Hans-Günther Winkler	FRG	32	Frank Chapot Kathryn Kusner Neal Shapiro William Steinkraus	USA	32.25	Piero D'Inzeo Raimondo D'Inzeo Graziano Mancinelli Vittorio Orlandi	ITA	48
1976	Hubert Parot Michel Roche Marc Roguet Marcel Rozier	FRA	40	Alwin Schockemohle Paul Schockemohle Sönke Sönksen Hans-Günther Winkler	FRG	44	Edgar Gupper François Mathy Stanny van Paeschen Eric Wauters	BEL	63
1980	Viktor Asmaev Viacheslav Chukanov Nikolai Korolkov Viktor Poganovski	URS	20.25	Janusz Bobik Wiesław Hartman Jan Kowalczyk Marian Kozicki	POL	56	Valencia Gerardo Tazzer Jesus Gomez Portugal Joaquin Perez Heras Alberto Valdes Lacarra	MEX	59.75
1984	Leslie Burr Joe Fargis Conrad Homfeld Melanie Smith	USA	12	Timothy Grubb Steven Smith John Whitaker Michael Whitaker	USA	36.75	Fritz Ligges Peter Luther Paul Schockemöhle Franke Sloothaak	FRG	39.25
1988	Ludger Beerbaum Wolfgang Brinkmann Dirk Hafemeister Franke Sloothaak	FRG	17.25	Greg Best Joe Fargis Lisa Jacquin Anne Kursinski	USA	20.5	Hubert Bourdy Frédéric Cottier Pierre Durand Michel Robert	FRA	27.5
1992	Jos Lansink Piet Raymakers Bert Romp Jan Tops	NED	12	Boris Boor Thomas Fruhmann Jorg Muntzner Hugo Simon	AUT	16.75	Hubert Bourdy Herve Godignon Eric Navet Michel Robert	FRA	24.75
1996									

Fencing

Stars to Watch

by Graham Morrison

Landmark women's épée

ERIC Srecki of France, the reigning men's épée Olympic and world champion, and Germany's Arnd Schmitt, the 1988 Olympic winner, look set to generate the most interest amongst the two to three dozen fencers with serious expectations of medals in Atlanta.

France has invested heavily in Srecki and clearly expects him to deliver gold. The 30 year old Schmitt, meanwhile, topped world cup rankings in the 1994/95 season, featuring in virtually every important final and now looks ready to retake the title. Yet Sandro Cuomo, of Italy, with his spectacular flying attacks, and Russia's Pavel Kolobkov as well as Spaniard Fernando Pena could all have a chance.

A Contemporary Hero ★★★★★★★★★★★★★★★★★★★★★★★★★★★★★★★★★★★★

Eric Srecki *(France)*

Reigning men's Olympic and world épée champion, Eric Srecki, is by far the most successful of the current crop of French fencers. He took up fencing in 1970 and entered the French national squad in 1985. In that same year he won his first of four French national championships titles. A powerful left-hander, since 1987 he has collected four gold, three silver and one bronze medal at world and Olympic level.

Srecki is now 31 years old, married with two children and works for a leading French bank in Paris where he lives and trains. Atlanta could be his last Games and he clearly intends to end at the top with a successful defence of the title. In the 1994/95 season he won the world cup and ended no.3 on the world rankings list. During that season he won competitions in Montreal, Berne and Lugano and finished second in Venezuela.

Atlanta is a landmark for the sport as women's épée will be contested for the first time at the Games. And predictions of the inaugural winners are made more complicated by the fact that the 1995 world championships in The Hague, Holland, did not reflect that season's performances as world no.1 and

★★★★★★★★★★★★★★★★★★★★★★★★★★★★ **A Contemporary Heroine**

Taymi Chappe *(Cuba)*

Taymi Chappe, the 1994/95 season world cup winner and world no.1 at women's épée, surprised herself when she won the 1990 world championships in spectacular style in Lyon, France, fencing for Cuba, her country of origin. Then four years ago, Chappe, of African descent, married a Spaniard and moved to Madrid.

After her 1990 win and her marriage, Chappe dropped out of sight for a while. But in 1994 she returned with some impressively consistent performances which brought four gold medals in world cup events (in Brazil, Holland, Portugal and Italy) and two bronze medals (in Australia and Switzerland).

Fencing for the "Sala de Armas de Madrid" club, 27 year old Chappe has matured as a fencer but lost none of her competitiveness, settling into the Spanish circuit to end the 1994/95 season at the top of the domestic rankings. In addition, she took the Spanish national women's épée crown and a team gold for her club.

world cup holder Taymi Chappe crashed to 17th place while eventual winner Joanna Jakimiuk of Poland had to settle for 50th place in the world rankings.

Leading Olympic performances can be expected from both. But first they must overcome the defensive style of Gyongyi Szalay, who leads the tough Hungarian squad and the petite Swiss fencer Gianna Buerki, a specialist in ducking the longer reach of taller opponents. Other contenders include Laura Flessel and Sophie Moresee of France, Kim of Korea and China's Gao Huigi.

Four years ago, in Barcelona, Giovanna Trillini won the women's foil gold. She returns to the Olympic scene in Atlanta at the head of a highly competitive Italian squad who have focused their whole effort on Trillini's defence. In Barcelona, though, Trillini had a near miss as China's Wang Huifeng came within an ace of gold.

1988 Olympic winner Anja Fichtel-Mauritz of Germany will also challenge her strongly this time. And the home crowd will spur on the increasingly successful USA team. American Ann Marsh made 10th place in The Hague in July 1995 and was gold medallist in the 1995 Pan American Games held in Argentina. But they will all need to treat Romanian Laura Badea with respect. At the last world championships she surprised even herself by eliminating first Fichtel-Mauritz, then Italian world no.1, Valentina Vessali, before pushing Trillini into second place.

Current Olympic men's foil champion Phillipe Omnes of France has struggled since Barcelona. That leaves the reigning world champion Dmitri Chevtchenko of Russia, 1994 world champion Roland Tuckers, or Elvis Gregory Gil, both of

Cuba, amongst those fighting for the title. In the last world championships finals Tuckers and Gregory suffered surprise defeats by José Guerra who made history as the first Spanish men's foil world finalist. Although ultimately outclassed by Chevtchenko, Guerra cannot be ignored.

Recent rule changes, meanwhile, have transformed the sabre as a weapon and could make it the most exciting competition of all. The final stages will see Italy, Hungary, Russia and Germany fighting for supremacy. 1994 World champion Felix Becker will put up a strong defence of his title for Germany but the Russian Grigorii Kirienko, four times world champion (1989, '91, '93 and '95) and Barcelona team gold medallist, will want to add an individual Olympic gold to his medals tally. Hot on his heels will be the Italian Tohni Terenzi and defending Olympic champion Bence Szabó of Hungary, both popular with spectators.

G. M. □

Retrospective

Hungary's Aladár Gerevich won seven fencing gold medals in the sabre individual and team events between 1932 and '60 in six consecutive Games – a record length of Olympic medal-winning career for any athlete in any sport. And Hungary won every sabre team gold between 1928 and '60.

Another of the sport's all time greats was Edoardo Mangiarotti of Italy with 13 medals in total. He was naturally right-handed but was forced by his father to fence left-handed because it was felt to be an advantage.

Fencing, meanwhile, was one of the first sports in which professionals competed at the Games. There were competi-

A Sporting Legend ★★★★★★★★★★★★★★★★★★★★★★★★★★★★★★★★★★

Christian D'Oriola (France)

Most lists of post World War II sporting greats would include Christian D'Oriola of France representing the sport of fencing. Never far from the top, D'Oriola won a total of 19 world medals including four world championship individual foil golds (1947, '49, '53 and '54) as well as two Olympic individual golds (1952 and '56).

D'Oriola came from such a sporting family that another branch excelled in equestrian events. One of three children, he was made to start fencing in 1937 at the age of eight. At nine, he was given the option of stopping but declined and, at 18, won his first world foil title. He concentrated on international fencing winning more world titles than his own domestic French championships. Ill health kept him out of the sport in 1950 and '51 and after the 1956 Olympic Games he retired only to return in 1960 to finish eighth. But for these breaks, his tally of wins would have been greater. D'Oriola never won a bronze medal.

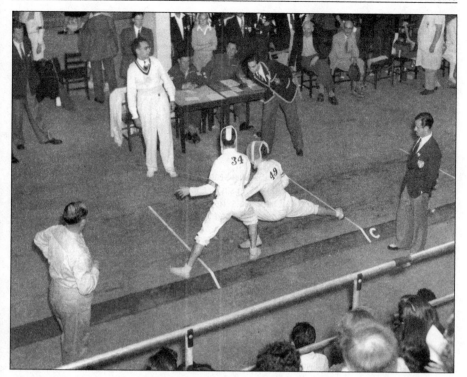

tions for fencing teachers or "masters" in both 1896 and 1900. Many of the rules for international fencing were codified in 1912. In the Olympic Games of that year France and Italy refused to enter some of the events because their suggested changes to the rules were rejected.

Passions in Olympic fencing have also been known to boil over. In 1924 a real-life duel was fought as a result of the sabre team final. A Hungarian judge called Kovács had an argument, during the final, with the Italian fencer Oreste Puliti. Puliti was disqualified as a result and struck Kovács a blow to the face. Months later the two fought a duel which only finished when spectators pulled the two apart. Both were badly wounded.

D'Oriola (France) and Zulfkar (Egypt) at Wembley 1948.

Background

Anyone brought up on a diet of old black-and-white "three musketeer" movies would expect the French to be near the top of the Olympic fencing medal tables. They would be right, together with Italy and Hungary. More recently Germany and the former Soviet Union have also had top international contenders. Of course, modern Olympic fencing with its protective clothing and electronic scoring is far removed from its dramatized counterpart.

FENCING

Sporting Legends ★★★★★★★★★★★★★★★★★★★★★★★★★★★★★★★★

Aldo and Nedo Nadi *(Italy)*

The Italian brothers Aldo and Nedo Nadi are strong candidates for the accolade of being the best fencers of all time. Aldo, born in 1899 and the son of a leading Italian fencing master, dominated the sport in the years around World War I. His older brother, Nedo, set an Olympic record for fencing golds in one Games that should stand for ever. In 1920, in Antwerp, he collected five first places – two individual (foil and épée) and three for team events. Aldo had to settle for three Olympic team gold medals and the individual sabre silver after which both brothers turned professional.

Had they remained amateur, their tally would have been staggering. Aldo seldom competed outside of professional events from then onwards but, in single encounters, remained undefeated in any weapon for 12 years until he ran out of opponents. He only fought his brother once, in 1935 in a demonstration match. Their father was spectating and Nedo insisted that it should end in a draw, which it did.

Fencing has been part of the Olympic Games of the modern era since the outset in 1896 with men's foil and sabre events followed by the épée in 1900. A women's foil event was added in 1924, a women's foil team event in 1960 and women's épée events will take place in 1996 for the first time. Electronic scoring was introduced for the épée as long ago as 1936 but came later for the foil (1956) and sabre (1992).

Some bygone fencing celebrities (but not Olympic competitors) include Winston Churchill, Douglas Fairbanks Jnr, and H.M. King Hussain of Jordan. Dame Mary Glen Haig, of Great Britain, was an Olympic fencer in 1956 and later became one of the first female members of the IOC.

There are examples of swords used as weapons dating back to the bronze age. In the Middle Ages swords were generally heavy and clumsy weapons because opponents wore heavy body armour. Only later, when they were used in close-quarter fighting did they become lighter and swordsmen needed to become more skilful.

From these origins, fencing grew first as an art, a duelling weapon and then as a modern competitive sport. Masks were added in the eighteenth century. Fencing schools sprang up around Europe and then the British army adopted fencing as part of its physical training in 1861. The FEI (International Fencing Federation) was formed in 1913 continuing the process of standardizing international rules for the sport.

Equipment

Fencing takes place on a piste which is 1.8m (5ft 10in.) wide and 14m (over 45ft) long. Its surface is smooth, even and generally made of wood covered by a plastic or rubber synthetic. This is covered by a compound with a metallic base in order to neutralize the scoring system if a weapon hits the floor. There are various boundary markings on the piste (see diagram).

The three fencing weapons or swords are called the foil, épée and sabre. Each has a flexible steel blade which fencers hold by its "hilt" or handle which is itself covered by a convex metal guard to protect the fencing hand. The foil and épée are very similar-shaped weapons although the latter is a little heavier and stiffer and its blade is triangular in section rather than the rectangular section of the foil. Sabres, meanwhile, are turned over on themselves at the far end of the blade. Each weapon is wired to record hits electrically.

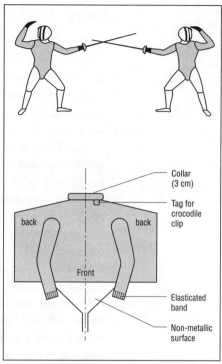

Electric sabre target and metallic vest

Fencers wear white clothing including a jacket, breeches, long white socks, a mask (of fine wire mesh which also has a protective "bib"), a glove and, in the case of the foil and sabre events, a metallic overjacket which conducts electricity as part of the scoring system and is worn over the jacket, covering the valid target area. A wire leads from this garment to the scoring device and is called the "body wire". Spectators can see when a hit has been scored because a lamp lights up on the scoring equipment.

Fencing piste

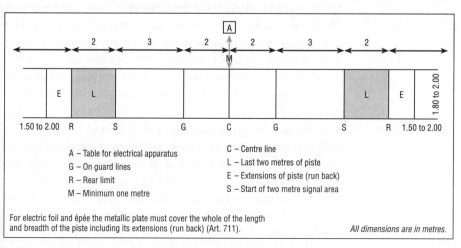

A – Table for electrical apparatus
G – On guard lines
R – Rear limit
M – Minimum one metre

C – Centre line
L – Last two metres of piste
E – Extensions of piste (run back)
S – Start of two metre signal area

For electric foil and épée the metallic plate must cover the whole of the length and breadth of the piste including its extensions (run back) (Art. 711).

All dimensions are in metres.

Rules

At foil and épée hits are only recorded with the point of the weapon whereas the cutting edge also counts in sabre events. Target areas also vary for each weapon. Only hits to the opponent's torso count at foil whilst sabre exponents can also score by hitting the arms or head. In the épée, fencers can score by hitting any part of the body.

Each bout or encounter is controlled by a referee and a timekeeper and scorer. An equipment check is carried out before each bout. The referee calls the fencers to order with the words – immortalized in swashbuckling Hollywood film epics – "on guard" followed by "ready" and then "play". He decides whether a hit is valid or not and makes sure that the other officials keep the score correctly.

During a bout every thrust or cut must hit the target area clearly to register a hit. Fencers may duck as a means of defence but cannot turn their back on their opponent. If a fencer is forced back over the piste's end boundary a penalty hit is recorded and fencing is resumed from the "on guard" position. There are no penalties for stepping over the side boundaries of the piste.

Atlanta format

Each nation can enter a maximum of three competitors per event up to a maximum of 20. For the first time, at the 1996 Games, there have been qualifying events in fencing to give a starting total of 220 fencers – 132 men and 88 women. A women's individual and team épée have been added to the programme since 1992.

The individual events at the Olympic Games are fought on the basis of a knock-out – or direct elimination – draw. The first fencer to score 15 hits on his or her opponent wins. Each bout is limited to a maximum of nine minutes actual fencing time. The eventual two finalists compete for the gold and silver medals whilst the losing semi-finalists contest the bronze medal.

There are also team events at foil, épée and sabre for men, and at épée for women with a maximum of twelve countries entered in each. Each team has three fencers. The teams are seeded on the basis of an individual's world-ranking at the end of the preceding world championships and, as in the individual event, the losing semi-finalists compete for the bronze medal.

In a team match each fencer fences the three opponents in the facing team – a total of nine bouts. But the match is scored as a relay. The first two fencers fight until one of them scores five hits. The next pair take over the score at this point and continue until one of them has ten hits. This continues until the ninth bout when the team first reaching 45 hits is the winner. This formula, only introduced for the 1994-95 season, has proved extremely exciting.

For both individual and team events, in the case of a draw at the end of regulation time, a further one minute is fenced and the first fencer to score one hit wins the contest.

Venue

Fencing at the 1996 Olympic Games takes place at the Georgia World Congress Center. This is the second largest convention centre in the USA. During the Games it will play host to seven different sports. For the fencing events there will be a spectator capacity of 5,200. The Center is located 3.2km (2 miles) from the Olympic Village.

MEDALLISTS (by nation)

	Men's			Women's			
	Gold	Silver	Bronze	Gold	Silver	Bronze	Total
France	34	34	24	2	1	2	97
Italy	30	32	19	4	2	3	90
Hungary	27	13	19	5	6	5	75
Soviet Union	14	14	15	5	3	3	54
United States [1]	2	6	11	-	-	-	19
Germany	2	5	3	2	4	2	18
Poland	4	6	7	-	-	1	18
FRG	4	6	-	3	1	1	15
Belgium	5	3	5	-	-	-	13
Great Britain	-	6	-	1	3	-	10
Romania	1	-	2	-	2	4	9
Cuba	5	2	1	-	-	-	8
Greece	3	3	2	-	-	-	8
Netherlands	-	1	7	-	-	-	8
Sweden	2	3	2	-	-	-	7
Austria	-	1	3	1	-	2	7
Denmark	-	1	1	1	1	2	6
Switzerland	-	2	3	-	-	-	5
Bohemia	-	-	2	-	-	-	2
China	-	-	-	1	1	-	2
GDR	-	1	-	-	-	-	1
Mexico	-	-	-	-	1	-	1
Argentina	-	-	1	-	-	-	1
Portugal	-	-	1	-	-	-	1
	133	139	128	25	25	25	475

[1] Double counting for 1904 foil team gold medal

ATLANTA SCHEDULE

Venue: Georgia World Congress Center, Hall F

Date	Description	Round	Start	End
20 Jul	ind épée (m)	Last 64	10:00	13:00
		Last 32		
		Last 16		
		q/finals		
		s/finals	15:00	16:40
		fence-off (bronze)		
		FINAL		
21 Jul	ind épée (w)	Last 64	8:00	12:50
		Last 32		
		Last 16		
		q/finals		
	ind sabre (m)	Last 64		
		Last 32		
		Last 16		
		q/finals		
	ind épée (w)	s/finals	15:00	18:00
		fence-off (bronze)		
		FINAL		
	ind sabre (m)	s/finals		
		fence-off (bronze)		
		FINAL		
22 Jul	ind foil (w)	Last 64	8:00	13:55
		Last 32		
		Last 16		
		q/finals		
	ind foil (m)	Last 64		
		Last 32		
		Last 16		
		q/finals		
	ind foil (w)	s/finals	15:00	18:45
		fence-off (bronze)		
		FINAL		
	ind foil (m)	s/finals		
		fence-off (bronze)		
		FINAL		
23 Jul	team épée (m)	Last 16	10:00	13:45
		q/finals		
		fence-off (11-12 place)		
		fence-off (9-10 place)		
		s/finals		
		fence-off (5-8 place)		
		fence-off (9-10 place)		
		fence-off (11-12 place)		
		fence-off (5-6 place)		

Date	Description	Round	Start	End
		fence-off (7-8 place)		
		fence-off (bronze)	15:00	17:00
		FINAL		
24 Jul	team épée (w)	Last 16	8:00	13:45
		q/finals		
		fence-off (9-12 place)		
		s/finals		
		fence-off (5-8 place)		
		fence-off (9-10 place)		
		fence-off (11-12 place)		
		fence-off (5-6 place)		
		fence-off (7-8 place)		
	team sabre (m)	Last 16		
		q/finals		
		fence-off (9-12 place)		
		s/finals		
		fence-off (5-8 place)		
		fence-off (9-10 place)		
		fence-off (11-12 place)		
		fence-off (5-6 place)		
		fence-off (7-8 place)		
	team épée (w)	fence-off (bronze)	15:00	19:10
		FINAL		
	team sabre (m)	fence-off (bronze)		
		FINAL		
25 Jul	team foil (w)	Last 16	8:00	14:45
		q/finals		
		fence-off (9-12 place)		
		s/finals		
		fence-off (5-8 place)		
		fence-off (9-10 place)		
		fence-off (11-12 place)		
		fence-off (5-6 place)		
		fence-off (7-8 place)		
	team foil (m)	Last 16		
		q/finals		
		fence-off (9-12 place)		
		s/finals		
		fence-off (5-8 place)		
		fence-off (9-10 place)		
		fence-off (11-12 place)		
		fence-off (5-6 place)		
		fence-off (7-8 place)		
	team foil (w)	fence-off (bronze)	15:00	19:10
		FINAL		
	team foil (m)	fence-off (bronze)		
		FINAL		

MEDALLISTS

FENCING (Men)

Year	Gold	C'ntry	Silver	C'ntry	Bronze	C'ntry

Foil Individual

Year	Gold	C'ntry	Silver	C'ntry	Bronze	C'ntry
1896	Eugene-Henri Gravelotte	FRA	Henri Callot	FRA	Perikles Pierrakos-Mavromichalis	GRE
1900	Emile Coste	FRA	Henri Masson	FRA	Marcel Boulenger	FRA
1904	Ramón Fonst	CUB	Albertson Van Zo Post	USA	Charles Tatham	USA
1912	Nedo Nadi	ITA	Pietro Speciale	ITA	Richard Verderber	AUT
1920	Nedo Nadi	ITA	Philippe Cattiau	FRA	Roger Ducret	FRA
1924	Roger Ducret	FRA	Philippe Cattiau	FRA	Maurice van Damme	BEL
1928	Lucien Gaudin	FRA	Erwin Casmir	GER	Giulio Gaudini	ITA
1932	Gustavo Marzi	ITA	Joseph Levis	USA	Giulio Gaudini	ITA
1936	Giulio Gaudini	ITA	Edward Gardère	FRA	Giorgio Bocchino	ITA
1948	Jehan Buhan	FRA	Christian D'Oriola	FRA	Lajos Maszlay	HUN
1952	Christian D'Oriola	FRA	Edoardo Mangiarotti	ITA	Manlio Di Rosa	ITA
1956	Christian D'Oriola	FRA	Giancarlo Bergamini	ITA	Antonio Spallino	ITA
1960	Viktor Zhdanovich	URS	Yuri Sisikin	URS	Albert Axelrod	USA
1964	Egon Franke	POL	Jean-Claude Magnan	FRA	Daniel Revenu	FRA
1968	Ion Drimbă	ROM	Jenő Kamuti	HUN	Daniel Revenu	FRA
1972	Witold Wojda	POL	Jenő Kamuti	HUN	Christian Noël	FRA
1976	Fabio dal Zotto	ITA	Alexander Romankov	URS	Bernard Talvard	FRA
1980	Vladimir Smirnov	URS	Pascal Jolyot	FRA	Alexander Romankov	URS
1984	Mauro Numa	ITA	Matthias Behr	FRG	Stefano Cerioni	ITA
1988	Stefano Cerioni	ITA	Udo Wagner	GDR	Alexander Romankov	URS
1992	Phillipe Omnes	FRA	Sergei Goloubitski	EUN	Elvis Gregory Gil	CUB
1996						

Sabre Individual

Year	Gold	C'ntry	Silver	C'ntry	Bronze	C'ntry
1896	Ioannis Georgiadis	GRE	Telemachos Karakalos	GRE	Holger Nielsen	DEN
1900	Georges de la Falaise	FRA	Leon Thiebaut	FRA	Siegfried Flesch	AUT
1904	Manuel Diaz	CUB	William Grebe	USA	Albertson Van Zo Post	USA
1908	Jenő Fuchs	HUN	Béla Zulavszky	HUN	Vilém Goppold de Lobsdorf	BOH
1912	Jenő Fuchs	HUN	Béla Békessy	HUN	Ervin Mészáros	HUN
1920	Nedo Nadi	ITA	Aldo Nadi	ITA	Adrianus De Jong	NED
1924	Sándor Posta	HUN	Roger Ducret	FRA	János Garai	HUN
1928	E Vitez Tersánszky	HUN	Attila Petschauer	HUN	Bino Bini	ITA
1932	György Piller	HUN	Giulio Gaudini	ITA	Endre Kabos	HUN
1936	Endre Kabos	HUN	Gustavo Marzi	ITA	Aladar Gerey	HUN
1948	Aladár Gerevich	HUN	Vincenzo Pinton	ITA	Pál Kovács	HUN
1952	Pál Kovács	HUN	Aladár Gerevich	HUN	Tibor Berczelli	HUN
1956	Rudolph Kárpáti	HUN	Jerzy Pawłowski	POL	Lev Kouznetsov	URS
1960	Rudolph Kárpáti	HUN	Zoltán Horváth	HUN	Wladimiro Calarese	ITA
1964	Tibor Pézsa	HUN	Claude Arabo	FRA	Umar Mavlikhanov	URS
1968	Jerzy Pawłowski	POL	Mark Rakita	URS	Tibor Pézsa	HUN
1972	Viktor Sidiak	URS	Péter Maróth	HUN	Vladimir Nazlymov	URS
1976	Viktor Krovopouskov	URS	Vladimir Nazlymov	URS	Viktor Sidiak	URS
1980	Viktor Krovopouskov	URS	Mikhail Burtsev	URS	Imre Gedövári	HUN
1984	Jean-François Lamour	FRA	Marco Marin	ITA	Peter Westbrook	USA
1988	Jean-François Lamour	FRA	Janusz Olech	POL	Giovanni Scalzo	ITA
1992	Bence Szabó	HUN	Marco Marin	ITA	Jean-François Lamour	FRA
1996						

Épée Individual

Year	Gold	C'ntry	Silver	C'ntry	Bronze	C'ntry
1900	Ramón Fonst	CUB	Louis Perree	FRA	León Sée	FRA
1904	Ramón Fonst	CUB	Charles Tatham	USA	Albertson Van Zo Post	USA
1908	Gaston Alibert	FRA	Alexandre Lippmann	FRA	Eugène Olivier	FRA
1912	Paul Anspach	BEL	Ivan Ossiier	DEN	Philippe le Hardy de Beaulieu	BEL
1920	Armand Massard	FRA	Alexandre Lippman	FRA	Gustave Buchard	FRA
1924	Charles Delporte	BEL	Roger Ducret	FRA	Nils Hellsten	SWE
1928	Lucien Gaudin	FRA	Georges Buchard	FRA	George Calnan	USA
1932	Giancarlo Cornaggia-Medici	ITA	Georges Buchard	FRA	Carlo Agostini	ITA
1936	Franco Riccardi	ITA	Saverio Ragno	ITA	Giancarlo Cornaggia-Medici	ITA
1948	Luigi Cantone	ITA	Oswald Zappelli	SUI	Edoardo Maniarotti	ITA

/continued on next page 229

Year	Gold	C'ntry	Silver	C'ntry	Bronze	C'ntry
1952	Edoardo Mangiarotti	ITA	Dario Mangiarotti	ITA	Oswald Zappelli	SUI
1956	Carlo Pavesi	ITA	Giuseppe Delfino	ITA	Edoardo Mangiarotti	ITA
1960	Giuseppe Delfino	ITA	Allan Jay	GBR	Bruno Khabarov	URS
1964	Grigory Kriss	URS	Henry William Hoskyns	GBR	Guram Kostava	URS
1968	Győső Kulcsar	HUN	Grigory Kriss	URS	Gianluigi Saccaro	ITA
1972	Csaba Fenyvesi	HUN	Jacques Ladegaillerie	FRA	Győző Kulcsár	HUN
1976	Alexander Pusch	FRG	Jürgen Hehn	FRG	Győző Kulcsár	HUN
1980	Johan Harmenberg	SWE	Ernő Kolczonai	HUN	Philippe Riboud	FRA
1984	Philippe Boisse	FRA	Björne Väggö	SWE	Philippe Riboud	FRA
1988	Arnd Schmitt	FRG	Philippe Riboud	FRA	Andrei Chouvalov	URS
1992	Eric Srecki	FRA	Pavel Kolobkov	EUN	Jean-Michel Henry	FRA
1996						

Foil Team

Year	Gold	C'ntry	Silver	C'ntry	Bronze	C'ntry
1904	Manuel Diaz	CUB	Arthur Fox	USA		
	Ramón Fonst	CUB	Charles Tatham			
	Albertson Van Zo Post	USA	Charles Fitzhugh Townsend			
1920	Baldo Baldi	ITA	Gaston Amson	FRA	Henry Breckinridge	USA
	Tommaso Costantino		Philippe Cattiau		Francis Honeycutt	
	Aldo Nadi		Lionel Bony de Castellane		Arthur St Clair Lyon	
	Nedo Nadi		Roger Ducret		Harold Rayner	
	Abelardo Olivier		Lucien Gaudin		Robert Sears	
	Oreste Puliti		André Labatut			
	Pietro Speciale		Marcel Perrot			
	Rodolfo Terlizzi		Georges Trombert			
1924	Philippe Cattiau	FRA	Désiré Beaurain	BEL	László Berti	HUN
	Jacques Coutrot		Marcel Bérré		István Licteneckert	
	Guy de Luget		Charles Crahay		Sándor Posta	
	Roger Ducret		Fernand de Montigny		Zoltán Schenker	
	Lucien Gaudin		Albert de Roocker		Ödön von Tersánszky	
	Henri Jobier		Maurice van Damme			
	André Labatut					
	Joseph Peroteaux					
1928	Giorgio Chiavacci	ITA	Philippe Cattiau	FRA	Raúl Anganuzzi	ARG
	Giulio Gaudini		Roger Ducret		Carmelo Camet	
	Gioacchino Guaragna		Raymond Flacher		Roberto Larraz	
	Giorgio Pessina		André Gaboriaud		Hector Lucchetti	
	Ugo Pignotti		Lucien Gaudin		Luis Lucchetti	
	Oreste Puliti		André Labatut			
1932	René Bondoux	FRA	Giulio Gaudini	ITA	Hugh Alessandroni	USA
	René Bougnol		Gioacchino Guaragna		George Calnan	
	Philippe Cattiau		Gustavo Marzi		Dernell Every	
	Edward Gardère		Giorgio Pessina		Joseph Levis	
	René Lemoine		Ugo Pignotti		Frank Righeimer	
	Jean Piot		Rodolfo Terlizzi		Richard Steere	
1936	Giorgio Bocchino	ITA	René Bondoux	FRA	Otto Adam	GER
	Manlio di Rosa		René Bougnol		Erwin Casmir	
	Giulio Gaudini		Jacques Coutrot		Julius Eisenecker	
	Gioacchino Guaragna		André Gardère		August Heim	
	Gustavo Marzi		Edward Gardère		Siegfried Lerdon	
	Ciro Verratti		René Lemoine		Stefan Rosenbauer	
1948	André Bonin	FRA	Manlio di Rosa	ITA	Raymond Bru	BEL
	René Bougnol		Edoardo Mangiarotti		Georges de Bourguignon	
	Jehan Buhan		Renzo Nostini		Henri Paternoster	
	Jacques Lataste		Giuliano Nostini		Paul Valcke	
	Christian D'Oriola		Giorgio Pellini		André van de Werwe de Vorsselaere	
	Adrien Rommel		Saverio Ragno		Edouard Yves	
1952	Jehan Buhan	FRA	Giancarlo Bergamini	ITA	Tibor Berczelly	HUN
	Jacques Lataste		Manlio di Rosa		Aladár Gerevich	
	Claude Netter		Edoardo Mangiarotti		Lajos Maszlay	
	Jacques Noël		Renzo Nostini		Endre Palócz	
	Christian D'Oriola		Giorgio Pellini		József Sakovics	
	Adrien Rommel		Antonio Spallino		Endre Tilli	

Year	Gold	C'ntry	Silver	C'ntry	Bronze	C'ntry
1956	Giancarlo Bergamini	ITA	Bernard Baudoux	FRA	Mihály Fülöp	HUN
	Luigi Carpaneda		Roger Closset		József Gyuricza	
	Manlio di Rosa		René Coicaud		József Marosi	
	Vittorio Lucarelli		Jacques Lataste		József Sakovics	
	Edoardo Mangiarotti		Claude Netter		Lajos Somodi	
	Antonio Spallino		Christian D'Oriola		Endre Tilli	
1960	Mark Midler	URS	Aldo Aureggio	ITA	Jürgen Brecht	GER
	Yuri Rudov		Luigi Carpaneda		Tim Gerresheim	
	Yuri Sisikin		Mario Curletto		Eberhard Mehl	
	German Sveshnikov		Edoardo Mangiarotti		Jürgen Theuerkauff	
	Viktor Zhdanovich		Alberto Pellegrino			
1964	Mark Midler	URS	Egon Franke	POL	Jacky Courtillat	FRA
	Yuri Sisikin		Ryszard Parulski		Christian Noël	
	German Sveshnikov		Zbigniew Skrudlik		Daniel Revenu	
	Viktor Zhdanovich		Witold Wojda		Pierre Rodocanachi	
1968	Gilles Berolatti	FRA	Viktor Putiatin	URS	Egon Franke	POL
	Jacques Dimont		Yuri Sharov		Adam Lisewski	
	Jean Magnan		Yuri Sisikin		Ryszard Parulski	
	Christian Noël		Vasily Stankovich		Zbigniew Skrudlik	
	Daniel Revenu		German Sveshnikov		Witold Wojda	
1972	Marek Dąbrowski	POL	Vladimir Denissov	URS	Jean-Claude Magnan	FRA
	Jerzy Kaczmarek		Anatoli Kotescev		Christian Noël	
	Lech Koziejowski		Leonid Romanov		Daniel Revenu	
	Witold Wojda		Vassily Stankovich		Bernard Talvard	
1976	Thomas Bach	FRG	Giovan Battista Coletti	ITA	Didier Flamet	FRA
	Matthias Behr		Carlo Montano		Christian Noël	
	Harald Hein		Stefano Simoncelli		Frédérick Pietruszka	
	Klaus Reichert		Fabio Dal Zotto		Bernard Talvard	
1980	Philippe Bonin	FRA	Ashot Karagian	URS	Lech Koziejowski	POL
	Bruno Boscherie		Vladimir Lapitski		Adam Robak	
	Didier Flament		Alexander Romankov		Marian Sypniewski	
	Pascal Jolyot		Sabirzhan Ruziev		Bogusław Zych	
			Vladimir Smirnov			
1984	Andrea Borella	ITA	Frank Beck	FRG	Marc Cerboni	FRA
	Stefano Cerioni		Matthias Behr		Patrick Groc	
	Andrea Cipressa		Mathias Gey		Pascal Jolyot	
	Mauro Numa		Harald Hein		Philippe Omnes	
	Angelo Scuri		Klaus Reichert		Frédérick Pietruszka	
1988	Vladimir Aptsiaouri	URS	Matthias Behr	FRG	Istvan Busa	HUN
	Anvar Ibraguimov		Thomas Endres		Zsolt Érsek	
	Boris Koretskü		Mathias Gey		Robert Gatai	
	Ilgar Mamedov		Ulrich Schreck		Pál Szekeres	
	Alexander Romankov		Thorsten Weidner		István Szelei	
1992	Alexander Koch	GER	Tulio Diaz Babier	CUB	Piotr Kiełpikowski	POL
	Ulrich Rainer Schreck		Elvis Gregory Gil		Adam Krzesiński	
	Udo Wagner		Hermenegildo Garcia Marturell		Cezary Siess	
	Thorsten Weidner		Oscar Garcia Perez		Ryszard Sobczak	
	Ingo Weissenborn		Guillermo Betancourt Scull		Marian Sypniewski	
1996						

Sabre Team

1908	Dezső Földes	HUN	Marcello Bertinetti	ITA	Vilém Goppold de Lobsdorf	BOH
	Jenő Fuchs		Sante Ceccherini		Otakar Lada	
	Oszkár Gerde		Riccardo Nowak		Vlastimil Lada-Sažavsky	
	Péter Tóth		Abelardo Olivier		Bedřich Schejbal	
	Lajos Werkner		Alessandro Pirzio-Biroli		Jaroslav Tuček	
1912	László Berti	HUN	Albert Bogen	AUT	Adrianus de Jong	NED
	Dezső Földes		Rudolf Cvetko		Hendrik de Iongh	
	Jenő Fuchs		Friedrich Golling		Jetze Doorman	
	Oszkár Gerde		Otto Herschmann		Dirk Scalongne	
	Ervin Mészáros		Andreas Suttner		Willém Hubert van Blijenburgh	
	Zoltán Schenker		Reinhold Trampler		George van Rossem	
	Péter Tóth		Richard Verderber			
	Lajos Werkner					

/continued on next page

Year	Gold	C'ntry	Silver	C'ntry	Bronze	C'ntry
1920	Baldo Baldi	ITA	Henri de Saint Germain	FRA	Adrianus de Jong	NED
	Francesco Gargano		Jean Lacroix		Louis Delaunoij	
	Nedo Nadi		Jean Margraff		Jetze Doorman	
	Aldo Nadi		Jean Mondielli		William Hubert van Blijenburgh	
	Oreste Puliti		Marc Perrodon		Jan van der Wiel	
	Giorgio Santelli		Georges Trombert		Henri Wijnoldy-Daniels	
	Dino Urbani				Salomon Zeldenrust	
1924	Renato Anselmi	ITA	László Berti	HUN	Adrianus de Jong	NED
	Guido Balzarini		János Garai		Jetze Doorman	
	Marcello Bertinetti		Sándor Posta		Hendrik Scherpenhuijzen	
	Bino Bini		József Rády		Jan van der Wiel	
	Vincenzo Cuccia		Zoltán Schenker		Maarten van Dulm	
	Oreste Moricca		László Szechy		Henri Wijnoldy-Daniels	
	Oreste Puliti		Ödön von Tersztyanszky			
	Giulio Sarrocchi		Jenö Uhlyarik			
1928	János Garai	HUN	Renato Anselmi	ITA	Tadeusz Friedrich	POL
	Gyula Glykais		Bino Bini		Kazimierz Łaskowski	
	Sándor Gombos		Gustavo Marzi		Alexsander Malecki	
	Attila Petschauer		Oreste Puliti		Adam Papee	
	József Rády		Emilio Salafia		Władysław Segda	
	Ödön von Tersánszky		Giulio Sarrocchi		Jerzy Zabielski	
1932	Aladár Gerevich	HUN	Renato Anselmi	ITA	Władysław Doborowolski	POL
	Gyula Glykais		Arturo de Vecchi		Tadeusz Friedrich	
	Endre Kabos		Giulio Guadini		Leszek Lubicz-Nycz	
	Ernő Nagy		Gustavo Marzi		Adam Papée	
	Attila Petschauer		Ugo Pignotti		Wadysaw Segda	
	György Piller		Emilio Salafia		Marjan Suski	
1936	Tibor Berczelly	HUN	Giulio Gaudini	ITA	Erwin Casmir	GER
	Aladár Gerevich		Gustavo Marzi		Julius Eisenecker	
	Endre Kabos		Aldo Masciotta		Hans Esser	
	Pál Kovács		Aldo Montano		August Heim	
	László Rajcsányi		Vincenzo Pinton		Hans Jörger	
	Imre Rajczy		Athos Tanzini		Richard Wahl	
1948	Tibor Berczelly	HUN	Gastone Dare	ITA	Norman Armitage	USA
	Aladár Gerevich		Aldo Montano		Dean Cetrulo	
	Rudolf Kárpáti		Renzo Nostini		Miguel de Capriles	
	Pál Kovács		Vincenzo Pinton		James Flynn	
	Bertalan Papp		Mauro Racca		Tibor Nyilas	
	László Rajcsányi		Carlo Turcato		George Worth	
1952	Tibor Berczelly	HUN	Roberto Ferrari	ITA	Jean Laroyenne	FRA
	Aladár Gerevich		Gastone Dare		Jacques Lefèvre	
	Rudolf Kárpáti		Renzo Nostini		Jean Levavasseur	
	Pál Kovács		Giorgio Pellini		Bernard Morel	
	Bertalan Papp		Vincenzo Pinton		Maurice Piot	
	László Rajcsányi		Mauro Racca		Jean-François Tournon	
1956	Aladár Gerevich	HUN	Marek Kuszewski	POL	Leonid Bogdanov	URS
	Jenő Hámori		Zygmunt Pawłas		Evgeni Cherepovsky	
	Rudolf Kárpáti		Jerzy Pawłowski		Lev Kuznyetsov	
	Attila Keresztes		Andrzej Piątkowski		Yakov Rylsky	
	Pál Kovács		Wojciech Zabłocki		David Tyschler	
	Daniel Magai		Ryszard Żub			
1960	Gábor Delneki	HUN	Marek Kuszewski	POL	Giampaolo Calanchini	ITA
	Aladár Gerevich		Emil Ochyra		Wladimiro Calarese	
	Zoltán Horváth		Jerzy Pawłowski		Pierluigi Chicca	
	Rudolf Kárpáti		Andrzej Piątkowski		Roberto Ferrari	
	Pál Kovács		Wojciech Zabłocki		Mario Ravagnan	
	Tamás Mendelényi		Ryszard Żub			
1964	Nugzar Asatiani	URS	Giampaolo Calanchini	ITA	Emil Ochyra	POL
	Umar Mavlikhanov		Wladimiro Calarese		Jerzy Pawłowski	
	Boris Melnikov		Pierluigi Chicca		Andrzej Piątkowski	
	Mark Rakita		Mario Ravagnan		Wojciech Zabłocki	
	Yakov Rylsky		Cesare Salvadori		Ryszard Żub	
1968	Umar Mavlikhanov	URS	Wladimiro Calarese	ITA	Peter Bakonyi	HUN
	Vladimir Nazlymov		Pierluigi Chicca		János Kalmár	
	Mark Rakita		Michele Maffei		Tamas Kovacs	
	Viktor Sidiak		Rolando Rigoli		Miklós Meszéna	
	Eduard Vinokurov		Cesare Salvadori		Tibor Pézsa	

Year	Gold	C'ntry	Silver	C'ntry	Bronze	C'ntry
1972	Michele Maffei	ITA	Viktor Basenov	URS	Peter Bakonyi	HUN
	Mario Aldo Montano		Vladimir Nazlymov		Pál Gerevich	
	Mario Tullio Montano		Mark Rakita		Tamas Kovacs	
	Rolando Rigoli		Viktor Sidiak		Péter Maróth	
	Cesare Salvadori		Eduard Vinokurov		Tibor Pézsa	
1976	Mikhail Burtsev	URS	Angelo Arcidiacono	ITA	Dan Irimiciuc	ROM
	Viktor Krovopouskov		Michele Maffei		Cornel Marin	
	Vladimir Nazlymov		Mario Aldo Montano		Marin Mustaţă	
	Viktor Sidiak		Mario Tullio Montano		Alexandru Nilca	
	Edouard Vinokurov		Tommaso Montano		Ioan Pop	
1980	Nikolai Alekhin	URS	Michele Maffei	ITA	Imre Gedövári	HUN
	Mikhail Burtsev		Ferdinando Meglio		Pál Gerevich	
	Viktor Krovopuskov		Mario Aldo Montano		Ferenc Hammang	
	Vladimir Nazlymov		Marco Romano		György Nébald	
	Viktor Sidiak		Giovanni Scalzo		Rudolf Nébald	
1984	Angelo Arcidiacono	ITA	Philippe Delrieu	FRA	Alexandru Chiculita	ROM
	Gianfranco dalla Barba		Franck Ducheix		Corneliu Marin	
	Marco Marin		Hervé Granger-Veyron		Marin Mustaţă	
	Ferdinando Meglio		Pierre Guichot		Ioan Pop	
	Giovanni Scalzo		Jean-François Lamour		Vilmos Szabo	
1988	Imre Bujdosó	HUN	Andrei Alchan	URS	Massimo Cavaliere	ITA
	László Csongrádi		Mikhail Bourtsev		Gianfranco dalla Barba	
	Imre Gedövári		Sergei Koriakin		Marco Marin	
	György Nébald		Sergei Mindirgassov		Ferdinando Meglio	
	Bence Szabó		Giorgi Pogossov		Giovanni Scalzo	
1992	Alexander Chirchov	EUN	Péter Abay	HUN	Jean-Phillippe Daurelle	FRA
	Vadim Gouttsait		Imre Bujdosó		Franck Ducheix	
	Grigorij Kirienko		Csaba Kőves		Hervé Granger-Veyron	
	Gueorgui Pogossov		György Nébald		Pierre Guichot	
	Stanislav Pozdniakov		Bence Szabó		Jean-François Lamour	
1996						

Épée Team

Year	Gold	C'ntry	Silver	C'ntry	Bronze	C'ntry
1908	Gaston Alibert	FRA	Edgar Amphlett	GBR	Paul Anspach	BEL
	Henri Georges Berger		John Blake		Desiré Beaurain	
	Charles Collignon		Charles Leaf Daniell		Fernand Bosmans	
	Bernard Gravier		Percival Davson		Orphile Fernand de Montigny	
	Alexandre Lippmann		Arthur Everitt		Ferdinand Feyerick	
	Eugène Olivier		Cecil Haig		François Rom	
	Jean Stern		Martin Holt		Victor Willems	
			Sydney Martineau			
			Robert Montgomerie			
1912	Henri Anspach	BEL	Edgar Amphlett	GBR	Adrianus de Jong	NED
	Paul Anspach		John Blake		Jetze Doorman	
	Orphile Fernand de Montigny		Percival Davson		Leonardus Salomonson	
	Robert Hennet		Arthur Everitt		Willem Hubert van Blijenburgh	
	Jacques Ochs		Martin Holt		George van Rossem	
	François Rom		Sydney Martineau			
	Gaston Salmon		Robert Montgomerie			
	Victor Willems		Edgar Seligman			
1920	Antonio Allocchio	ITA	Paul Anspach	BEL	Gaston Amson	FRA
	Tullio Bozza		Victor Boin		Gustave Buchard	
	Giovanni Canova		Joseph de Craecker		Georges Casanova	
	Tommaso Costantino		Maurice Dewée		Alexandre Lippmann	
	Paolo Thaon di Revel		Ernest Gevers		Armand Massard	
	Andrea Marrazi		Félix Goblet d'Alviella		Emile Moureau	
	Aldo Nadi		Philippe Le Hardy de Beaulieu		Georges Trombert	
	Nedo Nadi		Léon Tom			
	Abelardo Olivier					
	Dino Urbani					

/continued on next page 233

Year	Gold	C'ntry	Silver	C'ntry	Bronze	C'ntry
1924	Georges Buchard	FRA	Paul Anspach	BEL	Giulio Basletta	ITA
	Roger Ducret		Joseph de Craecker		Marcello Bertinetti	
	Lucien Gaudin		Charles Delporte		Giovanni Canova	
	André Labatut		Orphile Fernand de Montigny		Vincenzo Cuccia	
	Lionel Liottel		Ernest Gevers		Virgilio Mantegazza	
	Alexandre Lippmann		Léon Tom		Oreste Moricca	
	Georges Tainturier					
1928	Carlo Agostoni	ITA	Gaston Amson	FRA	Jorge de Paiva	POR
	Giulio Basletta		René Barbier		Henrique de Silveira	
	Marcello Bertinetti		Georges Buchard		Paulo Eca Leal	
	Giancarlo Cornaggia-Medici		Emile Cornic		Mário de Noronha	
	Renzo Minoli		Armand Massard		Frederico Paredes	
	Franco Riccardi		Bernard Schmetz		João Sassetti	
1932	Georges Buchard	FRA	Carlo Agostoni	ITA	George Calnan	USA
	Philippe Cattiau		Giancarlo Cornaggia-Medici		Miguel de Caprilles	
	Fernand Jourdant		Renzo Minoli		Gustave Heiss	
	Jean Piot		Saverio Ragno		Tracy Jaeckel	
	Bernard Schmetz		Franco Riccardi		Frank Righeimer	
	Georges Tainturier				Curtis Shears	
1936	Giancarlo Brusati	ITA	Gösta Almgren	SWE	Georges Buchard	FRA
	Giancarlo Cornaggia-Medici		Birger Cederin		Philippe Cattiau	
	Edoardo Mangiarotti		Hans Drakenberg		Henri Dulieux	
	Alfredo Pezzana		Gustaf Dyrssen		Michel Pécheux	
	Saverio Ragno		Hans Granfelt		Bernard Schmetz	
	Franco Riccardi		Sven Thofelt		Paul Wormser	
1948	Edouard Artigas	FRA	Carlo Agostoni	ITA	Per Carleson	SWE
	Marcel Desprets		Luigi Cantone		Frank Cervell	
	Henri Guérin		Marc Antonio Mandruzzato		Carl Forssell	
	Maurice Huet		Dario Mangiarotti		Bengt Ljungquist	
	Henri Lepage		Edoardo Mangiarotti		Sven Thofelt	
	Michel Pécheux		Fiorenzo Marini		Arne Tollbom	
1952	Roberto Battaglia	ITA	Per Carleson	SWE	Paul Barth	SUI
	Franco Bertinetti		Sven Fahlman		Willy Fitting	
	Giuseppe Delfino		Carl Forssell		Paul Meister	
	Dario Mangiarotti		Bengt Ljungquist		Otto Rüfenacht	
	Edoardo Mangiarotti		Lennart Magnusson		Mario Valota	
	Carlo Pavesi		Berndt-Otto Rehbinder		Oswald Zappelli	
1956	Giorgio Anglesio	ITA	Lajos Balthazár	HUN	Daniel Dagallier	FRA
	Franco Bertinetti		Barnabás Berzsenyi		Yves Dreyfus	
	Giuseppe Delfino		József Marosi		Armand Mouyal	
	Edoardo Mangiarotti		Ambrus Nagy		Claude Nigon	
	Carlo Pavesi		Béla Rerrich		René Queyroux	
	Alberto Pellegrino		József Sakovics			
1960	Giuseppe Delfino	ITA	Michael Alexander	GBR	Valentin Chernikov	URS
	Edoardo Mangiarotti		Raymond Harrison		Arnold Chernushevich	
	Fiorenzo Marini		Henry Hoskyns		Bruno Habarovs	
	Carlo Pavesi		Michael Howard		Guram Kostava	
	Alberto Pellegrino		Allan Jay		Alexander Pavlovski	
	Gianluigi Saccaro		John Pelling			
1964	Tamás Gábor	HUN	Giambattista Breda	ITA	Claude Bourquard	FRA
	István Kausz		Giuseppe Delfino		Jacques Brodin	
	Győző Kulcsar		Gianfranco Paolucci		Yves Dreyfus	
	Zoltán Nemere		Gianluigi Saccaro		Jacques Guittet	
1968	Csaba Fenyvesi	HUN	Grigory Kriss	URS	Bohdan Andrzejewski	POL
	Győző Kulcsar		Viktor Modzolevsky		Kazimierz Barburski	
	Pál Nagy		Alexei Nikanchikov		Michał Butkiewicz	
	Zoltán Nemere		Yuri Smoliakov		Bogdan Gonsior	
	Pál Schmitt		Iosif Vitebsky		Henryk Nielaba	
1972	Sandor Erdős	HUN	Guy Evéquoz	SUI	Viktor Modzolevsky	URS
	Csaba Fenyvesi		Daniel Giger		Sergei Paramonov	
	Győző Kulcsár		Christian Kauter		Igor Valetov	
	István Osztrics		Peter Lötscher		Georgy Zajítsky	
	Pál Schmitt		François Suchanecki			

Year	Gold	C'ntry	Silver	C'ntry	Bronze	C'ntry
1976	Rolf Edling	SWE	Reinhold Behr	FRG	Jean-Blaise Evéquoz	SUI
	Göran Flodström		Volker Fischer		Daniel Giger	
	Leif Högström		Jürgen Hehn		Christian Kauter	
	Hans Jacobson		Hanns Jana		Michel Poffet	
	Orvar Jonsson		Alexander Pusch		François Suchanecki	
	Carl von Essen					
1980	Philippe Boisse	FRA	Ludomir Chronowski	POL	Alexander Abushakhmetov	URS
	Hubert Gardas		Piotr Jabłkowski		Ashot Karagan	
	Patrick Picot		Andrzej Lis		Boris Lukomski	
	Philippe Riboud		Mariusz Strzałka		Alexander Mozhaev	
	Michel Salesse		Leszek Swornowski		Vladimir Smirnov	
1984	Elmar Borrmann	FRG	Philippe Boisse	FRA	Stefano Bellone	ITA
	Volker Fischer		Jean-Michel Henry		Sandro Cuomo	
	Gerhard Heer		Olivier Lenglet		Cosimo Ferro	
	Rafael Nickel		Philippe Riboud		Roberto Manzi	
	Alexander Pusch		Michel Salesse		Angelo Mazzoni	
1988	Frédéric Delpla	FRA	Elmar Borrmann	FRG	Andrei Chouvalov	URS
	Jean-Michel Henry		Volker Fischer		Pavel Kolobkov	
	Olivier Lenglet		Thomas Gerull		Vladimir Reznitchenko	
	Philippe Riboud		Alexander Pusch		Mikhail Tichko	
	Eric Srecki		Arnd Schmitt		Igor Tikhomirov	
1992	Elmar Borrmann	GER	Ferenc Hegedűs	HUN	Andrei Chouvalov	EUN
	Robert Felisiak		Ernő Kolczonay		Pavel Kolobkov	
	Uwe Proske		Iván Kovács		Sergei Kostarev	
	Vladimir Reznitchenko		Krisztián Kulcsár		Sergei Kravtchouk	
	Arnd Schmitt		Gábor Totola		Valeri Zakharevitch	
1996						

FENCING (Women)

Year	Gold	C'ntry	Silver	C'ntry	Bronze	C'ntry

Foil Individual

Year	Gold	C'ntry	Silver	C'ntry	Bronze	C'ntry
1924	Ellen Osiier	DEN	Gladis Davis	GBR	Grete Heckscher	DEN
1928	Helene Mayer	GER	Muriel Freeman	GBR	Olga Oelkers	GER
1932	Ellen Preis	AUT	Heather Guinness	GBR	Erna Bogen	HUN
1936	Ilona Elek-Schacherer	HUN	Helene Mayer	GER	Ellen Preis	AUT
1948	Ilona Elek	HUN	Karen Lachmann	DEN	Ellen Müller-Preis	AUT
1952	Irene Camber	ITA	Ilona Elek	HUN	Karen Lachmann	DEN
1956	Gillian Sheen	GBR	Olga Orban	ROM	Renée Garilhe	FRA
1960	Adelheid Schmid	GER	Valentina Rastvorova	URS	Maria Vicol	ROM
1964	Ildikó Rejtő	HUN	Helga Margot Mees	GER	Antonella Ragno	ITA
1968	Elena Novikova	URS	Pilar Roldán	MEX	Ildikó Rejtő	HUN
1972	Antonella Ragno Lonzi	ITA	Ildikó Bóbis	HUN	Galina Gorokhova	URS
1976	Ildikó Schwarczenberger	HUN	Maria Consolata Collino	ITA	Elena Belova	URS
1980	Pascale Trinquet	FRA	Magdolna Maros	HUN	Barbara Wysoczanska	POL
1984	Juje Luan	CHN	Cornelia Hanisch	FRG	Donna Vaccaroni	ITA
1988	Anja Fichtel	FRG	Sabine Bau	FRG	Zita Funkenhauser	FRG
1992	Giovanna Trillini	ITA	Wang Huifeng	CHN	Tatiana Sadovskaia	EUN
1996						

Foil Team

Year	Gold	C'ntry	Silver	C'ntry	Bronze	C'ntry
1960	Galina Gorokhova	URS	Lídia Dömölki	HUN	Irene Camber	ITA
	Tatiana Petrenko		Katalin Juhász		Velleda Cesari	
	Valentina Prudskova		Magda Kovacs		Bruna Colombetti	
	Valentina Rastvorova		Ildikó Rejtő		Claudia Pasini	
	Ludmila Shishova		Tiborne Szekely		Antonella Ragno	
	Alexandra Zabelina					
1964	Katalin Juhász	HUN	Galina Gorokhova	URS	Helga Mees	GER
	Judit Mendelényi-Agoston		Valentina Prudskova		Rosemarie Scherberger	
	Lídia Sakovics-Dömölki		Valentina Rastvorova		Adelheid Schmid	
	Ildikó Rejtő		Tatiana Samusenko		Gudrun Theuerkauff	
			Ludmila Shishova			

/continued on next page 235

Year	Gold	C'ntry	Silver	C'ntry	Bronze	C'ntry
1968	Svetlana Chirkova	URS	Ildikó Bóbis	HUN	Ileana Drimbă	ROM
	Galina Gorokhova		Maria Gulacsy		Ana Ene-Dersidan	
	Elena Novikova		Paula Marosi		Clara Stahl-Lencic	
	Tatiana Samusenko		Ildikó Rejtő		Olga Szabó	
	Alexandra Zabelina		Lídia Sakovics		Maria Vicol	
1972	Galina Gorokhova	URS	Ildikó Bóbis	HUN	Ileana Ghiulai	ROM
	Elena Novikova		Ildikó Rónay		Ana Pascu	
	Tatiana Semusenko		Ildikó Rejtő		Ecaterina Stahl	
	Alexandra Zabelina		Ildikó Schwarczenberger		Olga Szabó	
			Maria Szolnoki			
1976	Nailia Guiliazova	URS	Brigitte Dumont	FRA	Ildikó Bóbis	HUN
	Olga Kniazeva		Claudie Josland		Edit Kovacs	
	Valentina Nikonova		Brigitte Latrille-Gaudin		Magda Maros	
	Elena Novikova		Christine Muzio		Ildikó Rejtő	
	Valentina Sidorova		Véronique Trinquet		Ildikó Schwarczenberger	
1980	Véronique Brouquier	FRA	Elena Belova	URS	Edit Kovacs	HUN
	Brigitte Latrille-Gaudin		Nailia Giliazova		Magdolina Maros	
	Christine Muzio		Valentina Sidorova		Ildikó Schwarczenberger	
	Isabelle Regard		Larisa Tsagaraeva		Gertrud Stefanek	
	Pascale Trinquet		Irina Ushakova		Zsuzsa Szőcs	
1984	Sabine Bischoff	FRG	Aurora Dan	ROM	Véronique Brouqier	FRA
	Zita Funkenhauser		Elisabeta Guzganu		Brigitte Gaudin	
	Cornelia Hanisch		Rozalia Oros		Ann Meygret	
	Christiane Weber		Koszto Veber		Laurence Modaine	
	Ute Wessel		Marcela Zsak		Pascale Trinquet-Hachin	
1988	Sabine Bau	FRG	Francesca Bortolozzi	ITA	Zsuzsanna Jánosi	HUN
	Anja Fichtel		Annapia Gandolfi		Katalin Tuschak	
	Zita Funkenhauser		Lucia Traversa		Edit Kovacs	
	Annette Klug		Dorina Vaccaroni		Gertrud Stefanek	
	Christiane Weber		Margherita Zalaffi		Zsuzsa Szőcs	
1992	Diana Bianchedi	ITA	Sabine Christiane Bau	GER	Laura Gabriela Badea	ROM
	Francesca Bortolozzi		Annette Dobmeier		Roxana Dumitrescu	
	Giovanna Trillini		Anja Fichtel-Mauritz		Claudia Laura Grigorescu	
	Dorina Vaccaroni		Zita Funkenhauser		Reka Zsofia Szabó	
	Margherita Zalaffi		Monika Weber-Koszto		Elisabeta Tufan	
1996						

Épée Individual

1996

Épée Team

1996

Football (Soccer)

Stars to Watch

by Jerry Trecker

Soccer with a different formula

THE LAST Games of the 20th Century could point the way toward soccer's return as a dominant Olympic sport in the next millennium. The addition of women's soccer as a medal sport, coupled with a lengthy growth process in the men's game means that the United States of America will host its second major soccer extravaganza in the space of two years.

Women's soccer may not yet have the worldwide appeal of the men's game, but FIFA general secretary Joseph Blatter says that will change with the advent of the 21st century. Speaking at the second FIFA women's world championship in Sweden, Blatter proclaimed: "the women show us how the game should be played – with elegance, an attacking spirit and fair play."

The men's competition has undergone a major change since the state-supported sports systems of Eastern Europe dominated the competition between 1956 and 1980. Consistent with the transformation from pure amateurism to

---

★★★★★★★★★★★★★★★★★★★★★★★★★★★★★ **A Contemporary Heroine**

Michelle Akers *(USA)*

Michelle Akers could be excused if she simply sat back and counted the honours which have distinguished the career of someone described as the best female soccer player in the world. Instead, the 30 year old American goal-scoring star looks at the 1996 Olympic Games as a chance to return to centre stage after a women's World Cup last year that was ruined by injury.

Akers, who led the 1991 women's World Cup with ten goals, was knocked out in the opening game in Sweden when she suffered a second degree concussion in a goal-mouth collision. That, says the 1.78m (5ft 10in.), 68kg (10st 10lb) champion, has provided all the motivation she needed to remain in training for a shot at an Olympic Games gold medal. By the time they begin, Akers will be near the 100-game, 100-goal mark. She has twice been named United States' "Female Athlete of the Year".

controlled professionalism in other Olympic sports, men's soccer today offers a professional face. However, it is a face with a difference from the World Cup (held in the USA in 1994).

FIFA and the International Olympic Committee have agreed on a formula which puts the Olympic soccer tournament into the FIFA family of youth competitions. The 1996 qualifying competition was open only to players aged 23 and under, but once the final 16 qualifiers are known, each country will be allowed to add three players of any age. The outcome should be the appearance of some world-class stars in Atlanta adding experience and glamour to age-group squads. Amongst them could be France's Michel Platini.

A Sporting Legend ★★★★★★★★★★★★★★★★★★★★★★★★★★★★★★★★★★★★

Michel Platini (France)

Michel Platini, who turned 40 in 1995, has packed enough into his soccer lifetime to rank as one of the greatest players in the history of the game. The French star is not finished, however. Currently he is serving with his country's organizers as they prepare to host the 1998 World Cup.

Platini won a European championship with France in 1984 and was the star of two World Cup teams (1982, '86). He excelled at the French club St. Etienne before moving to Juventus, where he inspired that famous Italian club to a series of honours in the mid '80s. Before that, Platini had already made his first appearance on the world stage, as a youth star of the 1976 Montreal Games. In those days, only amateur players could represent Western European countries, so the 21 year old ace retained his Olympic eligibility in order to lead France. He did so with three goals in a tournament that helped to create today's rising soccer interest in North America.

It is certain who will participate in the women's eight-team event because those qualifiers were determined by the finish in the second Women's World Championship. The host USA team will be joined by world champions Norway, Brazil, China, Denmark, Germany, Japan and Sweden.

Unlike the men's event there are no restrictions on participants for the women's event. That should ensure the presence of the top female players, like Norway's Hege Ruse (the outstanding player in the second women's world championship), China's dynamic Fan Yungjie, Germany's star striker Heidi Mohr and the American midfield pair of Mia Hamm and Kristine Lilly.

Because the men's qualifying competition was not scheduled to conclude until the eve of the Games selections for the 16-team field will take place up to the last moment. It is expected that Argentina and Brazil will grab the two places for South America and that Africa will be represented by at least a couple of the nations that have done so well in FIFA youth tournaments. Cameroon, Ghana and Nigeria, for example, had all reached the final stages of African qualifying.

The European entry of five nations is determined by the UEFA Under-21 tournament and some surprises seem likely. Although the traditional powers Germany and Italy were well-placed to win their sections, the appearance of neither in America was certain. It looks far more likely, for example, that Norway, emerging as a world soccer power in the last decade, and Portugal, which won the FIFA youth championship tournaments in both 1991 and '93, could come to the USA as potential medal winners.

The rest of the men's field will include three teams from Asia, likely to be headed by always-powerful South Korea and the ever-growing Japan, and two from the CONCACAF (Central and North American) region. The hosts America have one of these automatically. The 16th team will be the winner of a play-off between a CONCACAF runner-up and the Oceania champions, likely to be Australia or New Zealand.

As in the 1984 Los Angeles Olympic Games, the soccer tournaments will not be played entirely in the host venue. Appreciating the fact that soccer was a huge national attraction when it was staged across the country, the Atlanta organizers have awarded soccer to Birmingham, Alabama, to Miami and Orlando, both in Florida, and to Washington, DC. The finals are to be staged at the University of Georgia's mammoth football stadium in Athens.

J. T. □

Retrospective

Soccer has arguably been the liveliest of all the Olympic sports. None of the others has generated such wayward signs of passion – crowd invasions, protests, controversies, fights, and even the declaration of a state of siege in one country after a bitterly disputed qualifying match!

This can all give the impression that soccer is a rowdy, ill-disciplined, unsporting affair unsuited to the special ethos of the Games. But, whilst this is almost certainly untrue, the deft and flowing skills which have made the game the most popular in the world have also helped set the stage for some extraordinary scenes.

The entire Czechoslovakian team walked off in protest against some controversial refereeing decisions in the 1920 final. The home team, Belgium, was 2-0 up before a partisan crowd at the time. Chaos resulted.

Czechoslovakia were disqualified and a play-off for second place was ordered. But France, who lost to Czechoslovakia in the semi-finals, refused to play because by then many of their best players had gone home. Eventually Spain beat Sweden and Italy to earn third place.

More controversy occurred in the 1924 final in Paris when Holland had a protest turned down after their 2-1 defeat to Uruguay. A Dutch referee was then assigned to the final and Uruguay's protest against this was accepted. They went on to beat Switzerland 3-0.

In 1936 in Berlin the referee ordered Italy's Achille Piccini off after two Americans were injured. Piccini refused and the Italians surrounded the referee and covered his mouth with their hands. The match went on with Piccini and Italy won 1-0.

Five days later a quarter-final was ordered to be replayed behind closed doors after Peruvian fans had rushed in and attacked an Austrian player. Amid the chaos Peru scored two quick goals and won 4-2, and when Austria protested a panel of five Europeans ordered a replay two days later. The Peruvians refused and withdrew. So did Columbia, in support of their fellow South Americans.

In Lima there were Peruvian demonstrations before the German consulate. However, this was mild compared with the Lima ructions of 1964 when 328 people were killed in fights in the streets after a qualifying match between Peru and Argentina.

This happened after the referee disallowed an equalizer in the last two minutes, two spectators attacked the official, both were arrested and the match was suspended. Demonstrators marched on the national palace demanding an end to police brutality and a declaration of a draw in the soccer, while the Peruvian government declared a state of siege and suspended the constitution.

In 1968 the Bulgarians were obliged to play the second half of the final with only eight players after three were sent off and the crowd invaded the pitch. Their opponents, Hungary, also had one sent off but won the final.

Most of the soccer over the years has been just as worthy of publicity as the occasional aggravation going on around it, with many tales of the heroic and the unusual. Among the best was the achievement of Yugoslavia in winning the 1960 final 3-1 against Denmark – with only ten men.

Had it not been for a sudden curiosity in the semi-finals Sweden might have found it more difficult to go on to win the 1948 final. One of their goals against their closest rivals Denmark would not have stood had their quick thinking centre-forward Gunnar Nordahl not leapt into the back of the Danish net to avoid being penalized for off-side!

Background

Soccer helped change the way people thought about the Olympic Games. It was the first team sport to be included on the programme. That happened in 1900 and its appearance in Paris that year was marked by the fact that the winners, a Danish team, beat Smyrna, a team from a Greek town, by 15-0. Amazingly, that score was bettered eight years later when Denmark beat France 17-1, with the Danish centre-forward Sofus Nielsen scoring a record ten goals. Nielsen still holds the record for the most goals in Olympic competition, 13.

Olympic soccer came under the control of the sport's international governing body, FIFA, after it was formed in 1904, and it steadily grew in importance. By 1922 there were 22 countries participating in the Games. However, Olympic soccer was weakened by the introduction of the World Cup in 1930 and by the exclusion of the sport from the 1932 Olympic Games.

There has also been much argument about the interpretation of the term "amateur" as applied to soccer.

★★★★★★★★★★★★★★★★★★★★★★★★★★★★★★ **A Sporting Legend**

Oleg Blokhin *(Soviet Union)*

Oleg Blokhin will be remembered alongside the giant goalkeeper Lev Yashin as one of the greatest players ever produced in the former Soviet Union. But the Ukrainian star's many honours never included an Olympic gold medal. Although there was Soviet dominance in many Olympic sports, the Olympic soccer gold eluded them despite Blokhin's leadership and brilliance on the wing. Blokhin's best Olympic chance might have come in 1976. However, the Soviet decision to have Dynamo Kiev double as the national team backfired, even though throughout Eastern Europe it was the finest club side of its era. It meant that they arrived in Montreal after a crushing burden of matches. Kiev won the European cup winners cup in 1975 and by the time Blokhin became the first Soviet star to play outside the country – with Olympiakos of Greece – he had played 107 full internationals for the Soviet Union.

FOOTBALL (SOCCER)

Shamateurism' (or secret payment) appeared to have come into the Olympic Arena with the appearance of certain Eastern European powers after 1948. The Games began to be dominated by state-sponsored teams.

In 1964 Italy withdrew after accusations that its players were professional (three played for the famous professional club, Inter Milan) and it became clear that legislation would have to change.

By this stage Olympic soccer had become even more popular, requiring the introduction of a pre-Olympic tournament (in 1952). It seemed only a matter of time before attitudes changed, although it required the Los Angeles Games of 1984 – the most commercially-oriented Games of them all up until that time – before professionals were allowed into soccer. More than 100,000 watched the final of that year, won by France.

After this happened only those professionals who had not played in professional soccer's showpiece event, the World Cup, were permitted to play in the Olympic Games. Later this rule was abolished and the only restriction became that players should be under 23. However, this has been modified for Atlanta (see later), which should see some famous names taking part.

There have been many outstanding teams, and the number of possible winners is gratifyingly large. However, Hungary had a wonderful run up until 1972 when they were beaten for only the second time in 21 matches as Poland overcame them 2-1 in the Munich final. Hungary still has the most golds, three.

The biggest shock? Probably when Italy was beaten 4-0 in a preliminary round by Zambia. And the greatest oddity? Possibly when the Soviet Union won the title in 1988 fully 14 minutes into extra time, denying Brazil the gold they have never taken.

Equipment

The ball, unlike that in American football, must be round. It is made of leather, with a circumference of not more than 71cm (28in.) and not less than 68cm (27in.). It must weigh not more than 453g (16oz).

The goal posts must be 7.32m (8yds) apart and the crossbar 2.44m (8ft) high with nets attached. There is considerable flexibility permitted in the size of the playing field, but the standard size for international matches is 105x68m (115x73yds).

Rules

The whole of the ball must pass over the goal-line between the posts for it to be a goal. A player can use the feet, the head and, if he or she wishes, any part of the body to propel the ball – except the arms and hands.

There are two teams of eleven players, of which one must be a goalkeeper (who can handle the ball within the penalty area). There are three substitutes on each side, who are allowed to replace an on-field player once. A substituted player cannot return and a match is played for two halves of 45 minutes each.

Atlanta Format

There is a qualifying competition which will result in 16 men's teams playing at the Olympic Games in four groups of four. Two progress from each group to a quarter-final knock-out stage, followed by semi-finals and a final. In the men's competition players must have been born on or after 1 January 1973 and must not have played in a previous Olympic Games. However, each team may have three players to whom these restrictions do not apply.

There is a women's competition for the first time, of eight teams. All players must be at least 16 years old. They will play in two groups of four with the top two in each group advancing to semi-finals and a final. And there is a third place play-off for the bronze medal in both competitions.

Venues

Sanford stadium will host the semi-finals and finals of the men's and women's competitions. It is the fourth largest college football stadium in the country, with a capacity of 85,000. The stadium has had its famous hedges bordering the field removed in order to accommodate a wider soccer pitch.

Four other cities throughout the south-east will provide the venues of first round and quarter-final matches. They are the Citrus Bowl in Orlando, Florida; the Legion Field in Birmingham, Alabama; the Orange Bowl, Miami, Florida; and the RFK Memorial Stadium in Washington DC.

The Citrus Bowl was one of the most popular venues for the 1994 World Cup in the United States and is 715 km (447 miles) south-east of Atlanta. The Legion Field holds 80,000 spectators, is one of the South's most historic stadia, and is

Sanford stadium

located 235 km (146 miles) west of Atlanta. The Orange Bowl has a capacity of 74,000 and is 1,072 km (670 miles) south of Atlanta. The RFK Memorial Stadium, the home of the Washington Redskins football team, has hosted many international soccer matches and is 1027 km (642 miles) from Atlanta, just a few miles from the US Capitol Building.

MEDALLISTS (by nation)

		Men's		
	Gold	Silver	Bronze	Total
Hungary	3	1	1	5
Soviet Union	2	-	3	5
Denmark	1	3	1	5
Yugoslavia	1	3	1	5
Great Britain	3	-	-	3
GDR	1	1	1	3
Poland	1	2	-	3
Sweden	1	-	2	3
Netherlands	-	-	3	3
Uruguay	2	-	-	2
Czechoslovakia	1	1	-	2
France	1	1	-	2
Belgium	1	-	1	2
Italy	1	-	1	2
Brazil	-	2	-	2
Bulgaria	-	1	1	2
Greece	-	1	1	2
Spain	1	1	-	2
United States	-	1	1	2
Canada	1	-	-	1
Argentina	-	1	-	1
Austria	-	1	-	1
Switzerland	-	1	-	1
FRG	-	-	1	1
Germany	-	-	1	1
Ghana	-	-	1	1
Japan	-	-	1	1
Norway	-	-	1	1
	21	21	22[1]	64

[1] Third place tie in 1972

ATLANTA SCHEDULE

Venues:
Sanford Stadium, Athens, Georgia = A
Florida Citrus Bowl, Orlando, Florida = O
Legion Field, Birmingham, Alabama = B
Orange Bowl, Miami, Florida = M
RFK Memorial Stadium, Washington, D.C. = W

Date	Round	Start	End	Venue
20 Jul	prelims (m)	15:00	17:00	W
		19:30	21:30	B
		18:30	20:30	O
		18:30	20:30	M

Date	Round	Start	End	Venue
21 Jul	prelims (w)	15:00	19:30	W
	prelims (m)			
	prelims (w)	14:30	19:00	B
	prelims (m)			
	prelims (w)	16:00	20:30	O
	prelims (m)			
	prelims (w)	16:00	20:30	M
	prelims (m)			
22 Jul	prelims (m)	19:30	21:30	B
	prelims (m)	19:30	21:30	W
	prelims (m)	19:00	21:00	M
	prelims (m)	19:00	21:00	O
23 Jul	prelims (w)	17:30	22:00	B
	prelims (m)			
	prelims (w)	18:30	23:00	W
	prelims (m)			
	prelims (w)	18:00	22:30	M
	prelims (m)			
	prelims (w)	18:00	22:30	O
	prelims (m)			
24 Jul	prelims (m)	19:30	21:30	B
	prelims (m)	19:30	21:30	W
	prelims (m)	19:00	21:00	M
	prelims (m)	19:00	21:00	O
25 Jul	prelims (w)	18:30	23:00	B
	prelims (m)			
	prelims (w)	18:30	23:00	W
	prelims (m)			
	prelims (w)	18:30	23:00	M
	prelims (m)			
	prelims (w)	18:30	23:00	O
	prelims (m)			
27 Jul	q/finals (m)	19:30	21:30	B
	q/finals (m)	18:00	20:00	M
28 Jul	s/finals (w)	15:00	19:30	A
	q/finals (m)	16:00	18:00	B
	q/finals (m)	18:00	20:00	M
31 Jul	s/finals (m)	15:00	17:00	A
	s/finals (m)	20:00	22:00	A
1 Aug	play-off (bronze) (w)	18:00	22:45	A
	FINAL (w)			A
2 Aug	play-off (bronze) (m)	20:00	22:00	A
3 Aug	FINAL (m)	15:30	17:45	A

MEDALLISTS

FOOTBALL

Year	Gold	C'ntry	Score	Silver	C'ntry	Bronze	C'ntry
1900	Claude Buckingham	GBR		Pierre Allemane	FRA	Albert Delbecque	BEL
	R E Barridge			Bach		R Kelecom	
	Alfred Chalk			Bloch		Marcel Leboutte	
	William Grosing			Fernand Canelle		Londot	
	A Haslam			Duparc		Ernest Moreau	
	J H Jones			Fraysse		Georges Pelgrims	
	J Nicholas			Gaillard		Alphonse Renier	
	William Quash			René Garnier		E Spannoghe	
	F G Spackman			Grandjean		Erich Thornton	
	R R Turner			Huteau		van Heuckelum	
	James Zealey			Lambert		C van Hoorden	
				Macaire			
				Peltier			
1904	George Ducker	CAN		Charles Bartliff	USA	Joseph Brady	USA
	John Fraser			Warren Brittingham		George Cooke	
	John Gourley			Oscar Brockmeyer		Thomas Cooke	
	Alexander Hall			Alexander Cudmore		Cormic Cosgrove	
	Albert Johnson			Charles January		Dierkes	
	Robert Lane			John January		Martin Dooling	
	Ernest Linton			Thomas January		Frank Frost	
	Gordon McDonald			Raymond Lawler		Henry Jameson	
	Frederick Steep			Joseph Lydon		Claude Jameson	
	Tom Taylor			Louis Menges		Johnson	
	William Twaits			Peter Ratican		O'Connell	
						Harry Tate	
1908	Horace Bailey	GBR	2-0	Harald Bohr	DEN	Reinier Beeuwkes	NED
	Arthur Berry			Charles Buchwald		George de Bruyn Kops	
	Frederick Chapman			Ludwig Drescher		Johannes de Korver	
	Walter Corbett			Harald Hansen		Karel Hejting	
	Harold Hardman			August Lindgreen		Emil Mundt	
	Robert Hawkes			Christian Middelboe		Louis Otten	
	Kenneth Hunt			Nils Middelboe		Gerard Reemen	
	Clyde Purnell			Niels Oscar Nielsen		Eduard Snetlage	
	Herbert Smith			Sofus Nielsen		Johan Sol	
	Henry Stapley			Björn Rasmussen		Ja Thomée	
	Vivian Woodward			Vilhelm Wolfhagen		Jan Welcker	
1912	Arthur Berry	GBR	4-2	Paul Berth	DEN	Johannes Boutmy	NED
	Ronald Brebner			Sofus Hansen		Nicolaas Bouvy	
	Thomas Burn			Harald Hansen		Henri de Groot	
	Joseph Dines			Emil Jörgensen		Nicolaas de Wolff	
	Gordon Hoare			Nils Middelboe		Constant Feith	
	Arthur Knight			Niels Oscar Nielsen		Gerardus Fortgens	
	Henry Littlewort			Sofus Nielsen		Marius Just Göbel	
	Douglas McWhirter			Anton Olsen		Dirk Lotsy	
	Ivor Sharpe			Axel Thufvason		Caesar ten Cate	
	Harold Walden			Vilhelm Wolfhagen		Jan van Bredakolff	
	Vivian Woodward					Jan van der Sluis	
						Jan Vos	
						David Wijnveldt	
1920	Félix Balyu	BEL	3-1	Patricio Arabolaza	ESP	Adrianus Bieshaar	NED
	Désiré Bastin			Aramburu		Leonard Bosschart	
	Mathieu Bragard			Mariano Arrate Esnaola		Evert Bulder	
	Robert Coppée			Juan Artola Letamendia		Jacob Bulder	
	Jean de Bie			José Maria Belaustequigoita Landaluce		Johannes de Natris	
	André Fierens			Sabino Bilbao Libano		Henri Denis	
	Emile Hanse			Ramón Eguiazábal Berroa		Bernardus Groosjohan	
	Georges Hebdin			Ramón Gil Fegueiros		Frederik Kuipers	
	Henri Larnoe			Domingo Gomez-AcedoVillaneuva		Richard MacNeill	
	Joseph Musch			Silverio Izaguirre Sorzabalbere		Hermanus Steeman	
	Fernand Nisot			Rafael Moreno Aranzadi		Jan van Dort	
	Armand Swartenbroeks			Luis Otero Sanchez		Hermanus van Heyden	
	Louis van Hege			Francisco Pagazaurtundúa Gonzalez		Oscar van Rappard	

Year	Gold	C'ntry	Score	Silver	C'ntry	Bronze	C'ntry
	Oscar Verbeeck			José Samitier Vilalta		Bernard Verheij	
				Agustin Sancho Agustina			
				Félix Sesúmaga Segura			
				Pedro Vallana Jeanguenat			
				Joaquin Vázquez Gonzalez			
				Ricardo Zamora Martinez			
1924	José Leandro Andrade	URU	3-0	Max Abegglen	SUI	Axel Alfredsson	SWE
	Pedro Arispe			Walter Dietrich		Albin C Dahl	
	Pedro Céa			Karl Ehrenbolger		Sven Friberg	
	Alfredo Ghierra			Paul Fässler		Fritjof Hillén	
	Andres Mazali			August Oberhauser		Gunnar Holmberg	
	José Nasazzi			Robert Pache		Per Kaufeldt	
	José Naya			Aron Pollitz		Tore Keller	
	Pedro Petrone			Hans Pulver		Rudolf Kock	
	Angel Romano			Rudolf Ramseyer		Sigfrid Lindberg	
	Hector Scarone			Adolphe Reymond		Evert Lundquist	
	Umberto Tomasina			Paul Schmiedlin		Sven Rydell	
	Antonio Urdinarán					Harry Sundberg	
	Santos Urdinarán						
	José Vidal						
	Alfredo Zibecchi						
1928	José Leandro Andrade	URU	2-1	Ludovico Bidoglio	ARG	Adolfo Baloncieri	ITA
	Pedro Arispe			Angel Bosio		Elvio Banchero	
	Juan Arremón			Saúl Calandra		Delfo Bellini	
	René Borjas			Alfredo Carricaberry		Fulvio Bernardini	
	Antonio Campolo			Roberto Cherro		Umberto Caligaris	
	Adhemar Canavesi			Octavio Diaz		Giampiero Combi	
	Hector Castro			Juan Evaristo		Peitro Genovesi	
	Pedro Cea			Manuel Ferreira		Virgilio Levratto	
	Lorenzo Fernández			Enrique Gainzarain		Mario Magnozzi	
	Roberto Figueroa			Segundo Medici		Alfredo Pitto	
	José Alvaro Gestido			Luis Monti		Angelo Schiavio	
	Andres Mazáli			Rudolfo Orlandini			
	José Nasazzi			Raimundo Orsi			
	Pedro Petrone			Fernando Paternoster			
	Juan Piriz			Feliciano Angel Perduca			
	Hector Scarone			Domingo Tarasconi			
	Santos Urdinarán						
1936	Giuseppe Baldo	ITA	2-1	Franz Fuchsberger	AUT	Arne Brustad	NOR
	Sergio Bertoni			Max Hofmeister		Nils Eriksen	
	Carlo Biagi			Eduard Kainberger		Odd Frantzen	
	Alfredo Foni			Karl Kainberger		Rolf Holmberg	
	Annibale Frossi			Martin Kargl		Öivind Holmsen	
	Francesco Gabriotti			Anton Krenn		Henry Johansen	
	Ugo Locatelli			Ernst Kúnz		Jörgen Juve	
	Libero Marchini			Adolf Laudon		Reidar Kvammen	
	Achille Piccini			Klement Steinmetz		Alf Martinsen	
	Pietro Rava			Karl Wahlmúller		Magdalon Monsen	
	Bruno Venturini			Walter Werginz		Fritjof Ulleberg	
1948	Sune Andersson	SWE	3-1	Alexander Atanacković	YUG	John Hansen	DEN
	Henry Carlsson			Stjepan Bobek		Viggo Jensen	
	Gunnar Gren			Miroslav Brozović		Tage Ivan Jensen	
	Nils Liedholm			Zeljko Čajkovski		Knud Lundberg	
	Torsten Lindberg			Zlatko Čajkovski		Eigil Nielsen	
	Erik Nilsson			Zvonko Cimermancić		Dion Örnvold	
	Bertil Nordahl			Miodrag Jovanović		Börge Overgaard	
	Gunnar Nordahl			Ljubomir Lovrić		Axel Pilmark	
	Knut Nordahl			Rajko Mitić		Johannes Plöger	
	Kjell Rosén			Branislav Stanković		Carl Aage Praest	
	Birger Rosengren			Bernard Vukas		Jörgen Sörensen	
1952	József Bozsik	HUN	2-0	Vladimir Beara	YUG	Olle Åhlund	SWE
	Jenő Buzánszky			Stjepan Bobek		Sylve Bengtsson	
	Zoltán Czibor			Vujadin Boškov		Yngve Brodd	
	Gyula Grosits			Zlatko Čajkovski		Bengt Gustavsson	
	Nándor Hidegkuti			Tomislav Crnković		Gösta Löfgren	
	Sándor Kocsis			Ivan Horvat		Erik Nilsson	

/continued on next page 247

Year	Gold	C'ntry	Score	Silver	C'ntry	Bronze	C'ntry
	Mihály Lantos			Rajko Mitić		Ingvar Rydell	
	Gyula Lorant			Tihomir Ognjanov		Lennart Samuelsson	
	Péter Palotás			Branislav Stanković		Gösta Sandberg	
	Ferenc Puskás			Bernard Vukas		Karl Svensson	
	Jozsef Zakariás			Branko Zebec			
1956	Anatoli Bachachkine	URS	1-0	Sava Antić	YUG	Todor Diev	BUL
	Anatoli Iliiune			Mladen Koscać		Ivan Kolev	
	Anatoli Issaev			Dobroslav Krstić		Nikolai Kovatchev	
	Lev Jasjin			Muhamed Mujić		Manol Manolov	
	Boris Kouznetsov			Zlatko Papec		Guerin Nikolov	
	Anatoli Maslenkine			Petar Radenković		Panayot Panayotov	
	Igor Netto			Nikola Radović		Kirill Rakarov	
	Mikhail Ogognikov			Ivan Santek		Stefan Stefanov	
	Sergei Salnikov			Dragoslav Šekularac		Gavril Stoyanov	
	Nikita Simonian			Ljubiša Spajić		Dimitre Stoyanov	
	Boris Tatouchine			Todor Veselinović			
1960	Andrija Anković	YUG	3-1	Paul Andersen	DEN	Flórian Albert	HUN
	Vladimir Durković			John Danielsen		Jenő Dálnoki	
	Milan Galić			Henning Enoksen		Zoltán Dudás	
	Fahrudin Jusufi			Henry From		János Dunai	
	Tomislav Knez			Bent Hansen		Lajos Faragó	
	Borivoje Kostić			Poul Jensen		János Gőrőcs	
	Alexander Kozlina			Flemming Nielsen		Ferenc Kovács	
	Dušan Maravić			Hans Nielsen		Dezső Novák	
	Željko Matus			Harald Nielsen		Pál Orosz	
	Željko Perusić			Poul Pedersen		László Pál	
	Novak Roganović			Jörn Sörensen		Tibor Pál	
	Velimir Sombolac			Tommy Troelsen		Gyula Rákosi	
	Milutin Šoškić					Imre Sátori	
	Silvester Takac					Ernő Solymosi	
	Blagoje Vidinić					Gábor Tőrők	
	Ante Zanetić					Pál Várhidi	
						Oszkár Vilezsál	
1964	Ferenc Bene	HUN	2-1	Jan Brumovskÿ	TCH	Wolfgang Barthels	GDR
	János Farkas			Ludovít Cvetler		Bernd Bauchspiess	
	József Gelei			Ján Geleta		Dieter Engelhardt	
	Tibor Gsernai			František Knebort		Otto Frössdorf	
	Kálmán Ihász			Karel Knesl		Henning Frenzel	
	Sándor Katona			Karel Lichtnegl		Manfred Geisler	
	Imre Komora			Vojtěch Masnÿ		Hans Jürgen Heinsch	
	Ferenc Nógrádi			Štefan Matlák		Gerhard Körner	
	Dezső Novák			Ivan Mráz		Klaus Lisiewicz	
	Arpád Orbán			Karel Nepomucký		Jürgen Nöldner	
	Károly Polotai			Zdeněk Pičman		Herbert Pankau	
	Antal Szentmihályi			František Schmucker		Peter Rock	
	Gusztáv Szepesi			Antonín Švajlen		Klaus-Dieter Seehaus	
	Zoltán Varga			Antonín Urban		Hermann Stöcker	
				František Valošek		Werner Unger	
				Josef Vojta		Klaus Urbanczyk	
				Vladimír Weiss		Eberhard Vogel	
						Manfred Walter	
						Horst Weigang	
1968	Istvàn Bàsti	HUN	4-1	Gueorgui Christakiev	BUL	Kunishige Kamamoto	JPN
	Lajos Drestÿak			Atanasse Christov		Mitsuo Kamata	
	Antal Dunai			Tzvetan Dimitrov		Hiroshi Katayama	
	Károly Fater			Asparoukh Donev		Yasuyuki Kuwahara	
	László Fazekas			Milko Gaidarski		Ikuo Matsumoto	
	István Juhász			Ivailo Gueorguiev		Teruki Miyamoto	
	László Keglovich			Atanasse Guerov		Masakatsu Miyamoto	
	Iván Menczel			Mikhail Guionine		Takaji Mori	
	László Nagy			Kiril Ivkov		Aritatsu Ogi	
	Ernő Noskó			Peter Jekov		Ryuichi Sugiyama	
	Dezső Novák			Georghi Vassilev		Masashi Watanabe	
	Miklós Páncsics			Tvetan Veselinov		Shigeo Yaegashi	
	Gabor Sarkőzi			Evgeni Yantchevski		Yoshitada Yamaguchi	
	Lajos Szűcs			Stoyan Yordanov		Kenzo Yokoyama	

Year	Gold	C'ntry	Score	Silver	C'ntry	Bronze	C'ntry
1972	Zygmunt Ańczok	POL	2-1	László Bálint	HUN	Bernd Bransch	GDR
	Lesław Ćmikiewicz			László Branikovits		Jürgen Croy	
	Kazimierz Dejna			Antal Dunai		Peter Ducke	
	Robert Gadocha			Ede Dunai		Frank Ganzera	
	Jerzy Gorgon			István Géczi		Reinhard Hafner	
	Zbigniew Gut			Péter Juhász		Harald Irmscher	
	Kazimierz Kmiecik			Lajos Kocsis		Hans-Jürgen Kreische	
	Hubert Kostka			Jósef Kovács		Lothar Kurbjuweit	
	Jerzy Kraśka			Mihály Kozma		Jürgen Pommerenke	
	Grzegorz Lato			Lajos Kű		Ralf Schulenberg	
	Wlodzimierz Lubański			Miklós Páncsics		Wolfgang Seguin	
	Joachim Marx			Ádám Rothermel		Jürgen Sparwasser	
	Zygmunt Maszczyk			Lajos Szűcs		Achim Streich	
	Marian Ostafiński			Kálmán Tóth		Eberhard Vogel	
	Zygfryd Szoltysik			Béla Váradi		Siegmar Watzlich	
	Antoni Szymanowski			Péter Vepi		Konrad Weise	
	Ryszard Szymczak			Csaba Vidacs		Manfred Zapf	
1976	Bernd Bransch	GDR	3-1	Jan Beniger	POL	Vladimir Astapovkski	URS
	Georg Buschner			Lestaw Ćmikiewicz		Oleg Blokhin	
	Jürgen Croy			Kazimierz Dejna		Leonid Buriak	
	Hans-Jürgen Dörner			Jerzy Gorgon		Vladimir Feodorov	
	Ullrich Grapenthin			Kazimier Gorski		Mikhail Fomenko	
	Wilfried Gröbner			Henryk Kasperczak		David Kipiani	
	Reinhard Häfner			Kazimierz Kmiecik		Viktor Kolotov	
	Gert Heidler			Grzegorz Lato		Anatoli Konkov	
	Martin Hoffman			Zygmunt Maszczyk		Valeri Lobanovski	
	Gerd Kische			Piotr Mowlik		Viktor Matvienko	
	Lothar Kurbjuweit			Roman Ogaza		Alexander Minaev	
	Reinhard Lauck			Wojciech Rudy		Leonid Nazarenko	
	Wolfram Löwe			Andrzej Szarmach		Vladimir Onischenko	
	Dieter Riedel			Antoni Szymanowski		Alexander Prokhorov	
	Hans-Jürgen Riediger			Jan Tomaszewski		Stefan Reshko	
	Hartmut Schade			Henryk Wawrowski		Vladimir Troshkin	
	Gerd Weber			Henryk Wieczorek		Vladimir Veremeev	
	Konrad Weise			Władysław Zmuda		Viktor Zviagintsev	
1980	Jan Berger	TCH	1-0	Jürgen Bähringer	GDR	Sergei Andreev	URS
	František Kunzo			Frank Baum		Sergei Baltacha	
	Werner Lička			Lothar Hause		Vladimir Bessonov	
	Luděk Macela			Bernd Jakubowski		Fiodor Cherenkov	
	Josef Mazura			Dieter Kühn		Alexander Chivadze	
	Petr Němec			Matthias Liebers		Rinat Dasaev	
	Jaroslav Netolička			Matthias Müller		Yuri Gavrilov	
	Luboš Pokluda			Wolf-Rüdiger Netz		Valeri Gazzaev	
	Libor Radimec			Werner Peter		Vagiz Khidiiatullin	
	Oldřich Rott			Bodo Rudwaleit		Sergei Nikulin	
	Zdeněk Rygel			Rüdiger Schnuphase		Khoren Oganesian	
	Stanislav Seman			Wolfgang Steinbach		Vladimir Pilgui	
	František Štambacher			Frank Terletzki		Alexander Prokopenko	
	Jindřich Svoboda			Norbert Trieloff		Oleg Romantsev	
	Rostislav Václavíček			Frank Uhlig		Sergei Shavlo	
	Ladislav Vízek			Artur Ullrich		Tengiz Sulakvelidze	
1984	William Ayache	FRA	2-0	Jorge Luiz Brum	BRA	Mirsad Baljić	YUG
	Michel Bensoussan			Milton Cruz		Mehmed Baždarević	
	Michel Bibard			Luis Dias		Vlado Čapljić	
	Dominique Bijotat			Andre Luiz Ferreira		Borislav Cvetković	
	Francois Brisson			Mauro Galvao		Stjepan Deverić	
	Patrick Cubaynes			Antonio José Gil		Milko Djurovski	
	Patrice Garande			Ademir Rock Kaeser		Marko Elsner	
	Philippe Jeannol			João Leiehardt Neto		Nenad Gračan	
	Guy Lacombe			Augilmar Oliveira		Tomislav Ivković	
	Jean-Claude Lemoult			Silvio Paiva		Srećko Katanec	
	Jean-Philippe Rohr			Gilmar Rinaldi		Branko Miljus	
	Albert Rust			Paulo Santos		Mitar Mrkela	
	Didier Sénac			Ronaldo Silva		Jovica Nikolić	
	Jean-Christoph Thouvenel			Davi Cortez Silva		Ivan Pudar	
	José Touré			Carlos Verri		Ljubomir Radanović	

/continued on next page 249

Year	Gold	C'ntry	Score	Silver	C'ntry	Bronze	C'ntry
	Daniel Xuereb			Francisco Vidal		Admir Smajić	
	Jean-Louis Zanon			Luiz Carlos Winck		Dragan Stojković	
1988	Alexander Borodiouk	URS	2-1	Aloisio Alves	BRA	Rudi Bommer	FRG
	Alexei Cherednik			José Araujo		Holger Fach	
	Igor Dobrovolski			Jorge Campos		Wolfgang Funkel	
	Sergei Fokine			Valdoo Candido		Armin Goertz	
	Sergei Gorloukovitch			Andre Cruz		Roland Grahammer	
	Arvidas Ianonis			Romario Farias		Thomas Hässler	
	Evgeni Iarovenko			José Ferreira		Thomas Hörster	
	Guela Ketachvili			Ademir Kaefer		Olaf Janssen	
	Dmitri Kharin			Sergio Luiz		Uwe Kamps	
	Evgeni Kouznetsov			Iomar Nascimento		Gerhard Kleppinger	
	Vladimir Lioutyi			José Oliveira		Jürgen Klinsmann	
	Viktor Lossev			Ricardo Raimundo		Frank Mill	
	Alexei Mikhailitchenko			João Santos		Oliver Reck	
	Arminas Narbekovas			Edmar Santos		Karlheinz Riedle	
	Igor Ponomarev			Geovani Silva		Gunnar Sauer	
	Alexei Proudnikov			Jorge Silva		Christian Schreier	
	Yuri Savitchev			Hamilton Souza		Michael Schulz	
	Igor Skliarov			Milton Souza		Ralf Sievers	
	Vladimir Tatartchouk			Claudio Taffarel		Fritz Walter	
	Vadim Tichtchenko			Luiz Winck		Wolfram Wuttke	
1992	José Amavisca Garate	ESP	3-2	Dariusz Adamczyk	POL	Joachin Yaw Acheampong	GHA
	Antonio Jimenez Sistachs			Tomasz Apiski		Simon Addo	
	Rafael Berges Marin			Marek Bajor		Sammi Adjei	
	José Santiago Canizares Ruiz			Jerzy Brzęczek		Mamood Amadu	
	Abelardo Fernandez Antuna			Dariusz Gęsior		Frank Amankwah	
	Albert Ferrer Llopis			Marcin Jałocha		Bernard Nii Aryee	
	Josep Guardiola Sala			Andrzej Juskowiak		Isaac Asare	
	Miguel Hernandez Sanchez			Alexander Kak		Kwame Ayew	
	Mikel Lasa Goicoechea			Andrzej Kobylański		Ibrahim Dossey	
	Juan Lopez Martinez			Dariusz Kosea		Robert Eshun	
	Javier Manjariin Pereda			Wojciech Kowalczyk		Mohammed Gargo	
	Luis Enrique Martinez Garcia			Marek Koźmiski		Mohammed Dramani Kalilu	
	Quico Narvaez			Grzegorz Mielcarski		Maxwell Konadu	
	Alfonso Perez Munoz			Arkadiusz Onyszko		Osei Kuffuor	
	Antonio Pinilla Miranda			Ryszard Staniek		Samuel Ablade Kumah	
	Francisco Soler Atencis			Piotr Świerczewski		Nii Odartey Lamptey	
	Roberto Solozabal Villanueva			Dariusz Szubert		Anthony Mensah	
	Francisco Veza Fragoso			Tomasz Wadoch		Alex Nyarko	
	Gabriel Vidal Nova			Mirostaw Waligora		Yaw Owusu	
	David Villabona Etxaleku			Tomasz Wieszczycki		Yaw Preko	
						Shamo Quaye	
						Oli Rahman	

Gymnastics

by Vera Marinova

A new age and geography for gymnastics

"WE USED to guess at just about everything. The whole world has improved in this sport and now we've caught up. From now on, all major competitions will be like golf tournaments. It will not be a certainty who is going to win. It will depend on the day!"

The words were from Abie Grossfield, the USA men's team coach, after the unexpected victory of his gymnasts over the much higher-ranked and more experienced Chinese and Japanese at the Los Angeles Olympic Games of 1984. Time has told just how farsighted this ex-Olympian (1956 and '60) and many times national coach turned out to be. In Atlanta, 12 years later, a new map of world gymnastics as well as a new minimum age could engender some dramatic changes.

All this means that making a gymnastics prognosis for the 1996 Atlanta Olympic Games is as easy as predicting the winner of a national lottery. The moment is long past when clear favourites existed in the sport. After Barcelona, in 1992, a new era began in world gymnastics. New nations, new teams and many new talents appeared on the world stage after the break up of the Soviet Union. The strength of these teams rearranged the world ranking list and the challenge at major competitions became tougher than ever before.

Svetlana Khorkina of Russia

Coaches (from Bulgaria, China, Romania and Russia) and gymnasts started to migrate from East to West influencing standards and rankings for their new homelands. In 1996 this has particularly affected the middle order of gymnasts but, a decade from now, could have a major impact at the very top as economic factors begin to bite in the ex-Soviet bloc countries.

Valeri Belenki (Azerbaijan) all-round

bronze medallist in Barcelona and Marius Toba (Romania) now represent Germany and could be joined by 1993 world silver medallist Sergei Kharkov. And the former world pommel horse 'king' Valentine Mogilny (Russia) is set to wear the French tricolour. One-time top Soviet junior, Alexei Demianov (Moldova), now represents, and brings home medals to, Croatia.

In Atlanta, too, a new minimum age limit of 15 for the women (to be achieved in the year of the Games) has been invoked for the first time by the FIG (International Gymnastics Federation). Countries had been constantly striving after higher technical difficulties with the attendant need for younger and younger gymnasts. The media and general public had become dissatisfied as they witnessed power gymnastics peformed by "kindergarten robots", replacing the grace, elegance and beauty they had learned to love.

In consequence, some of the "old" celebrities have decided to stage comebacks. Of these, the three best examples include 1989 world champion, Svetlana Boginskaya, 1991 world champion Kim Zmeskal of the USA and 1991 world floor exercises champion, Elena Chusovitina of Uzbekistan.

After a long period of hesitation the FIG has also at last taken the decision to remove the compulsory programme – Atlanta will be the last time the 'sets' will be performed. From 1997 onwards 'imagination time' will begin as only optional exercises will be used at major internationals and demonstrations.

But in Atlanta a new competition format means that the coach will need to be a strategist as well as a technician. A team consists of seven gymnasts: six to perform on each piece of apparatus with five scores to count. The coach's choice will, therefore, be all important in terms of the final result of the team.

At the 1995 world championships, held in October in Japan, the new world order in the men's team event became apparent. Strikingly, Russia finished fourth on the list of twelve qualifying teams from the event for Atlanta, with no team medal for the first time in the modern era of gymnastics.

Romania picked up a well-deserved but surprising bronze. Ukraine and Belarussia were sadly affected by injuries during the competition, finishing fifth and sixth respectively. Former world champion Igor Korobtchinski snapped his achilles tendon. China took gold with Japan in the silver medal position.

In the corresponding women's field the list of Olympic visa winners was topped by Romania, followed by China and the

USA. China proved excellent in the optional programme and could challenge the Romanians in Atlanta. Russia were fourth – again for the first time without a team medal – and were followed by France and Germany. In a remarkable feat Greece also qualified and this shows what can be achieved by centralized training and national support in a very short period of time.

The two new all-round world champions Li Xiaozhuang of China for the men and Lilla Podkopayeva (Ukraine) for the women will face severe challenges in Atlanta from the two silver medallists Vitali Scherbo (Belarus) and Svetlana Khorkina (Russia) who have both stood on the highest rostrum before and will wish to do so again.

Until recently the best results on the international stage of rhythmic gymnastics had been achieved by the mixed Soviet team and representatives of the traditionally very strong and original Bulgarian school. Since the break up of the Soviet Union, the field has multiplied. Russia, Belarus and Ukraine have been given the chance to show the world many more talents from their unfathomable reservoirs. And although other nations, such as Spain and France, have been improving quickly, they do not very often have the chance to break the wall of the 'big four'.

Whoever gets to the top Olympic podium in Atlanta will have a hard battle. First amongst the favourites must be the

★★★★★★★★★★★★★★★★★★★★★★★★★★★★★★ **A Contemporary Hero**

Vitali Scherbo *(Belarus)*

He was born in Minsk, Belarus. Both his parents were acrobats. He entered the gymnasium aged six. At 16 he was able to hold a crucifix on the rings. At 17 he took part in his first major competition, the Goodwill Games in Seattle (USA) 1990 and he won it, taking four gold medals. Within the next two years, Scherbo was inevitably on the rostrum at European and world championships sweeping titles on different apparatus.

Wherever and whenever he appears Scherbo is still a threat to his rivals. An exuberant, extroverted and impulsive 'steamroller' producing medals. In 1993 he became the first ever gymnast to be awarded the 'Jesse Owens' international trophy.

Now he lives in America together with his wife Irina and daughter Kristina and he still represents Belarussia at major competitions. Will he be able to approach and equalize Kato's record (eight gold medals) in Atlanta at 23? Very possible. Just wait and see.

GYMNASTICS

A Sporting Legend ★★★★★★★★★★★★★★★★★★★★★★★★★★★★★★★★★★★★★★

Alexandra Timoshenko *(Ukraine)*

No other rhythmic gymnast in the world has two separate Olympic medals in her collection other than Alexandra Timoshenko of the Ukraine. Her first came as a bronze in Seoul in 1988 in a competition which was won by Marina Lobatch of the Soviet Union with silver going to Adriana Dounavska of Bulgaria.

Timoshenko's second medal was a gold in Barcelona four years ago to mark the end of her career. The extremely creative Timoshenko was challenged for much of the way by her compatriot Oksana Skaldina. Both were trained in Kiev under the famous Albina and Irina Derjugini (Irina, herself, was world all-around champion in 1977 and '79).

Timoshenko burst into the limelight at the Helsinki European championships of 1988 and shared the title with Bulgarians Elizabeth Koleva and Adriana Dounavska. A year later in Sarajevo she became world champion. By the time she quit the competitive floor she had collected eight gold medals from the world championships (1989 and '91); nine European titles (two in the all-around – 1988 and '90 – the rest of them on different apparatus); two European cups 1989 and '90.

Born on 18 February 1971 in Bohuslav, in the Ukraine, Timoshenko's mother was a book-keeper and her father was an engineer. She also had a sister five years younger than her. Timoshenko turned out to be one of the brightest stars in the whole history of rhythmic gymnastics. Her new elements showed an extreme flexibility and her high leg scales brought a new dimension to the sport. Now she lives in Austria and works for a German club.

Bulgarian Maria Petrova who managed to equal the record of her compatriot Maria Gulgova (three all-round world titles) at the Vienna 1995 contest. Petrova's maturity, style and strong nerves are unbelievable and she could well resist the strong challenge of potential Olympic medallists Ekaterina Serebrianskaya and Elena Vitritchenko both of the Ukraine as well as Yana Batyrchina and Amina Zaripova (Russia), Larissa Lukianenko, Olga Gontar and Evgenia Pavlina (Bulgaria).

For the first time at the Games, the rhythmic discipline will also feature a contest of group exercises. Each team, at the qualifying event in Vienna in September of last year, featured five instead of six gymnasts providing coaches and choreographers with a test of their creativity. Seven teams won their Atlanta tickets led by Bulgaria, Spain and Belarussia who must all be favourites for the 1996 Olympic podium. Spain will have high hopes in the new group exercises. They won the world and European titles in 1992 and took world gold in the balls and two ribbons exercise in Vienna in 1995.

There is no doubt that rhythmic gymnastics will be one of the jewels in the Olympic crown in Atlanta, the brightest and most attractive. The results, meanwhile, will all be based on who can put in a flawless performance tinged with a little luck.

V. M. ☐

Retrospective

Four years ago, Barcelona, Spain. Those Games will be remembered for the incredible victory of Vitali Scherbo representing the "Unified Team" with his hoard of six Olympic gold medals. Tatiana Goutsou, also of the Unified Team, took the women's all-round title against the odds. Most people, before the Games, would have backed her compatriot Svetlana Boguinskaia or Kim Zmeskal of the USA who finished fifth and tenth respectively. But such multi-medallists and dramatic upsets as well as telegenic charm have been a feature of past Olympic Games gymnastics competitions.

In 1972 the elfin figure and mischievous smile of Olga Korbut captured the imagination of a television public world-wide and catapulted the sport into the limelight. The 17 year old Soviet competitor won three golds and stole everybody's heart but questions were raised about her technical proficiency by some experts who believed the judges might also have been swayed.

Ironically Korbut's exploits overshadowed those of her team-mate Ludmila Turisheva who took the overall title in that Games and joined her immortal predecessors Larissa Latynina and Věra Čáslavská. And, four years later, Korbut's compatriot Nelli Kim had improved sufficiently to score two perfect "10s" alongside the six recorded by the

---

★★★★★★★★★★★★★★★★★★★★★★★★★★★★★★ **A Sporting Legend**

Ludmila Turischeva *(Russia)*

She was the third Soviet female gymnast to become Olympic champion after Maria Gorovskaya (1952) and Larissa Latynina (1956 and '60). But Ludmila Turischeva's great coach Vladislav Rostorozki was deeply impressed more by her seriousness than her talent when she first appeared in the Groznil gymnastics hall, in Russia, at 12 years of age.

"Gymnastics is more hard work than talent", she stated at the end of her career. Total dedication and hard work were in fact the secret of her great achievements. She made her debut in the Mexico City Olympic Games, in 1968, finishing with a team gold medal and 24th place in the individual contest. Two years later, in Ljubljana, Slovenia, she achieved her first world crown and then reigned unbeaten until 1975.

Even when she was forced to yield her Olympic title to Nadia Comăneci, in Montreal, in 1976, before setting foot on the third place podium, she embraced Nadia cordially. Turischeva always showed great dignity and coolness. Qualities which proved essential when the uneven bars fell apart during the finish of her routine at a world cup competition in London in 1975.

As a performer she will always be remembered for her brilliant technique, balletic and highly artistic style. She was the leader of a great generation teaming with Olga Korbut, Elvira Saadi, Rusudan Siharulidze and Nelli Kim. Turischeva won a career total of nine Olympic medals (four gold), 11 world championships medals (seven gold) and two European titles.

A Sporting Legend ★★★★★★★★★★★★★★★★★★★★★★★★★★★★★★★★★★★★

Sawao Kato *(Japan)*

In the whole Olympic history of gymnastics since 1896, only three men have twice been Olympic all-round champions: Alberto Braglia of Italy in 1908 (London) and 1912 (Stockholm); Viktor Tchoukarine of the Soviet Union in 1951 (Helsinki) and 1956 (Melbourne) and Sawao Kato of Japan in 1968 (Mexico City) and 1972 (Munich).

But Kato, who also competed in 1976, is the one with the richest collection of Olympic gold – eight altogether (of a total 11 Olympic medals), and this record is unlikely to be beaten in the future although Vitali Scherbo might try in Atlanta. Ironically, Kato won only once at the world championships, with the team in 1974, which is a reminder of how difficult and painful the way of the elite competitor at times has been.

Kato tore his Achilles tendon in 1969 and was injured again at the 1970 worlds in Ljubljana. In Varna in 1974, after two falls from the high bar Kato's arm looked so bad that the audience expected a doctor and a stretcher to appear. Instead Kato went on to complete the remainder of his routine.

He was a typical representative of the Japanese self discipline, dedicated hard work, ability to concentrate and to overcome oneself in the most decisive moments. Most of all, he was a stylist – a perfect all-rounder who shone on all apparatus but was most famous on the parallel bars. At 31, Kato won his last prize, the bronze on parallel bars at the Oviedo world cup in Spain in 1977. Now Kato coaches the Japanese 1994 national champion and 1995 world parallel bars bronze medallist, Hikaru Tanaka.

unsmiling Romanian, Nadia Comăneci even if Comăneci snatched the headlines as the first to score a "10" in Olympic history.

Olympic men's gymnastics might not have had a Korbut-style phenomenon but it has still been populated with superb athletes achieving ever more difficult movements. It has also had its fair share of heroes such as Japan's Shun Fujimoto who hurt his knee whilst warming up for the team event in 1976. He insisted on competing for the first three events before limping away. His help ensured a gold medal for his team. Only later was it discovered that he had actually fractured the knee. 1976 marked the final team gold in a five Games run for the Japanese men.

Perhaps the most remarkable male Olympic gymnast, however, was the American George Eyser who won three gold – one joint – two silver and a bronze medal in 1904. He had a wooden leg.

Background

The sport of gymnastics was part of the first Olympic Games

of the modern era, in 1896, in Athens. It has remained on the programme ever since. Women first competed at the Games in 1928 in a team event. But they had to wait until 1952 for the introduction of individual apparatus. Rhythmic gymnastics made its Olympic debut in 1984 in a competition which was badly hit by the boycott of that year but which allowed the charming Canadian Lori Fung to win the first gold.

Gymnastics, because of the range of events, has produced its fair share of multi-medallists. These include Larissa Latynina, of the Soviet Union, who won nine golds, five silver and four bronze between 1956 and '64. And, for the men, Sawao Kato of Japan won eight golds, three silver and one bronze between 1968 and '76.

The sport dates back beyond even the Ancient Games of Greece. 2,000 years earlier the Chinese, for instance, used to practise ritual mass gymnastic exercise. They still do as part of the art of "Wushu". More recently, Germany and Scandinavia took the lead in the last century in the founding of modern gymnastics through the teachings of men such as Pehr Ling and Johan Ludwig Jahn. Britain formed the Amateur Gymnastics Association in 1888 but the sport did not find popularity there until the modern TV age.

Germany and the Scandinavian nations were gradually overtaken from the '40s onwards by Japan, Czechoslovakia, the Soviet Union and East Germany. Latterly, of course, Romania, Bulgaria, China and the USA have all made their mark followed by the "new" nations formed in the wake of

★★★★★★★★★★★★★★★★★★★★★★★★★★★★★★ **A Sporting Legend**

Larissa Latynina *(Ukraine)*

Nine Olympic gold medals – and, with the five silver and four bronze, 18 medals in total. No-one else has been able to equal Latynina's original record set after three consecutive Olympic Games in 1956, '60 and '64. By the time of her final gold, ten years had elapsed since her debut at the world championships in Rome. A decade in which this sensitive girl, born on December 27, 1935 in Cheson, Ukraine, had set new levels for world gymnastics.

Latynina, whose maiden name was Dirij, had dreamt as a child of becoming a ballerina like the great Maya Plissetzkaya. In fact, she all but realized that dream by becoming the first gymnast to bring her sport so close to the boundaries of art.

After having moved to Kiev at 16 in order to train under Alexander Mishakov (also the coach of Boris Shakhlin) she started a glorious career finishing as twice Olympic all-round champion – in Melbourne '56 and Rome '60. Latynina's Olympic gold medals also included three team and three floor exercise golds at each Games as well as gold in the vault in 1956. She was twice world and twice European all-round champion.

Moreover in Italy she competed as a young mother, after having given birth to Tatiana. Her daughter, incidentally, went on to fulfil her mother's dream, finishing ballet school and dancing with the Berioska Company for many years.

A Sporting Legend ★★★★★★★★★★★★★★★★★★★★★★★★★★★★★★★★★★★

Nikolai Andrianov *(Russia)*

If the number of Olympic medals is taken into account, then the record of Nikolai Andrianov (15 medals altogether – six of them gold – and seven in one and the same Olympic Games, Montreal '76) still waits to be bettered in the field of male gymnastics.

Andrianov started gymnastics very late – at 12 years of age. In March 1964, he had just decided to pop in and see what his close friend Eugeni Skurlov was doing in the gym of Vladimir (a town placed some 200 km [75miles] away from Moscow). There he met the young coach, Nikolai Tolkachov by chance just 28 days after the man who was to become his surrogate father had arrived in town. Six years later in 1971 Andrianov entered the national team and never left it until after the Moscow Olympic Games of 1980 where his brilliant career came to an end with victory on vault and with the team silver in the all-round and floor and bronze on high bar.

Andrianov's debut was in Munich, 1972, and brought him gold on floor. The very peak was in Montreal, 1976, where Andrianov celebrated with the all-round champion's title and first place on floor, rings and vault.

Technical perfection, self confidence, iron nerves and constant striving after innovation – these were Andrianov's hallmarks. He was the first to show the world a triple somersault dismount from the high bar at the world championships in Varna, Bulgaria, in 1974, and a double straight salto on the floor (in the world championship in Spain in 1977).

In between the Games of Munich and Montreal Andrianov married the beautiful Liubov Burda (Olympic champion with the Soviet team in 1968 and '72) and they have two sons Seriozja and Volodia. Both boys have been gymnasts and their parents work in their now-famous gymnastics school.

---

the break up of the Soviet Union.

When gymnastics appeared on the Olympic programme in the early years it included events such as rope-climbing and club-swinging. Modern gymnasts leave those to the realms of Tarzan films and instead demonstrate their incredible agility, speed, precision and courage over a range of apparatus.

Equipment

There are six apparatus in men's artistic gymnastics. They are the vault, pommel horse, high bar, rings, parallel bars and floor. The women compete on four apparatus: the asymmetric (or uneven) bars, vault, beam and floor.

The mat on which gymnasts complete their floor exercise is composed of several small squares linked together to form an area which is 12m (13yds) square (set inside a podium which is 14m (15yds) square). The men's vaulting horse is 1.35m (4ft 5in.) high whilst the women's equivalent is 1.08m (3ft 6in.) high. The men's pommel horse, which is leather covered, is 1.1m (3ft 7in.) high and has two handles or "pommels" set in the centre at 0.45m (1ft 6in.) apart.

Competitors perform a series of static and swinging movements on the men's rings apparatus. The rings are set at a maximum 2.55m (8ft 2in.) above the floor. The parallel bars are 1.75m (5ft 9in.) high and comprise two flexible wood bars with an oval cross-section set 0.48m (1ft 7in.) apart.

The women's asymmetric (or uneven) bars have a lower bar at 1.6m (5ft 3in.) and a higher bar at 2.4m (7ft 10in.) above the floor. The men's high bar is 2.55m (8ft 2in.) high. A wooden bar just 0.1m (4in.) wide comprises the women's beam and it is 5m (16ft 5in.) long, set 1.2m (3ft 11in.) above the ground.

Male gymnasts wear long white trousers, (sometimes braces) and a sleeveless vest whilst the women wear leotards. Both sexes can wear light slippers in which to compete and often use chalk-dust to assist their grip on the apparatus.

Rules and Regulations

Gymnastics at the Olympic Games is divided into artistic and rhythmic disciplines. In the artistic discipline there are seven gymnasts in each team for the team event. Six of them compete on each apparatus performing one compulsory and one optional series of exercises. Four judges mark each exercise out of ten. The top and bottom mark are discarded and the middle two are averaged to give the score. Only the best five gymnasts' scores count towards a team's overall total. The team scoring the most points wins.

From the team event, the top 36-scoring individuals (a maximum of three men and three women from any one country) go forward to the individual all-round event for men and women. This involves one optional exercise on each apparatus. The highest combined score wins. There is a final of one optional exercise on each of the individual apparatus contested by the top eight scoring gymnasts (a maximum of two per country) on each piece in the team event.

For the rhythmic discipline, 40 gymnasts take part in the individual all-round competition, consisting of preliminary rounds of one optional exercise to music on each of the apparatus – ball, club, rope and ribbon. Each exercise is marked out of a possible ten points. The top 20 gymnasts go through to the semi-final and from there the top ten gymnasts compete in the final. The gymnast with the highest number of points wins. Eight teams of six gymnasts begin the group exercises competition consisting of two exercises. The top six proceed to a final, again of two exercises and the winning team is that which scores the highest number of points.

A Sporting Legend ★★★★★★★★★★★★★★★★★★★★★★★★★★★★★★★★★★

Nadia Comăneci *(Romania)*

She did not just appear – she swooped down on the international gymnastics stage in 1975 at the European championships in Skien, Norway. Only 13 years old, Nadia Comăneci became a big star overnight. Then everybody waited eagerly to see what would happen at the Montreal Olympic Games of the following year.

In effect, Comăneci turned these into 'Nadia's Gala'. She swept to the all-round title and scored a perfect "10" for the first time in the history of Olympic gymnastics – not once but twice on the uneven bars and beam and added two further perfect scores by the end of the competition. Comăneci brought the Romanian team to the forefront and became an Olympic "great", inspiring thousands of girls around the globe to take up gymnastics.

Comăneci was born in the little industrial town of Onesti on 12 November 1961. She took up gymnastics at the age of six and fate put her together with coaches Bella and Martha Karoly. This famous trio strode a glorious path. Technically brilliant and mentally very strong, Nadia was born a tough competitor.

In 1977 and '78 she grew by ten centimetres (3in), causing her serious training difficulties. However, Nadia went on. Gone was the crowd's "tiny" darling to be replaced by a young lady doing the gymnastics of the future. In Moscow in 1980 she took Olympic gold again on the beam and floor bringing her total to nine Olympic medals (five gold), two world golds and three all-round European titles. Comăneci's last competition was in the world student games in July 1981. In 1984 she took a new way in life by fleeing from Romania. Her home is now in California.

Men's artistic gymnasts must be aged 16 and over, the women in both artistic and rhythmic events must be 15 and over and the rhythmic gymnasts 14 and over in the year of the Olympic Games.

Atlanta Format

There are eight Olympic gold medals at stake in artistic gymnastics for men: the team event, individual all-round and the apparatus finals in the rings, vault, horizontal bar, parallel bars, pommel horse and floor. For women the six medal events are the team, individual all-round and individual apparatus finals in the beam, asymmetric bars, vault and floor. There is also a rhythmic gymnastics discipline for women with a group and individual event. This features exercises to music with specified equipment such as the ball, hoop, clubs and ribbon.

108 men and 108 women will compete in artistic gymnastics and eight teams with a total of 88 women rhythmic gymnastics at the 1996 Olympic Games. They have qualified by means of their 1995 world championships results. The nations

who have qualified in men's gymnastics are: China, Japan, Romania, Russia, Ukraine, Belarussia, Germany, Korea, USA, Bulgaria, Italy and France. The women's list includes: Romania, China, USA, Russia, Ukraine, France, Germany, Belarussia, Hungary, Japan, Greece and Australia. A certain number of gymnasts from non-team qualifying nations will also take part in the individual events.

In rhythmic gymnastics the countries to compete in Atlanta are: Russia, Bulgaria, Spain, France, Japan, Belarussia and China. The eighth entering squad will be one of the host nation – the USA.

Venue

Artistic gymnastics at the Atlanta Games takes place at the Georgia Dome which has a spectator capacity of 35,400 and is situated 3.2km (2 miles) from the Olympic Village. This was opened in August 1992 and is the home of the National Football League's Atlanta Falcons. It is the largest cable-supported stadium in the world.

The rhythmic discipline will be housed at the University of Georgia, in Athens, which is 104km (65 miles) from the Olympic Village and has a spectator capacity of 10,500. The University's coliseum has been renovated for the Games and is next door to Sanford Stadium which will host the Olympic football final.

MEDALLISTS (by nation)

	Men			Women			
	Gold	Silver	Bronze	Gold	Silver	Bronze	Total
Soviet Union	45	42	19	38	30	30	204
Japan	27	28	30	-	-	1	86
United States[1]	22	16	19	2	5	8	72
Switzerland	15	19	13	-	-	-	47
Romania	-	-	2	15	11	13	41
Hungary	6	5	4	7	6	10	38
GDR	3	3	10	3	10	7	36
Czechoslovakia	3	7	9	9	6	1	35
Germany	11	8	12	1	1	-	33
Italy	12	7	9	-	1	-	29
Finland	8	5	12	-	-	-	25
China	6	7	4	2	1	1	21
France	4	7	9	-	-	-	20
Yugoslavia	5	2	4	-	-	-	11
Sweden	5	2	-	1	1	1	10
Greece	3	2	3	-	-	-	8
Bulgaria	2	-	2	-	1	1	6
Norway	2	2	1	-	-	-	5
Denmark	1	3	1	-	-	-	5
Austria[1]	2	1	-	-	-	-	3
Great Britain	-	1	1	-	-	1	3
Belgium	-	1	1	-	-	-	2
Korea	-	-	2	-	-	-	2
Poland	-	1	-	-	-	1	2
FRG	-	-	1	-	-	1	2
Canada	-	-	-	1	-	-	1
Netherlands	-	-	-	1	-	-	1
North Korea (PRK)	1	-	-	-	-	-	1
Spain	-	-	-	-	1	-	1
	183	169	168	80	74	76	750

[1] Double counting for 1904 men's team title.

ATLANTA SCHEDULE

Gymnastics – Artistic
Venue: Georgia Dome

Date	Description	Round	Start	End
20 Jul	team (m)	compulsory 1	9:15	11:23
		compulsory 2	12:30	14:38
		compulsory 3	16:30	18:38
21 Jul	team (w)	compulsory 1	9:30	13:05
		compulsory 2		
		compulsory 3	15:00	18:40
		compulsory 4		
22 Jul	team (m)	optional 1	9:15	11:23
		optional 2	12:30	14:50
		optional 3 (FINAL)	16:30	19:13
23 Jul	team (w)	optional 1	9:30	12:53
		optional 2		
		optional 3	15:00	19:03
		optional 4 (FINAL)		
24 Jul	ind all round (m)	FINAL	16:15	18:59
25 Jul	ind all round (w)	FINAL	16:15	19:06
28 Jul	floor (m)	FINALS	21:30	23:41
	vault (w)			
	pommel horse (m)			
	asymmetric bars (w)			
	rings (m)			
29 Jul	vault (m)	FINALS	20:30	23:10
	beam (w)			
	parallel bars (m)			
	floor (w)			
	high bar (m)			
30 Jul	gala event (m&w)	exhibition*	16:00	18:00

* no medals awarded

Gymnastics – Rhythmic
Venue: University of Georgia

Date	Description	Round	Start	End
1 Aug	ind	prelims	10:00	12:50
	group	prelims	15:00	16:40
2 Aug	ind	prelims	10:00	12:50
	group	FINAL	15:00	16:35
3 Aug	ind	s/finals	10:00	12:50
4 Aug	ind	FINAL	13:00	15:15

Competition in rhythmic gymnastics is open to women only

MEDALLISTS

GYMNASTICS (Men)

Year	Gold	C'ntry	Points	Silver	C'ntry	Points	Bronze	C'ntry	Points

Team Competition

Year	Gold	C'ntry	Points	Silver	C'ntry	Points	Bronze	C'ntry	Points
1904	John Grieb	USA/	370.13	Emil Beyer	USA	356.37	John Duha	USA	352.69
	Anton Heida	AUT		John Bissinger			Charles Krause		
	Max Hess			Arthur Rosenkampff			George Mayer		
	Phillip Kassell			Julian Schmitz			Robert Maysack		
	Julius Lenhart			Otto Steffen			Philip Schuster		
	Ernst Reckeweg			Max Wolf			Edward Siegler		
1908	Gösta Åsbrink	SWE	438	Arthur Amundsen	NOR	425	Eino Forsström	FIN	405
	Per Bertilsson			Carl Albert Andersen			Otto Granström		
	Hjalmar Cedercrona			Otto Authén			Johan Kemp		
	Andreas Cervin			Hermann Bohne			Iivan Kyykoski		
	Rudolf Degermark			Trygve Böysen			Heikki Lehmusto		
	Carl Folcker			Oskar Bye			Johan Lindroth		
	Sven Forssman			Conrad Carlsrud			Yrjö Linko		
	Eric Granfelt			Sverre Gröner			Edvard Linna		
	Carl Hårlemann			Harald Halvorsen			Martti Markanen		
	Nils Hellsten			Peter Hol			Kaarlo Mikkolainen		
	Arvid Holmberg			Eugene Ingebretsen			Veli Niëminen		
	Carl Holmberg			Ole Iversen			Kaarlo Kustaa Paasia		
	Osvald Holmberg			Per Mathias Jespersen			Arvo Pohjanpää		
	Gunnar Höjer			Sigurd Johannessen			Eino Railio		
	Hugo Jahnke			Nicolai Kiaer			Heikki Riipinen		
	John Jarlén			Carl Klaeth			Arno Saarinen		
	Gustaf Johnson			Thor Larsen			Einar Sahlsten		
	Rolf Jonsson			Rolf Lefdahl			Arne Salovaara		
	Sven Landberg			Anders Moen			Viktor Smeds		
	Olle Lanner			Frithjof Olsen			Kaarlo Soinio		
	Axel Ljung			Carl Pedersen			Kurt Enoch Stenberg		
	Osvald Moberg			Paul Pedersen			Väino Töri		
	Carl Norberg			Sigvard Sivertsen			Karl Magnus Wegelins		
	Thomas Norberg			John Skrataas					
	Thor Norberg			Harald Smedvik					
	Axel Norling			Andreas Strand					
	Daniel Norling			Olaf Syvertsen					
	Gustaf Olsen								
	Leonard Peterson								
	Sven Rosén								
	Gustaf Rosenquist								
	Carl Silfverstrand								
	Axel Sjöblom								
	Birger Sörvik								
	Haakon Sörvik								
	Karl Johan Svensson-Sarland								
	Karl-Gustaf Vingqvist								
	Nils Widforss								
1912	Pietro Bianchi	ITA	265.75	Lajos Aradi	HUN	227.25	Albert Betts	GBR	184.5
	Guido Boni			József Berkes			William Cowhig		
	Alberto Braglia			Imre Erdődy			Sydney Cross		
	Giuseppe Domenichelli			Samu Fóti			Harry Dickason		
	Carlo Fregosi			Imre Gellért			Herbert Drury		
	Alfredo Gollini			Győző Halmos			Bernard Franklin		
	Francesco Loy			Ottó Hellmich			Leonard Hanson		
	Giovanni Mangiante			István Herczeg			Samuel Hodgetts		
	Lorenzo Mangiante			József Keresztesi			Charles Luck		
	Serafino Mazzarochi			János Korponai			William MacKune		
	Guido Romano			Elemér Pászty			Ronald McLean		
	Paolo Salvi			Árpád Pétery			Alfred Messenger		
	Luciano Savorini			Jenő Réti			Henry Oberholzer		
	Adolfo Tunesi			Ferenc Szűcs			Edward Pepper		
	Giorgio Zampori			Ődön Téry			Edward Potts		
	Angelo Zorzi			Géza Tuli			Reginald Potts		

/continued on next page 263

Year	Gold	C'ntry	Points	Silver	C'ntry	Points	Bronze	C'ntry	Points
	Arnaldo Andreoli						George Ross		
	Ettore Bellotto						Charles Simmons		
							Arthur Southern		
							William Titt		
							Charles Vigurs		
							Samuel Walker		
							John Whitaker		
1920	Pietro Bianchi	ITA	359.885	Eugène Auwerkerken	BEL	346.785	Georges Berger	FRA	340.1
	Fernando Bonatti			Théophile Bauer			Emile Bouchés		
	Luigi Cambiaso			François Claessens			René Boulanger		
	Luigi Contessi			Augustus Cootmans			Alfred Buyenne		
	Carlo Costigliolo			François Gibens			Eugène Cordonnier		
	Luigi Costigliolo			Jean van Guysse			Léon Delsarte		
	Giuseppe Domenichelli			Albert Haepers			Georges Lucien Démanet		
	Roberto Ferrari			Dominique Jacobs			Paul Joseph Durin		
	Carlo Fregosi			Félicien Kempeneers			Georges Duvant		
	Romualdo Ghiglione			Jules Labéeu			Fernand Fauconnier		
	Ambrogio Levati			Hubert Lafortune			Arthur Hermann		
	Francesco Loy			Auguste Landrieu			Albert Hersoy		
	Vittorio Lucchetti			Charles Lannie			André Higelin		
	Luigi Maiocco			Constant Loriot			Auguste Hoël		
	Ferdinando Mandrini			Ferdinand Minnaert			Louis Kempe		
	Giovanni Mangiante			Nicolas Maerloos			Georges Lagouge		
	Lorenzo Mangiante			Louis Stoop			Paulin Alexandre Lemaire		
	Antonio Marovelli			Alphonse van Mele			Ernest Lespinasse		
	Michele Mastromarino			François Verboven			Emile Martel		
	Giuseppe Paris			Jean Verboven			Jules Pirard		
	Manlio Pastorini			Julien Verdonck			Eugène Pollet		
	Ezio Roselli			Joseph Verstraeten			Georges Thurnherr		
	Paolo Salvi			Georges Vivex			Julien Wartelle		
	Giovanni Battista Tubino			Julianus Wagemans			Paul Wartelle		
	Giorgio Zampori								
	Angelo Zorzi								
1924	Luigi Cambiasi	ITA	839.058	Eugène Cordonnier	FRA	820.528	Hans Grieder	SUI	816.661
	Mario Lertoara			Léon Delsarte			August Güttinger		
	Vittorio Lucchetti			François Gangloff			Jean Gutweniger		
	Luigi Maiocco			Jean Gounot			Georges Miez		
	Fernando Mandrini			Arthur Hermann			Otto Pfister		
	Francesco Martino			André Higelin			Antoine Rebetez		
	Giuseppe Paris			Joseph Huber			Carl Widmer		
	Giorgio Zampori			Albert Séguin			Josef Wilhelm		
1928	Hans Grieder	SUI	1718.63	Josef Effenberger	TCH	1712.25	Eduard Antosijević	YUG	1648.75
	August Güttinger			Jan Gajdoš			Dragutin Ciotti		
	Hermann Hänggi			Jan Koutný			Stane Derganc		
	Eugen Mack			Emanuel Löffler			Boris Gregorka		
	Georges Miez			Bedřich Šupčík			Antun Malej		
	Otto Pfister			Ladislav Tikal			Ivan Porenta		
	Eduard Steinemann			Ladislav Vácha			Josip Primozic		
	Melchior Wetzel			Vaclav Vesely			Leon Štukelj		
1932	Oreste Capuzzo	ITA	541.85	Frank Cumiskey	USA	522.275	Mauri Noroma	FIN	509.995
	Savino Guglielmetti			Frank Haubold			Veikko Pakarinen		
	Mario Lertora			Alfred Jochim			Heikki Savolainen		
	Romeo Neri			Frederick Meyer			Einar Teräsvirta		
1936	Franz Beckert	GER	657.43	Walter Bach	SUI	654.802	Mauri Noroma	FIN	638.468
	Konrad Frey			Albert Bachmann			Veikko Pakarinen		
	Alfred Schwarzmann			Eugen Mack			Aleksanteri Saarvala		
	Willi Stadel			Georges Miez			Heikki Savolainen		
	Walter Steffens			Michael Reusch			Esa Seeste		
	Matthias Volz			Eduard Steinemann			Martti Uosikkinen		
1948	Paavo Aaltonen	FIN	1358.3	Christian Kipfer	SUI	1356.7	László Baranyai	HUN	1330.85
	Veikko Huhtanen			Walter Lehmann			János Mogyorósi-Klencs		
	Kalevi Laitinen			Robert Lucy			Ferenc Pataki		
	Olavi Rove			Michael Reusch			Lajos Sántha		
	Heikki Savolainen			Josef Stalder			Lajos Tóth		
	Einari Teräsvirta			Emil Studer			Ferenc Várkői		
1952	Vladimir Beljakov	URS	574.4	Hans Eugster	SUI	567.5	Paavo Aaltonen	FIN	564.2
	Josif Berdijev			Ernst Fivian			Kalevi Laitinen		

Year	Gold	C'ntry	Points	Silver	C'ntry	Points	Bronze	C'ntry	Points
	Evgeni Koroljkov			Ernst Gebendinger			Onni Lappalainen		
	Dmitri Leonkin			Jack Günthard			Kaino Lempinen		
	Valentin Mouratov			Hans Schwarzentruber			Berndt Lindfors		
	Mikhail Pereljman			Josef Stalder			Olavi Rove		
	Grant Shaginjan			Melchoir Thälmann			Heikki Savolainen		
	Viktor Tchoukarine			Jean Tschabold			Kalevi Viskari		
1956	Albert Asaryan	URS	568.25	Nobuyuki Aihara	JPN	566.4	Raimo Heinonen	FIN	555.95
	Valentin Mouratov			Akira Kono			Onni Lappalainen		
	Boris Shakhlin			Masami Kubota			Olavi Leimuvirta		
	Pavel Stolbov			Takashi Ono			Berndt Lindfors		
	Viktor Tchoukarine			Masao Takemoto			Martti Mansikka		
	Yuri Titov			Shinsaku Tsukawaki			Kalevi Suoniemi		
1960	Nobuyuki Aihara	JPN	575.2	Albert Asaryan	URS	572.7	Giovanni Carminucci	ITA	559.05
	Yukis Endo			Valeri Kerdemilidi			Pasquale Carminucci		
	Takashi Mitsukuri			Nikolai Miligulo			Gianfranco Marzolla		
	Takashi Ono			Vladimir Portnoi			Franco Menichelli		
	Masao Takemoto			Boris Shakhlin			Orlando Polmonari		
	Shuji Tsurumi			Yuri Titov			Angelo Vicardi		
1964	Yukio Endo	JPN	577.95	Sergei Diomidov	URS	575.45	Siegfried Fülle	GER	565.1
	Takuji Hayata			Viktor Leontyev			Philipp Fürst		
	Takashi Mitsukuri			Viktor Lisitsky			Erwin Koppe		
	Takashi Ono			Boris Shakhlin			Klaus Köste		
	Shuji Tsurumi			Yuri Tsapenko			Günter Lyhs		
	Haruhiro Yamashita			Yuri Titov			Peter Weber		
1968	Yukio Endo	JPN	575.9	Sergei Diomidov	URS	571.1	Günter Beier	GDR	557.15
	Sawao Kato			Valeri Iljinykh			Matthias Brehme		
	Takeshi Kato			Valeri Karasev			Gerhard Dietrich		
	Eizo Kenmotsu			Vladimir Klimenko			Siegfried Fülle		
	Akinori Nakayama			Viktor Lisitsky			Klaus Köste		
	Mitsuo Tsukahara			Mikhail Voronin			Peter Weber		
1972	Shigeru Kasamatsu	JPN	571.25	Nikolai Andrianov	URS	564.05	Matthias Brehme	GDR	559.7
	Sawao Kato			Viktor Klimenko			Wolfgang Klotz		
	Eizo Kenmotsu			Alexander Maleev			Klaus Köste		
	Akinori Nakayama			Edvard Mikaelian			Jürgen Paeke		
	Teruichi Okamura			Vladimir Shukin			Reinhard Rychly		
	Mitsuo Tsukahara			Mikhail Voronin			Wolfgang Thüne		
1976	Shun Fujimoto	JPN	576.85	Nikolai Andrianov	URS	576.45	Roland Brückner	GDR	564.65
	Hisato Igarashi			Alexander Ditiatin			Rainer Hanschke		
	Hiroshi Kajiyama			Gennadi Kryssin			Bernd Jager		
	Sawao Kato			Vladimir Marchenko			Wolfgang Klotz		
	Eizo Kemmotsu			Vladimir Markelov			Lutz Mack		
	Mitsuo Tsukahara			Vladimir Tikhonov			Michael Nikolai		
1980	Nikolai Andrianov	URS	589.6	Andreas Bronst	GDR	581.15	Ferenc Donáth	HUN	575.0
	Eduard Azarian			Roland Brückner			György Guczoghy		
	Alexander Ditiatin			Ralf-Peter Hemmann			Zoltán Kelemen		
	Bogdan Makuts			Lutz Hoffmann			Petér Kovács		
	Vladimir Markelov			Lutz Mack			Zoltán Magyar		
	Alexander Tkachev			Michael Nikolay			István Vámos		
1984	Bart Conner	USA	591.4	Li Xiaoping	CHN	590.8	Koji Gushiken	JPN	586.7
	Timothy Daggett			Li Ning			Noritoshi Hirata		
	Mitchell Gaylord			Li Yuejiu			Nobuyuki Kajitani		
	James Hartung			Lou Yun			Shinji Morisue		
	Scott Johnson			Tong Fei			Koji Sotomura		
	Peter Vidmar			Xu Zhiqiang			Kyoji Yamawaki		
1988	Vladimir Artemov	URS	593.35	Holger Behrendt	GDR	588.45	Yukio Iketani	JPN	585.6
	Dmitri Bilozertchev			Ralf Büchner			Hiroyuki Konishi		
	Vladimir Gogoladze			Ulf Hoffmann			Koichi Mizushima		
	Sergei Kharikov			Silvio Kroll			Daisuke Nishikawa		
	Valeri Lioukine			Sven Tippelt			Toshiharu Sato		
	Vladimir Nouvikov			Andreas Wecker			Takahiro Yamada		
1992	Valeri Belenki	EUN	585.45	Guo Linyao	CHN	580.375	Yutaka Aihara	JPN	578.25
	Roustam Charipov			Li Chunyang			Takashi Chinen		
	Vitali Scherbo			Li Dashuang			Yoshiaki Hatakeda		
	Igor Korobtchinski			Li Ge			Yukio Iketani		
	Grigori Misioutine			Li Jing			Masayuki Matsunaga		
	Alexei Voropaev			Li Xiaozhuang			Daisuke Nishikawa		
1996									

GYMNASTICS

Year	Gold	C'ntry	Points	Silver	C'ntry	Points	Bronze	C'ntry	Points
		RA	302	Nöel Bas	FRA	295	Lucien Demanet	FRA	293
		USA	161	George Eyser	USA	152	William Merz	USA	135
		ITA	317	Stanley Walter Tysal	GBR	312	Louis Segurra	FRA	297
		ITA	135	Louis Ségura	FRA	132.5	Adolfo Tunesi	ITA	131.5
	...pori	ITA	88.35	Marco Torrès	FRA	87.62	Jean Gounot	FRA	87.45
	...kelj	YUG	110.34	Robert Pražák	TCH	110.323	Bedřich Šupčik	TCH	106.93
192.	...es Miez	SUI	247.5	Hermann Hänggi	SUI	246.625	Leon Štukelj	YUG	244.875
1932	...meo Neri	ITA	140.625	István Pelle	HUN	134.925	Heikki Savolainen	FIN	134.575
1936	Alfred Schwarzmann	GER	113.1	Eugen Mack	SUI	112.334	Konrad Frey	GER	111.532
1948	Veikko Huhtanen	FIN	229.7	Walter Lehmann	SUI	229	Paavo Aaltonen	FIN	228.8
1952	Viktor Tchoukarine	URS	115.7	Grant Shaginjan	URS	114.95	Josef Stalder	SUI	114.75
1956	Viktor Tchoukarine	URS	114.25	Takashi Ono	JPN	114.2	Yuri Titov	URS	113.8
1960	Boris Shakhlin	URS	115.95	Takashi Ono	JPN	115.9	Yuri Titov	URS	115.6
1964	Yukio Endo	JPN	115.95	Shuji Tsurumi	JAP	115.4			
				Boris Shakhlin	URS				
				Viktor Lisitsky	URS				
1968	Sawao Kato	JPN	115.9	Mikhail Voronin	URS	115.85	Akinori Nakayama	JPN	115.65
1972	Sawao Kato	JPN	114.65	Eizo Kenmotsu	JPN	114.575	Akinori Nakayama	JPN	114.325
1976	Nikolai Andrianov	URS	116.65	Sawao Kato	JPN	115.65	Mitsuo Tsukahara	JPN	115.575
1980	Alexander Ditiatin	URS	118.65	Nikolai Andrianov	URS	118.225	Stoian Delchev	BUL	118
1984	Koji Gushiken	JPN	118.7	Peter Vidmar	USA	118.675	Li Ning	CHN	118.575
1988	Vladimir Artemov	URS	119.125	Valeri Lioukine	URS	119.025	Dmitri Bilozertchev	URS	118.975
1992	Vitali Scherbo	EUN	59.025	Grigori Misioutine	EUN	58.925	Valeri Belenki	EUN	58.625
1996									

Floor Exercise

Year	Gold	C'ntry	Points	Silver	C'ntry	Points	Bronze	C'ntry	Points
1932	István Pelle	HUN	28.8	Georges Miez	SUI	28.3	Mario Lertora	ITA	27.7
1936	Georges Miez	SUI	18.666	Josef Walter	SUI	18.5	Eugen Mack	SUI	18.466
							Konrad Frey	GER	
1948	Ferenc Pataki	HUN	19.35	János Mogyorósi-Klencs	HUN	19.2	Zdenek Ružička	TCH	19.05
1952	William Thoresson	SWE	19.25	Tadao Uesako	JPN	19.15			
				Jerzy Jokiel	POL	19.15			
1956	Valentin Mouratov	URS	19.2	Nobuyuki Aihara	JPN	19.1			
				William Thoresson	SWE				
				Viktor Tchoukarine	URS				
1960	Nobuyuki Aihara	JPN	19.45	Yuri Titov	URS	19.325	Franco Menichelli	ITA	19.275
1964	Franco Menichelli	ITA	19.45	Viktor Lisitsky	URS	19.35	Yukio Endo	JPN	19.35
1968	Sawao Kato	JPN	19.475	Akinori Nakayama	JPN	19.4	Takeshi Kato	JPN	19.275
1972	Nikolai Andrianov	URS	19.175	Akinori Nakayama	JPN	19.125	Shigeru Kasamatsu	JPN	19.025
1976	Nikolai Andrianov	URS	19.45	Vladimir Marchenko	URS	19.425	Peter Kormann	USA	19.3
1980	Roland Brückner	GDR	19.75	Nikolai Andrianov	URS	19.725	Alexander Ditiatin	URS	19.7
1984	Li Ning	CHN	19.925	Lou Yun	CHN	19.775	Koji Sotomura	JPN	19.7
							Philippe Vatuone	FRA	
1988	Sergei Kharikov	URS	19.925	Vladimir Artemov	URS	19.9	Lou Yun	CHN	19.85
1992	Li Xiaozhuang	CHN	9.925	Grigori Misioutine	EUN	9.787			
				Yukio Iketani	JPN				
1996									

Pommel Horse

Year	Gold	C'ntry	Points	Silver	C'ntry	Points	Bronze	C'ntry	Points
1896	Louis Zutter	SUI		Hermann Weingartner	GER		Gyula Kakas	HUN	
1904	Anton Heida	USA	42	George Eyser	USA	33	William Merz	USA	29
1924	Josef Wilhelm	SUI	21.23	Jean Gutweninger	SUI	21.13	Antoine Rebetez	SUI	20.73
1928	Hermann Hänggi	SUI	19.75	Georges Miez	SUI	19.25	Heikki Savoiainen	FIN	18.83
1932	István Pelle	HUN	19.07	Omero Bonoli	ITA	18.87	Frank Haubold	USA	18.57
1936	Konrad Frey	GER	19.333	Eugen Mack	SUI	19.167	Albert Bachmann	SUI	19.067
1948	Veikko Huhtanen	FIN	19.35						
	Heike Savolainen	FIN							
	Paavo Aaltonen	FIN							
1952	Viktor Tchoukarine	URS	19.5	Grant Shaginjan	URS	19.4			
				Evgeni Koroljkov	URS				
1956	Boris Shakhlin	URS	19.25	Takashi Oni	JPN	19.2	Viktor Tchoukarine	URS	19.1
1960	Eugen Ekman	FIN	19.375	Boris Shakhlin	URS	19.375	Shuji Tsumuri	JPN	19.15
1964	Miroslav Cerar	YUG	19.525	Shuji Tsurumi	JPN	19.325	Yuri Tsapenko	URS	19.2

Year	Gold	C'ntry	Points	Silver	C'ntry	Points	Bronze	C'ntry	Points
1968	Miroslav Cerar	YUG	19.325	Oll Laiho	FIN	19.225	Mikhail Voronin	URS	19.2
1972	Viktor Klimenko	URS	19.125	Sawao Kato	JPN	19.00	Eizo Kenmotsu	JPN	18.95
1976	Zoltán Magyar	HUN	19.7	Eizo Kemmotsu	JPN	19.575	Nikolai Andrianov	URS	19.525
							Michael Nikolay	GDR	
1980	Zoltán Magyar	HUN	19.925	Alexander Ditiatin	URS	19.8	Michael Nikolay	GDR	19.775
1984	Li Ning	CHN	19.95				Timothy Daggett	USA	19.825
	Peter Vidmar	USA							
1988	Lyubomir Gueraskov	BUL	19.95						
	Zsolt Borkai	HUN							
	Dmitri Bilozertchev	URS							
1992	Vitali Scherbo	EUN	9.925				Andreas Wecker	GER	9.887
	Pae Gil-su	PRK							
1996									

Rings

Year	Gold	C'ntry	Points	Silver	C'ntry	Points	Bronze	C'ntry	Points
1896	Ioannis Mitropoulos	GRE		Hermann Weingärtner	GER		Petros Persakis	GRE	
1904	Herman Glass	USA	45	William Merz	USA	35	Emil Voigt	USA	32
1924	Francesco Martino	ITA	21.553	Robert Pražák	TCH	21.483	Ladislav Vácha	TCH	21.43
1928	Leon Štukelj	YUG	19.25	Ladislav Vácha	TCH	19.17	Emanuel Löffler	TCH	18.83
1932	George Gulack	USA	19.433	William Denton	USA	18.6	Giovanni Lattuada	ITA	18.5
1936	Alois Hudeć	TCH	19.433	Leon Štukelj	YUG	18.867	Matthias Volz	GER	18.667
1948	Karl Frei	SUI	19.8	Michael Reusch	SUI	19.55	Zdenek Ružička	TCH	19.25
1952	Grant Shaginjan	URS	19.75	Viktor Tchoukarine	URS	19.55	Dimitri Leonkin	URS	19.4
							Hans Eugster	SUI	
1956	Albert Azaryan	URS	19.35	Valentin Mouratov	URS	19.15	Masao Takemoto	JPN	19.1
							Masami Kubota	JPN	
1960	Albert Azaryan	URS	19.725	Boris Shakhlin	URS	19.5	Takashi Ono	JPN	19.425
1964	Takuji Hayata	JPN	19.475	Franco Menichelli	ITA	19.425	Boris Shakhlin	URS	19.4
1968	Akinori Nakayama	JPN	19.45	Mikhail Voronin	URS	19.325	Sawao Kato	JPN	19.225
1972	Akinori Nakayama	JPN	19.35	Mikhail Voronin	URS	19.275	Mitsuo Tsukahara	JPN	19.225
1976	Nikolai Andrianov	URS	19.65	Alexander Ditiatin	URS	19.55	Dănut Grecu	ROM	19.5
1980	Alexander Ditiatin	URS	19.875	Alexander Tkachev	URS	19.725	Jiří Tabák	TCH	19.6
1984	Koji Gushiken	JPN	19.85				Mitchell Gaylord	USA	19.825
	Li Ning	CHN							
1988	Holger Behrendt	GDR	19.925				Sven Tippelt	GDR	19.875
	Dmitri Bilozertchev	URS							
1992	Vitali Scherbo	EUN	9.937	Li Jing	CHN	9.875	Li Xiaozhuang	CHN	9.862
							Andreas Wecker	FRG	
1996									

Horse Vault

Year	Gold	C'ntry	Points	Silver	C'ntry	Points	Bronze	C'ntry	Points
1896	Karl Schuhmann	GER		Louis Zutter	SUI		Hermann Weingäartner	GER	
1904	Anton Heida	USA	36				William Merz	USA	31
	George Eyser	USA							
1924	Frank Kriz	USA	9.98	Jan Koutný	TCH	9.97	Bohumil Mořkovský	TCH	9.93
1928	Eugen Mack	SUI	28.75	Emanuel Löffler	TCH	28.5	Stane Derganc	YUG	28.375
1932	Savino Guglielmetti	ITA	54.1	Alfred Joachim	USA	53.3	Edward Carmichael	USA	52.6
1936	Alfred Schwarzmann	GER	19.2	Eugen Mack	SUI	18.967	Matthias Volz	GER	18.467
1948	Paavo Aaltonen	FIN	19.55	Olavi Rove	FIN	19.5	Ferenc Pataki	HUN	19.25
							János Mogroyósi-	HUN	
							Klencs		
							Leo Sotorník	TCH	
1952	Viktor Tchoukarine	URS	19.2	Masao Takimoto	JPN	19.15	Takashi Ono	JPN	19.1
							Tadeo Uesako	JPN	
1956	Helmuth Bantz	GER	18.85				Yuri Titov	URS	18.75
	Valentin Mouratov	URS							
1960	Boris Shakhlin	URS	19.35	Takashi Ono	JPN	19.35	Vladimir Portnoi	URS	19.225
1964	Haruhiro Yamashita	JPN	19.6	Viktor Lisitski	URS	19.325	Hannu Rantakari	FIN	19.3
1968	Mikhail Voronin	URS	19	Yukio Endo	JPN	18.95	Sergei Diomidov	URS	18.925
1972	Klaus Köste	GDR	18.85	Viktor Klimenko	URS	18.825	Nikolai Andrianov	URS	18.8
1976	Nikolai Andrianov	URS	19.45	Mitsuo Tsukahara	JPN	19.375	Hiroshi Kajiyama	JPN	19.275
1980	Nikolai Andrianov	URS	19.825	Alexander Ditiatin	URS	19.8	Roland Brückner	GDR	19.775

/continued on next page

Year	Gold	C'ntry	Points	Silver	C'ntry	Points	Bronze	C'ntry	Points
1984	Lou Yun	CHN	19.95	Li Ning	CHN	19.825			
				Koji Gushiken	JPN				
				Mitchell Gaylord	USA				
				Shinji Morisue	JPN				
1988	Lou Yun	CHN	19.875	Sylvio Kroll	GDR	19.862	Park Jong Hoon	KOR	19.775
1992	Vitali Scherbo	EUN	9.856	Grigori Misioutine	EUN	9.781	Yoo Ok Ryul	KOR	9.762
1996									

Parallel Bars

Year	Gold	C'ntry	Points	Silver	C'ntry	Points	Bronze	C'ntry	Points
1896	Alfred Flatow	GER		Louis Zutter	SUI		Hermann Weingartner	GER	
1904	George Eyser	USA	44	Anton Heida	USA	43	John Duha	USA	40
1924	August Güttinger	SUI	21.63	Robert Pražák	TCH	21.61	Giorgio Zampori	ITA	21.45
1928	Ladislav Vácha	TCH	18.83	Josep Primožić	YUG	18.5	Hermann Hänggi	SUI	18.08
1932	Romeo Neri	ITA	18.97	István Pelle	HUN	18.6	Heikki Savolainen	FIN	18.27
1936	Konrad Frey	GER	19.067	Michael Reusch	SUI	19.034	Alfred Schwarzmann	GER	18.967
1948	Michael Reusch	SUI	19.75	Veikko Huhtanen	FIN	19.65	Josef Stalder	SUI	19.55
							Christian Kipfer	SUI	
1952	Hans Eugster	SUI	19.65	Viktor Tchoukarine	URS	19.6	Josef Stalder	SUI	19.5
1956	Viktor Tchoukarine	URS	19.2	Masami Kubota	JPN	19.15	Takashi Ono	JPN	19.1
							Masao Takemoto	JPN	
1960	Boris Shakhlin	URS	19.4	Giovanni Carminucci	ITA	19.375	Takashi Ono	JPN	19.35
1964	Yukio Endo	JPN	19.675	Shuji Tsurumi	JPN	19.45	Franco Menichelli	ITA	19.35
1968	Akinori Nakayama	JPN	19.475	Mikhail Voronin	URS	19.425	Vladimir Klimenko	URS	19.225
1972	Sawao Kato	JPN	19.475	Shigeru Kasamatsu	JPN	19.375	Eizo Kenmotsu	JPN	19.25
1976	Sawao Kato	JPN	19.675	Nikolai Andrianov	URS	19.5	Mitsuo Tsukahara	JPN	19.475
1980	Alexander Tkachev	URS	19.775	Alexander Ditiatin	URS	19.75	Roland Brückner	GDR	19.65
1984	Bart Conner	USA	19.95	Nobuyuki Kajitani	JPN	19.925	Mitchell Gaylord	USA	19.85
1988	Vladimir Artemov	URS	19.925	Valeri Lioukine	URS	19.9	Sven Tippelt	GDR	19.75
1992	Vitali Scherbo	EUN	9.9	Li Jing	CHN	9.812	Guo Linyao	CHN	9.8
							Igor Korobtchinski	EUN	
							Masayuki Matsunaga	JPN	
1996									

Horizontal Bars

Year	Gold	C'ntry	Points	Silver	C'ntry	Points	Bronze	C'ntry	Points
1896	Hermann Weingärtner	GER		Alfred Flatow	GER		Aristovophoulos	GRE	
							Petmetsas		
1904	Anton Heida	USA	40				George Eyser	USA	39
	Edward Hennig	USA							
1924	Leon Štukelj	YUG	19.73	Jean Gutweninger	SUI	19.236	André Higelin	FRA	19.163
1928	Georges Miez	SUI	19.17	Romeo Neri	ITA	19	Eugen Mack	SUI	18.92
1932	Dallas Bixler	USA	18.33	Heikki Savolainen	FIN	18.07	Einar Teräsvirta	FIN	18.07
1936	Aleksanteri Saarvala	FIN	19.367	Konrad Frey	GER	19.267	Alfred Schwarzmann	GER	19.233
1948	Josef Stalder	SUI	19.85	Walter Lehmann	SUI	19.7	Veikko Huhtanen	FIN	19.6
1952	Jack Günthard	SUI	19.55	Josef Stalder	SUI	19.5	Alfred Schwarzmann	GER	19.5
1956	Takashi Ono	JPN	19.6	Yuri Titov	URS	19.4	Masao Takemoto	JPN	19.3
1960	Takashi Ono	JPN	19.6	Masao Takemoto	JPN	19.525	Boris Shakhlin	URS	19.475
1964	Boris Shakhlin	USR	19.625	Yuri Titov	URS	19.55	Miroslav Cerar	YUG	19.5
1968	Mikhail Voronin	URS	19.55				Elzo Kenmotsu	JPN	19.375
	Akinori Nakayama	JPN							
1972	Mitsuo Tsukahara	JPN	19.725	Sawao Kato	JPN	19.525	Shigeru Kasamatsu	JPN	19.45
1976	Mitsuo Tsukahara	JPN	19.675	Eizo Kemmotsu	JPN	19.5	Eberhard Gienger	GER	19.475
							Henri Boerio	FRA	
1980	Stoian Delchev	BUL	19.825	Alexsandr Ditiatin	URS	19.75	Nikolai Andrianov	URS	19.675
1984	Shinji Morisue	JPN	20	Tong Fei	CHN	19.975	Koji Gushiken	JPN	19.95
1988	Vladimir Artemov	URS	19.9				Holger Behrendt	GDR	19.8
	Valeri Lioukine	URS							
1992	Trent Dimas	USA	9.875	Grigori Misioutine	EUN	9.837			
				Andreas Wecker	GER	9.837			
1996									

GYMNASTICS (Women)

Year	Gold	C'ntry	Points	Silver	C'ntry	Points	Bronze	C'ntry	Points

Team Competition

Year	Gold	C'ntry	Points	Silver	C'ntry	Points	Bronze	C'ntry	Points
1928	Estella Agsteribbe	NED	316.75	Bianca Ambrosetti	ITA	289.00	Anne Broadbent	GBR	258.25
	Petronella Burgerhof			Lavinia Gianoni			Lucille Desmond		
	Elka de Levie			Luigina Giavotti			Margaret Hartley		
	Helena Nordheim			Virginia Giorgi			Amy Jagger		
	Annie Polak			Germana Malabarba			Isobel Judd		
	Jud Simons			Clara Marangoni			Jessica Kite		
	Jacoba Stelma			Luigina Perversi			Madge Moreman		
	Jacomina van den Berg			Diana Pizzavini			Edith Pickles		
	Alida van den Bos			Anna Tanzini			Ethel Seymour		
	Anna van der Vegt			Carolina Tronconi			Ada Smith		
	Petronella van Randwijk			Ines Vercesi			Hilda Smith		
	Hendrika van Rumt			Rita Vittadini			Doris Woods		
1936	Trudi Meyer	GER	506.5	Marie Bajerová	TCH	503.6	Margit Csillik	HUN	499.00
	Erna Bürger			Vlasta Dekanova			Margit Kalocsai		
	Käthe Sohnemann			Božena Dobešová			Ilona Madary		
	Isolde Frölian			Vlasta Foltova			Gabriella Mészáros		
	Anita Bärwirth			Anna Hřebřinová			Margit Sándor-Nagy		
	Paula Pöhlsen			Matylda Pálfyová			Olga Tőrős		
	Friedel Iby			Zdenka Vermirovská			Judit Tóth		
	Julie Schmitt			Marie Vetrovská			Eszter Voit		
1948	Zdenka Honsová	TCH	445.45	Anna Fehér	HUN	440.55	Ladislava Bakanic	USA	422.6
	Marie Kovářová			Erzsébet Gulyás			Marian Barone		
	Miloslava Misáková			Irén Karcsics			Dorothy Dalton		
	Milena Müllerová			Mária Kővi			Meta Elste		
	Věra Ružičková			Margit Sándor			Helen Schifano		
	Olga Šilhánová			Erzsébet Sarkany			Clara Schroth		
	Božena Srncová			Olga Tass			Anita Simonis		
	Zdenka Veřmiřovská			Edit Vásárhelyi					
1952	Nina Botscharova	URS	527.03	Andrea Bodó	HUN	520.96	Hana Bobková-	TCH	503.32
	Pelageja Danilova			Erzsébet Gulyás			Marejková		
	Marja Gorovskaya			Irén Karcsics-Daruházi			Alena Chadimová		
	Ekaterina Kalintshuk			Ágnes Keleti			Jana Rabasová		
	Galina Minaitscheva			Margit Korondi			Alena Reichová		
	Galina Shamrai			Károlyne Perényi			Matylda Šínová		
	Galina Urbanovitsh			Olga Tass			Božena Srncová		
				Mária Zalai			Věra Vančurová-		
							Rylichová		
							Eva Vechtová		
1956	Polina Astakhova	URS	444.8	Andrea Bodó	HUN	443.5	Gheorgheta	ROM	438.2
	Ludmila Egorova			Erzsébet Gulyás			Hurmuzachi		
	Lidia Kalinina			Ágnes Keleti			Sonia Iovan		
	Larissa Latynina			Aliz Kertész			Elena Leusteanu		
	Tamara Manina			Margit Korondi			Elena Margarit		
	Sofia Mouratova			Olga Tass			Elena Sačalici		
							Emilia Vătăşoiu		
1960	Polina Astakhova	URS	382.32	Eva Vechtová-	TCH	373.323	Sonia Iovan	ROM	372.053
	Lidia Kalinina Ivanova			Bosáková			Atanasia Ionescu		
	Larissa Latynina			Věra Čáslavská			Elena Leusteanu		
	Tamara Lyukhina			Matylda Sínová-Matoušková			Emilia Liţă		
	Sofia Muratova			Hana Ružičková			Elena Niculescu		
	Margarita Nikolaeva			Ludmila Svédová			Uta Poreceanu		
				Adolfina Tačová					
1964	Polina Astakhova	URS	380.89	Věra Čáslavská	TCH	379.989	Toshiko Aihara	JPN	377.889
	Ludmila Gromova			Mariana Krajčiřová-Némethová			Ginko Chiba		
	Larissa Latynina			Jana Posnerová			Keiko Ikeda		
	Tamara Manina			Hana Ružičková			Taniko Nakamura		
	Elena Volchetskaya			Jaroslava Sedláčková			Kiyoko Ono		
	Tamara Zamotailova			Adolfina Tkačíková			Hiroko Tsuji		
1968	Liubov Burda	URS	382.85	Věra Čáslavská	TCH	382.2	Maritta Bauerschmidt	GDR	379.1
	Olga Kareseva			Mariana Krajčiřová-Némethová			Karin Janz		
	Natalia Kuchinskaya			Jana Posnerova-Kubičková			Marianne Noack		

/continued on next page 269

Year	Gold	C'ntry	Points	Silver	C'ntry	Points	Bronze	C'ntry	Points
	Larissa Petrik			Hana Lišková			Magdalena Schmidt		
	Ludmila Turischeva			Bohumila Řimnáčová			Ute Starke		
	Zinaida Voronina			Miroslava Skleničková			Erika Zuchold		
1972	Liubov Burda	URS	380.5	Irene Abel	GDR	376.55	Ilona Békési	HUN	368.25
	Olga Korbut			Angelika Hellmann			Mónika Császár		
	Antonina Koshel			Karin Janz			Márta Kelemen		
	Tamara Lazakovitch			Richarda Schmeisser			Anikó Kéry		
	Elvira Saadi			Christine Schmitt			Krisztina Medveczky		
	Ludmila Turischeva			Erika Zuchold			Zsuzsan Nagy		
1976	Maria Filatova	URS	390.35	Nadia Comăneci	ROM	387.15	Carola Dombeck	GDR	385.1
	Svetlana Grozdova			Mariana Constantin			Gitta Escher		
	Nelli Kim			Georgeta Gabor			Kerstin Gerschau		
	Olga Korbut			Anca Grigoraş			Angelika Hellmann		
	Elvira Saadi			Gabriela Trusca			Marion Kische		
	Ludmila Turischeva			Teodora Ungureanu			Steffi Kräker		
1980	Elena Davydova	URS	394.9	Nadia Comăneci	ROM	393.5	Maxi Gnauck	GDR	392.55
	Maria Filatova			Rodica Dunka			Silvia Hindorff		
	Nelli Kim			Emilia Eberle			Steffi Kräker		
	Elena Naimushina			Cristina Elena Grigoraş			Katharina Rensch		
	Natalia Shaposhnikova			Melita Rühn			Karola Sube		
	Stella Zakharova			Dumitrita Turner			Birgit Süss		
1984	Lavinia Agache	ROM	392.2	Pamela Bileck	USA	391.2	Zhou Ping	CHN	388.6
	Laura Cutina			Michelle Dusserre			Wu Jiani		
	Cristina Grigoras			Kathy Johnson			Zhou Qiurui		
	Simona Pauca			Julianne McNamara			Huang Qun		
	Mihaela Stanulet			Mary Lou Retton			Ma Yanhong		
	Ecaterina Szabó			Tracee Talavera			Chen Yongyan		
1988	Svetlana Baitova	URS	395.475	Aurelia Dobre	ROM	394.125	Gabriele Fähnrich	GDR	390.875
	Svetlana Boginskaya			Eugenia Golea			Martina Jentsch		
	Elena Chevtchenko			Celestina Popa			Dagmar Kersten		
	Elena Chouchounova			Gabriela Potorac			Ulrike Klotz		
	Natalia Lachtchenova			Daniela Silivas			Betti Schieferdecker		
	Olga Strajeva			Camelia Voinea			Dörte Thümmler		
1992	Svetlana Boginskaya	EUN	395.666	Cristina Bontas	ROM	395.079	Wendy Bruce	USA	394.704
	Roza Galieva			Gina Gogean			Dominique Dawes		
	Tatiana Goutsou			Vanda Hadarean			Shannon Miller		
	Elena Groudneva			Lavinia Milosovici			Elizabeth Okino		
	Tatiana Lyssenko			Maria Neculita			Kerri Strug		
	Oxana Tchoussovitina			Mirela Pasca			Kim Zmeskal		
1996									

Ind All Round

Year	Gold	C'ntry	Points	Silver	C'ntry	Points	Bronze	C'ntry	Points
1952	Marija Gorovskaya	URS	76.78	Nina Botsharova	URS	75.94	Margit Korondi	HUN	75.82
1956	Larissa Latynina	URS	74.933	Ágnes Keleti	HUN	74.633	Sofia Mouratova	URS	74.466
1960	Larissa Latynina	URS	77.031	Sofia Muratova	URS	76.696	Polina Astakhova	URS	76.164
1964	Věra Čáslavská	TCH	77.564	Larissa Latynina	URS	76.998	Polina Astakhova	URS	76.965
1968	Věra Čáslavská	TCH	78.25	Zinaida Voronina	URS	76.85	Natalia Kuchinskaya	URS	76.75
1972	Ludmila Turischeva	URS	77.025	Karin Janz	GDR	76.875	Tamara Lazakovitch	URS	76.85
1976	Nadia Comăneci	ROM	79.275	Nelli Kim	URS	78.675	Ludmila Turischeva	URS	78.625
1980	Elena Davydova	URS	79.15	Maxi Gnauck	GDR	79.075	Nadia Comăneci	ROM	79.075
1984	Mary Lou Retton	USA	79.175	Ecaterina Szabó	ROM	79.125	Simona Pauca	ROM	78.675
1988	Elena Chouchounova	URS	79.662	Daniela Silivas	ROM	76.637	Svetlana Boginskaya	URS	79.4
1992	Tatiana Goutsou	EUN	39.737	Shannon Miller	USA	39.725	Lavinia Milosovici	ROM	39.687
1996									

Horse Vault

Year	Gold	C'ntry	Points	Silver	C'ntry	Points	Bronze	C'ntry	Points
1952	Ekaterina Kalintshuk	URS	19.2	Marija Gorovskaya	URS	19.19	Galina Minaitsheva	URS	19.16
1956	Larissa Latynina	URS	18.833	Tamara Manina	URS	18.8	Olga Tass	HUN	18.733
							Ann-Sofi Colling	SWE	18.733
1960	Margarita Nikolaeva	URS	19.316	Sofia Muratova	URS	19.049	Larissa Latynina	URS	19.016
1964	Věra Čáslavská	TCH	19.483	Larissa Latynina	URS	19.283	Birgit Radochla	GER	19.283
1968	Věra Čáslavská	TCH	19.775	Erika Zuchold	GDR	19.625	Zinaida Voronina	URS	19.5
1972	Karin Janz	GDR	19.525	Erika Zuchold	GDR	19.275	Ludmila Turischeva	URS	19.25
1976	Nelli Kim	URS	19.8	Ludmila Turischeva	URS	19.65			
				Carola Dombeck	GDR				
1980	Natalia Shaposhnikova	URS	19.725	Steffi Kräker	GDR	19.675	Melita Rühn	ROM	19.65

Year	Gold	C'ntry	Points	Silver	C'ntry	Points	Bronze	C'ntry	Points
1984	Ecaterina Szabó	ROM	19.875	Mary Lou Retton	USA	19.85	Lavinia Agache	ROM	19.75
1988	Svetlana Boginskaya	URS	19.905	Gabriela Potorac	ROM	19.83	Daniela Silivas	ROM	19.818
1992	Henrietta Ønodi	HUN	9.925				Tatiana Lyssenko	EUN	9.912
	Lavinia Milosovici	ROM							
1996									

Asymmetric Bars

Year	Gold	C'ntry	Points	Silver	C'ntry	Points	Bronze	C'ntry	Points
1952	Margit Korondi	HUN	19.4	Marija Gorovskaya	URS	19.26	Ágnes Keleti	HUN	19.16
1956	Ágnes Keleti	HUN	18.966	Larissa Latynina	URS	18.833	Sofia Mouratova	URS	18.8
1960	Polina Astakhova	URS	19.616	Larissa Latynina	URS	19.416	Tamara Ljukhina	URS	19.399
1964	Polina Astakhova	URS	19.332	Katalin Makray	HUN	19.216	Larissa Latynina	URS	19.199
1968	Věra Čáslavská	TCH	19.65	Karin Janz	GDR	19.5	Zinaida Voronina	URS	19.42
1972	Karin Janz	GDR	19.675	Olga Korbut	URS	19.45			
				Erika Zuchold	GDR				
1976	Nadia Comăneci	ROM	20	Teodora Ungureanu	ROM	19.8	Márta Egerváry	HUN	19.775
1980	Maxi Gnauck	GDR	19.875	Emilie Eberle	ROM	19.85	Steffi Kräker	GDR	19.775
1984	Ma Yanhong	CHN	19.95				Mary Lou Retton	USA	19.8
	Julianne McNamara	USA							
1988	Daniela Silivas	ROM	20	Dagmar Kersten	GDR	19.987	Elena Chouchounova	URS	19.962
1992	Li Lu	CHN	10	Tatiana Goutsou	EUN	9.975	Shannon Miller	USA	9.962
1996									

Beam

Year	Gold	C'ntry	Points	Silver	C'ntry	Points	Bronze	C'ntry	Points
1952	Nina Botsharova	URS	19.22	Marija Gorovskaya	URS	19.13	Margit Korondi	HUN	19.02
1956	Ágnes Keleti	HUN	18.8	Eva Bosáková	TCH	18.633			
				Tamara Manina	URS				
1960	Eva Bosáková	TCH	19.283	Larissa Latynina	URS	19.233	Sofia Mouratova	URS	19.232
1964	Věra Čáslavská	TCH	19.449	Tamara Manina	URS	19.399	Larissa Latynina	URS	19.382
1968	Natalia Kuchinskaya	URS	19.65	Věra Čáslavská	TCH	19.575	Larissa Petrik	URS	19.25
1972	Olga Korbut	URS	19.4	Tamara Lazakovitch	URS	19.375	Karin Janz	GDR	18.975
1976	Nadia Comăneci	ROM	19.95	Olga Korbut	URS	19.725	Teodora Ungureanu	ROM	19.7
1980	Nadia Comăneci	ROM	19.8	Elena Davydova	URS	19.75	Natalia Shaposhnikova	URS	19.725
1984	Simona Pauca	ROM	19.8				Kathy Johnson	USA	19.65
	Ecaterina Szabó	ROM							
1988	Daniela Silivas	ROM	19.924	Elena Chouchounova	URS	19.875	Gabriela Potorac	ROM	19.837
1992	Tatiana Lyssenko	EUN	9.975	Li Lu	CHN	9.912			
				Shannon Miller	USA				
1996									

Floor Exercise

Year	Gold	C'ntry	Points	Silver	C'ntry	Points	Bronze	C'ntry	Points
1952	Ágnes Keleti	HUN	19.36	Marija Gorovskaya	URS	19.2	Margit Korondi	HUN	19
1956	Ágnes Keleti	HUN	18.733				Elena Leuştean	ROM	18.7
	Larissa Latynina	URS							
1960	Larissa Latynina	URS	19.583	Polina Astakhova	URS	19.532	Tamara Ljukhina	URS	19.449
1964	Larissa Latynina	URS	19.599	Polina Astakhova	URS	19.5	Anikó Ducza	HUN	19.3
1968	Larissa Petrik	URS	19.675				Natalia Kuchinskaya	URS	19.65
	Věra Čáslavská	TCH							
1972	Olga Korbut	URS	19.575	Ludmila Turischeva	URS	19.55	Tamara Lazakovitch	URS	19.45
1976	Nelli Kim	URS	19.85	Ludmila Turischeva	URS	19.825	Nadia Comăneci	ROM	19.75
1980	Nelli Kim	URS	19.875				Natalia Shaposhnikova	URS	19.825
	Nadia Comăneci	ROM							
1984	Ecaterina Szabó	ROM	19.975	Julianne McNamara	USA	19.95	Mary Lou Retton	USA	19.775
1988	Daniela Silivas	ROM	19.937	Svetlana Boginskaya	URS	19.887	Diana Doudeva	BUL	19.85
1992	Lavinia Milosovici	ROM	10	Henrietta Ónodi	HUN	9.95	Tatiana Goutsou	EUN	9.912
							Shannon Miller	USA	
							Cristina Bontas	ROM	
1996									

GYMNASTICS

Year	Gold	C'ntry	Points	Silver	C'ntry	Points	Bronze	C'ntry	Points

RHYTHMIC

Individual

Year	Gold	C'ntry	Points	Silver	C'ntry	Points	Bronze	C'ntry	Points
1984	Lori Fung	CAN	57.95	Doina Staiculescu	ROM	57.9	Regina Weber	FRG	57.7
1988	Marina Lobatch	URS	60	Adriana Dounavska	BUL	59.95	Alexandra Timochenko	URS	59.875
1992	Alexandra Timoshenko	EUN	59.037	Carolina Pascual Garcia	ESP	58.1	Oksana Skaldina	EUN	57.912
1996									

Team

Year	Gold	C'ntry	Points	Silver	C'ntry	Points	Bronze	C'ntry	Points
1996									

Handball

Stars to Watch

Time to change the handball pattern?

THERE is no doubt that the 1996 Olympic men's handball tournament will provide a new gold medallist. For the past three Games, the Soviet Union have reigned supreme – the last time as the Unified Team in Barcelona four years ago when they beat the favourites, Sweden, by 22–20 in the final.

Sweden v France, 1992

At the end of the 1992 tournament the Unified Team coach, Spartak Mironovitch, made an emotional speech in which he thanked the players of the Ukraine and Belarus for taking part. Will either feature on the medal rostrum in 1996 or will the winners be Russia, the 1993 world champions? Or will Sweden, 1995 world champions, turn silver into gold?

France were the surprise 1992 package and it will be interesting to see what a difference four years has made to the bronze medallists. They qualified in 1992 from the European zone only because Spain took an automatic place as hosts. Germany and Romania are also teams to watch as are Iceland. And the USA, as host nation would, no doubt, like to reach the later stages or even win a medal for the first time in Olympic history.

Korea v Norway, 1992 (Women)

In the recent Olympic past there has been a stable pattern to Olympic women's handball. The Koreans won gold in Seoul, beating Norway. Four years later the same two teams featured in the final and Korea won once more by a similar score. At both Games the Soviet Union were third. That, at least, is set to change with Germany and

273

Austria as potential medal contenders. It would be foolish, however, to discount the USA on their home territory. They finished sixth in 1992.

☐

Retrospective

Milan Lazarević, a 24 year-old from Belgrade, was the hero when handball re-entered the Olympic fray after an absence of nearly 40 years in 1972. He scored six goals for Yugoslavia against both Romania and Czechoslovakia to assure his team of their gold medal. The tournament itself was marked by quirky scoring systems. Romania only lost once in the 11-day event but were awarded bronze whilst Czechoslovakia, with only three wins from six matches, won silver. Yugoslavia beat Czechoslovakia 21–16 in the final.

A Contemporary Hero ★★★★★★★★★★★★★★★★★★★★★★★★★★★★★★★★★

Talant Douichebaev *(Soviet Union and Spain)*

Talant Douichebaev won Olympic gold in Barcelona, four years ago, with the Unified team when they defeated the more-favoured Swedish team in the final. In 1993 he went on to win a world title with the Russian team.

This former ZSKA Moscow player moved to Spain in 1991 where he has been actively playing for the last five years. On February 10, 1994, he became a Spanish citizen and has done much to make them one of the stronger teams in the world. This exceptional 29-year-old was declared handballer of the year in 1995.

The Soviet Union won the inaugural women's Olympic tournament in 1976. Six of their players went on to win a second gold in 1980. Romania twice started the Olympic tournament as reigning men's world champions – in 1972 and '76 – but were unable to take Olympic gold. In 1984 tiny Iceland drew its opening game with the mighty Yugoslavia having only been invited to participate at the last moment due to the boycott.

East Germany's Hans-Georg Beyer was part of the winning men's team in 1980. His brother Udo won the shot put in 1976 and took a bronze in the same event in 1980 whilst their sister Gisela was a discus competitor in 1980.

Background

Handball made its Olympic debut for men in 1936. At that time the Olympic discipline consisted of "full field" handball. This was played by eleven players on turf football pitches.

The sport returned in 1972 as a seven-a-side indoor game and, four years later, a women's tournament was introduced.

However there are records of handball-style games going back to antiquity. The sport is depicted in a tombstone carving in Athens dated at 600BC. As a modern sport it began to emerge in Germany in the late nineteenth century, gaining major popularity after World War I. The world governing body – now called the International Handball Federation – was first formed in 1928 and took its current name in 1946. Its first president was Avery Brundage – an American who went on to become president of the IOC. The current IHF has 133 member nations. Europe is the strongest continent with teams such as the former Soviet Union and Sweden as well as Yugoslavia and Hungary, followed closely by Africa.

★★★★★★★★★★★★★★★★★★★★★★★★★★★★★★ **A Contemporary Hero**

Magnus Wislander *(Sweden)*

This Swedish world champion plays in the German league for the European cup champions Kiel. In 1992 he took part in the Olympic Games handball tournament – an event which Sweden were expected to win but in which they finished up silver medallists following a final round defeat by the Unified Team. That followed his role in Sweden's fifth place at the 1988 Games.

In 1996, Wislander still plays for his German club and for his national team. Such is his presence on court that both function well with him but suffer in his absence. He is the brains of the field and could well prove difficult to replace when he finally decides to retire.

The first handball matches of the modern era are thought to have taken place in Berlin in 1917. Certainly, there are minutes of a match taking place on 29 October of that year. By 1925 several teams were taking part in a "workers Olympiad" in Frankfurt. The growth of the sport has since been rapid and the speed of the sport itself increased with the move from larger pitches to indoor, smaller courts.

Equipment

A handball court is 40m (131ft 3in.) long and 20m (65 ft 7in.) wide. It is divided in half by a centre line (see diagram) and has goals at either end which measure 3m (9ft 9in) in width and 2m (6ft 6in.) in height. Each goal has a net to stop the ball, when thrown into it, rebounding directly into the court. There are semi-circular goal area lines in front of each goal as well as a free throw line marked, again in a semi-circle, 9m (29ft 6in.) out from the goal-line. Penalties are taken from a horizontal line, a metre (3ft 3in.) in length, marked 7m (22ft 11in) out from the goal.

HANDBALL

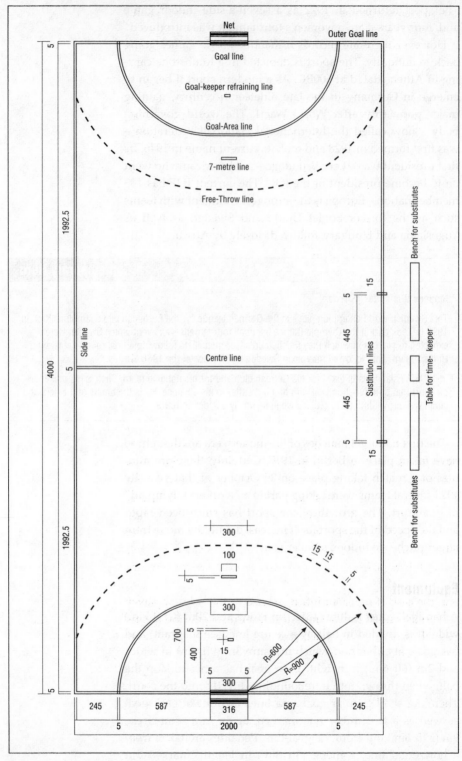

The playing court

A regulation handball has a circumference of 56cms (22in.) and is made of leather or synthetic materials.

Rules

Matches, for both men and women, are played in two halves of 30 minutes each with a ten-minute half-time interval. Teams change ends at half-time. Play begins, on the referee's whistle, with a throw-off from centre court. In the event of a draw at the end of full-time, extra time (consisting of two halves of five minutes) is played.

Each team can have twelve players, a maximum of seven on court at any one time of which one must be the goalkeeper. Substitutes can be made on a rolling basis. Only the goal-keeper is allowed in the goal area. A goal-keeper may touch the ball with any part of the body in the act of defence when inside the goal-area. Other players, during normal play, can throw, catch, stop, push or hit the ball using the hands, arms, head, torso, thigh and knees. They can hold the ball for a maximum of three seconds and take a maximum of three steps when in possession as well as bouncing the ball or rolling it with one hand. They are not allowed to kick the ball.

It is not permitted to obstruct or push an opponent with the body, arms or legs. Nor is it allowed to hit the ball out of an opponent's hands. Many of the rules governing handball and, in particular, free-throws, goal-throws and penalty-throws are similar to Association football. Rule infringements are penalized by free throws and, for more serious offences, penalty throws. A goal is scored when the whole of the ball crosses the goal-line between the uprights of the goal. The team scoring the most goals wins. As in Association football (soccer), it is possible for a defender or goal-keeper to score an "own-goal".

In the case of repeated infringements to the rules, a player can be suspended for two minutes. A third suspension means disqualification. Each match has two referees, a scorer and timekeeper. Both referees have equal authority.

Atlanta Format

Eight women's and 12 men's teams – a total of 192 male and 128 female athletes – will take part in the 1996 Olympic handball tournaments. The host nation has an automatic place in both draws. Other teams have qualified by means of the preceding world championships and continental qualifying events.

The men play in two preliminary groups of six followed by cross-over semi-finals and a final. Two groups of four contest the early rounds of the women's event followed, again, by semi-finals and a final. There is a bronze medal play-off in both events as well as classification matches for the lower ranks.

Venue

Handball, at the 1996 Olympic Games, will be played in two venues – the Georgia World Congress Center and the Georgia Dome. The former has a capacity of 7,900 whilst the Dome has 35,500 seats. Both are located within the Olympic Center cluster of venues which is 3.2km (2 miles) from the Olympic Village.

Atlanta's NFL team – the Falcons – normally play at the Dome which will witness the handball finals in half of the venue. The other half will be devoted to gymnastics. The World Congress Center, meanwhile, is the second largest convention centre in the USA and six other sports will be joining handball there during the Games.

MEDALLISTS (by nation)

| | Men | | | Women | | | |
	Gold	Silver	Bronze	Gold	Silver	Bronze	Total
Soviet Union	3	1	-	2	-	2	8
Yugoslavia	2	-	1	1	1	-	5
Korea	-	1	-	2	1	-	4
Romania	-	1	3	-	-	-	4
GDR	1	-	-	-	1	1	3
Norway	-	-	-	-	2	-	2
Germany	1	-	-	-	-	-	1
Austria	-	1	-	-	-	-	1
Czechoslovakia	-	1	-	-	-	-	1
FRG	-	1	-	-	-	-	1
China	-	-	-	-	-	1	1
France	-	-	1	-	-	-	1
Hungary	-	-	-	-	-	1	1
Poland	-	-	1	-	-	-	1
Sweden	-	1	-	-	-	-	1
Switzerland	-	-	1	-	-	-	1
	7	7	7	5	5	5	36

ATLANTA SCHEDULE

Venue: All matches played at Georgia World Congress Center, Hall G, except for 4 Aug (men's bronze play-off and FINAL) which will be played at the Georgia Dome

Date	Round	Start	End
24,25,27,29,	prelims (m)	10:00	13:00
31 July		14:30	17:30
		19:00	22:00
26,28,30 July	prelims (w)	10:00	13:00
		17:30	
		14:30	
1 Aug	play-off (7-8 place) (w)	10:00	13:00
	s/finals (w)		
	play-off (5-6 place) (w)	14:30	17:30
	s/finals (w)		
2 Aug	play-off (11-12 place) (m)	10:00	13:00
	play-off (9-10 place) (m)		
	play-off (7-8 place) (m)	14:30	17:30
	s/finals (m)		
	play-off (5-6 place) (m)	19:00	22:00
	s/finals (m)		
3 Aug	play-off (bronze) (w)	15:30	18:45
	FINAL (w)		
4 Aug	play-off (bronze) (m)	15:00	18:15
	FINAL (m)		

MEDALLISTS

HANDBALL (Men)

Year	Gold	C'ntry	Points	Silver	C'ntry	Bronze	C'ntry	Points
1936	Willi Bandholz	GER	10-6	Franz Bartl	AUT	Max Bloesch	SUI	10-5
	Wilhelm Baumann			Franz Berghammer		Rolf Faes		(v HUN)
	Helmut Berthold			Franz Bistricky		Burkhard Gantenbein		
	Helmuth Braselmann			Franz Brunner		Willy Gysi		
	Wilhelm Brinkmann			Hans Houschka		Erland Herkenrath		
	Georg Dascher			Emil Juracka		Ernst Hufschmid		
	Kurt Dossin			Ferdinand Kiefler		Willy Hufschmid		
	Fritz Fromm			Josef Kreci		Werner Meyer		
	Hermann Hansen			Otto Licha		Georg Mischon		
	Erich Hermann			Friedrich Maurer		Willy Schafer		
	Heinrich Keimig			Anton Perwein		Werner Scheurmann		
	Hans Keiter			Siegfried Powolny		Eduard Schmid		
	Alfred Klingler			Siegfried Purner		Erich Schmitt		
	Arthur Knautz			Walter Reisp		Eugen Seiterle		
	Heinz Körvers			Alfred Schmalzer		Max Streib		
	Carl Kreutzberg			Alois Schnabel		Robert Studer		
	Wilhelm Müller			Ludwig Schuberth		Rudolf Wirz		
	Günther Ortmann			Johann Tauscher				
	Edgar Reinhardt			Jaroslav Volak				
	Fritz Spengler			Leopold Wohlrab				
	Rudolf Stahl			Friedrich Wurmböck				
	Hans Theilig			Hans Zehetner				
1972	Abaz Arslanagić	YUG	21-16	Ladislav Beneš	TCH	Alexandru Dinca	ROM	19-16
	Petar Fajfrić			František Brůna		Ştefan Birtalan		(v GDR)
	Hrvoje Horvat			Vladimír Habr		Gavril Chicsid		
	Milorad Karalić			Vladimír Jarý		Adrian Cosma		
	Djoko Lavrnić			Jiří Kavan		Cristian Gatu		
	Milan Lazarević			Jaroslav Konečný		Gheorghe Gruia		
	Zdravko Miljak			František Králík		Roland Gunes		
	Slobodan Mišković			Jindřich Krepindl		Ghita Licu		
	Branislav Pokrajać			Vincent Lafko		Dan Marin		
	Nebojša Popović			Arnošt Klimčík		Cornel Penu		
	Miroslav Pribanić			Andrej Lukošík		Valentin Samungi		
	Albin Vidović			Pavel Mikeš		Simion Sobel		
	Zoran Živković			Pter Pospíšil		Werner Stockl		
	Zdenko Zorko			Ivan Satrapa		Constantin Tudosie		
				Zdeněk Škára		Radu Voinea		
				Jaroslav Škarvan				
1976	Alexander Anpilogov	URS	19-15	Ştefan Birtalan	ROM	Zdzisław Antczak	POL	21-18
	Anatoli Fedjukin			Adrian Cosma		Janusz Brzozowski		(v GER)
	Valeri Gassiy			Cezar Draganita		Piotr Ciesła		
	Vasili Iljin			Alexandru Folker		Jan Gmyrek		
	Mikhail Istchenko			Cristian Gatu		Alfred Kałuziński		
	Yuri Kidjaev			Mircea Grabovschi		Jerzy Klempel		
	Yuri Klimov			Roland Gunes		Zygfryd Kuchta		
	Vladimir Kravsov			Gabriel Kicsid		Jerzy Melcer		
	Sergei Kuschniriuk			Ghita Licu		Ryszard Przbysz		
	Yuri Lagutin			Nicolae Munteanu		Henryk Rozmiarek		
	Vladimir Makimov			Cornel Penu		Andrzej Sokolowski		
	Alexander Resanov			Werner Stockl		Andrzej Szymczak		
	Evgeni Tchernyschov			Constantin Tudosie		Mieczysław Wojczak		
	Anatoli Tomin			Radu Voina		Włodzimierz Zieliński		
1980	Hans-Georg Beyer	GDR	23-22	Alexander Anpilogov	URS	Nicolae Munteanu	ROM	20-18
	Lothar Doering			Vladimir Belov		Marian Dumitru		(v HUN)
	Günter Dreibrodt			Anatoli Fediukin		Iosef Boroş		
	Ernst Gerlach			Mikhail Istchenko		Maricel Voinea		
	Klaus Gruner			Alexander Karshakevish		Vasile Stîngă		
	Rainer Höft			Yuri Kidiaev		Radu Voina		
	Hans-Georg Jaunich			Vladimir Kravtsov		Cezar Draganiţă		
	Hartmut Krüger			Sergei Kushniriuk		Cornel Durău		
	Peter Rost			Viktor Makhorin		Ştefan Birtalan		

/continued on next page 279

HANDBALL

Year	Gold	C'ntry	Points	Silver	C'ntry	Bronze	C'ntry	Points
	Dietmar Schmidt			Valdemar Novitski		Alexandru Fölker		
	Wieland Schmidt			Vladimir Repiev		Neculai Vasilca		
	Siegfried Voigt			Evgeni Chernyschov		Adrian Cosma		
	Frank-Michael Wahl			Anatoli Tomin		Claudiu Eugen Ionescu		
	Ingolf Wiegert			Alexei Zhuk				
1984	Zlatan Arnautović	YUG	18-17	Jochen Fraatz	FRG	Mircea Bedivan	ROM	23-19
	Mirko Bašić			Thomas Happe		Iosif Boroş		(v DEN)
	Jovan Elezović			Arnulf Meffle		Alexandru Buligan		
	Mile Isaković			Rüdiger Neitzel		Gheorghe Covaciu		
	Pavo Jurina			Michael Paul		George Dogarescu		
	Milan Kalina			Dirk Rauin		Marian Dumitru		
	Slobodan Kuzmanovski			Siegfried Roch		Cornel Durău		
	Dragan Mladenović			Ulrich Roth		Alexandru Fölker		
	Zdravko Radjenović			Michael Roth		Nicolae Munteanu		
	Momir Rnić			Martin Schwalb		Vasile Oprea		
	Branko Štrbać			Uwe Schwenker		Adrian Simion		
	Veselin Vujović			Thomas Springel		Vasile Stîngă		
	Veselin Vuković			Andreas Thiel		Neculai Vasilca		
	Zdravko Zovko			Klaus Wöller		Maricel Voinea		
				Erhard Wunderlich				
1988	Viacheslav Atavin	URS	32-25	Choi Suk Jae	KOR	Mirko Bašić	YUG	27-23
	Yuri Chevtsov			Kang Jae Won		Jozef Holpert		(v HUN)
	Alexander Karchakevish			Kim Jae Hwan		Slobodan Kuzmanovski		
	Andrei Lavrov			Koh Suk Chang		Alvaro Načinović		
	Yuri Nesterov			Lee Sang Hyo		Goran Perkovač		
	Valdemar Novitski			Lim Jin Suk		Žlatko Portner		
	Alexander Rymanov			Oh Young Ki		Iztok Puć		
	Konstantin Charovarov			Park Do Hun		Momir Rnić		
	Giorgi Sviridenko			Park Young Dae		Žlatko Saračević		
	Igor Tchoumak			Roh Hyun Suk		Irfan Smajlagić		
	Andrei Tioumentsev			Shim Jae Hong		Ermin Velić		
	Alexander Toutchkine			Sin Young Suk		Veselin Vujović		
	Mikhail Vassiliev			Yoon Tai II				
1992	Andrei Barbachinski	EUN	22-20	Robert Andersson	SWE	Philippe Debureau	FRA	24-20
	Sergei Bebechko			Magnus Andersson		Philippe Gardent		(v ISR)
	Talant Douichebaev			Anders Bäckegren		Denis Lathoud		
	Dmitri Filioppov			Per Carlén		Pascal Mahé		
	Iouri Gavrilov			Magnus Cato		Philippe Médard		
	Valeri Gopine			Erik Hajas		Gaél Monthurel		
	Viacheslav Gorpishin			Robert Hedin		Laurent Munier		
	Oleg Grebnev			Patrik Liljestrand		Frédéric Perez		
	Mikhail Iakimovitch			Ola Lindgren		Thierry Perreux		
	Oleg Kisilev			Mats Olsson		Alain Portes		
	Vassili Koudinov			Steffan Olsson		Eric Quintin		
	Andrei Lavrov			Axel Sjöblad		Jackson Richardson		
	Andrei Minevski			Tommy Suoraniemi		Stéphane Stoecklin		
	Igor Tchoumak			Tomas Svensson		Jean-Luc Thiebaut		
	Igor Vassiliev			Pierre Thorsson		Denis Tristant		
				Magnus Wislander		Frédéric Volle		

HANDBALL (Women)

Year	Gold	C'ntry	Points	Silver	C'ntry	Bronze	C'ntry	Points
1976	Lubov Berezhnaja	URS	14-11	Gabriele Badorek	GDR	Éva Angyal	HUN	20-15
	Ludmila Bobrus			Hannelore Burosch		Mária Berzsenyi		(v ROM)
	Aldona Chesaitite			Roswitha Krause		Agota Bujdosó		
	Tatiana Glustchenko			Waltraud Kretzschmar		Klára Csík		
	Larisa Karlova			Evelyn Matz		Zsuzsa Kezi		
	Maria Litoschenko			Liane Michaelis		Katalin Laki		
	Nina Lobova			Eva Paskuy		Rozália Lelkes		
	Tatiana Makarets			Kristina Richter		Márta Megyeri		
	Ludmila Pantchuk			Christina Rost		Ilona Nagy		
	Rafiga Schabanova			Silvia Siefert		Marianna Nagy		
	Natalia Sherstjuk			Marion Tietz		Erzsébet Németh		
	Ludmila Shubina			Petra Uhlig		Amália Sterbinszky		
	Zinaida Turchina			Christina Voss		Borbála Tóth-Harsányi		

Year	Gold	C'ntry	Points	Silver	C'ntry	Bronze	C'ntry	Points
	Galina Zakharova			Hannelore Zober		Mária Vadász		
1980	Lubov Berezhnaja-	URS	18-9	Svetlana Anastasovski	YUG	Birgit Heinecke	GDR	19-9
	Odinokova			Mirjana Djurica		Roswitha Krause		(v HUN)
	Ludmila Bobrus-Poradnik			Radmila Drljača		Waltraud Kretzschmar		
	Larisa Karlova			Katica Ileš		Katrin Krüger		
	Valentina Lutaieva			Slavica Jeremić		Kornelia Kunisch		
	Tatiana Makarets-Koschergina			Svetlana Kitić		Evelyn Matz		
	Aldona Nenenene			Jasna Merdan		Kristina Richter		
	Irina Palchikova			Vesna Milošević		Christina Rost		
	Yulia Safina			Mirjana Ognjenović		Sabine Röther		
	Larisa Savkina			Vesna Radović		Renate Rudolph		
	Natalia Scherstjuk-Timoshkina			Rada Savić		Marion Tietz		
	Sigita Strechen			Ana Titlić		Petra Uhlig		
	Zinaida Turchina			Biserka Višnjić		Claudia Wunderlilch		
	Olga Zubareva			Zorica Vojinović		Hannelore Zober		
1984	Alenka Cuderman	YUG	29-23	Han Hwa Soon	KOR	Chen Zhen	CHN	20-19
	Svetlana Anastasovski			Jeong Hyoi Soon		Gao Xiumin		(v FRG)
	Svetlana Dašić-Kitić			Jeung Soon Bok		He Jianping		
	Slavica Djukić			Kim Choon Yei		Li Lan		
	Dragica Djurić			Kim Kyung Soon		Liu Liping		
	Mirjana Djurica			Kim Mi Sook		Liu Yumei		
	Emilija Erčić			Kim Ok Hwa		Sun Xiulan		
	Ljubinka Janković			Lee Soon Ei		Wang Linwei		
	Jasna Kolar-Merdan			Lee Young Ja		Wang Mingxing		
	Svetlana Mugoša			Son Mi Na		Wu Xingjiang		
	Ljijana Mugoša			Sung Kyung Hwa		Zhang Peijun		
	Mirjana Ognjenović			Yoon Byung Soon		Zhang Weihong		
	Zorica Pavisević			Youn Soo Kyung		Zhu Juefeng		
	Jasna Ptujeć							
	Biserka Višnjić							
1988	Han Hyun Sook	KOR	23-20	Kjerstin Andersen	NOR	Natalia Anissimova	URS	18-15
	Kim Choon Rye			Berit Digre		Marina Bazanova		(v YUG)
	Kim Hyun Mee			Marte Eliasson		Tatiana Djandjgava		
	Kim Kyung Soon			Susann Goksor		Tatiana Gorb		
	Kim Mi Sook			Trine Haltvik		Elina Gousoeva		
	Kim Myung Soon			Hanne Hegh		Larisa Karlova		
	Lee Ki Soon			Hanne Hogness		Natalia Lapitskaia		
	Lim Mi Kyung			Vibeke Johnsen		Svetlana Mankova		
	Son Mi Na			Kristin Midthun		Natalia Mitruiuk		
	Song Ji Hyun			Karin Pettersen		Natalia Morskova		
	Suk Min Hee			Karin Singstao		Elena Nemachkalo		
	Sung Kyung Hwa			Annette Skottvoll		Natalia Rusnatchenko		
				Ingrid Steen		Olga Semenova		
				Heidi Sundal		Evgeni Tovstogan		
				Cathrine Svendsen		Zinaida Tourtchina		
1992	Cha Jae Kyung	KOR	28-21	Mona Dahle	NOR	Natalia Anissimova	EUN	24-20
	Han Hyun Sook			Kristine Duvholt		Marina Bazanova		(v GER)
	Han Sun Hi			Siri Eftedal		Svetlana Bogdanova		
	Hong Jeong Ho			Hege Kirsti Fröseth		Galina Borzenkova		
	Hwang Sun Hee			Susann Goksor		Natalia Deriouguina		
	Jang Ri Ra			Henriette Henriksen		Tatiana Djandjgava		
	Kim Hwa Sook			Hanne Hogness		Tatiana Gorb		
	Lee Ho Youn			Hege Kristine Luno Kvitsano		Ludmila Goudz		
	Lee Mi Young			Karin Pettersen		Elina Gousseva		
	Lim O Kyung			Tonje Sagstuen		Larisa Kisseleva		
	Min Hye Sook			Anne Brit Skartein		Natalia Morskova		
	Moon Hyang Ja			Annette Skotvoll		Galina Onoprienko		
	Nam Eun Young			Ingrid Steen		Svetlana Priahina		
	Oh Sung Ok			Heidi Sundal		Svetlana Rozintseva		
	Park Jeong Lim			Cathrine Svendsen		Raissa Verakso		
	Park Kap Sook			Heidi Marie Tjugum				

Hockey

Stars to Watch

by Sydney Friskin

A game of musical chairs?

IF THE followers of Olympic men's hockey are looking to Atlanta for a tale of the unexpected they are unlikely to find it. No new forces have emerged in the preparation for this event and the awesome gap between the stronger and weaker teams remains.

The balance of power tilted sharply in favour of Europe in 1988 at Seoul where the three prizes at stake were seized by Great Britain, Germany and The Netherlands. The position was altered somewhat at Barcelona in 1992 when Germany won the gold medal, Australia the silver and Pakistan the bronze.

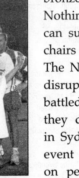

German team, 1992

Nothing that has happened since 1992 can suggest that the game of musical chairs involving Germany, Australia, The Netherlands and Pakistan will be disrupted in Atlanta. These four teams battled for the medals in Barcelona and they did so again in the world cup in Sydney at the end of 1994. In that event Pakistan beat The Netherlands on penalty strokes in the final and Australia won the bronze medal after defeating Germany 5-2 in the play-off for third place.

Australia, having been runners-up three times, in Mexico City (1968), Montreal (1976) and Barcelona (1992), will double their effort to fulfil their ambition. So, too, will The Netherlands who have never won the gold medal. Germany, with confidence renewed after retaining the European Nations Cup in Dublin, will strive mightily to keep the Olympic title and Pakistan, with their world cup triumph in Sydney behind them, will be seeking to become Olympic champions for the fourth time. They were previously successful in 1960, '68 and '84. These, initially, will be the teams to watch in Atlanta.

Two other sides worthy of attention are South Korea and Argentina. The Koreans, winners of the Asian Games title at

★★★★★★★★★★★★★★★★★★★★★★★★★★★★★ **A Contemporary Hero**

Mark Hager *(Australia)*

If Mark Hager had played rugby league as his father had suggested instead of hockey he would not have become an outstanding centre forward and the proud possessor of a world cup gold medal won in 1986. Originally from Queensland, he was given the opportunity to study at the Australian Institute of Sports where his international career began to blossom. After Australia had won the world cup in London the retirement of Terry Walsh left the way open for Hager to become the spearhead of their attack, a role he has successfully filled with his penetrating runs and goals of high quality. At the 1988 Olympic Games in Seoul, Hager was joint second with Sean Kerly of Great Britain in the scorers' list with eight goals.

At the 17th Champions Trophy tournament which ended in Berlin on October 1, 1995, Hager, as captain of Australia, scored three goals in helping his side to finish runners-up to Germany. He had by then scored 164 goals in international matches which topped the 200 mark. Injury kept him out of the 1992 Olympic Games in Barcelona but Atlanta beckons for what appears to be his last chance of an Olympic gold medal.

Seoul in 1986 and again at Hiroshima in October 1994, have brought a new dimension to the game in Asia. Impelled by a keen sense of positioning and a deep understanding of one another's methods they can make inroads into the best defences. They missed the 1992 Games in Barcelona and finished a disappointing eighth in the World Cup at Sydney. But winning the Indira Gandhi Gold Cup at New Delhi in February 1995, with a 3-1 win over India in the final has given them fresh hope.

Argentina, winners of the Pan-American Games title at Mar del Plata with a 1-0 victory over Canada in the final in March 1995, could be the joker in the pack. Combining athleticism with an artistic touch they are capable of beating the best and yet quite tantalizingly can lose to a weaker side. Despite finishing 11th in Barcelona they can cause a few upsets in Atlanta.

The overall picture for Atlanta is one of contrasting styles. Australia with a full complement of five fast and skilful forwards emulate India and Pakistan in presenting an effective counter to the European framework of firm defences and bustling forwards, usually three. Spain and Argentina offer an attractive blend of both patterns of play.

The big question is whether the Asian subcontinent can regain its lost glory but few, if any, can foresee an India-Pakistan final. If they do meet at any time in the tournament they will probably play to a packed house.

South Africa gained automatic qualification for Atlanta by winning the All African Games hockey title in Harare in September, 1995, finishing ahead of Egypt, Kenya, Zimbabwe, Nigeria and Namibia.

A Contemporary Hero ★★★★★★★★★★★★★★★★★★★★★★★★★★★★★

Floris Jan Bovelander *(The Netherlands)*

Floris Jan Bovelander of The Netherlands has been at the top of the scorers' list in the past two Olympic Games with nine and 11 goals, respectively. A penalty corner expert of worldwide repute, he has since 1986 been a matchwinner for the Dutch team and the linchpin of its defence. By the end of the 1994 world cup in Sydney, where The Netherlands won the silver medal, Bovelander had made 226 international appearances and scored 208 goals.

At the 1988 Olympic Games in Seoul he scored both goals from penalty corners against Australia for a 2-1 win in the play-off for the bronze medal and he remains one of The Netherlands' brightest hopes in Atlanta. Bovelander is best remembered for his magnificent feat in the 1990 world cup final at Lahore when his conversion of penalty corners in the 12th and 14th minute turned the match in favour of The Netherlands after Pakistan had taken the lead in the fifth minute. The Dutch eventually won 3-1.

Although South Africa finished tenth overall in the world cup at Sydney they drew 1-1 with Germany in the pool series and held South Korea goalless. By virtue of their fast and open style of play they could be one of the more attractive sides to watch.

In the women's tournament, meanwhile, all eyes will be on the host nation. The USA, not a major recent hockey force, gathered their team together in 1995 to live and train together intensively for months on end at the National Training Centre. It is a tactic which proved successful for the Spanish winners in 1992 as well as the Korean hosts of 1988. And the USA shocked some of the more established nations at the 1995 world cup with their athletic and competitive, even if technically raw, style.

Australia won that world cup and must start as favourites in Atlanta but, interestingly, Argentina emerged with a young side to take the silver medal whilst Great Britain, 1992 Olympic bronze medallists, faded to 9th place. The Netherlands, a previous but recently-fallen "great", are beginning to re-build their side and the Germans, whose skills are honed at an early age through indoor hockey, are technically very good. They also have Becker on their side – not Boris but a dazzling youngster called Britta.

S. F. □

Retrospective

India and Pakistan have dominated much of Olympic hockey history. One of their most famous players was Dhyan Chand. He first played in the 1928 tournament aged 22 and went on to win three golds. But he will mainly be remembered for playing barefoot in the 1936 final against Germany. And he

★★★★★★★★★★★★★★★★★★★★★★★★★★★★★★★★★ **A Sporting Legend**

Balbir Singh *(India)*

In India's heyday there emerged from the playing fields of the Punjab a centre forward of exceptional quality, Balbir Singh. He was the first in a line of five players bearing the same name all of whom shot into prominence. The senior Balbir became famous for his stickwork and acceleration which, coupled with timely body-swerve, enabled him to bemuse defenders particularly goalkeepers.

These attributes made Balbir an automatic choice for the Indian team in which he had a glittering career. He achieved the unique record of winning gold medals in three successive Olympic Games in 1948 (London), 1952 (Helsinki) and 1956 (Melbourne) in all of which he demonstrated the advantage of close-passing with inside forwards. He was at his brilliant best in the 1952 Olympic final at Helsinki when he scored five of India's goals in a 6-1 victory over The Netherlands, the last three in a row. He was captain of the Indian team in 1956 at Melbourne where in the final India beat Pakistan 1-0.

featured in the highest scoring match of Olympic history when India beat their American hosts 24-1 in 1932.

In 1972, however, Germany won the tournament beating Pakistan 1-0 in the final. Pakistan, it seemed, took defeat very badly. They mocked the medal ceremony, assaulted a doping control doctor and the players involved were banned from the Olympic Movement for life.

Four years later the first artifical pitch was used at the Games. Surprisingly India failed to even reach the semi-finals and New Zealand were the shock winners. But the upset of all time must have been the Zimbabwean women's gold medal at the 1980 Games. Invited as a last-minute substitute because of the boycott, they selected their team (incidentally all-white) over the weekend before the Games and had to have their travelling expenses paid by the International Olympic Committee. Members of the winning team were rewarded with an ox by a grateful Zimbabwean Sports Minister.

★★★★★★★★★★★★★★★★★★★★★★★★★★★★★★★★ **A Contemporary Hero**

Carsten Fischer *(Germany)*

Carsten Fischer, who announced his retirement from international hockey after the 1992 Olympic Games, was recalled by Germany in September 1995 for the sixth time after beating Australia on penalty strokes in the final at the end of which the scores were tied at 2-2. Fischer is regarded as a Colossus among full backs with the remarkable ability to transform defence into counter-attack. He is also adept at converting penalty corners.

Fischer made his mark at international level in 1982 in the second junior world cup in Kuala Lumpur. In the final against Australia, who were leading 1-0 at one stage, he inspired the Germans to a 4-1 win after converting a penalty corner. He won Olympic silver medals at Los Angeles in 1984 and Seoul in 1988. Treatment for a diabetic condition caused him to lose his blond hair before he reached Barcelona where he achieved his much cherished gold medal, pulling Germany out of a tight spot in the semi-final against Pakistan. He scored the equalizer from a penalty stroke in the 46th minute and the winning goal from a penalty corner in extra time for a 2-1 victory.

Background

Hockey first appeared on the Olympic programme in 1908 but a women's event was not added until 1980. India and Pakistan's joint winning streak is legendary. India took the title from 1928 to '56 as well as in 1964 and '80. Pakistan, meanwhile, won in 1960, '68 and '84. Germany were the team to spoil the sequence on home territory at the 1972 Munich Games.

Without doubt, the sport of hockey has been passed down from the earliest civilizations. There are drawings in the ancient tombs of the Nile valley depicting men playing sport with curved sticks and a round object. The Romans also played a game called "paganica" in which a feather-filled ball was hit with a club. And there are records of a similar game played by Argentinian Indians in the sixteenth century.

In its more modern version the sport became popular in the late nineteenth century in Britain with a national association, called the Hockey Association, being formed in 1886. The first international matches took place in the last few years of the last century. British servicemen were thought to have taken the modern sport to India at about the same time. And the International Hockey Federation was formed in 1924 at the behest of the IOC. Hockey quickly became one of the largest participation sports in the world and in 1970 a world cup was introduced. One of the other prestigious events is the "Champions Trophy". Women's hockey was hindered at first by the restrictive attitudes prevalent at the turn of the last century but quickly gained momentum with the earliest international matches around 1914.

Equipment

Hockey sticks are a maximum of 5.10cm (2in.) in diameter with a curved head of wood. They have a flat side and a rounded side. The ball is hard and just over 7.6cm (3in.) in diameter. Hockey pitches at the Olympic Games have a synthetic surface and are 91.40m (300ft) long and 55m (180ft) wide (see diagram). The goals are 2.14m (7ft) high and 3.66m (12ft) wide with a back net and stop boards at ground level.

Hockey goalkeepers need upper body protectors and must wear protective headgear as well as a different colour shirt to the rest of their team.

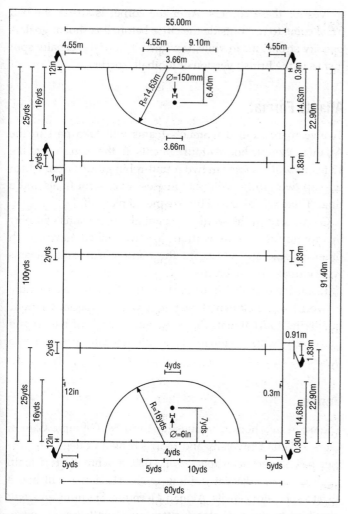

Hockey pitch

Rules

The object of the sport is to win by scoring more goals than the opposition. Each team has 11 players on the pitch at one time but can have up to five substitutes on a rolling basis. And a match lasts 70 minutes in two halves of 35 minutes with a half-time interval of ten minutes. Play is controlled by two umpires who enforce penalties, keep the time and signal goals. A goal can only be scored from inside the circle.

During a match players must not play the ball with the rounded side of the stick or play the ball with their stick above shoulder height. Nor can they stop or hit the ball with any part of their body, nor obstruct other players. Many goals are scored from penalty corners which are given for intentional fouls by the defence within the "25 yard" line or for unintentional fouls within the circle. Teams practise set moves for these corners. After the corner is struck the ball must come to rest outside the circle before it is shot at goal. A penalty stroke, meanwhile, is a free hit from the penalty spot just as in the British version of football (soccer).

Atlanta Format

Twelve men's and 8 women's teams will take part in the Atlanta Olympic hockey tournaments. In the men's event the 12 teams will compete in two round-robin groups from which the top two groups will play in cross-over semi-finals and a final. There will also be a bronze medal play-off.

Conversely, in the women's event all eight teams will play in a round-robin group with the top two ranked playing each other for gold and silver. The third and fourth ranked teams will compete for the bronze.

Teams have qualified for the Olympic Games via a mixture of world and continental events as well as special Olympic qualifying tournaments. In both events the host nation and the 1992 Olympic winners have automatically been given a place.

Venue

There are two hockey venues for the 1996 Olympic Games: Clark Atlanta University and Morris Brown College. The former has a spectator capacity of 5,000, a synthetic turf main pitch with an adjacent training pitch. The latter will house 15,000 spectators in its Alonzo Herndon Stadium and will play host to the final stages again on a synthetic turf pitch. Both are 4.8km (3 miles) from the Olympic Village.

MEDALLISTS (by nation)

	Men			Women			
	Gold	Silver	Bronze	Gold	Silver	Bronze	Total
India	8	1	2	-	-	-	11
Great Britain	3	2	4	-	-	1	10
Pakistan	3	3	2	-	-	-	8
Netherlands	-	2	3	1	-	1	7
Germany	1	1	2	-	1	-	5
Australia	-	3	1	1	-	-	5
FRG	1	2	-	-	1	-	4
Spain	1	1	1	-	-	-	3
Soviet Union	-	-	1	-	-	1	2
United States	-	-	1	-	-	1	2
New Zealand	1	-	-	-	-	-	1
Zimbabwe	-	-	-	1	-	-	1
Czechoslovakia	-	-	-	-	1	-	1
Denmark	-	1	-	-	-	-	1
Japan	-	1	-	-	-	-	1
Korea	-	-	-	-	1	-	1
Belgium	-	-	1	-	-	-	1
	18	17	18	3	4	4	64

ATLANTA SCHEDULE

Venues: Morris Brown College = MBC
Clark Atlanta University = CAU

Date	Round	Start	End	Venue
20 Jul	prelims (w)	8:30	13:00	MBC
	prelims (m)	8:30	10:30	CAU
	prelims (w)	17:30	22:00	MBC
	prelims (m)	17:30	22:00	CAU
21 Jul	prelims (m)	8:30	10:30	MBC
	prelims (m)	17:30	22:00	MBC
	prelims (w)	17:30	22:00	CAU
22 Jul	prelims (m)	8:30	10:30	MBC
	prelims (w)	8:30	13:00	CAU
	prelims (m)	17:30	22:00	MBC

Date	Round	Start	End	Venue
23 Jul	prelims (w)	8:30	13:00	MBC
	prelims (m)	8:30	10:30	CAU
	prelims (w)	17:30	22:00	MBC
	prelims (m)	17:30	22:00	CAU
24 Jul	prelims (m)	8:30	10:30	MBC
	prelims (m)	17:30	22:00	MBC
25 Jul	prelims (w)	8:30	13:00	MBC
	prelims (m)	8:30	10:30	CAU
	prelims (w)	17:30	22:00	MBC
	prelims (m)	17:30	22:00	CAU
26 Jul	prelims (m)	8:30	10:30	MBC
	prelims (m)	17:30	22:00	MBC
	prelims (w)	17:30	22:00	CAU
27 Jul	prelims (m)	8:30	10:30	MBC
	prelims (w)	8:30	13:00	CAU
	prelims (m)	17:30	22:00	MBC
28 Jul	prelims (w)	8:30	13:00	MBC
	prelims (m)	8:30	10:30	CAU
	prelims (w)	17:30	22:00	MBC
	prelims (m)	17:30	22:00	CAU
29 Jul	prelims (m)	8:30	10:30	MBC
	prelims (m)	17:30	22:00	MBC
30 Jul	prelims (w)	8:30	13:00	MBC
	prelims (w)	17:30	22:00	MBC
31 Jul	classification (m)	8:30	13:00	MBC
	classification (m)	8:30	13:00	CAU
	s/finals	17:30	22:00	MBC
1 Aug	play-off (9-10 place) (m)	8:30	13:00	MBC
	play-off (7-8 place) (m)			
	play-off (11-12 place) (m)	8:30	10:30	CAU
	play-off (bronze) (w)	17:00	21:45	MBC
	FINAL (w)			
2 Aug	play-off (5-6 place) (m)	8:30	10:30	MBC
	play-off (bronze) (m)	17:00	21:45	MBC
	FINAL (m)			

MEDALLISTS

HOCKEY (Men)

Year	Gold	C'ntry	Score	Silver	C'ntry	Bronze	C'ntry
1908	Louis Baillon	GBR	8-1	Edward Allman-Smith	GBR	Alexander Burt	GBR
(Eng)	Harold Freeman			Henry Brown	(Irl)	John Burt	(Scot)
	Eric Green			Walter Campbell		Andrew Dennistoun	
	Gerald Logan			William Graham		Charles Foulkes	
	Alan Noble			Richard Gregg		Hew Fraser	
	Edgar Page			Edward Holmes		John Harper-Orr	
	Reginald Pridmore			Robert Kennedy		Ivan Laing	
	Percy Rees			William McCormick		Hugh Neilson	
	John Robinson			Henry Murphy		William Orchardson	
	Stanley Shoveller			Walter Peterson		Norman Stevenson	
	Harvey Wood			Charles Power		Hugh Walker	
				Frank Robinson			
1920	Charles Atkins	GBR		Hans Adolf Bjerrum	DEN	André Becquet	BEL
	John Bennett			Ejvind Blach		Pierre Chibert	
	Harold Kennedy Cassels			Svend Blach		Raoul Daufresne de la Chevalerie	
	Harold Cooke			Steen Due		Orphile Fernand de Montigny	
	Eric Crockford			Thorvald Eigenbrod		Charles Delelienne	
	Reginald Crummack			Frands Faber		Louis Diercxens	
	Harry Haslam			Hans Jörgen Hansen		Robert Gevers	
	Arthur Leighton			Hans Christian Herlak		Adolphe Goemaere	
	Charles Marcon			Henning Holst		Raymond Keppens	
	John McBryan			Erik Husted		René Strauwen	
	George McGrath			Andreas Rasmussen		Pierre Valcke	
	Stanley Shoveller					Maurice van den Bemdem	
	William Smith					Jean van Nerom	
	Cyril Wilkinson						
1928	Richard Allen	IND	3-0	Jan Akkerman	NED	Bruno Boche	GER
	Dhyan Chand Bais			Johannes Brand		Georg Brunner	
	Maurice Gateley			Reindert de Waal		Heinz Förstendorff	
	William Cullen-Goodsir			Emile Duson		Erwin Franzkowiak	
	Leslie Hammond			Hendrik Visser 't Hooft		Werner Freyberg	
	Feroze Khan			Gerrit Jannink		Theodor Haag	
	George Martins			Adriaan Katte		Heinrich Haussmann	
	Rex Norris			August Kop		Kurt Haverbeck	
	Broome Eric Pinniger			Albert Tresling		Aribert Heymann	
	Michael Rocque			Paulus van de Rovaert		Herbert Hobein	
	Frederick Seaman			Robert van der Veen		Fritz Horn	
	Ali Shaukat					Karl-Heinz Irmer	
	Sayed Yusuf					Herbert Kemmer	
						Herbert Müller	
						Werner Proft	
						Gerd Strantzen	
						Rolf Wollner	
						Heinz Wöltje	
						Erich Zander	
1932	Richard Allen	IND	11-1	Shunkichi Hamada	JPN	William Boddington	USA
	Lal Shah Bokhari			Junzo Inohara		Harold Brewster	
	Richard Carr			Sadayoshi Kobayashi		Amos Deacon	
	Dhyan Chand Bais			Haruhiko Kon		Horace Disston	
	Leslie Hammond			Kenichi Konishi		Samuel Ewing	
	Arthur Hind			Hiroshi Nagata		James Gentle	
	Sayed Mohd Jaffar			Eiichi Nakamura		Henry Greer	
	Gurmit Singh Kullar			Yoshio Sakai		Laurence Knapp	
	Masude Minhas			Katsumi Shibata		David McMullin	
	Broome Eric Pinniger			Akio Sohda		Leonard O'Brien	
	Roop Singh			Toshio Usami		Charles Shaeffer	
	Carlyle Tapsell					Frederick Wolters	
1936	Richard Allen	IND	8-1	Ludwig Beisiegel	GER	Jan de Looper	NED
	Dhyan Chand Bais			Erich Cuntz		Hendrik de Looper	
	Roop Singh Bais			Karl Dröse		Agathon de Roos	
	Lionel Emmett			Alfred Gerdes		Reindert de Waal	
	Paul Peter Fernandes			Werner Hamel		Pieter Gunning	
	Joseph Galibardy			Hermann Auf Der Heide		Carl Heybroek	

Year	Gold	C'ntry	Score	Silver	C'ntry	Bronze	C'ntry
	Gurcharan Singh Garewal			Harald Huffmann		Henri Schnitger	
	Ernest Goodsir-Cullen			Erwin Keller		René Sparenberg	
	Sayed Mohomed Hussain			Herbert Kemmer		Ernst Willem van den Berg	
	Sayed Mohomed Jaffar			Werner Kubitzki		Rudolf van der Haar	
	Ahsan Mohomed Khan			Paul Mehlitz		Antoine van Lierop	
	Ahmed Sher Khan			Carl Menke		Max Westerkamp	
	Mirza Nasir-Ud-Din Masood			Fritz Messner			
	Cyril Michie			Detlef Okrent			
	Baboo Narsoo Nimal			Heinrich Peter			
	Joseph Phillip			Heinz Raack			
	Shabab-Ud-Din Shabban			Karl Ruck			
	Dara Singh			Hans Scherbart			
	Carlyle Tapsell			Heinrich Schmalix			
				Rudolf (Tito) Warnholtz			
				Kurt Weiss			
				Erich Zander			
1948	Hussain Ahktar	IND	4-0	Robert Adlard	GBR	Andries Boerstra	NED
	Leslie Claudius			Norman Borrett		Hendricus Bouwman	
	Walter d'Souza			David Brodie		Pieter Johan Bromberg	
	Keshava Dutt			Ronald Davies		Henri Derckx	
	Lawrence Fernandes			William Griffiths		Johan Drijver	
	Ranganandhan Francis			Frederich Robin Lindsay		Rius Esser	
	Randhir Singh Gentle			William Lindsay		Jan Kruize	
	Gerald Glacken			John Peake		Jenne Langhout	
	Patrick Jansen			Frank Reynolds		Hermanus Loggere	
	Amir Chand Kumar			George Sime		Antonius Richter	
	Kishan Lal			Michael Walford		Edouard Tiel	
	Leo Pinto			William Neil White		Willem van Heel	
	Jaswant Rajput						
	Latifur Rehaman						
	Reginald Rodrigues						
	Trilochan Singh						
	Grahanandan Nandy Singh						
	Kunwar Digvijai Singh						
	Balbir Dosanjh Singh						
	Max Vaz						
1952	Leslie Claudius	IND	6-1	Julius Ancion	NED	Denys Carnill	GBR
	Chinadori Deshmuthu			Andries Boerstra		John Cockett	
	Balbir Dosanjh Singh			Henri Derckx		John Conroy	
	Keshava Dutt			Dirk		Graham Dadds	
	Ranganandhan Francis			Johan Drijver		Derek Day	
	Randhir Singh Gentle			Rius Esser		Dennis Eagan	
	Udham Singh Kullar			Willem van Heel		Robin Fletcher	
	Govind Perumal			Jan Kruize		Roger Midgley	
	Muniswamy Rajagopal			Hermanus Loggere		Richard Norris	
	Raghbir Lal Sharma			Laurentz Mulder		Nigel Nugent	
	Dharam Singh			Edouard Tiel		Anthony Nunn	
	Grahanandan Singh			Leonard Wery		Anthony Robinson	
	Kunwar Digvijai Singh					John Taylor	
1956	Amit Singh Bakshi	IND	1-0	Hamid Abdul	PAK	Günter Brennecke	GER
	Raghbir Singh Bhola			Hussain Akhtar		Hugo Budinger	
	Leslie Claudius			Munir Ahmad Dar		Werner Delmes	
	Balbir Dosanjh Singh			Rasul Ghulam		Hugo Dollheiser	
	Ranganandhan Francis			Rehman Habib		Eberhard Ferstl	
	Hardyal Singh Garchey			Anwar Ahmad Khan		Alfred Lücker	
	Randhir Singh Gentle			Habib Ali Kiddi		Helmut Nonn	
	Balkishnan Singh Greval			Rehman Latif		Wolfgang Nonn	
	Hari Pal Kaushik			Hussain Atif Manzoor		Heinz Radzikowski	
	Gurdev Singh Kullar			Hussain Mussarat		Werner Rosenbaum	
	Udham Singh Kullar			Ullah Mutih		Günther Ullerich	
	Amir Chand Kumar			Ahmad Nasir			
	Shankar Laxman			Alam Noor			
	Govind Perumal			Hussain Zakir			
	Raghbir Lal Sharma						
	Bakshish Singh						
	Charles Stephen						

/continued on next page

Year	Gold	C'ntry	Score	Silver	C'ntry	Bronze	C'ntry
1960	Hamid Abdul	PAK	1-0	Joseph Antic	IND	Pedro Amat Fontanals	ESP
	Rashid Abdul			Raghbir Singh Bhola		Francisco Caballer Soteras	
	Waheed Abdul			Leslie Claudius		Juan Calzado de Castro	
	Bashir Ahmed			Udham Singh Kullar		José Colomer Rivas	
	Munir Ahmad Dar			Mohinder Lal		Carlos Del Coso Iglesias	
	Rasul Ghulan			Shankar Laxman		José Dinares Massagué	
	Anwar Ahmad Khan			John Victor Peter		Eduardo Dualde Santos de la Madrid	
	Aslam Khurshid			Govind Sawant		Joaquin Dualde Santos de la Madrid	
	Habib Ali Kidi			Jaman Lal Sharma		Rafael Egusquiza Basterra	
	Hussain Atif Manzoor			Charanjit Singh		Ignacio Macaya Santos de la Madrid	
	Ahmed Mushtav			Jaswant Singh		Pedro Murúa Leguizamon	
	Ullah Motih			Joginder Singh		Pedro Roig Junyent	
	Alam Noor			Prithipal Singh		Luis Usoz Quintana	
						Narciso Ventalió Surralles	
1964	Hari Pal Kaushik	IND	1-0	Muhammad Afzal	PAK	Mervyn Crossman	AUS
	Mohinder Lal			Manna		Paul Dearing	
	Shankar Laxman			Munir Ahmad Dar		Raymond Evans	
	Bandu Patil			Anwar Ahmad Khan		Brian Glencross	
	John Victor Peter			Saeed Anwar		Robin Hodder	
	Ali Sayeed			Mohammad Asad Malik		John McBryde	
	Charanjit Singh			Khurshid Azam		Donald McWatters	
	Darshan Singh			Tariq Aziz		Patrick Nilan	
	Dharam Singh			Abdul Hamid		Julian Pearce	
	Gurbux Singh			Zafar Hayat		Eric Pearce	
	Harbinder Singh			Manzoor Hussain Atif		Desmond Piper	
	Jagjit Singh			Khalid Mahmood		Donald Smart	
	Joginder Singh			Khizar Nawaz		Antony Waters	
	Prithipal Singh			Tariq Niazi		Graham Wood	
	Udham Singh			Muhammad Rashid			
				Mutih Ullah			
				Zaka-ud-Din			
1968	Riaz Ahmed	PAK	2-1	Paul Dearing	AUS	Rajendra Christy	IND
	Gulrez Akhtar			Raymond Evans		Perumal Krishnamurthy	
	Saeed Anwar			Brian Glencross		John Victor Peter	
	Mohammad Ashfaq			Robert Haigh		Inamur Rehman	
	Tariq Aziz			Donald Martin		Munir Sait	
	Jehangir Butt			James Mason		Ajitpal Singh	
	Tanvir Dar			Patrick Nilan		Balbir Singh I	
	Zakir Hussain			Gordon Pearce		Balbir Singh II	
	Khalid Hussain			Julian Pearce		Balbir Singh III	
	Asad Malik			Ronald Riley		Gurbaksh Singh	
	Abdul Rashid			Donald Smart		Gurbux Singh	
						Harbinder Singh	
						Harmik Singh	
						Inder Singh	
						Jagjit Singh	
						Prithipal Singh	
						Tarsem Singh	
1972	Wolfgang Baumgart	FRG	1-0	Iftikhar Ahmed	PAK	Kumar Ashok	IND
	Horst Dröse			Riaz Ahmed		Govinda Billimogaputtaswamy	
	Dieter Freise			Rasool Akhtar		Cornelius Charles	
	Werner Kaessmann			Saeed Anwar		Manuel Frederick	
	Carsten Keller			Mudassar Asghar		Michael Kindo	
	Detlef Kittstein			Jahangir Butt		Perumal Krishnamurthy	
	Ulrich Klaes			Islahud Din		Ganesh Mollerapoovayya	
	Peter Kraus			Akhtarul Islam		Ajitpal Singh	
	Michael Krause			Asad Malik		Harbinder Singh	
	Michael Peter			Abdur Rashid		Harcharan Singh	
	Wolfgang Rott			Fazalur Rehman		Harmik Singh	
	Fritz Schmidt			Mohammad Shahnaz		Kulwant Singh	
	Rainer Seifert			Saleem Sherwani		Mukhbain Singh	
	Wolfgang Strödter			Muhammad Zahid		Virinder Singh	
	Eckart Suhl			Munawaruz Zaman			
	Eduard Thelen						
	Peter Trump						
	Uli Vos						

Year	Gold	C'ntry	Score	Silver	C'ntry	Bronze	C'ntry
1976	Arthur Parkin	NZL	1-0	David Bell	AUS	Mudassar Asghar	PAK
	Paul Ackerley			Gregory Browning		Arshad Ali Chaudry	
	Jeff Archibald			Richard Charlesworth		Manzoor Hassan	
	Thur Borren			Ian Cooke		Manzoor Hussain	
	Alan Chesney			Barry Dancer		Islah Islahuddin	
	John Christensen			Douglas Golder		Munawar Zaman Khan	
	Greg Dayman			Graham Reid		Samiulah Khan	
	Tony Ineson			Robert Haigh		Haneef Khan	
	Barry Maister			Wayne Hammond		Arshad Mahmood	
	Selwyn Maister			James Irvine		Saleem Nazim	
	Trevor Manning			Stephen Marshall		Abdul Rashid	
	Alan McIntyre			Malcolm Poole		Akhtar Rasool	
	Neil McLeod			Robert Proctor		Shanaz Sheikh	
	Mohan Patel			Ronald Riley		Saleem Sherwani	
	Ramesh Patel			Trevor Smith		Iftikhar Syed	
	Les Wilson			Terry Walsh		Qamar Zia	
1980	Chettri Bir Bhadur	IND	4-3	Juan Amat	ESP	Sos Airapetian	URS
	Mervyn Fernandis			Jaime Arbos		Minneula Azizov	
	Zafar Iqbal			Juan Arbos		Valeri Beliakov	
	Maharajh Krishon Kaushik			Ricardo Cabot		Viktor Deputatov	
	Charanjit Kumar			Javier Cabot		Alexander Goncharov	
	Somaya Maneypanda			Miguel Chave		Alexander Gusev	
	Allan Schofield			Juan Luis Coghen		Sergei Klevtsov	
	Mohamed Shahid			Miguel de Paz		Viacheslav Lampeev	
	Rajinder Singh			Francisco Fábregas		Alexander Miasnikov	
	Deavinder Singh			José Garcia		Mikhail Nichepurenko	
	Gurmail Singh			Rafael Garralda		Leonid Pavlovski	
	Ravinder Pal Singh			Santiago Malgósa		Vladimir Pleshakov	
	Amarjit Rana Singh			Paulino Monsalve		Sergei Pleshakov	
	Surinder Singh			Juan Pellon		Alexander Syschev	
	Dung Dung Sylvanus			Carlos Roca		Oleg Zagorodnev	
	Baskaran Vasudevan			Jaime Zumalacarregui		Farit Zigangirov	
1984	Ishtiaq Ahmed	PAK	2-1	Christian Bassemir	FRG	Paul Barber	GBR
	Mushtaq Ahmad			Stefan Blöcher		Stephen Batchelor	
	Naeem Akhtar			Drik Brinkmann		Kulbir Bhaura	
	Nasir Ali			Heiner Dopp		Robert Cattrall	
	Tauqeer Dar			Carsten Fischer		Richard Dodds	
	Khalid Hameed			Tobias Frank		James Duthie	
	Manzoor Hussain			Volker Fried		Norman Hughes	
	Kaleemullah			Thomas Gunst		Sean Kerly	
	Hanir Khan			Horst-Ulrich Hänel		Richard Leman	
	Shahid Ali Khan			Karl-Joachim Hürter		Stephan Martin	
	Ayaz Mehmood			Andreas Keller		William McConnell	
	G Moinuddin			Reinhard Krull		Veryan Pappin	
	Abdul Rashid			Michael Peter		Jonathon Potter	
	Hasan Sardar			Ekkhard Schmidt-Oppet		Mark Precious	
	Salleem Sherwani			Maekku Slawyk		Ian Taylor	
	Qasim Zia			Thomas Reck		David Westcott	
1988	Paul Barber	GBR	3-1	Stefan Blöcher	FRG	Marc Benninga	NED
	Stephen Batchelor			Dirk Brinkmann		Jacques Brinkman	
	Dulbir Bhaura			Thomas Brinkmann		Maurits Crucg	
	Robert Clift			Heiner Dopp		Marc Delissen	
	Richard Dodds			Hanns-Henning Fastrich		Cees Jan Diepeveen	
	David Faulkner			Carsten Fischer		Patrick Faber	
	Russell Garcia			Tobias Frank		Ronald Jansen	
	Martyn Grimley			Volker Fried		Rene Klaassen	
	Sean Kerly			Horst-Ulrich Hänel		Hendrik Jan Kooijman	
	James Kirkwood			Michael Hilgers		Jan Hidde Kruize	
	Richard Leman			Andreas Keller		Floris Jan Bovelander	
	Stephen Martin			Michael Metz		Prank Leistra	
	Veryan Pappin			Andreas Mollandin		Erik Parlevliet	
	Jonathan Potter			Thomas Reck		Gerrit Jan Schlatmann	
	Imran Sherwani			Christian Schliemann		Tim Steens	
	Ian Taylor			Ekkhard Schmidt-Oppet		Taco van den Honert	

/continued on next page 293

Year	Gold	C'ntry	Score	Silver	C'ntry	Bronze	C'ntry
1992	Andreas Becker	GER	2-1	John Roderick Bestall	AUS	Ali Khan Shahid	PAK
	Christian Blunck			Warren Birmingham		Saeed Anjum	
	Carsten Fischer			Lee Bodimeade		Hasan Khan Farhat	
	Volker Fried			Ashley Carey		Bashsir Khalid	
	Michael Hilgers			Gregory Corbitt		Muhammad Junaid Khawaja	
	Andreas Keller			Stephen Davies		Ahmed Mansoor	
	Michael Knauth			Damon Diletti		Asif Bajwa Muhammad	
	Oliver Kurtz			Lachlan Dreher		Ikhlaq Muhammad	
	Christian Mayerhofer			Lachlan Elmer		Khalid Muhammad	
	Sven Meinhardt			Dean Evans		Qamar Ibrahim Muhammad	
	Michael Metz			Paul Snowden Lewis		Shehbaz Muhammad	
	Klaus Michler			Graham Reid		Hussain Musaddaq	
	Christopher Reitz			Jay Stacey		Mujahid Ali Rana	
	Stefan Saliger			David Wansbrough		Ahmed Shahbaz	
	Jan-Peter Tewes			Kenneth Wark		Zaman Tahir	
	Stefan Tewes			Michael York		Feroz Wasim	
1996							

HOCKEY (Women)

Year	Gold	C'ntry	Score	Silver	C'ntry	Bronze	C'ntry
1980	Arlene Boxhall	ZIM	4-1	Milada Blažková	TCH	Liailia Akhmerova	URS
	Elizabeth Chase			Jiřina Čermáková		Natalia Buzunova	
	Sandra Chick			Jiřina Hájková		Natalia Bykova	
	Gillian Cowley			Berta Hrubá		Tatiana Embakhtova	
	Patricia Davies			Ida Hubáčková		Nadezhda Filippova	
	Sarah English			Jiřina Kadlecová		Ludmila Frolova	
	Maureen George			Jarmila Králíčkova		Lidia Glubokova	
	Ann Grant			Jiřina Křížová		Nelli Gorbatkova	
	Susan Huggett			Alena Kyseličova		Elena Guryeva	
	Patricia McKillop			Jana Lahodová		Galina Inzhuvatova	
	Brenda Phillips			Květa Petříčková		Alina Kham	
	Christine Prinsloo			Viera Podhanyiová		Natella Krasnikova	
	Sonia Robertson			Yveta Šranková		Nadezhda Ovechkina	
	Anthea Stewart			Marie Sykorová		Tatiana Shvyganova	
	Helen Volk			Marta Urbanová		Galina Viuzhanina	
	Linda Watson			Lenka Vymazalová		Valentina Zazdravnykh	
1984	Carina Benninga	NED	2-0	Gabriele Appel	FRG	Beth Anders	USA
	Josephine Boekhorst			Dagmar Breiken		Beth Beglin	
	Bernadette de Beus			Beate Deininger		Regina Buggy	
	Marjolein Eysvogel			Elke Drüll		Gwen Cheeseman	
	Irene Hendriks			Birgit Hagen		Sheryl Johnson	
	Francisca Hillen			Birgit Hahn		Christine Larson-Mason	
	Anneloes Nieuwenhuizen			Martina Koch		Kathleen McGahey	
	Martine Ohr			Sigrid Landgraf		Anita Miller	
	Alexandra le Poole			Andrea Leitz-Weiermann		Leslie Milne	
	Alette Pos			Corinna Lingnau		Charlene Morett	
	Elisabeth Sevens			Christina Moser		Diane Moyer	
	Marieke van Doorn			Patricia Ott		Marcella Place	
	Aletta van Manen			Hella Roth		Karen Shelton	
	Sophie von Weiler			Gabriele Schley		Brenda Stauffer	
	Laurien Willemse			Susanne Schmid		Julie Staver	
	Margriet Zegers			Ursula Thielemann		Judy Strong	

Year	Gold	C'ntry	Score	Silver	C'ntry	Bronze	C'ntry
1988	Tracey Belbin	AUS	6-5	Chang Eun Jung	KOR	Bernadette de Beus	NED
	Deborah Bowman			Cho Ki Hyang		Yvonne Buter	
	Michelle Capes			Choi Choon Ok		Willemien Aardenburg	
	Lee Capes			Chung Eun Kyung		Laurien Willemse	
	Sally Carbon			Chung Sang Hyun		Marjolein Bolhuis	
	Elspeth Clement			Han Keum Sil		Lisanne Lejeune	
	Loretta Dorman			Han Ok Kyung		Carina Benninga	
	Maree Fish			Hwang Keum Sook		Annemieke Fokke	
	Rechelle Hawkes			Jin Won Sim		Ingrid Wolff	
	Lorraine Hillas			Kim Mi Sun		Marieke van Doorn	
	Kathleen Partridge			Kim Soon Duk		Sophie von Weiler	
	Sharon Patmore			Kim Young Sook		Aletta van Manen	
	Jacqueline Pereira			Lim Kye Sook		Noor Holsboer	
	Sandra Pisani			Park Soon Ja		Helen van der Ben	
	Kim Small			Seo Hyo Sun		Martine Ohr	
	Liane Tooth			Seo Kwang Mi		Anneloes Nieuwenhuizen	
1992	Sonia Barrio Gutierrez	ESP	2-1	Britta Becker	GER	Gillian Atkins	GBR
	Maria Del Carmen Cobos			Tanja Roswitha Dickenscheid		Lisa Bayliss	
	Mercedes Coghen Alberdingo			Nadine Ernsting		Wendy Fraser	
	Celia Corres Giner			Christina Stephanie Ferneck		Susan Fraser	
	Natalia Dorado Gomez			Eva Hagenbaumer		Kathryn Johnson	
	Nagore Gabellanes Marieta			Franziska Hentschel		Karen Brown	
	Maria V Gonzalez Laguillo			Caren Jungjohann		Sandie Lister	
	Ana Maiques Dern			Katrin Kauschke		Jackie McWilliams	
	Silvia Manrique Perez			Irina Kuhnt		Helen Morgan	
	Elisabeth Maragall Verge			Heike Latzsch		Mayr Nevill	
	M Martinez de Murguia			Susanne Muller		Mandy Nicholls	
	Teresa Motos Iceta			Kristina Peters		Alison Ramsay	
	Nuria Olive Vancells			Simone Heike Thomaschinski		Jane Sixsmith	
	Virginia Ramirez Merino			Bianca Margot Weiss		Tammy Miller	
	Maria Rodriguez Suarez			Anke Wild		Joanne Thompson	
	Maider Telleria Goni			Susanne Wollschlaeger		Victoria Dixon	
1996							

Judo

Stars to Watch

by Oon Oon Yeoh

The best the world has ever seen

AN OLYMPIC gold medal is considered to be the ultimate prize in judo. A world championship gold medal is a great achievement but in terms of prestige, honour and glory it can never quite match an Olympic gold medal. The international judo community eagerly awaits the Atlanta Olympic judo competition, for it will surely feature some of the best judo the world has ever seen.

Since the introduction of the sport, in 1964, in Tokyo, the standard of world judo has increased by leaps and bounds. The Japanese still produce some of the best judo players although the rest of the world is quickly catching up. Among the 1996 men's favourites in the Japanese team are: Toshihiko Koga, at under 78 kg, Hidehiko Yoshida, at under 86 kg and, in the women's events, Ryoko Tamura, at under 48 kg. Both Koga and Yoshida are defending Olympic champions.

A Contemporary Heroine ★★★★★★★★★★★★★★★★★★★★★★★★★★★★★★

Ryoko Tamura (Japan)

Diminutive Ryoko Tamura – just 1.44m (4ft 8.5 in.) and weighing 45 kg (7st 1lb) – is the smallest player in judo's lightest division (under 48 kg). However, what she lacks in size, she more than makes up for with speed, agility and technique.

"Yawara Chan" or "Miss Martial Artist", as she is affectionately referred to in Japan, first took up judo in the second year of primary school. She says she was attracted to the sport because she liked the idea of "throwing the boys around". Four months later, she actually sent two of them to the hospital with concussion!

In December 1994, Tamura suffered a serious illness – an abdominal abscess. This resulted in a long lay-off from the sport. However, when she came back, she did so convincingly, winning the 1995 All-Japan weight class competition.

Since 1991, this 19 year old sophomore from Teikyo University has won no fewer than 70 consecutive matches including victories over four-time world champion, Karen Briggs of Britain. Tamura is rightly regarded as Japan's best hope for an Olympic gold medal.

However, Tamura, while not an Olympic gold medallist, is regarded by experts to be the hottest prospect of all for a Japanese victory.

The other Asian powerhouse of the sport is, of course, South Korea. They have a strong contender in double world champion Jeon Ki Young who, in two consecutive world championships, defeated Japanese champion Yoshida. His compatriot, Yoon Dong Sik, at under 78 kg, is also a top prospect. He has replaced 1993 world champion, Chun Ki Young, as his country's top under 78 kg player. He is also the only player in the past five years to have beaten Koga in an international competition. South Korea also has a top female player in Cho Min Sun, a world champion at under 66 kg. She has a very sharp "ouchi-gari" (major inner leg reap) which she can seemingly execute from any grip.

European judo players are known for their power and for their unusual techniques. One of the strongest and most unorthodox players is Russia's Sergei Kossorotov who fights at over 95 kg. Although relatively light for his size, Kossorotov is extremely athletic and skilful. He has proven that he can defeat larger players by winning two European titles and a world title, all against considerably larger opponents.

The under 95 kg weight class has been dominated by Europeans for many years. It will be one of the most exciting divisions to watch as there are more top contenders in this division than any other. Amongst the leading favourites are: double European champion, Paweł Nastula of Poland – a canny, tactical player; Dmitri Sergeev of Russia – a very strong yet technically proficient player and Stephane Traineau of France – a complete player who is as strong at throwing as he is at ground work.

Ulla Werbrouck, Belgium's under 72 kg representative is probably the most likely European woman to win a gold medal. She is physically very strong and has an unstoppable "uchimata" (inner thigh throw). Her opponents will be hard pressed to find a counter or a block that will work against her favourite technique.

The Pan-American Judo Union (which covers all of North, Central and South America) is not particularly known for its judo but it does have a handful of individuals who are world class. Canada's Nicolas Gill is a former under 86 kg world silver medallist. He has a wide range of techniques and fears no one – a formidable combination. The USA's top hope is James Pedro who recently moved up to under 71 kg. Like

A Contemporary Hero ★★★★★★★★★★★★★★★★★★★★★★★★★★★★★★

Stephane Traineau *(France)*

"La Tornade" as Stephane Traineau is commonly known in France, is one of the most popular figures in French judo.

He has a strange habit of winning against top opponents but losing to underdogs. In the 1988 Seoul Olympic Games, he defeated double world champion, Hitoshi Sugai of Japan – the favourite – but failed to win a medal. He defeated Sugai again, at the 1989 Belgrade world championships. However, as before, he failed to win a medal.

In 1991, his judo reached full maturity and he took the world title in Barcelona, winning all of his matches by "ippon" (a winning throw – see later under rules). He was expected to win the 1992 Olympic title but he lost to the unfancied Leo White of the USA. Traineau was spectacularly caught by a sacrifice technique called "soto-makikomi" (outer winding) which was White's favourite, and only, technique.

However, in Atlanta, Traineau will be all set for another shot at the gold. He has already defeated Poland's Pawel Nastula and Dmitri Sergeev, the other leading contenders, in past world championships.

Gill, Pedro has a wide range of techniques and is extremely proficient on the ground.

The 1992 Barcelona Games was the first in which Cuba participated since 1980 and they made the biggest impact with their women's team. Verdecia Rodriguez at under 52 kg, a former world champion, and Odalis Reve at under 66 kg, a former Olympic champion, are their best hopes for Atlanta.

A Contemporary Hero ★★★★★★★★★★★★★★★★★★★★★★★★★★★★★★

James Pedro *(USA)*

James Pedro comes from a judo family. His father is a former competitor and is currently part of the American national coaching squad.

Pedro has recently moved up to the under 71 kg weight class after years of struggling to make the weight at the lower class of under 65 kg. Many observers felt that losing the weight necessary to qualify for the lower division had been detrimental to Pedro's performance. This observation seems to be correct. Since he moved up to his new weight, Pedro's results have improved significantly.

In 1994, he won the "German world masters", a top international tournament, where he defeated the top German player, Martin Schmidt, himself a European gold medallist and "Jigoro Kano Cup" winner.

Pedro, whose style is an unusual mix of classical judo throws and unorthodox take-downs, recently won a gold medal at the 1995 Pan-Am Games and the 1995 U.S. Open which was held in Atlanta.

Anton Geesink *(the Netherlands)*

Anton Geesink, of the Netherlands, was the first Western player to beat a Japanese player at the world championships. His remarkable achievement against the nation which gave birth to the sport came in 1961 when he defeated Koji Sone.

Three years later, at the 1964 Olympic Games, in Tokyo, he repeated the feat. Japan, meanwhile, had had a clean sweep of the other three divisions. Although Geesink was, by then, twice world champion – and certainly a force to be reckoned with – his victory was a shocking blow to the Japanese, who until then, had considered themselves to be nothing short of invincible.

The towering Dutchman with the ready wit won one more world championship title, in Rio de Janeiro in 1965, before retiring from competition. He went on to write several books on judo, did some professional wrestling in Japan, waged a campaign for the introduction of coloured judo uniforms, and has served as a member of the International Olympic Committee for many years. 30 years after his last world title, Anton Geesink remains as one of the most recognized figures in world judo.

These may all be the leading contenders but history has shown that Olympic judo results are incredibly difficult to predict.

O. O. Y. □

Retrospective

Judo is one of the most exciting and unpredictable of all Olympic sports. It has often been peppered with almost unbelievable upsets like the final-round defeat handed out in 1984 to the seemingly unassailable favourite in the under 78 kg category, Neil Adams, of Great Britain, by the previously unknown German, Frank Wieneke.

Imagine, too, the shock waves in Tokyo in 1964 when massive Dutchman Anton Geesink won the Open category gold medal in a sport which the host nation considered its own.

Peter Seisenbacher *(Austria)*

Peter Seisenbacher of Austria has the honour of being the first man to win two consecutive Olympic gold medals -in the Los Angeles Games in 1984, and four years later in Seoul. Only Hiroshi Saito of Japan has equalled the feat again in 1984 and '88.

Seisenbacher was a complete player, capable of powerful throwing techniques and devastating ground work. Coached by Britain's George Kerr, Seisenbacher combined his hard, physical style of judo with a shrewd tactical approach to competition to win almost every available major medal in judo. He was world champion in 1985 in Seoul and European champion in 1986 in Liège (that year, he even won a silver medal in the Open division although he was only an under 86 kg player).

Upon retirement from competition, Seisenbacher toured the world giving judo seminars, leading training camps, and briefly worked for the Austrian Ministry of Sports, developing junior judo programmes.

A Sporting Legend ★★★★★★★★★★★★★★★★★★★★★★★★★★★★★★★★★

Yasuhiro Yamashita *(Japan)*

Yasuhiro Yamashita is unanimously regarded as the greatest judo player of all time. Undefeated throughout his eight years of international competition – from 1977 to '84 – Yamashita capped his career with the title that he prized the most: Olympic champion.

He was too young to be selected for the 1976 Montreal Games, and Japan boycotted the 1980 Moscow Games. The 1984 Los Angeles Games was to be his moment of glory. Yet, it almost did not happen.

During his second bout, against Artur Schnabel of Germany, Yamashita tore his right calf muscle while attempting one of his favourite techniques, "uchimata" (inner thigh throw). This affected his subsequent matches. He nearly lost his semi-final bout against a lanky Frenchman, Laurent del Colombo. Yamashita eventually relied on groundwork to ensure victory. In the final, he faced the big Egyptian, Mohamed Rashwan, who had earlier won all his matches leading to the final by "ippon".

Rashwan did not hesitate to attack Yamashita's injured leg. Yamashita, fully expecting this, countered Rashwan with a hand technique, and took him straight to the ground where he secured a tight hold-down to gain victory. And thus, he fulfilled his childhood dream of winning an Olympic gold medal. Yamashita's victory made him a popular national hero in Japan.

After his retirement from competition he went abroad for a year, to England, to learn English. He also took the opportunity to study the various training methods and judo styles of the West. Yamashita left Europe with a good impression, stating that he admired some of the European training techniques. He felt they were very scientific and declared that he would try to implement some of the best elements of those techniques in Japan. And it is Yasuhiro Yamashita who, as manager of the Japanese national squad, leads his country's judo team to Atlanta.

Little matter that Geesink, now an IOC member, had earlier proved his capabilities by taking the world title in 1961. He was the first Westerner to inflict such defeats on the Japanese.

Another Dutchman, Wilhelm Ruska is the only man to have won two golds in one Games – the Open and over 93 kg categories in 1972. He attributed his strength – he was not particularly tall or heavy for the categories – to helping his

A Sporting Legend ★★★★★★★★★★★★★★★★★★★★★★★★★★★★★★★★★

Angelo Parisi *(Great Britain and France)*

Angelo Parisi was born in Italy and brought up in Great Britain. He began his long and illustrious career fighting for Great Britain. However, he later switched nationalities after marrying a Frenchwoman and becoming a French citizen in 1973.

Parisi was ambidextrous – which, in judo terms, means that he possessed the rare ability to throw both to the left and to the right, with equal facility. His flowing style of judo was greatly admired by all who watched him, including the great champion, Yasuhiro Yamashita, who proclaimed in 1980 that the only player worth watching at the Moscow Games was Angelo Parisi. An unusual but very flattering comment.

Parisi has won more Olympic medals than any player in history. His first medal was a bronze for Great Britain at the 1972 Munich Games. At the 1980 Moscow Games he fought in both the over 95 kg and the Open divisions, and won himself a gold and a silver medal respectively for France. He ended his career with a creditable silver medal at the 1984 Los Angeles Games, again for France.

Karen Briggs

mother, a cleaner, carry 40 buckets of water every morning when he was young. His feat is now unrepeatable since the abolition of the Open class.

Bakhaavaa Buidaa of Mongolia, a silver medallist in 1972, was the first judoka to be disqualified after failing a dope test. He was followed, in 1988, by Britain's Kerrith Brown.

Some Olympic champions, meanwhile, have taken a shaky path to victory via the former repechage system. This happened, for instance, to Shota Chochosvili of the Soviet Union who lost to Britain's David Starbrook in the 1972 preliminary rounds, fought through the repechage, won his semi-final and then beat Starbrook in the final to take gold.

Feats of immense bravery and courage are also part of Olympic judo. None more so than from Karen Briggs, Britain's four times world champion at under 48 kg. In her contest with Japan's Ryoko Tamura in 1992, Briggs dislocated her shoulder in almost the first exchange but insisted on continuing the fight only to be eventually disqualified for passivity. A sad end to the career of one of the sports "greats".

Background

Fittingly, for a sport which was born in Japan and whose Japanese terminology can seem like a string of unpronounceables to the uninitiated Westerner, judo made its Olympic debut in 1964 in Tokyo. It has been part of every Games since then apart from 1968. Women first competed in 1992 after a successful demonstration event in 1988.

Agreement on standardization of weight categories had to be reached before the sport entered the Games. At that time the Japanese had their own system as did the Americans and Europeans. Eventually, the European system was adopted – four categories – under 68 kg, under 80 kg, over 80 kg and Open. The weight categories have since evolved to give today's standard list of seven apiece for men and women. In the past three decades the duration of Olympic contests has gradually diminished from the early length of ten minutes (15 for finals) to today's standard of five minutes for men and four minutes for women.

Judo was first developed in Japan by Dr Jigoro Kano who, late in the last century, moulded the unarmed sections of the ancient Chinese art of Ju-Jitsu (part of Samurai training) into a new school called Kodokan judo in 1882. The sport subsequently spread to other areas of the globe via travelling pupils. Kano insisted that judo made the maximum use of the mind and body and, even today, the sport is based on a series of such principles.

The first European judo club was the Budokwai which opened in London in 1918 but the sport did not really flourish outside Japan until after World War II. Judo's first world championships were held in 1957.

Japan, understandably with eight million participants, was orginally dominant internationally. Although still strong, their influence has waned with France, Germany, the ex-Soviet Union, Cuba and Britain all hard on their heels.

Equipment

As previously intimated, to understand the sport of judo it helps to learn a few Japanese terms, starting with "Tatamis". These are the green, covered mats of pressed foam which are laid together over a raised, wooden platform (16m x 16m or 52.4 x 52.4ft) to provide judo's competition area. The action, however, takes place only over a central contest area 10m x 10m (32.8 x 32.8ft) together with a one metre (3.28ft) wide red border called the "danger zone", added in 1972. The remainder of the competition area at the edges is called the "safety zone" – a very necessary provision when several competition mats are used next to each other as contests have a habit of spilling over.

Competitors wear "judogis" or white judo uniforms tied with either a red or white sash. You could be forgiven for thinking that these resemble unstructured, heavy-cotton pyjamas but the regulations governing their size, length, width and fastenings are very strict. For instance the trousers have to fall within at least five centimetres of the ankle bone and must give between ten and 15 centimetres of room between the "judoka's" or judo player's leg and the material. Female competitors must also wear a white T-shirt beneath their judogi.

Judo court

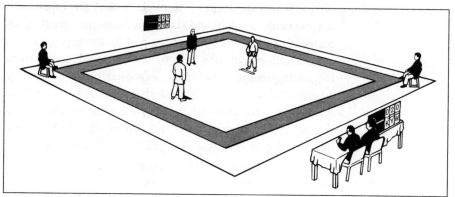

Rules

Olympic judo spectators get a taste of the sport's Japanese origins when they witness the sometimes elaborate bowing procedures which take place between officials prior to competition to show respect. Even the players begin and end each contest by standing and bowing to each other from two taped lines – one red and the other white corresponding to their sashes – laid in the centre of the contest zone four metres apart.

Contests are controlled by a referee, two judges, two time-keepers and a list-writer (who records the flow of the contest). The referee works from the mat. He uses hand signals to show results and infringements. But his decisions must be adjusted if the judges, who sit at two opposite corners of the mat, both think they should be higher or lower. If one judge thinks a decision should be higher and the other thinks the same decision should be lower, the referee's decision prevails. The judges also use hand signals to express their opinions and must make sure that the score is kept correctly.

Judo players attempt to win contests by scoring "ippon". This is the term used to describe four ultimate winning situations: throwing an opponent onto their back with considerable force and speed; holding an opponent down on their back (or both or one shoulder) for 30 seconds; forcing an opponent to surrender by tapping the mat twice or saying "maitta" ("I give up"); and, as delicately worded in the rule book, "making the effects of a stranglehold obvious". A contest ends automatically, with the referee holding up one arm palm outward, when ippon is scored

Below ippon, there are a number of moves and holds with which competitors can register a score. These are graded downwards from "waza-ari" (basically almost an ippon, two of which win the contest), through "yuko" (an ippon with two elements missing) and "koka" (a throw onto the thigh or buttocks or a hold for between ten and 20 seconds).

Competitors may also have scores registered against them for infringements – called in ascending order of severity "shido", "chui", "keikosu" and "hansoku make" – such as false attacks, non-combativity, illegal leg and arm holds and any move which may cause the danger of spinal or neck injury to the opponents. A "hansoku make" offence is serious enough to merit immediate disqualification and the termination of the contest.

At the end of a contest where ippon or a double "waza-ari" has not been scored, the score is evaluated by the referee and judges and the referee indicates the winner by raising his hand on the winner's side with the palm inwards.

Atlanta format

A total of 400 competitors will take part in the Atlanta Olympic judo tournament – 200 men and 200 women. There will be seven weight categories each for men and women. Each weight category will take place over a single day in a direct elimination draw format with a repechage system which gives a second chance of reaching at least the bronze medal fight.

Contests for men will last five minutes and, for women, four minutes of "real" time. "Real" time is the actual contest time and does not include time for stoppages or for the duration of holds.

Venue

The Georgia World Congress Center will play host to the judo tournament during the Atlanta Games. Situated just 3.2km (2 miles) from the Olympic Village, the Center has a spectator capacity of 7,500 for judo but will also house six other sports during the Games. It is the second largest convention centre in the USA.

MEDALLISTS (by nation)

	Men			Women			
	Gold	Silver	Bronze	Gold	Silver	Bronze	Total
Japan	16	3	8	-	3	2	32
USSR	7	5	14	-	-	1	27
France	3	3	10	2	-	2	20
Korea	4	5	7	1	-	-	17
Great Britain	-	5	7	-	1	2	15
Cuba	1	3	1	1	1	2	9
GDR	1	2	6	-	-	-	9
FRG	1	4	3	-	-	-	8
Netherlands	3	-	3	-	-	1	7
Hungary	1	2	4	-	-	-	7
USA	-	3	4	-	-	-	7
Poland	2	2	2	-	-	-	6
Brazil	2	1	3	-	-	-	6
Italy	1	1	1	-	1	-	4
Germany	-	1	3	-	-	-	4
Austria	2	-	1	-	-	-	3
Switzerland	1	1	1	-	-	-	3
Belgium	1	-	1	-	-	1	3
Canada	-	1	2	-	-	-	3
China	-	-	-	1	-	2	3
Bulgaria	-	1	1	-	-	-	2
Mongolia	-	1	1	-	-	-	2
Spain	-	-	-	2	-	-	2
Romania	-	-	2	-	-	-	2
Yugoslavia	-	-	2	-	-	-	2
Israel	-	-	1	-	1	-	2
Egypt	-	1	-	-	-	-	1
Australia	-	-	1	-	-	-	1
Czechoslovakia	-	-	1	-	-	-	1
Iceland	-	-	1	-	-	-	1
North Korea	-	-	1	-	-	-	1
Turkey	-	-	-	-	-	1	1
	46	45[1]	92	7	7	14	211

[1] 1972 silver medal withheld due to disqualification

ATLANTA SCHEDULE

Venue: Georgia World Congress Center, Hall H

Weight Class	Men	Women
Extra lightweight	60kg	48kg
Half-lightweight	65kg	52kg
Lightweight	71kg	56kg
Half-middleweight	78kg	61kg
Middleweight	86kg	66kg
Half-heavyweight	95kg	72kg
Heavyweight	+95kg	+72kg

Date	Description	Round	Start	End
20 Jul	heavyweight (m&w)	prelims	9:30	13:23
		repechage		
		FINALS	15:00	16:27
21 Jul	half-heavyweight (m&w)	prelims	9:30	13:23
		repechage		
		FINALS	15:00	16:27
22 Jul	middleweight (m&w)	prelims	9:30	13:23
		repechage		
		FINALS	15:00	16:27
23 Jul	half-middleweight (m&w)	prelims	9:30	13:23
		repechage		
		FINALS	15:00	16:27
24 Jul	lightweight (m&w)	prelims	9:30	13:23
		repechage		
		FINALS	15:00	16:27
25 Jul	half-lightweight (m&w)	prelims	9:30	13:23
		repechage		
		FINALS	15:00	16:27
26 Jul	extra-lightweight (m&w)	prelims	9:30	13:23
		repechage		
		FINALS	15:00	16:27

MEDALLISTS

JUDO (Men)

Extra Lightweight (−60kg)*

Year	Gold	C'ntry	Silver	C'ntry	Bronze	C'ntry
1964	Takehide Nakatani	JPN	Eric Hänni	SUI	Oleg Stepanov	URS
					Aron Bdgolubov	URS
1972	Takao Kawaguchi	JPN	—	DQ	Kim Yong Ik	PRK
					Jean-Jacques Mounier	FRA
1976	Hector Rodriquez	CUB	Chang Eun Kyung	KOR	Felice Mariani	ITA
					József Tuncsik	HUN
1980	Thierry Rey	FRA	José Rodriquez	CUB	Tibor Kincses	HUN
					Arambi Emizh	URS
1984	Shinji Hosokawa	JPN	Kim Jae Yup	KOR	Edward Liddle	USA
					Neil Eckersley	GBR
1988	Kim Jae Yup	KOR	Kevin Asano	USA	Amiran Totikachvili	URS
					Shinji Hosokawa	JPN
1992	Nazim Gousseinov	EUN	Yoon Hyun	KOR	Tadanori Koshino	JPN
					Richard Trautmann	GER
1996						

*(−63kg 1964–'76)

Half Lightweight (−65kg)

Year	Gold	C'ntry	Silver	C'ntry	Bronze	C'ntry
1980	Nikolai Solodukhin	URS	Tsendying Damdin	MGL	Ilian Nedkov	BUL
					Janusz Pawłowski	POL
1984	Yoshiyuki Matsuoka	JPN	Hwang Jung Oh	KOR	Josef Reiter	AUT
					Marc Alexandre	FRA
1988	Lee Kyung Keun	KOR	Janusz Pawłowski	POL	Bruno Carabetta	FRA
					Yosuke Yamamoto	JPN
1992	Rogerio Sampaio	BRA	József Csák	HUN	Udo Quellmalz	GER
	Cardoso				Israel Hernández Planas	CUB
1996						

Lightweight (−71kg)*

Year	Gold	C'ntry	Silver	C'ntry	Bronze	C'ntry
1972	Toyojazu Nomura	JPN	Anton Zajkowski	POL	Dietmar Hötger	GDR
					Anatoli Novikov	URS
1976	Vladimir Nevzorov	URS	Koji Kuramoto	JPN	Patrick Vial	FRA
					Marian Talaj	POL
1980	Ezio Gamba	ITA	Neil Adams	GBR	Karl-Heinz Lehmann	GDR
					Ravdan Davaadalai	MGL
1984	Ahn Byeong Keun	KOR	Ezio Gamba	ITA	Luis Onmura	BRA
					Kerrith Brown	GBR
1988	Marc Alexandre	FRA	Sven Loll	GDR	Michael Swain	USA
					Giorgi Tenadze	URS
1992	Toshihiko Koga	JPN	Bertalan Hajtós	HUN	Chung Hoon	KOR
					Shay Oren Smadga	ISR
1996						

*(up to 70kg in 1972 and '76)

Half Middleweight (−78kg)

Year	Gold	C'ntry	Silver	C'ntry	Bronze	C'ntry
1980	Shoto Khabareli	URS	Juan Ferrer	CUB	Bernard Tchoullouyan	FRA
					Harald Heinke	GDR
1984	Frank Wieneke	FRG	Neil Adams	GBR	Michel Nowak	FRA
					Mircea Fratiçă	ROM
1988	Waldemar Legień	POL	Frank Wieneke	FRG	Bachir Varaev	URS
					Torsten Bréchôt	GDR
1992	Hidehiko Yoshida	JPN	Jason Morris	USA	Bertrand Damaisin	FRA
					Kim Byung Joo	KOR
1996						

Middleweight (−86kg)*

Year	Gold	C'ntry	Silver	C'ntry	Bronze	C'ntry
1964	Isao Okano	JPN	Wolfgang Hofmann	GER	Kim Eui Tae	KOR
					James Steven Bregman	USA
1972	Shinobu Sekine	JPN	Oh Seung Lip	KOR	Brian Jacks	GBR
					Jean-Paul Coché	FRA
1976	Isamu Sonoda	JPN	Valeri Dvoinikov	URS	Slavko Obadov	YUG
					Park Young Chul	KOR
1980	Jürg Röthlisberger	SUI	Isaac Azcuy	CUB	Alexander Yatskevich	URS
					Detlef Ultsch	GDR
1984	Peter Seisenbacher	AUT	Robert Berland	USA	Seiki Nose	JPN
					Walter Carmona	BRA
1988	Peter Seisenbacher	AUT	Vladimir Chestakov	URS	Ben Spijkers	NED
					Akinobu Osako	JPN
1992	Waldemar Legien	POL	Pascal Tayot	FRA	Hirotaka Okada	JPN
					Nicolas Gill	CAN
1996						

*(up to 80kg in 1964–'76)

Half Heavyweight (−95kg)*

Year	Gold	C'ntry	Silver	C'ntry	Bronze	C'ntry
1972	Shota Chochoshvili	URS	David Starbrook	GBR	Chiaki Ishii	BRA
					Paul Barth	FRG
1976	Kazuhiro Ninomiya	JPN	Ramaz Narshiladze	URS	David Starbrook	GBR
					Jürg Röthlisberger	SUI
1980	Robert van de Walle	BEL	Tengiz Khubuluri	URS	Dietmar Lorenz	GDR
					Henk Numan	NED
1984	Ha Young Zoo	KOR	Douglas Vieira	BRA	Bjarni Fridriksson	ISL
					Gunter Neureuther	FRG
1988	Aurelio Miguel	BRA	Marc Meiling	FRG	Dennis Stewart	GBR
					Robert van de Walle	BEL
1992	Antal Kovács	HUN	Raymond Stevens	GBR	Dmitri Sergeev	EUN
					Theo Meijer	NED
1996						

*(up to 93kg in 1972 and '76)

Heavyweight (+95kg)*

Year	Gold	C'ntry	Silver	C'ntry	Bronze	C'ntry
1964	Isao Inokuma	JPN	Alfred Rogers	CAN	Anzor Kiknadze	URS
					Parnaoz Chikviladze	URS
1972	Wilhelm Ruska	NED	Klaus Glahn	FRG	Givi Onashvili	URS
					Motoki Nishimura	JPN
1976	Sergei Novikov	URS	Günther Neureuther	FRG	Sumio Endo	JPN
					Allen Coage	USA
1980	Angelo Parisi	FRA	Dimitr Zaprianov	BUL	Vladimír Kocman	TCH
					Radomir Kovačević	YUG
1984	Hitoshi Saito	JPN	Angelo Parisi	FRA	Cho Yong Chul	KOR
					Mark Berger	CAN
1988	Hitoshi Saito	JAP	Henry Stöhr	GDR	Cho Yong Chul	KOR
					Grigori Veritchev	URS
1992	David Khakhaleichvili	EUN	Naoya Ogawa	JPN	David Douillet	FRA
					Imre Csősz	HUN
1996						

* (over 93kg in 1964–'76)

/continued on next page

JUDO (Women)

Extra Lightweight (−48kg)

Year	Gold	C'ntry	Silver	C'ntry	Bronze	C'ntry
1992	Cecile Nowak	FRA	Ryoko Tamura	JPN	Hulya Senyurt	TUR
					Amarilis Savon Carmenaty	CUB
1996						

Half Lightweight (−52kg)

Year	Gold	C'ntry	Silver	C'ntry	Bronze	C'ntry
1992	Almudena Muñoz Martinez	ESP	Noriko Mizoguchi	JPN	Li Zhongyun	CHN
					Sharon Rendle	GBR
1996						

Lightweight (−56kg)

Year	Gold	C'ntry	Silver	C'ntry	Bronze	C'ntry
1992	Miriam Blasco Soto	ESP	Nicola Fairbrother	GBR	Chiyori Tateno	JPN
					Driulis Gonzalez Morales	CUB
1996						

Half Middleweight (−61kg)

Year	Gold	C'ntry	Silver	C'ntry	Bronze	C'ntry
1992	Catherine Fleury	FRA	Yael Arad	ISR	Zhang Di	CHN
					Elena Petrova	EUN
1996						

Middleweight (−66kg)

Year	Gold	C'ntry	Silver	C'ntry	Bronze	C'ntry
1992	Odalis Reve Jimenez	CUB	Emanuela Pierantozzi	ITA	Kate Howey	GBR
					Heidi Rakels	BEL
1996						

Half Heavyweight (−72kg)

Year	Gold	C'ntry	Silver	C'ntry	Bronze	C'ntry
1992	Kim Mi Jung	KOR	Yoko Tanabe	JPN	Irene de Kok	NED
					Laetitia Meignan	FRA
1996						

Heavyweight (+72kg)

Year	Gold	C'ntry	Silver	C'ntry	Bronze	C'ntry
1992	Zhuang Xiaoyan	CHN	Estela Rodriguez Villanueva	CUB	Natalia Lupino	FRA
					Yoko Sakaue	JPN
1996						

Modern Pentathlon

Stars to Watch

by John Goodbody

New format to test complete athlete

FEW SPORTS at Atlanta will have changed so dramatically during the previous Olympiad than Modern Pentathlon, which has responded quickly to criticisms about its accessibility for both competitors and spectators. The event, which was invented by Baron de Courbertin, now fulfils even more comprehensively the opinion of the founder of the modern Olympic Games that it "tested man's moral qualities as much as his physical resources and skills, producing thereby the ideal complete athlete."

For Atlanta, the shooting, swimming, fencing, riding and running will be compressed into one hectic day of activity, whereas previously the disciplines had been spread out over several days. There is now, therefore, an even greater emphasis on stamina.

The pistol-shooting is also now contested with air-guns at static targets rather than .22s on turning targets, making the sport more acceptable to newcomers but also putting an even greater premium on precision and coolness. The competition still ends with the cross-country running but now competitors start in their ranking order after the first four disciplines. The first man to finish is, therefore, the overall winner.

One man who has revelled in the new format is Dmitri Svatkovski, world champion in 1994 and '95 and also the reigning world cup holder. The 22 year old Russian has fulfilled all the promise he displayed when taking the world junior title in 1991. Nicknamed 'Tarzan' because of the long hair he originally wore, he has much of the athleticism and ruthlessness of his namesake. Remarkably solid all-round, his only weakness might be on the riding, were he to draw a particularly frisky horse.

Svatkovski, Akos Hanzely of Hungary, and Cesare Toraldo of Italy, the top three in the 1995 world championships in Basle, will automatically be able to take part at the Olympic Games. Although the three-man team event has been abandoned for Atlanta, the result from last year's world

1992 Olympic Champion Arkadiusz Skrzypaszek

championships means that Russia, Hungary and Italy are still able to field a maximum of three Olympic competitors this year. Other nations have been restricted to two each who have emerged via qualifying events.

Hanzely is the successor to his compatriots Attila Mizsér, the 1992 Olympic silver medallist, and László Fabian, the former world champion, who have both retired. Toraldo has been a consistent competitor in recent years and, although he will be 33 years old in Atlanta, experience is invaluable in modern pentathlon. Richard Phelps, of Britain, became world champion in 1993 at the age of 32 and was eighth in 1995.

One competitor to challenge for a medal in Atlanta is the young Latvian Vlachelsav Duhanov, who may become that most dangerous of all Olympic athletes, the man who is fulfilling his potential in the year of the Games.

J. G. □

Retrospective

Ironically, in a sport designed to test the all-round athlete, it is often the horses which seem to have a vital impact. Each competitor draws the horse he rides and only has a limited practice time. At the 1956 Games this obviously led to problems when four riders were hospitalized after falls during the riding event. Those were the Games, too, where the sport's scoring system was changed from points for placings to points against international scoring tables for various levels of performance in each of the events.

Modern pentathlon also demands stamina and commitment. In 1948 Captain Karacson of Hungary took it all a little too far. He broke his collarbone in the riding event but went on to compete left-handed in the fencing and shooting. Karacson was only forced to retire when he missed a shooting target completely.

Two unsavoury incidents marked the sport's Olympic history in 1968 and 1972. At the former Games, Hans Gunnar Liljeavall of Sweden was disqualified for consuming alcohol during the competition. Then, in 1972, a dispute opened up between the IOC and the UIPMB (the International Union of Modern Pentathlon and Biathlon) when 14 competitors were found to have taken tranquillizers which were banned by the

★★★★★★★★★★★★★★★★★★★★★★★★★★★★★★ **A Sporting Legend**

Boris Onishenko *(Soviet Union)*

Boris Onishenko was the man at the centre of the most notorious controversy in the Olympic history of modern pentathlon. Nothing that had occurred in his long and distinguished career prepared anyone for the incident in 1976.

A major in the Red Army, who represented Dynamo Kiev, Onishenko had won every honour in the sport except for the individual Olympic title. At the Games, he was a member of the Soviet teams, which finished second in 1968 and first in 1972, when he also took the individual silver medal.

In 1976, he was the reigning world champion and desperate for the Olympic crown because he was planning to retire after Montreal. However, while he was fencing against two British athletes, Adrian Parker and Jim Fox, the recording lights, indicating hits, unexpectedly came on although contact had not taken place.

Fox, an old friend of Onishenko, asked for the épée to be examined, believing it to be short-circuiting. Instead it was found that the Soviet competitor had tampered with the weapon, allowing him to register a hit even when it had not occurred.

Onishenko was disqualified and was sent home in disgrace and subsequently banned for life from all competitions. It was the saddest of ends for such a celebrated athlete.

★★★★★★★★★★★★★★★★★★★★★★★★★★★★★★ **A Sporting Legend**

Lars-Goran Hall *(Sweden)*

Lars-Goran Hall, a carpenter from Gothenburg, has a formidable claim to be the greatest Olympic competitor ever in modern pentathlon. A superbly balanced athlete, he is the only man to have won two Olympic individual titles.

Born in Karlskrona on April 30, 1927, he was first in the world championships in 1950 and 1951, making him favourite for the 1952 Olympic Games. However, his victory in Helsinki had two pieces of luck. First, the horse, which he drew for the riding event, was lame and its substitute turned out to be the best in the competition. This more than compensated for having to complete the course in teeming rain and he ended the discipline in first place.

Two days later, Hall was nearly 25 minutes late for the pistol shooting but was not disqualified because the competition had been held up while officials discussed a protest from the Soviet team.

A superb 300m swim and a solid run made certain that he finally finished seven place points clear of his nearest rival, Gábor Benedek, of Hungary. Hall also received a silver medal as a member of the Swedish team, the runners-up to Hungary. In winning individual gold he became the first non-military winner in the sport's history.

Four years later, he suffered from a particularly bad shoot, in which he finished 24th, in a discipline that was affected by both the wind and the length of the competition. However, just as in Helsinki, his prowess at swimming, and, to a lesser extent, in running brought him victory, this time by 58.5 points.

A Sporting Legend ★★★★★★★★★★★★★★★★★★★★★★★★★★★★★★★★★

András Balczó *(Hungary)*

The Hungarians have always had a particular talent for modern pentathlon and probably their supreme competitor has been András Balczó, who after so many years of trying, finally secured, in 1972, the Olympic individual title for which he craved.

He first competed in the Games in 1960 at the age of 22, where his three minutes 45 seconds swim was easily the fastest of the competition and he was also second in the cross-country event. However, a poor shoot cost him not only a medal but probably the title. He eventually finished fourth, with two of his compatriots, Ferenc Németh and Imre Nagy, taking the top two places. The trio easily captured the team title.

Balczó, a mechanic, was the most successful modern pentathlete of the 1960s, capturing five world titles, although he missed the 1964 Olympic Games and was upset by Björn Ferm of Sweden in 1968. Ferm was consistent and calm – even reading detective novels during the fencing event – and produced an outstanding swim and run to snatch the title by 11 points. The poker-faced Balczó's consolation was another team gold medal.

However, in 1972, Balczó, now 34 years old, mounted a last effort for the one title that had eluded him, had a heroic run and took the gold medal by 77 points from Boris Onishenko. His three gold medals are the most won by any athlete in the sport.

sport's ruling body but not by the IOC whose rules prevailed at the Games.

Modern pentathlon made its Olympic debut in 1912 and in that year a certain George Patton featured in the USA team – the very Patton who was to become famous as a World War II General. He finished fifth and would have done better if he had not been so poor in the shooting event.

Since 1912 there have been several changes to the competition format. In 1952 a team event was added. And in 1984 the sport was shortened from a five-day to a four-day format with the cross-country race on the final day being raced on a staggered start basis so that the first to cross the line won the individual gold medal. In Atlanta, however, all five disciplines take place on one day and there is no team event.

Background

As legend has it, the sport of modern pentathlon is based on the feats of a soldier messenger who started out on horseback to deliver his general's orders. His horse is killed behind enemy lines but he fights his way clear first with a sword, then with a pistol before swimming across a river and finally running to his destination. It is a test of speed, stamina, skill and steadiness under pressure.

There was a "Pentathlon" in the Ancient Games which consisted of running, jumping, spear and discus throwing and wrestling. When Baron Pierre de Coubertin battled for the introduction of the Pentathlon as part of the modern Games in 1912, the contemporary disciplines of shooting, swimming, fencing and horse riding were chosen to complement the original running event. Not surprisingly, the military enthusiastically adopted this new sport which was used as part of final examinations at a number of military academies.

Modern pentathlon was administered directly by the IOC until 1948 when the UIPM (International Union of Modern Pentathlon) was formed during the London Olympic Games with the 1920 Olympic champion Gustaf Dyrssen as its first president. The Olympic Winter Games sport of Biathlon (skiing and shooting) joined the Union in 1960 which then became the UIPMB. An earlier practical embodiment of the two disciplines came from Captain Willie Grut of Sweden. He won three of the five disciplines in the 1948 Games to win overall and had already achieved second place in the Olympic Winter Games demonstration event of "Winter Pentathlon" in that year. Biathlon broke away again in 1993 to form a separate international body.

Hungary have always been a strong nation in the sport but so, too, have Sweden who dominated many of the early events. More recently, athletes from the former communist bloc countries emerged. Britain's Richard Phelps was the 1993 world champion. He only took up the sport after watching his uncle on the televison. Robert Phelps competed in 1964, '68 and '72 and coached his nephew to Olympic team bronze in 1988.

Equipment

Air pistols will be used in the 1996 Games shooting event (as a change from the previous .22 calibre pistols) fired at

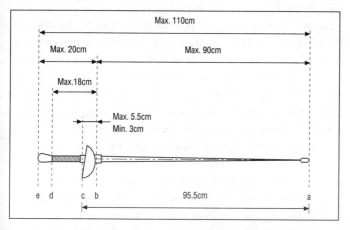

Épée

155cm (61in.) diameter centre-fire targets marked out in concentric rings at a distance of 10m (32ft 10in.). In the fencing discipline, competitors use épée swords. These have a maximum length of 110cm (43in.) with a stiff triangular, fluted blade and are electrically wired at the point to connect with the scoring system. The épée developed from the old duelling swords.

Athletes and horses in the riding event negotiate a course of between 350 – 450m (382 – 492yds) in length over 15 obstacles of a maximum height of 1.2m (3ft 11in.). The course includes one double and one triple combination. For the running event, a cross country course of 4,000m (4,376yds) is marked out over undulating territory.

Rules

For the shooting event each competitor is given 40 seconds to fire each of 20 shots at the target whose concentric rings score from one point on the outside to ten points for a bullseye. A score of 172 out of a possible 200 is worth 1,000 pentathlon points. Every point scored above or below 172 is worth plus or minus 12 pentathlon points.

In the fencing discipline athletes must fence every other competitor. The first to score a hit within the one minute time limit wins. If no hit is scored both athletes register a defeat. The target area is the whole body and a total score of 70% victories gives 1,000 pentathlon points with differing points scores below and above this average.

A time of 3:54.00 for the 300m freestyle swimming race would give 1,000 points and every half-second below or above this time equals plus or minus four points. Pentathletes swim the race in heats which are seeded according to their previously-registered personal best time.

In the riding event, competitors draw lots for horses and are then given just 20 minutes to get to know them using five practice jumps. Each rider starts with 1,100 points and loses 30 for each knockdown, 40 for a refusal, 60 points for falling off and three points for every second over the time limit – unless the final time is twice the limit in which case the competitor is eliminated altogether from the sport.

The final running event generates great excitement because the athletes set off at intervals which correspond in seconds to the pentathlon points difference between them after the first four events. This "chase" start means that the first athlete across the line wins the individual gold medal.

Atlanta Format

For the first time since 1952 there will be no team event in the sport of modern pentathlon at the 1996 Games. 32 athletes – all men and selected via three qualifying tournaments which took place in the Spring of this year – will contest the individual event which takes place in the space of one day. Of the 32 starters only the top three from the 1995 world championships were pre-selected. At world level there are well-established women's events but women do not yet feature on the Olympic programme.

Venue

The 1996 competition venues are as follows: shooting (currently scheduled for Wolf Creek shooting complex, 33.7km, 21 miles, from the Olympic Village with a spectator capacity of 1,100 but this may change); fencing (Georgia World Congress Center, 3.2km, 2 miles, from the Olympic Village with a spectator capacity of 5,200); Swimming (Georgia Tech Aquatic Center adjacent to the Olympic Village and with a spectator capacity of 14,600); riding and running (Georgia International Horse Park) 53km, 33 miles from the Olympic Village and with a spectator capacity of 29,700).

MODERN PENTATHLON – current Olympic records

Highest Score in Measurable Events

Event	Name	Country	Time/Result	Games	Year
Total	Anatoli Starostin	URS	5568	Moscow	1980
Shooting	Charles Leonard	USA	200	Berlin	1936
	Charles Horvath	SWE	200 (1132)	Moscow	1980
Swimming	Gintaras Staskevicius	LTU	3:10.47 (1352)	Barcelona	1992
Running*	Adrian Parker	GBR	12:09.50 (1378)	Montreal	1976

*The cross-country courses vary in difficulty, so no "true' record can exist for this event. The above is the best time recorded.

MEDALLISTS (by nation)

	Gold	Silver	Bronze	Total
Sweden	9	7	5	21
Hungary	8	7	3	18
Soviet Union	5	6	6	17
United States	-	5	3	8
Italy	2	2	3	7
Finland	-	1	4	5
Poland	3	-	-	3
Germany	1	-	1	2
Great Britain	1	-	1	2
Czechoslovakia	-	1	1	2
France	-	-	2	2
Total	29	29	29	87

ATLANTA SCHEDULE

Date	Description	Start	End	Venue
30 Jul	shooting	7:30	8:00	Wolf Creek Shooting Complex
	fencing	9:15	12:30	Georgia World Congress Center
	swimming	13:45	14:25	Georgia Tech Aquatic Center
	riding	17:00	18:30	Georgia International Horse Park
	running	19:00	19:27	Georgia International Horse Park

Competition in this sport is open to men only

MEDALLISTS

MODERN PENTATHLON

Year	Gold	C'ntry	Points	Silver	C'ntry	Points	Bronze	C'ntry	Points
Individual									
1912	Gösta Lilliehöök	SWE	27	Gösta Åsbrink	SWE	28	Georg de Laval	SWE	30
1920	Gustaf Dyrssen	SWE	18	Erik de Laval	SWE	23	Gösta Runö	SWE	27
1924	Bo Lindman	SWE	18	Gustaf Dyrssen	SWE	39.5	Bertil Uggla	SWE	45
1928	Sven Thofelt	SWE	47	Bo Lindman	SWE	50	Helmuth Kahl	GER	52
1932	Johan Oxenstiernna	SWE	32	Bo Lindman	SWE	35.5	Richard Mayo	USA	38.5
1936	Gotthardt Handrick	GER	31.5	Charles Leonard	USA	39.5	Silvano Abba	ITA	45.5
1948	William Grut	SWE	16	George Moore	USA	47	Gösta Gärdin	SWE	49
1952	Lars-Goran Hall	SWE	32	Gábor Benedek	HUN	39	István Szondi	HUN	41
1956	Lars-Goran Hall	SWE	4833	Olavi Mannonen	FIN	4774.5	Väinö Korhonen	FIN	4750
1960	Ferenc Németh	HUN	5024	Imre Nagy	HUN	4988	Robert Beck	USA	4981
1964	Ferenc Török	HUN	5116	Igor Novikov	URS	5067	Albert Mokeev	URS	5039
1968	Björn Ferm	SWE	4964	András Balczó	HUN	4953	Pavel Lednev	URS	4795
1972	András Balczó	HUN	5412	Boris Onishenko	URS	5335	Pavel Lednev	URS	5328
1976	Janusz Pyciak-Peciak	POL	5520	Pavel Lednev	URS	5485	Jan Bartů	TCH	5466
1980	Anatoli Starostin	URS	5568	Tamás Szombathelyi	HUN	5502	Pavel Lednev	URS	5382
1984	Daniele Masala	ITA	5469	Svante Rasmuson	SWE	5456	Carlo Massullo	ITA	5406
1988	János Martinek	HUN	5404	Carlo Massullo	ITA	5379	Vakhtang Iagorachvili	URS	5367
1992	Arkadiusz Skrzypaszek	POL	5559	Attila Mizsér	HUN	5446	Eduard Zenovka	EUN	5361
1996									

Rowing

Stars to Watch

by Dan Topolski

Redgrave attempts legendary feat

BRITAIN'S Steven Redgrave is likely to be the star turn at the 1996 Olympic regatta as he bids to win an unprecedented fourth gold medal at successive Games. The 34 year old Olympic champion, with his 24 year old partner Matthew Pinsent, will attempt a defence of their coxless pairs title, an event in which they are unbeaten since 1992 and in which Redgrave won his sixth consecutive world championship title last year in Tampere, Finland.

In fact 1996 looks set to be a year for the "old stagers" as the legendary Abbagnale brothers (Carmine and Giuseppe) of Italy – twice Olympic champions in the now defunct coxed pairs and seven times world title-holders – bid for further golden glory in the eights. Russia's Nikolai Pimenov is following the same route, while the exceptional 40 year old Italian lightweight, Francesco Esposito, contests the new lightweight double sculls event in which he was

Steven Redgrave (right) and Matthew Pinsent

★★★★★★★★★★★★★★★★★★★★★★★★★★★★★★★ **A Contemporary Hero**

Francesco Esposito *(Italy)*

The introduction to the Olympic programme of a new lightweight double sculls event has brought the extraordinary Italian Francesco Esposito into the spotlight.

Esposito has won seven world lightweight doubles titles, first with Ruggero Verroca, then with Enrico Gandola and now with Michelangelo Crispi, and two quadruple sculling titles. The diminutive 1.68m (5ft 5in.) 41 year old 'Ciccio' Esposito has regularly outperformed heavyweight athletes 30 kg (4st 11lb) heavier and over 0.3m (1ft) taller than himself. Also winner of silver and bronze medals, a fifth place in Los Angeles in the heavyweight double and national open weight singles champion throughout the eighties, Esposito has been one of the sport's most enduring performers.

A sports stadium clerk from Castellamare di Stabin, near Pompeii, where he lives with his wife and child, Esposito came from a poor background and found rowing an escape from a difficult environment. He flourished under the tutelage of the great coach Giuseppe La Mura in Naples, training with the Abbagnale brothers and participating in a great resurgence of Italian rowing during the last 15 years which has been masterminded by the Norwegian Thor Nilsen.

world champion with Michelangelo Crispi in 1994. They must be gold medal prospects even if Switzerland's Gier brothers (Michael and Markus) took away the world title last year.

The American eight ruled the world in 1994 and, though beaten last year by Germany, are determined to regain the 'blue riband' event of Olympic rowing which they dominated in all but three of the Games between 1900 and 1964. Since then, however, they have been eclipsed by Canada and Germany and have every motivation to win on their home waters. Holland, too, are a serious threat.

The rest of the US men's team, however, struggled to make last year's world championship finals and their best medal hopes now rest with their women. The eight won last year's world title and the coxless pair were second to Australia.

Australia's self-styled 'awesome foursome' who won the coxless fours in Barcelona at the 1992 Olympic Games, have recently taken up their oars again after a two-year break. They finished fifth in Tampere and have found that the standard has risen dramatically. Lining up against them are the strong Italian four, the 1994 and 1995 world champions, and the British crew which has the 1992 Olympic coxed pair winners, Greg and Jonny Searle, on board.

Canada's women rowers are strong, too, especially their double scullers Wendy Wiebe and Colleen Miller in the new

A Sporting Legend ★★★★★★★★★★★★★★★★★★★★★★★★★★★★★★★★★★★

Pertti Karppinen *(Finland)*

Pertti Karppinen, the "floating Finn", who was born in 1953, raced in five Olympic Games from 1976 to 1992 and won the coveted single sculling title three times in succession. His height – 2.05m (6ft 9in) – gave him the essential long levers to produce great stroke length without strain and, coupled with exceptional strength, made him a deadly sprint finisher.

His trademark was to hang at the back of the field, "easy and long", and then attack in the last

500m (547yds). Karppinen's great rival during those years was Germany's Peter-Michael Kolbe, five times world champion, who never managed to hold him off in an Olympic final.

Karppinen, who lives with his wife and two daughters in Raisio on the south coast of Finland, now works as a sports masseur. He also won the world title twice and raced a double with his brother for a world silver and won two further world silvers as well as a bronze medal.

He was also national champion for 18 years and would now like to turn his hand to coaching.

★★★★★★★★★★★★★★★★★★★★★★★★★★★★★★★★ **A Sporting Legend**

Birgit Peter *(German Democratic Republic)*

No analysis of world rowing would be complete without mention of the outstanding achievements of the former East German who became one of the sport's greats in the '80s. Few records can match Birgit Peter from Potsdam who won the Olympic double sculls title in 1988 and the quadruple sculls gold medal in Barcelona.

Between 1985 and 1990 she won four world titles including the single sculls in 1990, and was a quad crew member with another German star Jutte Behrendt Hampe.

Coached by Jutte Lan, the great Olympian of the '70s, Peter was remarkable not so much for her physical power but for exceptional technique. She was, according to her coaches, a great mover and very strong willed, successfully making the transition to play a prominent sporting role in the newly united Germany.

Peter, now 31, is a lab technician. She and fellow team member Christian Handle were married secretly in Indianapolis after the world championships – and retired from rowing. They live near Bremen.

lightweight event in which they are current world champions. Their heavyweight counterparts Marnie McBean and Kathleen Heddle won the Olympic coxless pairs title in Barcelona. These two were also in the winning eight then and remarkably are now intent on the double sculls title. They are the current world champions and also won the silver medal in the quadruple sculls last year behind the powerful Germans. Holland will also be strong in both these events.

The men's lightweight fours makes its debut in 1996 as an Olympic programme event and has a high quality field with world champions, Italy, once again the favourites. Only Denmark or Britain seem likely to threaten Italy, currently the world's leading rowing nation. Italy are also tipped to win the men's quadruple sculls.

The men's single sculls line-up is outstanding, with Germany's Thomas Lange seeking a third successive Olympic title after a two year break. His main rivals include the 1995 world champion from Slovenia, Iztok Cop, the 1993 world champion Derek Porter of Canada, the 1990 winner Estonia's Juri Jaanson, who was second last year, the perennial runner-up, Vaclav Chalupa of the Czech Republic, and the world record-holder, Switzerland's Xeno Muller. Lange also won world titles in 1987, '89 and '91 and had to beat the 1994 world champion Andre Willms to secure his Atlanta selection. He is a consummate sculler and a fine inheritor of the coveted mantle held by all time greats, Pertti Karppinen, Russia's Ivanov and John Kelly (father of the late actress Grace Kelly who became Princess Grace of Monaco).

Sweden's Maria Brandin won the world singles title last year from Silken Laumann of Canada and must start favourite here. But Germany has always been strong in this event and will be determined to regain the title they last held in 1988 with Jutta Behrendt.

The biggest teams are those of Germany, with 13 crews qualified in 14 events, and of the USA with 11.

D. T. □

Retrospective

Rowing was due to be a sport at the first of the modern Games, at Athens in 1896, but two days of bad weather made it impossible – the course was on the sea.

When rowing did begin it was in an extremely modest way with only four events – single sculls, coxed pairs, coxed fours and eights. Even more remarkable, it was another 76 years before the first women's races were held at the Games.

Even then for the first four Games which included women, they only raced over 1,000m, a much shorter distance than the various lengths of course used by the men. It was not until the Barcelona Games in 1992 that this was standardized, with both men and women rowing over 2,000m.

The first Olympic rowing also saw probably the youngest ever gold medallist. He was an unknown French boy and was recruited in an extraordinary way. The Dutch pair believed that their cox in the heats, Hermanus Brockmann, was too heavy and so they pulled a lad out of the spectators to do the job instead! He is thought to have been under ten.

By contrast both Robert Zimonyi and Guy Nickalls were over 40 when they set age records at the Games. Zimonyi, 46, became the oldest gold medallist when he coxed the United States eight to victory in 1964, and Nickalls, 41, was the oldest oarsman to win gold when he was part of the winning British eight in 1908.

United States eights went on to achieve other records between 1920 and 1956 when they won eight straight titles, and in the year of 1920 there was also a special American personality.

He was John Kelly senior, notable not only because he won both the single and doubles sculls, but because he was father of the actress Grace Kelly (later Princess Grace of Monaco). He also had a son, John Kelly junior, who competed in the Olympic Games four times.

Despite those wonderful United States achievements, it is a

Briton who has won the most medals. He is Jack Beresford, who took golds in 1924, 1932 and 1936, even though in two of those years he had to qualify for the finals through the repechage races. He also won two silver medals, in 1920 and 1928.

Five others have won three gold medals, including another Briton, Steve Redgrave, who could set another record by taking a fourth gold in Atlanta.

Sometimes the joy of achievement has got the better of oarsmen. In 1956 Viacheslav Ivanov of the Soviet Union jumped up and down with excitement after winning the singles sculls, and dropped his gold medal into Lake Wendouree!

It was never recovered. Davide Tizzano, an Italian quadruple sculler who dropped his medal into the lake in 1988 suffered less torment of disappointment. A Korean diver retrieved it. However, Ivanov was later given a replacement gold by the IOC, and he certainly learned a lesson. He went on to win a third consecutive gold medal in 1964, and the last two stayed completely dry.

Background

Rowing started on a 1,750m course when it made its Olympic debut in Paris in 1900 and was tried over four different distances for men and two for women before uniformity was achieved in the last Olympic Games – 2,000m for both sexes.

The sport grew in popularity after World War I to such an extent that repechage races to establish qualifiers for the finals were begun in 1924.

Much of the present system of race control is taken for granted these days, but it was not until after World War II that the chances of human error were greatly reduced. In 1948 for the first time there was a starter in a purpose built tower next to the River Thames. He pushed a button which was connected to stop watches in the finish area. The London Games also had photographic finish equipment.

Over the years there were changes in the design of boats, too. The German boat in 1956 had a cox steering whilst lying down inside the bow, thus reducing wind resistance. It was invented by the car magnate, von Opel.

Many oarsmen had difficulties in funding their training and competition, most notably the New Zealand eight in 1972, who had to raise about $32,000 themselves to get fit for Munich. They won the gold but their situation was starkly contrasting with that of the East Germans eight years later in Moscow.

They were state-funded and state-organized, making a nonsense of the amateur category. Their results also raised as many questions as they did cheers. Every single oarsman and woman they brought to the Soviet Union in 1980, all 54 of them, went back with a medal!

The altitude of Mexico turned the form book inside out in 1968, but one big change in 1976 at Montreal was less quirky and more surprising. For the first time the United States did not make the final of the eights.

However, this was also the year that women's races started, and one of the American women's eight which won a bronze in 1976, Anita Defrantz, went on to become the first black woman member of the IOC.

Since the collapse of the former East Germany things have changed again. The United States has regained much of its traditional strength, although the accolade of the strongest rowing nation has passed to Italy.

Equipment

Construction designs for the boats are unrestricted but the dimensions range from a shell about 8.2m (27ft) long for a singles sculls race to approximately 18.9m (62ft) long for a coxed eights race.

Oars are 3.82m (12ft 6in.) long and sculls are 2.98m (9ft 9in.). The blades must be painted with national colours.

Lake Lanier

Rules

Events are confined to boats of identical types and in rowing each oarsman or woman uses one oar. In sculling each sculler uses two sculls. The seats in both types of boat are fitted on runners and slide back and forth in unison with the rowing motion. A coxswain or "cox" steers the boat. In "coxless" events one of the rowers has rudder lines attached to a pivoting shoe with which he or she steers.

Boats race in six lanes over 2,000m. The recommended width is 13.5m (44ft 2in).

About three-quarters of the Olympic competitors qualified through their 1995 world championship results. The rest have acquired their places in Atlanta through qualification regattas in 1996 in Europe, Asia, Latin America and Africa.

It is the National Olympic Committee of the country concerned which qualifies for the Games in each case, not the individual rowers. This means the committee can then enter a crew with different oarsmen or women from those in the qualifying boat.

Atlanta Format

There are eight events for men and six for women. In general, the eight fastest qualifiers from preliminary heats go directly to the semi-finals and four more come through in extra races at Atlanta – called repechages. Six then race in each semi-final and the three fastest of each of these make up a six-boat race in the final. Although this overall system can vary depending on the initial number of entries.

There have been significant changes to the racing since Barcelona in 1992. The men's coxed pair and coxed four and the women's coxed four events have been deleted and three other events have replaced them. They are the men's lightweight double sculls, the men's lightweight coxless fours and the women's lightweight double sculls.

Venue

The rowing will take place at Lake Lanier in north Georgia, near Gainesville in Hall County, which is 88km (55 miles) north-east of Atlanta. It has 1,500 permanent seats and 18,500 temporary ones, as well as two boat houses and ramps and docks.

ROWING & SCULLING – current Olympic records

The standard men's course is 2000m in length. In 1900, rowing was held on the Seine over 1750m. In 1904 and 1908, the rowing course measured 1.5 miles (2814m). In 1906, the courses measured either 1000m or 1 mile (1609m.) In 1948 the rowing course measured 1 mile, 300 yards (1883m). The following Olympic record progressions for men only consider times rowed over 2000m. Women began Olympic rowing in 1976 over 1000m. in 1988, the women's courses changed to the men's distance of 2000m. Progressions are given for both distances.

Event	Name	Country	Time/Result	Games	Year
Men					
Single Sculls	Thomas Lange	GDR	6:49.86	Seoul	1988
Double Sculls	Alf Hansen	NOR	6:12.48	Montreal	1976
	Frank Hansen				
Men Quadruple Sculls	Andreas Hajek	GER	5:45.17	Barcelona	1992
	Michael Steinbach				
	Stephan Volkert				
	Andre Willms				
Men Coxless Pairs	Matthew Pinsent	GBR	6:27.72	Barcelona	1992
	Steven Redgrave				
Men Coxless Fours	Siegfried Brietzke	GDR	5:53.65	Montreal	1976
	Andreas Decker				
	Wolfgang Mager				
	Stefan Semmler				
Coxed Eights	Darren Barber	CAN	5:29.53	Barcelona	1992
	Andrew Crosby				
	Michael Forgeron				
	Robert Marland				
	Terrence Paul				
	Derek Porter				
	Michael Rascher				
	Bruce Robertson				
	John Wallace				
Women					
Single Sculls	Christine Scheiblich	GDR	3:36.09	Montreal	1976
	Elisabeta Lipa-Oleniuc	ROM	7:25.54	Barcelona	1992
Double Sculls	Elena Khloptseva	URS	3:16.27	Moscow	1980
	Larissa Popova				
	Kathrin Boron	GER	6:49.00	Barcelona	1992
	Kerstin Koeppen				
Quadruple Sculls	Kerstin Müller	GER	6:20.18	Barcelona	1992
	Kristina Mundt				
	Birgit Peter				
	Sybille Schmidt				
Coxless Pairs	Cornelia Klier	GDR	3:30.49	Moscow	1980
	Ute Steindorf				
	Kathleen Heddle	CAN	7:06.22	Barcelona	1992
	Marnie McBean				
Women Coxed Fours	Gerlinde Doberschutz	GDR	6:56.00	Seoul	1988
	Carola Hornig				
	Sylvia Rose				
	Birte Siech				
	Martina Walther				
Women Coxed Eights	Betsy Beard	USA	2:59.80	Los Angeles	1984
	Caroll Bower				
	Jeanne Flanagan				
	Carie Graves				
	Kathryn Keeler				
	Harriet Metcalf				
	Kristine Norellus				
	Shyril O'Steen				
	Kristen Thorsness				
	Kirsten Barnes	CAN	6:02.62	Barcelona	1992
	Shannon Crawford				
	Megan Delehanty				
	Kathleen Heddle				
	Marnie McBean				
	Jessica Monroe				
	Brenda Taylor				
	Lesley Thompson				
	Kay Worthington				

MEDALLISTS (by nation)

| | Men | | | Women | | | |
	Gold	Silver	Bronze	Gold	Silver	Bronze	Total
United States	28	20	16	1	5	2	72
GDR	20	4	7	13	3	1	48
Soviet Union	11	14	6	1	6	5	43
Great Britain	18	15	6	-	-	-	39
Germany	15	10	8	2	1	2	38
Italy	12	11	9	-	-	-	32
Romania	2	4	2	8	6	5	27
Canada	4	6	9	3	2	2	26
France	4	13	9	-	-	-	26
Switzerland	4	7	9	-	-	-	20
Australia	5	4	4	-	-	1	14
Netherlands	4	4	6	-	-	-	14
FRG	4	4	4	-	-	2	14
Denmark	3	3	6	-	-	1	13
Czechoslovakia	2	2	7	-	-	-	11
New Zealand	3	2	5	-	-	1	11
Norway	1	4	6	-	-	-	11
Poland	-	1	9	-	1	-	11
Bulgaria	-	-	1	2	3	4	10
Belgium	-	6	1	-	1	1	9
Finland	3	-	3	-	-	-	6
Austria	-	3	2	-	-	-	5
Yugoslavia	1	1	3	-	-	-	5
Greece	1	2	1	-	-	-	4
Argentina	1	1	2	-	-	-	4
Uruguay	-	1	3	-	-	-	4
Hungary	-	1	2	-	-	-	3
Slovenia	-	-	2	-	-	-	2
Sweden	-	2	-	-	-	-	2
China	-	-	-	-	-	2	2
Spain	-	1	-	-	-	-	1
Russia	-	-	1	-	-	-	1
	146	146	149	30	30	30	531

ATLANTA SCHEDULE

Venue: Lake Lanier, Gainesville/Hall County, Georgia

Date	Description	Round	Start	End
21 Jul	coxless pairs (m)	prelims	9:00	12:40
	coxless pairs (w)			
	l/wt double sculls (m)			
	l/wt double sculls (w)			
	coxless fours (m)			
	single sculls (w)			
	single sculls (m)			
22 Jul	double sculls (m)	prelims	9:00	12:00
	double sculls (w)			
	l/wt coxless fours (m)			
	quadruple sculls (w)			
	quadruple sculls (m)			
	eight (w)			
	eight (m)			

Date	Description	Round	Start	End
23 Jul	coxless pairs (m)	repechage	9:00	11:40
	coxless pairs (w)			
	double sculls (m)			
	double sculls (w)			
	coxless fours (m)			
	single sculls (w)			
	single sculls (m)			
24 Jul	l/wt double sculls (m)	repechage	9:00	11:30
	l/wt double sculls (w)			
	l/wt coxless fours (m)			
	quadruple sculls (w)			
	quadruple sculls (m)			
	eight (w)			
	eight (m)			
25 Jul	coxless pairs (m)	s/finals	9:00	11:40
	coxless pairs (w)			
	double sculls (m)			
	double sculls (w)			
	coxless fours (m)			
	single sculls (w)			
	single sculls (m)			
26 Jul	l/wt double sculls (m)	s/finals	9:00	11:30
	l/wt double sculls (w)			
	l/wt coxless fours (m)			
	quadruple sculls (m)			
	coxless pairs (m)	C FINAL		
	double sculls (m)			
	single sculls (w)			
	single sculls (m)			
	l/wt double sculls (m)			
	l/wt double sculls (w)			
	l/wt coxless fours (m)			
27 Jul	coxless pairs (m)	B FINAL	9:00	12:10
	coxless pairs (w)			
	double sculls (m)			
	double sculls (w)			
	coxless fours (m)			
	single sculls (w)			
	single sculls (m)			
	coxless pairs (m)	FINALS		
	coxless pairs (w)			
	double sculls (m)			
	double sculls (w)			
	coxless fours (m)			
	single sculls (w)			
	single sculls (m)			
28 Jul	l/wt double sculls (m)	B FINAL	9:00	12:10
	l/wt double sculls (w)			
	l/wt coxless fours (m)			
	quadruple sculls (w)			
	quadruple sculls (m)			
	eight (w)			
	eight (m)			
	l/wt double sculls (m)	FINALS		
	l/wt double sculls (w)			
	l/wt coxless fours (m)			
	quadruple sculls (w)			
	quadruple sculls (m)			
	eight (w)			
	eight (m)			

MEDALLISTS

ROWING (Men)

Year	Gold	C'ntry	Time	Silver	C'ntry	Time	Bronze	C'ntry	Time

HEAVYWEIGHT

Single Sculls

Year	Gold	C'ntry	Time	Silver	C'ntry	Time	Bronze	C'ntry	Time
1900	Henri Barrelet	FRA	7:35.6	André Gaudin	FRA	7:41.6	St George Ashe	GBR	8:15.6
1904	Frank Greer	USA	10:08.5	James Juvenal	USA		Constance Titus	USA	
1908	Harry Blackstaffe	GBR	9:26	Alexander McCulloch	GBR		Bernhard von Gaza	GER	
1912	William Kinnear	GBR	7:47.6	Polydore Veirman	BEL	7:56.0	Everard Butler	CAN	
1920	John Kelly Sr	USA	7:35.0	Jack Beresford	GBR	7:36.0	David Clarence Hadfield d'Arcy	NZL	7:48.0
1924	Jack Beresford	GBR	7:49.2	William Garrett Gilmore	USA	7:54.0	Josef Schneider	SUI	8:01.1
1928	Henry Pearce	AUS	7:11.0	Kenneth Myers	USA	7:20.8	Theodore Collet	GBR	7:19.8
1932	Henry Pearce	AUS	7:44.4	William Miller	USA	7:45.2	Guillermo Douglas	URG	8:13.6
1936	Gustav Shafer	GER	8:21.5	Josef Hasenöhrl	AUT	8:25.8	Daniel Barrow	USA	8:28.0
1948	Mervyn Wood	AUS	7:24.4	Eduardo Risso	URG	7:38.2	Romolo Catasta	ITA	7:51.4
1952	Yuri Tshukalov	URS	8:12.8	Mervyn Wood	AUS	8:14.5	Teodor Kocerka	POL	8:19.4
1956	Viacheslav Ivanov	URS	8:02.5	Stuart MacKenzie	AUS	8:07.7	John Kelly Jr	USA	8:11.8
1960	Viacheslav Ivanov	URS	7:13.96	Achim Hill	GER	7:20.21	Teodor Kocerka	POL	7:21.26
1964	Viacheslav Ivanov	URS	8:22.51	Achim Hill	GER	8:26.24	Gottfried Kottmann	SUI	8:29.68
1968	Henri Wienese	NED	7:47.80	Jochen Meissner	FRG	7:52.00	Alberto Demiddi	ARG	7:57.19
1972	Yuri Malishev	URS	7:10.12	Alberto Demiddi	ARG	7:11.53	Wolfgang Güldenpfennig	GDR	7:14.45
1976	Pertti Karppinen	FIN	7:29.03	Peter-Michael Kolbe	FRG	7:31.67	Joachim Dreifke	GDR	7:38.03
1980	Pertti Karppinen	FIN	7:09.61	Vasili Yakusha	URS	7:11.66	Peter Kersten	GDR	7:14.88
1984	Pertti Karppinen	FIN	7:00.24	Peter-Michael Kolbe	FRG	7:02.19	Robert Mills	CAN	7:10.38
1988	Thomas Lange	GDR	6:49.86	Peter-Michael Kolbe	GDR	6:54.77	Eric Verdonk	NZL	6:58.66
1992	Thomas Lange	GER	6:51.40	Václav Chalupa	TCH	6:52.93	Kajetan Broniewski	POL	6:56.82
1996									

Double Sculls

Year	Gold	C'ntry	Time	Silver	C'ntry	Time	Bronze	C'ntry	Time
1904	John Mulcahy William Varley	USA	10:03.2	John Hoben James McLaughlin	USA		Joseph Ravanack John Wells	USA	
1920	Paul Costello John Kelly Sr	USA	7:09.0	Pietro Annoni Erminio Dones	ITA	7:19.0	Gaston Giran Alfred Plé	FRA	7:21.0
1924	Paul Costello John Kelly Sr	USA	6:34.0	Marc Detton Jean-Pierre Stock	FRA	6:38.0	Rudolf Bosshard Heinrich Thoma	SUI	
1928	Paul Costello Charles McIlvaine	USA	6:41.4	John Guest Joseph Wright	CAN	6:51.0	Viktor Flessl Leo Losert	AUT	6:48.8
1932	William Garrett Gilmore Kenneth Myers	USA	7:17.4	Gerhard Boetzelen Herbert Buhtz	GER	7:22.8	Noël de Mille Charles Pratt	CAN	7:27.6
1936	Jack Beresford Leslie Southwood	GBR	7:20.8	Willy Kaidel Joachim Pirsch	GER	7:26.2	Jersy Ustupski Roger Verey	POL	7:36.2
1948	Richard Burnell Herbert Bushnell	GBR	6:51.3	Aage Larsen Ebbe Parsner	DEN	6:55.3	William Jones Juan Rodriguez	URG	7:12.4
1952	Tranquilo Cappozzo Eduardo Guerrero	ARG	7:32.2	Igor Emtchuk Giorgi Zilin	URS	7:38.3	Juan Rodriguez Miguel Seijas	URG	7:43.7
1956	Alexander Berkotov Yuri Tiukalov	URS	7:24.0	Bernard Costello Jr James Gardiner	USA	7:32.2	Murray Riley Merwyn Wood	AUS	6:37.4
1960	Václav Kozák Pavel Schmidt	TCH	6:47.50	Alexander Berkotov Yuri Tiukalov	URS	6:50.49	Ernst Hürlimann Rolf Larcher	SUI	6:50.59
1964	Boris Dubrovsky Oleg Tiurin	URS	7:10.66	Seymour Cromwell James Storm	USA	7:13.16	Vladimír Andrs Pavel Hofman	TCH	7:14.23
1968	Anatoli Sass Alexander Timoshinin	URS	6:51.82	Henricus Droog Leendert van Dis	NED	6:52.80	William Maher John Nunn	USA	6:54.21
1972	Gennadi Korshikov Alexander Timoshinin	URS	7:01.77	Frank Hansen Svein Thøgersen	NOR	7:02.58	Joachim Böhmer Hans-Ulrich Schmied	GDR	7:05.55
1976	Alf Hansen Frank Hansen	NOR	7:13.20	Chris Baillieu Michael Hart	GBR	7:15.26	Jürgen Bertow Hans-Ulrich Schmied	GDR	7:17.45
1980	Joachim Dreifke Klaus Kroppelien	GDR	6:24.33	Zoran Pančić Milorad Stanulov	YUG	6:26.34	Zdeněk Pecka Václav Vochoska	TCH	6:29.07
1984	Paul Enquist	USA	6:36.87	Pierre-Marie Deloof	BEL	6:38.19	Zoran Pančić	YUG	6:39.59

Year	Gold	C'ntry	Time	Silver	C'ntry	Time	Bronze	C'ntry	Time
1988	Bradley Lewis Ronald Florijn Nicolaas Rienks	NED	6:21.13	Dirk Crois Ueli Bodenmann Beat Schwerzmann	SUI	6:22.59	Milorad Stanulov Vassily Iakoucha Alexander Martchenko	URS	6:22.87
1992	Peter Antonie Stephen Hawkins	AUS	6:17.32	Arnold Jonke Christoph Zerbst	AUT	6:18.42	Nico Rienks Henk-Jan Zwolle	NED	6:22.82
1996									

Quadruple Sculls

Year	Gold	C'ntry	Time	Silver	C'ntry	Time	Bronze	C'ntry	Time
1976	Karl-Heinz Bussert Wolgang Güldenpfennig Rüdiger Reiche Michael Wolfgramm	GDR	6:18.65	Vitautas Butkus Evgeni Duleev Aivars Lazdenieks Yuri Yakimov	URS	6:19.89	Jaroslav Hellebrand Vladek Lacina Zdeněk Pecka Václav Vochoska	TCH	6:21.77
1980	Karsten Bunk Frank Dundr Uwe Heppner Martin Winter	GDR	5:49.81	Evgeni Barbakov Nikolai Dovgan Valeri Kleshnev Yuri Shapochka	URS	5:51.47	Bogdan Dobrev Mincho Nikolov Liubomir Petrov Ivo Rusev	BUL	5:52.38
1984	Michael Dursch Albert Hedderich Raimund Hörmann Dieter Wiedenmann	FRG	5:57.55	Gary Gullock Anthony Lovrich Timothy Mclaren Paul Reedy	AUS	5:57.98	Bruce Ford Doug Hamilton Mike Hughes Phil Monckton	CAN	5:59.07
1988	Agostino Abbagnale Gianluca Farina Piero Poli Davide Tizzano	ITA	5:53.37	Lars Bjönness Alf Hansen Rolf Thorsen Vetle Vinje	NOR	5:55.08	Steffen Bogs Heiko Habermann Jens Köppen Steffen Zühlke	GDR	5:56.13
1992	Andreas Hajek Michael Steinbach Stephan Volkert Andre Willms	GER	5:45.17	Lars Bjönness Per Albert Sätersdal Rolf Thorsen Kjetil Undset	NOR	5:47.09	Alessandro Corona Gianluca Farina Rossano Galtarossa Filippo Soffici	ITA	5:47.33
1996									

Coxless Pairs

Year	Gold	C'ntry	Time	Silver	C'ntry	Time	Bronze	C'ntry	Time
1904	Robert Farnam Joseph Ryan	USA	10:57.0	John Mulcahy William Varley	USA		John Joseph Buerger John Joachim	USA	
1908	John Fenning Gordon Thomson	GBR	9:41.0	George Fairbairn Philip Verdon	GBR				
1924	Antonie Beijnen Wilhelm Rösingh	NED	8:19.4	Maurice Bouton Georges Piot	FRA	8:21.6			
1928	Kurt Möschter Bruno Müller	GER	7:06.4	Archibald Nisbet Terence O'Brien	GBR	7:08.8	Paul McDowell John Schmitt	USA	7:20.4
1932	Lewis Clive Hugh Edwards	GBR	8:00.0	Cyril Stiles Frederick Thompson	NZL	8:02.4	Henryk Budziński Janusz Mikolajczak	POL	8:08.2
1936	Willi Eichhorn Hugo Strauss	GER	8:16.1	Harry Larsen Rickardt Olsen	DEN	8:19.2	Julio Curatella Horacio Podestá	ARG	8:23.0
1948	William Laurie John Wilson	GBR	7:21.1	Hans Kalt Josef Kalt	SUI	7:23.9	Bruno Boni Felice Fanetti	ITA	7:31.5
1952	Charles Logg Thomas Price	USA	8:20.7	Robert Baetens Michel Knuysen	BEL	8:23.5	Hans Kalt Kurt Schmid	SUI	8:32.7
1956	James Fifer Duvall Hecht	USA	7:55.4	Igor Boldakov Viktor Ivanov	URS	8:03.9	Josef Kloimstein Alfred Sageder	AUT	8:11.8
1960	Valentin Boreyko Oleg Golovanov	URS	7:02.01	Josef Kloimstein Alfred Sageder	AUT	7:03.69	Veli Lehtelä Toimi Pitkänen	FIN	7:03.80
1964	George Hungerford Roger Jackson	CAN	7:32.94	Steven Blaisse Ernst Veenemans	NED	7:33.40	Wolfgang Hottenrott Michael Schwan	GER	7:38.63
1968	Hans-Jörg Bothe Jörg Lucke	GDR	7:26.56	Lawrence Hough Philip Johnson	USA	7:26.71	Peter Christiansen Ivan Larsen	DEN	7:31.84
1972	Siegfried Brietzke Wolfgang Mager	GDR	6:53.16	Alfred Bachmann Heinrich Fischer	SUI	6:57.06	Roelof Luynenburg Ruud Stokvis	NED	6:58.70
1976	Bernd Landvoigt Jörg Landvoigt	GDR	7:23.31	Calvin Coffey Michael Staines	USA	7:26.73	Thomas Strauss Peter Vanroye	GDR	7:30.03
1980	Bernd Landvoigt Jörg Landvoigt	GDR	6:48.01	Nikolai Pimenov Yuri Pimenov	URS	6:50.50	Malcolm Carmichael Charles Wiggin	GBR	6:51.47
1984	Petru Iosub	ROM	6:45.39	Fernando Climent	ESP	6:48.47	Hans Magnus Grepperud	NOR	6:51.81

/continued on next page 327

Year	Gold	C'ntry	Time	Silver	C'ntry	Time	Bronze	C'ntry	Time
1988	Valer Toma Andrew Holmes Steven Redgrave	GBR	6:36.84	Luis Lasurtegui Danut Dobre Dragos Neagu	ROM	6:38.06	Sverre Loken Sadik Mujkić Bojan Presern	YUG	6:41.01
1992	Matthew Pinsent Steven Redgrave	GBR	6:27.72	Colin von Ettingshausen Peter Hoeltzenbein	GER	6:32.68	Iztok Cop Denis Zvegelj	SLO	6:33.43
1996									

Coxless Fours

Year	Gold	C'ntry	Time	Silver	C'ntry	Time	Bronze	C'ntry	Time
1904	George Dietz August Erker Albert Nasse Arthur Stockhoff	USA	9:05.8	Charles Aman Michael Begley Martin Fromanack Frederick Suerig	USA		Frank Dummerth John Freitag Louis Helm Gustav Voerg	USA	
1908	Robert Cudmore James Gillan Duncan MacKinnon John Somers-Smith	GBR	8:34.0	Harold Barker John Fenning Philip Filleul Gordon Thomson	GBR				
1924	Charles Eley James MacNabb Robert Morrison Terence Sanders	GBR	7:08.6	Archibald Black George Mackay A Mariacher William Wood	CAN	7:18.0	Emile Albrecht Alfred Probst Eugen Sigg Hans Walther	SUI	
1928	Richard Beesly Edward Bevan John Lander Michael Warriner	GBR	6:36.0	Ernest Bayer George Healis Charles Karle William Miller	USA	6:37.0	Umberto Bonadè Pietro Freschi Paolo Gennari Cesare Rossi	ITA	6:31.6
1932	John Babcock Jack Beresford Hugh Edwards Rowland George	GBR	6:58.2	Karl Aletter Walter Flinsch Ernst Gaber Hans Maier	GER	7:03.0	Francesco Cossu Giliante D'Este Antonio Ghiardello Antonio Provenzani	ITA	7:04.0
1936	Rudi Eckstein Martin Karl Willi Menne Toni Rom	GER	7:01.8	Alan Barrett Thomas Bristow Peter Jackson John Sturrock	GBR	7:06.5	Hermann Betschart Alex Homberger Hans Homberger Karl Schmid	SUI	7:10.6
1948	Francesco Faggi Giovanni Invernizzi Giuseppe Moioli Elio Morille	ITA	6:39.0	Helge Halkjaer Aksel Hansen J Storm Larsen Helge Schröder	DEN	6:43.5	Gregory Gates Stuart Griffing Frederick Kingsbury Roben Perew	USA	6:47.7
1952	Duje Bonačić Petar Šegvić Mateuz Trojanović Velomir Valenta	YUG	7:16.0	Pierre Blondiaux Marc Bouissou Roger Gautier Jacques Guissart	FRA	7:18.9	Oiva Lommi Veikko Lommi Lauri Nevalainen Kauko Wahlsten	FIN	7:23.3
1956	Donald Arnold Walter D'Hondt Lorne Loomer Archibald MacKinnon	CAN	7:08.8	James McIntosh Arthur McKinlay John McKinlay John Welchli	USA	7:18.4	Yves Delacour Guy Guillabert René Guissart Gaston Mercier	FRA	7:20.9
1960	Arthur Ayrault Theodore Nash John Sayre Richard Wailes	USA	6:26.26	Tullio Baraglia Renato Bosatta Giancarlo Crosta Giuseppe Galante	ITA	6:28.78	Igor Akhremchik Yuri Bachurov Valentin Morkovkin Anatoli Tarabrin	URS	6:29.62
1964	John Hansen Björn Haslöv Kurt Helmudt Erik Petersen	DEN	6:59.30	William Barry John James John Russell Hugh Wardell-Yerburgh	GBR	7:00.47	Richard Lyon Theodore Mittet Ted Nash Geoffrey Picard	USA	7:01.37
1968	Frank Forberger Dieter Grahn Frank Rühle Dieter Schubert	GDR	6:39.18	József Csermely Antal Melis Zoltán Melis György Sarlós	HUN	6:41.64	Abramo Albini Tullio Baraglia Renato Bosatta Pier Conti-Manzini	ITA	6:44.01
1972	Frank Forberger Dieter Grahn Frank Rühle Dieter Schubert	GDR	6:24.27	Ross Collinge Noel Mills Dudley Storey Dick Tonks	NZL	6:25.64	Joachim Ehrig Peter Funnekötter Franz Held Wolfgang Plottke	FRG	6:28.41
1976	Siegfried Brietzke Andreas Decker Wolfgang Mager Stefan Semmler	GDR	6:37.42	Rolf Andreassen Arne Bergodd Ole Nafstad Finn Tveter	NOR	6:41.22	Raul Arnemann Valeri Dolinin Anushavan Gasan-Dzhalalov Nikolai Kuznetsov	URS	6:42.52

Year	Gold	C'ntry	Time	Silver	C'ntry	Time	Bronze	C'ntry	Time
1980	Siegfried Brietzke	GDR	6:08.17	Valeri Dolinin	URS	6:11.81	John Beattie	GBR	6:16.58
	Andreas Decker			Vitali Eliseev			Martin Cross		
	Stefan Semmler			Alexei Kamkin			Ian McNuff		
	Jürgen Thiele			Alexander Kulagin			David Townsend		
1984	Shane O'Brien	NZL	6:03.48	David Clark	USA	6:06.10	Erik Christiansen	DEN	6:07.72
	Leslie O'Connell			Alan Forney			Michael Jessen		
	Conrad Robertson			Jonathan Smith			Lars Nielsen		
	Keith Trask			Philip Stekl			Per Rasmussen		
1988	Ralf Brudel	GDR	6:03.11	Thomas Bohrer	USA	6:05.53	Guido Grabow	FRG	6:06.22
	Olaf Förster			Richard Kennelly			Volker Grabow		
	Thomas Greiner			David Krmpotich			Norbert Kesslau		
	Roland Schröder			Raoul Rodriguez			Jörg Puttlitz		
1992	Andrew Cooper	AUS	5:55.04	Thomas Bohrer	USA	5:56.68	Milan Jansa	SLO	5:58.24
	Nicholas Green			William Burden			Janez Klemencić		
	Michael Scott McKay			Patrick Manning			Saso Mirjanić		
	James Tomkins			Jeffrey McLaughlin			Sadik Mujkić		
1996									

Coxed Eights

Year	Gold	C'ntry	Time	Silver	C'ntry	Time	Bronze	C'ntry	Time
1900	Louis Abell	USA	6:09.8	Prospère Bruggeman	BEL	6:13.8	François Brandt	NED	6:23.0
	William Carr			Jules de Bisschop			Hermanus Brockmann		
	Harry de Baecke			Oscar de Cock			Roelof Klein		
	John Exley			Oscar de Somville			Ruurd Leegstra		
	John Geiger			Maurice Hemelsoet			Walter Middelberg		
	Edwin Hedley			Frank Odberg			Hendrik Offerhaus		
	James Juvenal			Marcel van Crombrugghe			Walter Thijssen		
	Roscoe Lockwood			Alfred van Landeghem			Henricus Tromp		
	Edward Marsh			Maurice Verdonck			Johannes van Dijk		
1904	Louis Abell	USA	7:50.0	Arthur Bailey	CAN				
	Charles Armstrong			Philip Boyd					
	Frederick Cresser			Thomas Loudon					
	Joseph Dempsey			Donald McKenzie					
	John Exley			George Reiffenstein					
	James Flanagan			William Rice					
	Michael Gleason			George Strange					
	Harry Lott			William Wadsworth					
	Frank Schell			Joseph Wright					
1908	Henry Bucknall	GBR	7:52.0	Oscar de Somville	BEL		Gordon Balfour	CAN	
	Charles Burnell			Georges Mijs			Becher Gale		
	Raymond Etherington-Smith			Marcel Morimont			Douglas Kertland		
	Albert Gladstone			Rémy Orban			Walter Lewis		
	Banner Johnstone			Rodolphe Poma			Charles Riddy		
	Frederick Kelly			Oscar Taelman			Irving Robertson		
	G Maclagan			Alfred van Landeghem			Geoffrey Taylor		
	Guy Nickalls Sr			Polydore Veirman			Julius Thomson		
	Ronald Sanderson			François Vergucht			Joseph George Wright		
1912	Edgar Burgess	GBR	6:15.0	Robert Bourne	GBR		Fritz Bartholomae	GER	
	Philip Fleming			Beaufort Burdekin			Willi Bartholomae		
	Arthur Garton			William Fison			Max Broeske		
	James Gillan			Thomas Gillespie			Werner Dehn		
	Ewart Horsfall			Charles Littlejohn			Otto Liebing		
	Alistair Kirby			William Parker			Hans Matthiae		
	Sidney Swann			Frederick Pitman			Rudolf Reichelt		
	Henry Wells			John Walker			Kurt Runge		
	Leslie Wormald			Arthur Wiggins			Max Vetter		
1920	Sherman Clark	USA	6:02.6	John Campbell	GBR	6:05.0	Haakon Ellingsen	NOR	6:36.0
	Vincent Gallagher			Sebastian Earl			Thoralf Hagen		
	Edwin Graves			Ewart Horsfall			Thore Michelsen		
	Virgil Jacomini			Walter James			Arne Mortensen		
	Donald Johnston			Robin Johnstone			Karl Nag		
	William Jordan			Richard Lucas			Theodor Nag		
	Clyde King			Guy Nickalls Jr			Adolf Nilsen		
	Edward Moore			Ralph Shove			Conrad Olsen		
	Alden Sanborn			Sidney Swann			Tollef Tollefsen		

/continued on next page

Year	Gold	C'ntry	Time	Silver	C'ntry	Time	Bronze	C'ntry	Time
1924	Leonard Carpenter	USA	6:33.4	Arthur Bell	CAN		Antonio Cattalinich	ITA	
	Howard Kingsbury			Ivor Campbell			Francesco Cattalinich		
	Alfred Lindley			Robert Hunter			Simeone Cattalinich		
	John Miller			William Langford			Giuseppe Crivelli		
	James Rockefeller			Harold Little			Latino Gallasso		
	Frederick Sheffield			John Smith			Vittorio Gliubich		
	Benjamin Spock			Warren Snyder			Pietro Ivanov		
	Laurence Stoddard			Norman Taylor			Bruno Sorich		
	Alfred Wilson			William Wallace			Carlo Toniatti		
1928	Donald Blessing	USA	6:03.2	John Badcock	GBR	6:05.6	John Donnelly	CAN	6:03.8
	John Brinck			Jack Beresford			Frank Fiddes		
	Hubert Caldwell			Donald Gollan			John Hand		
	William Dally			James Hamilton			Frederick Hedges		
	Peter Donlon			Gordon Killick			Athol Meech		
	Francis Frederick			Harold Lane			John Murdoch		
	Marvin Stalder			Guy Nickalls			Edgar Norris		
	William Thompson			Arthur Sulley			Herbert Richardson		
	James Workman			Harold West			William Ross		
1932	James Blair	USA	6:37.6	Mario Balleri	ITA	6:37.8	Donald Boal	CAN	6:40:4
	Charles Chandler			Renato Barbieri			Earl Eastwood		
	David Dunlap			Dino Barsotti			Harry Fry		
	Norris Graham			Renato Bracci			Joseph Harris		
	Duncan Gregg			Vittorio Cioni			Cedric Liddell		
	Winslow Hall			Guglielmo del Bimbo			George MacDonald		
	Burton Jastram			Enrico Garzelli			Stanley Stanyar		
	Edwin Salisbury			Cesare Milani			Albert Taylor		
	Harold Tower			Roberto Vestrini			William Thoburn		
1936	Gordon Adam	USA	6:25.4	Dino Barsotti	ITA	6:26.0	Hans-Joachim	GER	6:26.4
	Charles Day			Enzo Bartolini			Hannemann		
	Donald Hume			Mario Checcacci			Heinz Kaufmann		
	George Hunt			Guglielmo del Bimbo			Hans Kuschke		
	James McMillin			Enrico Garzelli			Werner Löckle		
	Robert Moch			Oreste Grossi			Wilhelm Mahlow		
	Herbert Morris			Cesare Milani			Helmut Radach		
	Joseph Rantz			Ottorino Quaglierini			Alfred Rieck		
	John White			Dante Secchi			Herbert Schmidt		
							Gerd Völs		
1948	George Ahlgren	USA	5:56.7	Christopher Barton	GBR	6:06.9	Halfdan Gran-Olsen	NOR	6:10.3
	David Brown			Ernest Bircher			Hans Hansen		
	Lloyd Butler			Jack Dearlove			Harald Kraakenes		
	James Hardy			Michael Lapage			Thorstein Kraakenes		
	Ralph Purchase			Brian Lloyd			Kristoffer Lepsöe		
	Justus Smith			Paul Massey			Carl Monssen		
	John Stack			Alfred Mellows			Sigurd Monssen		
	David Turner			David Meyrick			Leif Naess		
	Ian Turner			Guy Richardson			Thor Pedersen		
1952	Robert Detweiler	USA	6:25.9	Slava Amiragov	URS	6:31.2	David Anderson	AUS	6:33.1
	James Dunbar			Igor Borisov			Phillip Cayser		
	William Fields			Evgeni Brago			Ernest Chapman		
	Wayne Frye			Leonid Gissen			Thomas Chessel		
	Charles Manning			Alexei Komarov			Merwyn Finlay		
	Richard Murphy			Vladimir Krjukov			Nimrod Greenwood		
	Henry Proctor			Igor Polyakov			Edward Pain		
	Franklin Shakespeare			Vladimir Rodimushkin			Robert Tinning		
	Edward Stevens			Evgeni Samsonov			Geoffrey Williamson		
1956	William Becklean	USA	6:35.2	David Helliwell	CAN	6:37.1	Michael Aikman	AUS	6:39.2
	Donald Beer			Philip Kueber			Angus Benfield		
	Thomas Charlton			Richard McClure			David Boykett		
	John Cooke			Douglas McDonald			Bryan Doyle		
	Caldwell Esselstyn			William McKerlich			Harold Hewitt		
	Charles Grimes			Carlton Ogawa			James Howden		
	Robert Morey			Donald Pretty			Walter Howell		
	Richard Wailes			Lawrence West			Garth Manton		
	David Wight			Robert Wilson			Adrian Monger		
1960	Klaus Bittner	GER	5:57.18	Donald Arnold	CAN	6:01.52	Bohumil Janoušek	TCH	6:04.84
	Karl-Heinz Hopp			Sohen Biln			Jan Jindra		
	Hans Lenk			Walter D'Hondt			Miroslav Koníček		

Year	Gold	C'ntry	Time	Silver	C'ntry	Time	Bronze	C'ntry	Time
	Willi Padge			Nelson Kuhn			Jiří Lundák		
	Manfred Ruilffs			John Lecky			Stanislav Lusk		
	Frank Schepke			Lorne Loomer			Václav Pavkovič		
	Kraft Schepke			William McKerlich			Luděk Pojezný		
	Walter Schröder			Archibald MacKinnon			Jan Švéda		
	Karl-Heinrich von Groddeck			Glenn Merwyn			Josef Věntus		
1964	Joseph Amlong	USA	6:18.23	Harold Dimke	GER	6:23.29	Petr Čermák	TCH	6:25.11
	Thomas Amlong			Thomas Ahrens			Bohumil Janoušek		
	Harold Budd			Klaus Behrens			Miroslav Koníček		
	Emory Clark			Klaus Bittner			Jiří Lundák		
	Stanley Cwiklinski			Horst Meyer			Jan Mrvík		
	Hugh Foley			Jürgen Plagemann			Richard Nový		
	William Knecht			Jürgen Schroeder			Luděk Pojezný		
	William Stowe			Karl-Heinrich von Groddeck			Julius Toček		
	Robert Zimonyi			Hans-Jürgen Wallbrecht			Josef Věntus		
1968	Rüdiger Henning	FRG	6:07.00	Peter Dickson	AUS	6:07.98	Antanas	URS	6:09.11
	Egbert Hirschfelder			David Douglas			Bogdanavichus		
	Wolfang Hottenrott			Alfred Duval			Vitautas Briedis		
	Horst Meyer			Joseph Fazio			Zugmas Jukna		
	Nikolaus Ott			Alan Grover			Valentin Kravchuk		
	Dirk Schreyer			Michael Morgan			Yuri Lorentsson		
	Jörg Siebert			Gary Pearce			Alexander Matryshkin		
	Günther Tiersch			John Ranch			Vladimir Sterlik		
	Lutz Ulbricht			Robert Shirlaw			Viktor Suslin		
							Iozapas Yagelavichus		
1972	Trevor Coker	NZL	6:08.94	Eugene Clapp	USA	6:11.61	Hans-Joachim Borzym	GDR	6:11.67
	Simon Dickie			Franklin Hobbs			Harold Dimke		
	Athol Earl			William Hobbs			Bernd Landvoigt		
	John Hunter			Paul Hoffman			Jörg Landvoigt		
	Tony Hurt			John Livingston			Heinrich Mederow		
	Dick Joyce			Michael Livingston			Manfred Schmorde		
	Gary Robertson			Timothy Mickelson			Manfred Schneider		
	Wybo Veldman			Peter Raymond			Hartmut Schreiber		
	Lindsay Wilson			Lawrence Terry			Dietmar Schwarz		
1976	Bernd Baumgart	GDR	5:58.29	James Clark	GBR	6:00.82	Trevor Coker	NZL	6:03.51
	Karl-Heinz Danielowski			Timothy Crooks			Simon Dickie		
	Gottfried Döhn			Richard Lester			Peter Dignan		
	Ulrich Karnatz			Hugh Matheson			Athol Earl		
	Werner Klatt			David Maxwell			Tony Hurt		
	Roland Kostulski			Leonard Robertson			Alexander Mclean		
	Hans-Joachim Lück			Fred Smallbone			Dave Rodger		
	Karl-Heinz Prudöhl			Patrick Sweeney			Ivan Sutherland		
	Dieter Wendisch			John Yallop			Lindsay Wilson		
1980	Jens Doberschütz	GDR	5:49.05	Henry Clay	GBR	5:51.92	Grigory Dmitrienko	URS	5:52.66
	Uwe Dühring			Andrew Justice			Viktor Kokoshin		
	Jörg Friedrich			Chris Mahoney			Andrei Lugin		
	Bernd Höing			Duncan McDougall			Igor Maistrenko		
	Ulrich Karnatz			Malcolm McGowan			Alexander Mantsevich		
	Ulrich Kons			Colin Moynihan			Ionas Normantas		
	Hans-Peter Koppe			John Pritchard			Ionas Pintskus		
	Bernd Krauss			Richard Stanhope			Andrei Tischchenko		
	Klaus-Dieter Ludwig			Allan Whitwell			Alexander Tkachenko		
1984	Dean Crawford	CAN	5:41.32	Earl Borchelt	USA	5:41.74	James Battersby	AUS	5:43.40
	Mark Evans			Charles Clapp			Ian Edmunds		
	Michael Evans			Thomas Darling			Steve Evans		
	Blair Horm			Bruce Ibbetson			Clyde Hefer		
	Grant Main			Robert Jaugstetter			Craig Muller		
	Brian McMahon			Walter Lubsen			Sam Patten		
	Kevin Neufeld			Christopher Penny			Ion Popa		
	Paul Steele			Andrew Sudduth			Gavin Thredgold		
	Patrick Turner			John Terwilliger			Timothy Willoughby		
1988	Thomas Domian	GDR	5:46.05	Veneamine Bout	URS	5:48.01	Seth Bauer	USA	5:48.26
	Armin Eichholz			Viktor Didouk			Doug Burden		
	Manfred Klein			Alexander Doumtchev			Jeff McLaughlin		
	Wolfgang Maennig			Pavel Gourkovsky			Peter Nordell		
	Matthias Mellinghaus			Nikolai Komarov			Ted Patton		

/continued on next page

Year	Gold	C'ntry	Time	Silver	C'ntry	Time	Bronze	C'ntry	Time
	Thomas Möllenkamp			Alexander Loukianov			John Pescatore		
	Bahne Rabe			Viktor Omelianovitch			John Rusher		
	Eckhardt Schultz			Vassili Tikhanov			John Smith		
	Ansgar Wessling			Andrei Vassiliev			Mike Teti		
1992	Darren Barber	CAN	5:29.53	Danut Dobre	ROM	5:29.67	Roland Baar	GER	5:31.00
	Andrew Crosby			Marin Gheorghe			Armin Eichholz		
	Michael Forgeron			Claudiu Gabriel Marin			Detlef Kirchhoff		
	Robert Marland			Vasile Ionel Mastacan			Manfred Willi Klein		
	Terrence Paul			Vasile Dorel Nastase			Bahne Rabe		
	Derek Porter			Valentin Robu			Frank Jörg Richter		
	Michael Rascher			Iulica Ruican			Hans Sennewald		
	Bruce Robertson			Viorel Talapan			Thorsten Streppelhoff		
	John Wallace			Ioan Iulian Vizitiu			Ansgar Wessling		
1996									

ROWING (Women)

Year	Gold	C'ntry	Time	Silver	C'ntry	Time	Bronze	C'ntry	Time

Single Sculls

Year	Gold	C'ntry	Time	Silver	C'ntry	Time	Bronze	C'ntry	Time
1976	Christine Scheiblich	GDR	4:05.56	Joan Lind	USA	4:06.21	Elena Antonova	URS	4:10.24
1980	Sanda Toma	ROM	3:40.69	Antonina Makhina	URS	3:41.65	Martina Schröter	GDR	3:43.54
1984	Valeria Račilă	ROM	3:40.68	Charlotte Geer	USA	3:43.89	Ann Haesebrouck	BEL	3:45.72
1988	Jutta Behrendt	GDR	7:47.19	Anne Marden	USA	7:50.28	Magdalena Gueorguieva	BUL	7:53.65
1992	Elisabeta Lipa Oleniuc	ROM	7:25.54	Annelies Bredael	BEL	7:26.64	Silken Laumann	CAN	7:28.85
1996									

Double Sculls

Year	Gold	C'ntry	Time	Silver	C'ntry	Time	Bronze	C'ntry	Time
1976	Svetla Otzetova	BUL	3:44.36	Sabine Jahn	GDR	3:47.86	Leonora Kaminskaite	URS	3:49.93
	Zdravka Yordanova			Petra Boesler			Genovaite Ramoshkene		
1980	Elena Khloptseva	URS	3:16.27	Cornelia Linse	GDR	3:17.63	Olga Homeghi	ROM	3:18.91
	Larissa Popova			Heidi Westphal			Valeria Roşca		
1984	Elisabeta Oleniuc	ROM	3:26.75	Greet Hellemans	NED	3:29.13	Daniele Laumann	CAN	3:29.82
	Marioara Popescu			Nicolette Hellemans			Silken Laumann		
1988	Birgit Peter	GDR	7:00.48	Veronica Cogeanu	ROM	7:04.36	Stefka Madina	BUL	7:06.03
	Martina Schröter			Elisabeta Lipa Oleniuc			Violeta Ninova		
1992	Kathrin Boron	GER	6:49.00	Veronica Cochelea	ROM	6:51.47	Gu Xiaoli	CHN	6:55.16
	Kerstin Köppen			Elisabeta Lipa Oleniuc			Lu Huali		
1996									

Quadruple Sculls

Year	Gold	C'ntry	Time	Silver	C'ntry	Time	Bronze	C'ntry	Time
1988	Kerstin Förster	GDR	6:21.06	Antonina Dumcheva	URS	6:23.47	Anişoara Balan	ROM	6:23.81
	Kristina Mundt			Inna Frolova			Veronica Cogeanu		
	Beate Schramm			Irina Kalimbet			Elisabeta Lipa		
	Jana Sorgers			Svetlana Mazy			Anişoara Minea		
1992	Kerstin Müller	GER	6:20.18	Veronica Cochelea	ROM	6:24.34	Elena Khloptseva	EUN	6:25.07
	Kristina Mundt			Anişoara Dobre			Ekaterina Khodotovitch		
	Birgit Peter			Doina Ignat			Tatiana Oustioujanina		
	Sybille Schmidt			Constanta Pipota			Antonina Zelikovitch		
1996									

Year	Gold	C'ntry	Time	Silver	C'ntry	Time	Bronze	C'ntry	Time

Coxless Pairs

Year	Gold	C'ntry	Time	Silver	C'ntry	Time	Bronze	C'ntry	Time
1976	Stoyanka Grouitcheva Siika Kelbetcheva	BUL	4:01.22	Sabine Dähne Angelika Noack	GDR	4:01.64	Edith Eckbauer Thea Einöder	FRG	4:02.35
1980	Cornelia Klier Ute Steindorf	GDR	3:30.49	Malgorzata Dluzewska Czesława Kościańska	POL	3:30.95	Siika Barbulova Stoianka Kurbatova	BUL	3:32.39
1984	Rodica Arba Elena Horvat	ROM	3:32.60	Betty Craig Tricia Smith	CAN	3:36.06	Ellen Becker Iris Vollener	FRG	3:40.50
1988	Rodica Arba Olga Homeghi	ROM	7:28.13	Lalka Berberova Radka Stoyanova	BUL	7:31.95	Lynley Hannen Nicola Payne	NZL	7:35.68
1992	Kathleen Heddle Marnie McBean	CAN	7:06.22	Ingeburg Schwerzmann Stefani Werremeier	GER	7:07.96	Stephanie Pierson Anna Seaton	USA	7:08.11
1996									

Coxed Eights

Year	Gold	C'ntry	Time	Silver	C'ntry	Time	Bronze	C'ntry	Time
1976	Brigitte Ahrenholz Henrietta Ebert Viola Goretzki Monika Kallies Christiane Knetsch Helma Lehmann Irina Müller Ilona Richter Marina Wilke	GDR	3:33.32	Olga Guzenko Olga Kolkova Klavdiya Kozenkova Olga Pugovskaya Nadezda Roshchina Nadezhda Rozgon Lyubov Talalaeva Nelli Tarakanova Elena Zubko	URS	3:36.17	Carol Brown Anita Defrantz Carie Graves Marion Greig Peggy McCarthy Gail Ricketson Lynn Silliman Anne Warner Jacqueli Zoch	USA	3:38.68
1980	Martina Boesler Christiane Köpke Gabriele Kühn Karin Metze Kersten Neisser Ilona Richter Marita Sandig Birgit Schütz Marina Wilke	GDR	3:03.32	Nina Frolova Maria Paziun Olga Pivovarova Nina Preobrazhenskaia Nadezhda Prishchepa Tatiana Stetsenko Elena Tereshina Nina Umanets Valentina Zhulina	URS	3:04.29	Angelica Aposteanu Elena Bondar Florica Bucur Maria Constantinesu Elena Dobriţoiu Rodica Frintu Ana Iliuta Rodica Puscatu Marlena Zagoni	ROM	3:05.63
1984	Betsy Beard Caroll Bower Jeanne Flanagan Carie Graves Kathryn Keeler Harriet Metcalf Kristine Norellus Shyril O'Steen Kristen Thorsness	USA	2:59.80	Mihaela Armasescu Doina Balan Adriana Chelariu Camelia Diaconescu Viorica Ioja Aneta Mihaly Aurora Plesca Lucia Sauca Marioara Trasca	ROM	3:00.87	Lynda Cornet Greet Hellemans Nicolette Hellemans Martha Laurijsen Catharina Neelissen Anne Marie Quist Willemien Vaandrager Marieke van Drogenbroek Harriet van Ettekoven	NED	3:02.92
1988	Ramona Balthasar Kathrin Haacker Anja Kluge Daniela Neunast Beatrix Schröer Uta Stange Annegret Strauch Ute Wild Judith Zeidler	GDR	6:15.17	Herta Anitas Rodica Arba Mihaela Armasescu Doina Balan Adriana Bazon Olga Homeghi Veronica Necula Ecaterina Oancia Marioara Trasca	ROM	6:17.44	Han Yagin He Yanwen Hu Yadong Li Ronghua Yang Xiao Zhang Wiznghua Zhang Yali Zhou Shouying Zhou Xiuhua	CHN	6:21.83
1992	Kirsten Barnes Shannon Crawford Megan Delehanty Kathleen Heddle Marnie McBean Jessica Monroe Brenda Taylor Lesley Thompson Kay Worthington	CAN	6:02.62	Adriana Bazon Iulia Bobeica Elena Georgescu Victoria Lepadatu Viorica Neculai Ioana Olteanu Maria Padurariu Doina Robu Doina Snep	ROM	6:06.26	Sylvia Doerdelmann Kathrin Haacker Christiane Harzendorf Daniela Neunast Cerstin Petersmann Dana Pyritz Annegret Strauch Ute Wagner Judith Zeidler	GER	6:07.80
1996									

/continued on next page 333

Coxless Fours

Year	Gold	C'ntry	Time	Silver	C'ntry	Time	Bronze	C'ntry	Time
1992	Kirsten Barnes	CAN	6:30.85	Shelagh Donohoe	USA	6:31.86	Antje Frank	GER	6:32.34
	Jessica Monroe			Cindy Eckert			Annette Hohn		
	Brenda Taylor			Carol Feeney			Gabriele Mehl		
	Kay Worthington			Amy Fuller			Birte Siech		
1996									

ROWING (Men)

LIGHTWEIGHT
Coxless Fours

Year	Gold	C'ntry	Time	Silver	C'ntry	Time	Bronze	C'ntry	Time
1996									

Double Sculls

Year	Gold	C'ntry	Time	Silver	C'ntry	Time	Bronze	C'ntry	Time
1996									

ROWING (Women)

Double Sculls

Year	Gold	C'ntry	Time	Silver	C'ntry	Time	Bronze	C'ntry	Time
1996									

Shooting

Stars to Watch

by Sarah Cooper

Consistency, ability and experience required

S HOOTING is a real test of the human machine in the truest of Olympic spirits. To succeed, a shooter must provide the best performance on the most important day in four years and do it alone, without knowing how the competitors alongside are doing. If a shooter has trained hard enough and developed the mind strength, if a shooter's performance capability is high enough and if it is that shooter's day, they may just win a gold medal when the last shot is fired.

430 athletes in 15 shooting events – all of which will be decided within the first week of the 1996 Games – will be hoping that they have produced just that mixture. Simply because there are so many entries and countries, and because competition is more or less equal, it is surprisingly difficult to predict winners. However, in several disciplines one particular shooter – or group of shooters – stand out because of their particularly high level of consistency, ability and experience.

One such man is Harald Stenvaag from Norway in the smallbore rifle (prone). He has been at the top consistently for nearly a decade. In the last few years he has won many world and European cups – a remarkable feat in this particularly fiercely-contested discipline. He still has to add a gold and this could be his year. Sergei Beliaev of Kazakhstan, Kurt Koch from Switzerland and Hubert Bichler of Germany will all be hoping to usurp him.

Raymond Debevec of Slovenia holds the world record in the smallbore rifle three positions event. He is capable of shooting "unbelievable" scores every now and again and experts describe his record for this event as truly "out of this world". But, like Stenvaag (who could also be a medal contender in this event), the big one has evaded him so far. He could be challenged by Russia's Gennadi Petikian, Petre Kúrka of Czechoslovakia as well as Glen Dubis, for the host nation, Norbert Sturney of Switzerland and Jean Pierre Amat of France.

In the men's air rifle the 1988 gold medallist from the

former Yugoslavia, Goran Maksimović must be one of the main contenders. He finished fifth in Barcelona and has shown great consistency ever since. But challenges could come from Wolfrom Waibel of Austria, Russia's Sergei Marinov, Boris Polak of Israel and Torsten Krebs of Germany – without mentioning that man Stenvaag of Norway again.

Shooters from China and the former Soviet Union will prove strong in the 10m running target event. They include Rus and Oleg Moldovan and Juy Ermolenko as well as Yang Lin and Fan Yandu. But Lubos Račanský from Czechoslovakia is probably the favourite for the title.

The USA's women's team may come to the fore in the air rifle 10m event. But the favourite for this event, and the smallbore rifle three positions event, must be Vesela Letcheva of Bulgaria, the current world record holder, who finished second in Seoul, in 1988, and sixth in Barcelona four years later. She has won more major rifle competitions than any other female shooter. Her challengers in both events could come from a range of nations including Russia, Hungary, Germany, China, Korea and the Ukraine as well as her own compatriot Nonka Matova.

In the women's pistol events (sport and air pistol) Jasna Šekarić of the former Yugoslavia has been dominant for almost a decade. She won gold and bronze in 1988 followed by sixth place and silver in 1992. Her consistency of performance is outstanding and Russia's Olga Klochneva, Bulgaria's Diana Jorgova, China's Li Duihong and South Korea's Soon Hee Boo will all find it difficult to beat her in both events whilst Margit Stein of Germany could be a challenger in the air pistol.

Marina Logvinenko (EUN) 1992 Gold medallist

German Ralf Schumann won the men's rapid fire pistol gold in 1992 after finishing with the silver medal four years earlier. He had a good 1995 and must be the man to beat in Atlanta. His main opposition is likely to come from Emil Milev of Bulgaria and Poland's Krzyszt Kucharczyk, the current world champion.

The air and free pistol events for men will feature many of the same names. China are certain to be strong, as are shooters from the former Soviet Union countries. Hot favourite for the air pistol must be Igor Bassinski from Belarussia but Sweden's Ragnar

★★★★★★★★★★★★★★★★★★★★★★★★★★★★★ **A Contemporary Hero**

Ragnar Skanåker *(Sweden)*

For Ragnar Skanåker of Sweden Atlanta spells a seventh Olympic Games. He has followed in the footsteps of his countryman and all-time "great", Torsten Ullman. But his specialization in the Olympic Games has been free pistol (although he often makes his national team for air pistol and rapid fire pistol as well).

Born in Stora Skedvi in June 1934, Skanåker has been a familiar face internationally for over two decades. He won Olympic free pistol gold in 1972, silver in 1984 and '88 and bronze in 1992. For years he had his peers guessing how he could perform so well every time it came to the big events.

More remarkably, Skanåker was entirely self-trained and motivated and beat off ranks of brilliant young shooters from the former Soviet Union, East Germany, Bulgaria, China and the USA.

In 1995, at 61 years of age, he competed at several of the World Cup Olympic qualifiers successfully. Skanåker, though, still has some way to go to beat his compatriot, Oscar Swahn, who won Olympic gold in the running deer team event in 1912 aged 64 and went on to win silver in the same event in 1920.

Skanåker, Skari Paosonen of Finland and Italy's Roberto Di Donna will all be medal contenders. They will be joined in the free pistol by Germany's Artur Gevorgian and Britain's Michael Gault.

The shotgun events of skeet, Olympic trap and double trap – the last with separate competitions for men and women and the former two for men only – complete the Atlanta Games shooting programme. Skeet, in particular, has an overabundance of talented shooters at the moment and the event is likely to be won by a margin of just one target. Two Italians, Bruno Rossetti, the Barcelona bronze medallist, and Andrea Benelli, must start as narrow favourites from strong Chinese and German contingents in particular.

Italy is the outstanding current nation, too, in Olympic trap with the USA and Canada both in contention. Marco Venturini of Italy is probably the favourite but, on the day, a winner could come from any one of ten nations.

S. C. □

Retrospective

Two Hungarians have provided a pair of truly remarkable Olympic tales. Károly Takács won the rapid fire pistol in 1948 and 1952 with his left hand. In 1938 a grenade had exploded in his right hand, his shooting hand, and shattered it forcing him to retrain completely with the other hand. Another Károly, Varga this time, won the smallbore rifle prone event in 1980 despite breaking his hand playing in a football match two days previously.

A Sporting Legend ★★★★★★★★★★★★★★★★★★★★★★★★★★★★★★

Malcolm Cooper *(Great Britain)*

Born on 20 December, 1947, in Camberley, England, Malcolm Cooper won the Olympic smallbore rifle (three positions) title in 1984. In doing so, he became the first British Olympic champion for rifle shooting since the London Games of 1908. He went on to defend successfully his title four years later, the first and only such defence in his chosen discipline.

An international competitor continually from 1970 to 1991, Malcolm started winning in 1977 and never really stopped until his retirement. By then, over 160 international medals were taken including 13 European, eight world and two Olympic titles as well as many Commonwealth Games medals and world records along the way. He was also one of the key players in the rankings rise, from the near bottom, of the British rifle team in the '70s and '80s.

His feats were all the more remarkable for being achieved when his event was for the most part dominated by the massively-resourced, full time competitors of the old Eastern Bloc and the USA. In comparison Cooper had to hold down a full-time job to finance his training, equipment and travel as well as contending with poor national facilities.

"My only unachieved ambition at the end of my career", he said, "was to have gone into full-time training to see what I could really have done".

Then there is the story of the Canadian, Gerald Ouellette, who won the smallbore rifle prone event in 1956. He was delighted with his world record of a maximum possible 600 points only to be later stripped of the record when it was discovered that the range was 1.5m short of the regulation distance.

On a more sinister note James Snook, a member of the 1920 USA gold-medal free pistol team in 1920, was put to death in the electric chair ten years later accused of murder. Ma Chin Shan, who competed in the rapid fire pistol at the 1964 Olympic Games in Tokyo for Chinese Taipei, afterwards defected to China – the only Olympic athlete to defect to, rather than from, a communist country.

Malcolm Cooper of Great Britain is one of the few shooters to have retained successfully an Olympic title. He won the smallbore rifle three positions event in 1984 and 1988. Who can say what might have happened if Britain had not boycotted the shooting event in 1980? Equally, disaster almost struck again in 1988 when, during a media conference at the range a day prior to competition, a BBC radio reporter kicked over and damaged Cooper's favourite rifle. Fortunately, he was able to repair it and go on to the gold.

Background

Baron Pierre de Coubertin was no mean pistol-shot himself. So it is, perhaps, fitting that shooting is celebrating its hundredth birthday as a programme sport at the centenary Games and could provide the first Atlanta gold medallist of all the sports when the men's air pistol takes place on the opening morning. And shooting, with its eight or six-person final shoot-outs (introduced in 1988), electronic scoreboards and shot by shot updates on TV is now one of the most exciting of Olympic sports.

It has been in the top four in terms of participant numbers and countries represented at the Games throughout the last century – even if it missed out on the Games of 1904 and 1928. It is a sport of great diversity of human shapes and sizes. Not surprisingly, then, most shooters get annoyed at the lack of media understanding and coverage of their sport.

A series of women's events has been added in recent years to encourage female participation. Women first competed at the Games, though, in mixed events from 1968 onwards. The first woman to win an "open" event was China's Zhang Shan who won the 1992 skeet title. America's Margaret Murdock, however, was the first woman to win an Olympic shooting medal – silver in 1976 in the smallbore rifle three positions event.

The events of the shooting programme have been changed several times over the past 100 years. So, too, have the methods of scoring and the competition formats.

Shooting's origins as a sport go back to the Middle Ages. The St Sebastianus Shooting Club in Cologne, Germany, was formed in 1463. Early air rifles had a large bulbous section which stored the compressed air. Air rifle shooting has been popular in many countries as a competitive sport since the 1900s. The International Shooting Union (UIT) was formed in 1965 but by that time there had been 39 "unofficial" world championships.

The Olympic disciplines of skeet and trap stem from "clay pigeon" shooting. The sport has been popular since the late 18th century. Live pigeons were once used, before the switch to the clay variety, and participants were called "old hats" because they kept the birds under their headgear before releasing them. Competition pistol shooting, meanwhile, dates from the late 1800s. The British National Rifle Association first introduced the weapon to their championships in 1885 with the American Association following suit a year later.

Equipment

On shooting ranges, safety is of obvious importance and there are strict regulations for lay-out and operation. Competitors are urged to wear ear-protectors and shatterproof, protective shooting glasses. There is also a series of rules governing the clothing which they can wear in rifle events. Shooters compete at a series of stations on the ranges.

Shooting targets vary in size from event to event but they are all (except skeet and trap) marked out in concentric rings to give scoring zones (from one point for the outer ring to ten points for the inner bullseye) and have two different background colours – white on the outside and black on the inside. The target paper must be non-reflecting. If a shot hits the line between two zones then it scores as the higher zone.

A 50m smallbore rifle target scoring area is 154.4mm (6in.) in diameter and the innermost ring – the bullseye – is 10.4mm (4.1in.) in diameter. For the 10m air rifle event, however, the target scoring zone is 45.5mm (1.8in.) in diameter and the "Ten" is a white dot just 0.5mm (0.01in.) wide. The running target event is the only one to have two target scoring areas and one aiming dot.

Targets in the skeet and trap events are saucer-shaped "clays" which can be black, white, yellow or orange and are 110mm (4.3in.) in diameter. They are thrown out, for trap events, at pre-determined trajectories from a pit by a machine which has a pivotal arm. And they must be capable of flying a distance of 75m from the pit. In the skeet event the targets are projected from two houses (or towers) at different heights and called the "low" and "high" houses. There are a number of shooting stations in skeet set in a semi-circle between the two houses.

The UIT sets regulations for the weapons and ammunition which are used for each event. Rapid-fire, free and sport pistols as well as small-bore rifles are all 5.6mm (.22 calibre) guns. The air pistol and air rifle are 4.5mm. In the skeet and trap events all types of smooth-bore shotguns are permissible provided that they do not exceed 12 gauge.

Rules and Regulations

There are 15 events on the Olympic shooting programme in 1996 for the three main classes of rifle, pistol and shotgun. The targets are set at a distance of 50m for the small-bore rifle events and the free pistol, at 25m for the rapid fire and sport pistol events and at 10m for the air pistol, running target and air rifle events. Clay targets are launched, singly for trap and two at a time for double trap, in front of shooting stations set in a row. Shooting stations for the skeet event are set in a semi-circle and targets are released singly or as doubles from two different level "houses". In all three events shooters have to move from station to station.

Each competition begins with a preliminary round followed by a shoot-out final. Eight shooters qualify for the final in all events except the trap, double trap and skeet where the top six go through. Scores in the final are added to each shooter's preliminary total and the winner is the shooter with the most points (or "clays" hit). In the case of ties there are sudden-death, shot-by-shot tie-breakers.

In the men's free pistol preliminaries each competitor has 60 shots at the target in a time limit of two hours. The final consists of ten shots, released one at a time by each competitor, in a time limit for each shot of 75 seconds. In the air pistol, men have an hour and 45 minutes to complete 60 shots whilst the women have an hour and 15 minutes for 40 shots. Perhaps the most exciting pistol event, however, is the rapid fire which features targets which are only exposed for mere seconds by red/green lights. Each competitor fires 60 shots in different series with target exposures varying between eight, six and four seconds. The final consists of two competition series of five shots at each target with four seconds per shot.

There is also a rapid fire section of the women's sport pistol. The first 30 shots must be released in a time limit of 6 minutes per 5 shots series but the second "rapid fire" 30 shots series gives just three seconds per shot. Magnified sights can be used at the Olympic Games in the running target event – a discipline which was re-introduced in 1972 after an absence of 70 years. In 1992 the targets were set at 10m rather than the previous 50m. This event incorporates a double target at which the men shoot a slow series of 30 shots each in five seconds and a second series of 30 shots each in 2.5 seconds. The final consists of 10 shots – five in each of the targets – in 2.5 seconds each.

Men and women compete in separate smallbore rifle events. Both have a three positions competition whilst the men also have a prone event called the "English Match" because it was first introduced in 1948 at the London Olympic Games. The men fire 60 shots in the prone event in a time limit of one hour 30 minutes. Women fire 20 shots in each of the three positions – prone, standing and kneeling – whilst men fire 40 shots in each and their event has been called the "marathon" of shooting lasting over four hours.

The air rifle, with a target set at 10m, was introduced as separate events for men and women at the 1984 Games because of the intensive use of air rifles for training and competition around the world as well as the relatively inexpensive ammunition and the ease of arranging facilities. The men shoot 60 shots in the standing position in an hour and 45 minutes and the women 40 shots in an hour and 15 minutes. All five rifle finals consist of ten shots each in a time limit of 75 seconds per shot in a standing position.

In the skeet and men's trap events there are 125 targets in the preliminary rounds shot in series of 25 followed by six-person finals. The double trap for men has 150 targets whilst that for women has 120 targets.

Atlanta Format

A total of 430 athletes – 300 men and 130 women – will take part in the sport of shooting at the 1996 Olympic Games. They have qualified for the Games via a series of international competitions.

Since 1992 a men's and women's double trap event has been added to the programme whilst the mixed or "open" trap and skeet events have been changed to men-only events.

Venue

Shooting at the Centennial Games will be located at the Wolf Creek Shooting Complex which is 33.7km (21 miles) from the Olympic Village in the south-west of Fulton County and near Atlanta's airport. It has an indoor 10m rifle and pistol range, a semi-enclosed 25m pistol range and three outdoor combined international trap and skeet ranges. The total seating capacity is 10,900 divided over all the ranges.

SHOOTING – current Olympic records

Many of the rules for Olympic shooting have changed over the years. The following Olympic record progressions pertain only to those years which in the events have been contested in the manner currently in use. In addition, in Barcelona many of the target sizes were smaller than in previous Olympics, thus new Olympic records were automatically set in many of the events. This progression lists only those records pertaining to the exact format and target sizes currently used. Current Olympic shooting consists of preliminary rounds, followed by one round shoot-offs for semi-finals (in some events) and finals. Records are listed both for the preliminaries and the semi-finals, and finals, where applicable.

Event	Name	Round	Country	Points	Games	Year
Men						
Rapid Fire Pistol	Ralf Schumann	1	GER	885	Barcelona	1992
Free Pistol	Alexander Melentiev	1	URS	581	Moscow	1980
	Sorin Babii	1	ROM	660	Seoul	1988
Smallbore Rifle, Prone	Hubert Bichler	4	GER	598	Barcelona	1992
(English Match)	Lee Eun Chul	1	KOR	702.5	Barcelona	1992
Smallbore Rifle,	Juha Hirvj	4	FIN	1172	Barcelona	1992
Three Positions	Gratchia Petikiane	1	EUN	12667.4	Barcelona	1992
Olympic Trap	Pavel Kubec	5	TCH	196	Barcelona	1992
	Kazumi Watanabe	2	JPN	219	Barcelona	1992
	Petr Hrdlička	1	TCH	219	Barcelona	1992
Skeet	Zhang Shan	1	CHN	200	Barcelona	1992
	Axel Wegner	1	GDR	222	Seoul	1988
	Zhang Shan	1	CHN	223	Barcelona	1992
Air Rifle	Yuri Fedkin	1	EUN	593	Barcelona	1992
	Yuri Fedkin	1	EUN	695.3	Barcelona	1992
Air Pistol	Sorin Babii	3	ROM	586	Barcelona	1992
	Wang Yifu	1	CHN	684.8	Barcelona	1992
10m Running Target	Michael Jakosits	1	GER	580	Barcelona	1992
	Michael Jakosits	1	GER	673	Barcelona	1992
Women						
Sport Pistol	Marina Logvinenko-Dobrantcheva	1	EUN	587	Barcelona	1992
	Marina Logvinenko-Dobrantcheva	1	EUN	684	Barcelona	1992
Air Rifle	Yeo Kab Soon	1	KOR	396	Barcelona	1992
	Yeo Kab Soon	1	KOR	498.2	Barcelona	1992
Air Pistol	Jasna Šekarić	2	YUG	389	Barcelona	1992
	Jasna Šekarić	2	YUG	486.4	Barcelona	1992
	Marina Logvinenko-Dobrancheva	1	EUN	486.4	Barcelona	1992
Smallbore Rifle,	Launi Meili	1	USA	587	Barcelona	1992
Three Positions	Launi Meili	1	USA	684.3	Barcelona	1992

MEDALLISTS (by nation)

	Men[1]			Women			
	Gold	Silver	Bronze	Gold	Silver	Bronze	Total
United States	42	24	19	2	1	1	89
Soviet Union	18	16	15	4	1	3	57
Sweden	13	23	19	-	-	-	55
Great Britain	13	14	18	-	-	-	45
France	12	16	12	-	-	-	40
Norway	16	9	11	-	-	-	36
Switzerland	11	11	12	-	-	-	34
Greece	5	7	7	-	-	-	19
Italy	6	3	8	-	1	-	18
Finland	3	5	9	-	-	-	17
Denmark	3	8	5	-	-	-	16
GDR	3	8	5	-	-	-	16
Hungary	6	3	6	-	-	-	15
Romania	5	4	4	-	-	-	13
China	3	2	3	2	1	1	12
Germany	4	4	3	-	-	-	11
FRG	3	2	3	1	2	-	11
Canada	3	3	2	1	-	-	9
Czechoslovakia	4	3	2	-	-	-	9
Belgium	2	3	3	-	-	-	8
Bulgaria	1	1	2	-	3	1	8
Poland	2	1	3	-	-	1	7
Japan	1	1	3	-	-	1	6
Yugoslavia	1	-	1	1	1	2	6
Austria	1	1	3	-	-	-	5
Brazil	1	1	1	-	-	-	3
Korea	1	1	-	1	-	-	3
Peru	1	2	-	-	-	-	3
Colombia	-	2	-	-	-	-	2
Netherlands	-	1	1	-	-	-	2
Russia	-	1	1	-	-	-	2
Spain	-	1	1	-	-	-	2
Australia	-	-	1	-	-	1	2
North Korea (PRK)	1	-	-	-	-	-	1
Argentina	-	1	-	-	-	-	1
Chile	-	1	-	-	-	-	1
Mexico	-	1	-	-	-	-	1
Portugal	-	1	-	-	-	-	1
South Africa	-	1	-	-	-	-	1
Latvia	-	1	-	-	-	-	1
Cuba	-	-	1	-	-	-	1
Haiti	-	-	1	-	-	-	1
New Zealand	-	-	1	-	-	-	1
Mongolia	-	-	-	-	1	-	1
Venezuela	-	-	1	-	-	-	1
	185	187	187	12[2]	11	11	593

[1] Including female medallists prior to 1984
[2] Including female winner of 1992 open Skeet competition

ATLANTA SCHEDULE

Venue: Wolf Creek Shooting Complex

Date	Description	Round	Start	End
20 Jul	10m air rifle (w)	prelims	9:00	15:15
	trap (m)	prelims		
	10m air rifle (w)	FINAL		
	10m air pistol (m)	prelims		
	10m air pistol (m)	FINAL		
21 Jul	trap (m)	prelims	9:00	15:25
	10m air pistol (w)			
	10m air pistol (w)	FINAL		
	trap (m)			
22 Jul	10m air rifle (m)	prelims	10:00	13:45
		FINAL		
23 Jul	50m free pistol (m)	prelims	9:00	15:25
	double trap (w)			
	50m free pistol (m)	FINAL		
	double trap (w)			
24 Jul	50m standard rifle (3 pos) (w)	prelims	8:30	15:25
	double trap (m)			
	25m rapid fire pistol (m)			
	50m standard rifle (3 pos) (w)	FINAL		
	double trap (m)			
25 Jul	50m free rifle prone (m)	prelims	8:30	15:25
	10m running target (m)			
	25m rapid fire pistol (m)			
	50m free rifle prone (m)	FINAL		
	25m rapid fire pistol (m)			
26 Jul	25m sport pistol (w)	prelims (precision)	8:30	15:25
	25m sport pistol (w)	prelims (rapid fire)		
	10m running target (m)	prelims		
	skeet (m)			
	25m sport pistol (w)	FINAL		
	10m running target (m)			
27 Jul	50m free rifle (3 pos) (m)	prelims	8:30	15:15
	skeet (m)			
	skeet (m)	FINAL		
	50m free rifle (3 pos) (m)			

MEDALLISTS

SHOOTING

Year	Gold	C'ntry	Points	Silver	C'ntry	Points	Bronze	C'ntry	Points
Olympic Trap									
1900	Roger de Barbarin	FRA	17	René Guyot	FRA	17	Justinien de Clary	FRA	17
1908	Walter Ewing	CAN	72	George Beattie	CAN	60	Alexander Maunder	GBR	57
							A Metaxas	GRE	
1912	James Graham	USA	96	Alfred Göldel	GER	94	Harry Blau	URS	91
1920	Mark Arie	USA	95	Frank Troeh	USA	93	Frank Wright	USA	87
1924	Gyula Halasy	HUN	98	Conrad-Walentin Huber	FIN	98	Frank Hughes	USA	97
1952	George Généreux	CAN	192	Knut Holmqvist	SWE	191	Hans Liljedahl	SWE	190
1956	Galliano Rossini	ITA	195	Adam Smelczyński	POL	190	Alessandro Ciceri	ITA	188
1960	Ion Dumitrescu	ROM	192	Galliano Rossini	ITA	191	Sergei Kalinin	URS	190
1964	Ennio Mattarelli	ITA	198	Pavel Senichev	URS	194	William Morris	USA	194
1968	John Braithwaite	GBR	198	Thomas Garrigus	USA	196	Kurt Czekalla	GDR	196
1972	Angelo Scalzone	ITA	199	Michel Carrega	FRA	198	Silvano Basagni	ITA	195
1976	Donald Haldeman	USA	190	Armando Silva Marques	POR	189	Ubaldesco Baldi	ITA	189
1980	Luciano Giovannetti	ITA	198	Rustam Yambulatov	URS	196	Jörg Damme	GDR	196
1984	Luciano Giovannetti	ITA	192	Francisco Boza	PER	192	Daniel Carlisle	USA	192
1988	Dmitri Monakov	URS	222	Miroslav Bednařík	TCH	222	Frans Peeters	BEL	219
1992	Petr Hrdlička	TCH	219	Kazumi Watanabe	JPN	219	Marco Venturini	ITA	218
1996*									

*Mixed from 1968–'92. Men only in 1996 and prior to '68

Skeet – Mixed

Year	Gold	C'ntry	Points	Silver	C'ntry	Points	Bronze	C'ntry	Points
1968	Evgeni Petrov	URS	198	Romano Garagnani	ITA	198	Konrad Wirnhier	FRG	198
1972	Konrad Wirnhier	FRG	195	Evgeni Petrov	URS	195	Michael Buchheim	GDR	195
1976	Josef Panáček	TCH	198	Eric Swinkels	NED	198	Wiesław Gawlikowski	POL	196
1980	Hans Kjeld Rasmussen	DEN	196	Lars-Göran Carlsson	SWE	196	Roberto Castrillo	CUB	196
1984	Matthew Dryke	USA	198	Ole Riber Rasmussen	DEN	196	Luca Scribani Rossi	ITA	196
1988	Axel Wegner	GDR	222	Alfonso De Iruarrizaga	CHI	221	Jorge Guardiola	ESP	220
1992	Zhang Shan	CHN	223	Juan Jorge Giha Yarur	PER	222	Bruno Mario Rossetti	ITA	222
1996*									

*In 1996 a men-only event

SHOOTING (Men)

Year	Gold	C'ntry	Points	Silver	C'ntry	Points	Bronze	C'ntry	Points
Double Trap									
1996									
Rapid Fire Pistol									
1896	Joannis Phrangudis	GRE	344	Georgios Orphanidis	GRE	249	Holger Nielsen	DEN	
1900	Maurice Larouy	FRA	58	Léon Moreaux	FRA	57	Eugène Balme	FRA	57
1908	Paul van Asbrock	BEL	490	Réginald Storms	BEL	487	James Gorman	USA	485
1912	Alfred Lane	USA	287	Paul Palén	SWE	286	Hübner von Holst	SWE	283
1920	N Paraines	BRA	274	Raymond Bracken	USA	272	Fritz Zulauf	SUI	269
1924	Henry Bailey	USA	18	Wilhelm Carlberg	SWE	18	Lennart Hannelius	FIN	18
1932	Renzo Morigi	ITA	36	Heinz Hax	GER	36	Domenico Matteucci	ITA	36
1936	Cornelius van Oyen	GER	30/6	Heinz Hax	GER	30/5	Torsten Ullman	SWE	4/30/04
1948	Károly Takács	HUN	580	Diaz Sáenz Valiente	ARG	571	Sven Lundqvist	SWE	569
1952	Károly Takács	HUN	579/60	Szilárd Kun	HUN	578/60	Gheorghe Lichiardopol	ROM	578/60
1956	Stefan Petrescu	ROM	587/60	Evguenti Tcherkassov	URS	585/60	Gheorghe Lichiardopol	ROM	581/60
1960	William McMillan	USA	587/147	Pentti Linnosvuo	FIN	587/139	Alexander Zabelin	URS	587/135
1964	Pentti Tapio Linnosvuop	FIN	592	Ion Tripşa	ROM	591	Lubomír Nácovský	TCH	590
1968	Józef Zapędzki	POL	593	Marcel Roşca	ROM	591	Renart Suleimanov	URS	591
1972	Józef Zapędski	POL	595	Ladislav Falta	TCH	594	Viktor Torshin	URS	593

/continued on next page **345**

Year	Gold	C'ntry	Points	Silver	C'ntry	Points	Bronze	C'ntry	Points
1976	Norbert Klaar	GDR	597	Jürgen Wiefel	GDR	596	Roberto Farraris	ITA	595
1980	Corneliu Ion	ROM	596	Jürgen Wiefel	GDR	596	Gerhard Petritsch	AUT	596
1984	Takeo Kamachi	JPN	595	Corneliu Ion	ROM	593	Rauno Bies	FIN	591
1988	Afanasi Kouzmine	URS	698	Ralf Schumann	GDR	696	Zoltán Kovács	HUN	693
1992	Ralf Schumann	GER	885	Afanasijs Kuzmins	LAT	882	Vladimir Vokhmianine	EUN	882
1996									

Free Pistol

Year	Gold	C'ntry	Points	Silver	C'ntry	Points	Bronze	C'ntry	Points
1896	Sumner Paine	USA	442	Viggo Jensen	DEN	285	Holger Nielsen	DEN	
1900	Karl Konrad Böderer	SUI	503	Achille Paroche	FRA	466	Konrad Stäheli	SUI	453
1912	Alfred Lane	USA	499	Peter Dolfen	USA	474	Charles Stewart	GBR	470
1920	Carl Frederick	USA	496	Afrani da Costa	BRA	489	Alfred Lane	USA	481
1936	Torsten Ullman	SWE	559	Erich Krempel	GER	544	Charles des Jamonnières	FRA	540
1948	Edwin Vasquez Cam	PER	545	Rodolphe Schnyder	SUI	539	Torsten Ullman	SWE	539
1952	Huelet Benner	USA	553	Angel León	ESP	550	Ambrus Balogh	HUN	549
1956	Pentti Tapio Linnosvuo	FIN	556	Makhmoul Umarov	URS	556	Offutt Pinion	USA	551
1960	Alexei Gustchin	URS	560	Makhmoul Umarov	URS	552	Yoshihisa Yoshikawa	JPN	552
1964	Vainö Johannes Markkanen	FIN	560	Franklin Green	USA	557	Yoshihisa Yoshikawa	JPN	554
1968	Grigory Kosykh	URS	562	Heinz Mertel	FRG	562	Harald Vollmar	GDR	560
1972	Ragnar Skanåker	SWE	567	Dan Iuga	ROM	562	Rudolf Dollinger	AUT	560
1976	Uwe Potteck	GDR	573	Harald Vollmar	GDR	567	Rudolf Dollinger	AUT	562
1980	Alexander Malentiev	URS	581	Harald Vollmar	GDR	568	Lubcho Diakov	BUL	565
1984	Xu Haifeng	CHN	566	Ragnar Skanåker	SWE	565	Wang Yifu	CHN	564
1988	Sorin Babii	ROM	660	Ragnar Skanåker	SWE	657	Igor Bassinski	URS	657
1992	Konstantine Loukachik	EUN	658	Wang Yifu	CHN	657	Ragnar Skanåker	SWE	657
1996									

Air Pistol

Year	Gold	C'ntry	Points	Silver	C'ntry	Points	Bronze	C'ntry	Points
1988	Taniou Kiriakov	BUL	687.90	Erich Buljung	USA	687.90	Xu Haifeng	CHN	684.50
1992	Wang Yifu	CHN	684.80	Sergei Pyjianov	EUN	684.10	Sorin Babii	ROM	684.10
1996									

Running Target

Year	Gold	C'ntry	Points	Silver	C'ntry	Points	Bronze	C'ntry	Points
1900	Louis Debray	FRA	20	Pierre Nivet	FRA	20	Georges Comte de Lambert	FRA	19
1972	Iakov Zhelezniak	URS	569	Helmut Bellingrodt	COL	565	John Kynoch	GBR	562
1976	Alexander Gazov	URS	579	Alexander Kedyarov	URS	576	Jerzy Greszkiewicz	POL	571
1980	Igor Sokolov	URS	589	Thomas Pfeffer	GDR	589	Alexander Gazov	URS	587
1984	Li Yuwei	CHN	587	Helmut Bellingrodt	COL	584	Huang Shiping	CHN	581
1988	Tor Heiestad	NOR	689	Huang Shiping	CHN	687	Gennadi Avramenko	URS	686
1992	Michael Jakosits	GER	673	Anatoli Asrabaev	EUN	672	Lubos Račanský	TCH	670
1996									

Smallbore Rifle (3 positions)

Year	Gold	C'ntry	Points	Silver	C'ntry	Points	Bronze	C'ntry	Points
1952	Erling Kongshaug	NOR	1164	Villio Ylönen	FIN	1164	Boris Andrejev	URS	1163
1956	Anatoli Bogdanov	URS	1172	Otakar Hořínek	TCH	1172	Nils Sundberg	SWE	1167
1960	Viktor Shamburkin	URS	1149	Marat Niasov	URS	1145	Klaus Zähringer	GER	1139
1964	Lones Wesley Wigger	USA	1164	Velitchko Hristov	BUL	1152	László Hammerl	HUN	1151
1968	Bernd Klingner	FRD	1157	John Writer	USA	1156	Vitali Parkhimovich	URS	1154
1972	John Writer	USA	1166	Lanny Bassham	USA	1157	Werner Lippoldt	GDR	1153
1976	Lanny Bassham	USA	1162	Margaret Murdock	USA	1162	Werner Seibold	FRG	1160
1980	Viktor Vlasov	URS	1173	Bernd Hartstein	GDR	1166	Sven Johansson	SWE	1165
1984	Malcolm Cooper	GBR	1173	Daniel Nipkow	SUI	1163	Alister Allan	GBR	1162
1988	Malcolm Cooper	GBR	1279.3	Alister Allan	GBR	1275.6	Kirill Ivanov	URS	1275
1992	Gratchia Petikiane	EUN	1267.4	Robert Foth	USA	1266.6	Ryohei Koba	JPN	1265.9
1996									

Smallbore Rifle – Prone

Year	Gold	C'ntry	Points	Silver	C'ntry	Points	Bronze	C'ntry	Points
1908	Arthur Ashton Carnell	GBR	387	Harry Humby	GBR	386	George Barnes	GBR	385
1912	Frederick Hird	USA	194	William Milne	GBR	193	Harry Burt	GBR	192
1920	Lawrence Nuesslein	USA	391	Arthur Rothrock	USA	386	Dennis Fenton	USA	385
1924	Pierre Coquelin de Lisle	FRA	398	Marcus Dinwiddie	USA	396	Josias Hartmann	SUI	394

Year	Gold	C'ntry	Points	Silver	C'ntry	Points	Bronze	C'ntry	Points
1932	Bertil Rönnmark	SWE	294	Gustavo Huet	MEX	294	Zoltan Hradetzky Soós-Ruszka	HUN	293
1936	Willy Røgeberg	NOR	300	Ralph Berzsenyi	HUN	296	Władysław Karas	POL	296
1948	Arthur Cook	USA	599	Walter Tomsen	USA	599	Jonas Jonsson	SWE	597
1952	Iosif Sârbu	ROM	400	Boris Andrejev	URS	400	Arthur Jackson	USA	399
1956	Gerald Ouellette	CAN	600	Vasilli Borissov	URS	599	Gilmour Stuart Boa	CAN	598
1960	Peter Kohnke	GER	590	James Hill	USA	589	Forcella Pelliccioni	VEN	587
1964	László Hammerl	HUN	597	Lones Wesley Wigger	USA	597	Tommy Gayle Rool	USA	596
1968	Jan Kúrka	TCH	598	László Hammerl	HUN	598	Roy Ballinger	NZL	597
1972	Ho Jun Li	PRK	599	Viktor Auer	USA	598	Nicolae Rotaru	ROM	598
1976	Karlheinz Smieszek	GER	599	Ulrich Lind	GER	597	Gennady Lushchikov	URS	595
1980	Károly Varga	HUN	599	Hellfried Heilfort	GDR	599	Petr Zaprianov	BUL	598
1984	Edward Etzel	USA	599	Michel Bury	FRA	596	Michael Sullivan	GBR	596
1988	Mirsolav Varga	TCH	703.9	Cha Young Chul	KOR	702.8	Attila Záhonyi	HUN	701.9
1992	Lee Eun Chul	KOR	702.5	Harald Stenvaag	NOR	701.4	Stevan Pletikosic	IOP	701.1
1996									

Air Rifle

Year	Gold	C'ntry	Points	Silver	C'ntry	Points	Bronze	C'ntry	Points
1984	Philippe Heberle	FRA	589	Andreas Kronthaler	AUT	587	Barry Dagger	GBR	587
1988	Goran Maksimović	YUG	695.6	Nicolas Berthelot	FRA	694.2	Johann Riederer	FRA	694
1992	Yuri Fedkine	EUN	695.3	Franck Badiou	FRA	691.9	Johann Riederer	GER	691.7
1996									

SHOOTING (Women)

Air Rifle

Year	Gold	C'ntry	Points	Silver	C'ntry	Points	Bronze	C'ntry	Points
1984	Pat Spurgin	USA	393	Edith Gufler	ITA	391	Wu Xiaoxuan	CHN	389
1988	Irina Chilova	URS	498.50	Silvia Sperber	FRG	497.50	Anna Maloukhina	URS	495.80
1992	Yeo Kab Soon	KOR	498.20	Vesela Letcheva	BUL	495.30	Aranka Binder	IOP	495.10
1996									

Smallbore – 3 positions

Year	Gold	C'ntry	Points	Silver	C'ntry	Points	Bronze	C'ntry	Points
1984	Wu Xiaoxuan	CHN	581	Ulrike Holmer	FRG	578	Wanda Jewell	USA	578
1988	Silvia Sperber	FRG	685.60	Vesela Letcheva	BUL	683.20	Valentina Tcherka Ssova	URS	681.40
1992	Launi Meili	USA	684.30	Nonka Matova	BUL	682.70	Malgorzata Ksiazkiewicz	POL	681.50
1996									

Sport Pistol

Year	Gold	C'ntry	Points	Silver	C'ntry	Points	Bronze	C'ntry	Points
1984	Linda Thom	CAN	585	Ruby Fox	USA	585	Patricia Dench	AUS	583
1988	Nino Saloukvadze	URS	690.00	Tomoko Hasegawa	JPN	686.00	Jasna Šekarić	YUG	686.00
1992	Marina Logvinenko	EUN	684.00	Li Duihong	CHN	680.00	Dorzhsuren Munkhbayar	MGL	679.00
1996									

Air Pistol

Year	Gold	C'ntry	Points	Silver	C'ntry	Points	Bronze	C'ntry	Points
1988	Jasna Šekarić	YUG	489.50	Nino Saloukvadze	URS	487.90	Marina Dobrantcheva	URS	485.20
1992	Marina Logvinenko	EUN	486.40	Jasna Šekarić	IOP	486.40	Maria Grousdeva	BUL	481.60
1996									

Double Trap

1996

Softball

Stars to Watch

by Bill Plummer III

Can America be beaten?

WHEN women's major fast pitch softball makes its long-awaited and long-anticipated debut in the Olympic Games at Columbus, Georgia, in July of 1996, there will not be any doubt as to which country will be the odds-on favourite to capture the gold medal – the United States of America.

Past history has shown the USA has dominated softball internationally and there is no reason to believe that they will not do the same when the competition begins on 21 July in Golden Park, Columbus. Any other result would be as dramatic as the first discoveries by the legendary seafarer of the same name.

In just about every international competition it has entered in recent years, the USA has come home with a medal. This includes a gold medal in the Superball Classic, which was a pre-Olympic event held in Columbus, in 1995, and which featured six of the countries competing in the Games this year. The only countries missing were the Netherlands and Canada.

In March of 1995, the USA national team captured a third consecutive gold medal in the Pan American Games, held in Parana, Argentina, sweeping through a six-team field and capping a 12-0 run with a 4-0 victory over Puerto Rico in the championship game. And although the USA's international win streak of 106 consecutive games was snapped by China, 1-0, in the Superball Classic, the USA regained its composure to win the gold medal easily, 8-0 behind the standout hurling of Lisa Fernandez to beat China and avenge the earlier defeat.

Lisa Fernandez (USA)

China, who lost to the USA 6-0 in the ISF women's world fast pitch championship in 1994 in St John's, Newfoundland, Canada, seems to be one of the only teams able to contend for the gold medal. But if they are to succeed, they must play better defence than in the Superball Classic, especially in the gold medal game when they made five errors and lost composure early – after the USA offense had put the game away, scoring four times in the first three innings.

At least seven to eight members of the Chinese team have played together since 1987 but there is a possibility that three or four new players may be introduced to the team for the Olympic Games. One player expected to retain her spot, however, is catcher An Zhongxin whose .467 batting average led all hitters in the Superball Classic.

Australia, who finished third in the ISF world championship and won a bronze medal in the Superball, must overcome base running lapses and have more of a consistent offense if they want to contend for a medal at Columbus. The Aussies blew an early lead against Chinese Taipei in the Superball Classic, then fought back to take a 9-4 win in ten innings. While most of the Olympic teams were

---

★★★★★★★★★★★★★★★★★★★★★★★★★★ **A Contemporary Heroine**

Michele Smith *(USA)*

If perseverance is one of the qualities needed to make the Olympic softball team, then Michele Smith has certainly got more than her share of it. Smith is not only an outstanding pitcher but is an excellent hitter who overcame a serious injury earlier in her career to accomplish one of her goals: play softball in the Olympic Games.

In 1986 her athletic career almost came to an end when she fell out of a moving vehicle just after her freshman year at Oklahoma State University. The accident detached the triceps from the bone in her left arm and chopped off the tip of her elbow. At that time the last thing on Smith's mind was pitching a softball. She knew she was lucky to be alive. The accident helped Smith put her life into perspective because she was taking things too seriously.

"It (the accident) put my life in perspective," she said. "I lost my identity as a person, because I was just a softball player. It made me a better player because I enjoy it more. I had a good sophomore year because I put so much time into rehabilitation."

Smith compiled a 19-5 record in her sophomore year and improved that to 26-6 in her junior year. She lost only three of 29 games in her senior year and finished her college career with an overall 82-20 record. Since college, Smith has continued to work and train with the same determination she had when she was recovering from the arm injury. This has propelled her into one of the top players in the world, let alone the USA.

She has won the Bertha Tickey Award four times as the outstanding pitcher in the Amateur Softball Association women's major fast pitch national championship. In March of 1995, she compiled a 3-0 record on the mound and batted .429 in leading the USA team to its third consecutive Pan Am gold medal. Now that she has reached one of her goals (making the Olympic team), Smith will put her other goal of becoming a doctor on the back burner until the Games are over.

announced in early 1995, Australia held back until late November.

Japan were surprised by Chinese Taipei in the world championship and had to defeat New Zealand in a qualifier to earn an Olympic berth. Chinese Taipei, Canada, Puerto Rico and the Netherlands complete the field, all hoping to win a medal.

These are the eight best teams in the world, but only one will emerge with a gold medal on July 30. No one knows who it will be, but the USA has combined power pitching with a potent attacking power offense, plus a razor-sharp defence and the ability to play well under pressure. It is hoping to do just that in Columbus to take the gold.

B. P. □

Retrospective

The International Olympic Committee approved the addition of women's softball to the Olympic programme in June 1991. It will make its debut in Atlanta during the Centennial Games.

Background

It is thought that softball emerged as a recreational sport when baseball was moved indoors. Credit for the first developments has been given to Hancock of the Farragut Boat

A Contemporary Heroine ★★★★★★★★★★★★★★★★★★★★★★★★★★★★★★★★★

Dot Richardson *(USA)*

When shortstop Dot Richardson was growing up in Orlando, Florida, her dream was to play for the USA in the Olympic Games. On September 4th, 1995, the 33 year old Richardson realized her dream when she was one of 15 players named to the first-ever USA Olympic team.

Considered one of the best players in the world, Richardson had considered retiring from softball not long ago to devote her time and unlimited energy to her medical career at the Los Angeles County – USC Medical Center's orthopaedic surgeon residency programme.

"I was prepared not to play any longer," Richardson said. "In fact, when I was in medical school I was thinking: This is it. I've been to the Pan American Games and been all over the world playing softball, and I was prepared to say that I had gone the farthest I could go."

Her mind changed both when the International Olympic Committee approved softball as an Olympic sport in June of 1991 and on finding that the staff and people at Los Angeles County – USC were supportive of her dream to play softball at the Games. Richardson, who was granted a year off from her residency programme to pursue her Olympic dream, has no regrets about her career, although juggling the two has never been easy. "There have been times when I've had to hop back and forth on planes going from school to competitions. It got crazy. There have been times when I just felt like I couldn't take it any more and I would ask myself what I was doing." In fact, what she was doing was turning a dream into reality.

Club in Chicago in the late 1880s. Ironically, having established itself indoors, it also became a popular outdoor game in parks and recreation areas.

A variety of rules existed until 1933 when an international committee was set up to standardize them. By the early '50s softball was becoming well-established as a competitive sport as well as being the leading participation sport in the USA. The first world championships for women were in 1965 in Melbourne, Australia, and for men in 1966 in Mexico City.

Equipment

Softball's playing field is diamond shaped and with a grass surface. The infield, which may be bare of grass, is the area inside the diamond and has a pitching mound and four bases – home, first, second and third. Bases are 18.3m (60ft) apart and each one forms one of the angles of the diamond. The area outside the bases is called the outfield.

Players hit the ball with a wooden bat which is 86.36cm (34in.) long with a diameter of 5.7cm (2.25in.). The ball itself is heavier and larger than a baseball but it is hard, not soft.

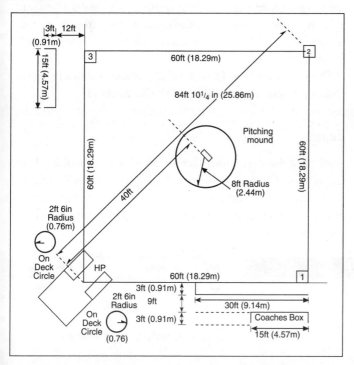

Softball court

Rules

Softball is played by two teams of nine players. Due to a shorter distance between the bases and a shorter pitching distance, it is generally faster than baseball. The aim is to score more runs than the opposition. A run is scored when a batter hits the ball into the field without it being caught before it bounces and the batter runs around the bases before being tagged by the ball. A player can be caught or tagged "out". If a team has three "outs" their opponents come into bat. When both teams have had three "outs" the inning is over and another one begins. There are seven innings in a complete game.

Four of the defensive players play in the in-field, with two between first and second base. The catcher stands behind home base. There are three outfield players. One of the main differences with baseball is that the pitcher must pitch the ball at the batter underhand rather than overhand.

Atlanta Format

Eight fast pitch teams, incorporating 120 athletes – all women – will take part in the 1996 Olympic Games softball tournament. They will play an initial round-robin group from which the top four teams will emerge to play semi-finals, a final and a bronze medal match. Qualification for Atlanta was by means of zonal tournaments, and the 1994 women's world championships.

The teams are: the USA, Canada, China, Australia, Japan, Chinese Taipei, Puerto Rico and the Netherlands.

Venue

Softball at the Centennial Games takes place at Golden Park, Columbus, Georgia, which is 168km (105 miles) from the main Olympic Village. This is southwest of Atlanta and will also incorporate a satellite athletes' Village. The stadium has a capacity of 8,500.

ATLANTA SCHEDULE

Venue: Golden Park, Columbus, Georgia

Date	Round	Start	End
21 - 27 Jul	prelims	9:00	13:00
		18:30	22:30

Date	Round	Start	End
29 Jul	s/finals	18:30	22:30
30 Jul	play-off (bronze)	18:30	22:30
	FINAL	16:30	20:45

Competition in this sport is open to women only.

Swimming

Stars to Watch

by Andrew Jameson

Perkins, Popov and a peculiarity

WILL Alexander Popov achieve sporting immortality? He can in Atlanta if he breaks the 100m freestyle world record and retains his Olympic title. Almost as fascinating a question is how much faster Kieren Perkins, of Australia, can go. Bet your bottom dollar he can win golds in the 400m and 1500m freestyle but the trickier guess is whether or not he can win them in world record times. And who, from such a wide field of favourites will win the men's breaststroke titles?

These are the burning issues for Atlanta. None greater, however, than the initial one – of whether Popov will live up to his reputation as the king of sprint. As reigning world, European and Olympic champion in both 50m and 100m freestyle the Russian rules supreme and is very much the man for the big occasion. It is difficult to see who would upset him in the 50m but there are thoroughbred sprinters from many countries including the USA, France, Great Britain, Lithuania, Brazil, Poland and Israel.

The 100m looks to be even more his domain. After setting the world record in Monte Carlo, Popov vowed he would swim faster still in Atlanta! The United States' Gary Hall finished second in the 1994 world championships and looks likely to be the one closest to the king. Other attempts to dethrone him will probably come from Gustavo Borges of Brazil and the French "come-back" kid Stéphan Caron, silver and bronze medallists in the Barcelona Olympic Games.

Move up a distance to the 200m, however, and the picture changes completely. This is expected to be one of the closest races of the Games. Difficult to pick who has the best shot at winning, therefore, but it may be Finland's Antti Kasvio.

There should be similar competition in the 400m – but mostly among those keen to qualify for the final in a lane not next to Kieren Perkins. This is the man who destroyed the world record at the last world championships with an awesome time of 3:48.80.

A Contemporary Hero ★★★★★★★★★★★★★★★★★★★★★★★★★★★★★★

Alexander Popov *(Russia)*

If the movie Tarzan was remade, Alexander Popov would undoubtedly be cast in the starring role, following in the footsteps of the greats such as Johnny Weissmuller and Clarence 'Buster' Crabbe. And if Popov repeats his 1992 Olympic gold medal performance in the 100m freestyle in Atlanta, he will join Weissmuller (1924 and 1928) and Hawaiian Duke Kahanamoku (1912 and 1920) as the only men to win the race twice.

Popov won two individual gold medals at the Barcelona Games, taking on the traditional might of the USA in both. In the 50m he faced the double team of Matt Biondi and Tom Jager. In the 100m, Biondi had held the world record for the previous nine years. Few would have thought that the 20 year old member of the new Unified Team (formerly the Soviet Union) would emerge as double Olympic gold medallist. However, his awesome underwater strength, mixed with supreme self confidence, swept him to victory at both disciplines.

As Olympic and European champion, Popov undertakes a tremendously busy schedule keeping him on the road up to nine months a year. In Monte Carlo in June 1994, Popov shattered Biondi's 100m record, setting a staggering new world mark of 48.21. Later that year he completed the set by adding the world championship title to his Olympic and European crowns.

Popov and Biondi remain the only two men in history to have swum the 100m in under 49 seconds. If Popov breaks his own world record in Atlanta and becomes the first human to dip under the 48 second barrier he will become one of the true greats and should, by rights, be one step closer to Hollywood.

The Australian will be favourite to knock more chunks out of his world record in the 1500m freestyle as well, although a couple of his compatriots should push him hard. Both Glen Housman and Dan Kowalski have broken 15 minutes for this event and so has the former world record-holder from Germany, Joerg Hoffmann.

Butterfly racing, meanwhile, has spawned a new style. A "breathing to the right-hand side" stroke is the peculiar technique which Russia's Denis Pankratov shares with the American 200m defending Olympic champion Melvin Stewart. Swimming a full 25m underwater at the start, Pankratov employed his breathing oddity and shocked the world by breaking the 100m and 200m world records within the space of three months in 1995. If he is not at his majestic best then Stewart and the Australian Scott Miller will probably have the best chances.

Majesty was certainly associated with the 200m backstroke world record-holder Martin Lopez-Zubero when he won the gold at Barcelona four years ago. The Spaniard took the title in front of his country's popular monarch King

Kieren Perkins

★★★★★★★★★★★★★★★★★★★★★★★★★★★★ **A Contemporary Hero**

Denis Pankratov *(Russia)*
In the space of three short months during 1995, Russia's Denis Pankratov rewrote the butterfly history books. On the Mediterranean shores of Southern France one sunny afternoon in June, the 200m world record was destroyed setting up a fascinating dual for Atlanta. America's Melvin Stewart wants his record back and has cut short his retirement to retrieve it.

Three months later at the European championships in Vienna, the 21 year old student from Volgograd turned his attention to the 100m. Few presented with the privilege of watching will ever forget it. Swimming the first 25m under the water, hitting the turn right on world record pace, he returned in an amazing 52.32 seconds, over half a second faster than Pablo Morales' nine year old world record.

In Atlanta, the blond Russian must surely be the favourite to take gold in both butterfly events, and has a great chance of a third gold in Russia's phenomenal medley relay team.

Juan Carlos. Lopez-Zubero returns to defend it in Atlanta, but the world and European champion Vladimir Selkov always attacks this event hard and will almost certainly be leading at the halfway turn. However, the surprise of the Olympics could spring up after that in what should be an excellent race. Watch out for the fast-finishing Nicolae Butacu of Romania.

The backstroke sprint may well produce racing of a different character. The United States' Jeff Rouse should add an Olympic gold to his world record and Barcelona Olympic silver.

Martin Lopez-Zubero

At least two of those who believe they have a realistic chance of winning the gold in the 100m breaststroke will not even qualify for the final. That is because there are at least ten of them and there are only eight places! European champion Fred de Burghgraeve, Australian Phil Rogers and Hungary's Károly Güttler all have a chance. The 200m will be extremely competitive as well, pitting Britain's Nick Gillingham against the two top Russians and Hungarians.

Tamás Darnyi

Two men, who between them have systematically wiped off the name of the great Tamás Darnyi from the world record lists, should cause trouble for each other in the 200m and 400m individual medley. They are Jani Sievinen of Finland and Tom Dolan of the USA, who will clearly be leading contenders.

A Contemporary Hero ★★★★★★★★★★★★★★★★★★★★★★★★★★★★★★★

Jeff Rouse *(USA)*

Quietly spoken, and quietly confident, Jeff Rouse represents one of America's biggest gold medal prospects at the 1996 Atlanta Olympic Games. He has one Olympic gold medal already. In leading off the USA 4x100m medley relay team four years ago, he reduced his own world record to 52.86, helping the USA to equal the world record. His greatest regret? Missing out on the individual 100m backstroke title in Barcelona to Canada's Mark Tewksbury by just six hundredths of a second.

A graduate of America's Stanford University, a hot house of Olympic gold medallists over the past 25 years, Rouse shines as arguably the world's greatest backstroke sprinter right from the gun. Renowned as an explosive starter, Rouse made a painful mistake which cost him the last world championships. Attempting to turn too close to the wall he was forced to tumble with his nose almost touching the wall. Lesson learnt, Rouse will be striving to be king of the backstroke sprinters in Atlanta.

Whether Darnyi will compete one more time has been a subject of speculation.

More battles loom between the Russians and the Americans in the relays. The final swimming event of the Olympics, the 4x100m should be of special interest. The USA should be comfortably ahead by halfway, but then be ready for Pankratov and Popov to bring Mother Russia home.

Nobody had ever had a butterfly career like Mary T. Meagher and whether or not anyone can get near her world records will be one of the great questions of the women's events. The greatest swimmer – or at least the one voted the greatest for the second year in a row – Krisztina Egerszegi of Hungary, may be able to win her fifth, sixth or even seventh gold medals in Atlanta. But an even bigger effect upon the destination of the women's medals could be caused by which swimmers the Chinese will enter – particularly in the sprints. Here, in the 50m and the 100m it should be China versus the USA, but the German Franziska Van Almsick should be very

A Contemporary Hero ★★★★★★★★★★★★★★★★★★★★★★★★★★★★★★

Tom Dolan *(USA)*

In reducing his personal best time by over eight seconds in 12 months, Tom Dolan achieved the improbable by breaking the world record in the 400m individual medley. It was improbable not just because the broken record had been set by a swimming legend, Támas Darnyi, but because Dolan suffers from exercise-induced asthma.

As with all great medley swimmers, Dolan has no weak stroke. He may not be leading the final in Atlanta after the butterfly leg, nor may he be after the backstroke leg. But at 1.98m (6ft 6in.) tall, he piles on the pressure in the second half of the race, and is blessed with a wicked sprint finish. This junior from the University of Michigan remains relatively new to the international swimming scene, despite being world champion and world record holder. Yet if Dolan maintains his current astounding rate of improvement, the 400m individual medley gold medal in Atlanta must surely go to the USA.

close in the 100m, which should be a thriller.

Franzi is a superstar without an Olympic gold medal but she ought to put that right by changing 1992 silver for gold in Atlanta in the 200m in which she is the world record holder. She may also choose to add the 400m to her repertoire. If so she will create a strong German force along with Julia Lang in an event likely to be dominated by youngsters. The average age of the world's top six in this and in the 800m is just 18 years old.

The 800m will see Janet Evans return to attempt a hat-trick of golds, having won in 1988 and '92. But although she is still the world record-holder Evans will have a tough job to resist other challenges, with Australia's Barcelona silver medallist Hayley Lewis likely to provide one of the most potent.

Two American "come-back" girls could make the butterfly races especially interesting. Crissy Ahmann-Leighton completes her return to the world's élite in the 100m and Summer Sanders, who snatched gold from China and Australia in Barcelona, is in the 200m again.

★★★★★★★★★★★★★★★★★★★★★★★★★★★★ **A Contemporary Heroine**

Franziska Van Almsick *(Germany)*

At the age of 13, she was barred from both European senior and junior championships for being too young, despite having been placed second at the German championships. The child superstar had to wait - but not for long.

One year later, Franziska Van Almsick collected four Olympic medals in Barcelona, including a bronze and a silver in the 100m and 200m freestyle. The next year she plundered the treasure trove at the European championships, winning a record six gold medals and one silver, and for her troubles was voted 1993 "World Female Swimmer of the Year".

It was a gold again at the world championships in Rome 1994 in the 200m freestyle, this time in a world record time. In Germany, Van Almsick is as famous as Steffi Graf and Boris Becker, the darling of her nation, a fashion model, a sporting superstar and an 18 year old multi-millionaire. But she has no Olympic gold medal.

In Atlanta the versatile German freestyle and butterfly champion will probably compete in six events. This tall, powerful, highly-motivated thoroughbred of the swimming pool has every chance of winning medals in all of them. Yet her greatest chance of victory must be in the 200m freestyle, her favourite event.

To win, she must avenge the defeat in Barcelona by America's Nicole Haislett. Van Almsick now has experience on her side, will confront everyone with a stunning technique and enters the Games as both world champion and world record holder. The test will come when the young Berliner will experience the pressure-cooker environment of an American Olympic Games surrounded by 15,000 wildly passionate supporters. The task will not be simple but, if she is ready, the world record will fall again.

"The mouse" could win both backstroke events. Quiet girl, Krisztina Egerszegi, once the youngest swimming gold medallist in Olympic history, should make a successful second defence of the 200m. But the 100m will depend on whether she participates or not. She believes it may be too short a distance for her and a late decision is being made as to whether she should go for it.

There will be plenty of "going for it" in the breaststrokes, in which world records may tumble. At least three women are capable of breaking them. Samantha Riley is the world record-holder and favourite in the 100m but amazing scenes can be expected if the South African Penelope Heyns can steal victory at either distance.

Expect Egerszegi again in the 400m individual medley, perhaps with a world record but the 200m could go to swimmers from any of five nations. In the relays it will be the USA against China again. However, watch out for Australia in the medley relay and for Germany in both freestyle relays. And watch out for who the Chinese bring. That could decide a great deal.

DIVING

When Napoleon Bonaparte said: "Let China sleep, for when she awakes the world will tremble" he could have been returning from a diving competition. In particular he could have been watching the world cup at the Olympic pool last year which suggested that the diving at the XXVI Olympiad will provide four enthralling contests. China is the dominant force in both men's and women's competitions, although there is significant competition from Russia, Germany and Australia.

What Fu Mingxia did on the platform board in Barcelona four years ago she has an excellent chance of repeating from the springboard in Atlanta despite being a relative newcomer at world level to the lower board. But, even so, Fu was world cup springboard champion late in 1994 and the psychological advantage must lie in her camp. World champion Tan Shuping will probably provide Fu with strong competition.

And there could be a double Atlanta gold for Fu. The holder should also start as co-favourite with compatriot Chi Bin in the platform competition. This pair have dominated the event since Fu won the 1990 world championships at the age of 12. The fight to knock these two off their lofty perch

★★★★★★★★★★★★★★★★★★★★★★★★ **A Contemporary Heroine**

Fu Mingxia *(China)*

Nobody in the history of diving has had such a huge influence on the sport at such a young age as Fu Mingxia. As a tiny 12 year old, she launched her 41kg (6st 7lb) body into diving's history books by winning the 1991 world platform championship. After much debate, it was decided by diving's officialdom that hitting the water head first at such speeds put too great a strain on a young body and the minimum eligible age to compete at world level was raised to 14.

This rule was further qualified to permit an athlete "in their fourteenth year" to compete, and so it was that 13 year old Fu took Olympic gold high above the city of Barcelona.

Clearly her height and age are an advantage. Although she has grown 10 centimetres since first winning the world championship, at 1.5m tall (5ft at full stretch) her tiny body still holds the perfect physique for spins, and Fu uses the gift to full advantage. In defending her world platform title in 1994, Fu took on the most difficult list of dives of all the finalists.

With heavy strapping around both wrists to protect her joints from the ravages of the sport, Fu practised for over two hours prior to the competition, and again for over an hour after collecting her gold medal. Such focus on detail while at the championship event, coupled with the six hours per day training routine which she has maintained at her Sports School in Beijing since the age of eight, has moulded Fu Mingxia into the world's greatest female platform diver.

As the diving finals in Atlanta draw closer, Fu has a unique opportunity to defend her Olympic title as an 18 year old. The reigning world cup champion on the 3m springboard, Fu Mingxia may even emulate the great Greg Louganis by winning gold on both diving boards.

SWIMMING

will be led by Vyninka Arlow, a pupil at the Australian Institute of Sport. Although beaten into the bronze medal place in a recent competition the margin of defeat was only nine points. So Arlow may have a chance of pulling off one of the greatest upsets of the Olympic Games.

Amazing leg strength gives the Russian Dmitri Saoutine one of the greatest springs there have ever been from the 3m board. He also has a cool temperament in the boiling pot atmosphere of a major final as his world title in the platform event shows. It is this which gives him the chance of a remarkable victory on the Atlanta springboard if he can get rid of a severe wrist injury in time.

However, such is the mighty strength in depth of China that the world champion Yu Zhoucheng may not even qualify. Xiong Ni, platform silver medallist behind Greg Louganis in 1988 and another Chinese, Wang, were just one point behind Saoutine in their last head-to-head.

Pick China to win the men's platform as well. The consistency of the softly-spoken Sun Shuwei will elevate him to the position of favourite to defend successfully the Olympic title he won in devastating fashion high on the hill overlooking Barcelona. Although nobody expects a repeat of the 43-point margin of that occasion, the 20 year old Chinese "master of the tower" will be extremely difficult to beat.

SYNCHRONIZED SWIMMING

The Americans will be favourites to win the inaugural Olympic team event in Atlanta with their powerful style emphasizing the precise execution of technically difficult elements. The Canadians should provide a strong challenge to the Americans, but Russia and Japan will also be fighting for the medals. Russia tend to produce artistically choreographed routines whilst the Japanese show mastery of a different style, all their own.

From 1984, its debut year, to 1992 synchronized swimming at the Games comprised a solo and duet competition. The sport requires overall body strength, agility, flexibility, grace, split second timing, musical interpretation and a keen sense of drama. Combine the strengths of a 400m swimmer with the lifting power of a water polo player, add the elegance of a dancer and that is the bare minimum required.

The idea of a team performance is for a group of swimmers to give a slow or fast moving depiction of various specific images, which change in the manner of a kaleidoscope. Among those showing their own unique style will be France. They are challenging for a place in the top four, having been placed fifth in previous events and closing the points gap all the time. China, Italy and Mexico are also all up-and-coming teams.

A Contemporary Heroine ★★★★★★★★★★★★★★★★★★★★★★★★★★★★★

Sylvie Frechette *(Canada)*

Sylvie Frechette made her mark because of her strength and flexibility, and the originality of her routines. In 1986 she won a gold medal at the Commonwealth Games. And in 1991 at the World Aquatic Games in Australia, she set a new world record when she scored seven perfect tens.

From 1988 until the Barcelona Games in 1992 she finished first in all but one of the international competitions she entered. A judging error at the Barcelona Games cost her a gold medal but her modesty and courage in the face of this huge disappointment won her widespread public admiration. After reviewing the incident, the IOC finally presented Sylvie with her gold medal 16 months after the Games. After nearly two years of retirement from the sport Sylvie began training again to become a member of the Canadian team for the 1996 Olympic Games, and she will be striving for her second Olympic gold medal.

WATER POLO

Italy won the 1992 water polo gold in a bad-tempered final with Spain, the host nation, by 8-7. Bronze went to the Unified Team. Yugoslavia, the 1988 champions, were barred from competing in water polo (as in all team sports in Barcelona under the terms of the agreement between the United Nations and the IOC over world-wide sanctions against Serbia and Montenegro following the outbreak of war in Bosnia-Hercegovina).

In 1996 the USA could prove tough to beat on home territory and backed by a home crowd in the Georgia Tech Aquatic Center.

A. J. □

Retrospective

No competitor in any sport has bettered the seven gold medals Mark Spitz achieved in Munich in 1972. It more than made up for the boasts in Mexico City four years earlier which did not come about.

Spitz wanted to be the first to win five golds in one Games and then to go one better and add a sixth. More than that, though, he wanted to win everything he entered and take seven golds.

He had doubts about the last, because he was unsure of being able to beat Jerry Heidenreich in the 100m freestyle. He considered withdrawing and it was only after being told by his coach that he would be seen as "chicken" that Spitz decided to go for the incredible target. Spitz surprised Heidenreich by starting at full speed instead of saving himself as he usually did and, with 15 yards to go, suddenly lost his rhythm and appeared in danger of defeat. But he pulled himself together at the very end and reached the wall half a stroke ahead of the advancing Heidenreich.

Swimming has transcended itself in many other ways. Johnny Weismuller's much-publicized role as Tarzan in the famous film occurred after he had been spotted modelling underwear in 1932! Earlier in 1924 he had made his name as the first person to swim 100m in less than a minute. However, Clarence "Buster" Crabbe, the 1932 400m freestyle champion, attracted the attention of the Hollywood producers even more. They cast him not only in the role of Tarzan, but Buck Rogers and Flash Gordon as well.

Swimming has also been a sport to spawn novelty. By 1988

A Sporting Legend ★★★★★★★★★★★★★★★★★★★★★★★★★★★★★★★★★★★★

Mary T. Meagher *(USA)*

"Madame Butterfly" Mary T. Meagher was just 14 years old when she first broke the world record for the 200m butterfly. This happened only 12 months after wanting to quit the sport and failing to qualify for the final in either of the two butterfly events at the American National Championships. She broke the 200m world record twice more that summer. Thus began the greatest butterfly career ever.

Born and raised in Louisville in the USA, Meagher was one of 11 children. The 'T' was added to her name so her family could distinguish between her and an older sister also called Mary. In 1980 she lowered the 200m record a further second, but it was at the 1981 USA national championships in Brown Deer, Wisconsin, that she rewrote the record books.

In the 100m, her own world mark stood at 59.26. "Madame Butterfly" stormed to an incredible time of 57.93 seconds. No female was to come within a second of this outstanding swim for nine years, and nobody has ever bettered it.

The 200m event was a similar story. Having chopped more than 3.5 seconds off Tracey Caulkin's world record over the previous two years, Meagher set her fifth world mark, stopping the clock at a staggering 2.05.96. She was still just 16

Graduating from high school a year early Meagher mapped out her strategy to win gold in Los Angeles. She joined coach Mark Schubert at the Mission Viejo Club in California, less than an hour's journey from the site of the Los Angeles Olympic pool. After a gruelling preparation she took the Games by storm. Her victory in the 200m butterfly in a time of 2:06.90 is still the Olympic record. She won by a staggering seven metres! In the 100m butterfly the margin of victory was a mere two metres! A third gold came in the 4x100 medley relay in which the world's greatest 'fly' swimmer set the fastest butterfly split ever recorded.

Four years later she completed her Olympic career taking a bronze medal in the 200m fly in the 1988 Olympic Games. Mary T. Meagher remains the greatest female butterfly swimmer that ever lived.

swimmers were frequently using the submarine start in the 100m backstroke, swimming the first 30 or 35m underwater. The sport's governing body banned it after the Seoul Olympic Games. An even bigger rule change took place for the 1956 Games in Melbourne. Breaststroke swimmers had begun bringing their arms back above the surface, and from this a new stroke, the butterfly, was officially created.

Greg Louganis' accident, 1988

Quirkier than any of this was the second final added to the 400m freestyle at the 1984 Los Angeles Olympic Games. It was designed to determine the occupants of places nine through to 16. But it created doubts as to who was really the best. Thomas Fahrner of Germany won the race in a time faster than the gold medallist George Dicarlo of the United States!

Four years later in Seoul, Greg Louganis produced a moment always to be remembered. This superb athlete hit his head on the diving springboard during the final, requiring five stitches. Yet he still went on to become the first man to take both springboard and platform golds in successive Olympic Games.

The hardest of hard luck stories took place at the Munich Games of 1972 when another American, Rick De Mont, was obliged to return his gold medal – after he had taken it home to California. American doctors had failed to register his declared medication as on the IOC banned list and De Mont had no idea that the Martax he took for his asthma was an illegal substance. Nor was he told about the alternatives he might have taken and, after winning the 400m freestyle, he was disqualified for taking ephedrine.

Background

Swimming began at the Olympic Games in a remarkably modest way. The men's event started in 1896 at Athens with a 100m for sailors. Only three took part in the near-freezing water in the Bay of Zea near Piraeus.

The women's events began 16 years later in Stockholm with three competitions, the 100m freestyle, the 400m team and plain diving. In another 20 years the whole scene had changed dramatically. More than 150,000 spectators watched the swimming in Los Angeles in 1932. This was also extraordinary for the fact that the Japanese men's team was made up mostly of under 17 year olds and yet won six gold medals.

Standards rose steadily, too. By 1952 in Helsinki every Olympic record was broken at least once. In a remarkable career spanning the 1956, '60 and '64 Olympic Games, Dawn Fraser broke 39 world records. And by 1976 in Montreal all

★★★★★★★★★★★★★★★★★★★★★★★★★★★★★ **A Sporting Legend**

Michael Gross *(Germany)*

At 1.98m (6ft 7in) tall and 2.2m (7ft 2in) from finger-tip to finger-tip, Michael Gross became the first West German swimmer to win an Olympic gold medal. He lowered his own world record in the final of the 200m freestyle in Los Angeles in 1984.

With a giant arm span that earned him the nickname "The Albatross", Gross also had intelligence and cunning in planning a winning strategy. This was never clearer than while winning the 200m butterfly at the Seoul Games. Deciding that early speed would give him the element of surprise, Gross was 1.5 seconds ahead at the half way mark, and a full 5m ahead with 50m to go. Although desperately tired inside the final 25m, "The Albatross" went on to win gold.

With 12 world records at distances between 100m and 800m, five world championship titles and 24 European records, Michael Gross retired in 1991 as 200m butterfly champion of the world.

A Sporting Legend ★★★★★★★★★★★★★★★★★★★★★★★★★★★★★★★★★★★

Kristin Otto *(Germany)*

At the Games of the XXIV Olympiad, women's swimming was dominated by one country, the German Democratic Republic. Their star was 22 year old Kristin Otto.

Before 1988, the most gold medals ever won by a female at one Olympic Games was four, a record held by another East German, the great Kornelia Ender.

Otto entered six events, four individual and two relays. She did not have long to wait for the first victory. Day one, race one, the women's 100m freestyle – it could not have been a better event for Otto. As reigning world and European champion and world record holder, she won the race by almost a full body length. At 1.85m (6ft 1in) tall and supremely powerful, Kristin Otto marched through her events in almost military style.

Gold came in the 100m backstroke and in the 4x100m freestyle relay. Another gold came in the 100m butterfly in the second fastest time in history.

Yet her huge successes brought about their own unique problems. As Olympic Champion in the 100m backstroke, butterfly and freestyle, which leg of the relay should she swim? The GDR officials decided that she should take the "lead-off" backstroke leg. Otto obliged by setting off in world record pace and the team was never headed. This brought her gold medal tally to five but her toughest test was still to come.

On the sixth day she rose for the 50m freestyle to take on world champion Tamara Costache and world record-holder Yang Wenyi of China. Two false starts unsettled the other seven finalists but played straight into the hands of Otto. On the third start she powered home. Otto had won six gold medals in one Olympic Games, the most won by any female in Olympic history.

---

but four of the 26 world records were broken. Swimming's increasing importance within the Olympic movement was reflected by the decision in 1968 to add 11 extra events. And in 1964 electronic timing was introduced. That year Hans-Joachim Klein of Germany won a bronze in the 100m freestyle by a thousandth of a second.

But for a while the sport suffered for having one country with a dominance of the best talent. In 1964 Don Schollander of the United States won four gold medals, and in 1968 the USA won more medals than all the other countries put together. Although the United States is still a major force today, thankfully there is a far wider range of prominent nations in the sport than 30 years ago. In 1984, in Los Angeles, Michael Gross became the first West German swimmer to win gold and in Barcelona, four years ago, 18 countries won medals.

The issue of professionalism became increasingly prevalent, particularly in the '70s when Spitz waved brand shoes in the air after a victory ceremony. He is said to have been given contracts worth five million dollars after having won his seven golds in 1972. But for the intervention of Spitz's coach who persuaded him to go for the seventh gold, a woman swimmer would have figured in the records as one of the two

Vladimir Salnikov *(Russia)*

Johnny Weissmuller was the first human to swim 100m under the "magic minute". In the summer Games of 1980 the 20 year old Muscovite, Vladimir Salnikov, became the first human to swim the 1500m at an average speed of under 60 seconds for each 100m! Every coach, spectator and swimmer in the Olympic pool that evening rose to their feet and applauded for a full five minutes. The "impossible" had been achieved.

Between 1977 and 1986, Salnikov swam the 1500m freestyle 61 times at international level. He was unbeaten in every race. When in 1986 he was only able to finish fourth in the final of the world championships and failed to make the final of the European championships 12 months later, the swimming world bade farewell to a fallen hero.

However, coached by his wife Marina, Salnikov returned to his rigorous training regime. Approaching the Seoul Olympic Games the odds seemed stacked against him. Only two swimmers in Olympic history had won gold medals eight years apart. And the 1500m freestyle is arguably the toughest event in the programme.

The heats went to plan, with the Russian qualifying comfortably in second place behind Matt Cetlinski of the USA. The final was a dream. Again comfortable to 600m, Salnikov piled on the pressure and broke the back of the field, returning a time of 15:00.40 in front of an ecstatic crowd to win by over two seconds.

Vladimir Salnikov had become the oldest swimmer in 56 years to win a gold medal at the ripe old age of 28.

Later that evening after the obligatory drugs test and media call Salnikov returned to the Olympic village for dinner. On entering the dining area word spread that Salnikov had returned as champion. Every coach, athlete from every sport stood and applauded in recognition of the champions' champion. "I can now retire with pleasure" he said. "Citius, altius, fortius" – Salnikov had achieved them all.

SWIMMING

most successful athletes of all. Kristin Otto of Germany won a record six gold medals in Seoul in 1988.

Seoul was also the venue for the breaking of a stereotype, giving proof that swimming is not the monopoly of the very young. Before an ecstatic crowd Vladimir Salnikov, aged 28, became the oldest swimmer in 56 years to win a gold when he captured the 1500m freestyle.

When the swimming and the diving pool were put in the same building in Moscow in 1980 it led to an unusual and highly significant protest. The noise from the racing caused complaints that it disturbed the divers' concentration. Aleksander Portnov protested, gained a re-dive and went on to take the gold medal. Just as quirky was the water polo match between Norway and Yugoslavia in 1952. Norway won but Yugoslavia protested about the refereeing and got a replay but only after a whole day's arguing.

Water polo made its Olympic debut in 1900. Great Britain dominated the early years but were then superseded by other European nations, particularly Hungary, Italy and Yugoslavia as well as the Soviet Union.

Equipment

An Olympic swimming pool must be 50m (164ft) long and 25m (82ft) wide with adequate training and warm-up pools. It has eight lanes, each 2.5m (8ft) wide, with two spaces of the same width outside lanes one and eight. Lane ropes with floats extend the full length of the course.

There are electronic touch pads at each end of the pool which are used to time the competitors. This automatic equipment is used to determine the winners, the placings and the times and takes precedence over human judges and time-keeping. Humans are only entrusted with judging and time-keeping if the equipment breaks down.

In diving there are two heights: 3m springboard and 10m platform (9ft 8in. and 32ft 8in.). The board is sprung and the platform is firm. In water polo the goals are 3m (9ft 8in.) wide x 0.9m. (2ft 11in.).

In all of the aquatic disciplines new TV cameras and angles caused a revolution in coverage at the Barcelona Games four years ago. These included tracking cameras along the pool floor and poolside and under the water for the diving events, giving some of the most dramatic pictures yet.

Rules

Four different strokes are used in Olympic swimming – backstroke, breaststroke, butterfly and freestyle – and there are strict rules governing permitted leg and arm movements as well as starts and turns and the length of time which competitors can remain under the water.

For example, in the breaststroke, swimmers may take one leg kick and one arm stroke whilst submerged. Breaststroke is the slowest of the four strokes and swimmers must touch the wall with both hands at each turn and the finish. It is a power . stroke requiring strength and precise timing, combining a two-armed underwater pull with a frog kick.

In the backstroke competitors start in the water and have to finish the event remaining on their back. It has become a faster stroke since a rule change allowed swimmers to tumble turn at the ends and touch the wall only with their feet.

Butterfly is considered the most demanding of the strokes because of the arm strength necessary for its undulating movements. It has simultaneous overhead arm movement and dolphin kick demanding precise technique. A two-handed touch is required at the turns and the finish. In freestyle events swimmers are technically allowed to use any stroke, but the crawl is the fastest and always used.

For "medley" events, both individual and relay, all four strokes are incorporated in the race, testing the all-round ability of swimmers.

In all the swimming events, competitors take part in heats which determine the fastest eight swimmers for the final. The fastest swimmers are then placed in the middle four lanes, which is a slight advantage because there may be less water turbulence. There is also a "B" final to classify the swimmers ranked 9-16.

In water polo each team has seven players, one of which must be a goalkeeper, and six reserves which can be used as substitutes.

In diving different styles are allocated five different degrees of difficulty, A,B,C,D and E which are used in calculating scores. Styles of diving include front, back reverse, inward, twist and armstand, and points are awarded by seven judges according to technique and grace. This takes into account the starting position, the run, the take-off, the flight and the entry (which should be perpendicular). The marks awarded are then multiplied by the degree of difficulty to give the final score with the diver scoring highest winning. There is always a preliminary, semi-final and final competition.

Teams of eight swimmers compete in synchronized swimming. They are required to complete two routines. The first is the team preliminaries (technical programme) which comprises each team performing ten specified movements within a routine lasting two minutes 50 seconds and counts 35% towards the final score. The second event is the free programme which lasts for five minutes and counts 65% towards the final score. There is plenty of opportunity for creativity and self-expression with amazing strength needed to produce lifts within the routines. Four judges consider technical merit and artistic impression with scores from nought to ten. Between 5.0 and 6.9 is considered "satisfactory", between 7.0 and 8.9 is "good" and between 9.0 and 10.0 "very good".

Atlanta Format

Over 1200 athletes will compete in the four "aquatic" disciplines of swimming (900), synchronized swimming (80), diving (140) and water polo (156). For the swimming events each swimmer has met qualifying standards by time set by FINA (The International Amateur Swimming Federation) at two levels. Each country can enter two swimmers per event if they have reached the higher standard and one per event at the lower standard.

A women's 4x200m freestyle relay has been added to the programme for Atlanta, bringing the women's competitions into line with the men's.

In synchronized swimming there is a change in the format for Atlanta. Last time competitors took part in either solo or duet events. Now there will only be a team event. This involves eight athletes from each country.

A total of 12 teams featuring 156 athletes – all male – will take part in the 1996 Olympic water polo. They will play in two groups of six from which the top four teams from each pool advance to the quarter-finals, semi-finals and final, with a bronze play-off. There will also be classification rounds for the lower placings. Teams have qualified for the competition by means of continental events.

Venue

Swimming, diving, water polo and synchronized swimming are all housed in the Georgia Tech Aquatic Center, which has a diving pool, a water polo pool with a capacity for 4,000 spectators, and a 14,000-seater shaded outdoor main stadium.

It is within the Olympic "ring", on the north-west side, adjacent to the Olympic village and about three miles from the Olympic stadium.

SWIMMING – current Olympic records

Event	Name	Country	Time/Result	Games	Year
Men					
50m Freestyle	Alexander Popov	EUN	21.91	Barcelona	1992
100m Freestyle	Matthew Biondi	USA	48.63	Seoul	1988
200m Freestyle	Evgeni Sadovyi	EUN	49.02	Barcelona	1992
400m Freestyle	Evgeni Sadovyi	EUN	3:45.00	Barcelona	1992
1,500m Freestyle	Kieren Perkins	AUS	14:43.48	Barcelona	1992
4x100m Freestyle Relay	Matthew Biondi	USA	3:16.53	Seoul	1988
	Troy Dalbey				
	Christopher Jacobs				
	Thomas Jager				
4x200m Freestyle Relay	Dmitri Lepikov	EUN	7:11.95	Barcelona	1992
	Vladimir Pychnenko				
	Evgeni Sadovyi				
	Veniamin Taianovich				
100m Backstroke	Jeff Rouse	USA	53.86	Barcelona	1992
200m Backstroke	Martin Lopez-Zubero	ESP	1:58.47	Barcelona	1992
100m Breaststroke	Nelson Diebel	USA	1:01.50	Barcelona	1992
200m Breaststroke	Mike Barrowman	USA	2:10.16	Barcelona	1992
100m Butterfly	Anthony Nesty	SUR	53.00	Seoul	1988
200m Butterfly	Melvin Stewart	USA	1:56.26	Barcelona	1992
200m Individual Medley	Tamás Darnyi	HUN	2:00.17	Seoul	1988
400m Individual Medley	Tamás Darnyi	HUN	4:14.23	Barcelona	1992
4x100m Medley Relay	Nelson Diebel	USA	3:36.93	Barcelona	1992
	Pablo Morales				
	Jon Olsen				
	Jeff Rouse				
Women					
50m Freestyle	Yang Wenyi	CHN	24.79	Barcelona	1992
100m Freestyle	Zhuang Yong	CHN	54.51	Barcelona	1992
200m Freestyle	Heike Friedrich	GDR	1:57.65	Seoul	1988
400m Freestyle	Janet Evans	USA	4:03.85	Seoul	1988
800m Freestyle	Janet Evans	USA	8:20.20	Seoul	1988
4x100m Freestyle Relay	Nicole Haislett	USA	3:39.46	Barcelona	1992
	Angel Martino				
	Jennifer Thompson				
	Dara Torres				
100m Backstroke	Krisztina Egerszegi	HUN	1:00.68	Barcelona	1992
200m Backstroke	Krisztina Egerszegi	HUN	2:07.06	Barcelona	1992
100m Breaststroke	Tania Dangalakova-Bogomilova	BUL	1:07.95	Seoul	1988
200m Breaststroke	Kyoko Iwasaki	JPN	2:26.65	Barcelona	1992
100m Butterfly	Qian Hong	CHN	58.62	Barcelona	1992
Women 200m Butterfly	Mary Meagher	USA	2:06.90	Los Angeles	1984
Women 200m Individual Medley	Li Lin	CHN	2:11.65	Barcelona	1992
Women 400m Individual Medley	Petra Schneider	GDR	4:36.29	Moscow	1980
Women 4x100m Medley Relay	Christine Ahmann-Leighton	USA	4:02.54	Barcelona	1992
	Lea Loveless				
	Anita Nall				
	Jennifer Thompson				

MEDALLISTS (by nation)

Swimming

	Men			Women			
	Gold	Silver	Bronze	Gold	Silver	Bronze	Total
United States	97	73	51	68	46	40	375
Australia[1]	24	20	28	14	13	13	112
GDR	6	7	5	32	25	17	92
Soviet Union	14	17	18	4	7	9	69
Great Britain	10	12	13	4	9	12	60
Hungary	12	13	11	8	6	3	53
Germany	9	11	9	3	7	11	50
Japan	12	17	11	3	1	1	45
Canada	6	7	6	1	5	10	35
Netherlands	-	-	2	9	13	10	34
Sweden	7	9	10	-	2	2	30
FRG	3	4	7	-	1	7	22
France	2	5	9	-	1	3	20
China	-	-	-	4	8	1	13
Denmark	-	2	1	2	3	3	11
Austria	2	4	4	-	-	1	11
Greece	1	3	3	-	-	-	7
Italy	-	-	3	-	1	2	6
Brazil	-	2	3	-	-	-	5
New Zealand[1]	1	1	2	-	-	1	5
South Africa	-	-	-	1	-	3	4
Bulgaria	-	-	-	1	1	1	3
Belgium	-	1	1	-	-	1	3
Finland	-	-	3	-	-	-	3
Poland	-	1	1	-	-	1	3
Romania	-	-	-	-	1	2	3
Spain	1	0	2	-	-	-	3
Argentina	1	-	-	-	1	-	2
Yugoslavia	-	-	-	1	1	-	2
Mexico	1	-	-	-	-	1	2
Philippines	-	-	2	-	-	-	2
Surinam	1	-	1	-	-	-	2
Costa Rica	-	-	-	-	1	-	1
Switzerland	-	-	1	-	-	-	1
Venezuela	-	-	1	-	-	-	1
	210[1]	209	208[2]	155[3]	153	155[4]	1090

[1] Double counting of Australia/New Zealand relay team in 1912
[2] Third place in 1896 100m not known
[3] Two golds in 1984 100m freestyle
[4] Two bronzes in 1988 50m freestyle

Synchronized Swimming

Women	Gold	Silver	Bronze	Total
Canada	3	3	-	6
United States	4	2	-	6
Japan	-	-	6	6
	7[1]	5	6	18

[1] Tie for gold in 1992

Waterpolo

	Gold	Silver	Bronze	Total
Hungary	6	3	3	12
United States	1	4	3	8
Soviet Union	2	2	4	8
Yugoslavia	3	4	-	7
Belgium	-	4	2	6
Italy	3	1	1	5
Great Britain	4	-	-	4
France	1	-	3	4
Germany	1	2	-	3
Sweden	-	1	2	3
Netherlands	-	-	2	2
Spain	-	1	-	1
FRG	-	-	1	1
	21	22[1]	21[1]	64

[1] Two bronzes 1900; two silvers, no bronze 1904

Diving

	Men			Women			
	Gold	Silver	Bronze	Gold	Silver	Bronze	Total
United States	27	20	19	19	20	20	125
Sweden	4	5	4	2	3	3	21
Germany	3	5	5	3	1	2	19
Soviet Union	2	1	4	2	5	3	17
China	1	4	3	5	1	-	14
Italy	3	4	2	-	-	-	9
Mexico	1	3	4	-	-	-	8
GDR	1	-	-	1	2	3	7
Great Britain	-	-	2	-	1	2	5
Czechoslovakia	-	-	-	1	1	-	2
Canada	-	-	-	1	-	1	2
Denmark	-	-	-	1	-	1	2
Egypt	-	1	1	-	-	-	2
Australia	1	-	-	-	-	-	1
France	-	-	-	-	1	-	1
Austria	-	-	1	-	-	-	1
	43	43	45[1]	35	35	35	236

[1] Two bronzes awarded in a 1904 and 1908 event

ATLANTA SCHEDULE

Venue: Georgia Tech Aquatic Center

Date	Description	Round	Start	End
SWIMMING				
20 Jul	100m freestyle (w)	prelims	10:05	12:07
	100m breaststroke (m)			
	400m ind. medley (w)			
	200m freestyle (m)			
	100m freestyle (w)	FINALS	19:33	21:07
	100m breaststroke (m)	(A&B)		
	400m ind. medley (w)			
	200m freestyle (m)			
21 Jul	200m freestyle (w)	prelims	10:05	12:10
	400m ind medley (m)			
	100m breaststroke (w)			
	4x200m freestyle relay			
	200m freestyle (w)	FINALS	19:33	21:12
	400m ind medley (m)	(A&B)		
	100m breaststroke (w)			
	4x200 freestyle relay (m)			
22 Jul	400m freestyle (w)	prelims	10:05	12:26
	100m freestyle (m)			
	100m backstroke (w)			
	200m butterfly (m)			
	4x100m freestyle relay (w)			
	400m freestyle (w)	FINALS	19:33	21:27
	100m freestyle (m)	(A&B)		
	100m backstroke (w)			
	200m butterfly (m)			
	4x100m freestyle relay (w)	FINAL		
23 Jul	400m freestyle (m)	prelims	10:05	12:22
	200m breaststroke (w)			
	100m backstroke (m)			
	100m butterfly (w)			
	4x100m freestyle relay (m)			
	400m freestyle (m)	FINALS	19:33	21:25
	200m breaststroke (w)	(A&B)		
	100m backstroke (m)			
	100m butterfly (w)			
	4x100m freestyle relay (m)	FINAL		
24 Jul	200m breaststroke (m)	prelims	10:05	12:56
	200m ind medley (w)			
	100m butterfly (m)			
	4x100m medley relay (w)			
	800m freestyle (w)			
	200m breaststroke (m)	FINALS	19:33	21:05
	200m ind medley (w)	(A&B)		
	100m butterfly (m)			
	4x100m medley relay	FINAL		
25 Jul	50m freestyle (m)	prelims	10:05	13:44
	200m backstroke (w)			
	200m ind. medley (m)			
	4x200m freestyle relay (w)			
	1,500m freestyle (m)			

Date	Description	Round	Start	End
	800m freestyle (w)	FINAL	19:33	21:43
	50m freestyle (m)	FINALS		
	200m backstroke (w)	(A&B)		
	200m ind medley (m)			
	4x200m freestyle relay (w)	FINAL		
26 Jul	200m butterfly (w)	prelims	10:05	11:47
	200m backstroke (m)			
	50m freestyle (w)			
	4x100 medley relay (m)			
	200m butterfly (w)	FINALS		
	200m backstroke (m)	(A&B)	19:33	21:47
	50m freestyle (m)			
	1,500m freestyle (m)	FINAL		
	4x100m medley relay (m)	FINAL		
DIVING				
26 Jul	platform (w)	prelims	15:00	17:30
27 Jul	platform (w)	s/finals	11:30	12:45
	platform (w)	FINAL	22:00	23:45
28 Jul	springboard (m)	prelims	20:00	23:59
29 Jul	springboard (m)	s/finals	11:30	13:00
	springboard (m)	FINAL	22:00	23:59
30 Jul	springboard (w)	prelims	20:00	23:00
31 Jul	springboard (w)	s/finals	11:30	13:00
	springboard (w)	FINAL	22:00	23:45
1 Aug	platform (m)	prelims	20:00	23:59
2 Aug	platform (m)	s/finals	11:30	13:00
	platform (m)	FINAL	22:00	23:59
SYNCHRONIZED SWIMMING				
30 Jul	technical routine (w)		10:00	11:15
2 Aug	free routine (w)		17:00	18:45
WATER POLO				
20 – 24 Jul	prelims		11:00	13:40
			15:00	19:20
			22:00	23:00
26 Jul	classification		11:00	13:40
	q/finals		15:00	19:20
	q/finals		22:00	23:00
27 Jul	classification		11:00	13:40
	classification		15:00	17:40
	s/finals		19:00	21:40
	s/finals			
	classification			
28 Jul	play-off (11-12 place)		8:00	10:30
	play-off (9-10 place)			
	play-off (7-8 place)		11:30	14:00
	play-off (5-6 place)			
	play-off (bronze)		15:00	18:15
	FINAL			

SWIMMING

MEDALLISTS

SWIMMING (Men)

Year	Gold	C'ntry	Time	Silver	C'ntry	Time	Bronze	C'ntry	Time
50m Freestyle									
1988	Matthew Biondi	USA	0:22.14	Thomas Jager	USA	0:22.36	Gennadi Prigoda	URS	0:22.71
1992	Alexander Popov	EUN	0:21.91	Matthew Biondi	USA	0:22.09	Thomas Jager	USA	0:22.30
1996									

100m Freestyle

Year	Gold	C'ntry	Time	Silver	C'ntry	Time	Bronze	C'ntry	Time
1896	Alfréd Hajós	HUN	1:22.2	Otto Herschmann	AUT	1:22.8			
1904[1]	Zoltán von Halmay	HUN	1:02.8	Charles Daniels	USA		John Scott Leary	USA	
1908	Charles Daniels	USA	1:05.6	Zoltán von Halmay	HUN	1:06.2	Harald Julin	AUS	1:08.0
1912	Duke Pao Kahanamoku	USA	1:03.4	Cecil Healy	AUS	1:04.6	Kenneth Huszagh	USA	1:05.6
1920	Duke Pao Kahanamoku	USA	1:00.4	Pua Kele Kealoha	USA	1:02.2	William Harris	USA	1:03.2
1924	Johnny Weissmuller	USA	0:59.0	Duke Pao Kahanamoku	USA	1:01.4	Samuel Kahanamoku	USA	1:01.8
1928	Johnny Weissmuller	USA	0:58.6	István Bárány	HUN	0:59.8	Katsuo Takaishi	JPN	1.00.0
1932	Yasuji Miyazaki	JPN	0:58.2	Tatsugo Kawaishi	JPN	0:58.6	Albert Schwartz	USA	0:58.8
1936	Ferench Csík	HUN	0:57.6	Masanori Yusa	JPN	0:57.9	Shigeo Arai	JPN	0:58.0
1948	Walter Ris	USA	0:57.3	Alan Ford	USA	0:57.8	Géza Kádas	HUN	0:58.1
1952	Clark Scholes	USA	0:57.4	Hiroshi Suzuki	JPN	0:57.4	Göran Larsson	SWE	0:58.2
1956	John Henricks	AUS	0:55.4	John Devitt	AUS	0:55.8	Gary Chapman	AUS	0:56.7
1960	John Devitt	AUS	0:55.2	Lance Larson	USA	0:55.2	Manuel Dos Santos	BRA	0:55.4
1964	Donald Schollander	USA	0:53.4	Robert McGregor	GBR	0:53.5	Hans-Joachim Klein	GER	0:54.0
1968	Michael Wenden	AUS	0:52.2	Kenneth Walsh	USA	0:52.8	Mark Spitz	USA	0:53.0
1972	Mark Spitz	USA	0:51.22	Jerry Heidenreich	USA	0:51.65	Vladimir Bure	URS	0:51.77
1976	Jim Montgomery	USA	0:49.99	Jim Babashoff	USA	0:50.81	Peter Nocke	FRG	0:51.31
1980	Jörg Wöithe	GDR	0:50.40	Per Holmertz	SWE	0:50.91	Per Johansson	SWE	0:51.29
1984	Ambrose Gaines	USA	0:49.80	Mark Stockwell	AUS	0:50.24	Per Johansson	SWE	0:50.31
1988	Matthew Biondi	USA	0:48.63	Christopher Jacobs	USA	0:49.08	Stéphan Caron	FRA	0:49.62
1992	Alexander Popov	EUN	0:49.02	Gustavo Borges	BRA	0:49.43	Stéphan Caron	FRA	0:49.50
1996									

[1] 100 yards

200m Freestyle

Year	Gold	C'ntry	Time	Silver	C'ntry	Time	Bronze	C'ntry	Time
1900	Fred Lane	AUS	2:25.2	Zoltán von Halmay	HUN	2:31.4	Karl Ruberl	AUT	2:32.0
1904[2]	Charles Daniels	USA	2:44.2	Francis Gailey	USA	2:46.0	Emil Rausch	GER	2:56.0
1906-1964 not held									
1968	Michael Wenden	AUS	1:55.2	Donald Schollander	USA	1:55.8	John Nelson	USA	1:58.1
1972	Mark Spitz	USA	1:52.78	Steve Genter	USA	1:53.73	Werner Lampe	FRG	1:53.99
1976	Bruce Furniss	USA	1:50.29	John Naber	USA	1:50.50	Jim Montgomery	USA	1:50.58
1980	Sergei Kopliakov	URS	1:49.81	Andrei Krylov	URS	1:50.76	Graeme Brewer	AUS	1:51.60
1984	Michael Gross	FRG	1:47.44	Michael Heath	USA	1:49.10	Thomas Fahrner	FRG	1:49.69
1988	Duncan Armstrong	AUS	1:47.25	Anders Holmertz	SWE	1:47.89	Matthew Biondi	USA	1:47.99
1992	Evgeni Sadovyi	EUN	1:46.70	Anders Holmertz	SWE	1:46.86	Antti Kasvio	FIN	1:47.63
1996									

[2] 220 yards

400m Freestyle

Year	Gold	C'ntry	Time	Silver	C'ntry	Time	Bronze	C'ntry	Time
1896	Paul Neumann	AUT	8:12.6	Antonios Pepanos	GRE	9:57.6	Evstatios Korafas	GRE	
1904[3]	Charles Daniels	USA	6:16.2	Francis Gailey	USA	6:22.0	Otto Wahle	AUT	6:39.0
1908	Henry Taylor	GBR	5:36.8	Frank Beaurepaire	AUS	5:44.2	Otto Scheff	AUT	5:46.0
1912	George Hodgson	CAN	5:24.4	John Hatfield	GBR	5:25.8	Harold Hardwick	AUS	5:31.2
1920	Norman Ross	USA	5:26.8	Ludy Langer	USA	5:29.0	George Vernot	CAN	5:29.6
1924	Johnny Weissmuller	USA	5:04.2	Arne Borg	SWE	5:05.6	Andrew Charlton	AUS	5:06.6
1928	Victoriano Zorillo	ARG	5:01.6	Andrew Charlton	AUS	5:03.6	Arne Borg	SWE	5:04.6
1932	Clarence Crabbe	USA	4:48.4	Jean Taris	FRA	4:48.5	Tsutomu Oyokota	JPN	4:52.3
1936	Jack Medica	USA	4:44.5	Shunpei Uto	JPN	4:45.6	Shozo Makino	JPN	4:48.1
1948	William Smith	USA	4:41.0	James McLane	USA	4:43.4	John Marshall	AUS	4:47.7
1952	Jean Boiteux	FRA	4:30.7	Ford Konno	USA	4:31.3	Per-Olaf Östrand	SWE	4:35.2
1956	Murray Rose	AUS	4:27.3	Tsuyoshi Yamanaka	JPN	4:30.4	George Breen	USA	4:32.5
1960	Murray Rose	AUS	4:18.3	Tsuyoshi Yamanaka	JPN	4:21.4	John Konrads	AUS	4:21.8

Year	Gold	C'ntry	Time	Silver	C'ntry	Time	Bronze	C'ntry	Time
1964	Donald Schollander	USA	4:12.2	Frank Wiegand	GER	4:14.9	Allan Wood	AUS	4:15.1
1968	Michael Burton	USA	4:09.0	Ralph Hutton	CAN	4:11.7	Alain Mosconi	FRA	4:13.3
1972	Bradford Cooper	AUS	4:00.27	Steve Genter	USA	4:01.94	Tom McBreen	USA	4:02.64
1976	Brian Goodell	USA	3:51.93	Tim Shaw	USA	3:52.54	Vladimir Raskatov	URS	3:55.76
1980	Vladimir Salnikov	URS	3:51.31	Andrei Krylov	URS	3:53.24	Ivar Stukolkin	URS	3:53.95
1984	George Dicarlo	USA	3:51.23	John Mykkanen	USA	3:51.49	Justin Lemberg	AUS	3:51.79
1988	Uwe Dassier	GDR	3:46.95	Duncan Armstrong	AUS	3:47.15	Artur Wojdat	POL	3:47.34
1992	Evgeni Sadovyi	EUN	3:45.00	Kieren Perkins	AUS	3:45.16	Anders Holmertz	SWE	3:46.77
1996									

[3] 440 yards

1500m Freestyle

Year	Gold	C'ntry	Time	Silver	C'ntry	Time	Bronze	C'ntry	Time
1896[4]	Alfréd Hajós	HUN	18:22.2	Ioannis Andreou	GRE	21:03.4	Evstatios Korafas	GRE	
1900[5]	Johnny Arthur Jarvis	GBR	13:40.2	Otto Wahle	AUT	14:53.6	Zoltán von Halmay	HUN	15:16.4
1904[6]	Emil Rausch	GER	27:18.2	Géza Kiss	HUN	28:28.2	Francis Gailey	USA	28:54.0
1908	Henry Taylor	GBR	28:48.2	Thomas Battersby	GBR	22:51.2	Frank Beaurepaire	AUS	22:56.2
1912	George Hodgson	CAN	22:00.0	John Hatfield	GBR	22:39.0	Harold Hardwick	AUS	23:15.4
1920	Norman Ross	USA	22:23.2	George Vernot	CAN	22:36.4	Frank Beaurepaire	AUS	23:04.0
1924	Andrew Charlton	AUS	20:06.6	Arne Borg	SWE	20:41.4	Frank Beaurepaire	AUS	21:48.4
1928	Arne Borg	SWE	19:51.8	Andrew Charlton	AUS	20:02.6	Clarence Crabbe	USA	20:28.8
1932	Kusuo Kitamura	JPN	19:12.4	Shozo Makino	JPN	19:14.1	James Cristy	USA	19:39.5
1936	Noboru Terada	JPN	19:13.7	Jack Medica	USA	19:34.0	Shunpei Uto	JPN	19:34.5
1948	James McLane	USA	19:18.5	John Marshall	AUS	19:31.3	Giorgi Mitró	HUN	19:43.2
1952	Ford Konno	USA	18:30.3	Shiro Hashizume	JPN	18:41.4	Tetsuo Okamoto	BRA	18:51.3
1956	Murray Rose	AUS	17:58.9	Tsuyoshi Yamanaka	JPN	18:00.3	George Breen	USA	18:08.2
1960	John Konrads	AUS	17:19.6	Murray Rose	AUS	17:21.7	George Breen	USA	17:30.6
1964	Robert Windle	AUS	17:01.7	John Mauer Nelson	USA	17:03.0	Allan Wood	AUS	17:07.7
1968	Michael Burton	USA	16:38.9	John Kinsella	USA	16:57.3	Gregory Brough	AUS	17:04.7
1972	Michael Burton	USA	15:52.58	Graham Windeatt	AUS	15:58.48	Douglas Northway	USA	16:09.25
1976	Brian Goodell	USA	15:02.40	Bobby Hackett	USA	15:03.91	Stephen Holland	AUS	15:04.66
1980	Vladimir Salnikov	URS	14:58.27	Alexander Chaev	URS	15:14.30	Maxwell Metzker	AUS	15:14.49
1984	Michael O'Brien	USA	15:05.20	George Dicarlo	USA	15:10.59	Stefan Pfeiffer	FRG	15:12.11
1988	Vladimir Salnikov	URS	15:00.40	Stefan Pfeiffer	FRG	15:02.69	Uwe Dassler	GDR	15:06.15
1992	Kieren Perkins	AUS	14:43.48	Glen Housman	AUS	14:55.29	Joerg Hoffmann	GER	15:02.29
1996									

[4] 1200 m [5] 1000 m [6] 1 mile

100m Backstroke

Year	Gold	C'ntry	Time	Silver	C'ntry	Time	Bronze	C'ntry	Time
1904[7]	Walter Brack	GER	1:16.8	Georg Hoffmann	GER	-	Thomas Zacharias	GER	-
1908	Arno Bieberstein	GER	1:24.6	Ludvig Dam	DEN	1:26.6	Herbert Haresnape	GBR	1:27.0
1912	Harry Hebner	USA	1:21.2	Otto Fahr	GER	1:22.4	Paul Kellner	GER	1:24.0
1920	Warren Paoa Kealoha	USA	1:15.2	Raymond Kegeris	USA	1:16.2	Gérard Blitz	BEL	1:19.0
1924	Warren Paoa Kealoha	USA	1:13.2	Paul Wyatt	USA	1:15.4	Károly Bartha	HUN	1:17.8
1928	George Kojak	USA	1:08.2	Walter Laufer	USA	1:10.0	Paul Wyatt	USA	1:12.0
1932	Masaji Kiyokawa	JPN	1:08.6	Toshio Irie	JPN	1:09.8	Kentaro Kawatsu	JPN	1:10.0
1936	Adolph Kiefer	USA	1:05.9	Albert van de Weghe	USA	1:07.7	Masaji Kiyokawa	JPN	1:08.4
1948	Allen Stack	USA	1:06.4	Robert Cowell	USA	1:06.5	Georges Vallerey	FRA	1:07.8
1952	Yoshinobu Oyakawa	USA	1:05.4	Gilbert Bozon	FRA	1:06.2	Jack Taylor	USA	1:06.4
1956	David Theile	AUS	1:02.2	John Monckton	AUS	1:03.2	Frank McKinney	USA	1:04.5
1960	David Theile	AUS	1:01.9	Frank McKinney	USA	1:02.1	Robert Bennett	USA	1:02.3
1964	not held								
1968	Roland Matthes	GDR	0:58.7	Charles Hickcox	USA	1:00.2	Ronnie Mills	USA	1:00.5
1972	Roland Matthes	GDR	0:56.58	Mike Stamm	USA	0:57.7	John Murphy	USA	0:58.35
1976	John Naber	USA	0:55.49	Peter Rocca	USA	0:56.34	Roland Matthes	GDR	0:57.22
1980	Bengt Baron	SWE	0:56.53	Viktor Kusnetsov	URS	0:56.99	Vladimir Dolgov	URS	0:57.63
1984	Richard Carey	USA	0:55.79	David Wilson	USA	0:56.35	Mike West	CAN	0:56.49
1988	Daichi Suzuki	JPN	0:55.05	David Berkoff	USA	0:55.18	Igor Polianski	URS	0:55.20
1992	Mark Tewksbury	CAN	0:53.98	Jeff Rouse	USA	0:54.04	David Berkoff	USA	0:54.78
1996									

[7] 100 yards

200m Backstroke

Year	Gold	C'ntry	Time	Silver	C'ntry	Time	Bronze	C'ntry	Time
1900	Ernst Hoppenberg	GER	2:47.0	Karl Ruberl	AUT	2:56.0	Johannes Drost	NED	3:01.0
1904-1960 not held									
1964	Jed Graef	USA	2:10.3	Gary Dilley	USA	2:10.5	Robert Bennett	USA	2:13.1

/continued on next page 373

Year	Gold	C'ntry	Time	Silver	C'ntry	Time	Bronze	C'ntry	Time
1968	Roland Matthes	GDR	2:09.6	Mitchell Ivey	USA	2:10.6	Jack Horsley	USA	2:10.9
1972	Roland Matthes	GDR	2:02.82	Mike Stamm	USA	2:04.09	Mitchell Ivey	USA	2:04.33
1976	John Naber	USA	1:59.19	Peter Rocca	USA	2:00.55	Dan Harrigan	USA	2:01.35
1980	Sándor Vladár	HUN	2:01.93	Zoltán Verrasztó	HUN	2:02.40	Mark Kerry	AUS	2:03.14
1984	Richard Carey	USA	2:00.23	Frédéric Delcourt	FRA	2:01.75	Cameron Henning	CAN	2:02.37
1988	Igor Polianski	URS	1:59.37	Frank Baltrusch	GDR	1:59.60	Paul Kingsman	NZL	2:00.48
1992	Martin Lopez-Zubero	ESP	1:58.47	Vladimir Selkov	EUN	1:58.87	Stefano Battistelli	ITA	1:59.40
1996									

100m Breaststroke

Year	Gold	C'ntry	Time	Silver	C'ntry	Time	Bronze	C'ntry	Time
1968	Donald McKenzie	USA	1:07.7	Vladimir Kosinski	URS	1:08.0	Nickolai Pankin	URS	1:08.0
1972	Nobutaka Taguchi	JPN	1:04.94	Tom Bruce	USA	1:05.43	John Hencken	USA	1:05.61
1976	John Hencken	USA	1:03.11	David Wilkie	GBR	1:03.43	Arvidas Iuozaytis	URS	1:04.23
1980	Duncan Goodhew	GBR	1:03.34	Arsen Miskarov	URS	1:03.82	Peter Evans	AUS	1:03.96
1984	Steve Lindquist	USA	1:01.65	Victor Davis	CAN	1:01.99	Peter Evans	AUS	1:02.97
1988	Adrian Moorhouse	GBR	1:02.04	Károly Güttler	HUN	1:02.05	Dmitri Volkov	URS	1:02.20
1992	Nelson Diebel	USA	1:01.50	Norbert Rózsa	HUN	1:01.68	Philip Rogers	AUS	1:01.76
1996									

200m Breaststroke

Year	Gold	C'ntry	Time	Silver	C'ntry	Time	Bronze	C'ntry	Time
1908	Frederick Holman	GBR	3:09.2	William Robinson	GBR	3:12.8	Pontus Hanson	SWE	3:14.6
1912	Walter Bathe	GER	3:01.8	Willi Lützow	GER	3:05.0	Paul Malisch	GER	3:08.0
1920	Håkan Malmrot	SWE	3:04.4	Thor Henning	SWE	3:09.2	Arvo Aaltonen	FIN	3:12.2
1924	Robert Skelton	USA	2:56.6	Joseph de Combe	BEL	2:59.2	William Kirschbaum	USA	3:01.0
1928	Yoshiyuki Tsuruta	JPN	2:48.8	Erich Rademacher	GER	2:50.6	Teofilo Yldefonzo	PHI	2:56.4
1932	Yoshiyuki Tsuruta	JPN	2:45.4	Reizo Koike	JPN	2:46.6	Teofilo Yldefonzo	PHI	2:47.1
1936	Tetsuo Hamuro	JPN	2:42.5	Erwin Sietas	GER	2:42.9	Reizo Koike	JPN	2:44.2
1948	Joseph Verdeur	USA	2:39.3	Keith Carter	USA	2:40.2	Robert Sohl	USA	2:43.9
1956	Masaru Furukawa	JPN	2:34.7	Masahiro Yoshimura	JPN	2:36.7	Kharis Iounitchev	URS	2:36.8
1960	William Mulliken	USA	2:37.4	Yoshihiko Osaki	JPN	2:38.0	Wieger Mensonides	NED	2:39.7
1964	Ian Obrien	AUS	2:27.8	Georgi Prokopenko	URS	2:28.2	Chester Jastremski	USA	2:29.6
1968	Felipe Muñoz	MEX	2:28.7	Vladimir Kosinsky	URS	2:29.2	Brian Job	USA	2:29.9
1972	John Hencken	USA	2:21.55	David Wilkie	GBR	2:23.67	Nobutaka Taguchi	JPN	2:23.88
1976	David Wilkie	GBR	2:15.11	John Hencken	USA	2:17.26	Rick Colella	USA	2:19.20
1980	Robertas Zhulpa	URS	2:15.85	Albán Vermes	HUN	2:16.93	Arsen Miskarov	URS	2:17.28
1984	Victor Davis	CAN	2:13.34	Glenn Beringen	AUS	2:15.79	Etienne Dagon	SUI	2:17.41
1988	József Szabó	HUN	2:13.52	Nick Gillingham	GBR	2:14.12	Sergio Lopez	ESP	2:15.21
1992	Mike Barrowman	USA	2:10.16	Norbert Rózsa	HUN	2:11.23	Nick Gillingham	GBR	2:11.29
1996									

100m Butterfly

Year	Gold	C'ntry	Time	Silver	C'ntry	Time	Bronze	C'ntry	Time
1968	Douglas Russell	USA	0:55.9	Mark Spitz	USA	0:56.4	Ross Wales	USA	0:57.2
1972	Mark Spitz	USA	0:54.27	Bruce Robertson	CAN	0:55.56	Jerry Heidenreich	USA	0:55.74
1976	Matt Vogel	USA	0:54.35	Joseph Bottom	USA	0:54.5	Gary Hall	USA	0:54.65
1980	Pär Arvidsson	SWE	0:54.92	Roger Pyttel	GDR	0:54.94	David Lopez	ESP	0:55.13
1984	Michael Gross	FRG	0:53.08	Pablo Morales	USA	0:53.23	Glenn Buchanan	AUS	0:53.85
1988	Anthony Nesty	SUR	0:53.00	Matthew Biondi	USA	0:53.01	Andy Jameson	GBR	0:53.30
1992	Pablo Morales	USA	0:53.32	Rafał Szukała	POL	0:53.35	Anthony Nesty	SUR	0:53.41
1996									

200m Butterfly

Year	Gold	C'ntry	Time	Silver	C'ntry	Time	Bronze	C'ntry	Time
1956	William Yorzyk	USA	2:19.3	Takashi Ishimoto	JPN	2:23.8	György Tumpek	HUN	2:23.9
1960	Michael Troy	USA	2:12.8	Neville Hayes	AUS	2:14.6	John Gillanders	USA	2:15.3
1964	Kevin Berry	AUS	2:06.6	Carl Joseph Robie	USA	2:07.5	Fred Shmidt	USA	2:09.3
1968	Carl Robie	USA	2:08.7	Martyn Woodroffe	GBR	2:09.0	John Ferris	USA	2:09.3
1972	Mark Spitz	USA	2:00.70	Gary Hall	USA	2:02.86	Robin Backhaus	USA	2:03.23
1976	Mike Bruner	USA	1:59.23	Steven Gregg	USA	1:59.54	Bill Forrester	USA	1:59.96
1980	Sergei Fesenko	URS	1:59.76	Philip Hubble	GBR	2:01.20	Roger Pyttel	GDR	2:01.39
1984	Jonathan Sieben	AUS	1:57.04	Michael Gross	FRG	1:57.40	Rafael Vidal Castro	VEN	1:57.51
1988	Michael Gross	FRG	1:56.94	Benny Nielsen	DEN	1:58.24	Anthony Mosse	NZL	1:58.28
1992	Mel Stewart	USA	1:56.26	Danyon Loader	NZL	1:57.93	Franck Esposito	FRA	1:58.51
1996									

Year	Gold	C'ntry	Time	Silver	C'ntry	Time	Bronze	C'ntry	Time

200m Individual Medley

Year	Gold	C'ntry	Time	Silver	C'ntry	Time	Bronze	C'ntry	Time
1968	Charles Hickcox	USA	2:12.0	Gregory Buckingham	USA	2:13.0	John Ferris	USA	2:13.3
1972	Gunnar Larsson	SWE	2:07.17	Tim McKee	USA	2:08.37	Steven Furniss	USA	2:08.45
1976	not held								
1980	not held								
1984	Alex Baumann	CAN	2:01.42	Pedro Morales	USA	2:03.05	Neil Cochran	GBR	2:04.38
1988	Tamás Darnyi	HUN	2:00.17	Patrick Küehl	GDR	2:01.61	Vadim Izarochtchouk	URS	2:02.40
1992	Tamás Darnyi	HUN	2:00.76	Gregory Burgess	USA	2:00.97	Attila Czene	HUN	2:01.00
1996									

400m Individual Medley

Year	Gold	C'ntry	Time	Silver	C'ntry	Time	Bronze	C'ntry	Time
1964	Richard William Roth	USA	4:45.4	Roy Saari	USA	4:47.1	Gerhaad Herz	GER	4:51.0
1968	Charles Hickcox	USA	4:48.4	Gary Hall	USA	4:48.7	Michael Holthaus	FRG	4:51.4
1972	Gunnar Larsson	SWE	4:31.98	Tim McKee	USA	4:31.98	András Hargitay	HUN	4:32.70
1976	Rod Strachan	USA	4:23.68	Tim McKee	USA	4:26.62	Andrei Smirnov	URS	4:26.90
1980	Aleksandr Sidorenko	URS	4:22.89	Sergei Feseniko	URS	4:23.43	Zoltán Verrasztó	HUN	4:24.24
1984	Alex Baumann	CAN	4:17.41	Ricardo Prado	BRA	4:18.45	Robert Woodhouse	AUS	4:20.50
1988	Tamás Darnyi	HUN	4:14.75	David Wharton	USA	4:17.36	Stefano Battistelli	ITA	4:18.01
1992	Tamás Darnyi	HUN	4:14.23	Eric Namesnik	USA	4:15.57	Luca Sacchi	ITA	4:16.34
1996									

4 x 100m Medley Relay

Year	Gold	C'ntry	Time	Silver	C'ntry	Time	Bronze	C'ntry	Time
1960	Frank McKinney Paul Hait Lance Larson Felix Farrell	USA	4:05.4	David Theile Terence Gathercole Neville Hayes Geoffrey Shipton	AUS	4:12.0	Kazuo Tomita Koichi Hirakida Yoshihiko Osaki Keigo Shimizu	JPN	4:12.2
1964	Harold Mann William Craig Fred Schmidt Stephen Clark	USA	3:58.4	Ernst-Joachim Küppers Egon Henninger Horst-Günther Gregor Hans-Joachim Klein	GER	4:01.6	Peter Reynolds Ian Obrian Kevin Berry David Dickson	AUS	4:02.3
1968	Charles Hickcox Donald McKenzie Douglas Russell Kenneth Walsh	USA	3:54.9	Roland Matthes Egon Henninger Horst-Günther Gregor Frank Wiegand	GDR	3:57.5	Yuri Gromak Vladimir Kossinsky Vladimir Nemschilov Leonid Ilichev	URS	4:00.7
1972	Michael Stamm Thomas Bruce Mark Spitz Jerry Heidenreich	USA	3:48.16	Roland Matthes Klaus Katzur Hartmut Flöckner Lutz Unger	GDR	3:52.12	Eric Fish William Mahony Bruce Robertson Robert Kasting	CAN	3:52.26
1976	John Naber John Hencken Matt Vogel Jim Montgomery	USA	3:42.22	Stephen Pickell Graham Smith Clay Evans Gary MacDonald	CAN	3:45.94	Klaus Steinbach Walter Kusch Michael Kraus Peter Nocke	FRG	3:47.29
1980	Marcus Kerry Peter Evans Mark Tonelli Neil Brooks	AUS	3:45.70	Viktor Kuznetsov Arsen Miskarov Evgeni Seredin Sergei Kopliakov	URS	3:45.92	Gary Abraham Duncan Goodhew David Lowe Martin Smith	GBR	3:47.71
1984	Richard Carey Steve Lundquist Pablo Morales Ambrose Gaines	USA	3:39.30	Mike West Victor Davis Tom Ponting Sandy Goss	CAN	3:43.23	Mark Kerry Peter Evans Glenn Buchanan Mark Stockwell	AUS	3:43.25
1988	David Berkoff Richard Schroeder Matthew Biondi Christopher Jacobs	USA	3:36.93	Mark Tewksbury Victor Davis Thomas Ponting Donald Goss	CAN	3:39.28	Igor Polianski Dmitri Volkov Vadim Jaroschtchuk Gennadi Prigoda	URS	3:39.96
1992	Jeff Rouse Nelson Diebel Pablo Morales Jon Olsen	USA	3:36.93	Vladimir Selkov Alexander Popov Pavel Khnykine Vassili Ivanov	EUN	3:38.56	Mark Tewksbury Jonathan Cleveland Stephen Clarke Marcel Gery	CAN	3:39.66
1996									

Year	Gold	C'ntry	Time	Silver	C'ntry	Time	Bronze	C'ntry	Time

4 x 100 m Freestyle Relay

Year	Gold	C'ntry	Time	Silver	C'ntry	Time	Bronze	C'ntry	Time
1964	Stephen Clark Michael Austin Gary Ilman Donald Schollander	USA	3:33.2	Horst Löffler Frank Wiegand Uwe Jacobsen Hans-Joachim Klein	GER	3:37.2	David Dickson Peter Doak John Ryan Robert Windle	AUS	3:39.1
1968	Zachary Zorn Stephen Rerych Mark Spitz Kenneth Walsh	USA	3:31.7	Semyon Belitz-Geiman Viktor Mazanov Georgi Kulikov Leonid Ilichev	URS	3:34.2	Gregory Rogers Robert Windle Robert Cusack Michael Wenden	AUS	3:34.7
1972	David Edgar John Murphy Jerry Heidenreich Mark Spitz	USA	3:26.42	Vladimir Bure Viktor Mazanov Viktor Aboimov Igor Grivennikov	URS	3:29.72	Roland Matthes Wilfried Hartung Peter Bruch Lutz Unger	GDR	3:32.42
1976+1980 not held									
1984	Christopher Cavanaugh Michael Heath Matthew Biondi Ambrose Gaines	USA	3:19.03	Gregory Fasala Nigel Brooks Michael Delany Mark Stockwell	AUS	3:19.68	Thomas Leidstrom Bengt Baron Mikael Örn Per Johansson	SWE	3:22.69
1988	Christopher Jacobs Troy Dalbey Thomas Jager Matthew Biondi	USA	3:15.63	Gennadi Prigoda Yuri Bachkatov Nikolai Evseev Vladimir Tkashenko	URS	3:18.33	Dirk Richter Thomas Flemming Lars Hinneburg Steffen Zesner	GDR	3:19.82
1992	Joseph Hudepohl Matthew Biondi Tom Jager Jon Olsen	USA	3:16.74	Pavel Khnykine Gennadi Prigoda Yuri Bashkatov Alexander Popov	EUN	3:17.56	Christian Troeger Dirk Richter Steffen Zesner Mark Pinger	GER	3:17.90
1996									

4 x 200m Freestyle Relay

Year	Gold	C'ntry	Time	Silver	C'ntry	Time	Bronze	C'ntry	Time
1908	John Derbyshire Paul Radmilovic William Foster Henry Taylor	GBR	10:55.6	József Munk Imre Zachár Béla Las-Torres Zoltán von Halmay	HUN	10:59.0	Harry Hebner Leo Goodwin Charles Daniels Leslie Rich	USA	11:02.8
1912	Cecil Healy Malcolm Champion Leslie Boardman Harold Hardwick	AUS/ NZL	10:11.6	Kenneth Huszagh Harry Hebner Perry McGillivray Duke Paoa Kahanamoku	USA	10:20.2	William Foster Thomas Battersby John Hatfield Henry Taylor	GBR	10:28.2
1920	Perry McGillivray Pua Kele Kealoha Norman Ross Duke Pao Kahanamoku	USA	10:04.4	Henry Hay William Herald Ivan Stedman Frank Beaurepaire	AUS	10:25.4	Leslie Savage Edward Peter Henry Taylor Harold Annison	GBR	10:37.2
1924	James Wallace O'Connor Harrison Glancy Ralph Breyer Johnny Weissmuller	USA	9:53.4	Maurice Christie Ernest Henry Frank Beaurepaire Andrew Charlton	AUS	10:02.2	Georg Werner Orvar Trolle Åke Borg Arne Borg	SWE	10:06.8
1928	Austin Clapp Walter Laufer George Kojac Johnny Weissmuller	USA	9:36.2	Hiroshi Yoneyama Nobuo Arai Tokuhei Sata Katsuo Takaishi	JPN	9:41.4	Frederick Bourne James Thompson Garnet Ault Walter Spence	CAN	9:47.8
1932	Yasuji Miyazaki Masanori Yusa Takashi Yokoyama Hisakichi Toyoda	JPN	8:58.4	Frank Booth George Fissler Maiola Kalili Manuella Kalili	USA	9:10.5	András Wanié László Szabados András Székely István Bárány	HUN	9:31.4
1936	Masanori Yusa Shigeo Sugiura Masaharu Taguchi Shigeo Arai	JPN	8:51.5	Ralph Flanagan John Macionis Paul Wolf Jack Medica	USA	9:03.0	Árpád Lengyel Oszkár Abay-Nemes Ödön Gróf Ferenc Csík	HUN	9:12.3
1948	Walter Ris James McLane Wallace Wolf William Smith	USA	8:46.0	Elemér Szatmári György Mitró Imre Nyéki Géza Kádas	HUN	8:48.4	Joseph Bernardo Henri Padou Jr. René Cornu Alexandre Jany	FRA	9:08.0

Year	Gold	C'ntry	Time	Silver	C'ntry	Time	Bronze	C'ntry	Time
1952	Wayne Moore	USA	8:31.1	Hiroshi Suzuki	JPN	8:33.5	Joseph Bernardo	FRA	8:45.9
	William Woolsey			Yoshihiro Hamaguchi			Aldo Eminente		
	Ford Konno			Toru Goto			Alexandre Jany		
	James McLane			Teijiro Tanikawa			Jean Boiteux		
1956	Kevin O'Halloran	AUS	8:23.6	Richard Hanley	USA	8:31.5	Vitaly Sorokine	HUN	8:34.7
	John Devitt			George Breen			Vladimir Stroujanov		
	Murray Rose			William Woolsey			Gennady Nikolaev		
	Jon Henricks			Ford Konno			Boris Nikitine		
1960	George Harrison	USA	8:10.2	Makoto Fukui	JPN	8:13.2	David Dickson	AUS	8:13.8
	Richard Blick			Hiroshi Ishii			John Devitt		
	Michael Troy			Tsuyoshi Yamanaka			Murray Rose		
	Felix Farrell			Tatsuo Fujimoto			Jon Konrads		
1964	Stephen Clark	USA	7:52.1	Horst-Günther Gregor	GER	7:59.3	Makoto Fukui	JAP	8:03.8
	Roy Saari			Gerhard Hetz			Kunihiro Iwasaki		
	Gary Ilman			Frank Wiegand			Toshio Shoji		
	Donald Schollander			Hans-Joachim Klein			Yukiaki Okabe		
1968	John Nelson	USA	7:52.3	Gregory Rogers	AUS	7:53.7	Vladimir Bure	URS	8:01.6
	Stephen Rerych			Graham White			Semyon Belitz-Geiman		
	Mark Spitz			Robert Windle			Georgi Kulikov		
	Donald Schollander			Michael Wenden			Leonid Ilichev		
1972	John Kinsella	USA	7:35.78	Klaus Steinbach	FRG	7:41.69	Igor Grivennikov	URS	7:45.76
	Frederick Tyler			Werner Lampe			Viktor Mazanov		
	Steven Genter			Hans-Günther Vosseler			Georgi Kulikov		
	Mark Spitz			Hans-Joachim Fassnacht			Vladimir Bure		
1976	Mike Bruner	USA	7:23.22	Vladimir Raskatov	URS	7:27.97	Alan McClatchey	GBR	7:32.11
	Bruce Furniss			Andrei Bogdanov			David Dunne		
	John Naber			Sergei Kopliakov			Gordon Downie		
	Jim Montgomery			Andrei Krylov			Brian Brinkley		
1980	Sergei Kopliakov	URS	7:23.50	Frank Pfütze	GDR	7:28.6	Jorge Luiz Fernandes	BRA	7:29.30
	Vladimir Salnikov			Jörg Woithe			Marcus Laborne		
	Ivar Stukolkin			Detlev Grabs			Mattioli		
	Andrei Krylov			Rainer Strohbach			Ciro Marques Delgado		
							Djan Garrido Madruga		
1984	Michael Heath	USA	7:15.69	Thomas Fahrner	FRG	7:15.73	Neil Cochran	GBR	7:24.78
	David Larson			Dirk Korthals			Paul Easter		
	Jeffrey Float			Alexander Schowtka			Paul Howe		
	Lawrence Hayes			Michael Gross			Andrew Astbury		
1988	Troy Dalbey	USA	7:12.51	Uwe Dassler	GDR	7:13.68	Erik Hochstein	FRG	7:14.35
	Matthew Cetlinski			Sven Lodziewski			Thomas Fahrner		
	Douglas Gjertson			Thomas Flemming			Rainer Henkel		
	Matthew Biondi			Steffen Zesner			Michael Gross		
1992	Dmitri Lepikov	EUN	7:11.95	Christer Wallin	SWE	7:15.51	Mel Stewart	USA	7:16.23
	Vladimir Pychnenko			Anders Holmertz			Joseph Hudepohl		
	Evgeni Sadovyi			Tommy Werner			Jon Olsen		
	Venjamin Taianovitch			Lars Frölander			Doug Gjertsen		
1996									

SWIMMING (Women)

Year	Gold	C'ntry	Time	Silver	C'ntry	Time	Bronze	C'ntry	Time

50m Freestyle

Year	Gold	C'ntry	Time	Silver	C'ntry	Time	Bronze	C'ntry	Time
1988	Kristin Otto	GDR	25.49	Yang Wenyi	CHN	25.64	Katrin Meissner	GDR	25.71
1992	Yang Wenyi	CHN	24.79	Zhuang Yong	CHN	25.08	Angel Martino	USA	25.23
1996									

100m Freestyle

Year	Gold	C'ntry	Time	Silver	C'ntry	Time	Bronze	C'ntry	Time
1912	Fanny Durack	AUS	1:22.2	Wilhelmina Wylie	AUS	1:25.4	Jennie Fletcher	GBR	1:27.0
1920	Ethelda Bleiberey	USA	1:13.6	Irene Guest	USA	1:17.0	Frances Schroth	USA	1:17.2
1924	Ethel Lackie	USA	1:12.4	Mariechen Wehselau	USA	1:12.8	Gertrude Ederle	USA	1:14.2
1928	Albina Osipowich	USA	1:11.0	Eleanor Garatti-Saville	USA	1:11.4	Margaret Cooper	GBR	1:13.6
1932	Helene Madison	USA	1:06.8	Willemijntje den Ouden	NED	1:07.8	Eleanor Saville	USA	1:09.3
1936	Hendrika Mastenbroek	NED	1:05.9	Jeanette Campbell	ARG	1:06.4	Gisela Arendt	GER	1:06.6
1948	Greta Andersen	DEN	1:06.3	Ann Curtis	USA	1:06.5	Marie-Louise Vaessen	NED	1:07.6
1952	Katalin Szöke	HUN	1:06.8	Johanna Termeulen	NED	1:07.0	Judit Temes	HUN	1:07.1

/continued on next page

Year	Gold	C'ntry	Time	Silver	C'ntry	Time	Bronze	C'ntry	Time
1956	Dawn Fraser	AUS	1:02.0	Lorraine Crapp	AUS	1:02.3	Faith Leech	AUS	1:05.1
1960	Dawn Fraser	AUS	1:01.2	Susan Christina Von Saltza	USA	1:02.8	Natalie Steward	GBR	1:03.1
1964	Dawn Fraser	AUS	0:59.5	Sharon Stouder	USA	0:59.9	Kathleen Ellis	USA	1:00.8
1968	Jan Henne	USA	1:00.0	Susan Pedersen	USA	1:00.3	Linda Gustavson	USA	1:00.3
1972	Sandra Neilson	USA	0:58.59	Shirley Babashoff	USA	0:59.02	Shane Gould	AUS	0:59.06
1976	Kornelia Ender	GDR	0:55.65	Petra Priemar	GDR	0:56.49	Enith Brigitha	NED	0:56.65
1980	Barbara Krause	GDR	0:54.79	Caren Metschuck	GDR	0:55.16	Ines Diers	GDR	0:55.65
1984	Carrie Steinseifer	USA	0:55.92	Nancy Hogshead	USA	0:55.92	Annemarie Verstappen	NED	0:56.08
1988	Kristin Otto	GDR	0:54.93	Zhuang Yong	CHN	0:55.47	Catherine Plewinski	FRA	0:55.49
1992	Zhuang Yong	CHN	0:54.64	Jennifer Thompson	USA	0:54.84	Franziska Van Almsick	GER	0:54.94
1996									

200m Freestyle

Year	Gold	C'ntry	Time	Silver	C'ntry	Time	Bronze	C'ntry	Time
1968	Debbie Meyer	USA	2:10.5	Jan Henne	USA	2:11.0	Jane Barkman	USA	2:11.2
1972	Shane Gould	AUS	2:03.56	Shirley Babashoff	USA	2:04.33	Keena Rothhammer	USA	2:04.92
1976	Kornelia Ender	GDR	1:59.26	Shirley Babashoff	USA	2:01.22	Enith Brigitha	NED	2:01.40
1980	Barbara Krause	GDR	1:58.33	Ines Diers	GDR	1:59.64	Carmela Schmidt	GDR	2:01.44
1984	Mary Wayte	USA	1:59.23	Cynthia Woodhead	USA	1:59.50	Annemarie Verstappen	NED	1:59.69
1988	Heike Friedrich	GDR	1:57.65	Silvia Poll	CRC	1:58.67	Manuela Stellmach	GDR	1:59.01
1992	Nicole Haislett	USA	1:57.90	Franziska Van Almsick	GER	1:58.00	Kerstin Kielgass	GER	1:59.67
1996									

400m Freestyle

Year	Gold	C'ntry	Time	Silver	C'ntry	Time	Bronze	C'ntry	Time
1920[8]	Ethelda Bleibtrey	USA	4:34.0	Margaret Woodbridge	USA	4:42.8	Frances Schroth	USA	4:52.0
1924	Martha Norelius	USA	6:02.2	Helen Wainwright	USA	6:03.8	Gertrude Ederle	USA	6:04.8
1928	Martha Norelius	USA	5:42.8	Maria Braun	NED	5:57.8	Josephine McKim	USA	6:00.2
1932	Helene Madison	USA	5:28.5	Lenore Kight	USA	5:28.6	Jenny Maakal	SAF	5:47.3
1936	Hendrika Mastenbroek	NED	5:26.4	Ragnhild Hveger	DEN	5:27.5	Lenore Wingard	USA	not recorded
1948	Ann Curtis	USA	5:17.8	Karen-Margrethe Harup	DEN	5:21.2	Catherine Gibson	GBR	5:22.5
1952	Valéria Gyenge	HUN	5:12.1	Éva Novák	HUN	5:13.7	Evelyn Kawamoto	USA	5:14.6
1956	Lorraine Crapp	AUS	4:54.6	Dawn Fraser	AUS	5:02.5	Sylvia Ruuska	USA	5:07.1
1960	Susan Christina Von Saltza	USA	4:50.6	Jane Cederqvist	SWE	4:53.9	Catharina Lagerberg	NED	4:56.9
1964	Virginia Duenkel	USA	4:43.3	Marilyn Rmaenofsky	USA	4:44.6	Terri Lee Stickles	USA	4:47.2
1968	Debbie Meyer	USA	4:31.8	Linda Gustavson	USA	4:35.5	Karen Moras	AUS	4:37.0
1972	Shane Gould	AUS	4:19.04	Novella Calligaris	ITA	4:22.44	Gudrun Wegner	GDR	4:23.11
1976	Petra Thümer	GDR	4:09.89	Shirley Babashoff	USA	4:10.46	Shannon Smith	CAN	4:14.60
1980	Ines Diers	GDR	4:08.76	Petra Schneider	GDR	4:09.16	Carmela Schmidt	GDR	4:10.86
1984	Tiffany Cohen	USA	4:07.10	Sarah Hardcastle	GBR	4:10.27	June Croft	GBR	4:11.49
1988	Janet Evans	USA	4:03.85	Heike Friedrich	GDR	4:05.94	Anke Moehring	GDR	4:06.62
1992	Dagmar Hase	GER	4:07.18	Janet Evans	USA	4:07.37	Hayley Lewis	AUS	4:11.22
1996									

[8] 300 metres

800m Freestyle

Year	Gold	C'ntry	Time	Silver	C'ntry	Time	Bronze	C'ntry	Time
1968	Debbie Meyer	USA	9:24.0	Pamela Kruse	USA	9:35.7	Teresa Ramírez	MEX	9:38.5
1972	Keena Rothhammer	USA	8:53.68	Shane Gould	AUS	8:56.39	Novella Calligaris	ITA	8:57.46
1976	Petra Thümer	GDR	8:37.14	Shirley Babashoff	USA	8:37.59	Wendy Weinberg	USA	8:42.60
1980	Michelle Ford	AUS	8:28.90	Ines Diers	GDR	8:32.55	Heike Dähne	GDR	8:33.48
1984	Tiffany Cohen	USA	8:24.95	Michele Richardson	USA	8:30.73	Sarah Hardcastle	GBR	8:32.60
1988	Janet Evans	USA	8:20.20	Astrid Strauss	GDR	8:22.09	Julie Mcdonald	AUS	8:22.93
1992	Janet Evans	USA	8:25.52	Hayley Lewis	AUS	8:30.34	Jana Henke	GER	8:30.99
1996									

100m Backstroke

Year	Gold	C'ntry	Time	Silver	C'ntry	Time	Bronze	C'ntry	Time
1924	Sybil Bauer	USA	1:23.2	Phyllis Harding	GBR	1:27.4	Aileen Riggin	USA	1:28.2
1928	Maria Braun	NED	1:22.0	Ellen King	GBR	1:22.2	Margaret Cooper	GBR	1:22.8
1932	Eleanor Holm	USA	1:19.4	Philomena Mealing	AUS	1:21.3	Elizabeth Davies	GBR	1:22.5
1936	Dina Senff	HOL	1:18.9	Hendrika Mastenbroek	NED	1:19.2	Alice Bridges	USA	1:19.4
1948	Karen-Margrete Harup	DEN	1:14.4	Suzanne Zimmerman	USA	1:16.0	Judith Davies	AUS	1:16.7
1952	Joan Harrison	SAF	1:14.3	Geertje Wielema	NED	1:14.5	Jean Stewart	NZL	1:15.8
1956	Judith Grinham	GBR	1:12.9	Carla Cone	USA	1:12.9	Margaret Edwards	GBR	1:13.1

Year	Gold	C'ntry	Time	Silver	C'ntry	Time	Bronze	C'ntry	Time
1960	Lynn Burke	USA	1:09.3	Natalie Steward	GBR	1:10.8	Satoko Tanaka	JPN	1:11.4
1964	Cathy Ferguson	USA	1:07.7	Christine Caron	FRA	1:07.9	Virginia Duenkel	USA	1:08.0
1968	Kaye Hall	USA	1:06.2	Elaine Tanner	CAN	1:06.7	Jane Swagerty	USA	1:08.1
1972	Melissa Belote	USA	1:05.78	Andrea Gyarmati	HUN	1:06.26	Susan Atwood	USA	1:06.34
1976	Ulrike Richter	GDR	1:01.83	Birgit Treiber	GDR	1:03.41	Nancy Garapick	CAN	1:03.71
1980	Rica Reinisch	GDR	1:00.86	Ina Kleber	GDR	1:02.07	Petra Riedel	GDR	1:02.64
1984	Theresa Andrews	USA	1:02.55	Betsy Mitchell	USA	1:02.63	Jolanda De Rover	NED	1:02.91
1988	Kristin Otto	GDR	1:00.89	Krisztina Egerszegi	HUN	1:01.56	Cornelia Sirch	GDR	1:01.57
1992	Krisztina Egerszegi	HUN	1:00.68	Tünde Szabó	HUN	1:01.14	Lea Loveless	USA	1:01.43
1996									

200m Backstroke

Year	Gold	C'ntry	Time	Silver	C'ntry	Time	Bronze	C'ntry	Time
1968	Pokey Watson	USA	2:24.8	Elaine Tanner	CAN	2:27.4	Kaye Hall	USA	2:28.9
1972	Melissa Belote	USA	2:19.19	Susan Atwood	USA	2:20.38	Donna Marie Gurr	CAN	2:23.22
1976	Ulrike Richter	GDR	2:13.43	Birgit Treiber	GDR	2:14.97	Nancy Garapick	CAN	2:15.60
1980	Rica Reinisch	GDR	2:11.77	Cornelia Polit	GDR	2:13.75	Birgit Treiber	GDR	2:14.14
1984	Jolanda De Rover	NED	2:12.38	Amy White	USA	2:13.04	Aneta Patrascoiu	ROM	2:13.29
1988	Krisztina Egerszegi	HUN	2:09.29	Kathrin Zimmermann	GDR	2:10.61	Cornelia Sirch	GDR	2:11.45
1992	Krisztina Egerszegi	HUN	2:07.06	Dagmar Hase	GER	2:09.46	Nicole Stevenson	AUS	2:10.20
1996									

100m Breaststroke

Year	Gold	C'ntry	Time	Silver	C'ntry	Time	Bronze	C'ntry	Time
1968	Djurdjica Bjedov	YUG	1:15.8	Galina Prosumenschikova-Stepanova	URS	1:15.9	Sharon Wichmann	USA	1:16.1
1972	Cathy Carr	USA	1:13.58	Galina Prosumenschikova-Stepanova	URS	1:14.99	Beverley Whitfield	AUS	1:15.73
1976	Anka Hannelore	GDR	1:11.16	Liubov Rusanova	URS	1:13.04	Marina Koshevaia	URS	1:13.30
1980	Ute Geweniger	GDR	1:10.22	Elvira Vasilkova	URS	1:10.41	Susanne Schultz Nielsson	DEN	1:11.16
1984	Petra Van Staveren	NED	1:09.88	Anne Ottenbrite	CAN	1:10.69	Cathérine Poirot	FRA	1:10.70
1988	Tania Dangalakova	BUL	1:07.95	Antojaneta Frenkeva	BUL	1:08.74	Silke Hoerner	GDR	1:08.83
1992	Elena Rudskovskaia	EUN	1:08.00	Anita Nall	USA	1:08.17	Samantha Riley	AUS	1:09.25
1996									

200m Breaststroke

Year	Gold	C'ntry	Time	Silver	C'ntry	Time	Bronze	C'ntry	Time
1924	Lucy Morton	GBR	3:33.2	Agnes Geraghty	USA	3:34.0	Gladys Carson	GBR	3:35.4
1928	Hilde Shroder	GER	3:12.6	Mietje Baron	NED	3:15.2	Lotte Mühe	GER	3:17.6
1932	Claire Dennis	AUS	3:06.3	Hideko Maehata	JPN	3:06.4	Else Jacobsen	DEN	3:07.1
1936	Hideko Maehata	JPN	3:03.6	Martha Genenger	GER	3:04.2	Inge Sørensen	DEN	3:07.8
1948	Petronella van Vliet	NED	2:57.2	Beatrice Lyons	AUS	2:57.7	Éva Novák	HUN	3:00.2
1952	Éva Székely	HUN	2:51.7	Éva Novák	HUN	2:54.4	Helen Gordon	GBR	2:57.6
1956	Ursula Happe	GER	2:53.1	Éva Székely	HUN	2:54.8	Eva-Maria Ten Elsen	GER	2:55.1
1960	Anita Lonsbrough	GBR	2:49.5	Wiltrud Urselmann	GER	2:50.0	Barbara Göbel	GER	2:53.6
1964	Galina Prosumenschikova-Stepanova	URS	2:46.4	Claudia Kolb	USA	2:47.6	Svetlana Babanina	URS	2:48.6
1968	Sharon Wichmann	USA	2:44.4	Djurdjica Bjedov	YUG	2:46.4	Galina Prosumenschikova-Stepanova	URS	2:47.0
1972	Beverley Whitfield	AUS	2:41.71	Dana Schoenfield	USA	2:42.05	Galina Prosumenschikova-Stepanova	URS	2:42.36
1976	Marina Koshevaia	URS	2:33.35	Marina Iurchenia	URS	2:36.08	Liubov Rusanova	URS	2:36.22
1980	Lina Kochushite	URS	2:29.54	Svetlana Varganova	URS	2:29.61	Yulia Bogdanova	URS	2:32.39
1984	Anne Ottenbrite	CAN	2:30.38	Susan Rapp	USA	2:31.15	Ingrid Lempereur	BEL	2:31.40
1988	Silke Hoerner	GDR	2:26.71	Huang Xiaomin	CHN	2:27.49	Antoaneta Frenkeva	BUL	2:28.34
1992	Kyoko Iwasaki	JPN	2:26.65	Li Lin	CHN	2:26.85	Anita Nall	USA	2:26.88
1996									

100m Butterfly

Year	Gold	C'ntry	Time	Silver	C'ntry	Time	Bronze	C'ntry	Time
1956	Shelley Mann	USA	1:11.0	Nancy Ramey	USA	1:11.9	Mary Sears	USA	1:14.4
1960	Carolyn Schuler	USA	1:09.6	Marianne Heemskerk	NED	1:10.4	Janice Andrew	AUS	1:10.2
1964	Sharon Stouder	USA	1:04.7	Ada Kok	NED	1:05.6	Kathleen Ellis	USA	1:06.0
1968	Lynette McClements	AUS	1:05.5	Ellie Daniel	USA	1:05.8	Susie Shields	USA	1:06.2
1972	Mayumi Aoki	JPN	1:03.34	Roswitha Beyer	GDR	1:03.61	Andréa Gyarmati	HUN	1:03.73
1976	Kornelia Ender	GDR	1:00.13	Andrea Pollack	GDR	1:00.98	Wendy Boglioli	USA	1:01.17
1980	Caren Metschuck	GDR	1:00.42	Andrea Pollack	GDR	1:00.90	Christiane Knacke	GDR	1:01.44
1984	Mary T Meagher	USA	0:59.26	Jenna Johnson	USA	1:00.19	Karin Seick	FRG	1:01.36

/continued on next page 379

Year	Gold	C'ntry	Time	Silver	C'ntry	Time	Bronze	C'ntry	Time
1988	Kristin Otto	GDR	0:59.00	Birte Weigang	GDR	0:59.45	Qian Hong	CHN	0:59.52
1992	Qian Hong	CHN	0:58.62	Christine Ahmann-Leighton	USA	0:58.74	Cathérine Plewinski	FRA	0:59.01
1996									

200m Butterfly

Year	Gold	C'ntry	Time	Silver	C'ntry	Time	Bronze	C'ntry	Time
1968	Aagje Kok	NED	2:24.7	Helga Lindner	GDR	2:24.8	Ellie Daniel	USA	2:25.9
1972	Karen Moe	USA	2:15.57	Lynn Colella	USA	2:16.34	Ellie Daniel	USA	2:16.74
1976	Andrea Pollack	GDR	2:11.41	Ulrike Tauber	GDR	2:12.50	Rosemarie Garbriel	GDR	2:12.86
1980	Ines Geissler	GDR	2:10.44	Sybille Schönrock	GDR	2:10.45	Michelle Ford	AUS	2:11.66
1984	Mary T Meagher	USA	2:06.90	Karen Phillips	AUS	2:10.56	Ina Beyermann	FRG	2:11.91
1988	Kathleen Nord	GDR	2:09.51	Birte Weigang	GDR	2:09.91	Mary T Meagher	USA	2:10.80
1992	Summer Sanders	USA	2:08.67	Wang Xiaohong	CHN	2:09.01	Susan O'Neil	AUS	2:09.03
1996									

200m Individual Medley

Year	Gold	C'ntry	Time	Silver	C'ntry	Time	Bronze	C'ntry	Time
1968	Claudia Kolb	USA	2:24.7	Susan Pedersen	USA	2:28.8	Jan Henne	USA	2:31.4
1972	Shane Gould	AUS	2:23.07	Kornelia Ender	GDR	2:23.59	Lynn Vidali	USA	2:24.06
1976	not held								
1980	not held								
1984	Tracy Caulkins	USA	2:12.64	Nancy Hogshead	USA	2:15.17	Michele Pearson	AUS	2:15.92
1988	Daniela Hunger	GDR	2:12.59	Elena Dendeberova	URS	2:13.31	Noemi Ildiko Lung	ROM	2:14.85
1992	Li Lin	CHN	2:11.65	Summer Sanders	USA	2:11.91	Daniela Hunger	GER	2:13.92
1996									

400m Individual Medley

Year	Gold	C'ntry	Time	Silver	C'ntry	Time	Bronze	C'ntry	Time
1964	Donna De Varona	USA	5:18.7	Sharon Evans Finneran	USA	5:24.1	Martha Randall	USA	5:24.2
1968	Claudia Kolb	USA	5:08.5	Lynn Vidali	USA	5:22.2	Sabine Steinbach	GDR	5:25.3
1972	Gail Neal	AUS	5:02.97	Leslie Cliff	CAN	5:03.57	Novella Calligaris	ITA	5:03.99
1976	Ulrike Tauber	GDR	4:42.77	Cheryl Gibson	CAN	4:48.10	Becky Smith	CAN	4:50.48
1980	Petra Schneider	GDR	4:36.29	Sharron Davies	GBR	4:46.83	Agnieszka Czopek	POL	4:48.17
1984	Tracy Caulkins	USA	4:39.24	Suzanne Landells	AUS	4:48.30	Petra Zindler	FRG	4:48.57
1988	Janet Evans	USA	4:37.76	Noemi Ildiko Lung	ROM	4:39.46	Daniela Hunger	GDR	4:39.76
1992	Krisztina Egerszegi	HUN	4:36.54	Li Lin	CHN	4:36.73	Summer Sanders	USA	4:37.58
1996									

4 x 100m Medley Relay

Year	Gold	C'ntry	Time	Silver	C'ntry	Time	Bronze	C'ntry	Time
1960	Lynn Burke, Patricia Kempner, Carolyn Schuler, Susan Christina Von Saltza	USA	4:41.1	Maryleen Wilson, Rosemary Lassig, Janice Andrew, Dawn Fraser	AUS	4:45.9	Ingrid Schmidt, Ursula Küper, Bärbel Fuhrmann, Ursula Brunner	GER	4:47.6
1964	Cathy Ferguson, Cynthia Goyette, Sharon Stouder, Kathleen Ellis	USA	4:33.9	Kornelia Winkel, Clena Bimolt, Ada Kok, Erica Terpstra	NED	4:37.0	Tatiana Savelieva, Svetlana Babanina, Tatiana Deviatova, Natalia Ustinova	URS	4:39.2
1968	Kaye Hall, Catie Ball, Ellie Daniel, Susan Pedersen	USA	4:28.3	Lynette Watson, Lynette McClements, Judy Playfair, Janet Steinbeck	AUS	4:30.0	Angelika Kraus, Uta Frommater, Heike Hustede, Heidi Reineck	FRG	4:36.4
1972	Melissa Belote, Catherine Carr, Deena Deardruff, Sandra Neilson	USA	4:20.75	Christine Herbst, Renate Vogel, Roswitha Beyer, Kornelia Ender	GDR	4:24.91	Silke Pielen, Verena Eberle, Gudrun Beckmann, Heidi Reineck	FRG	4:26.46
1976	Ulrike Richter, Anke Hannelore, Andrea Pollack, Kornelia Ender	GDR	4:07.95	Linda Jezek, Lauri Siering, Camille Wright, Shirley Babashoff	USA	4:14.55	Wendy Hogg, Robin Corsiglia, Susan Sloan, Anne Jardin	CAN	4:15.22
1980	Rica Reinisch, Ute Geweniger, Andrea Pollack, Caren Metschuck	GDR	4:06.67	Helen Jameson, Margaret Kelly, Ann Osgerby, June Croft	GBR	4:12.24	Elena Kruglova, Elvira Vasilkova, Alla Grishchenkova, Natalia Strunnikova	URS	4:13.61
1984	Theresa Andrews, Tracy Caulkins, Mary T Meagher, Nancy Hogshead	USA	4:08.34	Svenja Schlicht, Ute Hasse, Ina Beyermann, Karin Seick	FRG	4:11.97	Reema Abdo, Anne Ottenbrite, Michelle MacPherson, Pamela Rai	CAN	4:12.98

Year	Gold	C'ntry	Time	Silver	C'ntry	Time	Bronze	C'ntry	Time
1988	Kristin Otto Silke Hoerner Birte Weigang Katrin Meissner	GDR	4:03.74	Beth Barr Tracey Mcfarlane Janel Jorgensen Mary Wayte	USA	4:07.90	Lori Melien Allison Higson Jane Kerr Andrea Nugent	CAN	4:10.49
1992	Lea Loveless Anita Nall Christine Ahmann-Leighton Jennifer Thompson	USA	4:02.54	Dagmar Hase Jana Doerries Franziska Van Almsick Daniela Hunger	GER	4:05.19	Nina Jivanevskaia Elena Roudkovskaia Olga Kiritchenko Natalia Mechtcheriakova	EUN	4:06.44
1996									

4 x 100m Freestyle Relay

Year	Gold	C'ntry	Time	Silver	C'ntry	Time	Bronze	C'ntry	Time
1912	Isabella Moore Jennie Fletcher Anny Speirs Irene Steer	GBR	5:52.8	Wally Dressel Louise Otto Hermine Stindt Grete Rosenberg	GER	6:04.6	Margarete Adler Klara Milch Josefine Sticker Bertha Zahourek	AUT	6:17.0
1920	Margaret Woodbridge Frances Schroth Irene Guest Ethelda Bleibtrey	USA	5:11.6	Hilda James Constance Mabel Jeans Charlotte Radcliffe Grace McKenzie	GBR	5:40.6	Aina Berg Emily Machnow Carin Nilsson Jane Gylling	SWE	5:43.6
1924	Gertrude Ederle Euphrasia Donnolly Ethel Lackie Mariechen Wehselau	USA	4:58.8	Florence Barker Grace McKenzie Irene Tanner Constance Mabel Jeans	GBR	5:17.0	Aina Berg Wivan Pettersson Gurli Ewerlund Hjördis Töpel	SWE	5:35.6
1928	Adelaide Lambert Eleanor Garatti-Saville Albina Osipowich Martha Norelius	USA	4:47.6	Margaret Cooper Sarah Stewart Irene Tanner Ellen King	GBR	5:02.8	Kathleen Russell Rhoda Rennie Marie Bedford Frederica van der Goes	SAF	5:13.4
1932	Josephine McKim Helen Johns Eleanor Saville Helene Madison	USA	4:38.0	Maria Vierdag Maria Oversloot Cornelia Laddé Willemijntje den Ouden	NED	4:47.5	Elizabeth Davies Helen Varcoe Margaret Cooper Edna Hughes	GBR	4:52.4
1936	Johanna Selbach Catherina Wagner Willemijntje den Ouden Hendrika Mastenbroek	NED	4:36.0	Ruth Halbsguth Leni Lohmar Ingeborg Schmitz Gisela Arendt	GER	4:36.8	Katherine Rawls Bernice Lapp Mavis Freeman Olive McKean	USA	4:40.2
1948	Marie Corridon Thelma Kalama Brenda Helser Ann Curtis	USA	4:29.2	Eva Riise Karen Margrethe Harup Greta Andersen Fritze Carstensen	DEN	4:29.6	Irma Schumacher Margot Marsman Marie-Louise Vaessen Johanna Termeulen	NED	4:31.6
1952	Ilona Novák Judit Temes Éva Novák Katalin Szöke	HUN	4:24.4	Marie-Louise Linssen-Vaessen Koosje van Voorn Johanna Termeulen Irma Heijting-Schuhmacher	NED	4:29.0	Jacqueline La Vine Mary Louise Stepan Joan Alderson-Rosazza Evelyn Kawamoto	USA	4:30.1
1956	Dawn Fraser Faith Leech Sandra Morgan Lorraine Crapp	AUS	4:17.1	Sylvia Ruuska Shelley Mann Nancy Simons Joan Alderson-Rosazza	USA	4:19.2	Jeanette Myburgh Susan Roberts Natalie Myburgh Moira Abernethy	SAF	4:25.7
1960	Joan Spillane Shirley Stobs Carolyn Wood Susan Christina Von Saltza	USA	4:08.9	Dawn Fraser Ilsa Konrads Lorraine Crapp Alva Colquhoun	AUS	4:11.3	Christel Steffin Heidi Pechstein Gisela Weiss Ursula Brunner	GER	4:19.7
1964	Sharon Stouder Donna De Varona Lillian Watson Kathleen Ellis	USA	4:03.8	Robyn Thorn Janice Murphy Lynette Bell Dawn Fraser	AUS	4:06.9	Paulina van der Wildt Catharina Beumer Wilhelmina van Weerdenburg Erica Terpstra	NED	4:12.0

/continued on next page

Year	Gold	C'ntry	Points	Silver	C'ntry	Points	Bronze	C'ntry	Points
1968	Jane Barkman Linda Gustavson Susan Pedersen Jan Henne	USA	4:02.5	Gabriele Wetzko Roswitha Krause Uta Schumck Martina Grunert	GDR	4:05.7	Angela Coughlaw Marilyn Corson Elaine Tanner Marion Lay	CAN	4:07.2
1972	Sandra Neilson Jennifer Kempf Jane Barkman Shirley Babashoff	USA	3:55.19	Gabriele Wetzko Andrea Eife Elke Sehmisch Kornelia Ender	GDR	3:55.55	Jutta Weber Heidemarie Reineck Gudrun Beckmann Angela Steinbach	FRG	3:57.93
1976	Kim Peyton Wendy Boglioli Jill Sterkel Shirly Babashoff	USA	3:44.82	Kornelia Ender Petra Priemer Andrea Pollack Claudia Hempel	GDR	3:45.50	Gail Amundrud Barbara Clark Becky Smith Anne Jardin	CAN	3:48.81
1980	Barbara Krause Caren Metschuck Ines Diers Sarina Hülsenbeck	GDR	3:42.71	Carina Ljungdahl Tina Gustafsson Agneta Mårtensson Agneta Eriksson	SWE	3:48.93	Cornelia van Bentum Wilma van Velsen Reggie de Jong Annelies Maas	NED	3:49.51
1984	Jenna Johnson Carrie Steinseifer Dara Torres Nancy Hogshead	USA	3:43.43	Annemarie Verstappen Elles Voskes Desi Reijers Connie Van Bentum	NED	3:44.40	Iris Zscherpe Susanne Schuster Christine Pielke Karin Seick	FRG	3:45.56
1988	Kristin Otto Katrin Meissner Daniela Hunger Manuela Stellmach	GDR	3:40.63	Marianne Muis Mildred Muis Connie Van Bentum Karin Brienesse	NED	3:43.39	Mary Wayte Mitzi Kremer Laura Walker Dara Torres	USA	3:44.25
1992	Dara Torres Jennifer Thompson Angel Martino Nicole Haislett	USA	3:39.46	Zhuang Yong Yang Wenyi Lu Bin Le Jingyi	CHN	3:40.12	Franziska Van Almsick Manuela Stellmach Simone Osygus Daniela Hunger	GER	3:41.60
1996									

4 x 200m Freestyle Relay

1996

SYNCHRONIZED SWIMMING (Women)

Year	Gold	C'ntry	Points	Silver	C'ntry	Points	Bronze	C'ntry	Points

Synchronized Team

1996

DIVING (Men)

Year	Gold	C'ntry	Points	Silver	C'ntry	Points	Bronze	C'ntry	Points

Springboard Diving

Year	Gold	C'ntry	Points	Silver	C'ntry	Points	Bronze	C'ntry	Points
1908	Albert Zürner	GER	85.5	Kurt Behrens	GER	85.3	George Gaidzik	USA	80.8
1912	Paul Günther	GER	79.23	Hans Luber	GER	76.78	Kurt Behrens	GER	73.73
1920	Louis Kuehn	USA	675.4	Clarence Pinkston	USA	655.3	Louis Balbach	USA	649.5
1924	Albert White	USA	696.4	Ulise Joseph Desjardins	USA	693.2	Clarence Pinkston	USA	653.0
1928	Ulise Joseph Desjardins	USA	185.04	Michael Galitzen	USA	174.06	Farid Simaika	EGY	172.46
1932	Michael Galitzen	USA	161.38	Harold Smith	USA	158.54	Richard Degener	USA	151.82
1936	Dick Degener	USA	163.57	Marshall Wayne	USA	159.56	Al Greene	USA	146.29
1948	Bruce Harlan	USA	163.64	Miller Anderson	USA	157.29	Samuel Lee	USA	145.52
1952	David Browning	USA	205.29	Miller Anderson	USA	199.84	Robert Clotworthy	USA	184.92
1956	Robert Clotworthy	USA	159.56	Donald Harper	USA	156.23	Joaquin Capilla Pérez	MEX	150.69
1960	Gary Tobian	USA	170.00	Samuel Hall	USA	167.08	Juan Botella	MEX	162.3
1964	Kenneth Sitzberger	USA	159.9	Francis Xavier Gorman	USA	157.63	Lawrence Edwin Andreasen	USA	143.77
1968	Bernard Wrightson	USA	170.15	Klaus Dibiasi	ITA	159.94	James Henry	USA	158.09
1972	Vladimir Vasin	URS	594.09	Franco Cagnotto	ITA	591.63	Craig Lincoln	USA	577.29

Year	Gold	C'ntry	Points	Silver	C'ntry	Points	Bronze	C'ntry	Points
1976	Philip Boggs	USA	619.05	Franco Cagnotto	ITA	570.48	Alexander Kosenkov	URS	567.24
1980	Alexander Portnov	URS	905.025	Carlos Giron	MEX	892.14	Franco Cagnotto	ITA	871.5
1984	Gregory Louganis	USA	754.41	Tan Liangde	CHN	662.31	Ronald Merriott	USA	661.32
1988	Gregory Louganis	USA	730.80	Tan Liangde	CHN	704.88	Li Deliang	CHN	665.28
1992	Mark Lenzi	USA	676.53	Tan Liangde	CHN	645.57	Dmitri Saoutine	EUN	627.78
1996									

Platform Diving

Year	Gold	C'ntry	Points	Silver	C'ntry	Points	Bronze	C'ntry	Points
1904	George Sheldon	USA	12.66	Georg Hoffmann	GER	11.66	Francis Kehoe	USA	11.33
1908	Hjalmar Johansson	SWE	83.75	Karl Malmström	SWE	78.73	Arvid Spångberg	SWE	74.00
1912	Erik Adlerz	SWE	73.94	Albert Zürner	GER	72.6	Gustaf Blomgren	SWE	69.56
1920	Clarence Pinkston	USA	100.67	Erik Adlerz	SWE	99.08	Harry Prieste	USA	93.73
1924	Albert White	USA	97.46	David Fall	USA	97.3	Clarence Pinkston	USA	94.6
1928	Ulise Joseph DesJardins	USA	98.74	Farid Simaika	EGY	99.58	Michael Galitzen	USA	92.34
1932	Harold Smith	USA	124.8	Michael Galitzen	USA	124.28	Frank Kurtz	USA	121.98
1936	Marshall Wayne	USA	113.58	Elbert Root	USA	110.6	Hermann Stork	GER	110.31
1948	Samuel Lee	USA	130.05	Bruce Harlan	USA	122.3	Joaquin Capilla Pérez	MEX	113.52
1952	Samuel Lee	USA	156.28	Joaquin Capilla Pérez	MEX	145.21	Günther Haase	GER	141.31
1956	Joaquin Capilla Pérez	MEX	152.44	Gary Tobian	USA	152.41	Richard Connor	USA	149.79
1960	Robert Webster	USA	165.56	Gary Tobian	USA	165.25	Brian Phelps	GBR	157.13
1964	Robert Webster	USA	148.58	Klaus Dibiasi	ITA	147.54	Thomas Gompf	USA	146.57
1968	Klaus Dibiasi	ITA	164.18	Alvaro Gaxiola	MEX	154.49	Edwin Young	USA	153.93
1972	Klaus Dibiasi	ITA	504.12	Richard Rydze	USA	480.75	Franco Cagnotto	ITA	475.83
1976	Klaus Dibiasi	ITA	600.51	Gregory Louganis	USA	576.99	Vladimir Aleynik	URS	548.61
1980	Falk Hoffmann	GDR	835.65	Vladimir Aleinik	URS	819.705	David Ambartsumian	URS	817.44
1984	Gregory Louganis	USA	710.91	Bruce Kimball	USA	643.5	Li Kongzheng	CHN	638.28
1988	Gregory Louganis	USA	638.61	Xiong Ni	CHN	637.47	Jesús Mena	MEX	594.39
1992	Sun Shuwei	CHN	677.31	Scott Donie	USA	633.63	Xiong Ni	CHN	600.15
1996									

DIVING (Women)

Year	Gold	C'ntry	Points	Silver	C'ntry	Points	Bronze	C'ntry	Points

Springboard Diving

Year	Gold	C'ntry	Points	Silver	C'ntry	Points	Bronze	C'ntry	Points
1920	Aileen Riggin	USA	539.9	Helen Wainwright	USA	534.8	Thelma Payne	USA	534.1
1924	Elizabeth Becker-Pinkton	USA	474.5	Aileen Riggin	USA	460.4	Caroline Fletcher	USA	436.4
1928	Helen Meany	USA	78.62	Georgia Coleman	USA	73.38	Dorothy Poynton-Hill	USA	75.62
1932	Georgia Coleman	USA	87.52	Katherine Rawls	USA	82.56	Jane Fauntz	USA	82.12
1936	Marjorie Gestring	USA	89.27	Katherine Rawls	USA	88.35	Dorothy Poynton-Hill	USA	82.36
1948	Victoria Draves	USA	108.74	Zoe-Ann Olsen-Jensen	USA	108.23	Patricia Elsener	USA	101.3
1952	Patricia McCormick	USA	147.3	Mady Moreau	FRA	139.34	Zoe-Ann Olsen-Jensen	USA	127.57
1956	Patricia McCormick	USA	142.36	Jeannie Stunyo	USA	125.89	Irene MacDonald	CAN	121.4
1960	Ingrid Krämer-Engel-Gulbin	GER	155.81	Paula Myers-Pope	USA	141.24	Elizabeth Ferris	GBR	139.09
1964	Ingrid Krämer-Engel-Gulbin	GER	145.00	Jeanne Collier	USA	138.36	Mary Willard	USA	138.18
1968	Sue Gossick	USA	150.77	Tamara Pogozheva	URS	145.3	Keala O'Sullivan	USA	145.23
1972	Micki King	USA	450.03	Ulrika Knape	SWE	434.19	Marina Janicke	GDR	430.92
1976	Jennifer Chandler	USA	506.19	Christa Köhler	GDR	469.41	Cynthia McIngvale	USA	466.83
1980	Irina Kalinina	URS	725.91	Martina Proeber	GDR	698.895	Karin Guthke	GDR	685.245
1984	Sylvie Bernier	CAN	530.7	Kelly McCormick	USA	527.46	Christina Seufert	USA	517.62
1988	Gao Min	CHN	580.23	Li Qing	CHN	534.33	Kelly McCormick	USA	533.19
1992	Gao Min	CHN	572.40	Irina Lachko	EUN	514.14	Brita Baldus	GER	503.07
1996									

Platform Diving

Year	Gold	C'ntry	Points	Silver	C'ntry	Points	Bronze	C'ntry	Points
1912	Gerda Johansson	SWE	39.9	Lisa Regnell	SWE	36	Isobel White	GBR	34
1920	Anna Stefanie Nanny Clausen	DEN	34.6	Eileen Armstrong	GBR	33.3	Eva Olliwier	SWE	33.3
1924	Caroline Smith	USA	33.2	Elizabeth Becker-Pinkton	USA	33.4	Hjördis Töpel	SWE	32.8

/continued on next page

Year	Gold	C'ntry	Points	Silver	C'ntry	Points	Bronze	C'ntry	Points
1928	Elizabeth Becker-Pinkton	USA	31.6	Georgia Coleman	USA	30.6	Laura Sjöquist	SWE	29.2
1932	Dorothy Poynton	USA	40.26	Georgia Coleman	USA	35.56	Marion Roper	USA	35.22
1936	Dorothy Poynton-Hill	USA	33.93	Velma Dunn	USA	33.63	Kate Köhler	GER	33.43
1948	Victoria Draves	USA	68.87	Patricia Elsener	USA	66.28	Birte Christoffersen	DEN	66.04
1952	Patricia McCormick	USA	79.37	Paula Myers-Pope	USA	71.63	Juno Irvin	USA	70.49
1956	Patricia McCormick	USA	84.85	Juno Irwin	USA	81.64	Paula Myers-Pope	USA	81.58
1960	Ingrid Krämer-Engel-Gulbin	GER	91.28	Paula Myers-Pope	USA	89.94	Ninelia Krutova	URS	86.99
1964	Lesley Leigh Bush	USA	99.8	Ingrid Engel-Krämer	GER	98.45	Galina Alekseeva	URS	97.6
1968	Milena Duchková	TCH	109.59	Natalia Lobanoa	URS	105.14	Ann Peterson	USA	101.11
1972	Ulrika Knape	SWE	390	Milena Duchková	TCH	370.92	Marina Janicke	GDR	360.54
1976	Elena Vaytsekhovskaia	URS	406.59	Ulrika Knape	SWE	402.6	Deborah Wilson	USA	401.07
1980	Martina Jäschke	GDR	596.25	Servard Emirzian	URS	576.465	Liana Tsotadze	URS	575.92
1984	Zhou Jihong	CHN	435.51	Michele Mitchell	USA	431.19	Wendy Wyland	USA	422.07
1988	Xu Yanmei	CHN	445.20	Michele Mitchell	USA	436.95	Wendy Williams	USA	400.44
1992	Fu Mingxia	CHN	461.43	Elena Mirochina	EUN	411.63	Mary Ellen Clark	USA	401.91
1996									

WATERPOLO

Year	Gold	C'ntry	Score	Silver	C'ntry	Bronze	C'ntry
1900	Thomas Coe	GBR	7-2	Henri Cohen	BEL	Thomas Burgess	FRA
	John Derbyshire			Jean de Backer		Alphonse de Cuyper	
	Peter Kemp			Victor de Behr		Devenot	
	William Lister			Fernand Feyaerts		Louis Lauffray	
	Arthur Robertson			Oscar Grégoire		Henri Peslier	
	Eric Robinson			Albert Michant		Pesloy	
	George Wilkinson			Victor Sonnemans		Paul Vasseur	
1904	David Bratton	USA		Rex Beach	USA	Gwynne Evans	USA
	Leo Goodwin			David Hammond		Augustus Goessling	
	Louis Handley			Charles Healy		John Meyers	
	David Hesser			Frank Kehoe		William Orthwein	
	Joseph Ruddy			Jerome Steever		Amedee Reyburn	
	James Steen			Edwin Swatek		Fred Schreiner	
	George van Cleaf			William Tuttle		Manfred Toeppen	
1908	George Cornet	GBR	9-2	Victor Boin	BEL	Robert Andersson	SWE
	Charles Forsyth			Herman Donners		Erik Bergvall	
	George Nevinson			Fernand Feyaerts		Pontus Hanson	
	Paul Radmilovic			Oscar Grégoire		Harald Julin	
	Charles Smith			Herman Meyboom		Torsten Kumfeldt	
	Thomas Thould			Albert Michant		A Runstrom	
	George Wilkinson			Joseph Pletincx		Gunnar Wennerström	
1912	Isaac Bentham	GBR	8-0	Vilhelm Andersson	SWE	Victor Boin	BEL
	Charles Bugbee			Robert Andersson		Félicien Courbet	
	George Cornet			Erik Bergqvist		Herman Donners	
	Arthur Hill			Max Gumpel		Albert Durant	
	Paul Radmilovic			Pontus Hanson		Oscar Grégoire	
	Charles Smith			Harald Julin		Jean Hoffman	
	George Wilkinson			Torsten Kumfeldt		Herman Meyboom	
						Léon Pierre Nijs	
						Joseph Pletincx	
1920	Charles Bugbee	GBR	3-2	René Bauwens	BEL	Robert Andersson	SWE
	William Dean			Gérard Blitz		Vilhelm Andersson	
	Christopher Jones			Pierre Dewin		Erik Andersson	
	William Peacock			Albert Durant		Nils Backlund	
	Noel Purcell			Paul Gailly		Erik Bergqvist	
	Paul Radmilovic			Léon Pierre Nijs		Max Gumpel	
	Charles Smith			Joseph Pletincx		Pontus Hanson	
						Harald Julin	
						Theodor Nauman	
1924	Noë Delberghe	FRA	3-0	Gérard Blitz	BEL	Arthur Austin	USA
	Albert Delborgies			Joseph Cludts		Oliver Horn	
	Robert Desmettre			Joseph de Combe		Frederick Lauer	
	Paul Dujardin			Pierre Dewin		George Mitchell	
	Albert Mayaud			Albert Durant		John Norton	

Year	Gold	C'ntry	Score	Silver	C'ntry	Bronze	C'ntry
	Henri Padou			Georges Fleurix		James Wallace O'Connor	
	Georges Rigal			Paul Gailly		George Schroth	
				Joseph Pletincx		Herbert Vollmer	
				Jules Thiry		Peter John Weissmuller	
				Jean Pierre Vermetten			
1928	Max Amann	GER	5-2	István Barta	HUN	Emile Bulteel	FRA
	K Bahre			Olivér Halasy		Henri Cuvelier	
	Emil Benecke			Márton Homonnai		Paul Dujardin	
	Johann Blank			Sándor Ivády		Jules Keignaert	
	Otto Cordes			Alajos Keserű		Henri Padou	
	Fritz Gunst			Ferenc Keserű		Ernest Rogez	
	Erich Rademacher			József Vértesi		Albert Thévenon	
	Joachim Rademacher					Achille Tribouillet	
						Albert Van de Plancke	
1932	István Barta	HUN		Emil Benecke	GER	Austin Clapp	USA
	György Bródy			Otto Cordes		Philip Daubenspeck	
	Olivér Halasy			Hans Eckstein		Charles Finn	
	Márton Homonnai			Fritz Gunst		C Harold McAllister	
	Sándor Ivády			Erich Rademacher		Wallace O'Connor	
	Ferenc Keserű			Joachim Rademacher		F Calvert Strong	
	Alajos Keserű			Hans Schulze		Herbert Wildman	
	János Németh			Heiko Schwartz			
	Miklós Sárkány						
	József Vértesi						
1936	Mihály Bozsi	HUN	2-2	Bernhard Baier	GER	Gérard Blitz	BEL
	Jenő Brandé			Fritz Gunst		Albert Castelyns	
	György Bródy			Josef Hauser		Pierre Coppieters	
	Olivér Halasy			Fritz Kienzle		Joseph de Combe	
	Kálmán Hazai			Paul Kingenburg		Henri de Pauw	
	Márton Homonnai			Heinrich Krug		Henri Disy	
	György Kutosi			Hans Schneider		Fernand Isselé	
	István Molnár			Hans Schulze		Edmond Michiels	
	János Németh			Gustav Schürger		Henri Stoelen	
	Miklós Sárkány			Helmuth Schwenn			
	Sándor Tarics			Fritz Stolze			
1948	Ermenegildo Arena	ITA		Jenő Brandé	HUN	Cornelis Braasem	NED
	Emilio Bulgarelli			Oszkár Csuvik		Hendrikus Keetelaar	
	Pasquale Buonocore			Desző Fábián		Cornelis Korevaar	
	Aldo Ghira			Dezső Gyarmati		Johannes Rohner	
	Mario Maioni			Endre Győrffi		Albert Ruimschotel	
	Geminio Ognio			Miklós Hölöp		Pieter Salomons	
	Gianfranco Pandolfini			László Jenei		Frits Smol	
	Tullio Pandolfini			Dezső Lemhényi		Hans Stam	
	Cesare Rubini			Károly Szittya		Rudolph van Feggelen	
				István Szivós			
1952	Róbert Antal	HUN	2-2	Veljko Bakašun	YUG	Ermenegildo Arena	ITA
	Antal Bolvári			Marko Brainović		Lucio Ceccarini	
	Dezső Fábián			Vladimir Ivković		Renato de Sanzuane	
	Dezső Gyarmati			Zdravko Ježić		Raffaello Gambino	
	István Hasznos			Zdravko Kovačić		Salvatore Gionta	
	László Jenei			Ivo Kurtini		Maurizio Mannelli	
	György Kárpáti			Lovro Radonjić		Geminio Ognio	
	Dezső Lemhényi			Ivo Štakula		Carlo Peretti	
	Kálmán Markovits			Boško Vuksanović		Vincenzo Polito	
	Miklós Martin					Cesare Rubini	
	Károly Szittya					Renato Traiola	
	István Szivós						
	György Vizvári						
1956	Antal Bolvári	HUN	4-0	Ivo Cipci	YUG	Viktor Ageyev	URS
	Ottó Boros			Tomislav Franjković		Pyotr Breus	
	Dezső Gyarmati			Vladimir Ivković		Boris Goikhman	
	István Hevesi			Zdravko Ježić		Nodar Gyakharia	
	László Jenei			Horivoje Kačić		Viatcheslav Kurennoi	
	Tivadar Kanizsa			Zdravko Kovačić		Boris Markarov	
	György Kárpáti			Lovro Radonjić		Pyotr Mshvenieradze	

/continued on next page 385

Year	Gold	C'ntry	Points	Silver	C'ntry	Points	Bronze	C'ntry	Points
	Kálmán Markovits			Marjan Zurej			Valentin Prokopov		
	Mihály Mayer						Mikhail Ryschak		
	István Szivós						Yuri Schlyapin		
	Ervin Zádor								
1960	Amedeo Ambron	ITA		Viktor Ageyev	URS		András Bodnár	HUN	
	Danilo Bardi			Givi Chikvanaya			Ottó Boros		
	Giuseppe d'Altrui			Leri Gogoladze			Zoltán Dömötör		
	Salvatore Gionta			Boris Goikhman			László Felkai		
	Giancarlo Guerrini			Yuri Grigorovsky			Dezső Gyarmati		
	Franco Lavoratori			Anatoli Kartashov			István Hevesi		
	Gianni Lonzi			Viatcheslav Kurennoi			László Jenei		
	Rosario Parmegiani			Pyotr Mshvenieradze			Tivadar Kanizsa		
	Eraldo Pizzo			Vladimir Novikov			György Kárpáti		
	Dante Rossi			Evgeni Salzyn			András Katona		
	Brunello Spinelli			Vladimir Semyonov			János Konrád		
							Kálmán Markovits		
							Péter Rusorán		
1964	Miklós Ambrus	HUN		Ozren Bonačić	YUG		Viktor Ageyev	URS	
	András Bodnár			Zoran Janković			Zenon Bortkevich		
	Ottó Boros			Milan Muškatirović			Igor Grabovsky		
	Zoltán Dömötör			Ante Nardeli			Boris Grishin		
	László Felkai			Frane Nonković			Nikolai Kalashnikov		
	Desző Gyarmati			Vinko Rosić			Vladimir Kuznyetsov		
	Tivadar Kanizsa			Mirko Sandić			Nikolai Kuzynetsov		
	György Kárpáti			Zlatko Šimenc			Leonid Osipov		
	János Konrád			Bozidar Stanišić			Boris Popov		
	Mihály Mayer			Karlo Stipanić			Vladimir Semyonov		
	Dénes Pócsik			Ivo Trumbić			Eduard Yegorov		
	Péter Rusorán								
1968	Ozren Bonačić	YUG	13-11	Alexei Barkalov	URS		András Bodnár	HUN	
	Dejan Dabović			Oleg Bovin			Zoltán Dömötör		
	Zdravko Hebel			Givi Chikvanaya			László Felkai		
	Zoran Janković			Alexander Dolgushin			János Konrád		
	Ronald Lopanty			Yuri Grigorovsky			Ferenc Konrád		
	Uroš Marović			Boris Grishin			Mihály Mayer		
	Djordje Perišić			Vadim Guljaev			Endre Molnár		
	Miroslav Poljak			Leonid Osipov			Dénes Pócsik		
	Mirko Sandić			Vladimir Semenov			János Steinmetz		
	Karlo Stipanić			Alexander Shidlovsky			István Szivós		
	Ivo Trumbić			Viacheslav Skok					
1972	Anatoli Akimov	URS		András Bodnár	HUN		Peter Asch	USA	
	Alexei Barkalov			Tibor Cservenyák			Steven Barnett		
	Alexander Dolgushin			Tamás Faragó			Bruce Bradley		
	Alexander Dreval			István Görgényi			Stanley Cole		
	Vadim Gulyaev			Zoltán Kásás			James Ferguson		
	Alexander Kabanov			Ferenc Konrád			Eric Lindroth		
	Nikolai Melnikov			István Magas			John Parker		
	Leonid Osipov			Endre Molnár			Gary Sheerer		
	Alexander Shidlovski			Dénes Pócsik			James Slatton		
	Vladimir Shmudski			László Sárosi			Russell Webb		
	Viacheslav Sobchenko			István Szivós			Barry Weitzenberg		
1976	Gábor Csapó	HUN		Alberto Alberani	ITA		Alex Boegschoten	NED	
	Tibor Cservenyák			Silvio Baracchini			Ton Buunk		
	Tamás Faragó			Vincenzo d'Angelo			Piet de Zwarte		
	György Gerendás			Gianni De Miagistris			Andy Hoepelman		
	György Horkai			Riccardo De Magistris			Evert Kroon		
	György Kenéz			Marcello Del Duc			Nicolaas Landeweerd		
	Ferenc Konrád			Alessandro Ghibellini			Hans Smits		
	Endre Molnár			Luigi Castagnola			Gyze Stroboer		
	László Sárosi			Sante Marsili			Rik Toonen		
	Attila Sudár			Umberto Panerai			Hans van Zeeland		
	István Szivós			Roldano Simeoni			Jan Evert Veer		
1980	Vladimir Akimov	URS	8-7	Milivoj Bebić	YUG		Gábor Csapó	HUN	
	Alexei Barkalov			Zoran Gopčević			Tamás Faragó		
	Erkin Shagaev			Milorad Krivokapić			György Gerendás		
	Giorgi Mshvenieradze			Boško Loziča			Károly Hauszler		
	Evgeni Grishin			Predrag Manojlović			György Horkai		

Year	Gold	C'ntry	Points	Silver	C'ntry	Points	Bronze	C'ntry	Points
	Mikhail Ivanov			Zoran Muštur			László Kuncz		
	Alexander Kabanov			Damir Polić			István Kiss		
	Sergei Kotenko			Zoran Roje			Andre Molnár		
	Mait Riisman			Ratko Rudić			Attila Sudár		
	Evgeni Sharonov			Slobodan Trifunović			István Szivós		
	Viacheslav Sobchenko			Luka Vezilić			István Udvardi		
1984	Dragan Andrić	YUG	5-5	Douglas Burke	USA		Santiago Chalmovsky	GER	
	Milivoj Bebić			Jody Campbell			Armando Fernandez		
	Perica Bukić			Peter Campbell			Roland Freund		
	Veselin Djuho			Gary Figueroa			Rainer Hoppe		
	Milorad Krivokapić			Andrew McDonald			Thomas Huber		
	Deni Lušić			Kevin Robertson			Thomas Loebb		
	Igor Malanović			Terry Schroeder			Werner Obschernikat		
	Zoran Petrović			Timothy Shaw			Rainer Osselmann		
	Zoran Roje			John Siman			Frank Otto		
	Goran Sukno			Jon Svendsen			Peter Röhle		
	Tomislav Paškvalin			Joseph Vargas			Jürgen Schröder		
	Božo Vuletić			Craig Wilson			Hagen Stamm		
							Dirk Theismann		
1988	Dragan Andrić	YUG	9-7	James Bergeson	USA		Dmitri Apanasenko	URS	
	Mislav Bezmalinović			Gregory Boyer			Viktor Berenduga		
	Perica Bukić			George Campbell			Mikhail Giorgadze		
	Veselin Djuho			Jeffrey Campbell			Evgeni Grishin		
	Igor Gočanin			Jody Campbell			Mikhail Ivanov		
	Deni Lusic			Christopher Duplanty			Alexander Kolotov		
	Igor Milanović			Michael Evans			Sergei Kotenko		
	Tomislav Paškvalin			Douglas Kimball			Sergei Markoch		
	Renco Posinković			Edward Klass			Nurlan Mendygaliev		
	Goran Radjenović			Alan Mouchawar			Giorgi Mshvenieradze		
	Dubravko Simenc			Kevin Robertson			Sergei Naumov		
	Alexander Sostar			Terry Schroeder			Evgeni Sharonov		
	Mirko Vičević			Craig Wilson			Nikolai Smirnov		
1992	Marco D'Altrui	ITA	9-8	Daniel Ballart Sans	ESP		Dmitri Apanassenko	EUN	
	Francesco Attolico			Manuel Estiarte Duocastella			Andrei Belofastov		
	Gianni Averaimo			Pedro Garcia Aguado			Evgeni Charonov		
	Alessandro Bovo			Salvador Gomez Aguera			Dmitri Gorchkov		
	Paolo Caldarella			Marco Gonzalez Junquera			Vladimir Karaboutov		
	Alessandro Campagna			Ruben Michavila Jover			Alexander Kolotov		
	Massimiliano Ferretti			Miguel Angel Oca Gaia			Andrei Kovalenko		
	Mario Fiorillo			Jose Pcio Llado			Nikolai Kozlov		
	Ferdinando Gandolfi			Sergio Pedrerol Cavalle			Sergei Markotch		
	Amedeo Pomilio			Jesus Miguel Rollan Prada			Sergei Naoumov		
	Giuseppe Porzio			Ricardo Sanchez Alarcon			Alexander Ogorodnikov		
	Francesco Porzio			Jordi Sans Juan			Alexander Tchiguir		
	Carlo Silipo			Manuel Silvestre Sanchez			Alexei Vdovine		
1996									

Table Tennis

Stars to Watch

by Richard Eaton

China's fortunes resurgent?

C AN "King Kong" climb the Atlanta skyscrapers? Kong Linghui burst on to the table tennis landscape with comparable force and shock to the screen monster after which he was nicknamed. At the beginning of 1995 he was not widely known, despite having become Asian champion at the age of 19. But by the end of it he was world champion.

Kong achieved that with wonderfully nimble movement, a potent forehand loop and a change of pace in attack that indicated maturity greater than the brief span of his career. Nevertheless there were some who argued that the Chinese teenager had had a touch of fortune in bringing about the greatest day of his life in Tianjin in May.

These critics claim that had the world championships not been held in "King Kong's" home country, he would not be the king; nor would China have done so sensationally well.

A Contemporary Hero ★★★★★★★★★★★★★★★★★★★★★★★★★★★★★

Jan-Ove Waldner *(Sweden)*

There will be many people who hope that Jan-Ove Waldner can retain the Olympic crown he won so majestically in Barcelona four years ago. They may partly want Waldner to succeed so that the increasing monopoly upon table tennis of one continent, Asia, can be resisted. But, perhaps most of all, because the languorously elegant Swede may well be the most talented player of all time.

Waldner is certainly not the most consistent. The Olympic champion sometimes seems too emotionally withdrawn to project his flowing forehand loops and velvety backhand counter-hits in all their brilliance. But at his best he is not merely entertaining, he is breathtaking.

His performance while beating Jean-Philippe Gatien of France in straight games in the last Olympic men's singles final was almost perfect: full of a genius's imagination and an artist's touch. A year later Gatien was to become world champion, placing Waldner's Olympic effort in exalted perspective.

It is incredible, therefore, that Waldner has won the world title only once, seven years ago, for he is surely more gifted than some who have won it several times. Atlanta anticipates.

★★★★★★★★★★★★★★★★★★★★★★★★★★★★★ **A Contemporary Heroine**

Qiao Hong *(China)*

Keep a close eye on the sometimes underestimated second best player in the Chinese women's squad. She deserves careful watching not only because at 1.6m (5ft 3in.) she may be easy to miss, but because her brilliance with a traditional western "shake-hands" style of attack can be overlooked by comparison with the even smaller and even more successful Chinese phenomenon Deng Yaping.

Qiao won the world women's singles title at the age of only 20, six years ago in Dortmund, but had to be content with one gold in Barcelona, the women's doubles with Deng. Her cause was hindered when she tripped over the mat coming into the Estacion del Nord, causing her to injure her ankle and creating worries that the women's singles final might not take place. She will be keen to erase the memory of that in Atlanta and prove that there is a major singles title left in her.

Although it had been on the cards that the world's most consistently successful table tennis nation would regain supremacy from Sweden in the men's game after an eight-year interval, it was something of a surprise that China should win every title for the first time since the world championships were held in Yugoslavia in 1981.

Winning all four Olympic titles in Atlanta will take a lot of doing. Defending men's singles champion Jan-Ove Waldner of Sweden is likely still to be a major influence with his silky touch and icy temperament, while Belgian Jean-Michel Saive's ferocious forehand loop and athleticism may help him recapture the consistent aggression which made him the world's number one player for much of 1994.

Perhaps most significant, neither Kong nor Wang Tao, nor Liu Guoliang nor others in the Chinese squad in Atlanta will have the tremendous support they had in Tianjin. Nevertheless, with or without the crowd on his side, you would back the stocky left-handed Wang, holder of the men's doubles with Lu Lin, and winner of world titles in both men's and mixed doubles last year, to be among the medals again.

Equally, you would bet all the banks on your main street to a China bull that players of Chinese origin would win the two women's gold medals. Quite possibly it will be a dual double for the 'pocket rocket' – Deng Yaping, winner of the women's singles and doubles last time in Barcelona.

Deng also won a pair of doubles titles in both the last two world championships, and makes up for being – at 1.47m (4ft 10in.) in height – the smallest ever world champion by being the bounciest and most relentless.

If there are to be surprises in Atlanta then it may well be emigrants from China who cause them. Chai Po Wa, the Commonwealth gold medallist, might give Hong

Kong one last projection of identity before her adopted country becomes subsumed by her country of origin next year.

The former women's singles world no.1 Geng Lijuan, a Canadian, played throughout 1995 better than at any time since she left China, while Japan's former Chinese international, Koyama Chire, has special reasons for coveting the Olympic title.

Her chances of this were denied her in 1988 by the Chinese authorities when she was deselected for the Games at Seoul. Koyama alleges that this was linked to her winning the world title in New Delhi in 1987 (under her then name of He Zhili) when one of her team-mates had been designated as the woman the Chinese expected instead to win.

A Contemporary Hero ★★★★★★★★★★★★★★★★★★★★★★★★★★★★

Chen Xinhua (Great Britain)

Chen was one of several hundred players and coaches who sought employment outside their native China during the '80s. But he is also unique amongst them in that his country of origin exercized its right to veto his country of domicile, Britain, at the Olympic Games.

That happened before Barcelona four years ago, when the Chinese thought, probably rightly, that the Yorkshire-based former World Cup winner from Fukien could still be good enough to deny one of their current players a medal.

They may also have thought that Chen's chances of ever taking part in an Olympic Games had thereby been quashed. However, this acrobatic and flamboyant itinerant has such a rare and versatile mixture of defence and attack that, at the age of 36, he is still going.

With the majority of the women's top ten players, then as now, being Chinese, it would almost have been possible to anticipate who would win the world title. Koyama defected, married her Japanese coach and resurrected her career. Any Olympic medal may look like gold to her after this.

Europeans, meanwhile, are hardly in contention in the women's events. Perhaps the closest to being a threat will be Jie Schopp, another former Chinese national, who now employs her defensive skills in the German cause.

It may, therefore, need a revival of the best form of the unpredictable Waldner or some of the flashing brilliance of the Frenchman known as "the matinee idol", 1993 men's singles world champion Jean-Philippe Gatien, if table tennis in Atlanta is not to become an Asian monopoly.

R. E. □

★★★★★★★★★★★★★★★★★★★★★★★★★★★★★★★ **A Sporting Legend**

Dragutin Surbek *(Croatia)*

Dragutin Surbek, already a table tennis legend, acquires his fame in different ways these days. In Atlanta, if he plays, he is likely to be the oldest man in the field. Approaching his 50th birthday, the dogged Croatian could also be the oldest man ever to play Olympic table tennis.

His age and his nationality have an important connection. Surbek had already done enough to establish himself as one of the "greats" of the sport when his country acquired independence. And, in the tragic atmosphere that has surrounded it, his table tennis acquired a new purpose.

At a ripe age he was able to win enough matches to attract considerable attention and to promote his country. His two world doubles titles and his European singles titles had been achieved primarily for himself. Now he was playing for Croatia – "a soldier with a bat", he described himself.

Although he no longer plunges around the barriers throwing up thrilling lobs quite in the way he used to, Surbek's forehand loop and fighting qualities can still make him dangerous. The legend is adding to his story.

Retrospective

In Olympic terms, table tennis is a mere stripling. It was recognized by the IOC in 1977 but did not make its debut as part of the sports programme until the Seoul Games of 1988. And the sport, which has also been known by its delightfully onomatopoeic name of "ping pong", made an immediate impact. The first Olympic men's singles final between two Koreans, Yoo Nam Kyu, the eventual champion, and Kim Ki Taek, was one of the most exciting contests in any sport of those Games, thrilling the home crowd as well as the TV audience.

Jean-Philippe Gatien

The inaugural Olympic tournament was marked, however, both by Asian dominance (China had been expected to win all four titles but took just the women's singles and men's doubles leaving South Korea to add the women's doubles crown to Yoo's men's singles success).

Four years later, however, things had changed partially. At least, in the men's singles. Sweden's Erik Lindh – conqueror of China's then world champion Jiang Jialiang in the quarter-finals – had been Europe's only men's singles medallist with a bronze in 1988. His compatriot, Jan-Ove Waldner, won the 1992 men's singles title in an all-European final with French world no.1 Jean-Philippe Gatien.

Other things, meanwhile, remained the same with China winning the other three titles including diminutive Deng Yaping's victory in the women's singles – a player once considered "too small to play for China". The men's doubles final – won by Lu Lin and Wang Tao of China – was marked by a stadium packed with supporters of their German opponents, Steffan Fetzner and Jorg Rosskopf, who only applauded their own pairing.

Background

At current elite level, the sport demands agility, athleticism and lightning reflexes and is played by millions of people worldwide. It has come a long way since its genesis late in the last century as both an after-dinner pastime and children's favourite – using the dining room table, wooden and velum bats and a variety of "nets" which could even simply consist of piles of books.

Originally popular in Britain, then Europe before spreading to Asia the sport has now developed worldwide due, partly, to the relative simplicity of its low-cost equipment and playing area but also because of its basic appeal. International events took place from the early part of this century onwards and the sport has often had great TV and spectator appeal.

Table tennis has also passed through a variety of equipment metamorphoses which have often dictated the fashionable playing styles of each period. Experimental gut or wire-strung bats displaced the original velum. In turn, these gave way in the '20s and '30s to experiments with pimpled rubber bat surfaces on a wooden blade – first tried as a one-off, shaved-down counting mat but later developed commercially – which gave greater spin and increased the excitement and skill level of the sport for the mass European crowds.

It was not unusual to see long rallies with one player in attack at the table and the other pinned back, defending from the barriers. Equally, and more negatively, two defensive players could play even longer rallies at the table in a "pushing" war of attrition waiting for each other to make mistakes. This style led to one world team final in the '30s lasting three days and a single point in one men's singles match lasting over an hour. Inevitably, the authorities were driven to introduce a time-limit rule called "expedite" which is still in existence today and is activated after 15 minutes of a game unless the score has already reached 19-all.

Since that time, however, equipment changes have often been considered controversial and potentially detrimental to spectator appeal by increasing players' ability to impart speed and spin and, thereby, shortening rallies.

These have included: the advent in the '50s of sponge layers between the bat's blade and rubber; the use of different rubbers of the same colour on either side of the bat in the late '70s and early '80s to allow players to "twiddle" the bat below the surface of the table and conceal the type of spin used until the last moment; and the current vogue for "fast glues" (adhesives which remain wet because they are used to fix the rubber to the bat just prior to play and are alleged to help attacking players impart greater speed to their shots but which have led to a ban on the most toxic glues because of the dangers of regularly breathing in adhesive fumes). Meanwhile, "twiddling" is permitted because bats must now have different colour rubbers on each side.

In the early years of international competition, Hungary, England, Czechoslovakia and Germany were the leading nations. After World War II, the Soviet Union, Sweden, Yugoslavia and Romania emerged in Europe and the sport also continued its spread into Africa, India and Asia. Japan became a dominant world force in the late '50s and early '60s to be replaced by China at the top in two periods – before the Cultural Revolution and on their return in 1970. Table tennis in the USA has remained more a popular pastime than a leading competitive sport.

Equipment

A modern-day competition table tennis table has standard dimensions (see diagram) but can have any material as its

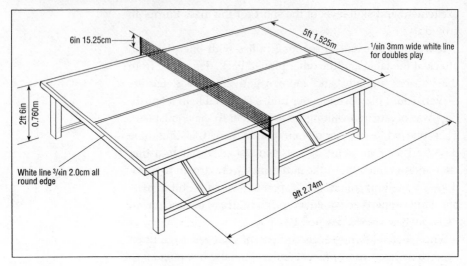

6in 15.25cm

5ft 1.525m

¹/₈in 3mm wide white line for doubles play

2ft 6in 0.760m

White line ³/₄in 2.0cm all round edge

9ft 2.74m

Table tennis table

surface as long as it is uniformly dark-coloured – most are blue or green – and gives an average bounce height of 23cm (9in.) when the ball is dropped onto it from a height of 30cm (12in.). The ball itself is made of celluloid, weighs 2.5gm (0.08 ounces) and can be white, yellow or orange. Bat blades must be at least 85% natural wood but can also have sandwich layers of other material such as adhesives or carbon fibre. A table tennis net is 15.25cm (6in.) high. The table is set within a playing area which, for Olympic competition, is 14 x 7m (46 x 23ft) and is delineated by a series of barriers.

Rules

Players toss to decide who serves first at the beginning of a match. The serve then changes from one player to another after every five points – unless the score in a game (also sometimes called a "set") reaches 20-all when the serve changes hands after every point. Throughout each game a point is scored for every rally won and matches can be the best of three or five games. Games are played up to 21 points unless both players reach the score of 20 in which case the game must be won by two clear points, i.e. 22-20, 23-21 etc. In doubles play, each player in a pairing must hit the ball alternately and the service must be made into one vertical half of the opponent's side of the table rather than the whole of the opponent's side as in singles.

A let is called and the point is replayed if a service ball touches the net before bouncing onto the opponent's side of the table but play continues if this happens at any other stage of a rally. The sides of the table top do not count as part of the playing surface but players often hit the edge of the top of the table with the ball leading to an awkward bounce and a difficult shot for an opponent to return.

Atlanta format

64 men and 64 women will compete in the Olympic tournament men's and women's singles events with 32 pairs in each of the men's and women's doubles. There is no mixed doubles event. Players are selected for the tournament by world ranking and continental qualifying tournaments and by invitation. A maximum of three singles players in each of the men's and women's singles and two doubles pairings in each of the doubles events is allowed from any one nation.

Each of the four events is decided by initial group and later knock-out stages. 16 groups of four players each in the early stages of the singles and eight groups of four pairs in the doubles events. The winners of each group then compete in a knock-out competition including a last 16 round, quarter-finals, semi-finals and finals. There is a play-off for the bronze medal between the losing semi-final players or pairs. All the group matches are the best of three games whilst those in the knock-out stages are the best of five games.

The Venue

Table tennis takes place in Atlanta at the Georgia World Congress Center just 3.2km (2 miles) from the Olympic Village and with a spectator capacity of 5,100. This venue is part of the Games' Olympic "Center" – the most concentrated cluster of venues in the city. It will house seven different sports during the Games and is the second largest convention centre in the USA.

MEDALLISTS (by nation)

	Men			Women			
	Gold	Silver	Bronze	Gold	Silver	Bronze	Total
China	2	-	1	3	4	1	11
Korea	1	1	4	1	-	2	9
Yugoslavia	-	1	-	-	-	1	2
Sweden	1	-	1	-	-	-	2
PRK	-	-	-	-	-	2	2
Germany	-	1	-	-	-	-	1
France	-	1	-	-	-	-	1
	4	4	6	4	4	6[1]	28

[1] Two bronze medals in 1992.

ATLANTA SCHEDULE

Venue: Georgia World Congress Center, Hall D

Date	Description	Round	Start	End
23 Jul	doubles (m&w)	prelims A-H	10:30	13:10
24 Jul	singles (w)	prelims A-P	10:30	13:10
	doubles (m&w)	prelims A-H	19:00	21:40

Date	Description	Round	Start	End
25 Jul	singles (w)	prelims A-P	10:00	14:00
	singles (m)	prelims A-H		
	doubles (m&w)	prelims A-H	19:00	23:00
	singles (m)	prelims I-P		
26 Jul	singles (m)	prelims A-H	10:00	14:00
	singles (w)	prelims A-P		
	doubles (w)	q/finals	19:00	21:20
	singles (m)	prelims I-P		
27 Jul	singles (m)	prelims A-P	10:00	14:40
	singles (w)	Last 16		
	doubles (m)	q/finals	19:00	22:00
	doubles (w)	s/finals		
28 Jul	singles (w)	Last 16	10:00	14:00
29 Jul	doubles (w)	FINAL	13:00	14:15
	singles (w)	q/finals	19:00	22:00
	doubles (m)	s/finals		
30 Jul	doubles (m)	FINAL	13:00	14:15
	singles (m)	q/finals	19:00	22:00
	singles (w)	s/finals		
31 Jul	singles (w)	FINAL	16:30	17:45
	singles (m)	s/finals	19:00	21:00
1 Aug	singles (m)	FINAL	16:30	17:45

MEDALLISTS

TABLE TENNIS (Men)

Year	Gold	C'ntry	Points	Silver	C'ntry	Points	Bronze	C'ntry	Points
Singles									
1988	Yoo Nam Kyu	KOR	17-21; 21-19; 21-11; 23-21	Kim Ki Taik	KOR		Erik Lindh	SWE	14-21; 21-17; 21-17; 21-16
1992	Jan-Ove Waldner	SWE	25-23; 21-18; 21-10	Jean-Philippe Gatien	FRA		Ma Wenge	CHN	
							Kim Taek Soo	KOR	
1996									

Year	Gold	C'ntry	Points	Silver	C'ntry	Points	Bronze	C'ntry	Points
Doubles									
1988	Chen Longcan Wei Qingguang	CHN	20-22; 21-8; 21-9	Ilija Lupulesku Zoran Primorac	YUG		Ahn Jae Hyung Yoo Nam Kyu	KOR	21-13; 21-16
1992	Lu Lin Wang Tao	CHN	26-24; 18-21; 21-18; 13-21; 21-14	Steffan Fetzner Jorg Rosskopf	GER		Kang Hee Chan Lee Chul Seung	KOR	
							Kim Taek Soo Yoo Nam Kyu	KOR	
1996									

TABLE TENNIS (Women)

Year	Gold	C'ntry	Points	Silver	C'ntry	Points	Bronze	C'ntry	Points
Singles									
1988	Chen Jing	CHN	21-17; 21-16; 21-23; 15-21; 21-15	Li Huifen	CHN		Jiao Zhimin	CHN	
1992	Deng Yaping	CHN	21-6; 21-8; 15-21; 23-21	Qiao Hong	CHN		Hyun Jung Hwa	KOR	
							Li Bun	PRK	
1996									

Year	Gold	C'ntry	Points	Silver	C'ntry	Points	Bronze	C'ntry	Points
Doubles									
1988	Hyun Jung Hwa Yang Young Ja	KOR	21-19; 16-21; 21-10	Chen Jing Jiao Zhimin	CHN		Jasna Fazlić Gordana Perkucin	YUG	
1992	Deng Yaping Qiao Hong	CHN	21-13; 14-21; 21-14; 21-19	Chen Zihe Gao Jun	CHN		Li Bun Yu Sun	PRK	
							Hong Cha Ok Hyun Jung Hwa	KOR	
1996									

Tennis

Stars to Watch

by John Oakley

Four players – one golden thought

WIMBLEDON is generally acclaimed as the major event in the tennis world but Steffi Graf, Boris Becker, Miloslav Mečíř and Ken Flach, all of whom have won Olympic Games titles, may be inclined to disagree.

Becker, the great German player, has won the men's singles at Wimbledon three times but still considers his men's doubles triumph at the Barcelona Games in 1992 as the highlight of his career. After he and Michael Stich had won the gold medal in Barcelona, a delighted Becker said: "You can't compare this with winning Wimbledon. There you play for yourself. Here you are playing for a land."

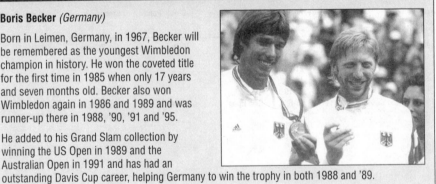

A Contemporary Hero ★★★★★★★★★★★★★★★★★★★★★★★★★★★★★★★

Boris Becker *(Germany)*

Born in Leimen, Germany, in 1967, Becker will be remembered as the youngest Wimbledon champion in history. He won the coveted title for the first time in 1985 when only 17 years and seven months old. Becker also won Wimbledon again in 1986 and 1989 and was runner-up there in 1988, '90, '91 and '95.

He added to his Grand Slam collection by winning the US Open in 1989 and the Australian Open in 1991 and has had an outstanding Davis Cup career, helping Germany to win the trophy in both 1988 and '89.

Becker possesses one of the biggest serves in the game, hits his ground strokes, smashes and volleys with great power and is at his best on fast surfaces, particularly grass and indoor carpets.

He won the Olympic men's doubles title with Michael Stich in Barcelona in 1992 and achieved one of his life's ambitions when he became world no.1 for 12 weeks during 1991.

Mečíř, one of the world's top players until back trouble forced him to retire in 1991, was even more emphatic. The artistic Czech, known as the "Big Cat", won the men's singles at the 1988 Seoul Games when tennis returned as an official sport at the Games for the first time since 1924. As he attended a press conference with his gold medal hanging proudly round his neck he said: "I have played in all the great championships like Wimbledon, Paris and Flushing Meadow. But for me the Olympic Games is the premier event. To win the Olympic title for my country is the proudest moment of my life."

Steffi Graf won the women's singles in Seoul and, with tears in her eyes, said later: "I have never felt so emotional at any other tournament. This was really special to me."

Flach, men's doubles champion at Wimbledon twice with fellow American Robert Seguso, carried off the doubles in Seoul with the same partner and had a change of mind. Before the Games began, he said: "I thought the Olympics was no big deal though I'm always glad to play for the United States." After winning the gold medal he stressed: "This is far, far better than winning Wimbledon. The Olympic Games beats anything I've played in."

Four top players with a single thought. The Olympic Games gold medal is the big one, the prize that tops all others.

Pete Sampras

So who will win the medals at the Atlanta Games this year? Andre Agassi or Pete Sampras, playing in their own country, will be expected to battle for the gold medal though surprises in the Olympic Games, especially in the men's events, are more than frequent. And it is often difficult to tell, right up to the last moment, who will appear in the various events.

Agassi and Sampras will almost certainly start favourites in the men's singles. Both were in stunning form last year and there could be no greater contrast between two great champions both in playing style and on-court demeanour. But other top players will all have medal hopes. Players like Goran Ivanišević, a fervent Croatian with a fiery temperament and equally hot serve, as well as Austrian Thomas Muster, a clay court specialist.

Stefan Edberg, winner of the demonstration event in 1984, cannot be ruled out entirely. Nor can his compatriot Magnus Larsson, the emerging though erratic Russian Yevgeny Kafelnikov, South African Wayne Ferreira and big serving Dutchman Richard Krajicek. Spaniards Sergi Bruguera and Alberto Berasategui and Germans Boris Becker and Michael Stich also look set to complete a star-studded cast.

Australians Todd Woodbridge and Mark Woodforde, the

TENNIS

reigning Wimbledon champions, will be favourites for the men's doubles with Dutch pair Jacco Eltingh and Paul Haarhuis strong contenders.

Among the women, Monica Seles, now an American citizen, has made a fascinating return to the game after being stabbed three years ago by a spectator. She is a fierce rival of Steffi Graf, the German who had her own problems last year with a back injury and her father jailed for alleged tax offences. Spaniard Arantxa Sanchez Vicario is a dogged fighter and her compatriot Conchita Martinez has the talent to do well.

A Contemporary Heroine ★★★★★★★★★★★★★★★★★★★★★★★★★★★★

Monica Seles *(USA)*

Just when she was at the height of her powers, Seles had more than two years out of the game after being stabbed by a deranged spectator at the Hamburg tournament in April, 1993. But, still only 22, she has returned to the sport and proved to be one of the greatest players in tennis history.

At the 1990 French Open Seles became the youngest winner of a Grand Slam title this century when only 16 years six months and has since won two more French titles, the Australian Open (three times) and two US Open crowns. More than that she became, with her infectious giggles and infamous on-court grunting, a worldwide star. For Seles, a baseliner with a devastating hit on both wings, the only missing link is the Wimbledon title though she was runner-up in 1992.

In March, 1994, Seles became an American citizen while still recuperating from the stabbing incident. She was born in Novi Sad, Yugoslavia, in 1973. But she made an astonishing return to the game last August by winning her first tournament, the Canadian Open, and then finishing runner-up to Steffi Graf at the US Open in a three-set final.

Finally, Jana Novotná, of Czechoslovakia and the Swiss teenage prodigy Martina Hingis will probably complete the list of the players to watch but what of Martina Navratilova? At 39 the legendary champion would like to compete though no longer full-time on the circuit. Should she be given a wild card? Sentiment says she should for it would be a fitting end to a great career.

J. O. □

Retrospective

TENNIS has only appeared on the Olympic programme in the modern era in both 1988 and '92. It was a demonstration event in 1984. Four years ago in Barcelona the tennis tournament was full of upsets. Stefan Edberg, the second seed, lost in the first round, Michael Chang, Guy Forget and Michael Stich were beaten in the second and Jim Courier, then the world's no.1, lost to the eventual champion in his first match. Pete Sampras and Boris ·Becker went down in the third. So seven of the top eight seeds were beaten before the quarter-finals and only Ivanišević, of the leading players, reached as far as the semi-finals.

Switzerland's Marc Rosset, ranked only 44 in the world and who had spent the previous week on a water skiing holiday because he thought he had no chance, was the shock gold medallist.

The women, in Barcelona, were more predictable with the top four seeds, Steffi Graf, Arantxa Sanchez Vicario, Jennifer Capriati and Mary Joe Fernandez reaching the semi-finals. But even this event provided a great shock with Capriati, only 16 at the time, beating Graf in the final to become the youngest ever Olympic tennis champion.

Stefan Edberg

Graf, therefore, added a silver medal to the gold she had won in 1988 when she became the first player – male or female – to complete the "Golden Slam", winning all the grand slam titles and the Olympic Games in one year. She also won the 1984 demonstration event marking her emergence on the international scene.

America took the 1992 women's doubles title through the unrelated Mary Joe and Gigi Fernandez who followed Pam Shriver and Zina Garrison's victory in the same event in 1988. Not surprisingly, given its world strength in depth, the USA leads the medal table since the sport's Olympic reintroduction in 1988 with four golds, a silver and three bronze medals. But it has not always been that way. In fact, the all time Olympic tennis medal table is led by Great Britain – now only famous in tennis circles for providing the home of the Wimbledon tennis championships where, incidentally, the 1908 Olympic tournament took place.

Background

Back in the early years of the modern Olympic era, between 1896 and 1924, Britain amassed 16 gold, 13 silver and 16 bronze medals. It will take some time to knock them off top spot in the medal table. Five of those golds came from Kitty McKane, later Kitty Godfree. She was also a Wimbledon champion and the IOC replaced her Olympic medals in

A Contemporary Heroine ★★★★★★★★★★★★★★★★★★★★★★★★★★★★★★

Steffi Graf *(Germany)*

Born in Bruhl, Germany, in 1969, Steffi Graf is one of the all-time greats of tennis and has won everything the sport has to offer in a glittering career. She has amassed 18 Grand Slam singles titles, four Australian Opens, four French Opens, four United States Opens and six Wimbledons and in 1988 she became only the third woman, after American Maureen Connolly (1953) and Australian Margaret Court (1970), to achieve the Grand Slam of all four titles in a calendar year.

But in 1988 Graf achieved the unique feat of not only winning all four Grand Slam titles but also the Olympic Games gold medal in Seoul to achieve what has become known as the "Golden Slam".

Right-handed with one of the most powerful serves in the women's game and possessor of a devastating forehand drive, she was taught by her father, Peter, from the age of four and quickly showed outstanding promise. Graf was first ranked by the Women's Tennis Association (WTA) in 1982 when she was only 13 years and four months old and has been a regular competitor on the WTA Tour ever since. For the past nine years she has been ranked either one or two in the world.

Graf has the best Olympic Games record, man or woman, of modern times, for she won the singles at Los Angeles in 1984 when tennis was a demonstration sport, won the singles again when tennis officially returned to the Olympic fold at Seoul in 1988 and was runner-up to Jennifer Capriati in the Barcelona Games.

She has been troubled by a back injury in recent years but was still good enough to win three of her 18 Grand Slam titles, the French Open, Wimbledon and the US Open, last year. She also set up the Steffi Graf Tennis Centre in Leipzig in 1991.

A Sporting Legend ★★★★★★★★★★★★★★★★★★★★★★★★★★★★★★★★

Suzanne Lenglen *(France)*

Suzanne Lenglen, born in 1899, was considered by many as the greatest woman player ever for she was beaten only once in her career, in the 1921 United States championships by American Molla Mallory when she was clearly unwell and retired after losing the first set.

Otherwise her tennis life was a complete success story for she won Wimbledon six times, five times running from 1919, and, after missing the 1924 championships through illness, again in 1925. She also won the French title six times between 1920 and 1926, missing only the 1924 event, again through illness.

Lenglen won the women's singles in her only Olympic Games appearance in Antwerp in 1920 and was likened to a ballerina because of her grace and artistry on the court. She turned professional in 1926 and also led the way in changing clothing fashions in women's tennis. She refused to wear the old fashioned corsets of the pre-World War I era and played in what were considered very daring dresses for her time.

1988 when she discovered that her original set had gone missing.

Another Briton, Charlotte Cooper, was the first female to win an Olympic title in any sport when she took the women's singles gold medal in 1900. Until Jennifer Capriati's win, at 16 years of age in 1992, the famous American eight times Wimbledon champion Helen Wills Moody was the youngest Olympic tennis title holder winning, aged 18 years and 288 days in 1924.

The first men's Olympic champion, Irish-born John Pius Boland, won his gold medal in the most casual fashion. He only entered the tournament because he happened to be visiting Athens on an archaeological quest. Boland also won the doubles event with a German partner.

In 1904 all the competitors were American apart from a lone German. And the 1908 and 1912 Games included indoor (or "covered court") competitions. The latter Games also clashed with Wimbledon.

Tennis, or "lawn tennis", first became popular midway through the reign of Queen Victoria (1837-1901). It was welcomed as a means of keeping young people from the English leisured classes occupied and was much simpler than Real (or Royal) tennis. Lawn tennis, as the name suggests, was played on courts marked out on garden lawns. Early versions of the same game are also recorded in France.

The first tennis club was formed in Warwickshire, England, in 1872. Then, in London, Major Wingfield established early rules and an hour-glass court. This was soon replaced by a rectangular version which was used at the first Wimbledon Championships in 1877. Tennis soon became a popular spectator sport and the first women's tournament took place in

★★★★★★★★★★★★★★★★★★★★★★★★★★★★ **A Sporting Legend**

Laurie Doherty *(Great Britain)*

Laurie Doherty, born in London in 1875, was the greatest tennis player when Britain ruled the sport in the early days of the century. He was Wimbledon champion five years running from 1902 to 1906 and was the men's doubles champion with older brother, Reggie, eight times in nine years from 1897.

He took part in only one Olympic Games, in Paris in 1900, and won both the singles, beating Irishman Harold Mahony in the final, and the doubles, with brother Reggie.

Celebrated for his smashing, volleying and speed about court, Doherty, despite the travelling difficulties of his day, became the first overseas winner of the US championships in 1903 and won the doubles twice with Reggie in 1902 and 1903.

And he had the greatest Davis Cup record of all time. Doherty played in five Challenge Rounds between 1902 and 1906 and was never beaten, winning seven singles and five doubles.

Dublin, Ireland, in 1879 – city which also played host to the first international match in 1892.

America was also emerging as a world force and in 1900 the Davis Cup, now a world team championships, was born as a match between England and the USA which the American hosts won 3-0. In 1913, the world governing body, now called the International Tennis Federation (ITF), was formed. Until the late '20s and early '30s tennis was an amateur sport but from then onwards it became a tradition for the great amateur champions eventually to turn professional. Disputes between various factions of the sport at world level began and culminated with the advent of "open" tennis in the late '60s and early '70s.

The modern sport is played worldwide – especially since the advent of ITF development programmes – with professional tours at various levels for both men and women together with "challenger" and "satellite" events at which emerging players battle for enough computer points to qualify for entry to the major events.

Equipment

Part of the early attraction of tennis derived from the simplicity of its equipment. Original rackets were heavy and wooden with gut strings. A steel racket was first introduced in 1930 but did not become popular until the '60s. From that point onwards technology began to transform the sport producing carbon fibre and graphite rackets which allowed the players to hit the ball much harder. Tennis balls are cloth-covered rubber and are pressurized. Much current debate surrounds the topic of trying to slow down the sport to protect spectator enjoyment, via ball or racket production technology, so that the men's game, in particular, does not become a procession of short rallies characterized by heavy serving.

Tennis court surfaces vary from grass to clay and from concrete to synthetic carpets with a whole range of alternatives in between. The 1996 Olympic Games tournament will be played on a surface called "Plexipave" – a medium-fast surface which should suit players of varying styles.

Rules

Olympic tennis features both singles and doubles competitions. The doubles court is wider than the singles court (see

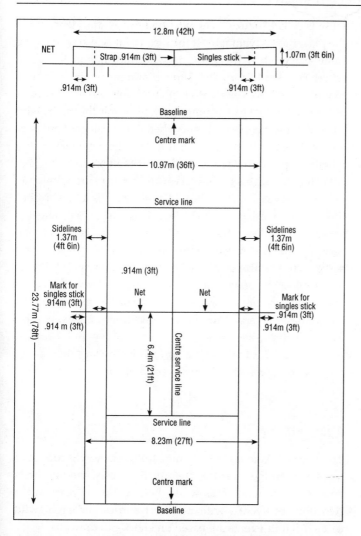

Tennis court

diagram). Each match is scored by points, games and sets and is played up to the best of three sets for all matches except the men's singles and doubles events which will be the best of five sets at the 1996 Games.

A set is won by the player who first secures six games, except after five-all when a clear margin of two games is required. At six-all in all but the final set of each match a special final and deciding game called the "tie-break" is played. The winner of the "tie-break" is the first to reach seven points unless the score reaches six-all after which play continues until one player establishes a two point margin.

In each tennis game points are awarded to either the server or the receiver based on who wins the point. Zero is called "love" in tennis and the subsequent scores for each point are 15, 30 and 40. If both players win three points each, 40-all, the score is called "deuce". The next point won after deuce takes the player to "advantage". If the next point is also won by the same player then the game is won, too. If not, the score reverts to deuce and the game continues again until one player wins two consecutive points. The server's score is always called first by the umpire who controls the match with a team of linespeople to decide whether the ball goes out over any of the court lines, whether it has hit the net on serve and whether a player has committed a foot-fault on serve.

Each point begins with a serve which must land within the opposite service court or "box". If a serve lands in the box but hits the net cord in the process it is called a "let" and the server is awarded a fresh start. If the ball lands outside the service court it is called a fault and the server gets a second serve. If this is also a fault the player loses the point. Points are also lost if a player fails to return the ball over the net or fails to hit it before it bounces twice, or hits a ball beyond the court lines. Players change ends after every odd game – i.e. after one, three, five games etc. There is a time limit between points to ensure that play is continuous during the games, and a 90 second interval after every odd game as the players change ends.

Atlanta format

This year, at Atlanta, the Olympic tournament will consist of 64 players in the men's and women's singles with 48 direct entries and 16 wild cards while there will be 32 pairs in the two doubles events, with 24 direct entries and eight wild cards. All four events are based on knock-out draws.

Players must have made themselves available for their nation's team for the Fed Cup (women's world team championship) or for the Davis Cup (men's equivalent) in any two of the last four years (one of which must have been either 1995 or '96) to be eligible for the Games. Selection for direct entries will then be based on computer rankings. Each nation can enter a maximum of three players in each singles event and two pairs in the doubles events to a maximum of four players per country. All four events are based on knock-out draws.

Venue

The 1996 Olympic tennis tournament will take place at Stone Mountain Park located 25.6km (16 miles) from the Olympic

Village. The centre court at the complex has 10,000 spectator seats. Two other courts have a spectator capacity of 5,000 and 3,000 respectively. In addition there are 13 courts with seating for 500 people. Stone Mountain Park is set against the dramatic backdrop of the world's largest exposed granite monolith. The tennis complex will remain once the Games close whereas the adjacent archery and cycling facilities will be dismantled.

MEDALLISTS (by nation)

Country	Gold	Silver	Bronze	Total
Great Britain	16	13	16	45
United States	11	5	7	23
France	8	7	6	21
Greece	1	5	3	9
Czechoslovakia	1	1	6	8
Germany	3	3	1	7
Sweden	-	2	5	7
South Africa	3	2	-	5
Spain	-	3	1	4
Australia	-	-	3	3
FRG	1	-	1	2
Japan	-	2	-	2
Argentina	-	1	1	2
Croatia	-	-	2	2
Soviet Union	-	-	2	2
Switzerland	1	-	-	1
Austria	-	1	-	1
Denmark	-	1	-	1
Bulgaria	-	-	1	1
Hungary	-	-	1	1
Italy	-	-	1	1
Netherlands	-	-	1	1
New Zealand	-	-	1	1
Norway	-	-	1	1
	45	46	60	151[1]

[1] Two-country pairs counted as two medals.

ATLANTA SCHEDULE

Venue: Stone Mountain Park

Date	Description	Round	Start	End
23-24 Jul	singles (m&w)	Rd 1	10:00	18:00
25-26 Jul	singles (m& w)	Rd 2	10:00	18:00
27 Jul	singles (m&w)	Rd 3	10:00	18:00
	doubles (m&w)	Rd 2		
28 Jul	singles (m)	Rd 3	10:00	16:00
	doubles (m&w)	Rd 2		
29 Jul	singles (w)	q/finals	11:00	19:00
	doubles (m)	q/finals		
30 Jul	singles (m)	q/finals	11:00	19:00
	doubles (w)	q/finals	11:00	19:00
31 Jul	singles (w)	s/finals	11:00	17:00
	doubles (m&w)	s/finals		
1 Aug	singles (m)	s/finals	11:00	19:00
	doubles (m&w)	play-offs (bronze)		
2 Aug	singles (w)	play-off (bronze) FINAL	10:00	18:30
	doubles (m)	FINAL		
3 Aug	singles (m)	play-off (bronze) FINAL	10:00	18:15
	doubles (w)	FINAL		

MEDALLISTS

TENNIS (Men)

Year	Gold	C'ntry	Points	Silver	C'ntry	Bronze	C'ntry

Singles

Year	Gold	C'ntry	Points	Silver	C'ntry	Bronze	C'ntry
1896	John Pius Boland	GBR/ IRL	6-3; 6-1	Dionysios Kasdaglis	GRE	Momcsillo Topavicz	HUN
						Constantinos Paspatis	GRE
1900	Hugh (Laurie) Doherty	GBR	6-4; 6-2 6-3	Harold Mahoney	GBR/IRL	Reginald Doherty	GBR
						Arthur Norris	GBR
1904	Beals Wright	USA	6-4; 6-4	Robert LeRoy	USA	Alphonzo Bell	USA
						Edgar Leonard	USA
1908	Josiah Ritchie	GBR	7-5; 6-3; 6-4	Otto Froitzheim	GER	Wilberforce Eaves	GBR
1908 Indoor	Arthur Gore	GBR	6-3; 7-5; 6-4	George Caridia	GBR	Major Josiah Ritchie	GBR
1912	Charles Winslow	SAF	7-5; 4-6 10-8; 8-6	Harry Kitson	SAF	Oscar Kreuzer	GER
1912 Indoor	André Gobert	FRA	8-6; 6-4; 6-4	Charles Dixon	GBR	Anthony Wilding	NZL
1920	Louis Raymond	SAF	5-7; 6-4; 7-5; 6-4	Ichiyo Kumagai	JPN	Charles Winslow	SAF
1924	Vincent Richards	USA	6-4; 6-4; 5-7; 4-6; 6-2	Henri Cochet	FRA	Umberto de Morpurgo	ITA
1928–1984 not held							
1988	Miloslav Mečíř	TCH	3-6; 6-2; 6-4; 62	Tim Mayotte	USA	Stefan Edberg	SWE
						Bradley Gilbert	USA
1992	Marc Rosset	SUI	7-6; 6-4; 3-6; 4-6;	Jordi Arrese Castané	ESP	Goran Ivanišević	CRO
						Andrei Tcherkasov	EUN
1996							

Doubles

Year	Gold	C'ntry	Points	Silver	C'ntry	Bronze	C'ntry
1896	John Pius Boland	GBR/ IRL	5-7; 6-4; 6-1	Dionysios Kasdaglis Demetrios Petrokokkinos	GRE	Edwin Flack George Robertson	AUS GBR
	Friedrich Traun	GER					
1900	Reginald Doherty Hugh (Laurie) Doherty	GBR	6-1; 6-1; 6-0	Basil Spalding de Garmendia Maxime Decugis	USA FRA	André Prévost Georges de la Chapelle	FRA
1904	Edgar Leonard Beals Wright	USA	6-4; 6-4; 6-2	Alphonzo Bell Robert LeRoy	USA	Joseph Wear Allen West	USA
1908	Reginald Doherty George Hillyard	GBR	9-7; 7-5; 9-7	James Parke Josiah Ritchie	GBR/ IRL	Clement Cazalet Charles Dixon	GBR
1908 Indoor	Herbert Roper Barrett Arthur Gore	GBR	6-2; 2-6; 6-3; 6-3	George Simond George Caridia	GBR	Wollmar Boström Gunnar Setterwall	SWE
1912	Harold Kitson Charles Winslow	SAF	4-6; 6-1; 6-2; 6-2	Fritz Pipes Arthur Zborzil	AUT	Albert Canet Eduard Marc Mény de Marangue	FRA
1912 Indoor	Maurice Germot André Gobert	FRA	6-4; 12-14; 6-2; 6-4	Carl Kempe Gunnar Setterwall	SWE	Alfred Ernest Beamish Charles Dixon	GBR
1920	Oswald Noel Turnbull Maxwell Woosnam	GBR	6-2; 5-7; 7-5; 7-5	Seiichiro Kashio Ichiyo Kumagai	JPN	Pierre Albarran Maxime Decugis	FRA
1924	Francis Hunter Vincent Richards	USA	4-6; 6-2; 6-3; 2-6; 6-3	Jacques Brugnon Henri Cochet	FRA	Jean Borotra Jean René Lacoste	FRA
1928–1984 not held							
1988	Kenneth Flach Robert Seguso	USA	6-3; 6-4; 6-7; 6-7; 9-7	Emilio Sanchez Sergio Casal Martinez	ESP	Stefan Edberg Anders Järryd Miloslav Mečíř Milan Srejber	SWE TCH
1992	Boris Becker Michael Stich	GER	7-6; 4-6; 7-6; 6-3	Wayne Ferreira Piet Norval	RSA	Goran Ivanišević Goran Prpić Javier Frana Christian Miniussi	CRO ARG

Year	Gold	C'ntry	Points	Silver	C'ntry	Bronze	C'ntry
1996							

TENNIS (Women)

Year	Gold	C'ntry	Points	Silver	C'ntry	Bronze	C'ntry

Singles

Year	Gold	C'ntry	Points	Silver	C'ntry	Bronze	C'ntry
1900	Charlotte Cooper	GBR	6-1; 6-4	Hélèn Prévost	FRA	Marion Jones	USA
1908	Dorothy Chambers	GBR	6-1; 7-5	Penelope Boothby	GBR	Ruth Winch	GBR
1908 Indoor	Gladys Eastlake-Smith	GBR	6-2; 4-6; 6-0	Alice Greene	GBR	Martha Adlerstråhle	SWE
1912	Marguerite Broquedis	FRA	4-6; 6-3; 6-4	Dora Köring	GER	Anne Bjurstedt-Mallory	NOR
1912 Indoor	Edith Hannam	GBR	6-4; 6-3	Thora Castenschiold	DEN	Mabel Parton	GBR
1920	Suzanne Lenglen	FRA	6-3; 6-0	Edith Dorothy Holman	GBR	Kathleen McKane	GBR
1924	Helen Wills-Moody	USA	6-2; 6-2	Julie Vlasto	FRA	Kathleen McKane	GBR
1928–1984 not held							
1988	Steffi Graf	FRG	6-3; 6-3	Gabriela Sabatini	ARG	Zina Garrison	USA
						Manuela Maleeva	BUL
1992	Jennifer Capriati	USA	3-6; 6-3; 6-4	Steffi Graf	GER	Mary Joe Fernandez	USA
						Arantxa Sanchez Vicario	ESP
1996							

Doubles

Year	Gold	C'ntry	Points	Silver	C'ntry	Bronze	C'ntry
1920	Kathleen McKane Winifred Margaret McNair	GBR	8-6; 6-4	Winifred Beamish Edith Dorothy Holman	GBR	Elisabeth d'Ayen Suzanne Lenglen	FRA
1924	Hazel Wightman Helen Wills-Moody	USA	7-5; 8-6	Phyllis Covell Kathleen McKane	GBR	Dorothy Shepherd-Barron Evelyn Colyer	GBR
1928–1984 not held							
1988	Zina Garrison Pamela Shriver	USA	4-6; 6-2; 10-8	Jana Novotná Helena Suková	TCH	Elizabeth Smylie Wendy Turnbull	AUS
						Steffi Graf Claudia Kohde-Kilsch	FRG
1992	Mary Joe Fernandez Gigi Fernandez	USA	7-5; 2-6; 6-2	Conchita Martinez Bernar Arantxa Sanchez Vicario	ESP	Rachel Mcquillan Nicole Provis	AUS
						Leila Meschki Natalia Zvereva	EUN
1996							

Volleyball

Stars to Watch

by Paddy Murphy

Four events under five rings

VOLLEYBALL will make a spectacular impact at these Atlanta Games. Four events under five Olympic rings. As hosts, the USA are first qualified and natural favourites for the indoor more traditional version. But in these Games, too, beach volleyball joins the full Olympic programme and again the USA must start favourites.

Indoors, the 12 men's and women's teams in Atlanta will be the best in the world. The men's holders, Brazil, stand in the way of a third USA men's Olympic title, while Cuba will be seeking to hold on to their women's crown and prevent a USA first.

Cuba, women's world champions and defending Olympic champions (with Mireya Luis Hernandez in their team) will also face the challenge of Brazil, winners of the 1994 world grand prix, but beaten for bronze by the USA in Barcelona.

For China's women, winners of the 1995 world student games, these Olympic Games may come too soon for them to win their 1984 title back again. Russia, meanwhile, may be inspired by the former Soviet Union's tradition in the sport in which it won four Olympic titles. Japan, winners in 1964 and 1976, and Korea, both bring fervour and verve and can never be ruled out.

In the Barcelona men's event, Brazil beat The Netherlands in the final, and the USA beat Cuba for bronze. Missing from this quartet is Italy who are the world and European champions, and the five-time winners of the world league.

A Contemporary Heroine ★★★★★★★★★★★★★★★★★★★★★★★★★★

Mireya Luis Hernandez *(Cuba)* Indoor

Once called 'the spiker with wings', this Camaguey born Angel won her first award as best all-round player aged 18 years at the 1985 junior world championships. Although she is only 1.75m (5ft 9in.) tall and with a nine year old son, and recovered from a broken knee cap, Hernandez' fantastic leaping brought Olympic success to Cuba in Barcelona. Afterwards she said: "I will be looking forward to new conquests." Atlanta gold is her next goal.

Atlanta is located on the Piedmont Plateau of the Blue Ridge Mountains, so will the Italian connection of that region and the mountains' colour matching that of the "azzurri" help inspire the Italian squad to their first Olympic gold? The USA were the team to beat in the '80s – Italy is the team everyone has to beat in the '90s.

Brazil were silver medallists at the Los Angeles Olympic Games in 1984, and could find the warm southern state of Georgia conducive to their attempts to retain the Olympic title. The Cuban men have been top ranked for decades and may also find Atlanta to their liking.

Korea vs. China

Barcelona was hailed as having been the most evenly balanced of Olympic volleyball competitions. The tall Dutch were losing finalists there and again in both the 1994 world and 1995 European final – both held in Athens. Like Italy, the Dutch will want gold not silver in Atlanta.

The 24 men's and 16 women's teams who will contest the inaugural Olympic beach volleyball tournament bring to reality another dream of the visionary world volleyball president, Ruben Acosta, of Mexico. Forecasting the destinations of the first gold medals, though, is very difficult.

The Americans must be favoured. Despite double knee surgery veteran star Sinjin Smith and his most recent partner, Carl Henkel, as well as Carlos Briceno and Jeff Williams, will represent 'American Dreams'. But they face the challenge of Brazil with the pairings of Franco Nieto and Roberto Lopes, and Jose Marco De Melo and Emmanuel Rego, to name but two.

Nor should the names of Jan Kvallheim and Bjorn Maaseide be forgotten. Norwegians playing beach volleyball? Yes,

★★★★★★★★★★★★★★★★★★★★★★★★★ A Contemporary Hero

Ron Zwerver *(Netherlands)* Indoor

The 29 year old 'Flying Dutchman' has been consistently one of the best all-round players in the world for the past six years. His height of 2m (6ft 6in.) make him an average size player on the Orange squad but his talents make him a star among stars. He has played in the world class Italian league and his jump services and attacks from the back court may lead Netherlands to the elusive gold.

Brazilian team, 1992

and the world and European champions of 1994 will not be out of place in Atlanta.

In the women's competition American pairings such as Nancy Reno and Holly McPeak, and Liz Masakayan and Karolyn Kirby, will be the gold medal contenders. But there are world leaders Sandrinha Pires and Jacqui Silva of Brazil to consider, to admire, and to believe worthy of Olympic triumph. Their compatriots Adriana Samuel and Monica Rodrigues could also be close to the title when the final whistle blows.

A Contemporary Heroine ★★★★★★★★★★★★★★★★★★★★★★★★★★★★

Jacqui Silva *(Brazil)* Beach

A regular on the USA beach circuit for the past decade, she won the American nationals for the first three years and three US Opens subsequently, with American partners. Successes in the world series make Silva and compatriot partner Sandrinha Pires look unstoppable. Recovery from serious injury has motivated this player of speed and agility, talents most needed on sand.

Kerri Pottharst and Nathalie Cook of Australia have pushed the Americans hard recently, and some "Olde Worlde" magic may be brought to the sands of Atlanta beach by the Germans Beate Buhler and Danja Musch, by the current European champions Cordula Borger and Beate Paetow, or even by Britain's Amanda Glover and partner Audrey Cooper.

P. M. ☐

Retrospective

When volleyball made its Olympic debut in Tokyo (1964), the women's event nearly did not take place. That was because for a short while it did not have the requisite minimum number of six teams for an official tournament after a political dispute had led to the withdrawal of North Korea. The Japanese organizers came up with an enterprising solution. They successfully offered the South Koreans a million yen towards their costs for participating. It proved an excellent investment, the South Koreans came and played and the Japanese women went on to win gold.

The first men's gold only went to the Soviet Union on a better points ratio (for and against) after they had earlier lost to Japan.

Before the 1988 Games, the nation of Peru had only ever won one gold medal before, in pistol shooting 40 years earlier. Imagine, then, the excitement when their women's volleyball team reached the Olympic final in Seoul. They advanced to a two set lead over the Soviets and were 12-6 up in the third set before the Soviet coach called for a time-out and put three substitutes on court. It was a moment which changed the course and the character of the match. The Soviets clawed back and the match went to a fifth and final set. The ambitious Peruvians still got to match point just before the end, but saw their gold recede from them like a mirage 15-17.

Another drama involving the Soviet Union, took place in 1976 in Montreal when they led by two sets to one and 15-14 in the fourth against the Poles in the Olympic men's final. But a spectacular smash by Polish giant Tomasz Wojtowicz saved the match point and the Poles won the decider 19-17.

Women's volleyball has been hugely important in China, too. In the 1980s when the team needed a new coach the four contenders debated the role on television rather like Presidential candidates in America.

★★★★★★★★★★★★★★★★★★★★★★★★★★★★★★ **A Sporting Legend**

Alexander Savin *(USSR)* Indoor

After 500 games with the great Soviet team of the '70s and '80s, 'Czar' Alexander retired in 1987 as the best Soviet player ever. He left behind the awesome image of a leaping moustachioed giant measuring 2m (6ft 6in.), head and shoulders above the net, his block impossible to get round, his attack impossible to stop. A silver medallist in Montreal, he won gold in Moscow, was world champion in 1978 and 1982 and won many European, national and club titles.

It took a long time for the USA, the founders of the sport, to succeed at the Games. That happened in 1984 when their men took gold but their women failed in an unusual tale involving their Chinese opponents in the final. Three American players and their coach were spotted by the Chinese wearing gold medals on TV immediately prior to the match. It was enough to galvanize the Chinese into recording a straight sets victory.

Finally, a little romance has sometimes come to the sport at the Games, too. The captain of the 1964 Japanese women's team, Masae Kasai, told the prime minister of her country, Eisaku Sato, that such were her training demands that she had no time to meet any men and, at the age of 31, she wanted to marry. He introduced her to a man called Kazuo Nakamura and the pair promptly got married.

Background

Volleyball, like basketball, began in the USA. At Holyoke YMCA, Massachusetts, in 1895 to be more precise. Its inventor, W G Morgan, allegedly dreamt it up as a recreation for middle-aged men who found basketball too rigorous. Little did he know that his sport would later make such huge demands for speed, fitness and agility on court.

Morgan first used a basketball but found it too heavy and had a special, lighter ball manufactured. Inevitably, volleyball became a competitive sport, particularly after World War I. And it spread abroad wherever Americans travelled. It was a regular school sport as early as 1913 and was probably introduced to Europe after 1918. The International Volleyball Federation (FIVB) was formed in 1947.

America, the Soviet Union (who dominated the sport in the '60s and '70s), Poland, Czechoslovakia, Japan and Brazil have been among the top nations. The most successful Olympic player of all, inevitably, came from the Soviet Union – Inna Ryskal – who won two golds and two silvers between 1964 and 1976.

A Sporting Legend ★★★★★★★★★★★★★★★★★★★★★★★★★★★★★

Gene Selznik *(USA)*

The Californian 'King of the Beach' of the '50s and '60s, and a gifted all-round player indoors, Selznik was the first American volleyball player to win a "World's Best" award at the 1956 Paris championships. Often credited with creating the two-man service reception system, he is regarded by many as a visionary whose ideas are now the norm in today's game. Famed for his dancing, beach opponents ruefully called him the Joker – usually after having lost to him and his partner Bernie Holtzman during their unbeatable run between 1954 and 1956.

Beach volleyball has been popular as a competitive sport since the early '50s. But it will make its first Olympic appearance in Atlanta.

Equipment

Both volleyball and the debut discipline of beach volleyball have courts which are 18 m (59ft 8in.) long and 9m (29ft 6in.) wide. Each version of the game also has a free zone around the court, which varies but can be between 6m and 9m (19ft 6in. and 29ft 3in.) at the sides and ends (see diagram).

Indoor volleyball is played on a surface made of wood or synthetic substances. Beach volleyball is played on sand which must be levelled, and free of rocks, shells, stones or any other objects which may cause a risk of injury. Furthermore the sand must not be so fine as to cause dust or stick to the skin and must be at least 40cm (15.7in.) deep.

The ball is spherical, made of leather, and weighs between 260 and 280gm (9.2 and 9.9oz). The net is 9.5m long (31ft 1in.) and 1m wide (3ft

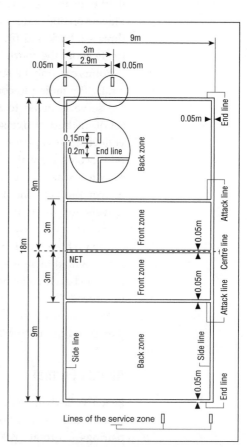

Volleyball court

3in.) for both types of volleyball but these nets are placed at different heights above the ground for men and women. They must be at 2.43m (7ft 11in.) high for men and 19cm (7.4in.) lower for women.

But perhaps the most conspicuous difference – and one that may well attract plenty of attention in these Games – is that beach volleyball players are allowed to wear bathing suits rather than the shorts and sports shirts of the indoor game.

Rules

Beach volleyball teams consist of two players with no substitutes whilst up to 12 players make up an indoor volleyball team of which six must be on the court at any time. A substitute may enter the game only once per set. In volleyball, players hit or tap the ball to keep it off the ground. They are not allowed to catch, hold or run with the ball.

A match (indoor version) starts with the back right-hand player serving the ball from the service area (behind the end line) over the net and into the opponents' side of the court. Players on both sides are arranged at this point in two rows of three – a back and front row. After the serve they can move freely about the court.

Points can only be scored by the serving team. Once it loses a rally (by failing to complete the serve, or to return the ball) the serve is given to the opposition. This applies for each set of the best of five set matches (best of three sets in beach volleyball) except for the final or deciding set when every rally scores regardless of serve. After the serve, in a rally, each team has three touches of the ball in which to return it over the net. The aim is to set the ball up for the front players to smash it to the ground within the opponents' court to score a point.

The first to score 15 points (12 in beach volleyball) wins the set, provided there is a minimum lead of two points. At 14-14 (11-11 in beach volleyball), play continues until there is a two-point lead. But at 16-16 (13-13 in beach volleyball) one point decides the set except, once more, in the deciding set where play continues until a two point margin is created.

Atlanta Format

Beach volleyball makes its first Olympic appearance of all time at the Atlanta Games with 24 men's and 16 women's pairings – a total of 80 athletes. They were selected via the FIVB world championships series and will play in a double elimination tournament until four teams qualify for the semi-finals – two each from the winners and losers brackets – and final. There will be a play-off for bronze.

For indoor volleyball, 144 athletes make up the 12 men's and 12 women's (an increase of four women's teams since 1992) teams. They compete in two groups of six teams from which the top eight teams play a knock-out tournament consisting of the quarter-finals, semi-finals, final and bronze medal match. Teams qualified for Atlanta via the world cup and continental qualifying events.

There have been some rule changes, too, for indoor volleyball in Atlanta. Among the most important is that the service zone will be increased from the 3m to 9m (9ft 10in to 29ft 6in.) behind the end line. Another concerns the ball touching the body. Previously it was not allowed to touch a ball with any part of the anatomy below the knee and remain legal. Now the whole body may be used, including the feet.

Venues

Beach volleyball will be played at Atlanta Beach which is in Clayton County International Park 32km (20 miles) south of the Olympic village. There is a 7,500 seat volleyball stadium. Indoor volleyball will be played at two venues – the University of Georgia's gym and the Omni Coliseum. The University, which will host the preliminary rounds, is 32km (20 miles) south of the Olympic village, and the Omni Coliseum is located in the Olympic centre. It is the home of the Atlanta Hawks basketball team and has a spectator capacity of 16,400. The University's capacity is 9,500 spectators.

MEDALLISTS (by nation)

Country	Men			Women			Total
	Gold	Silver	Bronze	Gold	Silver	Bronze	
Soviet Union	3	2	1	4	3	-	13
Japan	1	1	1	2	2	1	8
United States	2	-	1	-	1	1	5
Poland	1	-	-	-	-	2	3
China	-	-	-	1	-	1	2
GDR	-	1	-	-	1	-	2
Brazil	1	1	-	-	-	-	2
Bulgaria	-	1	-	-	-	1	2
Cuba	-	-	1	1	-	-	2
Czechoslovakia	-	1	1	-	-	-	2
Peru	-	-	-	-	1	-	1
Argentina	-	-	1	-	-	-	1
Italy	-	-	1	-	-	-	1
Netherlands	-	1	-	-	-	-	1
Korea	-	-	-	-	-	1	1
North Korea (PRK)	-	-	-	-	-	1	1
Romania	-	-	1	-	-	-	1
	8	8	8	8	8	8	48

ATLANTA SCHEDULE

Beach
Venue: Clayton County International Park

Date	Round	Start	End
23-25 Jul	prelims (m&w)	9:00	12:45
		14:00	17:45
26 Jul	prelims (m&w)	10:00	12:15
	prelims (m)	14:30	17:45
	s/finals (w)		

Date	Round	Start	End
27 Jul	s/finals (m) play-off (bronze) (w)	10:00	12:45
	s/finals (m) FINAL (w)	14:00	17:00
28 Jul	play-off (bronze) (m) FINAL (m)	11:30	15:15

Indoor
Venue: Omni Coliseum = OC
University of Georgia = UG

Date	Round	Start	End	Venue
20,22,24, 26,28 Jul	prelims (w)	10:00	14:30	OC
		16:00	20:30	UG
		19:30	23:59	OC
21,23,25, 27,29 Jul	prelims (m)	10:00	14:30	OC
		16:00	20:30	UG
		19:30	23:59	OC
30 Jul	q/finals (w)	12:00	16:30	OC
		19:30	23:59	
31 Jul	q/finals (m)	12:00	16:30	OC
		19:30	23:59	
1 Aug	play-offs (7-8 place) (w) play-offs (5-6place) (w)	12:00	16:30	
	s/finals (w)	19:30	23:59	OC
2 Aug	play-offs (7-8 place) (m) play-offs (5-6place) (m)	12:00	16:30	
	s/finals (m)	19:30	23:59	OC
3 Aug	play-off (bronze) (w) FINAL (w)	12:00	16:45	OC
4 Aug	play-off (bronze) (m) FINAL (m)	12:00	16:45	OC

MEDALLISTS

VOLLEYBALL (Men)

Year	Gold	C'ntry	Score	Silver	C'ntry	Bronze	C'ntry
1964	Ivan Bugaenkov	URS	15-9	Milan Cüda	TCH	Yutaka Demachi	JPN
	Nikolai Burobin		15-8	Bohumil Gollian		Tokihiko Higuchi	
	Yuri Chesnokov		5-15	Zdeněk Humhal		Naohiro Ikeda	
	Vazha Kacharava		10-15	Petr Kop		Toshiaki Kosedo	
	Valeri Kalachikhin		15-7	Josef Labuda		Tsutomu Koyama	
	Vitali Kovalenko			Josef Musil		Masayuki Minami	
	Stanislav Ljugailo			Karel Paulus		Teruhisa Moriyama	
	Giorgi Mondzolevsky			Boris Perušič		Yuzo Nakamura	
	Yuri Poiarkov			Pavel Schenk		Katsutoshi Nekoda	
	Eduard Sibiriakov			Václav Šmídl		Yasutaka Sato	
	Yuri Vengerovski			Josef Šorm		Sadatoshi Sugahara	
	Dmitri Voskoboinikov			Ladislav Toman		Takeshi Tokutomi	
1968	Oleg Antropov	URS	4-15	Kenji Kimura	JPN	Bohumil Gollian	TCH
	Vladimir Belyaev		15-13	Isao Koizumi		Zdeněk Gröessel	
	Ivan Bugaenkov		15-19	Masayuki Minami		Petr Kop	
	Vladimir Ivanov		15-13	Yasuaki Mitsumori		Drahomír Koudelka	
	Valeri Kravchenko			Jungo Morita		Josef Musil	
	Evgeni Lapinski			Katsutoshi Nekoda		Vladimír Petlák	
	Vasilijus Matushevas			Seiji Ohko		Antonín Procházka	
	Viktor Mikhalchuk			Tetsuo Sato		Pavel Schenk	
	Giorgi Mondzolevsky			Kenji Shimaoka		Josef Smolka	
	Eduard Sibiryakov			Mamoru Shiragami		František Sokol	
				Tadayoshi Yakota		Jiří Svoboda	
						Lubomír Zajíček	
1972	Yoshihide Fukao	JPN	11-15	Horst Hagen	GDR	Viktor Borsch	URS
	Kenji Kimura		15-2	Wolfgang Löwe		Viacheslav Domani	
	Masayuki Minami		15-10	Wolfgang Maibohm		Vladimir Kondra	
	Jungo Morita		15-10	Jürgen Maune		Valeri Kravchenko	
	Yuzo Nakamura			Horst Peter		Evgeni Lapinski	
	Katsutoshi Nekoda			Eckehard Pietzsch		Vladimir Patkin	
	Tetsuo Nishimoto			Siegfried Schneider		Yuri Poiarkov	
	Yasuhiro Noguchi			Arnold Schulz		Vladimir Putiatov	
	Seiji Oko			Rudi Schumann		Alexander Saprykinh	
	Tetsuo Sato			Rainer Tscharke		Yuri Starunskii	
	Kenji Shimaoka			Wolfgang Webner		Efim Tchulak	
	Tadayoshi Yokota			Wolfgang Weise		Leonid Zaiko	
1976	Bronisław Bebel	POL	11-15	Vladimir	URS	Alfredo Figueredo	CUB
	Ryszard Bosek		15-13	Chernyschovnischev		Viktor Garcia	
	Wiesław Gawłowski		12-15	Efim Chulak		Diego Lapera	
	Marek Karbarz		19-17	Vladimir Dorohov		Loenel Marshall	
	Lech Lasko		15-7	Alexander Ermilov		Ernesto Martinez	
	Zbigniew Lubiejewski			Vladimir Kondra		Lorenzo Martinez	
	Mirosław Rybaczewski			Oleg Moliboga		Jorge Perez	
	Wlodzimierz Sadalski			Anatoli Polishuk		Antonio Rodriguez	
	Edward Skorek			Alexander Salas		Carlos Salas	
	Włodzimierz Stefański			Pavel Selivanov		Victoriano Sarmientos	
	Tomasz Wójtowicz			Yuri Starunski		Jesus Savigne	
	Zbigniew Zarzycki			Yuri Tchesnokov		Raul Virches	
				Vladimir Ulanov			
				Viacheslav Zaitsev			
1980	Vladimir	URS	15-7	Yordan Angelov	BUL	Marius Căta-Chiţiga	ROM
	Chernyschovnischev		15-13	Stefan Dimitrov		Valter Corneliu Chifu	
	Vladimir Dorokov		14-16	Dimitr Dimitrov		Laurenţiu Dumanoiu	
	Alexander Jermilov		15-11	Stoian Gunchev		Günter Enescu	
	Vladimir Kondra			Khristo Iliev		Dan Gîrleanu	
	Valeri Krivov			Petko Petkov		Sorin Macavei	
	Fiodor Lashchenov			Kaspar Simeonov		Viorel Maniole	
	Viliar Loor			Khristo Stoianov		Florin Mina	
	Oleg Moliboga			Mitko Todorov		Corneliu Oros	
	Yuri Panchenko			Tsano Tsanov		Constantin Sterea	
	Alexander Savin			Emil Valchev		Nicu Stoian	
	Pavel Selivanov			Dimitr Zlatanov		Neculae Vasile Pop	
	Viacheslav Zaitsev						

Year	Gold	C'ntry	Score	Silver	C'ntry	Bronze	C'ntry
1984	Aldis Berzins	USA	15-6	Ruy Campos Nascimento	BRA	Franco Bertoli	ITA
	Craig Buck		15-6	Fernando D'Avila		Gian Carlo Dametto	
	Rich Duwelius		15-7	Marcus Freire		Giovanni Errichiello	
	Dusty Dvorak			Domingos Lampariello Neto		Giovanni Lanfranco	
	Karch Kiraly			José Montanaro		Andrea Lucchetta	
	Chris Marlowe			Mario Xando Oliviera Neto		Guido de Luigi	
	Pat Powers			Bernard Rajzman		Marco Negri	
	Steve Salmons			Bernardo Rezende		Francesco dall'Olio	
	Dave Saunders			Antonio Ribeiro		Pier Paolo Lucchetta	
	Paul Sunderland			Amauri Ribeiro		Piero Rebaudengo	
	Steve Timmons			William Silva		Paolo Vecchi	
	Marc Waldie			Ranan Zotto		Fabio Vullo	
1988	Craig Buck	USA	13-15	Iaroslav Antonov	URS	Daniel Castellani	ARG
	Robert Ctvrtlik		15-10	Vladimir Chkourikhine		Daniel Colla	
	Scott Fortune		15-4	Andrei Kouznetsov		Hugo Conte	
	Karch Kiraly		15-8	Evgeni Krasilnikov		Juan Cuminetti	
	Ricci Luyties			Valeri Lossev		Alejandro Diz	
	Robert Partie			Yuri Pantchenko		Waldo Kantor	
	Jon Root			Igor Rounov		Eduardo Martinez	
	Eric Sato			Yuri Sapega		Esteban de Palma	
	David Saunders			Alexander Sorokolet		Raul Quiroga	
	Jeffery Stork			Yuri Tcherednik		Jon Uriarte	
	Troy Tanner			Raimond Vilde		Carlos Weber	
	Stephen Timmons			Viacheslav Zaitsev		Claudio Zulianello	
1992	Antonio Carlos Aguiar	BRA	15-12	Edwin Benne	NED	Nick Becker	USA
	Gouveia		15-8	Peter Blange		Carlos Briceno	
	Mauricio Camargo		15-5	Ronald Boudrie		Robert Ctvrtlik	
	Lima			Henk-Jan Held		Scott Fortune	
	Douglas Chiarotti			Martin van der Horst		Daniel Greenbaum	
	Talmo Curto De Oliveira			Marko Klok		Brent Hilliard	
	Andre Felippe Falbo Ferreira			Roelof van der Meulen		Bryan Ivie	
	Giovane Farinazzo Gavio			Jan Posthuma		Robert Partie	
	Paulo Andre Juroski Silva			Avital Selinger		Robert Samuelson	
	Amauri Ribeiro			Martin Teffer		Eric Sato	
	Alexandre Samuel			Ronald Zoodsma		Jeffrey Stork	
	Janelson Santos Carvalho			Ronald Zwerver		Stephen Timmons	
	Jorge Edson Saouza De Brito						
	Marcelo Teles Negrao						
1996							

VOLLEYBALL (Women)

Year	Gold	C'ntry	Score	Silver	C'ntry	Bronze	C'ntry
1964	Yuko Fujimoto	JPN		Nelly Abramova	URS	Krystyna Czajkowska	POL
	Yuriko Handa			Astra Biltauer		Maria Golimowska	
	Sata Isobe			Ludmila Buldakova		Krystyna Jakubowska	
	Masae Kasai			Ludmila Gureeva		Danuta Kordaczuk	
	Masako Kondo			Valentina Kamenek		Krystyna Krupa	
	Yoshiko Matsumura			Marita Katuscheva		Józefa Ledwig	
	Katsumi Matsumura			Nelly Lukanina		Jadwiga Marko	
	Emiko Miyamoto			Valentina Mishak		Jadwiga Rutkowska	
	Setsuko Sasaki			Tatiana Roschina		Maria Śliwka	
	Ayano Shibuki			Inna Ryskal		Zofia Szcześniewska	
	Yoko Shinozaki			Antonina Ryzhova			
	Kinuko Tanida			Tamara Tikhonina			

/continued on next page

Year	Gold	C'ntry	Score	Silver	C'ntry	Bronze	C'ntry
1968	Ludmila Buldakova	URS	15-10	Sachiko Fukunaka	JPN	Halina Aszkielowicz	POL
	Vera Galushka		16-14	Makiko Furukawa		Lidia Chmielnicka	
	Vera Lantratova		3-15	Keiko Hama		Krystyna Czajkowska	
	Galina Leontieva		15-9	Setsuko Inoue		Krystyna Jakubowska	
	Ludmila Mikhailovskaya			Toyoko Iwahara		Krystyna Krup	
	Tatiana Ponyaeva			Youko Kasahara		Jadwiga Książek	
	Inna Ryskal			Yukiyo Kojima		Józefa Ledwig	
	Roza Salikhova			Sumie Oinuma		Barbara Niemczyk	
	Tatiana Sarycheva			Aiko Onozawa		Krystyna Ostromecka	
	Nina Smoleeva			Kunie Shishikura		Elżbieta Porzec	
	Tatiana Veinberg			Suzue Takayama		Zofia Szcześniewska	
	Valentina Vinogradova			Setsuko Yoshida		Wanda Wiecha	
1972	Ludmila Borozna	URS	15-11	Makiko Furukawa	JPN	Hwang He Suk	PRK
	Ludmila Buldakova		4-15	Keiko Hama		Jang Ok Rim	
	Vera Duiunova		15-11	Takako Iida		Jong Ok Jin	
	Tatiana Gonobobleva		9-15	Toyoko Iwahara		Kang Ok Sun	
	Galina Leontieva		15-11	Katsumi Matsumura		Kim Myong Suk	
	Inna Ryskal			Sumie Oinuma		Kim Su Dae	
	Roza Salikhova			Mariko Okamoto		Kim Yeun Ja	
	Tatiana Sarytcheva			Seiko Shimakage		Kim Zung Bok	
	Nina Smoleeva			Michiko Shiokawa		Paek Myong Suk	
	Tatiana Tretakovai			Takako Shirai		Ri Chun Ok	
	Lubov Turina			Noriko Yamashita		Ryom Chun Ja	
				Yaeko Yamazaki			
1976	Yuko Arakida	JPN	15-7	Larisa Bergen	URS	Baik Myung Sun	KOR
	Takako Iida		15-8	Ludmila Chernysheva		Byon Kyung Ja	
	Katsuko Kanesaka		15-2	Zoya Iusova		Chang Hee Sook	
	Kiyomi Kato			Olga Kozakova		Jo Hea Jung	
	Echiko Maeda			Natalia Kushnir		Jung Soon Ok	
	Noriko Matsuda			Nina Muradian		Lee Soo Nok	
	Mariko Okamoto			Lilia Osadtchaya		Lee Soon Book	
	Takako Shirai			Anna Rostova		Ma Kum Ja	
	Shoko Takayanagi			Lubov Rudovskaya		Park Mi Kum	
	Hiromi Yano			Inna Ryskal		Yu Jung Ye	
	Yuri Yokoyama			Ludmila Schetinina		Yu Kyung Hwa	
	Mariko Yoshida			Nina Smoleeva		Yun Young Nae	
1980	Elena Akhaminova	URS	15-12	Katharina Bullin	GDR	Verka Borisova	BUL
	Elena Andreiuk		11-15	Barbara Czekalla		Tzvetana Bozhurina	
	Svetlana Badulina		15-13	Brigitte Fetzer		Tania Dimitrova	
	Ludmila Chernysheva		15-7	Andrea Heim		Rositsa Dimitrova	
	Liubov Kozyreva			Ute Kostrzewa		Maia Georgieva	
	Lidia Loginova			Heike Lehmann		Margarita Gerasimova	
	Irina Makagonova			Christine Mummhardt		Tania Gogova	
	Svetlana Nikishina			Karin Püschel		Valentina Ilieva	
	Larisa Pavlova			Karla Roffeis		Rumiana Kaicheva	
	Nadezda Radzevich			Martina Schmidt		Anka Khristolova	
	Natalia Razumova			Annette Schultz		Silva Petrunova	
	Olga Solovova			Anke Westendorf		Galina Stancheva	
1984	Hou Yuzhu	CHN	16-14	Jeanne Beauprey	USA	Yumi Egami	JPN
	Jiang Ying		15-3	Carolyn Becker		Norie Hiro	
	Lang Ping		15-9	Linda Chisholm		Miyoko Hirose	
	Li Yanjun			Rita Crockett		Kyoko Ishida	
	Liang Yan			Laurie Flachmeier		Yoko Kagabu	
	Su Huijuan			Debbie Green		Yoko Mitsuya	
	Yang Xilan			Flora Hyman		Keiko Miyajima	
	Yang Xiaojun			Rose Magers		Kimie Morita	
	Zhang Rongfang			Kimberly Ruddins		Kumi Nakada	
	Zheng Meizhu			Julie Vollertsen		Emiko Odaka	
	Zhou Xiaolan			Paula Weishoff		Sachiko Otani	
	Zhu Ling			Susan Woodstra		Kayoki Sugiyama	
1988	Olga Chkournova	URS	10-15	Luisa Cervera	PER	Cui Yongmei	CHN
	Svetlana Korytova		12-15	Demisse Fajardo		Hou Yuzhu	
	Marina Koumych		15-13	Miriam Gallardo		Jiyang Ying	
	Tatiana Krainova		15-7	Rosa Garcia		Li Guojun	
	Olga Krivocheeva		17-15	Alejandra de la Guerra		Li Yueming	
	Marina Nikoulina			Isabel Heredia		Su Huijuan	
	Valentina Oguienko			Katherine Horny		Wu Dan	

Year	Gold	C'ntry	Score	Silver	C'ntry	Bronze	C'ntry
	Elena Ovtchinnikova			Natalia Malaga		Yang Xiaojun	
	Irina Parkhomtchouk			Gabriela Perez del Solar		Yang Xilan	
	Tatiana Sidorenko			Cecilia Tait		Zheng Meizhu	
	Irina Smirnova			Gina Torrealva			
	Elena Volkova			Cenaida Uribe			
1992	Regla Bell McKenzie	CUB	16-14	Evguenia Artamonova	EUN	Janet Cobbs	USA
	Mercedes Calderon Martinez		12-15	Elena Batukhtina		Tara Cross-Battle	
	Magaly Carvajal Rivera		15-12	Elena Chebukina		Lory Endicott	
	Marleny Costa Blanco		15-13	Svetlana Korytova		Caren Kemner	
	Ana Ibis Fernandez Valle			Galina Lebedeva		Ruth Lawanson	
	Idalmis Gato Moya			Tatiana Menshova		Tammy Liley	
	Lilia Izquierdo Aguirre			Natalia Morozova		Kimberly Oden	
	Norka Latamblet Daudinot			Marina Nikulina		Elaina Oden	
	Mireya Luis Hernandez			Valentina Oguienko		Tonya Sanders	
	Rais O'Farril Bolanos			Tatiana Sidorenko		Liane Sato	
	Tania Ortiz Calvo			Irina Smirnova		Paula Weishoff	
	Regla Torres Herrera			Svetlana Vasilevskaya		Yoko Zetterlund	
1996							

BEACH VOLLEYBALL (Men)

Year	Gold	C'ntry	Score	Silver	C'ntry	Bronze	C'ntry
1996							

BEACH VOLLEYBALL (Women)

Year	Gold	C'ntry	Score	Silver	C'ntry	Bronze	C'ntry
1996							

Weightlifting

Stars to Watch

by Jenō Boskovics

Two triples in store?

THERE IS a strong possibility that the sport of weight-lifting will create its first triple Olympic champions in Atlanta. The athletes likely to earn this honour are Turk, Naim Suleymanoğlü, in the 64 kg category or Belarus, Alexander Kourlovitch, in the over 108 kg class. Both won in Seoul, 1988, and Barcelona, 1992, and start favourites in their respective categories in 1996.

Turkey in recent years has emerged as a world power and its lifters, in general, are amongst the top contenders for the Atlanta Games. So, too, are Turkey's neighbours, Greece, who have recently captured world, and even Olympic, titles. The Germans could also rediscover their one-time success.

Halil Mutlu, Fedail Guler and, most of all, Naim Suley-manoğlü – all from Turkey – are the gold-medal favourites in the 54, 64 and 70 kg categories respectively. Another exceptional star is Kakhi Kakhiachvili who became Olympic champion in 1992 as a member of the "Unified Team" of the ex-Soviet republics but who has been representing Greece since 1994.

Suleymanoğlü

As always, the contest of the heaviest – the over 108 kg – is expected to attract the most interest. From Games to Games, this category has been dominated by the former Soviet Union "giants" like Vlasov, Zhabotinsky, Alexeyev, and Rakhmanov. In Atlanta, the scene is set for, perhaps, the biggest super heavyweight battle of all time between Kourlovitch and Andrei Chemerkin of Russia and Ronny Weller of Germany. Another young Russian, Alexei Petrov, who recently graduated a winner from the junior ranks to be a winner of senior world titles and holder of senior world records, may also be promoted to the club of great champions.

Atlanta could also achieve records for crowd figures and participating nations (69 took part in 1992) even if the maximum number of competitors in the overall competition has been cut back to 230 under new quotas for each of the Olympic sports in an effort to contain the size, but not the quality, of the Games.

J. B. □

Retrospective

Weightlifting is one of the Olympic Games' most popular TV spectacles with huge titans straining to lift and hold seemingly unimaginable weights. It has also proved a great spectator attraction on the spot. Even as far back as 1936, 20,000 spectators watched the heavyweight competition.

Meanwhile, by curtailing the sport's entries in 1996 the Atlanta hosts should avoid the kind of pressure of numbers competing which resulted in many events at the Games between 1936 and '60 carrying on until the small hours of the

★★★★★★★★★★★★★★★★★★★★★★★★★★★★ **A Sporting Legend**

Imre Földi *(Hungary)*

Standing a mere1.48m (4ft 10in.) tall, this "mini-super" athlete is the only weightlifter in the world to have participated in five Olympic Games. Imre Földi, born in 1938, marked his first Games in Rome, going on to Tokyo (1964), Mexico City (1968), Munich (1972) and even Montreal (1976). But Foldi is also one of the most ill-fated athletes in the world. With just a little help from fortune, he may well have become the first triple Olympic Champion in weightlifting history. Yet he missed out, literally, by a matter of mere grams.

In Tokyo, after setting a 357.5 kg world record, Földi almost felt the gold medal in his hands when the Soviet, Alexei Vakhonin, attempted to jerk the – at that time – incredible weight of 142.5 kg. He succeeded, and Földi missed the gold. In Mexico, the Hungarian wound up the competition again with a world record of 367.5 kg, but his total was tied by Iranian Nassiri and as the latter weighed 300 grams less, Földi had to cede the Olympic title once again. Nevertheless, Földi did not give up. In Munich he made yet another world record total of 377.5 kg and finally captured the Olympic championship.

His Olympic tally, then, is one gold and two silver medals, one fifth and one sixth place. Various scoring systems crown him as the most successful weightlifter of all times. In his career, Földi set 20 world records and won the world championships six times. Today, Földi's biggest joy is his daughter, Csilla. She, too, chose weightlifting as her sport and is already twelve-times European champion.

WEIGHTLIFTING

morning. Remarkably, at the 1948 Games every Olympic record was broken and seven world records were set.

Olympic weightlifters have often proved acrobatic – like Mohamed Nassiri of Iran, the 1968 bantamweight winner, who celebrated with a perfect back somersault, and Takoshi Ichiba of Japan who in 1984 did a black flip before each lift to warm up.

Past weightlifting competitions at the Olympic Games have had their lighter, petulant episodes when disgruntled judges have stormed off upset at having their decisions challenged or over-ruled by the jury as in 1960 and '68. But the sport has suffered its darker Olympic moments, too. Poland's Zbigniew Kaczmarek won the lightweight gold on his 30th birthday at the 1976 Games before being disqualified for drug abuse along with seven other lifters who had been taking either steroids or amphetamines.

Several other lifters at subsequent Games have also been banned for similar offences. This includes the bizarre cases in 1992 of two British weightlifters who were banned for taking an allegedly anabolic agent called Clenbuterol. They were disqualified from the Games but later re-instated by the sport after doubts over the illegality of the substance. Weightlifting authorities, meanwhile, continue to make concerted efforts to deter would-be culprits by instituting life bans for offenders.

Background

This sport is rightly proud of its Olympic heritage. As early as the first Olympic Games of the modern era in Athens, 1896, seven weightlifters competed as part of the sport of "athletics" – one of the nine "founding" sports. It reappeared in this way in 1904 and then, in 1920, it became a separate programme sport.

Amongst the events featuring in those first Olympic Games, weightlifting was the only one which had already conferred the title of world champion on a sportsman – on 28th March, 1891, in London. Atlanta will play host to the 20th Olympic weightlifting competition and during the event the 400th Olympic weightlifting medal will be awarded – the silver in the 91 kg category.

The profile of weightlifting has changed significantly since the first Olympic Games. The original one-hand and two-hand lifts were first replaced by a competition format consisting of three disciplines: press, snatch and clean and jerk.

Norair Nurikian *(Bulgaria)*

When Norair Nurikian reached the zenith of his career, Bulgaria did not yet count as a world power in weightlifting. They had plenty of talented athletes, yet Nurikian, who was born in 1948, was the first to win an Olympic title for Bulgaria. And, to the present day, remains the only Bulgarian to have won two Olympic gold medals.

He collected these honours in Munich (1972) and Montreal (1976). Unusually, he first excelled in the 60 kg class then, four years later in Montreal, won the contest for the up to 56 kg class. Weightlifters normally move upwards to bigger weight categories as they progress in their careers.

Nurikian still shudders at the mere mention of the 56 kg. He used to have to lose weight even to make it into the 60 kg category, let alone the 56 kg. Yet, shortly before Montreal, his coaches advised him to lift in the lighter class where he had a better chance of winning. So he lost more than five kilograms in a matter of weeks. "After all, it was worth the agony," he remembers today.

Nurikian was not keen on amassing world records. He set a total of four only. His philosophy was – and still is – that the focus must be on sufficient training for the next major challenge. He was true to this principle as a competitor and later as the chief coach to the Bulgarian team. Today, he works as General Secretary of the Bulgarian Weightlifting Federation as well as being a successful businessman.

Then, in 1972, the press was abolished and the Olympic result has since been the aggregate of the best poundage in the snatch and the clean and jerk.

Along with the progress of the Olympic competition format (today a crystallized, simple, yet comprehensive system which leaves minimum room for biased refereeing decisions), developments have also taken place in the top weightlifting nations. Early in this century, Austria, Germany, Switzerland and France were the most successful nations. Later on, the

Yoshinobu Miyake *(Japan)*

Yoshinobu Miyake was an outstanding weightlifter not just in Japanese and Asian terms but on a world scale as well. At the age of 21, he entered the Games in Rome and immediately won the silver medal. He was the undisputed champion of his bodyweight category (60 kg), winning Olympic laurels both in 1964 and 1968. He also took part in the 1972 Olympic Games of Munich, however, as he pointed out, he was too old, at 33, to be able to keep pace with the younger generation and finished in fourth position.

Parallel to this wonderful Olympic career, Miyake collected six world titles and established 25 world records. He is still closely in touch with weightlifting and enjoys a worldwide reputation. He maintains a school in Japan with 300 students and trusts that some of them may become Japan's future weightlifting champions. His favourite lifter is the current king of his former category, Naim Suleymanoğlü. According to Miyake's forecast of several years ago, Suleymanoğlü was always likely to become the sport's first ever triple Olympic Champion.

A Sporting Legend ★★★★★★★★★★★★★★★★★★★★★★★★★★★★★★★★★★

Vasili Alexeev *(Soviet Union)*

This Russian giant, whose body weighed 161.7kg (25st 6.5lb) at the last Olympic Games he attended (1980), had earlier emerged out of nowhere to become an overnight star.

Apart from his compatriots, no-one had suspected his brilliance until, on January 21, 1970, at the Soviet national championships, Alexeev seized world records in the press (210.5 kg), the clean and jerk (221.5 kg) and the Olympic total (592.5 kg) and was dubbed the "Strongest Man in the World". Just two months later, he broke the magic barrier of 600 kg with a new aggregate performance. In the course of years to come, Alexeev gradually improved this figure to 645 kg.

For many years he was unbeatable. His tally of world records is still unmatched: 80. Alexeev won two Olympic gold medals: Montreal (1976) and Munich (1972), and 22 world titles – another record. He was the sport's ultimate star and a favourite invitee at international contests. Whenever he accepted an invitation, the hosts could be sure of a capacity audience. For four years (up to and including Barcelona), Alexeev was the chief coach of the Soviet team. After Barcelona, the Unified Team broke up and Alexeev retired.

USA reigned supreme for many years. Then, from its appearance in 1952, until the late '70s, the Soviet Union was the sovereign power. In the '80s the Soviets met a major challenger, Bulgaria, only for both to be threatened even more recently by Turkey, Greece and Germany.

In the course of weightlifting's Olympic history a total of 115 countries have entered 1,836 competitors – many of whom have participated at two or more Games. And the 130 gold medals have been shared by 199 weightlifters from 14 nations.

Equipment

Competitors lift 450mm (18in.) diameter disc weights which are attached to a 2.2m (7ft 2in.) long metal bar at either end and fixed with metal collars. Discs vary in weight from 0.25 kg – 25 kg, are coloured according to weight (red is the heaviest at 25 kg and the 2.5 kg disc is black) and are fitted onto the bar from the heaviest on the inside to the lightest on the outside.

Weightlifters wear regulation leotards in competition. They also have the option of wearing a t-shirt (under the leotard), a white belt at the waist and fingerless gloves. Weightlifting shoes have a strap over the instep and must give the athlete a good grip on the raised competition platform of 4m x 4m (13ft x 13ft).

Each competitor's number, category, lifts attempted and final total are recorded on electronic scoreboards which also incorporate the three lights which are operated by the referees.

Rules

One of the most important pieces of equipment at the Olympic weightlifting tournament is a set of weighing scales as each competitor, two hours before competition, must be weighed to prove that they are within the weight limit for their chosen category. If they are "overweight" they may move up, as in boxing, to a higher weight class.

There are two lifts in each competition: the snatch; the clean and jerk. During competition a lifter may decide at which weight to enter the fray and at which of the subsequent 2.5 kg intervals to continue. He has three attempts in each lift and the decisions on when to enter the competition lead to great pyschological battles between pre-event favourites. The weights are lifted in progressive order, as defined by the rules. And the weightlifter lifting the highest aggregate total from the two lifts wins unless there is a tie in which case the lifter with the lowest bodyweight wins. This latter rule has been invoked several times in Olympic history with lifters missing out on gold medals by mere grams.

Each competitor is given 90 seconds to start the attempt once called to the platform. A signal of warning is given 30 seconds before the end of a lifter's allocated time. The correctness of the lift is adjudicated by three referees, each indicating their decision by giving a white light for a good lift and red for a failed one. Final decisions are made on a majority basis.

In the snatch a lifter must place the bar horizontally on the floor, lift it with two hands starting with the palms downwards to the full extent of his arms above his head in one movement while splitting or bending his legs. Then he must bring his feet back in line with one another and hold the weight motionless until the referee signals him to put it back down. If he drops the bar after this signal from any height above his waist the lift is disallowed.

For the clean and jerk the lifter starts in the same position but hoists the bar to rest against the chest or clavicles before performing the jerk during which the bar is lifted to the full stretch of the arms above the head. Once again the lifter must finish by holding the bar motionless with his feet in a line parallel to the plane of his trunk.

Competitors in each of the ten bodyweight categories are divided into a higher and lower group depending on previous performances. Pekka Niemi of Finland is the only lifter ever to win a medal from the "B" group. He took 1984 bronze in the 100 kg class.

Atlanta Format

240 athletes – all men – will take part in the 1996 Olympic weightlifting tournament. Since 1992 the ten weight categories have been altered slightly. The new classes start at under 54 kg, rather than the 52 kg of previous years, and finish with the over 108 kg class as a substitute for Barcelona's over 110 kg category. One weight category is decided per day with a rest day after five days.

Venue

The 1996 Olympic event takes place at the Georgia World Congress Center which is 3.2km (2 miles) from the Olympic Village and has a spectator capacity of 5,000. The venue is the second largest convention centre in the USA.

WEIGHTLIFTING – current Olympic records

Event	Name	Country	Time/Result	Games	Year
Snatch					
52 kg	Sevdalin Marinov	BUL	120	Seoul	1988
56 kg	Chun Byung-Kwang	KOR	132.5	Barcelona	1992
60 kg	Naim Suleymanoğlu	TUR	152.5	Seoul	1988
67.5 kg	Israel Militossian	URS	155	Seoul	1988
	Israel Militossian	CIS	155	Barcelona	1992
75 kg	Borislav Guidikov	BUL	157.5	Seoul	1988
82.5 kg	Yuri Vardanian	URS	177.5	Moscow	1980
90 kg	Anatoli Khrapatyi	URS	187.5	Seoul	1988
100 kg	Pavel Kouznetsov	URS	190	Seoul	1988
	Viktor Tregoubov	CIS	190	Barcelona	1992
110 kg	Yuri Zacharevitch	URS	210	Seoul	1988
110 kg+	Alexander Kourlovitch	URS	212.5	Seoul	1988
Clean & Jerk					
52 kg	Sevdalin Marinov	BUL	150	Seoul	1988
	Ivan Ivanov	BUL	150	Barcelona	1992
56 kg	Oxen Mirzoian	URS	165	Seoul	1988
60 kg	Naim Suleymanoğlu	TUR	190	Seoul	1988
67.5 kg	Yanko Rusev	BUL	195	Moscow	1980
75 kg	Borislav Guidikov	BUL	207.5	Seoul	1988
82.5 kg	Yuri Vardanian	URS	222.5	Moscow	1980
90 kg	Kakhi Kakhiachvili	CIS	235	Barcelona	1992
100 kg	Pavel Kouznetsov	URS	235	Seoul	1988
110 kg	Yuri Zakarevitch	URS	245	Seoul	1988
110 kg+	Vasili Alexeev	URS	255	Montreal	1976
Total					
52 kg	Sevdalin Marinov	BUL	270	Seoul	1988
56 kg	Oxen Mirzoian	URS	292.5	Seoul	1988
60 kg	Naim Suleymanoğlu	TUR	342.5	Seoul	1988
67.5 kg	Yanko Rusev	BUL	342.5	Moscow	1980
75 kg	Borislav Guidikov	BUL	375	Seoul	1988
82.5 kg	Yuri Vardanian	URS	400	Moscow	1980
90 kg	Anatoli Khrapatyi	URS	412.5	Seoul	1988
	Kakhi Kakhiachvili	CIS	412.5	Barcelona	1992
100 kg	Pavel Kouznetsov	URS	425	Seoul	1988
110 kg	Yuri Zakarevitch	URS	455	Seoul	1988
110 kg+	Alexander Kourlovitch	URS	462.5	Seoul	1988

MEDALLISTS (by nation)

Men

Country	Gold	Silver	Bronze	Total
Soviet Union	44	25	2	71
United States	15	16	10	41
Bulgaria	10	13	5	28
Poland	4	3	18	25
Hungary	2	7	9	18
Germany	5	3	10	18
France	9	2	4	15
Italy	5	5	5	15
China	4	5	6	15
Japan	2	2	8	12
Austria	4	5	2	11
GDR	1	4	6	11
Romania	2	6	2	10
Egypt	5	2	2	9
Iran	1	3	5	9
Czechoslovakia	3	2	3	8
FRG	2	2	3	7
Estonia	1	3	3	7
Great Britain	1	3	3	7
Greece	3	-	3	6
Korea	1	1	4	6
Belgium	1	2	1	4
Switzerland	-	2	2	4
Sweden	-	-	4	4
Denmark	1	2	-	3
Australia	1	1	1	3
Cuba	1	1	1	3
Finland	1	-	2	3
Trinidad	-	1	2	3
North Korea(PRK)	-	1	2	3
Netherlands	-	-	3	3
Turkey	2	-	-	2
Canada	-	2	-	2
Argentina	-	1	1	2
Norway	1	-	-	1
Lebanon	-	1	-	1
Luxembourg	-	1	-	1
Singapore	-	1	-	1
Iraq	-	-	1	1
Taipei	-	-	1	1
	132[1]	128	134[2,3,4]	394

[1] Tie for gold in 1928 and 1936 lightweight class
[2] Four-way tie for bronze in 1896
[3] Triple tie for bronze in 1906 heavyweight class
[4] No bronze in 1992 light-heavyweight class

ATLANTA SCHEDULE

Venue: Georgia World Congress Center, Hall E

Date	Description	Round	Start	End
20 Jul	54 kg	gp B	12:30	14:30
		gp A (FINAL)	15:30	17:30
21 Jul	59 kg	gp B	12:30	14:30
		gp A (FINAL)	15:30	17:30
22 Jul	64 kg	gp B	12:30	14:30
		gp A (FINAL)	15:30	17:30
23 Jul	70 kg	gp B	12:30	14:30
		gp A (FINAL)	15:30	17:30
24 Jul	76 kg	gp B	12:30	14:30
		gp A (FINAL)	15:30	17:30
26 Jul	83 kg	gp B	12:30	14:30
		gp A (FINAL)	15:30	17:30
27 Jul	91 kg	gp B	12:30	14:30
		gp A (FINAL)	15:30	17:30
28 Jul	99 kg	gp B	12:30	14:30
		gp A (FINAL)	15:30	17:30
29 Jul	108 kg	gp B	12:30	14:30
		gp A (FINAL)	15:30	17:30
30 Jul	+108 kg	gp B	12:30	14:30
		gp A (FINAL)	15:30	17:30

Competition in this sport is open to men only.

Note: There is a possibility that some "C" sessions may be added to the schedule. The addition of these sessions will be known by 15 June 1996. If these sessions are added, they will be held between 10:00 and 11:30.

MEDALLISTS

WEIGHTLIFTING

Year	Gold	C'ntry	Points	Silver	C'ntry	Points	Bronze	C'ntry	Points

–52 kg

Year	Gold	C'ntry	Points	Silver	C'ntry	Points	Bronze	C'ntry	Points
1972	Zygmunt Smalcerz	POL	337.5	Lajos Szücs	HUN	330	Sándor Holczreiter	HUN	327.5
1976	Alexander Voronin	URS	242.5	György Köszegi	HUN	237.5	Mohammad Nassiri	IRN	235
1980	Kanybek Osmonaliev	URS	245	Chol Ho Bong	PRK	245	Han Gyong Si	PRK	245
1984	Zeng Guoqiang	CHN	235	Zhou Peishun	CHN	235	Manabe Kazushito	JPN	232.5
1988	Sevdalin Marinov	BUL	270	Chun Byung Kwan	KOR	260	He Zhuoqiang	CHN	257.5
1992	Ivan Ivanov Ivanov	BUL	265	Lin Qisheng	CHN	262.5	Traian Cihaerean	ROM	252.5

–56 kg

Year	Gold	C'ntry	Points	Silver	C'ntry	Points	Bronze	C'ntry	Points
1948	Joseph De Pietro	USA	307.3	Julian Creus	GBR	297.5	Richard Tom	USA	295
1952	Ivan Udodov	URS	315	Mahmoud Namdjou	IRN	307.5	Ali Mirzai	IRN	300
1956	Charles Vinci	USA	342.5	Vladimir Stogov	URS	337.5	Mahmoud Namjou	IRN	332.5
1960	Charles Vinci	USA	345	Yoshinobu Miyake	JPN	337.5	Esmaiil Elm Khan	IRN	330
1964	Alexei Vakhonin	URS	357.5	Imre Földi	HUN	355	Shiro Ichinoseki	JPN	347.5
1968	Mohammad Nassiri	IRN	367.5	Imre Földi	HUN	367.5	Henryk Trębicki	POL	357.5
1972	Imre Földi	HUN	377.5	Mohamed Nassiri	IRN	370	Gennadi Chetin	URS	367.5
1976	Norair Nurikian	BUL	262.5	Grzegorz Cziura	POL	252.5	Kenkichi Ando	JPN	250
1980	Daniel Nuñez	CUB	275	Yuri Sarkisian	URS	270	Tadeusz Dembończyk	POL	265
1984	Wu Shude	CHN	267.5	Lai Runming	CHN	265	Masahiro Kotaka	JPN	252.5
1988	Oxen Mirzoian	URS	292.5	He Yingqiang	CHN	287.5	Liu Shoubin	CHN	267.5
1992	Chun Byung Kwang	KOR	287.5	Liu Shoubin	CHN	277.5	Luo Jianming	CHN	277.5

–60 kg

Year	Gold	C'ntry	Points	Silver	C'ntry	Points	Bronze	C'ntry	Points
1920	François Dehaes	BEL	220	Alfred Schmit	EST	212.5	Eugène Rither	SUI	210
1924	Pierino Gabetti	ITA	402.5	Andreas Stadler	AUT	385	Arthur Reinmann	SUI	382.5
1928	Franz Andrysek	AUT	287.5	Pierino Gabetti	ITA	282.5	Hans Wölpert	GER	282.5
1932	Raymond Suvigny	FRA	287.5	Hans Wölpert	GER	282.5	Anthony Terriazo	USA	280
1936	Anthony Terlazzo	USA	312.5	Saleh Moh, Soliman	EDY	305	Ibrahim Shams	EGY	300
1948	Mahmoud Fayad	EGY	332.5	Rodney Wilkes	TRI	317.5	Jaafar Saimassi	IRN	312.5
1952	Rafael Tshimishkjan	URS	337.5	Nikolai Saksonov	URS	332.5	Rodney Wilkes	TRI	322.5
1956	Isaac Berger	USA	352.5	Evgeni Minaev	URS	342.5	Marian Zieliński	POL	335
1960	Evguenni Minaev	URS	372.5	Isaac Berger	USA	362.5	Sebastiono Mannironi	ITA	352.5
1964	Yoshinobu Miyake	JPN	397.5	Isaac Berger	USA	382.5	Mieczysław Nowak	POL	377.5
1968	Yoshinobo Miyake	JPN	392.5	Dito Shanidze	URS	387.5	Yoshiyuki Miayake	JPN	385
1972	Norair Nurikian	BUL	402.5	Dito Shanidze	URS	400	János Benedek	HUN	390
1976	Nikolai Kolesnikov	URS	285	Georgi Todorov	BUL	280	Kazumasa Hirai	JPN	275
1980	Viktor Mazin	URS	290	Stefan Dimitrov	BUL	287.5	Marek Seweryn	POL	282.5
1984	Chen Weiqiang	CHN	282.5	Gelu Radu	ROM	280	Tsai Wen-Yee	TPE	272.5
1988	Naim Suleymanoğlü	TUR	342.5	Stefan Topourov	BUL	312.5	Ye Huanming	CHN	287.5
1992	Naim Suleymanoğlü	TUR	320	Nikolai Slavev Peshalov	BUL	305	He Yingqiang	CHN	295

–67.5 kg

Year	Gold	C'ntry	Points	Silver	C'ntry	Points	Bronze	C'ntry	Points
1920	Alfred Neuland	EST	257.5	Louis Wiliquet	BEL	240	Florimond Rooms	BEL	230
1924	Edmond Décottignies	FRA	440	Anton Zwerina	AUT	427.5	Bohumil Durdys	TCH	425
1928	Hans Haas	AUT	322.5	Kurt Helbig	GER	322.5	Fernand Arnout	FRA	302.5
1932	René Duverger	FRA	325	Hans Haas	AUT	307.5	Gastone Pierini	ITA	302.5
1936	Mohamed Ahmed Mesbah	EGY	342.5	Robert Fein	AUT	342.5	Karl Jansen	GER	327.5
1948	Ibrahim Shams	EGY	360	Appia Hamouda	EGY	360	James Halliday	GBR	340
1952	Tommy Kono	USA	362.5	Evgenij Lopatin	URS	350	Verdi Barberis	AUS	350
1956	Igor Rybak	URS	380	Ravil Khaboutdinov	URS	372.5	Kim Chang Hee	KOR	370
1960	Viktor Bushuev	URS	397.5	Tan Howe Liang	SIN	380	Abdul Wahid Aziz	IRQ	380
1964	Waldemar Baszanowski	POL	432.5	Vladimir Kaplunov	URS	432.5	Marian Zieliński	POL	420
1968	Waldemar Baszanowski	POL	437.5	Parviz Jalayer	IRN	422.5	Marian Zieliński	POL	420
1972	Mukharbi Kirzhinov	URS	460	Mladen Kuchev	BUL	450	Zbigniew Kaczmarek	POL	437.5
1976	Piotr Korol	URS	305	Daniel Senet	FRA	300	Kazimierz Czarnecki	POL	295
1980	Yanko Rusev	BUL	342.5	Joachim Kunz	GDR	335	Mincho Pashev	BUL	325

Year	Gold	C'ntry	Points	Silver	C'ntry	Points	Bronze	C'ntry	Points
1984	Yao Jingyuan	CHN	320	Andrei Socaci	ROM	312.5	Jouni Grönman	FIN	312.5
1988	Joachim Kunz	GDR	340	Israel Militossian	URS	337.5	Li Jinhe	CHN	325
1992	Israel Militossian	EUN	337.5	Yoto Vassilev Yotov	BUL	327.5	Andreas Behm	GER	320

−75 kg

Year	Gold	C'ntry	Points	Silver	C'ntry	Points	Bronze	C'ntry	Points
1920	Henri Gance	FRA	245	Pietro Bianchi	ITA	237.5	Albert Pettersson	SWE	237.5
1924	Carlo Galimberti	ITA	492.5	Alfred Neuland	EST	455	Jaan Kikkas	EST	450
1928	Roger François	FRA	335	Carlo Galimberti	ITA	332.5	August Scheffer	NED	327.5
1932	Rudolf Jsmayr	GER	345	Carlo Galimberti	ITA	340	Karl Hipfinger	AUT	337.5
1936	Khadr el Touni	EGY	387.5	Rudolf Ismayr	GER	352.5	Adolf Wagner	GER	352.5
1948	Frank Spellman	USA	390	Peter George	USA	382.5	Sung Jip Kim	KOR	380
1952	Peter George	USA	400	Gérald Gratton	CAN	390	Sung Jip Kim	KOR	382.5
1956	Fedor Bogdanovskii	URS	420	Peter George	USA	412.5	Ermanno Pignatti	ITA	382.5
1960	Alexander Kurynov	URS	437.5	Tommy Kono	USA	427.5	Gyözö Veres	HUN	405
1964	Hans Zdražila	TCH	445	Viktor Kurentsov	URS	440	Masashi Ohuchi	JPN	437.5
1968	Viktor Kurentsov	URS	475	Masashi Ohuchi	JPN	455	Károly Bakos	HUN	440
1972	Yordan Bikov	BUL	485	Mohamed Trabulsi	LIB	472.5	Anselmo Silvino	ITA	470
1976	Yordan Mitkov	BUL	335	Vartan Militosyan	URS	330	Peter Wenzel	GDR	327.5
1980	Asen Zlatev	BUL	360	Alexander Pervi	URS	357.5	Nedelcho Kolev	BUL	345
1984	Karl-Heinz Radschinsky	FRG	340	Jacques Demers	CAN	335	Dragomir Cioroslan	ROM	332.5
1988	Borislav Guidikov	BUL	375	Ingo Steinhöfel	GDR	360	Alexander Varbanov	BUL	357.5
1992	Fedor Kassapu	EUN	357.5	Pablo Lara Rodriguez	CUB	357.5	Myong Nam Kim	PRK	352.5

−82.5 kg

Year	Gold	C'ntry	Points	Silver	C'ntry	Points	Bronze	C'ntry	Points
1920	Ernest Cadine	FRA	295	Fritz Hünenberger	SUI	277.5	Erik Pettersson	SWE	267.5
1924	Charles Rigoulot	FRA	502.5	Fritz Hünenberger	SUI	490	Leopold Friedrich	AUT	490
1928	El Sayed Nosseir	EGY	355	Louis Hostin	FRA	352.5	Johannes Verheijen	NED	337.5
1932	Louis Hostin	FRA	365	Svend Olsen	DEN	360	Henry Duey	USA	330
1936	Louis Hostin	FRA	372.5	Eugen Deutsch	GER	365	Ibrahim Wasif	EGY	360
1948	Stanley Stanczyk	USA	417.5	Harold Sakata	USA	380	Gösta Magnusson	SWE	375
1952	Trofim Lomakin	URS	417.5	Stanley Stanczyk	USA	415	Arkadij Vorobjev	URS	407.5
1956	Tommy Kono	USA	447.5	Vassili Stepanov	URS	427.5	James George	USA	417.5
1960	Ireneusz Paliński	POL	442.5	James George	USA	430	Jan Bochenek	POL	420
1964	Rudolf Plyukfeider	URS	475	Géza Tóth	HUN	467.5	Gyözö Veres	HUN	467.5
1968	Boris Selitsky	URS	485	Vladimir Belyaev	URS	485	Norbert Ozimek	POL	472.5
1972	Leif Jenssen	NOR	507.5	Norbert Ozimek	POL	497.5	György Horváth	HUN	495
1976	Valeri Shary	URS	365	Trendafil Stoichev	BUL	360	Péter Baczakó	HUN	345
1980	Yuri Vardanian	URS	400	Blagoi Blagoev	BUL	372.5	Dušán Poliačik	TCH	367.5
1984	Petre Becheru	ROM	355	Robert Kabbas	AUS	342.5	Ryoji Isaoka	JPN	340
1988	Israil Arsamakov	URS	377.5	István Messzi	HUN	370	Lee Hyung Kun	KOR	367.5
1992	Pyrros Dimas	GRE	370	Krzysztof Siemion	POL	370	Ibragim Samadov	EUN	370

−90 kg

Year	Gold	C'ntry	Points	Silver	C'ntry	Points	Bronze	C'ntry	Points
1952	Norbert Schemansky	USA	445	Grigorij Novak	URS	410	Lennox Kilgour	TRI	402.5
1956	Arkadil Vorobiev	URS	462.5	Dave Sheppard	USA	442.5	Jean Debuf	FRA	425
1960	Arkadil Vorobiev	URS	472.5	Trofim Lomakin	URS	457.5	Louis Martin	GBR	445
1964	Vladimir Golovanov	URS	487.5	Louis George Martin	GBR	475	Ireneusz Paliński	POL	467.5
1968	Kaarlo Kangasniemi	FIN	518	Yan Talts	URS	507.5	Marek Golab	POL	495
1972	Andon Nikolov	BUL	525	Atanas Shopov	BUL	517.5	Hans Bettembourg	SWE	512.5
1976	David Rigert	URS	382.5	Lee James	USA	362.5	Atanas Shopov	BUL	360
1980	Péter Baczakó	HUN	377.5	Rumen Aleksandrov	BUL	375	Frank Mantek	GDR	370
1984	Nicu Vlad	ROM	392.5	Dumitru Petre	ROM	360	David Mercer	GBR	352.5
1988	Anatoli Khrapatyi	URS	412.5	Nail Moukhamediarov	URS	400	Slawomir Zawada	POL	400
1992	Kakhi Kakhiachvili	EUN	412.5	Sergei Syrtsov	EUN	412.5	Sergiusz Wolczaniecki	POL	392.5

−100 kg

Year	Gold	C'ntry	Points	Silver	C'ntry	Points	Bronze	C'ntry	Points
1980	Otakar Zaremba	TCH	395	Igor Nikitin	URS	392.5	Alberto Blanco	CUB	385
1984	Rolf Milser	FRG	385	Vasile Gropă	ROM	382.5	Pekka Niemi	FIN	367.5
1988	Pavel Kouznetsov	URS	425	Nicu Vlad	ROM	402.5	Peter Immesberger	FRG	395
1992	Viktor Tregoubov	EUN	410	Timour Taimazov	EUN	402.5	Waldemar Malak	POL	400

/continued on next page 431

Year	Gold	C'ntry	Points	Silver	C'ntry	Points	Bronze	C'ntry	Points

–110 kg

Year	Gold	C'ntry	Points	Silver	C'ntry	Points	Bronze	C'ntry	Points
1972	Jaan Talts	URS	580	Alexander Kratchev	BUL	562.5	Stefan Grützner	GDR	555
1976	Yuri Zaitsev	URS	385	Krastcho Semerdjiev	BUL	385	Tadeusz Rutkowski	POL	377.5
1980	Leonid Taranenko	URS	422.5	Valentin Christov	BUL	405	György Szalai	HUN	390
1984	Norberto Oberburger	ITA	390	Stefan Tasnadi	ROM	380	Guy Carlton	USA	377.5
1988	Yuri Zakarevitch	URS	455	József Jacsó	HUN	427.5	Ronny Weller	GDR	425
1992	Ronny Weller	GER	410	Timur Taimasov	UKR	402.5	Waldemar Malak	POL	400

Unlimited Weight (110 kg+)

Year	Gold	C'ntry	Points	Silver	C'ntry	Points	Bronze	C'ntry	Points
1920	Filippo Bottino	ITA	265	Joseph Alzin	LUX	260	Louis Bernet	FRA	255
1924	Giuseppe Tonani	ITA	517.5	Franz Aigner	AUT	515	Harald Tammer	EST	497.5
1928	Josef Strassberger	GER	372.5	Arnold Luohaäär	EST	360	Jaroslav Skobla	TCH	357.5
1932	Jaroslav Skobla	TCH	380	Václav Pšenička	TCH	377.5	Josef Strassberger	GER	377.5
1936	Josef Manger	GER	410	Václav Pšenička	TCH	402.5	Arnold Luohaäär	EST	400
1948	John Davis	USA	452.5	Norbert Schemansky	USA	425	Abram Charité	NED	412.5
1952	John Davis	USA	460	Jim Bradford	USA	437.5	Humberto Selvetti	ARG	432.5
1956	Paul Anderson	USA	500	Humberio Selvetti	ARG	500	Alberto Pigaiani	ITA	452.5
1960	Yuri Vlasov	URS	537.5	Jim Bradford	USA	512.5	Norbert Schemansky	USA	500
1964	Leonid Zhabotinsky	URS	572.5	Yuri Vlasov	URS	570	Norbert Schemansky	USA	537.5
1968	Leonid Zhabotinsky	URS	572.5	Serge Reding	BEL	555	Joseph Dube	USA	555
1972	Vasili Alexeev	URS	640	Rudolph Mang	GER	610	Gerd Bonk	GDR	572.5
1976	Vasili Alexeev	URS	440	Gerd Bonk	GDR	405	Helmut Losch	GDR	387.5
1980	Sultan Rakhmanov	URS	440	Jürgen Heuser	GDR	410	Tadeusz Rutkowski	POL	407.5
1984	Dinko Lukim	AUS	412.5	Mario Martinez	USA	410	Manfred Nerlinger	FRG	397.5
1988	Alexander Kourlovitch	URS	462.5	Manfred Nerlinger	FRG	430	Martin Zawieja	FRG	415
1992	Alexander Kourlovitch	EUN	450	Leonid Taranenko	EUN	425	Manfred Nerlinger	GER	412.5

* NB All weight categories change in 1996

–54 kg
1996

–59 kg
1996

–64 kg
1996

–70 kg
1996

–76 kg
1996

–83 kg
1996

–91 kg
1996

–99 kg
1996

–108 kg
1996

108 kg+
1996

Wrestling

Stars to Watch

by Togay Bayatli

Devastating power and technique

ATLANTA'S wrestling competition should provide a panoply of stars. But, the brightest and best, could well prove to be Russia's Alexander Kareline. He won gold in Barcelona in the 130 kg Greco-Roman competition. And Kareline is noted for both his power and his technique – a devastating combination. No-one has been able so far to pin him down in a competition.

Jack Jones (USA) 1992

In the freestyle disciplines, meanwhile, Bulgaria's seven-times world champion at 52 kg, Valentin Jordanov, will be looking to better his Barcelona bronze. His main rival could be Jack Jones of the USA. A Turk, Turan Ceylan, starts as favourite in the 74 kg category whilst his compatriot, Mahmut Demir is the leading contender at over 100 kg. Americans look set to dominate the 82 kg category through Kevin Jackson, a three-times world, and defending Olympic, champion.

The Greco-Roman honours could be spread wider. Russia's

★★★★★★★★★★★★★★★★★★★★★★★★★★★★★★ **A Sporting Legend**

Ahmet Ayik *(Turkey)*

To become Olympic and world champion in any sport is difficult enough. But Ahmet Ayik – often referred to as "the gentleman of the mat" – had greater obstacles than most as his career coincided with that of the widely-regarded master and three-times Olympic champion, Alexander Medved of the Soviet Union, as well of that of the tough Iranian opponent Tahti.

Indeed Ayik, the 1968 Olympic champion, never lost to the great Medved. In 1964 the two met in the final of the 97 kg category of the Olympic Games. At the end of competition time Ayik was 2-1 ahead. But under wrestling rules a victory can only be recorded if three points have been scored by one wrestler. So the situation went for arbitration to the mat officials who gave victory to Medved.

Ayik went to embrace and congratulate Medved with tears in his eyes as he collected his silver medal and vowed one day to beat the Soviet legend – a feat he later managed only once in competition. Ayik went on to win the world and European championships twice each.

Islam Dorusev is the favourite for the 68 kg category but looks set to face a challenge from Valouz Ghani of France. Cuba, Germany and Turkey are also leading nations in this classical sport.

T. B. □

Retrospective

Rumour has it that there were no time limits on wrestling contests in the early Olympic Games of the modern era. Yet some accounts of bouts also speak of final whistles after half an hour and others refer to just six minutes. Whatever the truth for each Games, we know that in 1912 one contest between Martin Klein, representing Russia, and Alpo Asikainen of Finland, lasted 11 hours and 40 minutes. Klein won but was too exhausted to continue in the next round.

Britain's 1984 bronze medallist Noel Loban was born in Wimbledon, raised in New York, before returning to his native London as a lay-preacher come teacher. He ran up the 180 emergency exit stairs in the British capital's Russell Square tube station ten times every day as part of his training. Another British wrestling bronze medallist, Ken Richmond from the 1952 Games, was famous as the well-honed man who struck the gong at the beginning of the Rank Company films.

In 1952 four Turkish Olympic champions were unable to defend their titles, won in 1948, because their entries were submitted after the deadline. Alexander Medved, of the

A Sporting Legend ★★★★★★★★★★★★★★★★★★★★★★★★★★★★★★★★★

Alexander Medved *(Soviet Union)*

Alexander Medved is the world's most revered and famous wrestler. He was born on September 16, 1937, in Belaya Tzerkov. After finishing school in 1954 he served in the Soviet Army for three years and later studied at the State Culture Institute until 1965. Today, Medved is the Head of the Sports Department at the Belarussian State University.

But it is as a three-times Olympic wrestling champion that he will be remembered. It was in Munich, in 1972, that Medved, by then a 35 year-old weighing 104.78 kg (16st 7lb), won his third successive Greco-Roman title. This time round it was in the super heavyweight division to add to his previous successes in lighter body-weight classes. It was a feat nothing short of remarkable in a sport which is gruelling in its physical demands.

This seven-times world champion and three times European champion was renowned for his power as well as his technique. In his wrestling days he competed for the Soviet Union and won nine national titles as well as being awarded the Order of Lenin for his achievements. But after the break-up of the Soviet bloc he was elected the first Vice-President of the Belarus National Olympic Committee. He was also awarded the IOC's Olympic Order and won UNESCO's prize "For Nobility in Sport".

Soviet Union, was a wrestling legend, winning three successive Olympic gold medals in 1964, '68 and '72.

In 1984 the wrestling competition was affected by the boycott and American brothers Mark and David Schultz became medal-contenders. Both won golds but not before they had been accused of "brutality" by some watching experts. According to the reports, David wrenched an opponent's knee and Mark broke an opponent's elbow.

Background

Wrestling as a sport and form of combat is probably as old as the Human Race. The famous Greek poet of *circa* 8th century BC, Homer, described epic wrestling matches and the sport was definitely part of the Ancient Games. Many different branches of the sport have grown up around the world including the famous "Sumo" wrestling in Japan.

The modern version of the sport is exciting and has thousands of participants particularly in Russia, Turkey, Japan and Iran. Scandinavia, too, has produced many good Greco-Roman exponents. After World War II, the Soviet-bloc nations began to emerge as major contenders at the Games.

As an Olympic sport, wrestling made its debut as an open bodyweight contest in the Greco-Roman style at the 1896 Games before the freestyle discipline joined the Olympic programme in 1904.

★★★★★★★★★★★★★★★★★★★★★★★★★★★★★★★ **A Sporting Legend**

Yasar Dogu *(Turkey)*

Imagine a sportsman whose career spanned several decades but who only lost once in senior competition. That is the story of Yasar Dogu, a Turkish wrestler, who understandably became a legend in his own country.

Dogu's one defeat came in Oslo at the 1939 European championships during his first Greco-Roman competition in which he won the silver medal. Born in a little village on the Black Sea in 1913, Dogu went on to become Olympic, world, European and Balkan champion. His titles began with the two European titles in 1947. Both were in the 73 kg class but the first, in Stockholm, was freestyle and the second, in Prague, was Greco-Roman. Dogu went on to win the Olympic freestyle title in the same division a year later in London and took the world title in 1951 in Helsinki at 87 kg.

As a wrestler, Dogu was famous for the power in his arms and, therefore, he was successful both in freestyle and Greco-Roman. After finishing his active life as a wrestler, he became the coach of the Turkish National Team which won six gold and two silver medals in 1960 at the Rome Games.

WRESTLING

Equipment

Wrestling takes place on a mat which looks a little like a "target" on the floor. It has a centre spot, and a red one-metre (3ft 3in.) wide band forming a circle of 7m (22ft 10in.) in diameter out from the centre (see diagram). The colours help mark out the competition zones. Each wrestler has a corner – coloured blue or red on the mat – for each bout and they must wear either the corresponding blue or red singlet. For Greco-Roman events this singlet can extend below the knees but in freestyle wrestling it must only reach to mid-thigh length.

Wrestlers also wear specially-designed shoes which have good ankle supports. They must be either clean-shaven or have a full beard – in-between measures are not permitted.

Wrestling mat

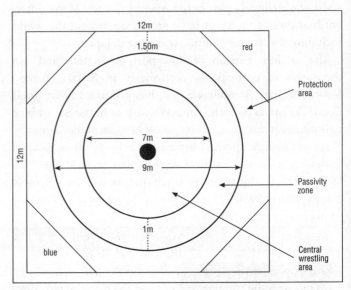

Rules

There are two types of wrestling style which have separate competitions and medals at the Olympic Games: Greco-Roman and freestyle. In the former, wrestlers can only attack and hold using their arms and upper body whereas they can also use their legs in freestyle.

For both types of competition each wrestler is weighed and must be within the permitted range for the weight class. Wrestlers are then paired off in the draw for the preliminary round and fight each other. The winners go into the "A" draw and the losers into the "B" draw. Winners progress through the "A" draw until there are only two wrestlers left who fight for the gold and silver medal in the final. In the "B" draw any wrestler who loses twice is eliminated. The remainder progress until there are only two remaining who compete for the bronze medal. There are also classification bouts for the other placings.

Each bout lasts for five minutes. After five minutes, if there is no winner, the competition will continue into overtime which lasts a maximum of three minutes. A wrestling bout is controlled by the referee on the mat. He wears a red cuff on one arm and a blue cuff on the other and uses his fingers to indicate the points scored by the relevant wrestler for holds and moves. These are then evaluated by the judge who, if in agreement, puts them on the electronic scoreboard. Where the referee and judge disagree it is up to the mat chairman to make the final decision.

A bout can be won by a wrestler who pins his opponent down so that both his shoulders come into contact with the mat. This is called a "fall" and the referee strikes the mat and blows his whistle to indicate that the bout is over. Wrestlers also win if they establish a margin of ten clear points over their rival – called "technical superiority". And a victory on "points" can be declared at the end of regulation time as long as the leading wrestler has scored at least three technical points. In overtime, the first wrestler to score a point wins as long as this brings his score to at least three points. If there is no clear winner on points even after overtime then the mat officials award a victory "by decision" in which they evaluate all the moves of the bout.

Wrestlers are penalized during competition for a variety of illegal holds and offences including "passivity". This means that a wrestler is being too defensive. If a bout spills out over the competition zone on the mat, the wrestlers are brought back to the centre to continue either in a standing position or on the ground. Different holds and attacks score differing points. These are called technical points. But a wrestler's final recorded score is logged in classification points. These include a 4-0 victory for a fall, 4-1 win for technical superiority, 3-0 for a win on points where the loser has no technical points, 3-1 for a win on points if the opponent has scored technical points and 3-1 for a win by decision.

Atlanta format

A total of 380 wrestlers – all men – will participate in the 1996 Olympic Games in Atlanta. There are ten weight categories in each style – freestyle and Greco-Roman – giving a total of 60 medals on offer. The competition is a knock-out draw with once-defeated athletes having the chance, via a "B" draw, to compete for the bronze medal. Wrestlers qualified for Atlanta through a series of continental championships and wild cards.

Venue

Wrestling takes place at the Georgia World Congress Center which is 3.2km (2 miles) from the Olympic Village. It has a spectator capacity of 5,000. This venue, which is the USA's second largest convention centre, will also host competitions in a variety of other sports during the Games.

MEDALLISTS (by nation)

	Freestyle			Greco-Roman			
	Gold	Silver	Bronze	Gold	Silver	Bronze	Total
Soviet Union	31	17	15	37	19	13	132
United States	41	32	21	2	2	3	101
Finland	8	7	10	19	20	18	82
Sweden	8	10	8	19	16	18	79
Bulgaria	6	15	9	8	14	7	59
Hungary	3	4	7	15	9	11	49
Turkey	15	11	6	9	4	2	47
Japan	16	9	7	4	4	2	42
Romania	1	-	4	6	8	13	32
Germany	1	3	2	4	12	7	29
Iran	3	8	11	-	1	1	24
Korea	4	4	6	1	1	5	21
Italy	1	-	-	5	4	9	19
Poland	-	1	3	2	7	5	18
Great Britain	3	4	10	-	-	-	17
Yugoslavia	1	1	2	3	5	4	16
Czechoslovakia	-	1	3	1	6	4	15
Switzerland	4	4	5	-	-	1	14
Denmark	-	-	-	2	3	7	12
France	2	2	3	1	1	2	11
Estonia	2	1	-	3	-	4	10
Canada	-	4	5	-	-	-	9
FRG	-	1	3	1	3	1	9
Greece	-	-	1	1	3	4	9
Mongolia	-	4	4	-	-	-	8
GDR	-	2	1	2	1	1	7
North Korea (PRK)	2	2	2	-	-	-	6
Cuba	1	-	1	1	-	2	5
Austria	-	-	1	1	2	1	5
Egypt (UAR)	-	-	-	1	2	2	5
Norway	-	1	-	2	1	1	5
Belgium	-	3	-	-	-	1	4
Australia	-	1	2	-	-	-	3
Russia	-	-	-	-	3	-	3
Lebanon	-	-	-	-	1	2	3
Latvia	-	-	-	-	1	-	1
Mexico	-	-	-	-	1	-	1
Syria	-	1	-	-	-	-	1
China	-	-	-	-	-	1	1
India	-	-	1	-	-	-	1
Pakistan	-	-	1	-	-	-	1
	153	153	154[1]	150[2]	154	152[3]	916

[1] Two bronzes in 1920 heavyweight class
[2] No gold in 1912 light-heavyweight class
[3] No bronze in 1906 all-round class

ATLANTA SCHEDULE

Venue: Georgia World Congress Center,
Hall G – Greco-Roman
Hall H – Freestyle

Date	Description	Round	Start	End
Greco-Roman				
20 Jul	48,57,68,82,100 kg	prelims	10:00	13:00
		classification	15:30	18:40
21 Jul	48,57,68,82,100 kg	classification	10:00	13:50
	48,57,68,82,100 kg	bronze matches	15:30	18:20
		FINALS		
22 Jul	52,62,74,90,130 kg	prelims	10:00	13:00
		classification	15:30	18:40
23 Jul	52,62,74,90,130 kg	classification	10:00	13:50
	52,62,74,90,130 kg	bronze matches	15:30	18:20
		FINALS		
Freestyle				
30 Jul	48,57,68,82,100 kg	prelims	9:30	13:00
		classification	15:30	18:40
31 Jul	48,57,68,82,100 kg	classification	9:30	13:20
	48,57,68,82,100 kg	bronze matches	15:30	18:20
		FINALS		
1 Aug	52,62,74,90,130 kg	prelims	9:30	13:00
		classification	15:30	18:40
2 Aug	52,62,74,90,130 kg	classification	9:30	13:20
	52,62,74,90,130 kg	bronze matches	15:30	18:20
		FINALS		

Competition in this sport is open to men only

MEDALLISTS

WRESTLING

Year	Gold	C'ntry	Silver	C'ntry	Bronze	C'ntry

Freestyle (–48 kg)*

Year	Gold	C'ntry	Silver	C'ntry	Bronze	C'ntry
1904	Robert Curry	USA	John Hein	USA	Gustav Thiefenthaler	USA
1972	Roman Dmitriev	URS	Ognian Nikolov	BUL	Ebrahim Javadpour	IRN
1976	Khassan Issaev	BUL	Roman Dmitriev	URS	Akira Kudo	JPN
1980	Claudio Pollio	ITA	Jang Se Hong	PRK	Sergei Kornilaev	URS
1984	Robert Weaver	USA	Takashi Irie	JPN	Son Gab Do	KOR
1988	Takashi Kobayshi	JPN	Ivan Tzonov	BUL	Sergei Karamtchakov	URS
1992	Kim Il	PRK	Kim Jong Shin	KOR	Vougar Oroudjov	EUN
1996						

Freestyle (–52 kg)

Year	Gold	C'ntry	Silver	C'ntry	Bronze	C'ntry
1904	George Mehnert	USA	Gustav Bauer	USA	William Nelson	USA
1948	Lennart Vitala	FIN	Halit Balamir	TUR	K R Johansson	SWE
1952	Hasan Gemici	TUR	Yushu Kitano	JPN	Mahmoud Mollaghassemi	IRN
1956	Mirian Tsalkalamanidze	URS	Mohamad-Ali Khojastehpour	IRN	Hüseyin Akbaş	TUR
1960	Ahmet Bilek	TUR	Masayuki Matsubara	JPN	Saidabaar Moha Safepow	IRN
1964	Yoshida Yoshikatsu	JPN	Chang Sun Chang	KOR	Said Aliakbar Haydari	IRN
1968	Shigeo Nakata	JPN	Richard Sanders	USA	Surenjav Sukhbaatar	MGL
1972	Kiyomi Kato	JPN	Arsen Alakhverdiev	URS	Kim Gwong-hyong	PRK
1976	Yuji Takada	JPN	Alexander Ivanov	URS	Jeon Hae Sup	KOR
1980	Anatoli Beloglazov	URS	Władysław Stecyk	POL	Nermedin Selimov	BUL
1984	Šaban Trstena	YUG	Kim Jong Kyu	KOR	Yuji Takada	JPN
1988	Mitsuru Sato	JPN	Šaban Trstena	YUG	Vladimir Togouzov	URS
1992	Hak-son Li	PRK	Larry Lee Jones	USA	Valentin Jordanov	BUL
1996						

Freestyle (–57 kg)

Year	Gold	C'ntry	Silver	C'ntry	Bronze	C'ntry
1904	Isidor 'Jack' Niflot	USA	August Wester	USA	Zenon B Strebler	USA
1908	N Mehnert	USA	William Press	GBR	Aubert Côté	CAN
1924	Kustaa Pihlajamäki	FIN	Kaarol Makinen	FIN	Bryan Hines	USA
1928	Kaarlo Mäkinen	FIN	C Spapen	BEL	James Trifunov	CAN
1932	Robert Pearce	USA	Ödön Zombori	HUN	Aatos Jaskari	FIN
1936	Ödön Zombory	HUN	Ross Flood	USA	Johannes Herbert	GER
1948	Nasuh Akar	TUR	Gerald Leeman	USA	Charles Kouyos	FRA
1952	Shohachi Ishii	JPN	Rashid Mamedbekov	URS	Kha-Shaba Jadav	IND
1956	Mustafa Dagistanli	TUR	Mohamad-Mehdi Yaghoubi	IRN	Mikhail Chatkov	URS
1960	Terence McCann	USA	Nejdet Zalev	BUL	Tadeusz Trojanowski	POL
1964	Yajiro Uetake	JPN	Huseyin Akbas	TUR	Aidyn Ali Ogly Ibragimov	URS
1968	Yochito Uetake	JPN	Donald Behm	USA	Gorgori Abutaleb	IRN
1972	Hideaki Yanagida	JPN	Richard Sanders	USA	László Klinga	HUN
1976	Vladimir Umin	URS	Hans-Dieter Bruchert	GDR	Masao Arai	JPN
1980	Sergei Beloglazov	URS	Li Ho-pyong	PRK	Dugarsuren Ouinbold	MGL
1984	Hideaki Tomiyama	JPN	Barry Davis	USA	Kim Eui Kon	KOR
1988	Sergei Beloglazov	URS	Askari Mohammadian	IRN	Noh Kyung Sun	KOR
1992	Alejandro Puerto Diaz	CUB	Sergei Smal	EUN	Kim Yong-sik	PRK
1996						

Freestyle (–62 kg)

Year	Gold	C'ntry	Silver	C'ntry	Bronze	C'ntry
1904	Benjamin Bradshaw	USA	Theodore McLear	USA	Charles Clapper	USA
1908	George Dole	USA	James Slim	GBR	William McKie	GBR
1920	Charles Ackerly	USA	Samuel Gerson	USA	Philip Bernard	GBR
1924	Robin Reed	USA	Chester Newton	USA	Katsutoshi Naitoh	JPN
1928	Allie Morrisson	USA	A Pihlajamäki	FIN	Hans Minder	AUI
1932	Herman Pihlajamäki	FIN	Edgar Nemir	USA	Einar Karlsson	SWE
1936	Kustaa Pihlajamäki	FIN	Francis Millard	USA	Gösta Jönsson	SWE
1948	Gazanfer Bilge	TUR	Ivar Sjölin	SWE	Adolf Müller	SUI
1952	Bayram Şit	TUR	Nasser Guivéhtchi	IRN	Josiah Henson	USA
1956	Shozo Sasahara	JPN	Joseph Mewis	BEL	Erkki Eino Penttilä	FIN
1960	Mustafa Dağistanli	TUR	Stancho Ivanov	BUL	Vladimir Rubashvili	URS
1964	Osamu Watanabe	JPN	Stantcho Kolev Ivanov	BUL	Nodar Khokhashvili	URS

*NB: all weight limits have varied slightly for each category in different Games

Year	Gold	C'ntry	Silver	C'ntry	Bronze	C'ntry
1968	Masaaki Kaneko	JPN	Todorov Enio	BUL	Shamseddin Seyed-Abbassi	IRN
1972	Zagalav Abdulbekov	URS	Vehbi Akdag	TUR	Ivan Krastev	BUL
1976	Yang Jung Mo	KOR	Zeveg Oidov	MGL	Gene Davis	USA
1980	Magomedgasan Abushev	URS	Mikho Dukov	BUL	Georges Hajiioannidis	GRE
1984	Randy Lewis	USA	Kosei Akaishi	JPN	Lee Jung Keun	KOR
1988	John Smith	USA	Stepan Sarkissian	URS	Simeon Chterev	BUL
1992	John Smith	USA	Asgari Mohammadian	IRN	Lozaro Reinoso Martinez	CUB
1996						

Freestyle (−68 kg)

Year	Gold	C'ntry	Silver	C'ntry	Bronze	C'ntry
1904	Otto Roehm	USA	Rudolph Tesing	USA	Albert Zirkel	USA
1908	George de Relwyskow	GBR	William Wood	GBR	Albert Gingell	GBR
1920	Kaarlo Anttila	FIN	Gottfrid Svensson	SWE	Peter Wright	GBR
1924	Russell Vis	USA	Volmari Wikström	FIN	Arvo Haavisto	FIN
1928	Osvald Käpp	EST	Charles Pacôme	FRA	Eino Leino	FIN
1932	Charles Pacome	FRA	Károly Kárpáti	HUN	Gustaf Klarén	SWE
1936	Károly Kárpáti	HUN	Wolfgang Ehrl	GER	Herman Pihlajamäki	FIN
1948	Celal Atik	TUR	Gösta Frändfors	SWE	Hermann Baumann	SUI
1952	Olle Anderberg	SWE	Thomas Evans	USA	Djahanbakte Tovfighe	IRN
1956	Emamali Habibi	IRN	Shigera Kasahara	JPN	Alimbeg Bestaev	URS
1960	Shelby Wilson	USA	Vladimir Sinyavskiy	URS	Enio Valtchev Dimov	BUL
1964	Enio Valtchev Dimov	BUL	Klaus Rost	GER	Iwao Horiuchi	JPN
1968	Abdollah Movahed	IRN	Enio Valtchev Dimov	BUL	Sereeter Danzandarjaa	MGL
1972	Dan Gable	USA	Kikuo Wada	JPN	Ruslan Ashuraliev	URS
1976	Pavel Pinigin	URS	Lloyd Keaser	USA	Yasaburo Sugawara	JPN
1980	Saipulla Absaidov	URS	Ivan Yankov	BUL	Šaban Sejdi	YUG
1984	You In Tak	KOR	Andrew Rein	USA	Jukka Rauhala	FIN
1988	Arsen Fadzaev	URS	Park Jang Soon	KOR	Nate Carr	USA
1992	Arsen Fadzaev	EUN	Valentin Getzov	BUL	Kosei Akaishi	JPN
1996						

Freestyle (−74 kg)

Year	Gold	C'ntry	Silver	C'ntry	Bronze	C'ntry
1904	Charles Ericksen	USA	William Beckmann	USA	Jerry Winholtz	USA
1924	Hermann Gehri	SUI	Eino Leino	FIN	Otto Muller	SUI
1928	Arvo Haavisto	FIN	Lloyd Appelton	USA	Maurice Letchford	CAN
1932	Jack van Bebber	USA	Daniel MacDonald	CAN	Eino Leino	FIN
1936	Frank Lewis	USA	Ture Andersson	SWE	Joe Schleimer	CAN
1948	Yaşar Doğu	TUR	Richard Garrard	AUS	Lelland Merrill	USA
1952	William Smith	USA	Per Gunnar Börje Berlin	SWE	Abdullah Modjtabavi	IRN
1956	Mitsuo Ikeda	JPN	Ibrahim Zengin	TUR	Vakhtang Balavadze	URS
1960	Douglas Blubaugh	USA	Ismail Ogan	TUR	Mohammad Bashir	PAK
1964	Ismail Ogan	TUR	Guliko Sagaradze	URS	Mohamad-Ali Sanatkaran	IRN
1968	Mahmut Atalay	TUR	Daniel Robin	FRA	Dagvasuren Purev	MGL
1972	Wayne Wells	USA	Jan Karlsson	SWE	Adolf Seger	FRG
1976	Jiichiro Date	JPN	Mansour Barzegar	IRN	Stanley Dziedzic	USA
1980	Valentin Raichev	BUL	Jamtsying Davaajav	MGL	Daniel Karabin	TCH
1984	David Schultz	USA	Martin Knosp	FRG	Šaban Sejdi	YUG
1988	Kenneth Monday	USA	Adlan Varaev	URS	Rakhmad Sofiadi	BUL
1992	Park Jang Soon	KOR	Kenneth Monday	USA	Amir Khadem Azghadi	IRN
1996						

Freestyle (−82 kg)

Year	Gold	C'ntry	Silver	C'ntry	Bronze	C'ntry
1908	Stanley Bacon	GBR	George de Rewylskow	GBR	Frederick Beck	GBR
1920	Eino Leino	FIN	Vaino Penttala	FIN	Charles Johnson	USA
1924	Fritz Haggmann	SUI	Pierre Ollivier	BEL	Vilho Pekkala	FIN
1928	Ernst Kyburz	SUI	Donald Stockton	CAN	Samuel Rabin	GBR
1932	Ivar Johansson	SWE	Kyösti Luukko	FIN	József Tunyogi	HUN
1936	Emile Poilvé	FRA	Richard Voliva	USA	Ahmet Kireçci	TUR
1948	Glenn Brand	USA	Adil Candemir	TUR	Erik Lindén	SWE
1952	David Cimakuridze	URS	Golamreza Takhty	IRN	György Gurics	HUN
1956	Nikola Stantchen Nikolov	BUL	Dan Allen Hodge	USA	Guergui Skhirtladze	URS
1960	Hazan Güngör	TUR	Gueorgui Skhirtladze	URS	Hans Antonsson	SWE
1964	Prodan Stoyanov Gardjev	BUL	Hasan Güngör	TUR	Daniel Oliver Brand	USA
1968	Boris Gurevitch	URS	Munkhbat Jigjid	MGL	Prodane Gardjev	BUL

/continued on next page 441

Year	Gold	C'ntry	Silver	C'ntry	Bronze	C'ntry
1972	Levan Tediashvili	URS	John Peterson	USA	Vasile Iorga	ROM
1976	John Peterson	USA	Viktor Novojilov	URS	Adolf Seger	FRG
1980	Ismail Abilov	BUL	Magomedkhan Aratsilov	URS	István Kovács	HUN
1984	Mark Schultz	USA	Hideyjuki Nagashima	JPN	Chris Rinke	CAN
1988	Han Myung Woo	KOR	Necmi Gencalp	TUR	Josef Lohyňa	TCH
1992	Kevin Jackson	USA	Elmadi Jabraijlov	EUN	Rasul Khadem Azghadi	IRN
1996						

Freestyle (–90 kg)

Year	Gold	C'ntry	Silver	C'ntry	Bronze	C'ntry
1920	Anders Larsson	SWE	Charles Courant	SUI	Walter Maurer	USA
1924	John Franklin Spellman	USA	Rudolf Svensson	SWE	Charles Courant	SUI
1928	Thure Sjöstedt	SWE	Arnold Bögli	SUI	Henri Lefèbvre	FRA
1932	Peter Mehringer	USA	Thure Sjöstedt	SWE	Eddie Scarf	AUS
1936	Knut Fridell	SWE	August Neo	EST	Erich Siebert	GER
1948	Henry Wittenberg	USA	Fritz Stöckli	SUI	Bengt Fahlkvist	SWE
1952	Bror Wiking Palm	SWE	Henry Wittenberg	USA	Adil Atan	TUR
1956	Gholam-Reza Takhti	IRN	Boris Koulaev	URS	Peter Steele Blair	USA
1960	Ismet Atli	TUR	Gholam-Reza Takhti	IRN	Anatoli Albul	URS
1964	Alexander Medved	URS	Ahmet Ayik	TUR	Said Mustafov Sherifov	BUL
1968	Ahmet Ayik	TUR	Shota Lomidze	URS	József Csatári	HUN
1972	Ben Peterson	USA	Gennadi Strakhov	URS	Károly Bajkó	HUN
1976	Levan Tediashvili	URS	Benjamin Peterson	USA	Stelica Morcov	ROM
1980	Sanasar Oganisian	URS	Uwe Neupert	GDR	Aleksander Cichon	POL
1984	Ed Banach	USA	Akira Ota	JPN	Noel Loban	GBR
1988	Makharbek Khadartsev	URS	Akira Ota	JPN	Kim Tae Woo	KOR
1992	Makharbek Khadartsev	EUN	Kenan Simsek	TUR	Christopher Campbell	USA
1996						

Freestyle (–100 kg)

Year	Gold	C'ntry	Silver	C'ntry	Bronze	C'ntry
1972	Ivan Yarygin	URS	Khorloo Baianmunkh	MGL	József Csatári	HUN
1976	Ivan Yarygin	URS	Russell Hellickson	USA	Dimo Kostov	BUL
1980	Ilia Mate	URS	Slavcho Chervenkov	BUL	Július Strnisko	TCH
1984	Lou Banach	USA	Joseph Atiyeh	SYR	Vasile Puşcaşu	ROM
1988	Vasile Puşcaşu	ROM	Leri Khabelov	URS	William Scherr	USA
1992	Leri Khabelov	EUN	Heiko Balz	GER	Ali Kayali	TUR
1996						

Freestyle (100+ kg)

Year	Gold	C'ntry	Silver	C'ntry	Bronze	C'ntry
1904	Bernhuff Hansen	USA	Frank Kungler	USA	Fred Warmboldt	USA
1908	George O'Kelly	GBR/IRL	Jacob Gundersen	NOR	Edward Barrett	GBR/IRL
1920	Robert Roth	SUI	Nathan Pendleton	USA	Frederick Meyer	USA
1924	Harry Steele	USA	Henri Wernli	SUI	Andrew MacDonald	GBR
1928	Johan Richthoff	SWE	Aukusti Sihvola	FIN	Edmond Dame	FRA
1932	Johan Richthoff	SWE	John Riley	USA	Nikolaus Hirschl	AUT
1936	Kristjan Palusalu	EST	Josef Klapuch	TCH	Hjalmar Nyström	FIN
1948	Gyula Bóbis	HUN	Bertil Antonsson	SWE	Joseph Armstrong	AUS
1952	Arsen Mekokishvili	URS	Bertil Antonsson	SWE	Kenneth Richmond	GBR
1956	Hamit Kaplan	TUR	Ussein Mehmedov Alichev	BUL	Taisto Ilmari Kangasniemi	FIN
1960	Wilfried Dietrich	GER	Hamit Kaplan	TUR	Savkuz Dzarasov	URS
1964	Alexander Ivanitsky	URS	Liutvi Ahmedov Djiber	BUL	Hamit Kaplan	TUR
1968	Alexander Medved	URS	Osman Duraliev	BUL	Wilfried Dietrich	FRG
1972	Alexander Medved	URS	Osman Duraliev	BUL	Chris Taylor	USA
1976	Soslan Andiev	URS	József Balla	HUN	Ladislau Simon	ROM
1980	Soslan Andiev	URS	József Balla	HUN	Adam Sandurski	POL
1984	Bruce Baumgartner	USA	Bob Molle	CAN	Ayhan Taskin	TUR
1988	David Gobejichvili	URS	Bruce Baumgartner	USA	Andreas Schröder	GDR
1992	Bruce Baumgartner	USA	Jeffrey Thue	CAN	David Gobedjichvili	EUN
1996						

Greco-Roman (–48 kg)

Year	Gold	C'ntry	Silver	C'ntry	Bronze	C'ntry
1972	Gheorghe Berceanu	ROM	Rahim Aliabadi	IRN	Stefan Angelov	BUL
1976	Alexei Shumakov	URS	Gheorghe Berceanu	ROM	Stefan Angelov	BUL
1980	Zhaksylyk Ushkempirov	URS	Constantin Alexandru	ROM	Ferenc Seres	HUN
1984	Vincenzo Maenza	ITA	Markus Scherer	FRG	Ikuzo Saito	JPN

Year	Gold	C'ntry	Silver	C'ntry	Bronze	C'ntry
1988	Vincenzo Maenza	ITA	Andrzej Głąb	POL	Bratan Tzenov	BUL
1992	Oleg Koutcherenko	EUN	Vincenzo Maenza	ITA	Wilber Sanchez Amita	CUB
1996						

Greco-Roman (–52 kg)

Year	Gold	C'ntry	Silver	C'ntry	Bronze	C'ntry
1948	Pietro Lombardi	ITA	Kenan Olcay	TUR	Reino Kangasmaki	FIN
1952	Boris Gurevitsh	URS	Ignazio Fabra	ITA	Leo Honkala	FIN
1956	Nikolai Soloviev	URS	Ignazio Fabra	ITA	Dursan Ali Egribaş	TUR
1960	Dumitru Pirvulescu	ROM	Osman Sayed	UAR	Mohammad Paziraye	IRN
1964	Tsutomu Hanahara	JPN	Angel Stoyanov Kerezov	BUL	Dumitru Pirvulescu	ROM
1968	Peter Kirov	BUL	Vladimir Bakuln	URS	Miroslav Zeman	TCH
1972	Peter Kirov	BUL	Koichiro Hirayama	JPN	Giuseppe Bognanni	ITA
1976	Vitali Konstantinov	URS	Nicu Ginga	ROM	Koichiro Hirayama	JPN
1980	Vakhtang Blagidze	URS	Lajos Rácz	HUN	Mladen Mladenov	BUL
1984	Atsuji Miyahara	JPN	Daniel Aceves	MEX	Bang Dae Du	KOR
1988	Jon Ronningen	NOR	Atsuji Miyahara	JPN	Lee Jae Suk	KOR
1992	Jon Ronningen	NOR	Alfred Ter-Mkrttchian	EUN	Min Kyung Kap	KOR
1996						

Greco-Roman (–57 kg)

Year	Gold	C'ntry	Silver	C'ntry	Bronze	C'ntry
1924	Eduard Pütsep	EST	Anselm Ahflors	FIN	Väinö Ikonen	FIN
1928	Kurt Leucht	GER	Jindřich Maudr	TCH	Giovanni Gozzi	ITA
1932	Jakob Brendel	GER	Marcello Nizzola	ITA	Louis François	FRA
1936	Márton Lőrincz	HUN	Egon Svennson	SWE	Jakob Brendel	GER
1948	Kurt Pettersén	SWE	Mahmoud Aly	EGY	Halil Kaya	TUR
1952	Imre Hódos	HUN	Zakaria Chihab	LEB	Artem Terjan	URS
1956	Konstantin Vyroupaev	URS	Edvin Vesterby	SWE	Francisc Horvat	ROM
1960	Oleg Karavaev	URS	Ion Cernea	ROM	Dinko Petrov	BUL
1964	Masamitsu Ichiguchi	JPN	Vladlen Trostiansky	URS	Ion Cernea	ROM
1968	János Varga	HUN	Ion Baciu	ROM	Ivan Kochergin	URS
1972	Rustem Kazakov	URS	Hans-Jürgen Veil	FRG	Risto Björlin	FIN
1976	Pertti Ukkola	FIN	Ivan Frgić	YUG	Farhat Mustafin	URS
1980	Shamil Serikov	URS	Józef Lipień	POL	Benni Ljungbek	SWE
1984	Pasquale Passarelli	FRG	Masaki Eto	JPN	Haralambos Holidis	GRE
1988	András Sike	HUN	Stoyan Balov	BUL	Haralambos Holidis	GRE
1992	An Han Bong	KOR	Rifat Yildiz	GER	Zetian Sheng	CHN
1996						

Greco-Roman (–62 kg)

Year	Gold	C'ntry	Silver	C'ntry	Bronze	C'ntry
1912	Kaarlo Koskelo	FIN	Georg Gerstäcker	GER	Otto Lasanen	FIN
1920	Oskar Friman	FIN	Heikki Kakhonen	SWE	Frithiof Svensson	SWE
1924	Kalle Anttila	FIN	Alexander Toivola	FIN	Eric Malmberg	SWE
1928	Voldemar Väli	EST	Erik Malmberg	SWE	Giacomo Quaglia	ITA
1932	Giovanni Gozzi	ITA	Wolfgang Ehrl	GER	Lauri Koskela	FIN
1936	Yaşar Erkan	TUR	Aarne Reini	FIN	Einar Karlsson	SWE
1948	Mehmet Oktav	TUR	Olle Anderberg	SWE	Ferenc Tóth	HUN
1952	Jakov Punkin	URS	Imre Polyák	HUN	Abdel Aal Ahmed Rashed	EGY
1956	Rauno Leonard Mäkinen	FIN	Imre Polyák	HUN	Roman Dzneladze	URS
1960	Müzahir Sille	TUR	Imre Polyák	HUN	Konstantin Vyrupaev	URS
1964	Imre Polyák	HUN	Roman Rurua	URS	Branko Martinovic	YUG
1968	Roman Rurua	URS	Hideo Fujimoto	JPN	Simion Popeşcu	ROM
1972	Georgi Markov	BUL	Heinz-Helmut Wehling	GDR	Kazimierz Lipień	POL
1976	Kazimier Lipień	POL	Nelson Davidian	URS	László Réczi	HUN
1980	Stilianos Migiakis	GRE	István Tóth	HUN	Boris Kramorenko	URS
1984	Kim Weon Kee	KOR	Kentolle Johansson	SWE	Hugo Dietsche	SUI
1988	Kamandar Madjhidov	URS	Jivko Vanguelov	BUL	An Dae Hyun	KOR
1992	Akif Pirim	TUR	Sergei Martynov	EUN	Juan Maren Delis	CUB
1996						

Greco-Roman (–68 kg)

Year	Gold	C'ntry	Silver	C'ntry	Bronze	C'ntry
1908	Enrico Porro	ITA	Nikolai Orloff	URS	Arvid Lindén	FIN
1912	Eemil Väre	FIN	Gustaf Maimström	SWE	Edvin Matiason	SWE
1920	Eemil Väre	FIN	Taavi Tamminen	FIN	Frithjof Andersen	NOR
1924	Oskar Friman	FIN	Lajos Keresztes	HUN	Karl Westerlund	FIN

/continued on next page 443

Year	Gold	C'ntry	Silver	C'ntry	Bronze	C'ntry
1928	Lajos Keresztes	HUN	Eduard Sperling	GER	Edward Westerlund	FIN
1932	Erik Malmberg	SWE	Abraham Kurland	DEN	Eduard Sperling	GER
1936	Lauri Koskela	FIN	Josef Herda	TCH	Voldermar Väli	EST
1948	Karl Freij	SWE	Aage Eriksen	NOR	Károly Ferencz	HUN
1952	Chasame Safin	URS	Karl Gustav Herbert Freij	SWE	Mikuláš Atanasov	TCH
1956	Kyösti Emil Lehtonen	FIN	Riza Dogan	TUR	Gyula Tóth	HUN
1960	Avtandil Koridze	URS	Branko Martinovič	YUG	Gustav Freij	SWE
1964	Kazim Ayvaz	TUR	Valeriu Bularcă	ROM	David Gvantseladze	URS
1968	Muneji Mumemura	JPN	Stevan Horvat	YUG	Petros Galaktopoulos	GRE
1972	Shamil Khisamutdinov	URS	Stoyan Apostolov	BUL	Gian Matteo Ranzi	ITA
1976	Suren Nalbandyan	URS	Ştefan Rusu	ROM	Heinz-Helmut Wehling	GDR
1980	Ştefan Rusu	ROM	Andrzej Supron	POL	Lars-Erik Skiöld	SWE
1984	Vlado Lisjak	YUG	Tapio Sipilä	FIN	James Martinez	USA
1988	Levon Djoulfalakian	URS	Kim Sung Moon	KOR	Tapio Sipilä	FIN
1992	Attila Repka	HUN	Islam Dougoutchiev	EUN	Rodney Stacy Smith	USA
1996						

Greco-Roman (−74 kg)

Year	Gold	C'ntry	Silver	C'ntry	Bronze	C'ntry
1932	Ivar Johannsson	SWE	Väinö Kajander	FIN	Ercole Gallegati	ITA
1936	Rodulf Svedberg	SWE	Fritz Schäfer	GER	Eino Virtanen	FIN
1948	Erik Gösta Andersson	SWE	Miklós Szilvási	HUN	Henrik Hansen	DEN
1952	Miklós Szilvási	HUN	Erik Gösta Andersson	SWE	Khalil Taha	LEB
1956	Mithat Bayrak	TUR	Vladimir Maneev	URS	Per Gunnar Börje Berlin	SWE
1960	Mithat Bayrak	TUR	Günter Maritschnizo	GER	René Schiermeyer	FRA
1964	Anatoli Kolesov	URS	Cyril Petkov Todorov	BUL	Bertil Alexis Nyström	SWE
1968	Rudolf Vesper	GDR	Daniel Robin	FRA	Károly Bajkó	HUN
1972	Vítězslav Mácha	TCH	Petros Galaktopoulos	GRE	Jan Karlsson	SWE
1976	Anatolyi Bykov	URS	Vítězslav Mácha	TCH	Karalheinz Helbing	GER
1980	Ferenc Kocsis	HUN	Anatoli Bykov	URS	Mikko Huhtala	FIN
1984	Jouko Salomäki	FIN	Roger Tallroth	SWE	Ştefan Ruso	ROM
1988	Kim Young Nam	KOR	Daulet Turlykhanov	URS	Józef Tracz	POL
1992	Mnatsakan Iskandarian	EUN	Józef Tracz	POL	Torbjörn Kornbakk	SWE
1996						

Greco-Roman (−82 kg)

Year	Gold	C'ntry	Silver	C'ntry	Bronze	C'ntry
1908	Frithiof Mårtensson	SWE	Mauritz Andersson	SWE	Anders Andersen	DEN
1912	Claes Johanson	SWE	Martin Klein	URS	Alfred Asikainen	FIN
1920	Carl Westergren	SWE	Arthur Lindfors	FIN	Matti Perttilä	FIN
1924	Edward Westerlund	FIN	Arthur Lindfors	FIN	Roman Steinberg	EST
1928	Väinö Kokkinen	FIN	László Papp	HUN	Albert Kusnets	EST
1932	Väinö Kokkinen	FIN	Jean Földeak	GER	Axel Cadier	SWE
1936	Ivar Johansson	SWE	Ludwig Schweickert	GER	József Palotás	HUN
1948	Rolf Axel Einar Grönberg	SWE	Muhlis Tayfur	TUR	Ercole Gallegati	ITA
1952	Rolf Axel Einar Grönberg	SWE	Kalervo Rauhala	FIN	Nicolaj Belov	URS
1956	Guivi Kartosia	URS	Dimitar Dimitrov Dobrev	BUL	Karl-Alex Rune Jansson	SWE
1960	Dimitar Dimitrov Dobrev	BUL	Lothar Metz	GER	Ion Tăranu	ROM
1964	Branislav Simić	YUG	Jiří Kormaník	TCH	Lothar Metz	GER
1968	Lothar Metz	GDR	Valentin Olenik	URS	Branislav Simić	YUG
1972	Csaba Hegedűs	HUN	Anatoli Nazarenko	URS	Milan Nenadić	YUG
1976	Momir Petković	YUG	Vladimir Cheboksarov	URS	Ivan Kolev	BUL
1980	Gennadi Korban	URS	Jan Dolgowicz	POL	Pavel Pavlov	BUL
1984	Ion Draica	ROM	Dino Thanopoulos	GRE	Soren Claeson	SWE
1988	Mikhail Mischler	URS	Tibor Komáromi	HUN	Kim Sang Kyu	KOR
1992	Péter Farkas	HUN	Piotr Stepień	POL	Daoulet Tourlykhaov	EUN
1996						

Greco-Roman (−90 kg)

Year	Gold	C'ntry	Silver	C'ntry	Bronze	C'ntry
1908	Werner Weckman	FIN	Urjö Saarela	FIN	Carl Jensen	DEN
1912	Anders Ahlgren	SWE	Ivar Böling	FIN	Béla Varga	HUN
1920	Claes Johanson	SWE	Edil Rosenqvist	FIN	Johannes Eriksen	DEN
1924	Carl Westergren	SWE	Rudolf Svensson	SWE	Onni Pellinen	FIN
1928	Ibrahim Moustafa	EGY	Adolf Rieger	GER	Onni Pellinen	FIN
1932	Rudolf Svenssen	SWE	Onni Pellinen	FIN	Mario Gruppioni	ITA
1936	Axel Cadier	SWE	Edvins Bietags	LAT	August Neo	EST
1948	Karl-Erik Nilsson	SWE	Kelpo Gröndahl	FIN	Ibrahim Orabi	EGY

Year	Gold	C'ntry	Silver	C'ntry	Bronze	C'ntry
1952	Kelpo Gröndahl	FIN	Chalva Tshihladze	URS	Karl-Erik Nilsson	SWE
1956	Valentine Nikolaev	URS	Petko Atanassov Sirakov	BUL	Karl-Erik Nilsson	SWE
1960	Tevfik Kis	TUR	Kralyu Bimbalov	BUL	Gulvi Kartozjia	URS
1964	Boyan Radev Alexandrov	BUL	Per Oskar Svensson	SWE	Heinz Kiehl	GER
1968	Boian Radev	BUL	Nikolai Yakoyenko	URS	Nicolas Martinescu	ROM
1972	Valeri Rezantsev	URS	Josip Čorak	YUG	Czesław Kwieciński	POL
1976	Valeri Rezantsev	URS	Stoyan Ivanov	BUL	Czesław Kwieciński	POL
1980	Norbert Nottny	HUN	Igor Kanyin	URS	Petre Dicu	ROM
1984	Steven Fraser	USA	Ilie Matei	ROM	Frank Andersson	SWE
1988	Atanas Komchev	URS	Harri Koskela	FIN	Vladimir Popov	URS
1992	Maik Bullman	GER	Hakki Basar	TUR	Gogui Kogouachvili	EUN
1996						

Greco-Roman (–100 kg)

Year	Gold	C'ntry	Silver	C'ntry	Bronze	C'ntry
1972	Nicolas Martinescu	ROM	Nikolai Iakovenko	URS	Ferenc Kiss	HUN
1976	Nikolai Bolboshin	URS	Kamen Goranov	BUL	Andrzej Skrzylewski	POL
1980	Georgi Raikov	BUL	Roman Bierła	POL	Vasile Andrei	ROM
1984	Vasile Andrei	ROM	Greg Gibson	USA	Jozef Tertelje	YUG
1988	Andrzej Wroński	POL	Gerhard Himmel	FRG	Dennis Koslowski	USA
1992	Hector Milian	CUB	Dennis Koslowski	USA	Seerguei Demiachkievitch	EUN
1996						

Greco-Roman (100+ kg)

Year	Gold	C'ntry	Silver	C'ntry	Bronze	C'ntry
1896	Karl Schumann	GER	Georgios Tsitas	GRE	Stephanos Christopoulos	GRE
1908	Richárd Weisz	HUN	Alexander Petroff	URS	Sören Marius Jensen	DEN
1912	Yrjö Saarela	FIN	Johan Olin	FIN	Sören Marius Jensen	DEN
1920	Adolf Lindfors	FIN	Poul Hansen	DEN	Martti Nieminen	FIN
1924	Henri Deglane	FRA	Edil Rosenqvist	FIN	Rajmund Badó	HUN
1928	Rudolf Svensson	SWE	Hjalmar Eemil Nyström	FIN	Georgi Gehring	GER
1932	Carl Westergren	SWE	Josef Urban	TCH	Nikolaus Hirschl	AUT
1936	Kristjan Palusalu	EST	John Nyman	SWE	Kurt Hornfischer	GER
1948	Ahmet Kireçci	TUR	Tor Nilsson	SWE	Guido Fantoni	ITA
1952	Johannes Kotkas	URS	Josef Růžička	TCH	Tauno Kovanen	FIN
1956	Anatolii Parfenov	URS	Wilfried Dietrich	GER	Adelmo Bulgarelli	ITA
1960	Ivan Bogdan	URS	Wilfried Dietrich	GER	Bohumil Kubát	TCH
1964	István Kozma	HUN	Anatoli Roschin	URS	Wilfried Dietrich	GER
1968	István Kozma	HUN	Anatoli Roshin	URS	Petr Kment	TCH
1972	Anatoli Roshin	URS	Alexander Tomov	BUL	Viktor Dolîpschi	ROM
1976	Alexander Kolchinski	URS	Alexander Tomov	BUL	Roman Codreanu	ROM
1980	Alexander Kolchinski	URS	Alexander Tomov	BUL	Hassan Bchara	LIB
1984	Jeffrey Blatnick	USA	Refik Memišević	YUG	Viktor Dolîpschi	ROM
1988	Alexander Kareline	URS	Ranguel Guerovski	BUL	Tomas Johansson	SWE
1992	Alexander Kareline	EUN	Tomas Johansson	SWE	Ioan Grigoras	ROM
1996						

Yachting

Stars to Watch

by Bryn Vaile

Savannah Showdown

THE HISTORIC city of Savannah lies far – 400km (250 miles) – from the hustle and bustle of Olympic Atlanta. But its quiet charm has done little to defuse a storm of controversy which brewed up over the logistical background to the 1996 Olympic Games yachting regatta. Nor will its distance from the Olympic hub detract from the intensity of top level competition on the water.

In fact, the whole Olympic experience threatened to pass Savannah by when would-be competitors, coaches and managers first discovered that they were to face a 30-minute long bus ride from their accommodation to the marina followed by another 30-minute water-taxi ride to a specially constructed floating day-base. And the keelboats would suffer a different kind of stress with a two hour tow every other day from the marina to and from their course areas.

Tempers frayed but were then calmed by the Organizing Committee and Savannah kept its Olympic status. The scene is now set for some stiff competition. None more so than in the Mistral class of boardsailing. It has been transformed by the introduction, for the first time at the Games, of a rule allowing unlimited "pumping" or fanning of the sail to increase speed substantially. In one swoop the racing both for men and women in this class has been turned into a battle of aerobic fitness as well as sailing skill.

Boardsailing fleet in competition

In the men's event the Greek Nicholas Kaklamanakis, world ranked no.1 in 1995, should be the main gold medal contender, but he will be chased hard by 1988 gold medallist, Bruce Kendall of New Zealand, and the winner of the hotly-contested French trials. The man with a home mission, however, will be American, Mike Gebhardt, who won bronze in 1988, silver in 1992 and would love to complete his Olympic set with gold in 1996.

The women's boardsailing will be a battle between 1992 bronze medallist Dorien de Vries of the Netherlands and either Anne François of France or Lee Lia Shan of Hong Kong. Norway's Jorunn Horgen also has an outside chance of a medal.

Mistral competitors use boards and rigs supplied by the organizers. So, too, do the Finn class sailors (men's single-handed dinghy) and Europe (women's single-handed) where the hulls are concerned but the sailors can use their own optimized rigs. Both rigs are very simi-

Finn single hander

lar and have recently seen the introduction of carbon fibre masts. This has caused an explosion of development and could significantly affect the outcome.

Front runners in the Finn should be 1992 Olympic and 1995 European champion José Maria Van Der Ploeg of Spain, and Fred Loof of Sweden, 1995 pre-Olympic winner and runner up in the 1995 European championship. Medal honours in the Europe should be between 1992 silver medallist, Natalia Dufresne of Spain, The Netherlands' Margriet Matthysse, who is quick in the waves, and former world ranked no. 1, Shirley Robertson of Great Britain.

Racing in the brand-new Olympic Laser class (open single-handed class with hull and rig supplied by the organizers) will be incredibly tight and could be decided by inches on the finish line. Whoever wins the Brazilian trial, Robert Scheidt,

470 dinghy planing to the downward mark at 1992 Olympics, Barcelona

1995 world champion, or pre-Olympic regatta runner up, Peter Tanscheit, will face a strong challenge from both New Zealand and Australia. The outside shot is world youth champion Ben Ainslie of Great Britain who has showed skill and maturity beyond his 19 years of age.

A four-way fight could develop in the men's 470 class (two-handed dinghy with competitor's own hull and rig used) between Andreas Kosmatopoulos and Kostas Trigonis of Greece, Britain's John Merricks and Ian Walker, Jordi

Calafat and Francisco Sánchez of Spain (who took gold in home water four years ago) and 1992 silver medallists, America's Morgan Reeser and Kevin Burnham. The British pair's outstanding team work and tactical skill have dominated the class for the past two years and they have only recently been challenged by the Greek pair's excellent boat speed in winds up to 12 knots.

The women's 470 class, meanwhile, looks set to be dominated by Theresa Zabell, the 1992 Olympic champion who has now teamed up with Begona Via Dufresne. The other medals are likely to be decided between Germany, the Ukraine and Japan.

Tornado doing the 'wild thing'

The Olympic speed machine, the Tornado (a catamaran class), could boil down to a fascinating battle between the "old boys" and a new emerging generation in the shape of 1995 world champions Walter and Marco Pirinoli of Italy and Germans Helge and Christian Sach, respectively. Both, however, could face challenges from the 1984 Olympic gold and silver medallists, Rex Sellers of New Zealand and Randy Smyth of America. France, winners of the class at the last two Games, may also have an outside chance of a medal.

With its match racing final, in which boats are pitched into one-on-one

★★★★★★★★★★★★★★★★★★★★★★★★★★★★ **Contemporary Heroes**

Mark Reynolds and Hal Haenel *(USA)*

For Californians Mark Reynolds and Hal Haenel, Atlanta offers up the opportunity for a record-breaking third consecutive Olympic medal in the Star class. Since Reynolds teamed up with Haenel in 1986, the pair have dominated the American star fleet and have won most of the top international events.

In the 1988 US Olympic trials, they defeated the, then, reigning world champions Paul Cayard and Steve Erikson and went on to take silver in a demanding strong-wind series in the waters off Pusan in South Korea. Their 1992 Olympic performance, however, was a classic. They took gold with a day of racing to spare.

Consistency is the hallmark of their sailing. They took the 1995 world championships title after previously finishing in the top five of the event on four occasions starting in 1987.

Reynolds, aged 40, is a lifetime resident of San Diego and a sailmaker by trade whilst Haenel came orginally from St. Louis, Missouri. He is the manager of a motion picture studio in Los Angeles and his other passion in life is collecting and restoring classic sports cars.

racing, the Soling class features possible winners from Denmark, Sweden, Australia, Spain and Britain. Sailors from these nations have all achieved impressive results in the past two years and it will all depend on who gets it right on the day. Intriguingly, there is also a possibility that one of the America's Cup skippers will make a last minute challenge. Russell Coutts of New Zealand and Dennis Connor and Jim Brady both of America, will be dangermen should they win an Atlanta place from their nations' trials.

Finally, the grand, old class of the Olympic Games, the Star. This two-handed dinghy with a keel and a truly massive rig has been part of the Games continuously since 1932 (except 1976). In 1996 Americans Mark Reynolds and Hal Haenel could add to their 1988 silver and 1992 gold. They have hit form again just at the right time, winning the 1995 world championships. Their consistency, team work and preparation give the opposition little chance.

However, they could be chased all the way by Australians Colin Beashel and David Giles, Ross MacDonald and Eric Jespersen of Canada who won bronze in 1992, and look out for one of the sport's great natural talents, Brazil's Torben Grael and Marcelo Ferreira. Grael took silver at the 1984 Games in the Soling and bronze in the Star class in 1988.

B. V. ☐

Retrospective

Once viewed as a sport for kings and the extravagantly rich, yachting has evolved in the past 20 years to widen its appeal and accessibility by introducing newer, more popular and exciting classes. One of the main tactics at the Games has been to reduce equipment costs by supplying boats and rigs. This started as far back as the 1948 Olympic Games for the men's single-handed class when yachting took place at Torquay, a town on the South West coast of Britain.

Equipment supply now covers all single-handed classes and has also eased the burden of boat and rig measurement which can take several days prior to the Olympic regatta and requires a veritable army of personnel – without mentioning the rows which can develop as competitors try to slip modifications of all types through the rules.

Legendary skippers from the very cream of the sport, including the America's Cup and the highest level of off-shore racing, have always been attracted by the Olympic regatta. Dennis Connor, of America's Cup winning fame, won bronze in 1976 (incidentally with Conn Findlay as crew – a man who had previously won two rowing golds) in the Tempest Class. While the man who beat him to take the 1983 Cup, John Bertrand of Australia, finished 4th in 1972 and then won bronze in 1976 in the Finn class. 1992 America's Cup helmsman Buddy Melges is a double Olympic medalist with a bronze in 1964 (Flying Dutchman) and a gold in Soling in 1972.

A Sporting Legend ★★★★★★★★★★★★★★★★★★★★★★★★★★★★★★★★★★

Rodney Pattison *(Great Britain)*

Rodney Pattison and crew Iain MacDonald-Smith's 1968 Olympic regatta started with disqualification (effectively using up their one discard). From there, though, they sailed an impeccable series of five straight wins and one second place to win the Flying Dutchman gold comfortably. Theirs was a great victory combining excellent boat speed, superb teamwork and tactical decision awareness and their performance was an inspiration to a generation of Olympic sailors.

Pattison, with a series of different crew, dominated the Flying Dutchman class for the next four years winning all the major regattas, including European and world titles. At the 1972 Olympic Games he won four of the seven races and did not even have to start the final race to win. Four years later, while not the fastest in any one wind condition, his tactical awareness and all round speed kept him in contention, to win the silver medal.

Pattisson's abilities have clearly been demonstrated in many areas of sailing including both the America's and Admirals Cup competitions. He has skippered world championship winning yachts at the Quarter Ton Cup in 1976 and the One Ton Cup in 1985 as well as being involved with offshore multi hulls. He was awarded the MBE, a British honour bestowed by the Queen, for services to yachting.

No aspect of Olympic sailing would be complete, however, without mentioning Paul Elvström, the 'Great Dane', who won four consecutive gold medals between 1948 and '60 in the Finn class and was still competing in 1988 in the Tornado class with his daughter Trine. Russian Valentin Mankin was also surely one of the world's most versatile sailors taking gold in the Finn in 1968, gold in the Tempest class in 1972, silver again in the Tempest in 1976, then gold in the Star class in 1980.

If single-minded dedication and technical brilliance count then Britain's Rodney Pattison was in a class of his own. He developed boat tuning to a new level of perfection and refinement in an eight year reign at the top of the highly technical Flying Dutchman class. His highly individual approach paid handsomely with gold in 1968 and '72 and a silver in 1976.

The introduction of a specific women's class in 1988 in the 470 dinghy has brought a new dimension to the regatta. And steely determination was shown in that year by the American winners, Alison Jolly and Lynne Jewell, who in the final race capsized their dinghy to repair a broken jib luff adjustment and then righted their craft in a 25 knot wind to finish ninth and take the gold medal.

Family ties do not hinder or prevent success, it would seem, at the Games. The three Swedish Sunelin brothers took gold in the 5.5 metre class in 1968. In 1920 Britain's Cyril Wright took 7 metre gold. One of the crew was his wife Dorothy and the yacht was co-owned by her father who, perhaps wisely, decided not to be part of the crew.

In 1948 the Star class gold was truly a family affair with Hilary and Paul Smart of America winning from Carlos de Cárdenas and Carlos Jr. of Cuba. In the American boat the son skipped while in the Cuban boat the father skipped. A unique family double was achieved in 1984 when Bill Buchan took gold in the Star class and son Carl won gold in the Flying Dutchman class.

Background

The sport of sailing has developed from the basic use of sailing boats as a means of transport and fishing. First scheduled to be held in 1896, but cancelled due to bad weather, Olympic yachting has gradually mirrored many of the changes in format and type of craft used throughout the world. Gone are the massive 'Metre' and 'Ton' keelboat class yachts of the pre-World War II era. These yachts were

A Contemporary Heroine ★★★★★★★★★★★★★★★★★★★★★★★★★★★★

Theresa Zabell *(Spain)*

Riding on the crest of Spain's recent sailing success came 30 year old Theresa Zabell. Born in Ipswich, England, in 1965 her sporting career began at the relatively old age of 14. Since then she has notched up an impressive record of 12 Spanish 470 class titles, three European championships and three world championships. She and crew Begona via Duffresne are world ranked no 1 and must be almost a sure fire bet for the women's 470 gold in Savannah.

Even when at home in Barcelona she is close to the water, her apartment is in the former Olympic Village overlooking the waters on which she won the women's 470 gold medal for the host nation four years ago.

the standard 'racing' classes of this period.

The first dinghy class to make its debut was a single-handed class in 1920. And while the ratio of keelboats to dinghies only improved slightly in the next 50 years, it was completely reversed in 1976 with the selection of five dinghy, one catamaran (for the first time) and two keelboat classes for the Games. Evolution continued with the introduction of board sailing in 1984.

For the past few Olympiads results have been dominated by three countries: New Zealand, USA and Spain. Both the USA and Spain have had the added advantage of sailing on home waters and have invested large amounts of money to achieve this level of success. New Zealand is a sailing-'mad' country and their success in the Olympic arena is a mirror of their sailors' ability in many other championships throughout the world. Four other nations have shown they have the consistent ability to win medals: Australia, Denmark, France and Great Britain.

Equipment

Gone are the days of wooden hulls and spars and of cotton sails. Modern racing craft make extensive use of the very latest man-made plastics and composite materials for the hulls. Their spars are either extruded aluminium or carbon-fibre. The sails are of either "dacron", "mylar" or nylon and are engineered for both strength and minimum weight.

Four types of craft are used at the Olympic.Games. The Mistral sailboard is a "surfboard" with a mast and sail and the sailor is an integral part of the craft controlling the rig (sail and mast) with the arms and steering with bodyweight and movement in a standing position. The dinghy classes are characterized by a lifting centreboard (or daggerboard) and have either a single sail (una) rig – for the Europe, Finn and

Laser events – or a two sail (sloop) rig – for the 470 class. This latter class also has an additional large downwind sail called a spinnaker. These craft are steered by a conventional rudder with the crew using their bodyweight as leverage to counterbalance the forces developed by the rig.

Keelboats – Soling and Star classes – have a ballasted fin that is fixed below the hull – in other words the keel. They are sailed in the same manner as the dinghies and the Soling has a spinnaker. Finally, the catamarans of the Tornado class are twin-hulled craft with a centreboard and rudder on each hull. They use a sloop rig which is characterized by a fully-battened mainsail.

Star keelboat class

In all the classes where competitors supply their own rigs, these are optimized for their bodyweight and for the conditions which are likely to prevail on a given day. In fact the different boats require sailors of differing physique for optimum performance so that the Finn class is likely to be populated by tall, heavy men whilst the 470 sailors are lighter.

Boat lengths vary from the 3.35m (11ft) Europe to the 8.2m (26ft 7in.) Soling. In the fastest class, the Tornado, boats can reach speeds of more than 20 knots.

Soling keelboat class

Rules

Each of the ten Olympic classes is governed and controlled by individual class rules covering the individual specification, shape and size of every piece of the craft's equipment. All equipment, either brought by an individual competitor or supplied by the organizing committee, is scrupulously measured to ensure that it is all within the rules and tolerances.

Of the classes used at the Olympic regatta four must be sailed by one person alone – the Mistral, the Laser, the Europe and the Finn. Three of the remaining classes are two-handed – the

470, Star and Tornado. The only three-person class is the Soling.

The competition rules are some of the most complex, developed after more than a hundred years of competition many of which started from international maritime law. They include who should give way in close encounters on the water and defining the rights and wrongs of any normal manoeuvre. Competitors who are penalized in certain circumstances may have to turn two full circles to exonerate themselves before continuing on the course. But there are also umpires who control the start and the racing on the water and any protests are heard after racing by the jury.

The newly-introduced scoring system of points for places (i.e. one point for first, two points for second etc.) has improved understanding of the results and reduced the sailors' need to perform complex mental computations on the water.

Atlanta Format

In 1996, of the eight boat types, four are "open" to both sexes to compete against each other: the Tornado, Soling, Star and Laser. The Mistral and 470 have separate classes for men and women. The Europe is for women only whilst the Finn is for men only. The Laser has replaced the Flying Dutchman class since 1992 and the Mistral has replaced the Division 2 sailboard.

In the past four years yachting has undergone a rapid metamorphosis both in format and style of competition. Gone are the silhouettes of craft competing on the horizon with courses that allowed competitors to spread out sometimes miles apart. Modern courses are set around inflatable marker buoys. Boats start on an upwind leg and then do a series of loops (upwind and downwind) on triangular or trapezoid shape courses. The new short races of between 35 and 90 minutes each have put a high premium on starting technique, good acceleration, boat handling, consistent boat speed and sharp tactical skills. Changes to the course set-ups have increased the opportunities to gain places and reduced the number of processional legs.

Each nation is allowed to select one entrant in each class for the Olympic regatta but they may have had to win a qualifying place via a continental qualification regatta if entry numbers exceeded the quota. In Savannah the fleet sizes (i.e. the number of boats) will be as follows: Mistral 45 men and 27 women; Laser 41; Finn 30; Europe 25; 470 35 men and 22 women; Soling, Star and Tornado 23 each. That means a total of 443 athletes.

All but one of the classes have an eleven race series of two races a day. Each entrant is allowed to discard their worst two results after nine races. The craft with the least points wins. The exception to this format is the Soling class. Here the top six yachts from the fleet racing go through to a final knock-out series. The top two go straight into the semi-finals whilst the remaining four are paired off to compete against each other in the best of five races. The winners go into the semi-finals. Both semi-finals and the final are also contested over the best of five races.

Venue

The waters off Savannah Wassaw Sound look likely to give some excellent conditions with 10-16 knot winds which could rise to 20 knots if thunderstorms are nearby. The current is predictable and, given the shorter races, should have no real effect on the outcome. The four course areas, "Alpha" in Wassaw Sound, and the three `ocean' courses, "Bravo", "Charlie" and "Delta", are located to the east/north east of the regatta day base.

Savannah itself is 400km (250 miles) East of Atlanta on the Atlantic coast and will also host extra athlete accommodation.

MEDALLISTS (by nation)

Country	Gold	Silver	Bronze	Total
United States	16	19	14	49
Great Britain	14	10	9	33
Sweden	9	11	9	29
Norway	16	11	1	28
France	12	6	9	27
Denmark	9	8	4	21
Netherlands	4	4	5	13
New Zealand	6	3	3	12
Soviet Union	4	5	3	12
Spain	7	2	1	10
Australia	3	1	6	10
Germany	2	3	3	8
Italy	2	1	5	8
Finland	1	1	6	8
Canada	-	2	6	8
Belgium	2	3	2	7
FRG	2	2	3	7
Brazil	2	1	4	7
GDR	2	2	2	6
Greece	1	1	1	3
Switzerland	1	1	1	3
Austria	-	3	-	3
Portugal	-	2	1	3
Bahamas	1	-	1	2
Argentina	-	2	-	2
Estonia	-	-	2	2
China	-	1	-	1
Cuba	-	1	-	1
Ireland	-	1	-	1
Netherlands Antilles	-	1	-	1
Virgin Islands	-	1	-	1
Hungary	-	-	1	1
Russia	-	-	1	1
	116	109[1]	103[1]	328

[1] Some events in the early Games had no silver and/or bronze

ATLANTA SCHEDULE

Venue: Wassaw Sound, Savannah, Georgia

Courses: Alpha – A, Bravo – B, Charlie – C, Delta – D

Date	Description	Round	Start	End	Course Area
22 Jul	Mistral (m)	R 1&2	13:00	18:00	A
	Mistral (w)				
	Laser (op)				B
	Europe (w)				
	Star (op)				C
	Finn (m)				
	Soling (op)				D
	Tornado (op)				

Date	Description	Round	Start	End	Course Area
23 Jul	Mistral (m)	R 3&4	13:00	18:00	A
	Mistral (w)				
	Laser (op)				B
	Europe (w)				
	Star (op)				C
	Finn (m)				
	Soling (op)				D
	Tornado (op)				
24 Jul	Mistral (m)	R 5&6	13:00	18:00	A
	Mistral (w)				
	Laser (op)				B
	Europe (w)				
	Star (op)				D
	Finn (m)				
	470 (m)	R 1&2			C
	470 (w)				
25 Jul	Europe (w)	R 7&8	13:00	18:00	B
	Laser (op)				
	470 (m)	R 3&4			C
	470 (w)				
	Star (op)	R 7&8			D
	Finn (m)				
26-Jul	Mistral (m)	R 7&8	13:00	18:00	A
	Mistral (w)				
	Soling (op)	R 5&6			D
	Tornado (op)				
27 Jul	Mistral (m)	R 9&10	13:00	18:00	A
	Mistral (w)				
	470 (m)	R 5&6			
	470 (w)				
	Finn (m)	R 9&10			C
	Star (op)				
	Soling (op)	R 7&8			D
	Tornado (op)				
28 Jul	Mistral (m)	R-FINAL	13:00	18:00	A
	Mistral (w)	R-FINAL			
	470 (m)	R 7&8			B
	470 (w)				
	Soling (op)	R 7&8			D
	Tornado (op)				
29 Jul	Laser (op)	R 9&10	13:00	18:00	B
	Europe (w)				
	Finn (m)	R-FINAL			C
	Star (op)	R-FINAL			C
30 Jul	470 (m)	R 9&10	13:00	18:00	C
	470 (w)				
	Tornado (op)	R-FINAL			D
31 Jul	Europe (w)	R-FINAL	13:00	18:00	B
	Laser (op)	R-FINAL			C
	Soling (op)	Rd 1 match races			D
1 Aug	470 (w)	R-FINAL	13:00	18:00	C
	470 (m)	R-FINAL	14:30	18:00	
	Soling (op)	Rd 2 match races (FINAL)			D
2-Aug	Soling (op)	match races (FINAL)		18:00	D

MEDALLISTS

WINDSURFING (Men)

Year	Gold	C'ntry	Points	Silver	C'ntry	Points	Bronze	C'ntry	Points
1984 (Windglider)	Stephan van den Berg	NED	27.7	Randall Scott Steele	USA	66	Bruce Kendall	NZL	46.4
1988 (Division II)	Bruce Kendall	NZE	35.4	Jan Boersma	NLA	42.7	Michael Gebhardt	USA	48
1992 (Lechner)	Franck David	FRA	70.7	Mike Gebhardt	USA	71.1	Lars Kleppich	AUS	98.7
1996 (Mistral)									

WINDSURFING (Women)

Year	Gold	C'ntry	Points	Silver	C'ntry	Points	Bronze	C'ntry	Points
1992 (Lechner)	Barbara Kendall	NZL	47.8	Zhang Xiaodong	CHN	65.8	Dorien de Vries	NED	68.7
1996 (Mistral)									

YACHTING (Men)

Year	Gold	C'ntry	Points	Silver	C'ntry	Points	Bronze	C'ntry	Points

Finn*

Year	Gold	C'ntry	Points	Silver	C'ntry	Points	Bronze	C'ntry	Points
1924	Léon Hubrechts	BEL	2	Henrik Robert	NOR	7	Hans-Erik Dittmar	FIN	8
1928	Sven Thorell	SWE		Henrik Robert	NOR		Bertel Broman	FIN	
1932	Jacques Lebrun	FRA	87	Adriaan Maas	NED	85	Santiago Amat Cansino	ESP	76
1936	Daniel Kagchelland	NED	163	Werner Krogmann	GER	150	Peter Scott	GBR	131
1948	Paul Elvström	DEN	5543	Ralph Evans	USA	5408	Jacobus de Jong	NED	5204
1952	Paul Elvström	DEN	8209	Charles Currey	GBR	5449	Rickard Sarby	SWE	5051
1956	Paul Elvström	DEN	7509	André Nelis	BEL	6254	John Marvin	USA	5953
1960	Paul Elvström	DEN	8171	Alexander Chuchelov	URS	6520	André Nelis	BEL	5934
1964	Wilhelm Kuhweide	GER	7638	Peter Barrett	USA	6373	Henning Norgaard Wind	DEN	6190
1968	Valentin Mankin	URS	11.7	Hubert Raudaschl	AUT	53.4	Fabio Albarelli	ITA	55.1
1972	Serge Maury	FRA	58	Ilias Hatzipavlis	GRE	71	Viktor Potapov	URS	74.7
1976	Jochen Schümann	GDR	35.4	Andrei Balashov	URS	39.7	John Bertrand	AUS	46.4
1980	Esko Rechardt	FIN	36.7	Wolfgang Mayrhofer	AUT	46.7	Andrei Balashov	URS	47.4
1984	Russell Coutts	NZL	34.7	John Bertrand	USA	37	Terry Neilson	CAN	37.7
1988	José Doreste	ESP	38.1	Peter Holmberg	ISV	40.4	John Cutler	NZL	45
1992	José van der Ploeg Garciá	ESP	33.4	Brian Ledbetter	USA	54.7	Craig Monk	NZL	64.7
1996									

*Results given are all for single-handed men's dinghy class. This became the Finn in 1952

470 Class

Year	Gold	C'ntry	Points	Silver	C'ntry	Points	Bronze	C'ntry	Points
1976	Frank Hübner Harro Bode	FRG	42.4	Antonio Gorostegui Pedro Millet	ESP	49.7	Ian Brown Ian Ruff	AUS	57
1980	Marcos Pinto Rizzo Soares Eduardo Penido	BRA	36.4	Jörn Borowski Egbert Swensson	GDR	38.7	Jouko Lindgren Georg Tallberg	FIN	39.7
1984	Luis Doreste Roberto Molina	ESP	33.7	Stephen Benjamin Christopher Steinfeld	USA	78	Thierry Peponnet Luc Pillot	FRA	69.4
1988	Thierry Peponnet Luc Pillot	FRA	34.7	Tonu Tyniste Toomas Tyniste	URS	46	John Shadden Charles McKee	USA	51
1992	Jordi Calafat Esterlich Francisco Sánchez Luna	ESP	50	Morgan Reeser Kevin Burnham	USA	66.7	Tonu Tyniste Toomas Tyniste	EST	68.7
1996									

YACHTING (Women)

Europe

Year	Gold	C'ntry	Points	Silver	C'ntry	Points	Bronze	C'ntry	Points
1992	Linda Andersen	NOR	48.7	Natalia Via Dufresne Pereña	ESP	57.4	Julia Trotman	USA	62.7
1996									

470

Year	Gold	C'ntry	Points	Silver	C'ntry	Points	Bronze	C'ntry	Points
1988	Allison Jolly Lynne Jewell	USA	26.7	Marit Söderström Birgitta Bengtsson	SWE	40	Larissa Moskalenko Irina Tchounikhovskaia	URS	45.4
1992	Theresa Zabell Lucas Patricia Guerra Cabrera	ESP	29.7	Leslie Egnot Janet Shearer	NZL	36.7	Jennifer Isler Pamela Healy	USA	40.7
1996									

YACHTING (Open)

Tornado

Year	Gold	C'ntry	Points	Silver	C'ntry	Points	Bronze	C'ntry	Points
1976	Reginald White John Osborn	GBR	18	David McFaull Michael Rothwell	USA	36	Jörg Spengler Jörg Schmall	FRG	37.7
1980	Alexandre Welter Lars Sigurd Björkström	BRA	21.4	Peter Due Per Kjergard	DEN	30.4	Göran Marström Jörgen Ragnarsson	SWE	33.7
1984	Rex Sellers Christopher Timms	NZL	14.7	Randy Smyth Jay Glaser	USA	37	Chris Cairns John Anderson	AUS	50.4
1988	Jean-Yves Le Déroff Nicolas Hénard	FRA	16	Rex Sellers Christopher Timms	NZL	35.4	Lars Grael Clinio Freitas	BRA	40.1
1992	Yves Loday Nicolas Henard	FRA	40.4	Randy Smyth Keith Notary	USA	42	Mitch Booth John Forbes	AUS	44.4
1996									

Soling

Year	Gold	C'ntry	Points	Silver	C'ntry	Points	Bronze	C'ntry	Points
1972	Harry Melges William Bentsen William Allen	USA	8.7	Stig Wennerström Bo Knape Stefan Krook	SWE	31.7	David Miller John Ekels Paul Cote	CAN	47.1
1976	Poul Jensen Valdemar Bandolowski Erik Hansen	DEN	46.7	John Kolius Walter Glasgow Richard Hoepfner	USA	47.4	Dieter Below Michael Zachries Olaf Engelhardt	GDR	47.4
1980	Poul Jensen Valdemar Bandolowski Erik Hansen	DEN	23	Boris Budnikov Alexander Budnikov Nikolai Poliakov	URS	30.4	Anastassios Boudouris Anastassios Gavrilis Aristidis Rapanakis	GRE	31.1
1984	Robert Haines Edward Trevelyan Roderick Davis	USA	33.7	Torben Grael Daniel Adler Ronaldo Senfft	BRA	43.4	Hans Fogh John Kerr Steve Calder	CAN	49.7
1988	Jochen Schümann Thomas Flach Bernd Jäkel	GDR	11.7	John Kostecki William Baylis Robert Billingham	USA	14	Jesper Bank Jan Mathiasen Steen Secher	DEN	52.7
1992*	Jesper Bank Steen Secher Jesper Seier	DEN		Kevin Mahaney Jim Brady Doug Kern	USA		Lawrie Smith Robert Cruikshank Ossie Stewart	GBR	
1996									

*1992 onwards Soling medals decided by match racing series following the fleet racing

Star Class

Year	Gold	C'ntry	Points	Silver	C'ntry	Points	Bronze	C'ntry	Points
1932	Gilbert Gray Andrew Libano	USA	46	Colin Ratsey Peter Jaffe	GBR	35	Gunnar Asther Hjalmar Sunden-Cullberg	SWE	28
1936	Peter Bischoff Hans Weise	GER	80	Arvid Laurin Uno Wallentin	SWE	64	Willem de Vries Lentsch Adriaan Maas	NED	

Year	Gold	C'ntry	Points	Silver	C'ntry	Points	Bronze	C'ntry	Points
1948	Hilary Smart Paul Smart	USA	5828	Carlos de Cárdenas Culmell Carlos de Cárdenas Pla	CUB	4949	Adriaan Maas Edward Stutterheim	NED	4731
1952	Nicolò Rode Agostino Straulino	ITA	7635	John Price John Reid	USA	7216	Francisco de Andrade Joaquim Fiuza	POR	4903
1956	Lawrence Low Herbert Williams	USA	5876	Nicolò Rode Agostino Straulino	ITA	5649	Durward Knowles Sloan Farrington	BAH	5223
1960	Timir Pinegin Fedor Shutkov	URS	7619	José Quina Mário Quina	POR	6665	William Parks Robert Halperin	USA	6269
1964	Durward Knowles Cecil Cooke	BAH	5664	Richard Stearns Lynn Williams	USA	5585	Pelle Pettersson Holger Sundström	SWE	5527
1968	Lowell North Peter Barrett	USA	14.4	Peder Lunde Per Wiken	NOR	43.7	Franco Cavallo Camilo Gargano	ITA	44.7
1972	David Forbes John Anderson	AUS	28.1	Pelle Petterson Stellan Westerdahl	SWE	44	Wilhelm Kuhweide Karsten Meyer	FRG	44.4
1980	Valentin Mankin Alexander Muzychenko	URS	24.7	Hubert Raudaschl Karl Fersti	AUT	31.7	Giorgio Gorla Alfio Peraboni	ITA	36.1
1984	William Buchan Stephen Erickson	USA	29.7	Joachim Griese Michael Marcour	FRG	41.4	Giorgio Gorla Alfio Peraboni	ITA	43.5
1988	Mike McIntyre Bryn Vaile	GBR	45.7	Mark Reynolds Hal Haenel	USA	48	Torben Grael Nelson Falcao	BRA	50
1992	Mark Reynolds Hal Haenel	USA	31.4	Roderick Davis Donald Cowie	NZL	58.4	Ross Macdonald Eric Jespersen	CAN	62.7
1996									

470

1996

Discontinued Sports

Sport	Year of Participation	Sport	Year of Participation
Cricket	1900	Motorboating	1908
Croquet	1900	Polo	1900, 1908, 1920, 1924 & 1936
Golf	1900, 1904	Roque	1904
Jeu de Paume ('Court Tennis')	1908	Rackets	1908
Lacrosse	1904, 1908	Rugby Union	1900, 1908, 1920 & 1924
		Tug of War	1900, 1904, 1908, 1912 & 1920

Discontinued Events

Events	Year of Final Games
Archery	
Men	
Au cordon dore – 50m	1900
Au chapelet – 50m	1900
Au cordon dore – 33m	1900
Au chapelet – 33m	1900
Sur la perche a la herse	1900
Double York Round	1904
Double American Round	1904
Team Round	1904
York Round	1908
Continental Style	1908
Moving Bird Target (28m, 33m, 50m)	1920
Teams (28m, 33m, 50m)	1920
Double FITA Round	1988
Women	
Double Columbia Round	1904
Double National Round	1904
National Round	1908
Double FITA Round	1988
Athletics	
Men	
60m	1904
5 miles	1908
Cross Country (ind.)	1924
Cross Country (team)	1924
200m Hurdles	1904
4,000m Steeplechase	1900
3,000m Walk	1920
3,500m Walk	1908
10,000m Walk	1952
10 mile Walk	1908
Standing High Jump	1912
Standing Long Jump	1912
Standing Triple Jump	1904
Shot Put (both hands)	1912
56lb Weight Throw	1920
Discus (Greek Style)	1908
Discus (both hands)	1912
Javelin (freestyle)	1908
Javelin (both hands)	1912
Triathlon	1904
This event was part of a combined gymnastics and track & field event.	
Pentathlon	1924
Women	
Pentathlon	1980
Canoeing	
Men	
Kayak singles 10,000m	1956
Folding Kayak singles 10,000m	1936
Kayak pairs 10,000m	1956
Folding Kayak pairs 10,000m	1936
Kayak singles relay 4x500m	1960
Canadian singles 10,000m	1956
Canadian pairs 10,000m	1956
Cycling	
Men	
One-lap race	1908

Events	Year of Final Games
5,000m track race	1908
10km track race	1896
20km track race	1908
50km track race	1924
100km track race	1908
12 hour race	1972
100km team time-trial (road)	1992
Equestrian	
High Jump	1900
Long Jump	1900
Figure Riding (ind. & team)	1920
Fencing	
Men	
Foil – Masters	1900
Épée – Masters	1900
Épée (combined amateur and masters event)	1900
Sabre – Masters	1900
Single sticks	1904
Gymnastics	
Men	
Combined competition (3 events)	1904
Combined competition (4 events)	1904
Rope Climbing	1932
Club Swinging	1932
Sidehorse Vaulting	1924
Tumbling	1932
Parallel Bars – team	1896
Horizontal Bar – team	1896
Free exercises & apparatus – team	1912
Swedish system – team	1912
Women	
Team exercises with portable apparatus	1956
Judo	
Men	
Open	1984
Modern Pentathlon	
Team event	1992
Rowing *	
Men	
Coxed fours-inriggers	1992
Coxed pairs	1992
Coxed fours	1992
Women	
Quadruple sculls with coxswain	1984
Four-oared shell with coxswain	1988
Coxless fours	1992
* All heavyweight categories	
Shooting	
Men	
Rapid-fire pistol teams	1920
Free pistol teams	1920
Military revolver	1896
Military revolver – teams	1912

Events	Year of Final Games
Free rifle	1908
Free rifle – teams	1924
Free rifle – 3 positions	1968
Military rifle	1920
Military rifle – teams	1920
Smallbore rifle	1920
Miniature rifle – teams	1920
Running deer	1956
Trap – teams	1924
Skeet – open	1992
Trap – open	1992
Swimming	
100m freestyle for sailors	1896
880yd freestyle	1904
4,000m freestyle	1900
400m breaststroke	1920
200m team	1900
4x50yd freestyle relay	1904
Obstacle race	1900
Underwater swimming	1900
Plunge for distance	1904
Plain high diving	1924
Synchronized swimming	
– ind.	1992
– duet	1992
Tennis	
Mixed doubles	1924
Yachting	
0.5 ton class	1900
0.5 – 1ton class	1900
1 – 2 ton class	1900
2 – 3 ton class	1900
3 – 10 ton class	1900
10 – 20 ton class	1900
Open class	1900
5.5m	1968
6m	1952
6m, 1907 rating	1920
6.5m	1920
7m	1920
8m	1936
8m, 1907 rating	1920
10m	1912
10m, 1907 rating	1920
10m, 1919 rating	1920
12m	1912
12m, 1907 rating	1920
12m, 1919 rating	1920
12ft dinghy	1920
18ft dinghy	1920
Meulan Class	1924
International 12ft Class	1928
Snowbird Class	1932
International Olympian Class	1936
Firefly Class	1948
Sharpie – 12 sq m	1956
30 sq m	1920
40 sq m	1920
Swallow	1972
Dragon	1976
Tempest	1976
Flying Dutchman	1992

460

PART 4
The Olympic Family and Movement

The Pursuit of Excellence

National Olympic Committees are able to provide their athletes with advanced training facilities and state of the art technical assistance. This universal sponsor support enables the world's athletes to compete in the spirit of friendship, solidarity and fair play synonymous with the Olympic Movement.

For many, the pursuit of excellence remains a distant dream. With the help of the Worldwide Olympic Sponsors, 10,000 athletes in Atlanta will realise that dream.

The Worldwide Olympic Sponsors

Panasonic

John Hancock

XEROX

IBM

UPS

The IOC: A Vast and Complex Global Organization

by Michèle Verdier

Introduction

What is the Olympic Movement? Who organizes the Organizing Committees? And who ensures that the Games are run in the best possible conditions for the athletes of the world? Who is responsible for promoting the ideals of Olympism worldwide on a permanent basis?

Inevitably the answers to such enormous questions lie within an interlocking series of vast and complex global organizations which make up the Olympic Movement.

The administrative structures of the International Olympic Committee (IOC) and the Olympic Movement have evolved parallel to the development of Olympic sport, now more than a century old. Over time, they have grown and adapted to the environment of the society in which sport exists, and have incorporated prevailing new technology and methods along every step of the way.

Today the IOC alone has a permanent headquarters split between Olympic House and the Château de Vidy in Lausanne, Switzerland, and employs around 80 full-time staff. It is equipped with the latest information technology, which enables it to follow events all over the world as they happen, around the clock. All a far cry from the days at the turn of the century when Baron Pierre de Coubertin, the man responsible for reviving the modern Olympic Games, worked single-handed from his home using just handwritten correspondence and the telegraph as means of communication.

The Olympic Movement is often graphically depicted as a pyramid. The IOC is at the tip. Two of the sides are occupied, one by the International Federations (IFs) governing a sport included on the programme of the Games of the Olympiad (summer) or Olympic Winter Games, the other by the National Olympic Committees (NOCs), which number 197. Inside this pyramid are the organizing committees elected by the IOC Session (or annual conference), whose task is to set up the practical side of the Games that they have been chosen to host. The pyramid also contains the organizations and the athletes who agree to be guided in their activities by the Olympic Charter.

The International Olympic Committee

The IOC is not a state but, in its operation, it possesses the structures of a typical modern democratic state. In the words of the "Olympic Charter", the set of rules which fixes and governs the activities of the Olympic Movement and which is to some extent its constitution, the IOC is the "supreme authority of the Olympic Movement".

It is a non-governmental, non-profit organization in the form of an association, with the status of a legal person. It is financed entirely by private income, essentially from the negotiation of exclusive television rights and marketing programmes, to the exclusion of any state subsidy. Moreover, the IOC retains only 10% of these revenues, and distributes the majority to its partners, namely the IFs and NOCs – through the so-called Olympic Solidarity fund – and the organizing committees (60%).

As the charter says, the IOC's role is, among other things, "to lead the promotion of Olympism; to encourage the organization and development of sport and sports competitions; to collaborate with the competent public or private organizations and authorities in the endeavour to place sport at the service of humanity; to ensure the regular celebration of the Olympic Games; to fight against any form of discrimination affecting the Olympic Movement; to lead the fight against doping in sport; to take measures, the goal of which is to prevent endangering the health of athletes; and to see to it that the Olympic Games are held in conditions which demonstrate a responsible concern for environmental issues".

The IOC fulfils these tasks through three elected elements: the Session (or annual conference), the Executive Board and the President himself – all supported by an administrative nerve-centre in Lausanne.

The Session is the "annual general assembly" or conference of all 96 IOC members. It constitutes the legislative power of the Movement, and as such is the supreme organ of the IOC, a kind of "Olympic parliament". Its agenda is established by the Executive Board and President. But its work generally revolves around adopting, modifying and interpreting the Olympic Charter. The Session may delegate all or some of its powers to the Executive Board. Any rule change or adoption of a new text requires the consent of at least two-thirds of the members present at the Session.

An IOC member is elected by all the existing members during the Session. They receive no salary for their work. In practical terms, to be chosen as an IOC member, a person must have had a career in sport (actively or as a voluntary or salaried administrator or senior office holder) or be a person of considerable influence within their own country. In reality, many IOC members fulfil both sets of criteria. They are generally recommended to the Session for membership by the President and Executive Board who will have researched them thoroughly in advance.

Members take an oath on joining the IOC and they must be able to speak at least one of the languages used at IOC meetings including French, English, German, Russian, Spanish and Arabic. The two official Olympic languages are French and English. Not every participating Olympic nation has a member. Some have two because they have organized an Olympic Games in the past such is the historical fashion in which membership has grown over the years. Baron Pierre de Coubertin's original inspiration for the IOC's membership was based on that used to select Stewards at Henley Royal Regatta – a rowing event in Britain.

Those members elected before 1966

are members for life. Members elected since 1966 must finish at the end of the year in which they celebrate their 80th birthday. Members may tender their resignation at any time. They are the IOC's ambassadors to their own country, and not the reverse. They must attend the Sessions, participate in the work of the Commissions to which they have been appointed, inform colleagues about the situation of Olympism in their country of origin and represent the President whenever asked to do so.

The Session also elects, through a secret ballot, eleven of the IOC members to form the Executive Board: the President, four vice presidents and six other members. A simple majority, that is to say half the members present plus one, is required. Together with the President, the Executive Board holds the executive power. It is the IOC's "government" or "cabinet", and its members begin their mandates at the end of the Session which elected them. They are elected for a four-year term.

An ordinary member of the Executive Board may stand for election as vice president. All outgoing members, including vice-presidents, must wait for one year before being eligible to seek a new term, whether as an ordinary member or directly as vice president. This rule was established to ensure two elements indispensable to the IOC: continuity of action (hence stability), and renewal (to bring in new blood and new ideas).

It is the Executive Board which has ultimate responsibility for the daily workings of the IOC, approves the internal organization, organization chart and administrative regulations; is responsible for financial management

and prepares the annual report. It establishes the agenda for the Sessions and recommends people for election as IOC members. Convened by the IOC President, the Executive Board meets four or five times a year.

Primus inter pares, the President is elected by secret ballot for an eight-year term by the IOC members. He or she may be re-elected for successive four-year terms. If he or she is prevented from fulfilling his or her duties, he or she is replaced by the most senior vice president until a new President is elected at the next Session. The President presides over all the activities of the IOC and represents it permanently. Since 1980 Juan Antonio Samaranch has been an executive President for the IOC because of the complexity of the post although he does not receive a salary.

To perform the tasks assigned to him by the Olympic Charter, the President sets up permanent or ad hoc Commissions and working groups whenever this appears necessary. These Commissions, often split into sub-commissions and working groups, meet at most once a year. The latest Commission to be set up by the IOC addresses issues related to sport and the environment. The President appoints the members, who do not have to be (and often are not) members of the IOC. Delegates of the IFs and NOCs also sit on the Commissions, together with representatives of the professions concerned, particularly for the media (press and radio/television) and medical Commissions. There is an athlete representative on every IOC Commission.

The Commissions are consultative bodies which give opinions and make recommendations. They have no decision-making powers. They submit reports to the Executive Board which examines these and in turn makes recommendations to the Session for a final decision.

The IOC also has a consultative body called the Congress. Convened by the President at fairly regular intervals, it is a discussion forum which brings together the IOC, IFs, NOCs, athletes, referees, media and all recognized associations dealing with sport or sports activities, in a format decided in advance by all the partners. This "university of ideas" allows the main orientation and development of the Olympic Movement to be identified. Its recommendations and final motions are studied by an ad hoc Commission, which reports to the Executive Board and Session. The resulting concrete measures are incorporated into the Olympic Charter, and thus allow the Olympic Movement to perpetuate itself and secure its permanence, while ensuring necessary renewal and progress.

The "IOC system" is vast and flexible in order to perform its mission, which is composite and on a global level. But it needs thorough coordination. This is provided by the central administration based in Lausanne, since 1915, and, more precisely, at the Château de Vidy since the end of 1967.

A director general (responsible more specifically for political, legal and financial issues), and a secretary general look after, among other things, general administration, protocol and the organization of all the meetings, and provide a link with the Olympic Museum. They are the right hand of the President. The director general and secretary general are assisted in their tasks by a team of directors responsible for specific areas.

The IOC has a permanent staff of around 80 people, representing some 15 nationalities and the administrative structure more or less parallels the Commissions, all the directors being responsible for one or more Commissions which correspond to their field of activity.

Equipped with a powerful data processing system and communications and information networks (in particular a wire to seven world and national agencies enabling it to follow global developments in real time 24 hours a day) linked to the four corners of the globe, the administration can perform the mission entrusted to it on behalf of the Movement, with maximum efficiency and a minimum number of permanent staff.

One of the key words of the Olympic Movement is independence. Each of its component parts, while included in a coherent whole, still retains its autonomy and sovereignty.

The International Federations

The International Federations governing a sport on the programme of the Games of the Olympiad and the Olympic Winter Games have an administrative structure comparable to that of the IOC, at least in terms of technical codification and rules of the sport in question. The IFs also have a permanent headquarters, an administration, executive board or committee and a general assembly or congress. They all have established constitutions, charters or rules which define their activities and missions as their sports have become codified and organized, some in a structured form even before the IOC was created.

They are also responsible for overseeing the technical correctness of the sports competitions at the Olympic Games. They help and advise the Organizing Committee as well as providing key technical personnel. They also set the competition rules and format.

Over the years, the winter and summer IFs have joined together within umbrella bodies promoting and safeguarding their common interests, particularly vis-à-vis the IOC and organizing committees. Thus the Association of Summer Olympic International Federations (ASOIF) and the Association of International Winter Sports Federations (AIWF) have come into being. It is through them that the funds from television rights are distributed among the IFs which form these associations, according to their own independently-formulated systems.

The National Olympic Committees

There are a total of 197 National Olympic Committees representing 197 countries. The NOCs represent the IOC in a given territory and their essential role is to form and enter the national teams which will represent them at the Olympic Games and to ensure the development of the Olympic Movement in the country for which they are recognized.

They are each vastly different in their size, scope and cultural background. Some NOCs are merged with the sports ministry, others are simply administered from the home of the president or secretary general whilst others again have their own administration and sophisticated technical, coaching, medical, marketing and sponsorship departments. They are similarly grouped together within an umbrella body, the Association of National Olympic Committees (ANOC), which provides an interface with the IOC and the organizing committees. In order to take into account regional and specific disparities, continental associations have also been set up for each of the continents: Africa, America, Asia, Europe and Oceania.

A permanent dialogue is maintained between the three pillars of the Olympic Movement, for organizing the Olympic Games but also for developing the Olympic Movement. Annual or two-yearly meetings are held between the IOC and ASOIF, IOC and AIWF and IOC and ANOC. All the problems of the Olympic Movement are discussed there, respecting the independence and autonomy of each partner, with the ultimate goal of working with the chosen organizing committees to stage the best summer and Winter Games possible for the athletes of the world.

Over the past 100 years the Olympic Movement has successfully ensured its survival by maintaining cohesion and unity. Only unity between the IOC, IFs and NOCs has enabled this atypical movement to run world sport in the service of the fundamental ideals on which the Olympic phenomenon is built. The Movement is now looking forward to the next Millennium.

100 Years of Olympic Marketing

by Michael Payne

I T WAS WITH some trepidation that the father of the modern Olympic Games, Baron Pierre de Coubertin, took the first historic steps towards the founding of the Olympic Movement one hundred years ago. "I was embarked on an adventure about whose immediate success I was far from feeling reassured", he said.

Were he alive today, de Coubertin would see that the flame of Olympism burns brighter than he could ever have imagined. The Olympic Movement has become the premier force for promoting the value of sport throughout the world, and the Olympic Games, the pinnacle of mankind's sporting achievement.

Financing the Games

In 1894 de Coubertin also worried about the problems of financing the Olympics and, as the Games have grown ever closer to achieving his goal of universality, so too have the financial challenges. No standard provisions were made in the development of the Olympic Charter for raising these funds. It was up to each Games Organizing Committee to generate the necessary revenue.

The 1896 Games were funded by stamps, ticket sales, commemorative medals, programme advertising and, above all, private donations. But the Official Report at the time makes it clear that such a huge undertaking could not rely merely on the voluntary general subscription of the host population: "Though it did all honour to the generosity of the public at large, it (the General Subscription) represented as yet an entirely inadequate sum for such a stupendous undertaking".

Without Mr George Averoff, the wealthy Greek benefactor who paid for the rebuilding of the Olympic Stadium, de Coubertin might never have achieved his ambition.

Games Comparison 1896/1996		
	Athens	**Atlanta**
Days	5	17
Sports	9	26
Events	32	271
Countries	13	200
Athletes	311	10,500
Tickets available	est. 60,000	11 million

Today the Olympic Games, and the Movement as a whole, are financed through the sale of TV rights, sponsorship, licensing, ticket sales, coins and stamps. The operation is controlled centrally by the IOC for the development of a long term global sponsor, supplier and broadcasting strategy. The IOC retains only 10% of total Olympic revenues, with the remaining 90% redirected to Organizing Committees of the Olympic Games (OCOGs) for the organization of the Games, International Sports Federations (IFs) and National Olympic Committees (NOCs). The arrangement ensures that even the smallest countries can send athletes or meet the cost of hosting the Games. Norway's achievement as host of the 1994 Lillehammer Winter Games bears testament to the value of this approach.

Sponsorship

Recognizing the value of the Olympic properties, early organizers licensed Olympic marks or logos/emblems for products and services provided to the OCOG.

- **1896 Athens Olympic Games:** current IOC sponsor Kodak was an advertiser in the first Olympic programme of 1896.
- **1912 Stockholm Olympic Games:** The OCOG sold the rights to take and sell photographs of the Games. Other agreements included the hiring out of field glasses, the sale of fans, purses and pocket books, and the right to place weighing machines in the grounds.
- **1932 Lake Placid Olympic Winter Games:** The OCOG organized tie-pins with US department stores which featured the Games in their window displays and advertising campaigns.
- **1932 Los Angeles Olympic Games:** Olympic funding by the Organizing Committee came of age with the Games achieving a financial surplus for the first time.
- **1952 Helsinki Olympic Games:** Helsinki marked the first attempt at an international marketing programme with companies from

11 countries giving value in kind ranging from food to carnations for medal winners. The Games also saw the first official Olympic Coin minted to help finance the Olympics.

- **1960 Rome Olympic Games:** Sponsor/supplier support was extended to include 46 companies providing perfume, chocolate, toothpaste, soap and maps of Olympic Rome.

Commercialism continued to grow, reaching a peak at the Montreal Games in 1976. Despite the participation of 628 sponsors and suppliers, the Games earned the reputation as "The Games that bankrupted a city."

The Los Angeles Games of 1984 marked a turning point in Olympic funding. Its marketing programme comprised 34 sponsors, 64 suppliers and 65 licensees, each with distinct rights and exclusivity and paved the way for the IOC to lead a move towards the modernization of Olympic financing through the 'TOP' (originally

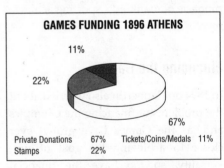

GAMES FUNDING 1896 ATHENS

11%
22%
67%

Private Donations	67%	Tickets/Coins/Medals	11%
Stamps	22%		

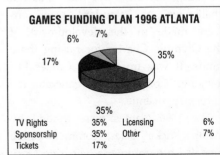

GAMES FUNDING PLAN 1996 ATLANTA

7%
6%
35%
17%
35%

TV Rights	35%	Licensing	6%
Sponsorship	35%	Other	7%
Tickets	17%		

meaning The Olympic Programme) Programme marketing initiative.

Launched in the 1985-1988 quadrennium of the Calgary and Seoul Games, TOP offered exclusive worldwide rights to a few international companies wishing to link their products with the Olympic themes of excellence, participation and fair play. In return, the Olympic Games received financial support and, more importantly, the technological and service support without which the modern Games could not take place.

Before TOP, and an organized marketing programme, the Olympic Movement had to rely on television rights fees as the major source of revenue and the major percentage of that revenue came from one country, the USA. Tickets were another major revenue source, but by the very nature of their limitations on space, they did not offer much growth possibility.

The need to modernize the funding of the Olympic Movement, and especially the Olympic Games, led to a concerted effort by the IOC to diversify revenue sources. Its actions included the establishment of the New Sources of Finance Commission, the development of TOP and efforts to increase broadcast rights outside North America.

TOP played a major role in diversifying the revenue base of the Olympic Games and in providing state-of-the-art technology to the Olympic Movement. The programme also ensured a balanced distribution of revenue throughout the Olympic Family, to OCOGs and NOCs. In addition it showed that sport and industry could work together to mutual advantage:

"As sponsoring companies began to understand the Olympic Movement, and as the IOC, the OCOGs and NOCs started to work with their sponsors, the companies became more involved, more committed, providing resources to the sport which went far beyond a straightforward commercial agenda," says IOC Marketing Director, Michael R Payne. *"The Olympic parties learned that the more they helped their sponsors to achieve their marketing objectives, to realize the benefits from their association with the Olympic Movement, the more sport received in return."*

Now in its third quadrennium, TOP enables sports organizations to retain their independence by harnessing the power of controlled sponsorship. It has become a model for sports organizations grappling with the problems of financing major events in a very different world from that of Baron de Coubertin, when competitive sport was open only to men wealthy enough to finance themselves.

To those who ask whether sponsorship poses a threat to the Olympic

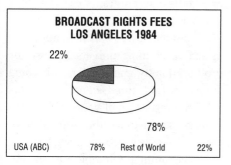

BROADCAST RIGHTS FEES LOS ANGELES 1984

22%

78%

| USA (ABC) | 78% | Rest of World | 22% |

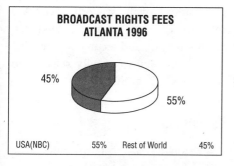

BROADCAST RIGHTS FEES ATLANTA 1996

45%

55%

| USA(NBC) | 55% | Rest of World | 45% |

Top 10 Sponsors	
1 Coca-Cola	Soft Drinks
2 Kodak	Film and Photographic Products
3 Visa	Consumer Payment Systems
4 Bausch & Lomb	Optical Products
5 Time/Sports Illustrated	Magazines
6 Xerox	Document Processing
7 Matsushita/ Panasonic	TV/Audio Entertainment
8 IBM	Data Processing
9 John Hancock	Life Insurance
10 United Parcel Service (UPS)	Express Mail; Regular & Express Package Delivery

Movement, the answer is, "No, provided we can work together with sponsors who understand what makes the Olympic Movement special and who want, as do the TOP sponsors, to keep it that way," says Richard W Pound, IOC member and Chairman of the Atlanta Coordination Commission.

"It is the respect and cooperation between the Olympic Movement and its sponsors which will lead to a long and mutually beneficial relationship. The progress of sport as an international phenomenon over the last 100 years could not have been possible without the support of sponsors and the business community. Take away sponsorship and commercialism from sport today and what is left? A large, unsophisticated, finely-tuned engine developed over a period of 100 years – with no fuel. To those who ask whether Olympic sponsorship is here to stay, the answer is "we certainly hope so"."

Licensing

Olympic licensing agreements have developed in tandem with sponsorship. The 1912 Stockholm Games represented the first concerted attempt to organize exclusive rights to sell memorabilia.

By the Tokyo Olympic Games of 1964 licensing had reached a level unimaginable under today's more controlled approach to Olympic financing. The Tokyo OCOG even sold an Olympic cigarette, "Olympia", which used the Olympic logo on its packaging. The brand generated over US$ 1 million for the OCOG. The tobacco category was later banned.

At the Munich Games in 1972 a private advertising agency acted as the "licensing agent" for the first time. Rights to the Olympic Rings were sold and several types of licensing and advertising agreements were made available. This was also the first Games at which an Olympic Mascot was licensed to private firms for sale.

Over time, it became clear that if licensing was to benefit the Games then there had to be a move away from "Trash and Trinkets" towards more controlled quality development and integrated design programmes. The 1994 Lillehammer Winter Games licensing programme showed this new approach in action, winning universal praise for product quality and design, to become the model for future Games.

With a record retail value of US$ 215 million (seven times the original forecast), sales of licensed products brought the Lillehammer Olympic Organizing Committee royalties worth over $20 million. The programme created 456 temporary jobs and secured another 291 at the companies carefully selected to make licensed products.

Television

Television is the means by which the

world experiences the Games and it is fundamental IOC policy that broadcasting rights are sold not to the highest bidders, but to those who guarantee the broadcast coverage. The IOC even helps 'subsidize' the rights fee with special programmes like barter in less well developed parts of the world to ensure coverage is universally maximized.

But the power of TV has not always been recognized. As recently as the 1956 Olympic Winter Games in Cortina the then president of the IOC, Avery Brundage, declared that "we in the IOC have done well without TV for 60 years and will do so certainly for the next 60." Despite Brundage's scepticism (and the fact that the last torch carrier at the Opening Ceremony of the Cortina Games tripped and fell over a TV cable) Olympic broadcasting proved enormously popular, going truly global eight years later with the first satellite relay of the Games from Tokyo.

As a measure of the popularity of Olympic programming, the US rights holder for the Lillehammer Winter Games, CBS, says the 1994 Games were the most watched event in US television history with 83.7% of potential viewers watching all or part of the Games. This success was worldwide, with, for example, viewing up over 14% in Japan to 760 million and up 31% in Great Britain versus 1992, although the latter may have been distorted by the popularity of retiring ice dancers, Christopher Dean and Jayne Torvill.

Such success was helped by production advances at the Lillehammer Games, ensuring coverage that was innovative and dynamic:
- Parallel-motion cable and rail tracking cameras conveyed the speed and drama of events like Freestyle

Moguls. Four panoramic cameras provided scenic views of the Olympic area and helicopter shots were offered daily.
- The broadcast showcased the successful wide scale use of digital technology. For the first time in Olympic history, the host broadcaster operation was based on an all digital distribution recording system.
- These were the first Olympics Games where the international radio and television sound was produced and delivered in stereo from all venues.

Advertising

The dangers of commercial clutter became apparent in the early Olympic years. Today the Olympic Games remains the only major sporting event where advertiser messages are prohibited both within the stadium and on athletes' clothing.
- **1920 Antwerp Olympic Games:** Programme advertising had grown to such an extent that there was little room for inclusion of material relating to the Games themselves.
- **1924 Paris Olympic Games:** Venue advertising was allowed for the first and only time.
- **1928 Amsterdam Olympic Games:** The IOC had begun to take steps to limit commercial clutter. Programme advertising was restricted and venue advertising banned in areas visible within and outside the stadium.

Tickets

IOC ticket policy is determined by two fundamental principles:
- Ticket prices must be reasonable, to ensure that attendance at the Games

is available to everyone.
- A proportion of tickets must be available internationally through NOCs.

Historically, tickets have been priced to allow maximum attendance:
- For the 1896 Olympic Games, the Greek Government passed legislation to allow tickets to be sold "tax free".
- Tickets were a major revenue source for Los Angeles, 1932, although the Organizing Committee decided that prices should be as low as possible. For example, opening ceremony tickets sold for US$3, morning athletics events were 50 cents, and children under 16 years could attend any event for only 50 cents. Over three million tickets were sold, generating almost US$1.5million
- The Rome Games in 1960 sold almost 1.5 million tickets, with 43% sold to international visitors from 76 countries.
- Lillehammer 1994 achieved record ticket sales. 1,207,396 tickets were sold, for a sales percentage of 87.2% – an all-time high for Olympic Winter Games.

The first official Olympic legal tender coins were minted for the 1952 Helsinki Olympic Games and soon became a popular souvenir and an important revenue source. The 1972 Munich Olympic Games coin programme generated over 50% of total revenue and at the Montreal Games four years later coins were marketed internationally for the first time, generating $127 million in sales.

Coin sales account for about 4% of Olympic revenue and remain a vital part of the Olympic cultural legacy. In 1992 the IOC introduced a Centennial Coin Collection to celebrate 100 years of Olympism. The collection is produced in association with the Mints of Canada, Australia, France, Austria and Greece.

Stamps

Stamps helped finance the first Olympic Games and through their use they acted as harbingers of the revival of Olympism around the world. They have continued to fulfil this dual role ever since, today generating about 4% of Olympic revenue. In 1928 Portugal was the first to issue stamps to help fund its team's participation in the Amsterdam Olympic Games of that year, and countries around the world have followed suit ever since. In 1992, 137 countries issued Olympic stamps.

Olympic Solidarity

by Dick Palmer

THE BEGINNINGS of Olympic Solidarity go back to 1961. Count Jean de Beaumont, one of the IOC Members in France, had the idea of an Olympic Aid Commission whose aim would be to assist those National Olympic Committees (NOCs) most in need. The notion was that a fund would be established to be supported by the IOC, donations from companies, organizations and individuals and by the richest NOCs. In 1963 the IOC created a Commission to assist underprivileged NOCs but later, sadly, due to lack of funds, it was decided not to continue.

In 1968 during a meeting of NOCs a programme described as Olympic Solidarity was formed. Thus began the movement and, of course, the name. The IOC after some initial misgivings adopted the concept in 1971 and set up an Olympic Solidarity Commission. Prominent in those early stages were Count Jean de Beaumont, Giulio Onesti of Italy and Raoul Mollet of Belgium (who developed a system of help and assistance, particularly by sports experts such as coaches for developing NOCs).

Olympic Solidarity had its first home in Rome under the guidance of Onesti, the then President of CONI (The Italian Olympic Committee) and the first President of ANOC (the worldwide Associa-tion of National Olympic Committees). Its first Director was Edward Wieztoric from Poland. However, in 1979, Wieztoric left and the offices of Solidarity moved to Lausanne, Switzerland.

In 1980 Juan Antonio Samaranch became President of the IOC. He quickly realized both the potential and importance of Olympic Solidarity. President Samaranch's philosophy was (and is) based on the strength of the three pillars of the Olympic Movement (the IOC, the International Federations and the NOCs) and Olympic Solidarity clearly had a pivotal role in strengthening the status, role and work of the NOCs.

Significantly President Samaranch, in 1981, appointed fellow Spaniard Anselmo Lopez to be the Director of Olympic Solidarity. He has been an inspired choice. A man of impeccable integrity, Lopez is himself a highly successful businessman who has brought his business acumen to bear on the development of Olympic Solidarity.

Continental Associations have been given a key role in the formation of Olympic Solidarity policies and on how the funds (made available through the television revenues for Olympic Games) are made available to NOCs. Each NOC in the Olympic Movement has benefited from Solidarity grants. Six athletes and two officials from each NOC have their expenses paid to the Games. Each NOC has an annual subvention for its administrative costs. NOCs are able to call on experts to run sports coaching courses in their countries for high level athletes and for national coaches. The Itinerant School for Sports Administration (a particular initiative of Anselmo Lopez) has run hundreds of courses to improve the efficiency and administrative skills of the NOCs. In many ways it is the Olympic Movement's most effective form of Olympic education.

But Olympic Solidarity has to cope with a changing world just like all other aspects of sport. Recently there has been a marketing initiative to try to improve the marketing skills of NOCs in the developing world to help them attract

further and vital funds from sponsors. Olympic Solidarity scholarships are now given to promising athletes, who lack opportunities in their own countries, to enable them to train and thus compete with the best in the world. Already results at recent Olympic Games and world championships give testimony to the benefits of this scheme.

And so from its early, perhaps tentative, beginnings Olympic Solidarity has become an indispensable part of the National Olympic Committees. By strengthening the work of the NOCs it is fortifying the basic framework of the Olympic Movement. Long may it play this vital role.

The Olympic Fight Against Drugs in Sport

by John Goodbody

THE INTERNATIONAL Olympic Committee (IOC) has struggled with persistent and lengthy determination to rid sport of drug-taking. As the guardian of the ethics of the Olympic Movement, it has been in the forefront of this battle, not only at the Games every four years but also for the panoply of sport, in all its variety of competitions across the world.

Quite rightly, the IOC has taken on itself the responsibility to co-ordinate the work against doping: to sponsor conferences; to accredit laboratories; to establish a definitive list of banned substances and, above all, to give sport the moral leadership which it has so desperately needed.

Because the Olympic Games are the most widely-publicized event on the sporting calendar, positive tests at the Games receive extraordinary publicity. The most notorious case of doping at the Games, the banning of Ben Johnson, of Canada, three days after his men's 100m victory in the sport of athletics over Carl Lewis in 1988, became such a "cause célèbre" only because it had taken place at the Olympic Games. Such global interest would not have occurred if this positive test had been recorded at even the world athletics championships, let alone a grand prix meeting.

Drug-taking in sport is not a new phenomenon. There had been reports of competitors using dope in the 19th century, pre-dating even the founding of the modern Olympic Games in 1896. These included canal swimmers in Amsterdam in 1865 and six-day cyclists 14 years later. It is believed that Dorando Pietri, the Italian who collapsed at the finish of the 1908 Olympic marathon, may have taken strychnine, then commonly used as a stimulant when taken in small doses. There were also reports that empty ampoules and syringes were found in the dressing-room at the 1952 Olympic Winter Games in Oslo during the skating events.

However, the decisive moment for the IOC occurred in 1960 when Knud Jensen, a Danish cyclist, died during the road race, a collapse almost certainly caused by taking stimulants. The following year, an IOC Medical Commission was set up in Athens under the presidency of Sir Arthur (later Lord) Porritt. Some drugs tests were carried out on cyclists at the 1964 Games, the first occasion these had occurred at the Games. Three years later, with the resignation of Sir Arthur and his replacement by Prince Alexandre de Merode of Belgium, the Commission was reconstituted. It was this Commission, which had charge of the first drugs tests to be carried out across the sports for the 1968 Games in Grenoble and Mexico.

The original impetus for instituting testing was to combat the growing use of stimulants. In 1967, Tommy Simpson, the 1965 world champion and Britain's greatest-ever cyclist, had died during the Tour de France on Mont Ventoux. Amphetamines were found in his clothing. However, properly regularized dope tests can easily identify whether competitors have taken stimulants and since the early '70s their use has declined. As Sir Arthur Gold, the former chairman of the British Olympic Association, said of testing at events: "Those who get caught are either the careless or the ill-advised."

The greatest problem that the IOC, and particularly the doping sub-commission of its Medical Commission, has faced has been the use of hormone drugs. They began to be widely employed in the early '60s. In 1973, Hal Connolly, the former Olympic hammer champion, wrote that from 1964 to '72: "like all my competitors I was using anabolic steroids as an integral part of my training in the hammer throw."

What was not perceived in the '70s was the widespread use to which anabolic steroids could be put. Initially, it was thought that only sports like the throwing events in athletics, weightlifters and the heavier divisions of the combat sports would benefit by adding increased muscle bulk. However, competitors in other disciplines found that the drugs enabled them to recover more quickly from intensive exercise, and that a whole range of activities could benefit, from long-distance running to swimming, from sprinting to cycling.

The first problem was one of detection. The IOC owed much to Professor Raymond Brooks of St. Thomas's Hospital, London, who discovered a fool-proof method of analysis. This was employed at the 1974 Commonwealth Games in New Zealand. The scientific results satisfied the IOC, who in April 1975, banned the use of anabolic steroids. In 1976, eight weightlifters were found positive for drug offences at the Montreal Games, seven of them for anabolic steroids.

However, there remained a further problem. That same year, Professor Arnold Beckett, then a member of the IOC Medical Commission, wrote: "A competitor may take anabolic steroids during training, discontinue their use a week or so before a particular event and still have an advantage at least in weight, from the drug misuse. Yet a urine sample collected at the event does not show a positive result. If international sports federations decide to introduce random testing at various events throughout the year, thereby making it difficult to establish a continuous anabolic steroid schedule, this should constitute a deterrent."

Sadly there was a lack of initiative for many years by the international federations to set up a programme of out-of-competition testing. In athletics, the centrepiece of the summer Games, there were more than 140 drug offences world-wide, many involving Olympic champions or world record-holders, even before the case of Ben Johnson focussed the minds of the officials of both the sport and the Olympic movement.

What was of such concern in the Johnson case was not that the sprinter was found positive, it was rather that at the subsequent judicial inquiry, Johnson and other leading Canadian athletes admitted that they had been taking hormone drugs for several years without being caught. They also disclosed what had been rumoured for several years: that competitors were now using substances like human growth hormone (HGH), which was not prohibited because no satisfactory test had been agreed.

The dismantling of the 'Iron Curtain' in 1989-90 provided further evidence of the extent of drug-taking in sport. Everyone had suspected that the former East Germans had been taking drugs but what was not fully understood was the extent of the state's involvement across the range of Olympic disciplines.

Since 1990 the IOC has made strenuous efforts to standardize penalties for drug abuse throughout the sports. It has also looked at a Court of Arbitration for sport to limit the need for expensive legal cases. And, as the international federations have begun increasing the number of out-of-competition tests, so some of the loopholes have begun to be closed.

Another would have been shut if the findings of Professor Manfred Donike of Germany had been accepted. The head of the Cologne laboratory believed he could identify whether someone had taken hormone drugs even if he had stopped taking them several months before a test. He called his method the 'steroid profile'. However, this stalwart of the IOC Medical Commission died in August 1995 before he was able to convince his colleagues on the unquestioned validity of his research.

What the IOC should now consider is the building of a laboratory at its HQ in Lausanne, where a team of technicians can continue both this work and other research initiatives to counter the increasingly sophisticated methods of the drug users. It would be a continuation of a duty which it has discharged so keenly over the last 35 years.

International Olympic Sports Federations

INTERNATIONAL OLYMPIC COMMITTEE

International Olympic Committee
Château de Vidy, 1007 Lausanne,
Switzerland
Tel.: (41.21) 621 61 11 *Fax:* (41.21) 621 62 16

Museum and Olympic Study Centre
Villa Olympique, 1, Quai d'Ouchy,
1006 Lausanne, Switzerland
Tel.: (41.21) 621 65 11 *Fax:* (41.21) 621 65 12

INTERNATIONAL OLYMPIC SPORTS FEDERATIONS (Summer Games)

*(Sequence: by sport. C = Founding date.
A = Number of affiliated national
organizations.)*

Archery
FITA: Fédération Internationale de Tir à l'Arc
(C: 1931 A: 103)
Via Bartolini 39, 20155 Milan, Italy
Tel.: (39.2) 39 21 56 13 *Fax:* (39.2) 39 21 56 37

Athletics
IAAF: International Amateur Athletic
Federation (C: 1912 A:204)
17, rue Princesse Florestine, BP 359,
98007 Monte Carlo, Monaco Cédex
Tel.: (33.93) 30 70 70 *Fax:* (33.93) 15 95 15

Badminton
IBF: The International Badminton
Federation (C: 1934 A: 122)
4, Manor Park, MacKenzie Way,
Cheltenham, Gloucestershire GL51 9TX, UK
Tel.: (44.1242) 23 49 04 *Fax:* (44.1242) 22 10 30

Baseball
IBA: International Baseball Association
(C: 1938 A: 89)
Avenue Mon-Repos 24, 1005 Lausanne,
Switzerland
Tel.: (41.21) 311 18 63 *Fax:* (41 21) 311 18 64

Basketball
FIBA: Fédération Internationale de Basketball
(C: 1932 A: 198)
P.O. Box 700607, 81306 Munich, Germany
Tel.: (49.89) 78 30 36/7/8
Fax: (49.89) 785 35 96

Boxing
AIBA: Association Internationale de Boxe
Amateur (C: 1946 A: 182)
P.O. Box 0141, 10321 Berlin, Germany
Tel.: (49.30) 423 67 66 *Fax:* (49.30) 423 59 43

Canoeing
FIC: Fédération Internationale de Canoë
(C: 1924 A: 86)
Dózsa György út 1-3, 1143 Budapest, Hungary
Tel.: (36.1) 163 48 32 *Fax:* (36.1) 157 56 43

Cycling
UCI: Union Cycliste Internationale
(C: 1900 A: 167)
Case postale, 1000 Lausanne 23, Switzerland
Tel.: (41.21) 626 00 80 *Fax:* (41.21) 626 00 88

Equestrian
FEI: Fédération Equestre Internationale
(C: 1921 A: 106)
C.P. 157, Avenue Mon-Repos 24,
1000 Lausanne 5, Switzerland
Tel.: (41.21) 312 56 56 *Fax:* (41.21) 312 86 77

Fencing
FIE: Fédération Internationale d'Escrime
(C: 1913 A: 95)
32, rue de la Boétie, 75008 Paris, France
Tel.: (33.1) 45 61 14 72/84
Fax: (33.1) 45 63 46 85

Football
FIFA: Fédération Internationale de Football
Association (C: 1904 A: 168)
Case postale 85, 8030 Zurich, Switzerland
Tel.: (41.1) 384 95 95 *Fax:* (41.1) 384 96 96

Gymnastics
FIG: Fédération Internationale de
Gymnastique (C: 1881 A: 117)
Rue des Oeuches 10, Case postale 359, 2740
Moutier 1, Switzerland
Tel.: (41.32) 93 66 66 *Fax:* (41.32) 93 66 71

Handball
IHF: Fédération Internationale de Handball
(C: 1946 A: 136)
B.P. 312, 4020 Bâle, Switzerland
Tel.: (41.61) 272 13 00 *Fax:* (41.61) 272 13 44

Hockey
FIH: Fédération Internationale de Hockey
(C: 1924 A: 120)
B.P. 5, Avenue des Arts 1, 1040 Bruxelles,
Belgium
Tel.: (32.2) 219 45 37 *Fax:* (32.2) 219 27 61

Judo
IJF: International Judo Federation
(C: 1951 A: 168)
Hortaleza 108, 28004 Madrid, Spain
Tel.: (34.1) 310 26 18 *Fax:* (34.1) 319 04 33

Modern Pentathlon
UIPMB: Union Internationale de Pentathlon
Moderne et Biathlon (C: 1948 A: 72)
Ekeby House, Luiksestraat 23, 2587 AL La
Haye, Netherlands
Tel.: (31.70) 351 27 74 *Fax:* (31.70) 350 99 11

Rowing
FISA: Fédération Internationale des Sociétés
d'Aviron (C: 1892 A: 94)
Blochstrasse 2, Postfach, 3653
Oberhofen/Thunersee, Switzerland
Tel.: (41.33) 43 50 53 *Fax:* (41.33) 43 50 73

Shooting
UIT: Union Internationale de Tir
(C: 1907 A: 148)
Bavariaring 21, 80336 Munich, Germany
Tel.: (49.89) 53 42 93/53 10 12
Fax: (49.89) 530 94 81

Softball
ISF: Fédération Internationale de Softball
(provisional) (C: 1952 A: 90)
2801 N.E. 50th Street, Oklahoma City,
Oklahoma 73111, USA
Tel.: (1.405) 424 67 14 *Fax:* (1.405) 427 57 00

Swimming
FINA: Fédération Internationale de Natation
Amateur (C: 1908 A: 155)
Avenue de Beaumont 9, Rez-de-Chaussée, 1012
Lausanne, Switzerland
Tel.: (41.21) 312 66 02 *Fax:* (41.21) 312 66 10

Table Tennis
ITTF: The International Table Tennis
Federation (C: 1926 A: 166)
53, London Road, St Leonards-on-Sea, East
Sussex TN37 6AY, UK
Tel.: (44.1424) 72 14 14 *Fax:* (44.1424) 43 18 71

Tennis
ITF: Fédération Internationale de Tennis
(C: 1913 A: 190)
Palliser Road, Barons Court, London W14 9EN,
UK
Tel.: (44.171) 381 80 60 *Fax:* (44.171) 381 39 89

Triathlon
ITU: International Triathlon Union
(provisional) (C: 1989 A: 94)
1154 West 24th Street, North Vancouver, B.C.,
V7P 2J2 Canada
Tel.: (1.604) 987 00 92 *Fax:* (1.604) 926 72 60

Volleyball
FIVB: Fédération Internationale de Volleyball
(C: 1947 A: 210)
Case postale, 1001 Lausanne, Switzerland
Tel.: (41.21) 320 89 32/3/4
Fax: (41.21) 320 88 65

Weightlifting
IWF: International Weightlifting Federation
(C: 1905 A: 156)
Hold u. 1, Pf. 614, 1374 Budapest, Hungary
Tel.: (36.1) 131 81 53/153 05 30
Fax: (36.1) 153 01 99

Wrestling
FILA: Fédération Internationale des Luttes
Associées (C: 1912 A:132)
Avenue Ruchonnet 3, 1003 Lausanne,
Switzerland
Tel.: (41.21) 312 84 26 *Fax:* (41.21) 323 60 73

Yacht Racing
IYRU: International Yacht Racing Union
(C: 1907 A: 113)
27 Broadwall, Waterloo, London SE1 9PL, UK
Tel.: (44.171) 928 66 11 *Fax:* (44.171) 401 83 04

NATIONAL OLYMPIC COMMITTEES
(for forthcoming Games)

*A complete list of National Olympic
Committees is available from the IOC.*

AUS: Australian Olympic Committee Inc.
Level 13, The Maritime Centre, 207, Kent
Street, Sydney NSW 2000
Tel.: (61.2) 931 20 75 *Fax:* (61.2) 931 20 98

JPN: The Japanese Olympic Committee:
Kishi Memorial Hall, 1-1-1, Jinnan,
Shibuya-ku, Tokyo 150
Tel.: (81.3) 34 81 22 86 *Fax:* (81.3) 34 81 09 77/34
81 22 92

USA: United States Olympic Committee
Olympic House, 1750, East Boulder Street,
Colorado Springs, Colorado 80909
Tel.: (1.719) 578 45 42 *Fax:* (1.719) 632 41 80

The Next Olympic Century*

by Richard Palfreyman and Hiroshi Takeuchi

SYDNEY, with its landmark Opera House, is set to take the Olympic Movement into the next century when it hosts the Games of the year 2000 from September 15 to October 1 during the normally mild and sunny antipodean Spring. The Australian city was chosen as host in September 1993 by the IOC during its Session in Monte Carlo.

Some 70% of the Sydney venues are already in place. An Aquatics centre was opened in October 1994 at Sydney Olympic Park. The area, at Homebush Bay, will also stage athletics, baseball, cycling, tennis and archery. It is being built on former industrial land whose rehabilitation is seen as a major environmental triumph. The Athletes' Village will be the first to house **all** the athletes from every sport in one place. It will feature recycling, improved energy efficiency and solar power.

Sydney Harbour is the focus of other venues including sailing, football, basketball, weightlifting, judo, table tennis, triathlon (making its Olympic debut) and taekwondo. Ferry services will link the venues. Visitors will be able to enjoy a range of accommodation as well as superb public transport networks. The cost of staging the Games is likely to be A\$2 billion but the Australian economy should benefit by A\$7.3 billion.

Meanwhile, in 1998 (7-22 February), the Olympic Family looks forward to the last Olympic Winter Games of this millennium in Nagano, Japan. Nagano is situated in a popular and beautiful Alpine ski district dubbed the "roof of Japan" with over 100 peaks. Nagano was selected as host city by the IOC during its Session of June 1991 in Birmingham, UK. Salt Lake City, USA, beaten in that Birmingham vote, was later selected to host the Olympic Winter Games of 2002.

Women's ice hockey and the sport of curling will both appear on the Olympic programme for the first time in Nagano. Snow-boarding could join them subject to a decision from the local organizing committee. Nagano is also taking great care of the environment. Two years ago rare Goshawks' nests were found at the scheduled biathlon venue and so biathlon will be moved to a new site 100 miles away. Similarly, the men's downhill start gate, if built where the sport believes appropriate for a suitably tough course, would encroach on a National Park. It is a dilemma which, no doubt, will be resolved in time for Nagano to provide a fitting close to an Olympic Century.

* More information on both venues will be available in the "IOC Official Companions" to both the Nagano and Sydney Games to be published by Brassey's Sports in late 1997 and mid 2000 respectively.

The Other Games

by Morley Myers

COMPETITION is the lifeblood of sport and while the world waits until the quadrennial global gathering of the Olympic Games comes around again, many athletes are helped to maintain the tempo by participating in regional multi-sport events.

These act as a stimulus, nurturing talent and providing a yardstick for comparative accomplishment with neighbouring countries. The criteria for membership of these various Games are wide-ranging: geographical, linguistic, occupational and physical. Just like the Olympic Games, the existence of these other events is a triumph of perseverance and the ability to overcome seemingly impossible obstacles. They form an integral part of the intricate jigsaw puzzle which makes up the Olympic Family.

Asian Games

From humble beginnings in 1951, the Asian Games has grown into the largest of the regional games. Less than 500 athletes from 11 National Olympic Committees (NOCs) competed in New Delhi at the inaugural Games, which had been postponed for one year at the request of India.

Since then there has been a steady growth in the size of the Games despite financial and political problems some-times forcing last-minute changes in the host nation. A record 7,300 competitors from 43 NOCs took part in the 12th Asian Games in Hiroshima in 1994 when no less than 34 sports were on the programme, including such 'esoteric' items as "kabbadi" and "sepak takraw" – traditional regional sports.

Bangkok, which has already hosted the event three times, is scheduled to stage the 13th edition in 1998. Asia also houses various sub-continental Games and their numbers were recently swelled by the inaugural Central Asian Games between the former Soviet Union republics of Uzbekistan, Kazakhstan, Krygysztan, Tajikistan and Turkmenistan.

African Games

Baron Pierre de Coubertin, founder of the Modern Olympic Games, first conceived the idea of an African Games in 1912 and there were failed attempts to stage the event in 1925 and 1927 where they met opposition from the colonial powers. The long-awaited inaugural Games finally took place in 1965 when 20 independent African states competed in Brazzaville, Congo.

But there were early hiccups and the second Games were not held until 1973 in Lagos, Nigeria. This was followed by a five-year interval before the African countries met again in Algiers in 1978. But it was not until the late 1980s that the Games managed to establish a regular four-year cycle with Nairobi hosting the event in 1987 followed four years later by Cairo and then Harare, Zimbabwe.

The Continent which has produced many of the greatest middle and long distance runners has now really hit its stride.

PanAm Games

Just like its African counterpart, the PanAm Games took a long time between conception and delivery. The first meeting of the Pan American Sports Congress was in Buenos Aires in 1940 when 16 nations voted to stage the PanAm Games every four years starting from 1942.

But World War II intervened and only a handful of countries were present when the PanAm Games was finally launched in Buenos Aires in 1951. Forty-four years later, 6,800 athletes from 42 NOCs participated in the 12th PanAm Games in Mar del Plata, Argentina.

Commonwealth Games

The Commonwealth Games, under various guises, has been staged every four years since 1930, apart from the wartime period covering 1942 and 1946.

The first British Empire Games – as it was then called – took place in Hamilton, Canada, with just 11 countries competing in six sports. The 1934 and 1938 editions showed an increase in numbers, but the 12 year interval had an adverse impact with only 12 countries taking part in the 4th Empire Games in

Auckland in 1950. However, the trend was reversed four years later in Vancouver, Canada, where 24 countries participated.

The 1958 Games in Cardiff, marked something of a political watershed. Before the Games, a clause was added to the constitution of the British Empire and Commonwealth Games Federation which read: "No discrimination against any country or person shall be permitted on the grounds of race, colour, religion or politics." Yet, South Africa, which fielded an all-white team, was allowed to compete. However, the Republic later withdrew from the Commonwealth, averting any subsequent confrontations because of its apartheid policies.

Despite the breaking up of the British Empire, the Commonwealth Games continues to flourish and 3,500 athletes took part in the 15th edition in Victoria, Canada, in 1994. These Games also marked South Africa's re-emergence.

More Games

Surprisingly there are no European Games, despite various promptings and the recent addition of European Youth Olympic Days. But countries from this Continent can also compete in such multi-national gatherings as the Mediterranean Games, the Games for French speaking nations or even the biennial Games of the Small States of Europe.

Outside regionally-constructed events, there are Games to fit all categories. The biggest is the Universiade, the World Student Games, which has been held every two years since 1959, although earlier less refined versions date from 1923.

The 1959 Universiade in Turin, Italy, attracted 985 athletes from 45 countries. In 1995, at the 18th Universiade in Fukuoka, Japan, the figures had swollen to more than 4,300 athletes from 163 nations.

The multi-national multi-sports calendar is also occupied by such high-profile events as the Goodwill Games, the brainchild of American media mogul Ted Turner, who wanted to bring US and Soviet athletes together following the boycotts of the 1980 and 1984 Olympic Games. There are also 'World Games' open to those sports which are not on the Olympic programme.

But the Games which, perhaps, most closely parallel the Olympic Games in their ideology, format and history are the Paralympic Games. These have been held once every four years since 1960 and involve elite athletes with a disability. Originally the brainchild of Dr Ludwig Guttmann in Britain to provide sporting competition as rehabilitation therapy for spinally-injured World War II service men, they have emerged into a 19-sport, 102-nation and 4,000 athlete Games. They take place once every four years in the same host city as the Olympic Games, almost immediately after the Olympic Games close. Athletes must reach international qualifying standards to participate and there is also a Paralympic Winter Games.

Finally, there are the Special Olympics, Games for athletes with a learning disability based on grassroots participation rather than elite sport as athletes from the latter category can now take part in the Paralympic Games.

Authors and Editors

Editors

Bryn Vaile won Olympic gold in yachting's Star class in Korea in 1988. He is a sports writer, sports marketing and PR consultant. **Caroline Searle** is a former sports journalist who worked for the British Olympic Association for seven years as the Association's Public Affairs Director. Both are partners in Matchtight Media – a sports publications, sponsorship and public relations agency.

100 Glorious Years section

Neil Wilson: Has covered every Games since 1972 for a variety of British national newspapers including *The Times*, *Daily Mail* and *Independent*. One of the world's best sportswriters.

Iain Macleod: Top national newspaper columnist on Olympic matters and athletics correspondent for the *Daily Telegraph*.

Michèle Verdier: The IOC's Information Director. A talented multi-linguist who has often been the IOC's public image in making media statements during the Games. She also handles all media accreditation and facilities provision at each Olympic Games.

Atlanta section

Bert Roughton: Olympic correspondent of the *Atlanta Constitution and Journal* who has covered the Atlanta story since the city first bid for the Games.

Nicola Fairbrother: A former world champion and 1992 Olympic silver medallist in judo.

Sportsfile section

Archery: **Richard Perelman** (USA) FITA spokesman who was part of the 1984 Olympic organizing committee and wrote a book of his experiences.

Athletics: **Ian Chadband** (GBR) Athletics correspondent of the *Sunday Times*

Badminton: **Hans Møller** (DEN) Senior writer for Denmark's Ritzau Agency and a renowned world authority on the sport.

Baseball: **Jim Callis** (USA) Managing editor of *Baseball America* magazine.

Basketball: **Skip Myslenski** (USA) Basketball correspondent of the *Chicago Tribune* who has covered several recent Olympic Games.

Boxing: **Neil Allen** (GBR) Veteran sports correspondent at four decades of Olympic Games for both *The Times* (of London) and the *London Evening Standard*. Expert in both athletics and boxing.

Canoeing: **Myriam Jerusalemi** (FRA)
World champion slalom canoeist.
Ivan Lawler (GBR) Olympic sprint racing
canoeist.

Cycling: **Peter Bryan** (GBR)
Cycling correspondent of *The Times* of
London.

Equestrian: **Dieter Hennig** (GER)
A leading German equestrian writer.

Fencing: **Graham Morrison** (GBR)
Editor of *The Sword* – a leading fencing
publication.

Football: **Jerry Trecker** (USA)
Top freelance writer on international soccer.

Gymnastics: **Vera Marinova** (BUL)
Former gymnast and Olympic team coach
who now also works as a TV commentator
at the Games.

Hockey: **Sydney Friskin** (GBR)
Hockey correspondent of *The Times* of
London

Judo: **Oon Oon Yeoh** (MAL)
A Malaysian journalist and author of judo
books.

Modern Pentathlon: **John Goodbody** (GBR)
Chief Sports News Correspondent of *The
Times* of London and a leading authority on
drugs in sport.

Rowing: **Dan Topolski** (GBR)
Oxford University rowing coach and
celebrated former international oarsman
and journalist.

Shooting: **Sarah Cooper** (GBR)
Former Olympic shooting competitor. This
section has been co-edited by Sarah's
husband, Malcolm, who won Olympic
shooting gold in 1984 and 1988.

Softball: **Bill Plummer** III (USA)
Director of PR and Media of the Amateur
Softball Association, Oklahoma City.

Swimming: **Andy Jameson** (GBR)
Olympic bronze medallist 100m butterfly
1988 Games. BBC TV swimming
commentator.

Table Tennis: **Richard Eaton** (GBR)
Table tennis correspondent of *The Times* of
London.

Tennis: **John Oakley** (GBR)
British national agency journalist who has
covered every Wimbledon since 1946 and
every Olympic Games since 1952.

Volleyball: **Paddy Murphy** (IRL)
Volleyball international referee and BBC TV
commentator.

Weightlifting: **Jenő Boskovics** (HUN)
Leading international journalist and
spokesperson for the International
Weightlifting Federation.

Wrestling: **Togay Bayatli** (TUR)
President of the Association of International
Sports Press (AIPS) and General Secretary of
the Turkish NOC. A leading sportswriter.

Yachting: **Neils Rasmussen** (DEN)
Sports correspondent for *Politiken* in
Copenhagen. Has supplied personality
piece on Paul Elvström.
Bryn Vaile (GBR) 1988 Olympic gold
medallist in the Star Class.

Olympic Movement section

Includes articles by **Michèle Verdier** and
John Goodbody (see above).

Dick Palmer: General Secretary of the
British Olympic Association and Britain's
Olympic Games Chef de Mission since 1976
who has worked for Olympic Solidarity for
two decades.

Michael Payne: Director of Marketing at the
IOC who has supplied an article on the
Games sponsorship, finances, licensing etc.

Richard Palfreyman: Sydney 2000
representative.
Hiroshi Takeuchi: Olympic correspondent
with the Japanese news agency (Kyodo).

Morley Myers: Olympic correspondent for
the last three decades. Now working for the
UPI news agency. Part of the IOC's Press
Commission.

Acknowledgements

The directors of Brassey's Sports, together with the editors Bryn Vaile and Caroline Searle, would like to acknowledge the invaluable help of the International Olympic Committee in compiling and editing "The IOC Official Olympic Companion" in its 1996 edition. They would also like to acknowledge the following:

Sports Federations:

A debt of gratitude is owed to the international federations of the following sports: archery, athletics, badminton, basketball, boxing, cycling, equestrian, fencing (especially Peter Jacobs), football, gymnastics, hockey, modern pentathlon, rowing, shooting, softball, swimming, table tennis, tennis, volleyball, weightlifting, wrestling and yachting. As well as the Association Internationale de la Presse Sportive (AIPS) who gave help in sourcing authors.

The editors have also been grateful for additional help from the British Olympic Association (for the use of its library and resources), the Badminton Association of England, the British Baseball Association, Ian Irwin of boxing, the British Canoe Union, the British Cycling Federation, the British Show Jumping Association, the Amateur Fencing Association, the Football Association, the Great Britain Hockey Board and Hockey Association, the British Judo Association, the Amateur Rowing Association, the Amateur Swimming Association, the Lawn Tennis Association, the British Amateur Weightlifting Association, the British Amateur Wrestling Association.

Editorial assistance:

Richard Eaton, a sports correspondent of the Times, provided editorial assistance for this volume. A great debt is owed to the editorial team – led by Pauline Turpitt (of Matchtight Media) and Sue Midgeley (of Brassey's) and including Cathy Green and Jennifer Steele for the many hours spent in inputting, checking and proof-reading all medallist data for the book. Matthew Brown also provided research for the Sportsfile. We are grateful, too, for the help given by embassies and individuals in checking the spelling and accenting of names.

Reference Sources:

The Official Reports – compiled by the relevant organizing committee – for every Games of the Olympiad since 1896.

The Official British Olympic Association Reports of every Games of the Olympiad since 1896.

The Olympic Review (October 1992. No.300)

IOC Complete results of the Games of 1896, 1900, 1908, 1920, 1924.

IOC Complete list of Olympic competitors since 1896 by nation – Wolf Lyberg

IOC Olympic Movement Directory 1995

ACOG Atlanta 1996 Press Guide (June 1995 version)

Bob Brennan, Jayne Pearce and Laurie Olsen of the ACOG Press Department

The Oxford Companion to Sports and Games – John Arlott (Paladin)

The Complete Book of the Olympics – David Wallechinsky

The Barcelona Bike Handbook – Mike Price

The International Gymnast

The World of Gymnastics

"Flick-flack – Weltbuhne des Turnens" – Sportverlag Berlin (1986)

The Sword – Malcolm Fare

The Olympic Games 1984 by Lord Killanin and John Rodda – Willow Books.

Medal tables by nation (Sportsfile section). Our grateful thanks go to Stan Greenberg, editor of the Guiness Olympics Fact Book, for providing up-to-date medal tables for each sport by nation.

Photographs

Allsport UK Ltd
Allsport/Hulton Deutsch
Atlanta Olympic Organising Committee (ACOG)
Royal Yachting Association (RYA)
Bryn Vaile